12TH EDITION

JOHN CAMPBELL
DAVID FOSKETT
NEIL RIPPINGTON
PATRICIA PASKINS

PRACTICAL COOKERY

FOR LEVEL 2 NVQ AND APPRENTICESHIPS

DYNAMIC
LEARNING

HODDER
EDUCATION
AN HACHETTE UK COMPANY

Orders: please contact Bookpoint Ltd, 130 Milton Park, Abingdon, Oxon OX14 4SB. Telephone: (44) 01235 827720. Fax: (44) 01235 400454. Lines are open from 9.00 - 5.00, Monday to Saturday, with a 24-hour message answering service. You can also order through our website www.hoddereducation.co.uk

If you have any comments to make about this, or any of our other titles, please send them to educationenquiries@hodder.co.uk

British Library Cataloguing in Publication Data

A catalogue record for this title is available from the British Library.
ISBN: 978 1444 17008 5
ISBN (HELPE): 978 1444 17682 7

First published 1962
Second edition 1967
Third edition 1972
Fourth edition 1974
Fifth edition 1981
Sixth edition 1987
Seventh edition 1990
Eighth edition 1995
Ninth edition 2000
Tenth edition 2004
Eleventh edition 2008

This edition published 2012

Impression number 10 9 8 7 6 5 4 3
Year   2015, 2014, 2013

Copyright © 2012 John Campbell, David Foskett, Neil Rippington and Patricia Paskins

Hachette UK's policy is to use papers that are natural, renewable and recyclable products and made from wood grown in sustainable forests. The logging and manufacturing processes are expected to conform to the environmental regulations of the country of origin.

Typeset by DC Graphic Design Limited, Swanley VIllage, Kent.

Printed in India for Hodder Education, an Hachette UK Company, 338 Euston Road, London NW1 3BH.

Contents

Preface

When David Foskett and Victor Ceserani invited me to join their writing team several years ago I jumped at the opportunity. Education has shaped the person I am today – through college and higher education where my skills were developed and nurtured by some inspirational teachers, and through the day-to-day contact I have with my staff and professional peers who continually help me to develop and refine my knowledge and skills in the profession I love.

At the heart of *Practical Cookery* is a strong partnership with industry. This close connection ensures that the book reflects modern practice and will effectively help prepare you for your career. It will also continue to support you long after your career has started, so keep it close to hand!

This book has been the product of a huge amount of work both by the authors and the supporting team. I hope it makes the theoretical parts of the course understandable and the practical elements truly inspiring. To play a part in helping to shape the education of students using this book is a privilege. It provides me with an opportunity to give something back in return for the education I have been lucky enough to receive. My hope is that this book will help motivate you to succeed in your studies and go on to have a rewarding and fulfilling career. We think it represents the best we can give you.

Good luck!
John Campbell

Introduction

'Practical Cookery is a must for all students of cookery. I still use my copy printed in 1981 when writing recipes, a great practical, reference book. Thank you Victor and Ronald.'
- Brian Turner, CBE

This book provides a sound foundation of professional cookery for catering students at all levels. Every student needs to:

- develop a professional attitude and appearance, acquire skills and behave professionally
- develop knowledge and understanding of all commodities – their cost, quality points and uses
- understand the methods of cookery and be able to produce a variety of dishes suitable for different types of establishment
- understand recipe balance and be able to produce dishes of the required quality, flavour, temperature, presentation and quantity
- gain the experience that will enable them to develop recipes from original ideas
- understand healthy eating and nutrition
- use healthy, hygienic and safe procedures for the storage, preparation, cooking and service of food – and understand why this matters.

To be creative, chefs must understand and acquire the basic skills and techniques of professional cookery. These skills must be supported by underpinning knowledge.

Basic skills and recipes are fundamental because they provide the framework for a successful career in professional cookery. *Practical Cookery* provides an invaluable foundation of professional skills and knowledge, balancing the traditional and the modern.

How to use this book

If you are a student taking the Level 2 NVQ Diploma in Food Production and Cooking you will find that the book has been carefully structured around the requirements of the course.

At the start of each chapter is a list telling you which specification units are covered in the chapter.

Each chapter includes some underpinning knowledge and theory. If the chapter topic is a food commodity, then the knowledge section is followed by recipes.

On the first page of the chapter is a list of the recipes within the chapter. There is also a complete index of recipes at the back of the book.

If you are a VRQ student, the unit that each chapter links to has also been detailed at the start of the chapter. There is additional knowledge for your course on the website:

- Investigating the catering and hospitality industry http://bit.ly/Abe3Cn
- Catering operations, costs and menu planning http://bit.ly/xICP9I
- Applying workplace skills http://bit.ly/w1WYvu

Using the recipes

Our recipes are full of helpful features:

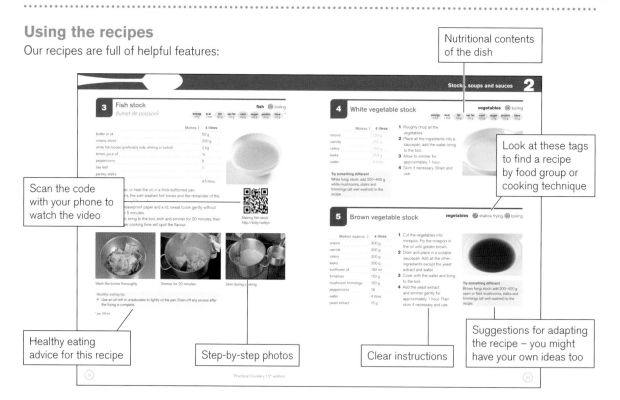

Nutritional contents of the dish

Look at these tags to find a recipe by food group or cooking technique

Scan the code with your phone to watch the video

Healthy eating advice for this recipe

Step-by-step photos

Clear instructions

Suggestions for adapting the recipe – you might have your own ideas too

To help make sure that you develop all the practical skills you need for your course, the recipes are tagged with the food groups and methods of cookery they use. The tags are at the top right of the recipe, just under the title. This makes it easy to look through the book and pick a recipe that meets your needs.

To make it even easier, the main methods of cookery are shown by icons. So if you want to practise shallow frying, look for that icon. They look like this:

- Boiling
- Steaming
- Poaching
- Stewing or casseroling
- Grilling
- Baking
- Roasting
- Shallow frying
- Deep frying

Keep an eye on the icons as you study, and you'll know exactly which skills you have been using.

Healthy catering

There is no such thing as unhealthy food, but eating in an unhealthy way may lead to obesity, ill health and even early death. Obesity is increasing in the UK, especially among young people.

Nutritional data is provided for some of the recipes in this book, to help you make informed choices about what to cook and eat. Look out for the Healthy Eating Tips in some recipes – these suggestions will help you to make the dish healthier and more balanced.

Nutritional data is provided per portion, except for loaves and flans (data provided per loaf) and where stated.

Free digital resources, any time, any place

There are free videos and recipes on the website. Look out for the QR codes throughout the book. They look like this.

Principles of poaching
http://bit.ly/wutwTE

To use the QR codes to view the videos you will need a QR code reader for your smartphone/tablet. There are many free readers available, depending on the smartphone/tablet you are using. We have supplied some suggestions below, but this is not an exhaustive list and you should only download software compatible with your device and operating system. We do not endorse any of the third-party products listed below and downloading them is at your own risk.

- for iPhone/iPad, Qrafter – http://itunes.apple.com/app/qrafter-qr-code-reader-generator/id416098700
- for Android, QR Droid – https://market.android.com/details?id=la.droid.qr&hl=en
- for Blackberry, QR Scanner Pro – http://appworld.blackberry.com/webstore/content/13962
- for Windows/Symbian, Upcode – http://www.upc.fi/en/upcode/download/

Once you have downloaded a QR code reader, simply open the reader app and use it to take a photo of the code. The video will then load on your smartphone/tablet.

If you cannot read the QR code or you are using a computer, the web link next to the code will take you directly to the same video.

There are also weblinks to the free extra recipes in the table at the start of Chapters 2 to 11.

The terms and conditions which govern these free online resources may be seen at http://bit.ly/yfVC0P

Even more digital resources are available to centres that purchase Practical Cookery Dynamic Learning – see page xiii for more information.

Conversion tables

In this book, metric weights and measures are used. All temperatures are given in degrees Celsius. You can use these tables to convert to other units.

Weights and measures

Imperial	Approx. metric equivalent
¼ oz	5 g
½ oz	10 g
1 oz	25 g
2 oz	50 g
3 oz	75 g
4 oz	100 g
5 oz	125 g
6 oz	150 g
7 oz	175 g
8 oz	200 g
9 oz	225 g
10 oz	250 g
11 oz	275 g
12 oz	300 g
13 oz	325 g
14 oz	350 g
15 oz	375 g
16 oz	400 g
2 lb	1 kg
¼ pt	125 ml
½ pt	250 ml
¾ pt	375 ml
1 pt	500 ml
1½ pt	750 ml
2 pt (1 qt)	1 litre

Imperial	Approx. metric equivalent
2 qt	2 litres
1 gal	4.5 litres
¼ in	0.5 cm
½ in	1 cm
1 in	2 cm
1½ in	4 cm
2 in	5 cm
2½ in	6 cm
3 in	8 cm
4 in	10 cm
5 in	12 cm
6 in	15 cm
6½ in	16 cm
7 in	18 cm
12 in	30 cm
18 in	45 cm
Spoons and cups	
1 teaspoon (tsp)	5 ml
1 dessertspoon (dsp)	10 ml
1 tablespoon (tbsp)	15 ml
¼ cup	60 ml
1/3 cup	80 ml
½ cup	125 ml
1 cup	250 ml

Oven temperatures

	°C	Gas regulo	°F
	110	¼	225
	130	½	250
slow (cool)	140	1	275
	150	2	300
	160	3	325
	180	4	350
moderate	190	5	375
	200	6	400
	220	7	425
hot	230	8	450
very hot	250	9	475

About this book

50 years of Practical Cookery

1960 Victor Ceserani and Ronald Kinton, junior lecturers in cookery at the Acton Hotel and Catering School, decide to write a book for students.

1962 *Practical Cookery* is published by Edward Arnold; in the first year it sells almost 10,000 copies.

1964 *The Theory of Catering*, by the same authors, is published.

1987 Edward Arnold Publishers becomes part of Hodder & Stoughton, and continues to publish the books.

1988 A book for more advanced students, *Contemporary Cookery*, is published. This later became *Advanced Practical Cookery* and then *Practical Cookery Level 3.*

1995 David Foskett becomes the third author for the 8th edition of *Practical Cookery*.
Practical Cookery is printed in colour for the first time.

2000 The one millionth copy of *Practical Cookery* is sold.

2008 Ronald Kinton retires from Practical Cookery. The 11th edition of *Practical Cookery*, by John Campbell, David Foskett and Victor Ceserani, is published.
The first Dynamic Learning resource is published to go with the book, providing a wealth of video and other extra content.

2009 *Foundation Practical Cookery* is published for Level 1 students, school pupils and everyone learning to cook.

2012 50 years after the first book, a new edition of *Practical Cookery* by John Campbell, David Foskett, Neil Rippington and Patricia Paskins is published. This is the book you are holding in your hands!

About the authors

Award-winning chef **John Campbell** runs John Campbell Restaurants and is an honorary professor at the University of West London. As Executive Head Chef at The Vineyard at Stockcross, he achieved two Michelin stars, and the Chef Award and Education and Training Award at the 2008 Cateys. John works in a consultative partnership with Baxter Storey, and set up their training academy. John opened Coworth Park in 2010 with the Dorchester Collection as Director of Food and Beverage, earning the fine dining restaurant a Michelin star in the first year of trading.

Professor **David Foskett** MBE CMA FIH is a best-selling author. He is Head of School at the London School of Hospitality and Tourism at the University of West London. He was awarded Catering Educator of the Year 2004 and, in 2008, received France's Agricultural Order of Merit for his work promoting French food and food education.

Neil Rippington is Dean of the College of Food at University College Birmingham. He has received awards for his part in developing the City & Guilds Diplomas in Professional Cookery, and is a consultant and examiner for two major awarding bodies.

Patricia Paskins MHCIMA is a Senior Hospitality Lecturer and Work-Based Learning Tutor at the London School of Hospitality and Tourism at the University of West London. She also leads all Food Safety areas within the university, as well as working with and advising a number of external agencies.

About the nutritional analysts

New nutritional analysis for this book was carried out by Joanne Tucker, Senior Lecturer at the University of West London.

Some of the nutritional data was created for earlier editions by Jenny Arthur, nutrition consultant, Dr Jenny Poulter, Jane Cliff and Pat Bacon.

Acknowledgements

We are most grateful to Booker plc, in particular Ron Hickey and Niall Brannigan, for their support in the development of the book, including the provision of much of the food shown in the photographs.

We are also very grateful to Watts Farms for providing some of the fruit and vegetables used in the photographs.

We would like to thank the following:

- Matthew Bellamy, Martin Houghton, David Leaf, Fran Victory and Paul Wood for their advice during market research
- Gary Farrelly at the University of West London for his help with many aspects of the book
- Russums Catering Clothing and Equipment
- Steve James, Dipna Anand, Joshua Kane, Charlotte Symons, Simon Mattock and Callum Farmer for their roles in the new videos for the Dynamic Learning resource, and Adrian Moss of Instructional Design Ltd for producing the videos
- Alexia Chan, Deborah Edwards Noble, Neil Fozzard and Joanna Walker at Hodder Education, and Clare Weaver and Katie Frederick.

This book has been endorsed by the Academy of Culinary Arts, Britain's leading professional association of Head Chefs, Pastry Chefs, Restaurant Managers and suppliers. Its objectives are primarily focused on the education and training of young people in the hospitality industry through the provision of career opportunities; recognising and rewarding talent and skill; and raising standards and awareness of food, food provenance, cooking and service. These objectives are realised through a number of core education and training initiatives aimed at all ages and stages of development from teaching school children through to the Continual Professional Development of established chefs, pastry chefs and waiters.

Photography

Most of the photos in this book are by Andrew Callaghan of Callaghan Studios. The photography work could not have been done without the generous help of the authors and their colleagues and students at the University of West London (UWL) and University College Birmingham (UCB). The publishers would particularly like to acknowledge the following.

John Campbell, Song Wong and Gary Farrelly organised the photography at UWL. They were assisted in the kitchen by:

- Mark Apsey
- Dominic Moszkal
- Miroslav Hristov
- Jan Honzak
- Peter Lambie
- Tarkan Nevzat
- Cho Kok Keong
- Sin Qi Ren
- Lim Shanqyann
- Ng Pei Wen
- Andy Chong Kai Siong
- Toon Ju Ken.

Baxter Storey very generously allowed Peter, Miro and Jan to participate in the photography.

Neil Rippington organised the photography at UCB with the kind assistance of:

- Chris Barker from the Colchester Institute
- Stephanie Conway from the Colchester Institute
- Mike Edwards from UCB
- Adam Pickett from UCB
- Matthew Shropshall from UCB
- Anthony Wright from UCB
- Jilisa Barnaby
- Christopher Cownden
- Sarah Dale
- Harry Dempster
- Chelsea Dore
- Thomas Downes
- Michael Francis
- Benjamin Machmichael
- Nicholas Rowland
- Steven Selway
- Ciara Trainor.

The authors and publishers are grateful to everyone involved for their hard work.

Picture credits

Every effort has been made to trace the copyright holders of material reproduced here. The authors and publishers would like to thank the following for permission to reproduce copyright illustrations.

pp.5, 14 © Sarah Bailey/Hodder Education; p.19 Compass; pp.97, 146 (bottom) © Sarah Bailey/Hodder Education; pp.239 (top and bottom right), 240 (top), 243 (bottom), 247 (bottom) © EBLEX; pp.249, 250 (middle, right) © BPEX; pp.251, 252 © EBLEX; pp.266 (bottom), 337 (bottom) © Sarah Bailey/Hodder Education; p.428 British Potato Council; p.602 Crown copyright; pp.608 (except bottom), 609 Russums; p.612 © Photodisc; pp.631, 633 (right) Russums.

The photos on pages 6, 13, 63, 66, 88, 92, 102, 110 (top), 118, 125, 136 (top), 138, 146 (top), 147, 159, 166, 172, 178, 185 (bottom), 187, 196, 216, 225, 240 (top), 262, 266 (top), 276 293 (top), 321, 322 (top), 331 (top), 334, 335 (bottom), 345 (bottom), 350, 352, 365, 377, 382 (top), 384 (top), 410, 416, 417, 419, 420, 424, 432 (top), 433 (middle), 516, 525 (bottom), 548, 554, 583, 598 (bottom), 604, 606, 608 (bottom), 626 are © Sam Bailey/Hodder Education.

Except where stated above, photographs are by Andrew Callaghan and illustrations by Barking Dog Art. Crown copyright material is licensed under the Open Government Licence v1.0.

Other books in the series

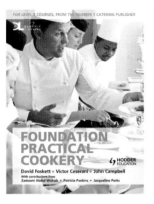

Also available from www.hoddereducation.co.uk:

- Foundation Practical Cookery
- Practical Cookery for Level 2 VRQ
- Practical Cookery Level 3 for VRQ and NVQ courses, 5th edition
- The Theory of Hospitality and Catering for Levels 3 and 4, 12th edition

Dynamic Learning: create outstanding lessons

Dynamic Learning is an online subscription solution that supports teaching and learning by providing quality content alongside easy-to-use tools.

Practical Cookery Dynamic Learning makes teaching easier and encourages students to develop, progress and achieve. Using the lesson maker tool tutors can:

- Create, organise and edit lessons
- Share plans, lessons and resources with colleagues
- Assign lessons and resources to students
- Export lessons and pre-tagged content to a VLE at the click of a button.

Tutors can also combine their own trusted resources with those from *Practical Cookery Dynamic Learning*, which has a whole host of informative, exciting and interactive resources including:

- Interactive quizzes
- Result tracking for tutors
- Videos of many cookery techniques
- Extra recipes
- Teaching resources such as worksheets and presentations.

Dynamic Learning is already being used by thousands of teachers around the world so make sure you don't miss out – to find out more and take out a free 60-day trial simply visit www.dynamic-learning.co.uk today.

Methods of cooking

The method chosen to cook various foods will greatly influence the finished product. Different foods can be cooked in different ways to:

- make food easy to digest and safe to eat
- make food pleasant to eat, with an agreeable flavour
- add the required colour and variety of colour
- give food a good texture – tender, slightly firm, crisp, depending on the food
- give variety to our menus and our diets.

What happens when food is cooked?

Heat can be applied directly to food, by **dry heat**, or by placing food in a hot cooking medium such as water or stock (**moist heat**).

This can take place in three ways, by **convection**, **conduction** and **radiation**. Each of these is explained below. In practice, most cooking uses a combination of all three. For example, a basic sponge is cooked by heat reflecting from the oven walls (radiation), heat circulating in the air within the oven (convection) and heat transferred from the cake tin to the cake mixture (conduction).

Convection

Convection occurs when a liquid or gas is heated causing hot air to rise and cooler air to sink, distributing the heat through the liquid or gas and into the food.

- Boiling food: the water is gradually heated by convection currents from the heat source and the hot water transfers heat to the food.
- Baking in an oven: the heat generated in the oven is transferred to the food.

Conduction

In conduction, heat passes through one solid to another. This can only be done with materials that are good conductors of heat, such as metals. The food needs to be in direct contact with a heated item in order to cook.

An example of cooking by conduction is food in direct contact with a griddle.

Radiation

Heat is transferred directly to food by electromagnetic waves, such as microwaves or infrared waves. These waves first heat the food and then cook it. Any object that is in the path of the waves, such as a salamander, will also become hot.

Examples of cooking by radiation include grilling, toasting, barbeque and microwaving.

The effect of cooking on food

In the process of cooking, heat affects the nutrients in food. These effects lead to changes in texture, appearance and flavour of the food.

Protein

Heat causes protein in liquids to coagulate (set or solidify). Examples in cookery include:

- Egg white: it thickens, becoming opaque and then firm, when it is cooked.
- Gluten (wheat protein): in bread it forms the crust on a loaf.
- Coatings on fried food (e.g. batter, breadcrumbs): these also contain gluten, which coagulates.

If protein is heated too much, it will become hard, tough, shrunken and unpalatable. Syneresis results from over-coagulated egg protein, which pushes out moisture; this can be seen in over-cooked scrambled egg.

Carbohydrates

Starches and sugars react differently to dry and moist heat, as shown in Table 1.1.

Table 1.1 How carbohydrates react to heat

	Starch	**Sugar**
Moist heat	Starch grains soften and swell. Near boiling point, the cellulose framework bursts, releasing the starch, which thickens the liquid.	Sugar dissolves in water. When heated it becomes syrup. Eventually it colours, then caramelises. Finally it will turn to carbon and ash.
Dry heat	Starch changes from creamy white to brown. It gives off water when heated. Starch on the surface of food changes to dextrin, a sugar – e.g. bread becoming toast. When overheated, starch will carbonise and burn.	Sugar caramelises quickly and then burns.

Fat

Fats melt into oils when heated. Water is given off with a bubbling noise. When all the water is gone, a faint blue haze appears; the fat itself will not evaporate. If the fat is heated even more, it will smoke and burn, giving an unpleasant smell caused by fatty acids. Fats within foods can cause a change in texture and flavour when heated: for example, melted cheese.

Vitamins

There will be some loss of water-soluble vitamins B and C when food is cooked in liquid such as in boiling. Some of the vitamins may also be lost by high temperatures, exposure to oxygen and enzyme action.

Vitamins in the A, D, E and K groups are not water soluble, so they will survive cooking in water; they are also not usually destroyed by heat.

To avoid loss of water-soluble vitamins:

- Do not prepare vegetables too far in advance and do not soak them in water.
- Cook vegetables in small quantities and as quickly as possible.
- Cover them with a lid during cooking, to speed up cooking time and minimise oxidation.
- Use foods that are as fresh as possible; do not store them for longer than necessary.
- Put green vegetables into boiling water to allow for rapid cooking.

Boiling, poaching and steaming

Table 1.2 explains the differences between boiling, poaching and steaming. It will help you to choose which method to use for a particular dish.

Table 1.2 Boiling, poaching and steaming

	Boiling	Poaching	Steaming
What exactly does it mean?	Food is immersed in liquid at 100°C. The temperature is then reduced slightly and maintained at the simmering point where the liquid is just moving.	Food is cooked in a liquid that is just below boiling point.	Food is often cooked under pressure in the steam produced by a boiling liquid.
Why use this method?	A healthy method of cookery: ● It does not use any fat. ● When done properly, it will keep the flavour and nutritional value is retained in the food but care must be taken not to lose water-soluble vitamins (see above). Some foods may also be parboiled (partly boiled) or blanched and finished using another method of cookery.	A gentle method, suitable for delicate foods such as eggs and fish. Used to cook food so that it is very tender and easy to eat and digest.	Steaming keeps most of the nutrients in the food. It is gentle, so it prevents the food from becoming too saturated with water.
What happens to the food as it is cooked?	Gentle boiling helps to break down the tough fibres of certain foods. When boiling meats, some of the meat extracts dissolve in the cooking liquid (see below).	Poaching helps to tenderise the food and improve the texture.	Steamed food will not take on any colour. The texture will vary according to the type of food, type of steamer and level of heat. Steamed sponges and puddings are light in texture.
Is it economical? Does it save on labour?	Older, tougher, cheaper joints of meat and poultry can be made tasty and tender. It is an economical way of cooking as it uses minimal fuel. It is labour saving, as boiling food needs little attention.	Poaching is economical as it does not require excessive heat and most foods cook quickly.	It is labour saving and suitable for cooking large quantities of food at one time, e.g. in schools. Smaller quantities can be economically cooked in a multi-tiered steamer on a stove top.
How does it affect nutrition?	Water-soluble vitamins, such as vitamins B and C, can be lost through excessive boiling.	A healthy method using water (or another liquid) without adding fats.	Steamed food tends to retain its nutritional value.
Other advantages	Nutritious, well-flavoured stock can be produced from the cooking liquor.	A quick, easy, uncomplicated cooking method.	It makes some foods lighter and easy to digest. Low-pressure steaming reduces the risk of overcooking, which can cause food to over soften. High-pressure steaming enables food to be cooked or reheated quickly.

Health and safety

● When you are boiling or poaching, you are dealing with hot/boiling water; work safely to avoid accidents.
● Make sure that the cooking pan is large enough, to avoid boiling water splashing over the edge.
● Lower food into boiling or poaching water gently so that the water does not splash up and scald you.
● When lifting the lid from the cooking pan, tilt it away from your face to avoid burns from the steam.

● When straining foods from boiling liquids do so carefully.
● When a pan of hot liquid is on the stove, make sure that the handle is turned in, so it is less likely to be knocked over and avoid carrying containers of very hot water from one place to another.
● When opening a steaming oven, open the door a little to allow some steam to escape then stand back as the door is opened fully.

Boiling

There are two ways of boiling, as described in Table 1.3.

Principles of boiling
http://bit.ly/A9UsQR

Table 1.3 Methods of boiling

Method of boiling	What is it used for?
Place the food in boiling liquid. The liquid will stop boiling when you put the food in, so heat to bring it back to boiling. Then reduce the heat so that the liquid just bubbles gently (simmering) and cooks the food.	● Cooking green vegetables – to retain maximum colour and nutritional value (when boiled for the shortest possible time) ● Meat ● Rice and pasta
Cover food with cold liquid. Heat it up and bring it to the boil, then reduce the heat to allow the food to simmer.	● Meat – to tenderise the fibrous structure ● Root, pulses and other vegetables ● Vegetable soups – to extract the starch ● Stocks – to extract flavour from the ingredients

Follow these guidelines when boiling food:

- Ensure that all pieces of food going in the same pan are of a similar size or density so they need the same cooking time.
- Foods that require different cooking times should not be cooked together. For example, the cooking time of potato is longer than that of cauliflower. Choose pans that are the right size to allow for the food and the boiling water.
- Use enough water to entirely cover the food throughout its cooking time. Use minimal amounts of water for green vegetables.
- Make sure that there is enough boiling liquid in the pan before you add the food to avoid lowering the temperature. This helps maintain the vitamins and colour of green vegetables.
- With meat and stock skim the surface of the liquid regularly during the cooking.
- Simmer rather than boil vigorously so that less water evaporates, and the food will not shrink too much or break up.

There are also guidelines for boiling certain foods:

- When you make stock, bring the ingredients to the boil from a cold start and skim off surface scum regularly.
- Pasta should not be overcooked but left slightly firm (called *al dente*).
- Meat and poultry should be well cooked and tender.
- Vegetables should not be overcooked but left slightly crisp.

- Tough meat must be cooked *slowly* so that there is time for the connective tissue to soften and change into gelatine. This dissolves in the cooking liquid and the fibres in the meat are released, making the meat tender. If this happens too fast, the meat will be tough and stringy. Gentle heat will allow the protein to coagulate without hardening.

Boiling spaghetti

Poaching

A poaching medium is the liquid in which the food is cooked. As well as water, different liquids can be used for specific dishes. Milk can be used to poach fish and also meringue for desserts. Suitable stocks can be used for fish or chicken and a court bouillon (see page 121) for fish. Fruit can be poached in a stock syrup or in a fruit juice.

A well-flavoured sauce can be made with the cooking liquid, such as from the milk in which fish is poached.

For most foods, heat the poaching liquid first. When it reaches a temperature just below boiling, lower the prepared food into the barely simmering liquid and allow it to cook in the gentle heat. The temperature must be controlled; there should be no sign of the liquid moving, except for the occasional bubble rising to the surface.

There are two ways of poaching: shallow and deep.

Shallow poaching

Foods such as cuts of fish and chicken are poached in a small amount of liquid and covered with silicone paper. Keep the liquid just below boiling point. A way to control the temperature when shallow poaching is to bring the liquid to the boil on top of the stove, place the food in the liquid, cover it and complete the cooking in a moderately hot oven, approximately 180°C.

Principles of poaching
http://bit.ly/wutwTE

Deep poaching

Poach eggs in approximately 8 cm of gently simmering water; a little acid such as vinegar may be added to stabilise the proteins and give the eggs a good shape. You can also deep poach whole fish (e.g. salmon), cuts of fish on or off the bone (e.g. turbot), cod and salmon, and whole chicken. All of these should be completely covered with the poaching liquid.

> **Note**
> When eggs are cooked in individual shallow metal pans over boiling water, this is actually steaming rather than poaching.

Time the cooking carefully to ensure the quality of the finished dish, retention of nutrients and for food safety reasons (for example, undercooked chicken can cause food poisoning). The time and temperature needed to cook the food correctly will vary slightly for different types of food.

Foods usually retain their shape during poaching, but they may look a little pale after cooking.

Poaching a chicken

Steaming

Principles of atmospheric steaming
http://bit.ly/ykv2E7

There are three main methods of steaming.

1 **Atmospheric steaming** – an atmospheric steamer is a closed 'oven' heated by steam generated by water boiling at the bottom. Food placed into the steamer is heated by direct conduction contact with the steam. They operate at normal atmospheric pressure and cook a little above 100°C. For small quantities, food can be steamed by boiling water in the bottom of a saucepan and with food in perforated containers above the boiling water. The steam from the boiling water heats the container and cooks the food inside it.

2 **High-pressure steaming** – this is done in high-pressure steamers working like pressure cookers. Steam in the sealed cooking chamber builds up pressure: high pressure produces higher temperatures, which makes the food cook faster.

A safety valve is used to control the pressure with maximum pressures pre-set. High-pressure steamers are also used for 'batch' cooking, where small quantities of vegetables are cooked frequently throughout the service. This means the vegetables are always freshly cooked, keep their colour, flavour and nutritional content.

3 **Combination steaming** – this is done in a combination ('combi') oven. Dry heat and steam are combined in the oven, adding a little moisture to the food as it cooks. As water vapour is added to a convection oven that uses a fan, the steam is distributed evenly and quickly. Although still only at 100°C, it will cook the food more quickly than in a conventional oven.

A commercial, pressureless steamer

When using steamers, timing and temperature are very important to make sure that the food is correctly cooked.

- Food cooks much faster in high-pressure steamers so it can overcook very quickly.
- When you are using a high-pressure steamer, wait until the pressure gauge shows that it has reached the correct pressure before you open the door very carefully, allowing some steam to escape before putting the food in. This means that the steamer will be at the correct cooking temperature, and the food will cook efficiently.

- Cooking times will vary according to the equipment used and the food to be steamed. It is essential that manufacturers' instructions are followed correctly.

The following notes apply to particular steamed dishes:
- The natural juices that result from steaming fish can be served with the fish or used to make the accompanying sauce.
- For meat or sweet steamed puddings, grease the basin before filling it. Make sure it is covered with greased greaseproof or silicone paper and foil to prevent moisture getting in and making the pudding soggy.

Steamers need to be cleaned and maintained, according to these guidelines:
- Before use, check that the steamer is clean and safe to use. Report any fault immediately.
- Steamer trays and runners should be washed in hot detergent water, rinsed and dried. Where applicable, drain, clean and refill the water-generating chamber. Door controls should be lightly greased occasionally. Leave the door slightly open to allow air to circulate when the steamer is not in use.
- Clean metal steamer trays and containers thoroughly using hot detergent water, rinse, then dry with kitchen paper/clean cloth.

> **Health and safety**
> The steam in steamers can be very dangerous as it is extremely hot and can cause serious burns and scalds. To avoid injuring yourself:
> - Make sure you are trained in how to use steamers and use them with great care.
> - Check the pressure in high-pressure steamers continually.
> - Allow the pressure to return to the correct level before opening doors or removing pressure cooker lids.
> - Allow time for the pressure to return to normal before opening commercial steamers. Then stand well away from the door as you open it, to avoid the full impact of the escaping steam.

Stewing/casseroling and braising

Stewing/casseroling and braising are slow, gentle methods of cookery using moist heat (see Table 1.4).

Table 1.4 Stewing and braising

	Stewing/casseroling	Braising
What exactly does it mean?	The food is completely covered by a liquid. Both the food and the sauce are served together. **Stews** are cooked on top of the stove. **Casseroles** are cooked in the oven. These methods use less liquid and a slightly lower cooking temperature than for boiling. Smaller pieces of meat are used than in braising and therefore take less time.	A method of cooking larger pieces of food. The food is only half covered with liquid and can be cooked on the stove top or in the oven. The food is cooked very slowly in a pan with a tight-fitting lid, using low temperatures. A combination of steaming and stewing cooks the food. Meat is usually cooked in large pieces and carved before serving.
Which foods are cooked in this way?	● Meat ● Poultry ● Vegetables ● Fruit	● Whole joints or large pieces of meat ● Tougher cuts of meat ● Poultry and poultry cuts, such as turkey breast ● Vegetables, sometimes with fillings (e.g. cabbage stuffed with rice) ● Furred game, such as hare and rabbit ● Most feathered game, such as pheasant, duck and goose
Why use this method?	● To cook cheaper cuts of meat and poultry in a way that makes them tender and palatable as well as producing a well-flavoured sauce. ● To give a rich flavour to the food.	● To tenderise some tougher joints of meat. ● To enhance the flavour and texture of food.
What happens to the food as it is cooked?	As the meat cooks slowly in gentle heat, the collagen (the protein in the connective tissue) changes into gelatine so the meat becomes tender. Protein coagulates without becoming tough. Flavours from the meat are released into the liquid, and flavours from the liquid and flavourings are absorbed by the meat. When fruit is stewed, pectin (a setting agent) is released into the cooking liquid, thickening it slightly and giving it flavour.	Braising breaks down the tissue fibre in certain foods, which softens them and makes them tender and edible. The collagen (the protein in the connective tissue) in meat changes into gelatine so that meat becomes tender. Cooking food in the braising liquid also improves the texture. Flavours from the meat are released into the liquid, and flavours from the liquid and other ingredients are absorbed by the meat.
Is it economical? Does it save on labour?	Stewing makes tougher cuts of meat and poultry tender and palatable. Usually, everything in a stew can be eaten so there is very little waste. Stews and casseroles are labour saving because foods can be cooked in bulk and do not need much attention.	Tougher, less expensive meats and poultry can be used.
How does it affect nutrition?	Some nutrients will escape from the food during cooking and will stay in the liquid. This means that nutrients are not lost, but become part of the sauce.	
Other advantages	If cooked correctly, very little liquid will evaporate, leaving sufficient sauce to serve as part of the stew. The food does not shrink much and keeps its flavour. Stews reheat easily. The tough cuts of meat that can be stewed are rich in flavour.	Maximum flavour is retained.

Stewing and casseroling

Principles of making a stew
http://bit.ly/yap1Ot

- **Stewing:** meat and vegetables are usually seared in hot oil/fat then placed in a saucepan and covered with liquid (water or stock). The liquid is brought to the boil, then turned down to a low simmer. A lid is placed on the pan and the food is left to cook slowly on the hob.
- **Casseroling:** this is the same process as cooking a stew, but in the oven. The term 'casserole' refers to both the cooking pot and the finished dish. Casserole pans are usually deep and ovenproof with handles and tight-fitting lids. They can be made of glass, metal, ceramic or any other heatproof material. Casserole ingredients may also include pulses and rice. A topping of cheese or breadcrumbs may also be added for texture and flavour.

The liquid for the stew should relate to the type of food you are cooking.

- For fruit, the liquid is usually fruit juice or syrup.
- For vegetables, use vegetable stock.
- For meat, chicken and fish use meat, chicken and fish stock, respectively.
- Wine or sherry may be added to the liquid for flavour, especially when stewing red meat.

Method

The process of stewing can be seen in some of the recipes in Chapter 7.

The stewing liquid can be **thickened**:

- by adding a thickening agent, such as flour, before cooking begins (for example, in blanquette)
- by adding a thickening agent later in the cooking process (for example, *beurre manié*, i.e. equal quantities of butter and flour kneaded together and added in small amounts)
- as a result of the cooking process reducing the liquid (for example, brown stew)

- as a result of the unpassed ingredients of the stew (such as potatoes in Irish stew).

However, stews should not be over-thickened and the sauce should stay light. Adjust the consistency at the end of cooking if necessary by adding more liquid or more thickening agent.

Good stews are cooked slowly, so it is important to control the temperature properly. The liquid should barely simmer (approximately 82°C). If cooking in the oven, the ideal temperature is 170°C. Cooking too fast or too hot will make the food tough, dry or stringy.

Use a tight-fitting lid to keep in the steam. This helps to keep the temperature correct and reduces evaporation.

Do not overcook stews as this:

- causes too much liquid to evaporate
- causes the food to break up
- causes the food to lose its colour
- spoils the flavour.

Expensive, tender cuts of meat are not suitable for a stew: the meat will become dry in the long cooking process.

> **Health and safety**
> - Place large pots of stew on the stove top carefully, to avoid splashing or spilling the liquid.
> - Take care when stirring a stew/casserole to avoid the risk of burns and scalds.
> - Lift the lid of the cooking pan away from you to avoid burns from the steam.
> - If you are using Bratt pans, be very careful when stirring the large quantity of hot, semi-liquid food.

Braising

Principles of braising
http://bit.ly/ykXwNB

There are two methods of braising:

1 **Brown braising** (for joints and cuts of meat): the meat is marinated, and may be larded (covered in strips of fatty bacon), before being cooked following the method given below.

2 **White braising** (for vegetables, such as celery or cabbage, and sweetbreads): the food is blanched and refreshed instead of being browned before braising; the cooking liquid is a white stock.

Foods should be braised in an appropriate liquid, such as:
● vegetable stock or vegetable juice, for vegetables
● stock, water, wine or beer for meat.

The process of braising can be seen in some of the recipes in Chapters 7, 8 and 9.

> **Health and safety**
> ● During cooking, the pan and its contents become extremely hot. Use thick, dry oven cloths whenever you remove the pot from the oven or lift the lid.
> ● The contents of the pan can become extremely hot, so take great care to lift the lid away from you to avoid burns and take care to prevent splashing yourself with hot liquid.

Baking and roasting

Baking and roasting are usually done in an oven (see Table 1.5), but food can also be roasted on a rotating spit. Low-temperature roasting is done in an oven, but this needs to be carefully controlled, and checked with a digital thermometer (food probe).

Table 1.5 Baking and roasting

	Baking	**Roasting**	**Low-temperature roasting**
What exactly does it mean?	Food is cooked in an oven using dry heat. The steam that is generated plays an important part in the process.	Food is cooked in dry heat with added fat or oil. Roasting can be done on a spit (by radiant heat) or in an oven with one of the following: ● applied dry heat ● forced-air convected heat ● convected heat combined with microwave energy.	Food is cooked in the oven at a lower temperature than for traditional roasting. Before roasting, the meat is browned all over in a frying pan over a high heat, with a little oil brushed over the lean surfaces.
Why use this method?	It is a traditional and accepted best method for some foods, e.g. bread. Baking can give foods an appealing colour and texture.	Roasting can make good-quality meat and poultry tender and succulent. Roasting gives a distinctive finish to food, e.g. roast beef or roast potatoes.	It will keep meat tender, as long as the oven temperature is strictly controlled. Most boneless cuts of meat are suitable for this method.
What happens to the food as it is cooked?	All products that are baked contain water. When heated, this will start to evaporate, creating steam. To ensure that the food is baked, not 'steamed', it must be evenly and well spaced in the oven. Certain ingredients, such as yeast and baking powder, are affected by heat, which chemically changes them, giving the structure of many foods, such as bread, an edible texture.	When roasting begins, the oven is very hot. This seals the surface protein of the food, keeping food moist and adding colour and flavour. Once the food is lightly browned, the oven temperature is reduced so that the inside of the food cooks without the surface becoming hard. During cooking, the product must be basted regularly with fat or oil and cooking juices; this helps to keep the food moist and caramelises the finished product.	The meat cooks slowly until the core reaches the required temperature. The fibrous structure of the meat is tenderised and the texture changes. Thicker cuts will take longer to roast. Meat that has a covering of fat will shrink during cooking and yield fewer portions.

	Baking	Roasting	Low-temperature roasting
Is it economical? Does it save on labour?	Bulk and batch cooking is possible, with products cooked uniformly and all to the same colour. Using full (not overfull) baking trays and use of all the oven shelves will save time and energy.	It is economical as roasting is a simple, uncomplicated method of cooking that does not require multiple ingredients. Labour saving as large numbers of meals can be produced efficiently, relatively quickly and easily with minimal attention.	Cheaper cuts of meat (e.g. pork belly) can be used, because this method will tenderise them. Slow roasting uses more energy than the traditional method, because it takes longer.
Other advantages	Suitable for a wide variety of foods. Baked products are appetising: they look and smell good. Ovens have effective manual or automatic temperature controls.	Continual basting with meat juices gives a distinctive flavour. Meat juices from the joint can also be used for gravy. Ovens have effective manual or automatic temperature controls. Transparent doors make it possible to check on food during cooking. Spit roasting can be a visual process for customers.	Gives a better yield (more portions) than traditional roasting.

Roast goose with traditional accompaniments

Baking

There are three methods of baking, as shown in Table 1.6.

Principles of baking
http://bit.ly/xZ76JY

Table 1.6 Methods of baking

Method	How it works	What it is used for
Dry baking in a preheated oven	The water in the food creates steam. This combines with the oven heat to cook the food.	Cakes, pastry, jacket potatoes
Baking with increased humidity	A bowl of water is placed in the oven, or steam is injected, to increase the humidity. This increases the water content and improves quality of some food.	Bread
Baking with heat modification: placing the container of food into a **bain marie** (tray of water) within the oven	The water modifies the heat that reaches the food. The food cooks more slowly and does not overheat or burn at the edges.	Baked egg custard (the slower cooking prevents it from overcooking)

When baking and roasting it is important to use the oven correctly:

- The oven must always be **preheated** to the required temperature before putting in any food, thus allowing it to start cooking at the correct temperature.
- Only open the oven door when it is essential. The temperature inside will fall, and the product can be spoiled, for example, Yorkshire puddings.
- When batches of food are being cooked, allow 'recovery time' for the oven to return to the correct temperature. When chilled or frozen items go into an oven 'recovery time' will be longer.
- In general-purpose ovens, the top part of the oven is the hottest. Position the oven shelves to suit the requirements of the food being cooked. In convection ovens, heat is even throughout the oven.
- Use baking trays that remain level in the oven. Foods will bake unevenly and liquids will spill if the tray is not level.
- Use the space in the oven efficiently but do not overcrowd it.

Roasting

Principles of roasting
http://bit.ly/z6HCDN

Follow these guidelines when roasting food:

- Use the oven temperature and shelf settings given in the recipe.
- Adjust the cooking time according to the weight of the food (see Table 1.7 for the cooking times for various meats).
- The shape, type, bone proportion and quality of the food will also affect the cooking time.
- The centre of meat must reach the required temperature (see Table 1.8). Use a meat thermometer or probe to check the temperature.

Table 1.7 Approximate cooking times, according to weight

Meat	Degree of cooking	Approximate cooking time
Beef	Underdone (medium)	15 minutes per 0.5 kg, plus 15 minutes over
	Well done	20 minutes per 0.5 kg, plus 20 minutes over
Lamb	Cooked pink	15 minutes per 0.5 kg, plus 15 minutes over
	Cooked through	20 minutes per 0.5 kg, plus 20 minutes over
Mutton	Cooked through	20 minutes per 0.5 kg, plus 20 minutes over
Veal	Cooked through	20 minutes per 0.5 kg, plus 25 minutes over
Pork	Cooked through	25 minutes per 0.5 kg, plus 25 minutes over

For food safety reasons joints of meat that have been boned and rolled or processed in any way should not be left underdone in the centre.

Table 1.8 Internal core temperatures

Meat	Core temperature
Beef (rare)	45–47°C
Beef (medium)	50–52°C
Beef (well done)	64–70°C
Lamb	55°C
Pork	60–65°C
Veal	60°C
Venison	60°C

Health and safety

- When removing trays from the oven, use thick, dry oven cloths to protect hands.
- Do not overload baking or roasting trays or use trays of food that are too heavy to lift easily.
- Open the oven door slowly – there is likely to be a lot of steam present, which can cause burns.
- When basting a joint, or removing it from the oven, be very careful. Hot fat around the joint could burn you if it splashes. Do not have too much fat in the roasting tray.

Grilling and barbecuing

Grilling is a fast method of cookery using radiant heat. It is also known as broiling. There are four ways of grilling, as described in Table 1.9.

Table 1.9 Methods of grilling

	Equipment	Method
Grilling over heat	Grills/griddles heated from below (under-fired grills) by charcoal, gas or electricity	Grill bars are preheated and greased so that food will not stick to them. Food starts on the hottest part of the grill, and is then moved to a cooler part. Cooking time varies according to the thickness of the food and the heat of the grill. The bars char the food to give a distinctive flavour and appearance; food is turned so that both sides are charred.
Barbecuing	A grill over a fierce heat fuelled by gas, charcoal or wood	As above. If using solid fuel, allow the flames and smoke to die down before placing food on the bars – otherwise the food will be tainted. Food may be marinated before cooking or brushed with barbecue sauce during cooking
Grilling under heat	Salamander (over-fired grill)	The salamander is preheated and the bars are greased. Food items that would break up easily, such as fish, can be held in a double-sided wire grid with a hinge and a handle; this should be greased. Also used for browning, gratinating or glazing some dishes.
Grilling between heat	Electrically heated grill bars or plates	Food is grilled between the grill bars or plates.

Principles of grilling
http://bit.ly/yywpge

Grilling is only suitable for best-quality, tender meat. Inferior meat will become tough and hard to eat after grilling.

Grilling is also useful for some vegetables.

- Fierce heat reaches the surface of the food. This rapidly coagulates and seals the surface protein, helping to keep meat moist and add good colour and flavour.
- As long as the food is not pierced, meat will retain more juices when grilled than in any other method of cooking.
- The food cooks quickly, so the maximum nutrients and flavour are retained.

Meat can be grilled to various degrees of cooking. To judge how well cooked the meat is, press it and look at the colour of the juices:

- red and bloody juice: rare meat
- reddish pink juice: underdone (medium) meat
- pink juice: just-done meat
- clear juice: well-done meat.

The advantages of grilling are that:

- it is a fast method and food can be cooked quickly to order
- grilled food has a distinctive appearance and flavour

- food is visible during cooking, which helps the chef to keep control
- grills can be used in view of the customer.

Follow these guidelines when grilling food:

- Small, thin items must be cooked quickly.
- Cook all items as quickly as possible; the slower they cook, the drier they will become.
- Oil the bars and baste/brush the food to prevent dryness.

Using an under-fired grill

> **Health and safety**
> - It is advisable to use tongs, slices or palette knives to turn or lift food: tongs for heavier items (e.g. steaks), slices for lighter or delicate items (e.g. fish).
> - When reaching over to food at the back of the grill/salamander take great care not to burn your arm or hands.
> - If food is marinated in oil, drain it well before cooking, as excess oil could catch fire on the grill.

Frying

Table 1.10 explains the differences between shallow and deep frying.

Table 1.10 Shallow and deep frying

	Shallow frying	Deep frying
What exactly does it mean?	Cooking food in a small amount of preheated fat or oil. Food can be fried in a shallow pan or on a flat surface (griddle plate).	Small pieces of food are completely immersed in hot fat or oil. The heat from the fat/oil penetrates into the food (by convection) as well as cooking the surface (by conduction). This is classified as a dry method of cookery, because no liquid is used and it has a drying effect on food; moisture in the oil is driven off as visible bubbles.
Why use this method?	To brown food and give a distinctive flavour.	To give food a golden-brown colour and a crisp texture.
What happens to the food as it is cooked?	A high temperature is used, so the surface protein of the food coagulates almost instantly. This means that natural juices/moisture is retained. The food absorbs some of the frying medium (fat or oil).	Some foods are precooked (e.g. fish cakes). Deep frying them seals the surface coating by coagulating the protein in the coating; it also reheats the interior. Uncoated foods (e.g. chipped potatoes) are cooked in the oil: they can absorb a large amount of the fat, which changes the texture and nutritional content.
Is it economical? Does it save on labour?	Shallow frying/pan frying can be a quick method of cookery, especially for tender, small cuts of meats and fish. It is most suitable for short order and à la carte service.	Food can be partially cooked (blanched) and then finished in hot oil later: this saves time during busy service, and also gives a good crisp quality to chips.
How does it affect nutrition?	Some of the fat or oil is absorbed by the food during cooking: this changes the nutritional content.	
Other advantages	A very quick method of cookery, suitable for prime cuts of meat, poultry, fish and also some vegetables. (Also see below.)	A quick and easy method of cooking. A wide variety of foods can be deep fried. Coated foods are sealed quickly, so the insides do not become greasy.

Shallow frying

There are four methods of shallow frying, as shown in Table 1.11.

Principles of shallow frying
http://bit.ly/x4E2br

Follow these guidelines when shallow frying food:
- Select the correct type and size of pan. If the pan is too small, food will not brown evenly and may break up; if too large, the parts not covered by food will burn, spoiling the flavour.
- Control the temperature carefully – it should be very hot to start with, then the heat reduced.
- Clean frying pans after every use.
- When shallow frying continuously over a busy period, work in an organised and systematic way.

Practical Cookery 12th edition

Table 1.11 Methods of shallow frying

	Method	What is it used for?
Shallow fry	Food is cooked with a small amount of fat or oil, in a frying pan or sauté pan. The presentation side of the food (the side that will be facing up) is fried first – it will look better, because the fat/oil is clean at this stage. Food is then turned so that the other side cooks and changes colour.	Small cuts of fish, meat or poultry Small whole fish (up to 400 g) Eggs Pancakes Some vegetables
Sauté	As for shallow frying (above), but with one of the following variations: ● The food is tossed in the fat/oil until golden brown and cooked. ● After cooking, food may be removed from the pan, the fat discarded and then the pan is deglazed with stock or wine to form part of the sauce.	Sliced/chopped potatoes, onions or other vegetables such as mushrooms or courgettes Tender cuts of meat or poultry, tender offal
Griddle	Food is cooked on a griddle (a solid metal plate), which has been lightly oiled and preheated. Food is turned during cooking.	Hamburgers, bacon or sausages Some fish Sliced onions and tomatoes Pancakes (turned once)
Stir fry	Food is fast-fried in a wok or frying pan with a little fat or oil.	Vegetables Strips of meat, fish or poultry Noodles

When shallow frying in butter, it is best to use **clarified butter (see page 27)**. This has had impurities removed and can be heated to a higher temperature without burning.

Health and safety
- Keep sleeves rolled down, as hot fat/oil could cause burns.
- Add food to the pan carefully, away from you, to reduce splashing.
- Use a thick, clean, dry cloth when handling pans.
- Move pans carefully to avoid spilling fat/oil onto the stove.

Deep frying

Principles of deep frying
http://bit.ly/zcs2Pl

Many foods can be deep fried, including:
- small pieces of lean meat
- chicken
- whole or filleted fish
- cheese
- vegetables
- prepared items such as fish cakes, fritters, samosas or spring rolls.

Conventional deep-fried foods, except potatoes, are coated in order to:
- protect the surface of the food from intense heat and from fat/oil penetrating the food
- prevent moisture and nutrients from escaping
- modify the rapid penetration of the intense heat.

The most common coatings are:
- milk and flour
- flour/egg/breadcrumbs
- batter
- pastry.

Crumbed food should be chilled before frying: this helps to keep the crumbs attached. Immediately before cooking, shake off any excess crumbs and pat the surface to make sure the coating is in contact with the food.

Battered food should be allowed to drain before cooking, so that there is no excess batter. It needs to be lowered carefully into the hot fat.

The purpose of the fat/oil in deep frying is to achieve the distinctive texture and flavour of deep-fried food. The fat/oil used depends on the food being cooked, the temperature required and the flavours desired. Suitable fats are:
- oils (soya, vegetable, sunflower, etc.)
- clarified butter (but remember this may burn at a much lower temperature than oil)

- animal fats, e.g. lard
- a mixture of oil and clarified butter.

If solid fat is used, it needs to melt in the fryer at a low temperature (so that it does not burn), before being brought up to a frying temperature.

Method

The process for deep frying food is as follows:

1 Cut the food into small pieces of uniform size.
2 Coat the food (see above).
3 Fill the fryer with oil or fat. Commercial fryers usually have a mark showing the required oil level: it is dangerous to overfill them. Any other pan or fryer should be filled between half and two-thirds full.
4 Preheat the oil to the correct temperature, normally between 175°C and 195°C. It is always best to use a thermostatically controlled fryer. As the oil gets close to this temperature, it will become quite still, with a little haze above it. (If it gets too hot, it may catch fire, so take care.)
5 Place the food carefully into the oil when the temperature is correct. (A frying basket may be used.)
6 Fry until cooked and golden brown.
7 Food can be turned with a spider (a wide, shallow mesh spoon with a long handle) during cooking, to help it cook evenly.
8 Remove and drain well before serving.
Timing and temperature are very important. Thicker pieces of food need to cook for longer without becoming over-coloured, so the oil should be at a lower temperature. The smaller the pieces of food, the hotter the oil and the shorter the cooking time. The recommended temperature also varies depending on the fat/oil used: most are used at 180°C but pure vegetable oil and dripping may be used at 170°C and olive oil at 175°C.

Smoking point occurs when oil is overheated: between 165°C and 224°C depending on the type of oil. **Flashpoint** is when oil catches on fire: between 270°C for olive oil and 324°C for vegetable oils. Always check oil packaging for temperature advice.

Follow these guidelines when deep frying food:
- Make sure that the fat/oil is hot enough before adding food. If it is too cool, the food will absorb extra fat/oil, making it greasy and unpalatable.

- Make sure that the fat/oil is not *too* hot or the surface of the food will burn, but the inside will stay raw. The food may become dry and tough.
- Never allow the fat/oil to smoke: this gives food a bad taste and smell as well as being dangerous as 'flashpoint' temperatures are close.
- If the fat starts to foam when food is added, lift out the food and allow the temperature to adjust.
- Do not deep fry too much food at once: it is better to fry food in batches. Adding too much food at once reduces the temperature drastically. If necessary, remove excess food from the fat.
- When frying continuous batches of food, allow the temperature of the fat to recover after each batch, before adding the next one. If this is not done, the food will be pale and soggy.
- Serve food as soon as possible after frying or it will lose its crisp texture.
- During cooking, skim off crumbs regularly using a spider. The fat will last longer if this is done. (Crumbs build up and cause the fat to go off, giving it a rancid taste.)
- Do not deep fry fatty foods. Do not add wet foods to the fryer.
- Any strongly flavoured food should be fried separately from other foods, or be the last thing fried before the fat is discarded. This is because the fat/oil will take on flavours from the food.
- Small, thin pieces of food can be deep fried from frozen. Fry frozen food in smaller quantities, as it will bring down the temperature of the oil.
- Turn down the temperature of the fryer during quiet periods, to save on fuel.

When you have finished frying:
- Allow the fat/oil to cool then strain it so that there are no food particles present next time it is heated up.
- Cover the fat/oil while the fryer is not in use, so that it does not oxidise (the oxygen in the air can turn the oil or fat rancid).

Some commercial fryers have a 'cool zone'. This is a section at the base where crumbs and food particles are collected, so that they do not overcook in the oil. These crumbs must be removed when the fat is cool.

Health and safety

Deep frying can be very dangerous. Hot fat/oil can cause serious burns.

- Only use a deep fryer after proper training.
- Use a thermostatically controlled fryer with oil-level indicators rather than heating oil on a stove.
- Never leave the fryer unattended. Keep a close eye on the temperature and do not let it get too hot: never let oil reach its smoke point. If it is smoking, it is very close to its flashpoint and could catch fire.

- If a fryer catches fire, switch off and cover with a lid if possible so that the fire does not get any more oxygen. Fire extinguishing equipment should be kept near the fryer. (Wet chemical extinguisher or fire blanket.) Only use these if you have been trained in their use and never use any other type of fire extinguisher on a fryer fire.
- Stand back when placing food into hot oil and avoid putting your face, arms or hands over the fryer.
- Do not move a pan of hot oil, leave where it is until cool.
- Avoid sudden movements around fryers and do not drop anything into the fryer.

Other methods of cooking

Table 1.12 describes three methods of cooking: pot roasting, tandoori cooking and paper bag cooking.

Table 1.13 describes sous vide and microwave cookery and explains their advantages and disadvantages.

Table 1.12 Pot roasting, tandoori and paper bag cooking

	Pot roasting (*poêlé*)	Tandoori cooking	Paper bag cooking (*en papillotte*)
What exactly does it mean?	Cooking food on a bed of root vegetables in a covered pan.	Cooking by dry heat at up to 375°C in a clay oven (tandoor). The heat source is at the base of the oven, but the clay radiates heat evenly throughout. Food is placed in vertically; no oil or fat is used. Naan (traditional Indian flat bread) is placed on the inside wall of the oven to cook.	Food is tightly sealed in oiled greaseproof paper or foil so that no steam escapes during cooking. The bags are tightly sealed, placed on a lightly greased tray and cooked in a hot oven. Food is served in the bag, to be opened by or in front of the customer.
Why use this method?	It retains the maximum flavour of all ingredients.	The cooking process and the marinade (if used) give a distinctive flavour. Food cooks quickly.	Maximum flavour and nutritional value are retained.
Preparing food for cooking	The meat is coated generously with oil or butter before the pan is covered.	Food may be marinated for between 20 minutes and 2 hours before cooking. It may also be brushed with marinade during cooking.	Thick items (e.g. red mullet) should be quickly partly precooked, usually by grilling or shallow frying.
Using herbs and spices	Mix herbs with the bed of root vegetables. These can be used with a good stock as a base for the sauce.	Marinades may include onions, garlic, herbs, spices and oil, yoghurt, wine or lemon juice. A red colouring agent may be used. Marinating tenderises the food.	Finely cut vegetables, herbs and spices may be placed in the bag.
Other guidelines	Use a pan of the correct size for the food to be cooked.	If a tandoor is not available, an oven, grill rotisserie or barbecue can be used, following the principles of tandoori cooking. In this case, the spices must be cooked briefly over a fierce heat before they are added to the marinade.	

Sealing a parcel for cooking *en papillotte*

Table 1.13 Sous vide and microwave cooking

	Sous vide	Microwave cooking
What exactly does it mean?	A professional cooking method in which food is vacuum-sealed and cooked in plastic pouches.	Cooking, defrosting or reheating food using electromagnetic waves (microwaves).
Why use this method?	It extends the useable shelf life of food. The final product retains its texture, flavour and appearance.	It is a quick and convenient way of defrosting/heating/cooking food.
What happens to the food as it is cooked?	It is pasteurised by being heated in a water bath to 75°C and then quickly cooled below 3°C: this process slows the multiplication of bacteria. It is stored chilled: the plastic barrier means that the food oxidises less, and there is less contact with possible contaminants. When required, the packet of food is reheated in a water bath.	The microwaves penetrate 5 cm from each side into the food. They agitate molecules of water and particles of food, making them move around. This causes friction among the particles, which generates heat in the food.
Is it economical? Does it save on labour?	Excellent for efficiency. Single servings of meals can be prepared one or two days in advance, and can be retrieved and heated quickly when needed. Standardised recipes may be used, ensuring quality regardless of individuals' cooking skills. Several meals can be pasteurised or regenerated in the same water bath, reducing the amount of pot washing. Traditional heat methods are not used, reducing kitchen temperatures and the cost of cooling.	It can be up to 70 per cent faster than other cooking methods, and it enables fast defrosting. It is economical on fuel. Food can also be cooked in the serving dish, which reduces the amount of dishwashing. Hot meals can be available all day, and can even be self-service, keeping costs down but customers satisfied.
How does it affect nutrition?	Certain nutrients, such as vitamins, can be lost by this method of cookery but others, such as water-soluble vitamins, may be retained.	Food is cooked very quickly, so nutrients and flavour are retained.
Other advantages		Minimises shrinkage and drying out of food.
Disadvantages	There are some food safety issues (see below).	Not suitable for some foods and some types of container such as metal. Microwave ovens are quite small and so only small quantities can be cooked. Food is not browned unless the microwave has a browning element.

Sous vide

Sous vide was developed by George Pralus at the Restaurant Troisgros in Roanne, France, in 1967. It is a technique that must be managed carefully, as there are some food safety risks. The key problems are:

- It is impossible to smell vacuum packaged food and judge whether it is fresh.
- It is impossible to check the core temperature of food that is hermetically sealed in a package.

Vacuum packaging prevents **aerobic bacteria** from growing on the food. However, some bacteria are of a different type: **anaerobic**. These multiply where there is a absence of oxygen, such as inside a vacuum pouch.

Sous vide uses relatively low temperatures, and anaerobic bacteria can thrive in these conditions.

To reduce the risk of food poisoning, follow these guidelines:

- Use the freshest, highest quality ingredients in sous vide packages. Fresh ingredients will have fewer bacteria to start with.
- Calibrate equipment every day.
- Check all seals and packages for leaks.
- Raw packages must not be kept for more than *two days* before they are pasteurised.
- Pasteurisation must take place above 75°C.
- Packages must be cooled to below 3°C within *two hours* of being pasteurised.
- Store packages below 3°C, in covered containers.
- Label packages with the date and time of packaging, pasteurisation and expiration.
- Use packages by the use by date or discard them.

Sous vide is widely used by industrial food producers: they can package food with a minimum of processing, and it will retain its flavour, texture and size.

Fresh sous vide is also used in some restaurants, mostly at the 'high end'. The technique is less popular in the majority of restaurant kitchens because of the cost of the equipment and complexity of the technique.

Microwave cooking

Microwaves are similar to the waves that carry television signals, but are at a higher frequency.

Follow these guidelines when using a microwave oven:

- Use glass, ceramic or plastic containers for food. Do *not* use metal unless the oven manufacturer states that you can.
- For the best results, use round, shallow containers with straight sides.
- Keep food level; do not pile it up in mounds.
- Leave enough space in the container to allow the food to be stirred.
- Cover most foods during cooking, e.g. with microwave clingfilm. This helps the food cook quickly and stay moist. It also prevents splashing and condensation in the oven.

- Some foods, and some container materials, absorb energy faster than others – this means they will heat up more quickly.
- Food with a high water content will cook more quickly than dry food.
- The colder the food is to start with, the longer it will take to heat up.
- The denser the food is, the longer it will take to heat up. Turn dense foods (e.g. potatoes) during cooking.

- Thick or deep food is more difficult to heat through, because microwaves only penetrate 5 cm from each side of the food.
- The weight or quantity of food in the oven will affect the cooking time necessary.
- The shape of the food (e.g. a liquid could be in a tall container or a low flat one) will affect the cooking time.
- Even-shaped items of food will cook uniformly throughout. If items are an uneven shape, arrange them with the thickest part at the outside of the dish.

If there is a large quantity of food, or it is very dense or frozen, it is a good idea to heat it in stages, with rest intervals in between.

Microwave ovens cook more quickly round the edges of the food than in the middle so food should be stirred during cooking, if possible, to ensure even cooking. For dishes that cannot be stirred:

- Rotate the dish by a quarter turn occasionally.
- Place small pieces of microwave clingfilm over the parts that are cooking before others.
- Use even-shaped containers and food of uniform thickness, no more than 5 cm.
- Arrange small items or dishes in a circle and turn each one during cooking.

Generally, it is better to undercook food than to overcook it. However, for food safety reasons items such as meat and poultry must reach the correct core temperature when they are cooked *and* reheated: *use a thermometer (probe) to check.*

There are particular issues when microwaving some foods. Examples are described in Table 1.14.

Health and safety
- Follow manufacturer's instructions.
- Do not run a microwave oven when it is empty.
- Remove clingfilm covers carefully from hot dishes as steam builds up under the film. Pull the clingfilm towards you, so that the steam escapes in the other direction.
- Microwavable plastic pouches need to be cut open after cooking. They will be hot and soft so need handling with care. Put the pouch on a plate before cutting it open.
- Microwave ovens should be inspected/tested regularly.
- If the door seal is damaged, do not use the microwave.

Table 1.14 Microwaving different foods

Food	Issues	Guidance for microwaving
Whole potatoes, tomatoes, peppers, unpeeled apples	Pressure may build up inside the item until it bursts.	Pierce or score the skin before cooking – this will release pressure.
Eggs	Eggs in their shells will burst in the microwave.	Never cook eggs in their shells. Poached or fried eggs (in a browning dish) can be cooked in the microwave: the yolk must be lightly pricked to release pressure. Scrambled eggs can be cooked, but stir frequently and remove them before they are done. Let them stand while they finish cooking.
Deep-fried food	It is impossible to deep fry in a microwave, because you cannot control the temperature of the fat.	Breadcrumbed food can be microwave cooked in a tablespoon of oil, which will give an acceptable but less crisp alternative.
Yorkshire puddings, choux pastry	It is impossible to produce a soft interior with a crispy crust.	Cannot be cooked in the microwave.
Meringue	Microwave cooking will not produce a crisp or coloured meringue.	Meringue toppings (e.g. lemon meringue pie) can be cooked in the microwave if required soft and uncoloured.
Kidney, liver	Thin membranes on the food may split with a popping sound during cooking.	The dish should be lightly covered to prevent spattering; the popping sound is not a problem.
Food with bones	Bones act as tunnels, storing up pressure, and the food around the bone pops and spits.	Only microwave with care and turn frequently.
Poultry with skin	Skin may split with a popping sound during cooking and does not colour.	Perforate with a fork and cover before cooking.
Fish	It is easy to overcook and become dry.	Stop cooking before the fish is done. Let it stand – it will finish cooking and change from opaque to flaky.
Joints of meat or chicken	These are large and dense and may need a longer cooking at a lower setting to allow heat to conduct.	Allow to stand for 10–15 minutes after microwaving. The food will continue to cook and heat will spread evenly throughout the food.
Moist food, e.g. stew	May cook/heat unevenly (edges cooking first).	Cover the food, e.g. with loose clingfilm. If there is a large proportion of liquid, stir during cooking – only cover three-quarters of the dish, so that you can stir through the gap.
Food containing sugar	Sugar heats slowly at first, then suddenly becomes very hot very quickly, especially if it is dissolved in liquid. It attracts microwaves.	Do not microwave these foods for too long: the sugar will burn.

2 Stocks, soups and sauces

This chapter is relevant to the following units:

- Prepare, cook and finish basic hot sauces (NVQ)
- Prepare, cook and finish basic soups (NVQ)
- Make basic stocks (NVQ)
- Prepare and cook stocks, soups and sauces (VRQ).

Health, safety and hygiene

For information on maintaining a safe and secure working environment, a professional and hygienic appearance, and clean food production areas, equipment and utensils, as well as food hygiene, please refer to Chapters 14 and 15. Additional health and safety points are as follows.

- After stock, sauces, gravies and soups have been rapidly cooled in a blast chiller they should be stored in a refrigerator at a temperature below 5°C.
- If they are to be deep-frozen they should be labelled and dated, and stored below -18°C.
- When taken from storage they must be boiled for at least 2 minutes before being used.

- They must not be reheated more than once.
- Ideally, stocks should be made fresh, and, if not used the same day, chilled rapidly and stored hygienically under refrigeration.
- If stocks are not given the correct care and attention, particularly with regard to the soundness of the ingredients used, they can easily become contaminated and a risk to health.
- Never store a stock, sauce, gravy or soup above eye level as this could lead to an accident by someone spilling the contents over themselves.

Stocks

Stock is the basis of all meat sauces, gravies, soups and purées. It is really just the flavour of meat extracted by long and gentle simmering, or the infusion/transfer of flavour from an ingredient such as fish, vegetables or shellfish. In making stock, it should be remembered that the objective is to draw the goodness out of the solids and into the liquor, imparting the desired level of flavour and other elements that are important to the end product, whether it be a soup, sauce or perhaps a reduction.

Stocks are the foundation of many important kitchen preparations; for this reason, the greatest possible care should be taken in their production, and stocks, bouillons and nages should only be made with high-quality ingredients. A good, well-flavoured stock cannot be made with inferior ingredients.

Key points to remember when making stocks

- Unsound meat or bones and decaying vegetables will give stock an unpleasant flavour and cause it to deteriorate quickly.
- Scum should be removed; otherwise it will boil into the stock and spoil the colour and flavour.
- Fat should be skimmed off, otherwise the stock will taste greasy.
- Stock should always simmer gently; if it is allowed to boil quickly, it will evaporate and go cloudy/milky.

- Salt should not be added to stock.
- When making chicken stock the bones will need to be soaked first to remove the blood that is in the cavity.
- If stock is to be kept, strain it and cool quickly, then place it in the refrigerator.

Nages

A nage is a light but well-flavoured stock, often used for cooking fish and other seafood. The nage will enhance the flavours of dishes.

Cooking stocks

When cooking predominantly meat stocks, be mindful that they will contain collagen. This is the main fibrous component of skin, tendons, connective tissue and bones. If you have cooked at higher temperatures (e.g. boiling), the collagen content of the sauce will be high, giving you a viscous sauce earlier in the reduction process; due to the thickness of such a sauce, it is impossible to reduce it further without burning.

When making a glaze ensure that the base stock used at the start has a medium extraction of collagen (not too thick). This will yield a more flavoursome result and the glaze will be less viscous.

Sauces

A sauce is a liquid that has been thickened by either:
- *beurre manié*
- egg yolks
- roux
- cornflour, arrowroot or starch
- cream and/or butter added to reduced stock
- rice (in the case of some shellfish bisques)
- reducing cooking liquor or stock.

We will take a closer look at some of these below.

All sauces should be smooth, glossy in appearance, definite in taste and light in texture; the thickening medium should be used in moderation.

Beurre manié

Beurre manié is a paste made from equal quantities of soft butter and flour, which is then added to a simmering liquid while whisking continuously to prevent lumps forming.

Egg yolks

Egg yolks are used as a basis for a liaison, which is traditionally used to thicken a classic velouté (see recipes 24 and 25). Both egg yolks and cream are mixed together and added to the sauce/velouté off the boil; this mixture is intended to thicken, however it is essential to keep stirring it, otherwise the eggs will curdle. Once thickening is achieved the sauce/velouté must be removed and served immediately. *The liquid must not be allowed to boil or simmer.*

Egg yolks are used in mayonnaise (page 97), hollandaise sauce (recipe 47) and custard sauces (page 486). Refer to the appropriate recipe, though, as the yolks are used in a different manner for each sauce. When making mayonnaise (where the yolks are not cooked) or hollandaise (where temperatures remain low), it is advisable to use pasteurised eggs for food safety reasons.

Sabayon

A sabayon is a mixture of egg yolks and a little water whisked to the ribbon stage over a gentle heat. The mixture should be the consistency of thick cream. It is added to sauces to assist their glazing.

Cornflour, arrowroot or starch

Cornflour, arrowroot or starch (such as potato starch) is used for thickening gravy and sauces. These are diluted with water, stock or milk, then stirred into the boiling liquid, allowed to reboil for a few minutes and then strained.

Roux

A roux is a combination of fat and flour, which are cooked together. There are three degrees to which a roux may be cooked (white, blond and brown) and one approach known as 'continental' roux style (see below).

A boiling liquid should never be added to a hot roux as the result may be lumpy and the person making the sauce may be scalded by the steam produced. If allowed to stand for a time over a moderate heat, a sauce made with a roux may become thin due to a chemical change (dextrinisation) in the flour.

White roux

This is used for white (béchamel) sauce and soups. Equal quantities of butter and flour are cooked together without colouring for a few minutes, to a sandy texture. Alternatively, use polyunsaturated vegetable margarine or make a roux with vegetable oil, using equal quantities of oil to flour. This does give a slack roux but enables the liquid to be incorporated easily.

Blond roux

This is used for veloutés, tomato sauce and soups. Equal quantities of butter or vegetable oil and flour are cooked for a little longer than a white roux, but without colouring, to a sandy texture.

Making a blond roux and a velouté http://bit.ly/weUClc

Brown roux

This was traditionally used for brown (espagnole) sauce and soups and is slightly browned at the roux-making stage.

Continental roux

This is a very easy and straightforward thickening agent that can be frozen and used as a quick thickener during service or à la minute.

Mix equal quantities of flour and vegetable oil together to a paste and place in the oven at 140°C. Cook the mixture, mixing it in on itself periodically until a sandy texture is achieved. Remove and allow to cool to room temperature. When it is cool enough to handle, form into a sausage shape using a double layer of cling film. Chill, then freeze.

To use, remove from the freezer and shave a little off the end of the log. Whisk it into the boiling sauce (as the flour is already cooked it is not necessary to add it slowly to prevent lumping as this will not occur). Once the desired thickness has been achieved, pass and serve.

Thickening sauces with sauce flour

Sauces may be thickened using this flour, which is a specially milled flour that does not require any addition of fat to prevent it from going lumpy. It is useful when making sauces for those on a low-fat diet.

Other sauces

- Vegetable or fruit purées are known as a coulis. No other thickening agent is used.
- Blood was traditionally used in recipes such as jugged hare, but is used rarely today.
- Cooking liquor from certain dishes and/or stock can be reduced to give a light sauce.

Espagnole

This is a traditional brown sauce made from brown roux and brown stock, simmered for several hours and skimmed frequently to produce a refined sauce. Because of the lengthy, time-consuming process and a move away from heavy flour-based sauces, in many kitchens a reduced veal stock (see recipe 30) is used as a base for most brown sauces.

Demi-glace

Demi-glace is used as the base for a number of derivative sauces. Current practice in most kitchens is to use either stock-reduced sauce, jus-lié or a commercially produced powder or granule-based product.

Salsa

Salsa is the Spanish word for a sauce. A wide variety of ingredients can be used and chunky mixtures made to serve with grilled or fried fish, meat and poultry dishes. Recipes 43 and 44 are for salsa.

Butter as a sauce

Clarified butter

Clarified butter is butter that has been melted and skimmed. After that, the fat element of the butter is carefully poured off, leaving the milky residue behind. This gives a clear fat that can reach higher temperatures than normal butter without burning, but that can also be used to nap over steamed vegetables, or poached or grilled fish.

Beurre noisette

Beurre noisette basically translates to 'nut butter', and its flavour comes from the caramelisation of the milk element in the butter solids. It is achieved by placing diced hard butter into a moderately hot pan and bringing to a foam (a good indication that it is ready). Like clarified butter, this can be served with poached or steamed vegetables and fish, but the classic use is with shallow-fried fish. If you take the butter a little further, however, and almost burn the sediment, then add a little vinegar, this is called black butter (*beurre noir*) and is traditionally served with skate.

Beurre fondu/emulsion

This is basically an emulsion between fat and liquid – for example, melted butter emulsified with any nage described above will give you a slightly thicker sauce that can be used to coat vegetables or fish. However, to intensify the flavour, if you were to add a *beurre noisette* to the pan, or your cooking medium was clarified butter, you could start cooking the product in the pan with the fat. Once it is half cooked, stop the cooking by adding a nage and then bring quickly to the boil. Through this boiling process the fat and the stock will become emulsified, which gives an emulsified sauce made in the pan, but with the cooking juices also added.

Compound butter sauces

Compound butters are made by mixing the flavouring ingredients (e.g. herbs) into softened butter, which can then be shaped into a roll 2 cm in diameter, placed in wet greaseproof paper, foil or clingfilm, hardened in a refrigerator and cut into 0.5 cm slices when required.

- Parsley butter: chopped parsley and lemon juice.
- Herb butter: mixed herbs (chives, tarragon, fennel, dill) and lemon juice.
- Garlic butter: mashed to a paste.

Compound butters are served with grilled and some fried fish, and with grilled meats.

Flavoured oils

Flavoured oils are used to enhance certain types of food and dishes, especially pasta, fish and salads. Recipes 49–57 are for flavoured oils.

Soups

There are many ways to classify soup, whether it be a classic velouté thickened with a liaison, a purée of lentils with ham hock stock or a broth with a clear liquid; even the crystal clarity of consommé still graces our modern restaurant tables. However, the fundamental foundation of today's dining is a lighter and more sophisticated approach. Therefore, a combination of the above, with a careful approach to thickening, will yield a light and flavoursome soup.

The principles of soup making

Though the perfection of soups can take experience, the basic principles of soup making are quite simple to follow.

Most soup making begins by preparing a stock (see above).

The underlying flavours of a broth's foundation ingredients are enhanced by the herbs and seasonings added. In many cases, this flavour base begins by preparing a mixture of flavouring elements cooked in a little fat or oil; because of their aromatic properties and flavours, most soups begin this phase with a combination of onion, garlic, leeks and carrots (this is called a mirepoix) or aromats. The resulting broth is the foundation of all soups.

Health-conscious eaters should look for clear broth soups containing vegetables, beans and lean protein like chicken, fish or lean beef. Italian minestrone, bouillabaisse and gazpacho are excellent choices. Cream-based soups can often be adapted by using yoghurt or low-fat crème fraiche to produce a soup that is lower in fat.

Types of soup

- Bisque: a very rich soup with a creamy consistency; usually made of lobster or shellfish (crab, shrimp, etc.).
- Bouillabaisse: a Mediterranean fish soup/stew, made of multiple types of seafood, olive oil, water, and seasonings like garlic, onions, tomato and parsley.
- Broth: an unpassed soup containing vegetables and sometimes meat or fish (e.g. Scotch broth).
- Chowder: a hearty North American soup, usually with a seafood base.
- Consommé: a clear, unthickened soup, with an intense flavour derived from meat or fish bones, or even a vegetable base, and a good stock, clarified by a process of careful straining.
- Cream: based on a velouté or purée, and finished with cream.
- Dashi: the Japanese equivalent of consommé; made of giant seaweed, or konbu, dried bonito and water.
- Gazpacho: a Spanish tomato-vegetable soup served ice cold.
- Minestrone: an Italian vegetable-based soup.
- Potage: a French term referring to a thick soup.
- Puréed soup: a soup of vegetable base that has been puréed in a food mill or blender; typically altered after milling with the addition of broth, cream, butter, sour cream or coconut milk.
- Velouté: a velvety French sauce made with stock; synonymous with soup in many cases and thickened with a liaison (see thickenings, below).
- Vichyssoise: a simple, flavourful puréed potato and leek soup, thickened with the potato itself. Traditionally this is leek and potato soup, if served hot a little cream or crème fraiche may be added to give a richness to the soup; however, served cold, it is classified as vichyssoise and if fat is added to this preparation the dish would leave a fatty residue on the palate and offer a less than clear mouth feel.

Soups may be served for luncheon, dinner, supper and snack meals. A portion is usually between 200 and 250 ml, depending on the type of soup and the number of courses to follow.

Table 3.1 Guide to soups, their preparation and presentation

Soup type	Base	Passed or unpassed?	Finish	Example
Clear	Stock	Strained	Usually garnished	Consommé (recipe 82)
Broth	Stock Cut vegetables	Unpassed	Chopped herbs	Scotch broth (recipe 58) Minestrone (recipe 60)
Purée	Stock Fresh vegetables Pulses	Passed	Croutons	Lentil soup (recipe 79) Potato soup (recipe 71)
Velouté	Blond roux Vegetables Stock	Passed	Liaison of yolk and cream	Pea velouté (recipe 80)
Cream	Stock and vegetables Vegetable purée	Passed	Cream, milk or yoghurt	Cream of vegetable (recipe 61) Cream of fresh pea (recipe 62) Cream of tomato (recipe 63)
Bisque	Shellfish Fish stock	Passed	Cream	Prawn bisque (recipe 84)
Miscellaneous				Clam chowder (recipe 83) Gazpacho (recipe 74)

White or brown stock

energy	kcal	fat	sat fat	carb	sugar	protein	fibre
4 KJ	1 kcal	0.0 g	0.0 g	0.2 g	0.0 g	0.0 g	0.0 g

	Makes ›	4 litres
raw meaty bones		1 kg
water		4 litres
onion, carrot, celery, leek		400 g
bouquet garni		1
peppercorns		8

For white stock

1. Chop the bones into small pieces, and remove any fat or marrow.
2. Place the bones in a large stock pot, cover with cold water and bring to the boil.
3. Drain. Wash off the bones under cold water, then clean the pot.
4. Return the bones to the cleaned pot, add fresh water and reboil.
5. Skim as and when required, wipe round inside the pot and simmer gently.
6. After 2 hours, add the washed, peeled whole vegetables, bouquet garni and peppercorns.
7. Simmer for 6–8 hours. Skim, strain and, if to be kept, cool quickly and refrigerate.

For brown stock

1. Chop the beef bones and brown well on all sides either by placing in a roasting tin in the oven, or carefully browning in a little fat in a frying pan.
2. Drain off any fat and place the bones in a stock pot.
3. Brown any sediment that may be in the bottom of the tray, deglaze (swill out) with 0.5 litres of boiling water, simmer for a few minutes and add to the bones.
4. Add the cold water, bring to the boil and skim. Simmer for 2 hours.
5. Wash, peel and roughly cut the vegetables, fry in a little fat until brown, strain and add to the bones.
6. Add the bouquet garni and peppercorns.
7. Simmer for 6–8 hours. Skim and strain.

> **Chef's tip**
> A few squashed tomatoes and washed mushroom trimmings can also be added to brown stocks to improve flavour, as can a calf's foot and/or a knuckle of bacon. If bacon is used, dishes made with the stock will not be suitable for some religious diets.

Making brown stock
http://bit.ly/A6F9q4

2 White chicken stock

Makes ⟩	4 litres
chicken carcass/wings	5 kg
onions, peeled	1½
carrots, peeled	2
cloves of garlic, crushed	2
leeks, washed and blemishes removed	1
celery sticks	2
bay leaf	1
sprigs of thyme, small	1
whole white peppercorns	5 g
water, cold	7 litres

1 Remove any excess fat from the chicken carcasses and wash off under cold water.

2 Place all the bones into a pot that will hold all the ingredients, leaving 5 cm at the top to skim.

3 Add all the other ingredients and cold water, and bring to a simmer; immediately skim all the fat that rises to the surface.

4 Turn the heat off and allow the bones and vegetables to sink. Once this has happened, turn the heat back on, skim and bring to just under a simmer, making as little movement as possible to create more of an infusion than a stock. Skim continuously.

5 Leave to simmer for 2 hours then pass through a fine sieve into a clean pan; reduce down rapidly, until you have about 4 litres remaining.

3 Fish stock
(fumet de poisson)

fish boiling

energy	kcal	fat	sat fat	carb	sugar	protein	fibre
4 KJ	1 kcal	0.0 g	0.0 g	0.2 g	0.2 g	0.0 g	0.0 g

*

	Makes ⟩	4 litres
butter or oil		50 g
onions, sliced		200 g
white fish bones (preferably sole, whiting or turbot)		2 kg
lemon, juice of		½
peppercorns		8
bay leaf		1
parsley stalks		
water		4.5 litres

1 Melt the butter, or heat the oil, in a thick-bottomed pan.

2 Add the onions, the well-washed fish bones and the remainder of the ingredients except the water.

3 Cover with greaseproof paper and a lid; sweat (cook gently without colouring) for 5 minutes.

4 Add the water, bring to the boil, skim and simmer for 20 minutes, then strain. A longer cooking time will spoil the flavour.

Making fish stock
http://bit.ly/xzrbyn

Wash the bones thoroughly

Simmer for 20 minutes

Skim during cooking

Healthy eating tip

- Use an oil rich in unsaturates to lightly oil the pan. Drain off any excess after the frying is complete.

* per 100 ml

4 White vegetable stock

vegetables boiling

energy	kcal	fat	sat fat	carb	sugar	protein	fibre
4 KJ	1 kcal	0.0 g	0.0 g	0.2 g	0.2g	0.0 g	0.0 g

Makes >	4 litres
onions	250 g
carrots	250 g
celery	250 g
leeks	250 g
water	4 litres

Try something different
White fungi stock: add 200–400 g white mushrooms, stalks and trimmings (all well washed) to the recipe.

1 Roughly chop all the vegetables.
2 Place all the ingredients into a saucepan, add the water, bring to the boil.
3 Allow to simmer for approximately 1 hour.
4 Skim if necessary. Strain and use.

5 Brown vegetable stock

vegetables shallow frying, boiling

Makes approx. >	4 litres
onions	300 g
carrots	300 g
celery	300 g
leeks	300 g
sunflower oil	180 ml
tomatoes	150 g
mushroom trimmings	150 g
peppercorns	18
water	4 litres
yeast extract	15 g

1 Cut the vegetables into mirepoix. Fry the mirepoix in the oil until golden brown.
2 Drain and place in a suitable saucepan. Add all the other ingredients except the yeast extract and water.
3 Cover with the water and bring to the boil.
4 Add the yeast extract and simmer gently for approximately 1 hour. Then skim if necessary and use.

Try something different
Brown fungi stock: add 200–400 g open or field mushrooms, stalks and trimmings (all well washed) to the recipe.

6 Beef jus

Makes approx. >	1 litre
mushrooms, finely sliced	750 g
butter	100 g
shallots, finely sliced	350 g
beef trim, diced	350 g
sherry vinegar	100 ml
red wine	700 ml
chicken stock	500 ml
beef stock	1 litre

1 Caramelise the mushrooms in foaming butter, strain, then put aside in a saucepan.

2 Caramelise the shallots in foaming butter, strain, then put in the same saucepan.

3 In another pan, caramelise the beef trim until golden brown.

4 Place the beef trim with the vegetables in the saucepan. Deglaze the frying pans with the vinegar, then add to the pan with the beef, shallots and mushrooms.

5 Reduce the wine by half and add to the other ingredients.

6 Add the stock, then reduce to sauce consistency.

7 Pass through a sieve, then chill and store until needed.

7 Lamb jus

Makes approx. >	1 litre
fresh thyme	50 g
bay leaves, fresh	2
garlic	1 bulb
red wine	500 ml
lamb bones	1 kg
veal bones	0.5 kg
white onions, peeled	3
large carrots, peeled	4
celery sticks	3
leeks, chopped	2
tomato puree	3 tbsp
water	approx. 3 litres

1 Pre-heat the oven to 175°C. Place the herbs, garlic and wine in a large, deep container. Place all the bones on a roasting rack on top of the container of herbs and wine, and roast in the oven for 50–60 minutes. When the bones are completely roasted and have taken on a dark golden-brown appearance, remove from oven.

2 Place all the ingredients in a large pot and cover with cold water. Put the pot onto the heat and bring to the simmer; immediately skim all fat that rises to the surface.

3 Turn the heat off and allow the bones and vegetables to sink. Once this has happened, turn the heat back on and bring to

just under a simmer, making as little movement as possible to create more of an infusion than a stock. Simmer for 6 hours, skimming regularly.

4 Pass through a fine sieve, place in the blast chiller until cold and then in the refrigerator overnight. Next day, reduce down rapidly, until you have about 1 litre remaining.

8 Chicken jus

chicken, lamb roasting, boiling, simmering

Makes approx. ⟩	1 litre
chicken stock	600 ml
lamb jus or stock	600 ml
chicken wings, chopped small	300 g
vegetable oil	60 ml
shallots, sliced	100 g
butter	50 g
tomatoes, chopped	200 g
white wine vinegar	40 ml
red wine vinegar	75 ml
tarragon	3 g
chervil	3 g

1 Put the lamb jus and chicken stock in a pan and reduce to 1 litre.
2 Roast the chicken wings in oil until slightly golden.
3 Add the shallots and butter, and cook until lightly browned (do not allow the butter to burn).
4 Strain off the butter and return the bones to the pan; deglaze with the vinegar and add tomatoes.
5 Ensure the bottom of the pan is clean. Add the reduced stock/ jus and simmer for 15 minutes.
6 Pass through a sieve, then reduce to sauce consistency.

7 Remove from the heat and infuse with the herbs for 5 minutes.
8 Pass through a chinois and then muslin cloth.

9 Red wine jus

 shallow frying, boiling, simmering

Makes approx. ⟩	1 litre
shallots, sliced	150 g
butter	50 g
garlic, halved	10 g
red wine vinegar	100 ml
red wine	500 ml
chicken stock	700 ml
lamb or beef jus	500 ml
bay leaves	2
sprig of thyme	1

1 Caramelise the shallots in foaming butter until golden, adding the garlic at the end.
2 Strain through a colander and then put back into the pan and deglaze with the vinegar.
3 Reduce the red wine by half along with the stock and jus, at the same time as colouring the shallots.
4 When everything is done, combine and simmer for 20 minutes.
5 Pass through a sieve and reduce to sauce consistency.

6 Infuse the herbs for 5 minutes.
7 Pass through muslin cloth and store until needed.

10 Reduction of stock (glaze)

boiling, simmering

A glaze is a stock, fond or nage that has been reduced: that is, much of the water content is removed by gently simmering. The solid residues, and all the flavour, stay in the glaze.

Any kind of stock can be used, but it is important to be careful if using meat stock. Meat stock contains collagen; if the stock is cooked at boiling temperature, there will be a lot of collagen in the glaze. This means the sauce will become thick more quickly than non-meat glazes. It will then be impossible to reduce it any more without burning it.

Glazes have a strong flavour and contain a lot of salt, so only use small amounts.

11 Roast gravy
(jus rôti)

beef, veal — roasting, boiling, simmering

energy	kcal	fat	sat fat	carb	sugar	protein	fibre	*
504 KJ	120 kcal	10.0 g	1.3 g	1.8 g	0.0g	5.6 g	0.0 g	

Makes >	1 litre
raw veal bones or beef and veal trimmings	500 g
stock or water	1.25 litres
onions, chopped	125 g
celery, chopped	60 g
carrots, chopped	125 g

Tip

For preference, use beef bones for roast beef gravy and the appropriate bones for lamb, veal, mutton and pork.

Healthy eating tips

- Use an unsaturated oil (sunflower or vegetable). Lightly oil the pan.
- Season with the minimum amount of salt.

1 Chop the bones and brown in the oven, or brown in a little oil on top of the stove in a frying pan. Drain off all the fat.
2 Place the bones in a saucepan with the stock or water.
3 Bring to the boil, skim and allow to simmer.
4 Lightly brown the vegetables, which may be fried in a little fat in a frying pan and then add to the bones.
5 Simmer for 1½–2 hours.
6 Correct the colour and seasoning. Strain and skim off all fat.

Roast gravy is usually produced by deglazing the roasting tin after the joint is cooked, during the relaxing period before carving. The gravy is enhanced by the meat sediment left in the roasting tin.

* Using sunflower oil, for 4 portions

12 Thickened gravy
(jus-lié)

boiling, simmering

1 Start with roast gravy (recipe 11) or reduced veal stock (recipe 30). Add 2 tsp tomato purée, a few mushroom trimmings and a pinch of thyme and simmer for 10–15 minutes.
2 Stir some arrowroot diluted in cold water into the simmering gravy.
3 Reboil, simmer for 5–10 minutes and pass through a strainer.

Try something different
Add a little rosemary, thyme or lavender.

13 Pepper sauce
(sauce poivrade)

shallow frying, simmering

energy	kcal	fat	sat fat	carb	sugar	protein	fibre
247 KJ	60 kcal	5.3 g	2.5 g	2.6 g	2.0g	0.5 g	0.6 g

Portions >	4	10
butter or oil	25 g	60 g
onions, chopped into mirepoix	50 g	125 g
carrots, chopped into mirepoix	50 g	125 g
celery, chopped into mirepoix	50 g	125 g
bay leaf	1	1
sprig of thyme		
white wine	2 tbsp	5 tbsp
vinegar	2 tbsp	5 tbsp
mignonette pepper	5 g	12 g
demi-glace, *jus-lié* or reduced stock	250 ml	625 ml
cream	25 ml	65 ml

1 Melt the butter or heat the oil in a small sauteuse.
2 Add the vegetables and herbs (mirepoix) and allow to brown.
3 Pour off the fat.
4 Add the wine, vinegar and pepper.
5 Reduce by half. Add the demi-glace and cream.
6 Simmer for 20–30 minutes. Correct the seasoning.

Note
Mignonette pepper is coarsely ground black pepper. The softer green or pink peppercorns may be used instead. Usually served with joints or cuts of venison.

Healthy eating tips
- Use an unsaturated oil (sunflower or vegetable). Lightly oil the pan.
- Skim the fat from the finished dish.
- Season with the minimum amount of salt.

14 Chasseur sauce
(sauce chasseur)

bulbs, fungi, vegetable fruits boiling, shallow frying

energy	kcal	fat	sat fat	carb	sugar	protein	fibre
227 KJ	55 kcal	5.3 g	2.5 g	1.4 g	1.2 g	0.5 g	0.5 g

Portions ⟩	4	10
butter or oil	25 g	60 g
shallots, chopped	10 g	25 g
garlic clove, chopped (optional)	1	1
button mushrooms, sliced	50 g	125 g
white wine, dry	60 ml	150 ml
tomatoes, skinned, deseeded, diced	100 g	250 g
demi-glace, *jus-lié* or reduced stock	250 ml	625 ml
parsley and tarragon, chopped		

1 Melt the butter or heat the oil in a small sauteuse.
2 Add the shallots and cook gently for 2–3 minutes without colour.
3 Add the garlic and the mushrooms, cover and cook gently for 2–3 minutes.
4 Strain off the fat.
5 Add the wine and reduce by half.
6 Add the demi-glace; simmer for 5–10 minutes. Add the tomatoes.
7 Correct the seasoning. Add the tarragon and parsley.

May be served with fried steaks, chops, chicken, etc.

Healthy eating tips
- Use an unsaturated oil (sunflower or vegetable). Lightly oil the pan.
- Skim the fat from the finished dish.
- Season with the minimum amount of salt.

Piquant   Robert   Chasseur

Italian   Madeira   Brown onion

Recipes 14 to 19

Practical Cookery 12th edition

15 Italian sauce
(sauce italienne)

pork, fungi, vegetable fruits  boiling, shallow frying

	energy 258 KJ	kcal 63 kcal	fat 5.6 g	sat fat 2.6 g	carb 1.3 g	sugar 1.2 g	protein 1.8 g	fibre 0.4 g

Portions ⟩	4	10
butter or oil	25 g	60 g
shallots, chopped	10 g	25 g
mushrooms, chopped	50 g	125 g
demi-glace, *jus-lié* or reduced stock	250 ml	625 ml
lean ham, chopped	25 g	60 g
tomatoes, skinned, de-seeded, diced	100 g	250 g
parsley, chervil and tarragon, chopped		

1 Melt the butter or heat the oil in a small sauteuse.
2 Add the shallots and cook gently for 2–3 minutes, then add the mushrooms and cook gently for a further 2–3 minutes.
3 Add the demi-glace, ham and tomatoes.
4 Simmer for 5–10 minutes. Correct the seasoning. Add the chopped herbs.

Usually served with fried cuts of veal, lamb or chicken.

Healthy eating tips
- Use an unsaturated oil (sunflower or vegetable). Lightly oil the pan and drain off any excess after the frying is complete.
- Trim as much fat as possible from the ham.
- The ham is salty, so do not add more salt; flavour will come from the herbs.
- Skim all fat from the finished sauce.

16 Brown onion sauce
(sauce lyonnaise)

bulbs boiling, shallow frying

	energy 240 KJ	kcal 58 kcal	fat 5.2 g	sat fat 2.5 g	carb 2.3 g	sugar 1.7 g	protein 0.3 g	fibre 0.4 g

Portions ⟩	4	10
butter or oil	25 g	60 g
onions, sliced	100 g	250 g
vinegar	2 tbsp	5 tbsp
demi-glace, *jus-lié* or reduced stock	250 ml	625 ml

1 Melt the butter or heat the oil in a sauteuse.
2 Add the onions, cover with a lid.
3 Cook gently until tender.
4 Remove the lid and colour lightly.
5 Add the vinegar and completely reduce.
6 Add the demi-glace; simmer for 5–10 minutes.
7 Skim and correct the seasoning.

May be served with burgers, fried liver or sausages.

Healthy eating tips
- Use an unsaturated oil (sunflower or vegetable). Lightly oil the pan and drain off any excess after the frying is complete, before adding the vinegar.
- Season with the minimum amount of salt.

17 Madeira sauce
(sauce Madère)

boiling

energy	kcal	fat	sat fat	carb	sugar	protein	fibre
43 KJ	10 kcal	0.1 g	0.0 g	1.6 g	1.2 g	0.3 g	0.4 g

Portions ⟩	4	10
demi-glace, *jus-lié* or reduced stock	250 ml	625 ml
Madeira wine	2 tbsp	5 tbsp
butter, cold, cubed (optional)	25 g	60 g

1 Boil the demi-glace in a small sauteuse.
2 Add the Madeira; reboil. Correct the seasoning.
3 Pass through a fine conical strainer. Gradually incorporate the butter, if required. Do not allow the sauce to reboil as the butter will split.

Tip
May be served with braised ox tongue or ham. Dry sherry or port wine may be substituted for Madeira and the sauce renamed accordingly. Butter may be used (but not oil or margarine) to enhance the flavour.

18 Piquant sauce
(sauce piquante)

vegetable fruits boiling

energy	kcal	fat	sat fat	carb	sugar	protein	fibre
197 KJ	48 kcal	5.1 g	3.3 g	0.3 g	0.3 g	0.0 g	0.0 g

Portions ⟩	4	10
vinegar	60 ml	150 ml
shallots, chopped	50 g	125 g
demi-glace, *jus-lié* or reduced stock	250 ml	625 ml
gherkins, chopped	25 g	60 g
capers, chopped	10 g	25 g
chervil, tarragon and parsley, chopped	½ tbsp	1½ tbsp

1 Place the vinegar and shallots in a small sauteuse and reduce by half.
2 Add the demi-glace; simmer for 15–20 minutes.
3 Add the rest of the ingredients. Skim and correct the seasoning.

May be served with made-up dishes, sausages and grilled meats.

19 Robert sauce
(sauce Robert)

boiling, shallow frying

energy	kcal	fat	sat fat	carb	sugar	protein	fibre
229 KJ	56 kcal	2.61 g	1.0 g	7.2 g	6.8 g	0.6 g	0.2 g

Portions ⟩	4	10
butter or oil	20 g	50 g
onions, finely chopped	10 g	25 g
vinegar	60 ml	150 ml
demi-glace, *jus-lié* or reduced stock	250 ml	625 ml
English or continental mustard	1 level tsp	2½ level tsp
caster sugar	1 level tbsp	2½ level tbsp

1 Melt the butter or heat the oil in a small sauteuse. Add the onions.
2 Cook gently without colour. Add the vinegar and reduce completely.
3 Add the demi-glace; simmer for 5–10 minutes.
4 Remove from the heat and add the mustard diluted with a little water and the sugar; do not boil. Skim and correct the seasoning.

May be served with fried sausages and burgers, or grilled pork chops.

Healthy eating tips
- Use an unsaturated oil (sunflower or vegetable). Lightly oil the pan and drain off any excess after the frying is complete and before adding the vinegar.
- Season with the minimum amount of salt.

20 Béchamel sauce
(white sauce)

dairy products  boiling

Makes ›	1 litre	4.5 litres
butter or oil	100 g	400 g
plain white flour	100 g	400 g
milk, warmed	1 litre	4.5 litres
onion, studded with cloves	1	2–3

1 Melt the butter or heat the oil in a thick-bottomed pan.
2 Mix in the flour with a heat-proof plastic spoon.
3 Cook for a few minutes, stirring frequently. As you are making a white roux, do not allow the mixture to colour.
4 Remove the pan from the heat to allow the roux to cool.
5 Return the pan to the stove and, over a low heat, gradually mix the milk into the roux.
6 Add the studded onion.
7 Allow the mixture to simmer gently for 30 minutes, stirring frequently to make sure the sauce does not burn on the bottom.
8 Remove the onion and pass the sauce through a conical strainer.

> **Tip**
> To prevent a skin from forming, brush the surface with melted butter. When ready to use, stir this into the sauce. Alternatively, cover the sauce with greaseproof paper.

21 Béchamel sauce
(reduced fat)

dairy products boiling

energy	kcal	fat	sat fat	carb	sugar	protein	fibre
302 KJ	73 kcal	1.8 g	1.1 g	10.9 g	4.8 g	4.2 g	0.3 g

Makes ›	1 litre
milk	1 litre
sauce flour	80 g
seasoning	

1 The milk may be first infused with an onion studded with cloves, a carrot and a bouquet garni. Allow to cool.
2 Place the milk in a suitable saucepan, gradually whisk in the sauce flour. Bring slowly to the boil until the sauce has thickened.
3 Season, simmer for approximately 5–10 minutes. Use as required.

> **Tip**
> Add a little blended cornflour prior to heating, to stabilise the sauce.

22 Mornay sauce

dairy products boiling

	Makes ⟩	500 ml
milk		500 ml
grated cheese		50 g
egg yolk (optional)		1
sauce flour		40 g

1 The milk may be first infused with an onion studded with cloves, a carrot and a bouquet garni. Allow to cool.
2 Place the milk in a suitable saucepan, gradually whisk in the sauce flour. Bring slowly to the boil until the sauce has thickened.
3 Mix in the cheese and egg yolk when the sauce is boiling.
4 Remove from the heat. Strain if necessary.
5 Do not allow the sauce to reboil at any time.

Mornay sauce (front) and parsley sauce (back)

> **Tip**
> Add a little cornflour prior to heating to stabilise the sauce.
> Mornay sauce can also be made using a traditional béchamel.

23 Parsley sauce

dairy products, herbs boiling

	Makes ⟩	500 ml
milk		500 ml
sauce flour		40 g
parsley, chopped		1 tbsp
seasoning		

1 The milk may be first infused with a studded onion clouté, carrot and a bouquet garni. Allow to cool.
2 Place the milk in a suitable saucepan, gradually whisk in the sauce flour. Bring slowly to the boil until the sauce has thickened.
3 Season, add the parsley and simmer for approximately 5–10 minutes. Use as required.

24 Velouté (chicken, veal, mutton)

boiling, making a roux

energy	kcal	fat	sat fat	carb	sugar	protein	fibre	*
4594 KJ	1094 kcal	82.6 g	35.4 g	79.0 g	1.6 g	13.3 g	3.6 g	

	Makes ⟩	1 litre
butter or oil		100 g
flour		100 g
stock (chicken, veal, mutton) as required		1 litre

1 Melt the butter or heat the oil in a thick-bottomed pan.
2 Add the flour and mix in.
3 Cook out to a sandy texture over gentle heat without colouring.
4 Allow the roux to cool.
5 Gradually add the boiling stock.
6 Stir until smooth and boiling.
7 Allow to simmer for approximately 1 hour.
8 Pass it through a fine conical strainer.

Note

This is a basic white sauce made from white stock and a blond roux.
A velouté sauce for chicken or veal dishes is usually finished with cream and, in some cases, egg yolks. The finished sauce should be of a light consistency, barely coating the back of a spoon.

Healthy eating tip

Make sure all the fat has been skimmed from the stock before adding it to the roux.

* Using hard margarine, for 1 litre. Using sunflower oil instead, this recipe provides, for 1 litre: 5304 kJ/ 1263 kcal energy; 101.5 g fat; 13.3 g sat fat; 78.9 g carb; 1.5 g sugar; 13.2 g protein; 3.6 g fibre

25 Fish velouté

fish boiling, making a roux, simmering

energy	kcal	fat	sat fat	carb	sugar	protein	fibre
4805 KJ	1144 kcal	90.4 g	39.0 g	77.8 g	1.6 g	9.5 g	3.6 g

	Makes ⟩	1 litre
butter		100 g
flour		100 g
fish stock		1 litre

1 Prepare a blond roux using the butter and flour.
2 Gradually add the stock, stirring continuously until boiling point is reached.
3 Simmer for approximately 1 hour.
4 Pass through a fine conical strainer.

Note

This will give a thick sauce that can be thinned down with the cooking liquor from the fish for which the sauce is intended.

Healthy eating tip

Make sure all the fat has been skimmed from the stock before adding it to the roux.

26 | *Sauce suprême*

boiling, making a roux, simmering

Portions ⟩	4	10
butter or oil	100 g	250 g
flour	100 g	250 g
stock (chicken, veal, fish, mutton) as required	1 litre	2.5 litres
mushroom trimmings	25 g	60 g
egg yolk (optional)	1	2
cream	60 ml	150 ml
lemon juice	2–3 drops	5–6 drops

1 Melt the butter or heat the oil in a thick-bottomed pan.
2 Add the flour and mix in.
3 Cook out to a sandy texture over gentle heat without colouring.
4 Allow the roux to cool.
5 Gradually add the boiling stock.
6 Stir until smooth and boiling.
7 Add the mushroom trimmings. Allow to simmer for approximately 1 hour.
8 Pass it through a fine conical strainer.
9 Finish with a liaison of the egg yolk, cream and lemon juice. Serve immediately; do not reboil.

27 Mushroom sauce

fungi boiling, making a roux, simmering

Makes ›	1 litre	4.5 litres
butter or oil	100 g	400 g
flour	100 g	400 g
stock (chicken, veal, fish, mutton) as required	1 litre	4.5 litres
mushroom trimmings	50 g	225 g
white button mushrooms, well-washed, sliced, sweated	200 g	900 g
cream	120 ml	540 ml
egg yolk (optional)	2	9
lemon, juice of	½	1

1 Melt the butter or heat the oil in a thick-bottomed pan.

2 Add the flour and mix in.

3 Cook out to a sandy texture over gentle heat without colouring.

4 Allow the roux to cool.

5 Gradually add the boiling stock.

6 Stir until smooth and boiling.

7 Add the mushrooms and trimmings. Allow to simmer for approximately 1 hour.

8 Pass it through a fine conical strainer.

9 Simmer for 10 minutes, then add the egg yolk, cream and lemon juice. Serve immediately; do not reboil.

28 White wine sauce
(sauce vin blanc)

fish · boiling

energy	kcal	fat	sat fat	carb	sugar	protein	fibre *
3255 KJ	775 kcal	73.7 g	42.2 g	21.0 g	2.0 g	3.3 g	1.1 g

Portions ⟩	4	10
fish velouté	250 ml	625 ml
white wine, dry	2 tbsp	5 tbsp
butter	50 g	125 g
cream	2 tbsp	5 tbsp
salt, cayenne		
few drops of lemon juice		

1 Boil the fish velouté. Whisk in the wine.
2 Remove from the heat.
3 Gradually add the butter. Stir in the cream.
4 Correct the seasoning (using the salt and cayenne) and consistency (using the lemon juice).
5 Pass through a double muslin or fine strainer.

Whisk the wine into the boiling velouté

Remove from the heat and add the butter gradually

Stir in the cream

Tip
If the sauce is to be used for a glazed fish dish then 1 egg yolk or 1 tbsp sabayon should be added as soon as the sauce is removed from the heat. (Trade practice sometimes is to whisk in 1 tbsp hollandaise sauce.)

Try something different
● Finely sliced button mushrooms and chopped parsley.
● Finely sliced button mushrooms and diced, peeled and deseeded tomato.
● Picked shrimps.
● A few strands of blanched saffron.

* 4 portions

29 Shrimp sauce

shellfish boiling

energy	kcal	fat	sat fat	carb	sugar	protein	fibre	*
1381 KJ	332 kcal	22.1 g	10.3 g	20.0 g	0.9 g	14.3 g	0.8 g	

Portions ›	4	10
fish velouté or béchamel	250 ml	625 ml
salt, cayenne		
shrimps	60 g	150 g
cream	60 ml	150 ml

Note

May be served with any poached or steamed fish.

1 Boil the fish velouté or béchamel.
2 Correct the seasoning and adjust the consistency by diluting with fish stock.
3 Pass through a double muslin or fine strainer. Mix in the shrimps. Finish with cream.

* Using margarine reduced to half

30 Reduced veal stock for sauce

veal roasting, simmering

energy	kcal	fat	sat fat	carb	sugar	protein	fibre
8 KJ	2 kcal	0.0 g	0.0 g	0.5 g	0.4 g	0.0 g	0.0 g

Makes ›	4 litres
veal bones	4 kg
water	4 litres
carrots	400 g
onions	200 g
celery	100 g
tomatoes, blanched, skinned, quartered	1 kg
mushrooms, chopped	200 g
bouquet garni	1 large
cloves of garlic, unpeeled (optional)	4

Healthy eating tip

Skim all fat from the stock as it simmers, and the fat from the finished product.

1 Brown the chopped bones on a roasting tray in the oven.
2 Place the browned bones in a stock pot, cover with cold water and bring to simmering point.
3 Roughly chop the carrots, onions and celery. Using the same roasting tray and the fat from the bones, brown them off.
4 Drain off the fat, add the vegetables to the stock and deglaze the tray.
5 Add the quartered tomatoes, chopped mushrooms, bouquet garni and garlic (if desired). Simmer gently for 4–5 hours. Skim frequently.
6 Strain the stock into a clean pan and reduce until a light consistency is achieved.

Making a reduced stock
http://bit.ly/AxITyH

Reduction of wine, stock and cream

boiling, simmering

Makes approx. >	250 ml
white stock	500 ml
white wine	125 ml
double or whipping cream	125 ml

1 Place the stock and white wine in a suitable saucepan.
2 Reduce by at least two thirds and finish with cream.

Key point
Reduce the stock and wine to a slightly syrupy consistency.

Measure out all the ingredients

Reduce the wine and stock

Add the cream

32 Smitaine sauce
(sauce smitaine)

dairy products  shallow frying, simmering

	Makes 〉	0.5 litres
butter		25 g
onion, finely chopped		50 g
white wine		60 ml
sour cream		0.5 litres
seasoning		
lemon, juice of		¼

1 Melt butter in a sauteuse and cook the onion without colour.
2 Add the white wine and reduce by half.
3 Add the sour cream and season lightly; reduce by one-third.
4 Pass through a fine strainer and finish with lemon juice.

Use with a hached or diced beef steak as shown here, or with sausages, shallow-fried lambs' kidneys, lightly sautéd slices of beef or pork fillet, etc.

33 Curry sauce
(sauce kari)

fruit, spices shallow frying, boiling, making a roux

energy	kcal	fat	sat fat	carb	sugar	protein	fibre
1092 KJ	260 kcal	14.1 g	4.1 g	30.3 g	19.9 g	4.9 g	4.1 g

Portions ⟩	4	10
onion, chopped	50 g	125 g
clove of garlic	¼	½
butter or oil	10 g	25 g
flour	10 g	25 g
curry powder	5 g	12 g
tomato purée	5 g	12 g
stock	375 ml	1 litre
apple, chopped	25 g	60 g
chutney, chopped	1 tbsp	2 tbsp
desiccated coconut	5 g	12 g
sultanas	10 g	25 g
ginger root, grated *or*	10 g	25 g
ground ginger	5 g	12 g
salt		

1 Gently cook the onion and garlic in the fat in a small sauteuse without colouring.
2 Mix in the flour and curry powder. Cook gently to a sandy mixture.
3 Mix in the tomato purée, cool.
4 Gradually add the boiling stock and mix to a smooth sauce.
5 Add the remainder of the ingredients; season with salt, and simmer for 30 minutes. Skim and correct the seasoning.

* Using sunflower oil, for 4 portions

Note

This sauce has a wide range of uses, with prawns, shrimps, vegetables, eggs, and so on. For use with poached or soft-boiled eggs it may be strained and for all purposes it may be finished with 2–3 tbsp cream or natural yoghurt. For a traditional recipe the curry powder would be replaced by either curry paste or a mixture of freshly ground spices such as turmeric, cumin, allspice, fresh ginger, chilli and clove.

Healthy eating tips
- Use a small amount of an unsaturated oil (e.g. sunflower or vegetable) to fry the onion and garlic.
- Add the minimum amount of salt, tasting first – there is already lots of flavour from the spices, ginger, etc.

34 Soubise sauce

 shallow frying,  boiling

Makes >	500 ml
onion, chopped or diced	100 g
milk	500 ml
sauce flour	40 g
seasoning	

1 Cook the onions without colouring them, either by boiling or sweating in butter.

2 The milk may be first infused with a studded onion clouté, carrot and a bouquet garni. Allow to cool.

3 Place the milk in a suitable saucepan, gradually whisk in the sauce flour. Bring slowly to the boil until the sauce has thickened.

4 Add the onions, season, simmer for approximately 5–10 minutes.

5 Blitz well. Pass through a strainer.

Soubise sauce may also be made using béchamel sauce.

35 Bread sauce

simmering

energy	kcal	fat	sat fat	carb	sugar	protein	fibre
318 KJ	77 kcal	3.8 g	2.3 g	7.6 g	4.6 g	3.8 g	0.1 g

Portions >	4	10
semi-skimmed milk	375 ml	1 litre
onion, small, studded with a clove	1	2
fresh white breadcrumbs	75 g	180 g
salt, cayenne pepper		
butter	10 g	25 g

1 Infuse the simmering milk with the studded onion for 15 minutes.

2 Remove the onion, mix in the breadcrumbs. Simmer for 2–3 minutes.

3 Season, correct the consistency.

4 Add the butter on top of the sauce to prevent a skin forming.

5 Mix well when serving.

Note
Served with roast chicken, turkey and roast game.

Healthy eating tip
Use the minimum amount of salt.

36 Tomato sauce
(sauce tomate)

vegetable fruits   shallow frying, simmering

Makes ❭	500 ml
carrots, chopped into mirepoix	90 g
celery, chopped into mirepoix	30g
clove garlic, chopped	½
vegetable oil	25 g
butter	25 g
thyme	1 g
bay leaf	½
tomato purée	12 g
plum tomatoes	200 g
chicken stock	750 ml
juniper berries	2
cream	75 g
gastric (50/50 gastric vinegar and sugar, heated to dissolve the sugar)	5 g

1 Sweat the carrots, celery and garlic in the oil and butter.
2 Add the thyme, bay and tomato purée.
3 Cook for 5 minutes.
4 Add the tomatoes.
5 Cook for 5 minutes.
6 Add the chicken stock and juniper berries, reduce by a third.
7 Finish with the cream, bring to the boil and blitz. Season with salt and gastric.

37 Pesto

herbs, cheese

Portions ❭	4	10
fresh basil leaves	4 small bunches	10 small bunches
garlic clove, chopped	1	2–3
salt to taste		
pine nuts, lightly toasted	2 tbsp	5 tbsp
Parmesan cheese, grated	2 tbsp	5 tbsp
extra virgin olive oil	2 tbsp	5 tbsp

1 Put the basil leaves, garlic, salt and pine nuts into a mortar (or use a food processor) and pound into a smooth paste.
2 Place in a bowl, mix in the cheese and sufficient olive oil to make a sauce-like consistency.

Note
Pesto is a green basil sauce used in some pasta dishes, salads and fish dishes.

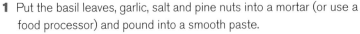

Practical Cookery 12th edition

38 Apple sauce

fruit

Portions ›	8
cooking apples	400 g
sugar	50 g
butter or margarine	25 g

1 Peel, core and wash the apples.
2 Place with other ingredients in a covered pan and cook to a purée.
3 Pass through a sieve or liquidise.

Traditionally an accompaniment to roast pork or duck.

39 Horseradish sauce

(sauce raifort)

root vegetables

energy	kcal	fat	sat fat	carb	sugar	protein	fibre	*
1807 KJ	430 kcal	43.8 g	27.8 g	6.0 g	5.0 g	3.6 g	2.1 g	

Portions ›	8
horseradish	25 g
vinegar or lemon juice	1 tbsp
salt, pepper	
cream or crème fraiche, lightly whipped	125 ml

1 Wash, peel and rewash the horseradish. Grate finely.
2 Mix all the ingredients together.

Serve with roast beef, smoked trout, eel or halibut.

> **Key point**
> It is essential to blend the ingredients without over-mixing them, in order to get a good flavour.

* For 8 portions

40 Cranberry sauce

fruit simmering

Portions ›	8
cranberries	400 g
water	100 ml
sugar	50 g

1 Simmer all ingredients together in a covered pan (not iron or aluminium) until soft.
2 The sauce may be sieved or liquidised if required.

Traditionally served with roast turkey.

Try something different
For a variation half orange juice and half water, plus some grated orange zest may be used.

41 Tartare sauce
(sauce tartare)

vegetable fruits

energy	kcal	fat	sat fat	carb	sugar	protein	fibre
938 KJ	228 kcal	24.8 g	3.6 g	0.3 g	0.3 g	0.7 g	0.1 g

Portions ❯	8
mayonnaise	250 ml
capers, chopped	25 g
gherkins, chopped	50 g
sprig of parsley, chopped	

Key point

Finely chop the gherkins and capers, and use a blender, to give the desired texture and consistency.

1 Combine all the ingredients.

This sauce is usually served with deep-fried fish.

Healthy eating tip

Proportionally reduce the fat by adding some low-fat yoghurt instead of some of the mayonnaise.

---

42 Mint sauce

herbs

energy	kcal	fat	sat fat	carb	sugar	protein	fibre
204 KJ	49 kcal	0.0 g	0.0 g	11.3 g	11.3 g	1.5 g	1.8 g *

Portions ❯	8
mint	2–3 tbsp
caster sugar	1 tsp
vinegar	125 ml

Note

Serve with roast lamb.
A less acid sauce can be produced by dissolving the sugar in 125 ml boiling water and, when cold, adding the chopped mint and 1–2 tablespoon vinegar to taste.

1 Chop the washed, picked mint and mix with the sugar.
2 Place in a china basin and add the vinegar.
3 If the vinegar is too sharp, dilute it with a little water.

* For 8 portions

43 Tomato and cucumber salsa

vegetable fruits

energy	kcal	fat	sat fat	carb	sugar	protein	fibre
202 KJ	49 kcal	4.3 g	0.7 g	2.0 g	2.0 g	0.6 g	0.7 g

Portions ⟩	8
ripe tomatoes, skinned, deseeded, chopped	400 g
cucumber, peeled, chopped	½
spring onions, chopped	6
fresh basil, chopped	1 tbsp
fresh parsley, chopped	1 tbsp
olive oil	3 tbsp
lemon or lime (juice of)	1
salt and pepper	

1 In a large bowl, mix all the ingredients together.

2 Correct seasoning and serve.

Healthy eating tip

Rely on the herbs for flavour, with the minimum amount of salt.

Try something different

This recipe may be varied by using any chopped salad ingredients and fresh herbs (e.g. tarragon, chervil). Do not be afraid to experiment.
Extra vegetables can be added and the salsa used liberally with grilled fish or chicken. Rice could be served with this, or the salsa used to fill a tortilla.

44 Salsa verde

herbs

energy	kcal	fat	sat fat	carb	sugar	protein	fibre	*
281 KJ	69 kcal	7.5 g	1.1 g	0.2 g	0.1 g	0.1 g	0.0 g	

	Portions ⟩	8
mint		1 tbsp
parsley	} coarsely chopped	3 tbsp
capers		3
garlic clove (optional)		1
Dijon mustard		1 tsp
lemon, juice of		½
extra virgin olive oil		120 ml
salt		

1 In a large bowl, mix all the ingredients together and check the seasoning.

Serve with grilled fish.

* Per tablespoon

Melted butter sauce
(beurre fondu)

dairy products boiling

energy	kcal	fat	sat fat	carb	sugar	protein	fibre *
388 KJ	94 kcal	10.3 g	6.5 g	0.1 g	0.1 g	0.1 g	0.0 g

Portions ›	4	10
butter	200 g	500 g
water or white wine	2 tbsp	5 tbsp

1 Boil the butter and water or wine together gently to emulsify until combined, then pass through a fine strainer.

Note

Usually served with poached fish and certain vegetables (e.g. blue trout, salmon; asparagus, sea kale). For butter sauce see recipe 46. For compound butter sauces see page 27.

* Per tablespoon

---

46 Butter sauce
(beurre blanc)

dairy products boiling

Portions ›	4	10
water	125 ml	300 ml
white wine vinegar	125 ml	300 ml
shallots, finely chopped	50 g	125 g
unsalted butter	200 g	500 g
lemon juice	1 tsp	2½ tsp
salt, pepper		

1 Reduce the water, vinegar and shallots in a thick-bottomed pan to approximately 62 ml, and allow to cool slightly.
2 Gradually whisk in the butter in small amounts, whisking continually until the mixture becomes creamy.
3 Whisk in the lemon juice, season lightly and keep warm in a bain-marie.

Key points

Once butter is added to a sauce, the sauce must not reboil, because it will split. The butter should be cold and sliced/cubed when it is mounted (monté) into the sauce, and the sauce should be kept moving to create a wave, skimming layers of the butter into the sauce.

Try something different

The sauce may be strained if desired. Variations include adding freshly shredded sorrel or spinach, blanched fine julienne of lemon or lime, or chopped fresh herbs.

Healthy eating tips

- Use the minimum amount of salt.
- Do not serve too much sauce with fish dishes.

47 Hollandaise sauce
(sauce hollandaise)

dairy products, eggs simmering

energy	kcal	fat	sat fat	carb	sugar	protein	fibre	*
6789 KJ	1616 kcal	176.2 g	107.9 g	0.1 g	0.1 g	7.3 g	0.0 g	

Portions ⟩	4	10
crushed peppercorn reduction (optional)	6	15
vinegar	1 tbsp	2½ tbsp
pasteurised egg yolks	2	5
butter or good-quality oil	200 g	500 g
lemon juice	1 tsp	2½ tsp
salt, cayenne pepper to taste		

1 Place the peppercorns and vinegar in a small sauteuse or stainless steel pan and reduce to one-third. Strain off.
2 Add 1 tbsp cold water; allow to cool.
3 Mix in the yolks with a whisk.
4 Return to a gentle heat over a bain marie and, whisking continuously, cook to a sabayon (this means cooking of the yolks to a thickened consistency, like cream, that will show the mark of the whisk).
5 Remove from the heat and cool slightly.
6 Whisk the melted warm butter in gradually, until thoroughly combined.
7 Correct the seasoning. If reduction is not used, add a few drops of lemon juice.
8 Pass through a fine conical strainer.
9 The sauce should be served warm within 2 hours of making.
10 Serve in a slightly warm sauceboat.

Served with hot fish (e.g. salmon, trout, turbot) and vegetables (e.g. asparagus, cauliflower, broccoli).

Key point

The cause of hollandaise sauce curdling is either that the butter has been added too quickly or that the sauce has been heated too much, which will cause the albumen in the eggs to harden, shrink and separate from the liquid.
Should the sauce curdle, place a teaspoon of boiling water in a clean sauteuse and gradually whisk in the curdled sauce. If this fails to reconstitute the sauce, then place an egg yolk in a clean sauteuse with 1 dessertspoon of water. Whisk lightly over a gentle heat until slightly thickened. Remove from the heat and gradually add the curdled sauce, whisking continuously. To stabilise the sauce during service, 60 ml thick béchamel sauce may be added before straining.

Food safety

To reduce the risk of salmonella infection, pasteurised egg yolks must be used. Do not keep the sauce for longer than 2 hours before discarding. This applies to all egg-based sauces.

Healthy eating tips

- This recipe is obviously high in saturated fat (butter, egg yolk).
- The fat is proportionally reduced when the sauce is served with grilled or baked fish and plenty of potatoes and other vegetables.
- Add the minimum of salt.

Making hollandaise sauce
http://bit.ly/wvtR4Q

* For 4 portions

Hollandaise

Béarnaise   Paloise

Recipes 47 and 48

48 Béarnaise sauce

dairy products, eggs boiling

energy	kcal	fat	sat fat	carb	sugar	protein	fibre
1728 KJ	420 kcal	45.2 g	27.2 g	0.6 g	0.5 g	2.6 g	0.0 g

Makes ›	500 g
shallots, chopped	50 g
tarragon	10 g
peppercorns, crushed	12
white wine vinegar	3 tbsp
egg yolks, pasteurised	6
melted butter	325 g
salt and cayenne pepper	
chervil and tarragon to finish, chopped	

1 Place the shallots, tarragon, peppercorns and vinegar in a small pan and reduce to one-third.
2 Add 1 tablespoon of cold water and allow to cool. Add the egg yolks.
3 Put on a bain-marie and whisk continuously to a sabayon consistency.
4 Remove from the heat and gradually whisk in the melted butter.
5 Add seasoning. Pass through muslin or a fine chinois.
6 To finish, add the chopped chervil and tarragon.

Key point

Egg-based sauces should not be kept warm for more than 2 hours. After this time, they should be thrown away, but are best made fresh to order.

Note

This is usually served with grilled meat and fish, e.g. Chateaubriand grillé, sauce béarnaise.
This sauce should be twice as thick as hollandaise.

Try something different

- **Choron sauce:** 200 g tomato concassée, well dried. Do not add the chopped tarragon and chervil to finish.
- **Foyot or valois sauce:** 25 g warm meat glaze.
- **Paloise sauce:** use chopped mint stalks in place of the tarragon in the reduction. To finish, add chopped mint instead of the chervil and tarragon.

49 Herb oil

herbs  boiling

Makes >	250 ml
picked flat leaf parsley	25 g
chives	10 g
picked basil leaves	10 g
picked spinach	100 g
corn oil	250 ml

1 Blanch all the herbs and spinach for 1½ minutes.

2 Drain well, place with the oil in a liquidiser and blitz for 2½ minutes. Pass and decant when rested.

Note
Uses include salads, salmon mi cuit and other fish dishes.

Herb   Lemon   Mint

Vanilla   Basil   Walnut

Flavoured oils (recipes 49, 50, 53, 55, 56 and 57)

50 Basil oil

herbs  boiling

Makes >	200 ml
fresh basil	25 g
oil	200 ml
salt, to taste	
mill pepper	

1 Blanch and refresh the basil; purée with the oil.

2 Allow to settle overnight and decant.

3 Store in bottles with a sprig of blanched basil.

Variations
Basil extract can be used in place of fresh basil; 50 g of grated Parmesan or Gorgonzola cheese may also be added to the basil oil.

51 Parsley oil

herbs **herbs**  boiling

Makes >	250 ml
picked flat leaf parsley	75 g
picked spinach	50 g
corn oil	250 ml

1 Blanch the parsley and spinach for 1½ minutes, drain well and place with the oil in a liquidiser.

2 Liquidise for 2½ minutes, place in the fridge and allow the sediment to settle overnight.

3 The next day, decant when rested and use.

> **Note**
> Uses include fish and meat dishes.

52 Garlic oil

bulbs shallow frying

Makes >	250 ml
vegetable, sunflower, soya and olive oil	250 ml
garlic, chopped and crushed	3 tbsp

1 Heat the oil in a suitable pan, add the crushed garlic, heat until the garlic is golden, allow to cool, add to the oil, store and use as required.

Garlic and sundried tomato oils (recipes 52 and 54)

53 Mint oil

herbs  boiling

Makes >	150 ml
mint	100 g
oil	150 ml
salt	3 tbsp

1 Blanch the mint for 30 seconds.

2 Refresh and squeeze the water out.

3 Place in a blender and slowly add the oil.

4 Allow to settle overnight and decant into bottles.

> **Note**
> Uses include lamb dishes, salads and fish dishes.

54   Sundried tomato oil

vegetable fruits

Makes ⟩	500 ml
olive oil	500 ml
sundried tomatoes	75 g
salt, to taste	
mill pepper	

1 Reconstitute the tomatoes in the olive oil.
2 Lightly warm the oil/tomatoes and purée in a liquidiser.
3 Add the mill pepper and salt.
4 Store in a bottle until required.

55   Lemon oil

Makes ⟩	250 ml
lemons, rind (with no pith – the whitish layer between skin and fruit)	3
lemon grass stick, cut lengthways and chopped into 2 cm strips	1
grapeseed oil	250 ml
olive oil	2 tbsp

1 Place all the ingredients into a food processor and pulse the mix until the lemon peel and grass are approximately 3 mm thick.
2 Allow to stand for 2 days. Decant and store in the fridge until ready for use (or you could freeze for longer if you wish).

56   Walnut oil

nuts, cheese

Makes ⟩	500 ml
olive or walnut oil	500 ml
walnuts, finely crushed	75 g
Parmesan cheese	75 g
salt, to taste	
mill pepper	

1 Mix all the ingredients together and bottle until required.

57 Vanilla oil

vanilla

	Makes ›	200 ml
vegetable oil		200 ml
vanilla pods, whole		5
vanilla pods, used		2
vanilla extract		50 ml

1 Warm the oil to around 60°C; add the vanilla in its various forms and infuse, scraping all the seeds into the oil. Store in a plastic bottle.

> **Note**
> Uses include salads, salmon mi cuit and other fish dishes.

58 Scotch broth

lamb boiling

	Portions ›	4	10
lean lamb or mutton		200 g	500 g
lamb stock		1 litre	2.5 litres
barley		25 g	60 g
vegetables (carrot, turnip, leek, celery, onion), cut into paysanne or gros brunoise		200 g	500 g
bouquet garni			
salt, pepper			
chopped parsley			

1 Place the lamb, free from fat, in a saucepan and cover with cold water.

2 Bring to the boil, then immediately wash off under running water.

3 Clean the pan, replace the meat, cover with cold water, bring to the boil and skim.

4 Add the washed barley, simmer for 1 hour.

5 Add the vegetables, bouquet garni and seasoning.

6 Skim when necessary; simmer for approximately 30 minutes, until tender.

7 Remove the meat, allow to cool and cut from the bone, remove all fat and cut the meat into neat dice the same size as the vegetables; return to the broth.

8 Correct the seasoning, skim off all the fat, add the chopped parsley and serve.

Healthy eating tips
- Remove all fat from the meat.
- Use only a small amount of salt.
- There are lots of healthy vegetables in this dish and the addition of a large bread roll will increase the starchy carbohydrate.

> **Note**
> Lamb is the traditional meat for a Scotch broth but it is often produced using beef.

59 Brown onion soup
(soupe à l'oignon)

bulbs shallow frying, boiling, simmering

energy	kcal	fat	sat fat	carb	sugar	protein	fibre	*
197 KJ	827 kcal	9.7 g	5.8 g	20.4 g	8.1 g	8.3 g	3.1 g	

Portions ⟩	4	10
onions	600 g	1.5 kg
butter	25 g	60 g
clove of garlic, chopped (optional)	1	3
flour, white or wholemeal	10 g	20 g
brown stock	1 litre	2.5 litres
salt, mill pepper		
flute (thin French stick)	¼	⅔
grated cheese	50 g	120 g

1 Peel the onions, halve and slice finely.
2 Melt the butter in a thick-bottomed pan, add the onions and garlic, and cook steadily over a good heat until cooked and well browned.

3 Mix in the flour and cook over a gentle heat, browning slightly.
4 Gradually mix in the stock, bring to the boil, skim and season.
5 Simmer for approximately 10 minutes until the onion is soft. Correct the seasoning.
6 Pour into an earthenware tureen or casserole, or individual dishes.
7 Cut the flute into 2 cm diameter slices and toast on both sides.
8 Sprinkle the toasted slices of bread liberally over the top of the soup.
9 Sprinkle with grated cheese and brown under the salamander.
10 Place on a dish and serve.

* Using butter

root vegetables, vegetable fruits 🍲 boiling, 🍳 shallow frying

energy	kcal	fat	sat fat	carb	sugar	protein	fibre	*
1115 KJ	22.9 kcal	22.9 g	5.8 g	11.9 g	4.2 g	3.8 g	4.1 g	

Portions >	4	10
mixed vegetables (onion, leek, celery, carrot, turnip, cabbage), peeled	300 g	750 g
butter or oil	50 g	125 g
white stock or water	1 litre	2 litres
bouquet garni		
salt, pepper		
peas	25 g	60 g
French beans	25 g	60 g
spaghetti	25 g	60 g
potatoes, peeled	50 g	125 g
tomato purée	1 tsp	3 tsp
tomatoes, skinned, deseeded, diced	100 g	250 g
fat bacon	50 g	125 g
parsley } optional		
clove of garlic	1	2½

1 Cut the peeled and washed mixed vegetables into paysanne.
2 Cook slowly without colour in the oil or butter in the pan with a lid on.
3 Add the stock, bouquet garni and seasoning; simmer for approximately 20 minutes.
4 Add the peas and the beans cut into diamonds and simmer for 10 minutes.
5 Add the spaghetti in 2 cm lengths, the potatoes cut into paysanne, the tomato purée and the tomatoes, and simmer gently until all the vegetables are cooked.
6 Meanwhile finely chop the fat bacon, parsley and garlic, and form into a paste.
7 Mould the paste into pellets the size of a pea and drop into the boiling soup.
8 Remove the bouquet garni, correct the seasoning.
9 Serve the soup topped with toasted flutes with Parmesan cheese. Alternatively, serve separately.

Vegetables chopped into paysanne

Fry or sweat the vegetables

Simmer the ingredients in the stock

Add the pellets of paste to the soup

Healthy eating tips
● Use an unsaturated oil (sunflower or vegetable) to lightly oil the pan. Drain off any excess after the frying is complete and skim the fat from the finished dish.
● Season with the minimum amount of salt as the bacon and cheese are high in salt.

* Using sunflower oil

61 Cream of vegetable soup

bulbs shallow frying, boiling

Portions ⟩	4	10
onions, leek and celery, sliced	100 g	250 g
other suitable vegetables,* sliced	200 g	500 g
butter or oil	50 g	125 g
flour	50 g	125 g
white stock or water	0.5 litres	1.5 litres
thin béchamel	0.5 litres	1 litre
bouquet garni		
salt, pepper		

*Suitable vegetables include Jerusalem artichokes, carrot, asparagus, mushrooms, cauliflower, parsnips, turnips and fennel

1 Gently cook all the sliced vegetables in the fat under a lid, without colour.
2 Mix in the flour and cook slowly for a few minutes without colour. Cool slightly.
3 Gradually mix in the hot stock. Stir to the boil.
4 Add the bouquet garni and season.
5 Simmer for approximately 45 minutes; skim when necessary.
6 Remove the bouquet garni; liquidise, blend or pass firmly through a sieve and then through a medium strainer.
7 Return to a clean pan, reboil, and correct the seasoning and consistency.

Making a cream soup
http://bit.ly/wsAsgc

Try something different
- Instead of using the béchamel, use an additional 250 ml of stock, and then finish the soup with 250 ml milk.
- Alternatively, do this with an additional 375 ml of stock and finish with 125 ml of cream.

62 Cream of green pea soup
(crème St Germain)

seeds and pods shallow frying, boiling

energy	kcal	fat	sat fat	carb	sugar	protein	fibre
1356 KJ	323 kcal	23.6 g	12.8 g	19.6 g	8.0 g	9.3 g	8.3 g

Portions ›	4	10
onion, chopped	25 g	60 g
leek, chopped	25 g	60 g
celery, chopped	25 g	60 g
butter or oil	25 g	60 g
water or white stock	500 ml	1.25 litres
peas, fresh (shelled) or frozen	250 ml	625 ml
sprig of mint		
bouquet garni		
thin béchamel	500 ml	1.25 litres
cream, natural yoghurt or fromage frais	60 ml	150 ml

1 Sweat the onion, leek and celery in the butter or oil.
2 Moisten with water or stock and bring to the boil.
3 Add the peas, mint and bouquet garni, and allow to boil for approximately 5 minutes.
4 Remove the bouquet garni, add the béchamel and bring to the boil.
5 Remove from the heat, liquidise and pass through a sieve. Skim off any fat.
6 Correct seasoning, pass through medium strainer.
7 Finish with cream, natural yoghurt or fromage frais.

> **Note**
> Fresh or frozen peas can be used.

Healthy eating tips
- Use an unsaturated oil (sunflower or vegetable). Lightly oil the pan and drain off any excess after the frying is complete.
- Season with the minimum amount of salt.

Try something different
Variations can be made with the addition of:
- a garnish of 25 g cooked and washed tapioca, added at the same time as the cream
- a garnish of 25 g cooked and washed vermicelli and julienne of sorrel cooked in butter
- natural yoghurt, skimmed milk or non-dairy cream may be used in place of cream

See also the variations listed under pulse soup (recipe 65).

63 Cream of tomato soup
(crème de tomates fraiche)

vegetable fruits boiling, shallow frying

Portions >	4	10
butter or oil	50 g	125 g
bacon trimmings, optional	25 g	60 g
onion, diced	100 g	250 g
carrot, diced	100 g	250 g
flour	50 g	125 g
fresh, fully ripe tomatoes	1 kg	2.5 kg
stock	0.5 litres	1.25 litres
tomato purée	½ tbsp	1 heaped tbsp
bouquet garni		
salt, pepper		
Croutons		
stale bread	1 slice	3 slices
butter, margarine or oil	50 g	125 g

1 Melt the butter or heat the oil in a thick-bottomed pan.
2 Add the bacon, onion and carrot (mirepoix) and brown lightly.
3 Mix in the flour and cook to a sandy texture.
4 Gradually add the hot stock.
5 Stir to the boil.
6 Remove the eyes from the tomatoes, wash them well, quarter them and add them to the soup after it has come to the boil.
7 If colour is lacking, add a little tomato purée soon after the soup comes to the boil.
8 Add the bouquet garni, season lightly.
9 Simmer for approximately 1 hour. Skim when required.
10 Remove the bouquet garni and mirepoix.
11 Liquidise or pass firmly through a sieve, then through a conical strainer.
12 Return to a clean pan, correct the seasoning and consistency. Bring to the boil.
13 Serve fried or toasted croutons separately.

Tips
- Flour may be omitted from the recipe if a thinner soup is required.
- A gastric may be added to give a sweet and sour aftertaste – reduce 2 tbsp vinegar and 25 g sugar to a syrup and add to the soup to finish.

Healthy eating tips
- Use soft margarine or sunflower/vegetable oil in place of the butter.
- Toast the croutons rather than frying them.
- Use the minimum amount of salt – there is plenty in the bacon.

Try something different
Variation without fresh tomatoes:
Substitute 150 g of tomato purée for the fresh tomatoes (375 g for 10 portions). When reboiling the soup (step 12), add 500 ml of milk or 125 ml of cream, yoghurt or fromage frais.

64 Mushroom soup
(crème de champignons)

fungi boiling, shallow frying

energy	kcal	fat	sat fat	carb	sugar	protein	fibre *
712 KJ	170 kcal	11.8 g	5.2 g	12.6 g	3.0 g	3.8 g	1.6 g

Portions ❭	4	10
onion, leek and celery, sliced	100 g	250 g
butter or oil	50 g	125 g
flour	50 g	125 g
white stock (preferably chicken)	1 litre	2.5 litres
white mushrooms, washed and chopped	200 g	500 g
bouquet garni		
salt, pepper		
milk or cream	125 ml (or 60 ml cream)	300 ml (or 150 ml cream)

1 Gently cook the sliced onions, leek and celery in the butter or oil in a thick-bottomed pan, without colouring.
2 Mix in the flour and cook over a gentle heat to a sandy texture without colouring.
3 Remove from the heat and cool slightly.
4 Gradually mix in the hot stock. Stir to the boil.
5 Add the well-washed, chopped mushrooms, the bouquet garni and season.
6 Simmer for 30–45 minutes. Skim when needed.
7 Remove the bouquet garni. Pass through a sieve or liquidise.
8 Pass through a medium strainer. Return to a clean saucepan.
9 Reboil, correct the seasoning and consistency; add the milk or cream.

* Using hard margarine

Note
Natural yoghurt, skimmed milk or non-dairy cream may be used in place of dairy cream. A garnish of thinly sliced mushrooms may be added. Wild mushrooms may also be used.

Healthy eating tips
● Use soft margarine or sunflower/vegetable oil in place of the butter.
● Use the minimum amount of salt.
● The least fatty option is to use a combination of semi-skimmed milk and yoghurt or fromage frais – not cream.

65 Pulse soup with croutons

pulses boiling

energy	kcal	fat	sat fat	carb	sugar	protein	fibre	*
728 KJ	177 kcal	1.3 g	0.2 g	32.0 g	3.3 g	11.3 g	3.6 g	

Portions ❯	4	10
pulses (soaked overnight if necessary)	200 g	500 g
white stock or water	1.5 litres	3.75 litres
onions, chopped	50 g	125 g
carrots, chopped	50 g	125 g
bouquet garni		
knuckle of ham or bacon (optional)	50 g	125 g
salt, pepper		
Croutons		
stale bread	1 slice	2½ slices
butter or oil	50 g	125 g

1 Wash the pulses (if pre-soaked, change the water and drain).
2 Place in a thick-bottomed pan; add the stock or water, bring to the boil and skim.
3 Add the remainder of ingredients, season lightly.
4 Simmer until tender; skim when necessary.
5 Remove the bouquet garni and ham.
6 Liquidise and pass through a conical strainer.
7 Return to a clean pan and reboil; correct the seasoning and consistency.
8 Serve accompanied by 0.5 cm diced bread croutons shallow-fried in butter or olive oil.

> **Note**
> Pulses are the dried seeds of plants that form pods. Any type of pulse can be made into soup – for example, split green and yellow peas, haricot beans and lentils.
> Pay particular attention to consistency as pulses absorb large quantities of water during cooking.

Healthy eating tips
- The fat and salt are reduced if the ham is omitted.
- Try lightly brushing the stale bread with olive oil and oven baking it with garlic and herbs. Alternatively, serve with sippets (see below).

Try something different
Variations can be made with the addition of:
- chopped fresh herbs (parsley, chervil, tarragon, coriander, chives, etc.)
- spice(s) (e.g. garam masala)
- crisp lardons of bacon
- sippets (small, thin pieces of bread, toasted or oven-baked).

* 1 portion (no croutons). 1 portion (with croutons) provides: 1223 kJ/291 kcal energy; 111.7 g fat; 6.8 g sat fat; 36.5 g carb; 3.6 g sugar; 12.1 g protein; 3.8 g fibre

66 Chicken soup
(crème de volaille or crème reine)

chicken boiling, shallow frying

energy	kcal	fat	sat fat	carb	sugar	protein	fibre	*
836 KJ	199 kcal	13.6 g	6.2 g	14.0 g	4.2 g	5.9 g	1.0 g	

Portions 〉	4	10
onion, leek and celery, sliced	100 g	250 g
butter or oil	50 g	125 g
flour	50 g	125 g
chicken stock	750 ml	1.75 litres
bouquet garni		
salt, pepper		
milk or cream	250 ml or 125 ml	625 ml or 300 ml
cooked dice or julienne of chicken (garnish)	25 g	60 g

1 Gently cook the sliced onions, leek and celery in a thick-bottomed pan, in the butter or oil, without colouring.
2 Mix in the flour; cook over a gentle heat to a sandy texture without colouring.
3 Cool slightly; gradually mix in the hot stock. Stir to the boil.
4 Add the bouquet garni and season.
5 Simmer for 30–45 minutes; skim when necessary. Remove the bouquet garni.
6 Liquidise or pass firmly through a fine strainer.
7 Return to a clean pan, reboil and finish with milk or cream; correct the seasoning.
8 Add the chicken garnish and serve.

* Using hard margarine

Note
Natural yoghurt, skimmed milk or non-dairy cream may be used in place of dairy cream. Add cooked small pasta or sliced mushrooms for variations.

Healthy eating tips
- Use soft margarine or sunflower/vegetable oil in place of the butter.
- Use the minimum amount of salt.
- The least fatty option is to use a combination of semi-skimmed milk and yoghurt or fromage frais – not cream.

67 Asparagus soup
(crème d'asperges)

energy	kcal	fat	sat fat	carb	sugar	protein	fibre	*
1515 KJ	361 kcal	25.3 g	11.9 g	27.1 g	8.1 g	7.7 g	2.5 g	

Portions ⟩	4	10
onion, sliced	50 g	125 g
celery, sliced	50 g	125 g
butter or oil	50 g	125 g
flour	50 g	125 g
white stock (preferably chicken)	1 litre	2.5 litres
asparagus stalk trimmings	200 g	500 g
or		
tin of asparagus	150 g	325 g
bouquet garni		
salt, pepper		
milk or cream	250 ml or 125 ml	625 ml or 300 ml

1 Gently sweat the onions and celery, without colouring, in the butter or oil.

2 Remove from the heat, mix in the flour, return to a low heat and cook out, without colouring, for a few minutes. Cool.

3 Gradually add the hot stock. Stir to the boil.

4 Add the well-washed asparagus trimmings, or the tin of asparagus, and bouquet garni. Season.

5 Simmer for 30–40 minutes, then remove bouquet garni.

6 Liquidise and pass through a strainer.

7 Return to a clean pan, reboil, correct seasoning and consistency. (Milk with a little cornflour can be added to adjust the consistency.)

8 Add the milk or cream and serve.

Healthy eating tips

● Use an unsaturated oil (sunflower/vegetable) to lightly oil the pan. Drain off any excess after the frying is complete and skim the fat from the finished dish.

● Season with the minimum amount of salt.

* Using hard margarine. Using butter, 1 portion provides: 919 kJ/223 kcal energy; 13.1 g fat; 8.0 g sat fat; 18.9 g carb; 8.8 g sugar; 8.4 g protein; 2.5 g fibre

68 Cream of spinach and celery soup

leafy vegetables  boiling, shallow frying

	energy 646 KJ	kcal 156 kcal	fat 9.3 g	sat fat 1.3 g	carb 9.0 g	sugar 4.1 g	protein 9.2 g	fibre 5.7 g	sodium 1.1 g *

Portions ❯	4	10
shallots, peeled and chopped (small mirepoix)	2	5
leeks, washed and chopped (small mirepoix)	1	2
cloves of garlic, peeled and chopped	5	7
corn oil	2 tbsp	5 tbsp
celery sticks, washed and chopped (small mirepoix)	4	10
flour	15 g	35 g
fresh spinach, well washed	500 g	1.25 kg
milk	600 ml	1.5 litres
vegetable stock (see recipe 4)	600 ml	1.5 litres
salt, to taste		

1 Cook the shallots, leeks and garlic in the oil for a few minutes, without colour.
2 Add the celery and cook for another few minutes until starting to soften.
3 Add the flour and mix well, then add the spinach and mix around. Add the milk and vegetable stock slowly, ensuring there are no lumps.
4 Stir continuously, bring to a simmer, then switch off and remove from heat. Cover and leave for a few minutes.
5 Blend until smooth in a food processor. Check seasoning and serve.

* Using unsweetened soya milk

69 Watercress soup

leafy vegetables 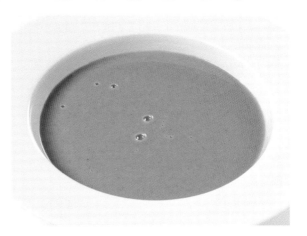 boiling, shallow frying

energy	kcal	fat	sat fat	carb	sugar	protein	fibre	sodium
1024 KJ	247 kcal	18.4 g	10.7 g	15.4 g	4.7 g	5.8 g	5.6 g	1.0 g

Portions ❯	4	Approx. 10
butter or oil	80 g	200 g
potatoes, chopped	240 g	600 g
leeks, chopped	100 g	250 g
shallots, chopped	120 g	300 g
cloves of garlic, peeled and chopped	1	2
vegetable stock or water	1 litre	2.5 litres
horseradish sauce	½ tbsp	1 ½ tbsp
spinach, picked and washed	300 g	750 g
watercress (ends trimmed)	150 g	375 g

1 Heat 50 g of the butter or oil in a thick-bottomed pan.
2 Add the potatoes and cook without colour for 2 minutes.
3 Add the leeks, shallots and garlic, and cook for a further 4 minutes without colour.
4 Add the stock and horseradish, bring to the boil and simmer for 6 minutes, then remove from the stove.
5 Heat a clean pan, add the remainder of the oil/ butter and wilt the spinach and watercress in a hot pan until the bitterness of the watercress is well rounded.
6 Add this to the liquid mix, liquidise until smooth and very green and pass through a conical strainer (not a chinois).
7 Allow to cool, then store.

70 Vegetable purée soup

bulbs 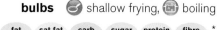 shallow frying, boiling

energy	kcal	fat	sat fat	carb	sugar	protein	fibre	*
601 KJ	143 kcal	10.3 g	4.4 g	11.4 g	1.8 g	1.9 g	1.9 g	

Portions >	4	Approx. 10
onions, leek and celery, sliced	100 g	250 g
other suitable vegetables,* sliced	200 g	500 g
butter or oil	50 g	125 g
flour	50 g	125 g
white stock or water	1 litre	2.5 litres
bouquet garni		
salt, pepper		

*Suitable vegetables include Jerusalem artichokes, carrots, asparagus, mushrooms, cauliflower, parsnips, turnips and fennel

1 Gently cook all the sliced vegetables in the fat under a lid, without colour.
2 Mix in the flour and cook slowly for a few minutes without colour. Cool slightly.
3 Gradually mix in the hot stock. Stir to the boil.
4 Add the bouquet garni and season.
5 Simmer for approximately 45 minutes; skim when necessary.
6 Remove the bouquet garni; liquidise or pass firmly through a sieve and then through a medium strainer.
7 Return to a clean pan, reboil, and correct the seasoning and consistency.

* Using hard margarine

Try something different
● Add a little spice, sufficient to give a subtle background flavour, e.g. garam masala with parsnip soup.
● Just before serving add a little freshly chopped herb(s), e.g. parsley, chervil, tarragon, coriander.

Healthy eating tips
● Use an unsaturated oil (sunflower or vegetable) to lightly oil the pan. Drain off any excess after the frying is complete and skim the fat from the finished dish.
● Season with the minimum amount of salt.
● Try using more vegetables to thicken the soup in place of the flour.

Making a purée soup
http://bit.ly/zp7WTh

71 Potato soup
(purée parmentier)

potatoes boiling, shallow frying

energy	kcal	fat	sat fat	carb	sugar	protein	fibre	*
1063 KJ	253 kcal	15.7 g	9.8 g	26.1 g	2.1 g	3.6 g	2.9 g	

Portions ⟩	4	10
butter or oil	25 g	60 g
onion, peeled and sliced	50 g	125 g
white of leek, sliced	50 g	125 g
white stock or water	1 litre	2.5 litres
potatoes, peeled	400 g	1.25 kg
bouquet garni		
salt, pepper		
parsley, chopped		
Croutons		
stale bread	1 slice	3 slices
butter, margarine or oil	50 g	125 g

1 Melt the butter or heat the oil in a thick-bottomed pan.
2 Add the peeled, washed and sliced onion and leek, cook for a few minutes without colour with the lid on.
3 Add the stock, the peeled, washed and sliced potatoes and the bouquet garni. Season.
4 Simmer for approximately 30 minutes. Remove the bouquet garni, skim off all fat.
5 Liquidise or pass the soup firmly through a sieve then pass through a medium conical strainer.
6 Return to a clean pan, reboil, correct the seasoning and consistency.
7 Sprinkle with chopped parsley.
8 Serve fried or toasted croutons separately.

* Using butter

Healthy eating tips
- Use an unsaturated oil (sunflower or vegetable). Lightly oil the pan and drain off any excess after the frying is complete.
- Season with the minimum amount of salt.
- Toast the croutons instead of frying them.

72 Potato and watercress soup

(purée cressonnière)

potatoes, leafy vegetables boiling, shallow frying

Portions ›	4	10
butter or oil	25 g	60 g
onion, peeled and sliced	50 g	125 g
white of leek, sliced	50 g	125 g
white stock or water	1 litre	2.5 litres
potatoes, peeled and sliced	400 g	1.5 kg
watercress	small bunch	small bunch
bouquet garni		
salt, pepper		
parsley, chopped		
Croutons		
stale bread	1 slice	3 slices
butter or oil	50 g	125 g

1 Pick off 12 neat leaves of watercress, plunge into a small pan of boiling water for 1–2 seconds. Refresh under cold water immediately; these leaves are to garnish the finished soup.
2 Melt the butter or heat the oil in a thick-bottomed pan.
3 Add the peeled and washed sliced onion and leek, cook for a few minutes without colour with the lid on.
4 Add the stock, the peeled, washed and sliced potatoes, the rest of the watercress, including the stalks, and the bouquet garni. Season.
5 Simmer for approximately 30 minutes. Remove the bouquet garni, skim off all fat.
6 Liquidise or pass the soup firmly through a sieve then pass through a medium conical strainer.
7 Return to a clean pan, reboil, correct the seasoning and consistency.
8 Garnish with watercress.
9 Serve fried or toasted croutons separately.

73 Chilled leek and potato soup
(vichyssoise)

potatoes, herbs  boiling, shallow frying

energy	kcal	fat	sat fat	carb	sugar	protein	fibre
949 KJ	228 kcal	15.0 g	9.3 g	20.3 g	3.2 g	4.1 g	1.8 g

*

Portions ›	4	10
butter or oil	25 g	60 g
onion, peeled, washed and sliced	50 g	125 g
white of leek, washed and sliced	50 g	125 g
white stock	1 litre	2.5 litres
potatoes, peeled, washed and sliced	400 g	1.5 kg
bouquet garni		
salt, pepper		
cream	125–250 ml	500 ml
chives, chopped		

Healthy eating tips

- Use an unsaturated oil (sunflower or vegetable). Lightly oil the pan and drain off any excess after the frying is complete.
- Season with the minimum amount of salt.
- Try using natural yoghurt or fromage frais instead of cream.

* Using 200 ml single cream

1 Melt the butter or heat the oil in a thick-bottomed pan.

2 Add the onion and leek, cook for a few minutes without colour, with the lid on.

3 Add the stock, potatoes and bouquet garni. Season.

4 Simmer for approximately 30 minutes. Remove the bouquet garni, skim.

5 Liquidise or pass the soup firmly through a sieve, then through a medium conical strainer.

6 Return to a clean pan and reboil; correct the seasoning and consistency, skim off any fat.

7 Finish with cream and garnish with chopped chives, either raw or cooked in a little butter. Usually served chilled.

74 Gazpacho

	energy	kcal	fat	sat fat	carb	sugar	protein	fibre	sodium
	861 KJ	203 kcal	2.7 g	0.8 g	40.5 g	38.7 g	6.7 g	12.5 g	3.2 g

Portions ❯	4	10
plum tomatoes, ripe	2.5 kg	6.25 kg
white onion, roughly chopped	1	2
cucumber, peeled and roughly chopped	1	2
garlic clove, crushed	½	1
red peppers, peeled and deseeded	550 g	1.3 kg
salt	40 g	80 g
cayenne pepper	2 g	5 g
Chardonnay vinegar or white wine vinegar	6 g	15 g
sugar (to taste, depending on season)	30 g	75 g

1 Mix all the ingredients together and leave to marinate overnight in the fridge.

2 Blitz the ingredients in a food processor and strain through a chinois.

3 Discard the remaining pulp into a colander lined with muslin (this is to catch the extra juices that will come from the pulp).

4 The juices from the pulp can be used to thin out the gazpacho until it reaches the correct consistency.

5 Check seasoning. Store in the refrigerator. Serve well chilled.

Note
This can be served unpassed for a different texture.

75 Tomato soup
(potage de tomates)

vegetable fruits boiling, shallow frying

| energy
1150 KJ | kcal
274 kcal | fat
21.3 g | sat fat
11.2 g | carb
17.1 g | sugar
3.7 g | protein
4.6 g | fibre
1.0 g | * |

Portions ❯	4	10
butter or oil	50 g	125 g
bacon trimmings, optional	25 g	60 g
onion, diced	100 g	250 g
carrot, diced	100 g	250 g
flour	50 g	125 g
tomato purée	150 g	375 g
stock	1.25 litres	3 litres
bouquet garni		
salt, pepper		
Croutons		
stale bread	1 slice	3 slices
butter or oil	50 g	125 g

1 Melt the butter or heat the oil in a thick-bottomed pan.
2 Add the bacon, onion and carrot (mirepoix) and brown lightly.
3 Mix in the flour and cook to a sandy texture.
4 Remove from the heat, mix in the tomato purée.
5 Return to heat. Gradually add the hot stock.
6 Stir to the boil. Add the bouquet garni, season lightly.
7 Simmer for approximately 1 hour. Skim when required.
8 Remove the bouquet garni and mirepoix.
9 Liquidise or pass firmly through a sieve, then through a conical strainer.
10 Return to a clean pan, correct the seasoning and consistency. Bring to the boil.
11 Serve fried or toasted croutons separately.

* Using hard margarine

Tip
If a slightly sweet/sour flavour is required, reduce 100 ml vinegar and 35 g caster sugar to a light caramel and mix into the completed soup.

Healthy eating tips
- Use soft margarine or sunflower/vegetable oil in place of the butter.
- Toast the croutons rather than frying them.
- Use the minimum amount of salt – there is plenty in the bacon.

Try something different
Variations can be made with the addition of:
- juice and lightly grated zest of 1–2 oranges
- tomato concassée
- cooked rice
- chopped fresh coriander, basil or chives
- 200 g peeled, sliced potatoes with the stock.

76 Roasted red pepper and tomato soup

vegetable fruits 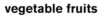 roasting, boiling, shallow frying

energy	kcal	fat	sat fat	carb	sugar	protein	fibre	salt
983 KJ	235 kcal	16.8 g	7.1 g	18.3 g	16.4 g	3.6 g	4.5 g	2.1 g

Portions ›	4	10
red peppers	4	10
plum tomatoes	400 g	1.25 kg
butter or oil	50 g	125 g
onion, chopped	100 g	250 g
carrot, chopped	100 g	250 g
stock	500 ml	1.5 litres
crème fraiche	2 tbsp	5 tbsp
basil	25 g	75 g
Croutons		
stale bread	1 slice	3 slices
butter or oil	50 g	125 g

1 Core and deseed the peppers, and halve the tomatoes.
2 Lightly sprinkle with oil, and place on a tray into a hot oven or under a grill until the pepper skins are blackened.
3 Allow the peppers to cool in a plastic bag.
4 Remove the skins and slice the flesh.
5 Place the butter or oil in a pan, add the onions and carrots and fry gently for 5 minutes.
6 Add the stock, peppers and tomatoes, and bring to the boil.
7 Simmer for 30 minutes, correct the seasoning and blend in a food processor until smooth.
8 Add crème fraiche and basil leaves torn into pieces, and serve with croutons.

77 Roasted butternut squash soup

vegetable fruits roasting, boiling, ⬤ shallow frying

energy	kcal	fat	sat fat	carb	sugar	protein	fibre
923 KJ	220 kcal	12.0 g	3.5 g	19.6 g	13.1 g	9.9 g	2.8 g

Portions ›	4	10
butternut squash, peeled and deseeded	600 g	2 kg
olive oil	2 tbsp	5 tbsp
onion, finely chopped	100 g	250 g
clove of garlic (optional), finely chopped	1	2
bacon, back rashers, in small pieces	4	10
chicken or vegetable stock	1 litre	2 litres
salt, pepper		
cream or thick natural yoghurt	6 tbsp	15 tbsp

1 Cut the squash into thick pieces, place on a lightly oiled baking sheet and roast for 20–25 minutes at 180°C until the flesh is soft and golden brown.

2 Sweat the onions and garlic without colouring (approx. 5 minutes).

3 Add the bacon and lightly brown.

4 Add the roasted squash, pour in the stock, bring to the boil and simmer for 20 minutes.

5 Allow to cool, then liquidise or blend until smooth.

6 Season lightly, add yoghurt or cream, reheat gently and serve.

Healthy eating tips

● Use an unsaturated oil (sunflower or vegetable) and lightly oil the pan. Drain off any excess fat after cooking the bacon.

● Use low-fat yoghurt to reduce the fat. Add a little cornflour to stabilise the yoghurt before adding to the soup.

Try something different

Add 3–4 saffron strands soaked in 1 tbsp hot water at point 4 in the recipe.

Carrot and butterbean soup

root vegetables, pulses boiling, shallow frying

energy	kcal	fat	sat fat	carb	sugar	protein	fibre	salt
891 KJ	213 kcal	5.9 g	0.7 g	33.4 g	19.3 g	8.5 g	8.1 g	3.6 g

Portions ❯	4	10
onions, peeled and chopped	1	2
cloves of garlic, chopped	2	5
sunflower oil	15 ml	35 ml
large to medium carrots, brunoise	6	15
carrot juice	500 ml	1.25 litres
vegetable stock	500 ml	1.25 litres
butter beans, cooked	400 g	1 kg
seasoning		

1 Cook the onion and garlic in the oil for a few minutes, without colour, then add the carrots and stir well.

2 Add the carrot juice and vegetable stock. Bring to the boil, turn down to a simmer and cook for about 15 minutes until the carrot is cooked through.

3 Add the beans and cook for a further 5 minutes or so until they are heated through.

4 Liquidise in a food processor until smooth; check seasoning.

Key point

With any soup recipe, it is important to simmer the soup gently. Do not let it boil vigorously, because too much water will evaporate. If the soup has boiled, add more stock or water to make up for this.

79	Lentil soup

pulses, pork boiling, shallow frying

energy	kcal	fat	sat fat	carb	sugar	protein	fibre	salt
1807 KJ	432 kcal	71.4 g	43.9 g	6.7 g	1.5 g	5.3 g	1.5 g	2.2 g

Portions ›	4	Approx. 10
For the ham hock		
ham hock	320 g	800 g
onion, peeled	25 g	60 g
whole carrot, peeled	½	1
For the soup		
baby shallots	1	3
leeks	50 g	125 g
celery	50 g	125 g
oil	40 ml	100 ml
red or yellow lentils	200 g	500 g
cooking liquid from the hock	1 litre	2.5 litres
milk, cream or crème fraiche	120 ml	300 ml

Try something different
Meat-free version: omit the ham hock, and use a vegetable stock or water instead of the cooking liquid.

1 Place the ham hock, onion and carrot in a pan and cover with about 3 litres of water.
2 Bring to the boil and then turn down to a slow simmer. (When the hock is cooked, the centre bone will slide out in one smooth motion.)
3 Slice the shallots, leek and celery into 1 cm dice.
4 Heat a pan with the oil, add the vegetables and cook until they are slightly coloured; add the lentils and cover them with the ham stock.
5 Bring to the boil, then turn the heat down to a very slow simmer.
6 Cook until all the lentils have broken down.
7 Allow to cool for 10 minutes and then purée until smooth.
8 Correct the consistency as necessary, and finish with boiled milk, cream or crème fraiche.

The ham hock can be shredded and used as a garnish.

80 Pea velouté

seeds and pods boiling, shallow frying

energy	kcal	fat	sat fat	carb	sugar	protein	fibre	sodium
984 KJ	237 kcal	17.8 g	9.6 g	12.2 g	5.5 g	7.7 g	6.9 g	0.1 g

Portions >	4	10
frozen peas	400 g	1 kg
vegetable oil	10 ml	25 ml
shallots, chopped	1	2
chicken or vegetable stock	700 ml	1.75 litres
milk	200 ml	500 ml
double cream	40 ml	100 ml
butter or margarine	40 g	100 g

1 Blanch the peas in a small pan of boiling water for 3 minutes, then drain.
2 Heat the oil in large saucepan and cook the shallots without letting them colour.
3 Add the peas to this pan, and cook for a further 2–3 minutes, again without colouring.
4 Add the stock and milk, bring to a simmer and cook until the peas are tender.

5 Cool the mixture slightly, then transfer to a food processor and liquidise until very smooth – this may take a while. At this point, the soup can be cooled completely then stored in an airtight container in the refrigerator until ready to serve.
6 Add the cream and butter just before serving.

81 Pumpkin velouté

vegetable fruits boiling, shallow frying

energy	kcal	fat	sat fat	carb	sugar	protein	fibre	salt	*
2883 KJ	689 kcal	71.4 g	43.9 g	6.7 g	1.5 g	5.3 g	1.5 g	3.0 g	

Portions >	4	10
shallots, sliced	1	3
butter	50 g	125 g
clove of garlic, sliced (optional)	½	1
large squash or pumpkin (300 g), flesh diced	1	2
Parmesan, grated	30 g	70 g
truffle oil	1 tbsp	2 tbsp
salt, pepper		
chicken stock	600 ml	1.5 litres

1 Sweat the shallots in butter, without colour, until cooked and soft.
2 Add the garlic, pumpkin, Parmesan and truffle oil. Correct the seasoning and cook for 5 minutes.

3 Add the chicken stock, bring to the boil, simmer for 5 minutes.
4 Blitz in a liquidiser, pass, correct the seasoning, then blast chill if to be stored.

* Using acorn squash and olive oil

82 Clear soup
(consommé)

beef boiling

energy	kcal	fat	sat fat	carb	sugar	protein	fibre
126 KJ	30 kcal	0.0 g	0.0 g	1.8 g	0.0 g	5.6 g	0.0 g

Portions ›	4	10
chopped or minced beef	200 g	500 g
salt, to taste		
egg whites	1–2	3–5
cold white or brown beef stock	1 litre	2.5 litres
mixed vegetables (onion, carrot, celery, leek)	100 g	250 g
bouquet garni		
peppercorns	3–4	8–10

1 Thoroughly mix the beef, salt, egg white and a quarter of the cold stock in a thick-bottomed pan.
2 Peel, wash and finely chop the vegetables.
3 Add to the beef with the remainder of the stock, the bouquet garni and the peppercorns.
4 Place over a gentle heat and bring slowly to the boil, stirring occasionally.
5 Allow to boil rapidly for 5–10 seconds. Give a final stir.
6 Lower the heat so that the consommé is simmering very gently.
7 Cook for 1½–2 hours without stirring.
8 Strain carefully through a double muslin.
9 Remove all fat, using both sides of 8 cm square pieces of kitchen paper.
10 Correct the seasoning and colour, which should be a delicate amber.
11 Degrease again, if necessary. Bring to the boil and serve.

Note

A consommé should be crystal clear. The clarification process is caused by the albumen of the egg white and meat coagulating, rising to the top of the liquid and carrying other solid ingredients. The remaining liquid beneath the coagulated surface should be gently simmering. Cloudiness is due to some or all of the following:
- poor-quality stock
- greasy stock
- unstrained stock
- imperfect coagulation of the clearing agent
- whisking after boiling point is reached, whereby the impurities mix with the liquid
- not allowing the soup to settle before straining
- lack of cleanliness of the pan or cloth
- any trace of grease or starch.

Healthy eating tips
- This soup is fat free!
- Keep the salt to a minimum and serve as a low-calorie starter for anyone wishing to reduce the fat in their diet.

Mix one quarter of the stock with the beef, salt and egg white

Once the remaining stock and the vegetables have been added, bring slowly to the boil

After the soup has simmered for at least 1½ hours, strain it carefully

83 New England clam chowder

shellfish, potatoes shallow frying, boiling

energy	kcal	fat	sat fat	carb	sugar	protein	fibre	*
1109 KJ	269 kcal	14.9 g	7.7 g	24.5 g	2.5 g	14.9 g	1.8 g	

Portions ❯	4	10
salt pork or bacon, cut into 0.5 cm dice	50 g	125 g
onion, finely chopped	50 g	125 g
fish stock or cold water	600 ml	1.5 litres
potatoes, cut into 0.5 cm dice	500 g	1.25 kg
fresh clams, steamed, shelled and trimmed	200 g	500 g
cream	180 ml	450 ml
thyme, crushed or chopped	1 g	2 g
salt, white pepper		
butter, softened	20 g	50 g
paprika		

1 Dry-fry the pork in a thick-bottomed saucepan for about 3 minutes, stirring constantly until a thin film of fat covers the bottom of the pan.
2 Stir in the chopped onion and cook gently until a light golden brown.
3 Add the water and potatoes, bring to the boil and simmer gently until the potatoes are cooked but not mushy.
4 Add the clams, the cream and thyme, and heat until almost boiling. Season with salt and pepper.
5 Correct the seasoning, stir in the softened butter and serve, dusting each soup bowl with a little paprika.

> **Note**
> The traditional accompaniment is salted cracker biscuits. An obvious variation would be to use scallops in place of clams.

* Using bacon or salt pork

84 Prawn bisque

shellfish  boiling, shallow frying

energy	kcal	fat	sat fat	carb	sugar	protein	fibre	sodium
1578 KJ	381 kcal	31.2 g	13.0 g	8.2 g	4.0 g	12.9 g	0.8 g	1.0 g

Portions >	4	10
oil	50 ml	125 ml
butter	30 g	75 g
shelled prawns (keep the shells)	250 g	625 g
flour	20 g	50 kg
tomato purée	1 tbsp	2 tbsp
shellfish nage	1 litre	2.5 litres
fish stock	150 ml	375 ml g
whipping cream	120 ml	300 ml
dry sherry	75 ml	180 ml
paprika, pinch		
seasoning		
chives, chopped		

1 Heat the oil and the butter. Add the prawns and cook for 3–4 minutes on a moderately high heat.
2 Sprinkle in the flour and cook for a further 2–3 minutes.
3 Add the tomato purée and cook for a further 2 minutes.
4 Meanwhile, bring the nage up to a simmer and, once the tomato purée has been cooked in, slowly add to the prawn mix, being mindful that you have formed a roux; stir in the fish stock to prevent lumping.
5 Once all the stock has been added, bring to the boil and simmer for 3–4 minutes.
6 Pass through a fine sieve, return the shells to the pan and pound to extract more flavour and more colour.
7 Pour over the fish stock, bring to the boil, then pass this back onto the already passed soup.
8 Bring to the boil, add the cream and sherry, correct the seasoning and served with chopped chives.

Cold preparation

This chapter is relevant to the following units:

- Prepare and present food for cold preparation (NVQ).

Cold food

Cold food is popular in every kind of food service operation for at least three good reasons:

1 Visual appeal: when the food is attractively displayed, carefully arranged and neatly garnished, the customers can have their appetites stimulated by seeing exactly what is being offered.

2 Efficiency: cold food can be prepared in advance, allowing a large number of people to be served in a short space of time. Self-service is also economic in terms of staffing.

3 Adaptability: if cold food is being served from a buffet, the range of foods can be simple or complex and wide-ranging, depending on the type of operation.

Cold foods can either be pre-plated or served from large dishes and bowls. In both cases presentation is important: the food should appear fresh, neatly arranged and not over-garnished.

Health, safety and hygiene

For information on maintaining a safe and secure working environment, a professional and hygienic appearance, and clean food production areas, equipment and utensils, as well as food safety, please refer to Chapters 14 and 15. Additional food safety points are as follows.

 Where possible, use latex gloves when handling food.

 Keep unprepared and prepared food under refrigeration at a temperature not exceeding 4°C. Refrigeration will not kill the bacteria that are present in the foods, but does help to prevent their growth.

● Whenever possible, the food on display to the public should be kept under refrigeration and the temperature should be checked to ensure that it is being maintained at a safe level.

- Where customers are viewing the food closely, ideally it should be displayed behind a sneeze screen.

- Dishes prepared in advance should be covered with film and refrigerated at 1–4°C to prevent them drying out.
- Personal, food and equipment hygiene of the highest order must be observed with all cold work.

Cold preparation

'Cold preparation' means the preparation of raw and/or cooked foods into a wide variety of cold items.

Cold food must look clean and fresh. Its presentation should be appealing to the eye.

Techniques

Techniques used in cold preparation include:

- peeling, chopping and cutting
- carving
- seasoning: the light addition of salt, pepper and possibly other flavouring agents
- dressing: this can either mean an accompanying salad dressing, such as vinaigrette, or the arrangement of food for presentation on plates, dishes or buffets
- garnishing: the final addition to the dish, such as lettuce, quarters of tomato and sliced cucumber added to egg mayonnaise
- marinade: a richly spiced pickling liquid used to give flavour and to assist in tenderising meats such as venison. Simple marinades (e.g. olive oil with herbs or soy sauce with herbs and/or spices) can be used with cuts of fish, chicken or meat.

Equipment

Bowls, tongs, whisks, spoons, and so on, as well as food processors, mixing machines and blenders are used with cold preparations.

Preparation for cold work

Well-planned organisation is essential to ensure adequate pre-preparation (*mise-en-place*), so that foods are assembled with a good work flow and are ready on time. Before, during and after assembling, and before final garnishing, foods must be kept in a cool place, cold room or refrigerator so as to minimise the risk of food contamination. Garnishing and final decoration should take place as close to the serving time as possible.

General rules

- Be aware of the texture and flavour of many raw foods that can be mixed together or combined with cooked foods (e.g. coleslaw, meat salad).
- Understand what combination of foods – for example, salads – is best suited to be served with other foods, such as cold meat or poultry.
- Develop simple artistic skills that require the minimum of time for preparation and assembly.
- Provide an attractive presentation of food at all times.
- Because of the requirements of food safety, cold foods are often served straight from the refrigerator. However, flavours will be better if the food is allowed to stand at room temperature for 5–10 minutes before serving.

Hors d'oeuvre and salads

The choice of a wide variety of foods, combination of foods and recipes is available for preparation and service as hors d'oeuvre and salads. Hors d'oeuvre can be divided into three categories:

1 single cold food items (smoked salmon, pâté, melon, etc.)
2 a selection of well-seasoned cold dishes
3 well-seasoned hot dishes.

Hors d'oeuvre may be served for luncheon, dinner or supper, and the wide choice, colour appeal and versatility of the dishes make many items and combinations of items suitable for snacks and salads at any time of day.

Salads may be served as an accompaniment to hot and cold foods and as dishes in their own right. They can be served for lunch, tea, high tea, dinner, supper and snack meals. Salads may be divided in two sections:

1 simple, using one ingredient
2 mixed, or composite, using more than one ingredient.

Some salads may form part of a composite hors d'oeuvre. Accompaniments include dressings and cold sauces.

Salads may be served as an accompaniment to hot and cold foods and as dishes in their own right.

Single-food hors d'oeuvre

Serve single-food hors d'oeuvre (e.g. smoked salmon or foie gras) with bread or toast, and butter separately. Add a salad garnish.

Terrines and pâté

A slice of terrine served with a suitable garnish (e.g. a small tossed salad dressed with vinaigrette and chopped fresh herbs) makes an ideal first course, or a small portion can form part of an hors d'oeuvre selection.

Pre-prepared pâtés or terrines are available in a wide variety of types and flavourings, which include liver (chicken, duck, etc.), poultry and game. Pâtés are usually cooked enclosed in a thin layer of bacon fat,

or they may be enclosed in hot water pastry within a special mould.

Pâtés and terrines must be kept under refrigeration at all times and should never be allowed to stand in a warm kitchen or dining room because they are easily contaminated by food poisoning bacteria.

Fish and vegetable pâtés and terrines are also available. When serving meat, poultry or game pâtés, a simple garnish and a little salad is sufficient.

The use of plastic gloves and tools such as palate knives and slices will reduce the risk of pâté contamination when cold foods are being handled. (See recipes 56–58.)

Cold meats

The typical meats or poultry for cold presentation are roast beef, boiled or honey roast ham or gammon, roast chicken or turkey, and boiled ox tongue. These can be cooked and cooled, or leftover joints from previous hot meals can be used. Cold meats can also be bought in ready cooked from suppliers. The various ways to present and serve cold meats are:

- sliced from whole joints on the bone in front of the customer (in which case all bones that may hinder carving must be removed first)
- sliced from boned joints, which in some cases may be rolled and stuffed (also in front of the customer)
- pre-sliced in the kitchen, in which case the meat or poultry should be cut as close to service time as possible, otherwise it will start to dry and curl up; pre-sliced meats or poultry can be neatly cut, dressed with the slices overlapping each other, placed on large dishes or individual plates, covered with clingfilm and kept under refrigeration; when large numbers of plated meals have to be prepared, plate rings or jackstands can be used and the plates stacked in sensible-sized numbers.

When roast chickens are required for serving cold, ideally they should be cooked 90 minutes before service, left to cool (preferably in a blast chiller) and then carved as required. In this way, the meat remains moist and succulent. Chickens can then be cut into pieces and the excess bones removed before serving.

Ham

Ham should not be confused with gammon. A gammon is the hind leg of a baconer pig and is cut from a side of bacon. A ham is the hind leg of a porker pig and is cut round from the side of pork with the aitch bone, and usually cured by dry salting. Ham is boiled and can be served hot or cold. Certain imported hams (Parma ham, Bayonne and Ardennes) are sliced thinly and eaten raw, generally as an hors d'oeuvre. In order to carve the ham efficiently it is necessary to remove the aitch bone after cooking. Traditional English hams include York and Bradenham.

Dressings, chutneys, relishes and pickles

Salad dressings

These dressings may be varied by the addition of other ingredients. Salads should be lightly dressed or the dressing offered separately to give the customer the choice.

Chutneys and relishes

Chutneys are made from a variety of ingredients, usually fruit, preserved in sugar and acid after careful cooking. They are flavoured with a range of spices.

Chutneys are served as an accompaniment to terrines and pâtés, salads, cold meats, poultry, game and cheese. They may also accompany a traditional curry (e.g. mango chutney).

Relishes are similar to chutneys except they are generally smoother and do not always contain as much sugar.

Fruits and vegetables for use in relishes and chutneys must be unblemished and well washed. Good-quality vinegars must be used at 5 per cent acetic acid.

Pickles

Vegetables to be pickled are usually brined (unless they are to be used in a chutney or similar mixture, then it is not necessary). Brining removes the surplus water that would otherwise dilute the vinegar and make it too weak to act as a preservative.

Dry brining is used for watery vegetables such as cucumbers, marrows and tomatoes. Place the prepared vegetables in a deep bowl, sprinkle salt between the layers, allowing about ½ tsp salt for each 500 g. Cover and leave overnight.

Wet brining is used for cauliflower, onions, etc. Allow 50 g salt to 500 ml water (sufficient for about 0.5 kg vegetables), place the prepared vegetables in a deep bowl, cover with the brine and leave overnight. Root vegetables such as artichokes, and sometimes beetroot, are cooked in half-strength brine until tender. After brining, rinse and drain the vegetables.

Spiced vinegar is used to cover most simple pickles; the vinegar used for this – and for all pickles – must be of high quality, with an acetic acid content of not less than 5 per cent. Brewed malt vinegar is most commonly used, but for onions, cauliflower and other light-coloured vegetables, white vinegar may be used.

1 Vinaigrette

	energy	kcal	fat	sat fat	carb	sugar	protein	fibre	*
	1740 KJ	415 kcal	45.5 g	6.3 g	0.5 g	0.1 g	0.6 g	0.0 g	

Portions 〉	4–6
olive oil, according to taste	3–6 tbsp
French mustard	1 tsp
vinegar	1 tbsp
salt, mill pepper, to taste	

Place the vinegar, mustard and seasoning in a bowl. Gradually whisk in the oil to make an emulsion.

The number of portions yielded will depend on how the vinaigrette is used.

Try something different

Variations to vinaigrette include:

- English mustard in place of French mustard
- chopped herbs (chives, parsley, tarragon, etc.)
- chopped hard-boiled egg
- other good-quality oils, e.g. sesame seed or walnut
- different flavoured vinegars or lemon juice.

* Using 3 tbsp oil, for 4–6 portions. Using 6 tbsp oil, this recipe provides for 4–6 portions: 3439 kJ/415 kcal energy; 90.5 g fat; 12.6 g sat fat; 0.5 g carb; 0.1 g sugar; 0.6 g protein; 0.0 g fibre

Making vinaigrette
http://bit.ly/AFhvFa

2 Balsamic vinegar and olive oil dressing

Makes 〉	300 ml
water	62 ml
olive oil	250 ml
balsamic vinegar	62 ml
sherry vinegar	2 tbsp
caster sugar	½ tsp
seasoning	

1 Whisk all ingredients together.
2 Correct the seasoning.

The amount of balsamic vinegar needed will depend on its quality, age, etc. Add more or less as required.

Key point

This dressing works well because it is not an emulsion. The oil and vinegar provide a stark contrast and can be stirred just before serving.

Portions >	4	10
tomatoes	200 g	500 g
caster sugar	½ tsp	1 ¼ tbsp
white wine vinegar	1 tbsp	2½ tbsp
extra virgin olive oil	3 tbsp	8 tbsp
seasoning		

1 Blanch and deseed the tomatoes; purée in a food processor.
2 Add the sugar, vinegar, olive oil and seasoning; whisk well to emulsify.
3 The vinaigrette should be smooth.

The number of portions yielded will depend on how the vinaigrette is used.

4 Thousand Island dressing

vegetable fruits, eggs

energy	kcal	fat	sat fat	carb	sugar	protein	fibre	*
15055 KJ	3584 kcal	38.7 g	56.5 g	10.2 g	9.8 g	16.1 g	1.8 g	

Portions ⟩	4–6
salt, pepper	
Tabasco sauce	3–4 drops
vinegar	125 ml
oil	375 ml
red pepper, chopped	50 g
green pepper, chopped	50 g
parsley, chopped	10 g
hard-boiled eggs, sieved	2
tomato ketchup (optional)	2 tbsp

1 Place the salt, pepper, Tabasco sauce and vinegar in a basin.
2 Mix well. Mix in the oil.
3 Add the chopped peppers and parsley.
4 Mix in the sieved hard-boiled eggs.
5 Mix in ketchup if desired.

The number of portions yielded will depend on how the dressing is used.

* For 4–6 portions

Finely chop the peppers and parsley

Sieve the hard-boiled eggs

Adjust the colour with ketchup as needed

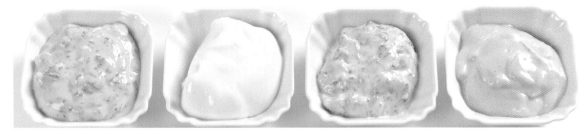
Recipes 4–6 and 8: Thousand Island dressing, mayonnaise, remoulade sauce and Andalusian sauce

5 Mayonnaise

energy	kcal	fat	sat fat	carb	sugar	protein	fibre
10030 KJ	2388 kcal	26.2 g	38.9 g	0.3 g	0.1 g	6.8 g	0.0 g

Portions >	8
egg yolks, pasteurised	2
vinegar	2 tsp
salt, ground white pepper	
English or continental mustard	1/8 tsp
corn oil	250 ml
boiling water	1 tsp (approx)

1 Place the yolks, vinegar and seasoning in a bowl and whisk well.
2 Gradually pour on the oil very slowly, whisking continuously.
3 Add the boiling water, whisking well. Correct the seasoning.

The number of portions yielded will depend on how the dressing is used.

Key points
- Gradually adding the oil to the beaten egg yolks forms an emulsion.
- This is a basic cold sauce and has a wide variety of uses, particularly in hors d'oeuvre dishes. It should always be available on any cold buffet.
- Because of the risk of salmonella food poisoning, it is strongly recommended that pasteurised egg yolks are used.

Beat the egg yolks and mix in the vinegar and seasoning

Begin whisking in the oil

Gradually add more oil

If, during the making of the sauce, it should become too thick, then a little vinegar or water may be added. Mayonnaise will turn or curdle for several reasons:
- if the oil is added too quickly
- if the oil is too cold
- if the sauce is insufficiently whisked
- if the yolk is stale and therefore weak.

The method used to rethicken a turned mayonnaise is either:
- by taking a clean basin, adding 1 teaspoon boiling water and gradually whisking in the curdled sauce, or
- by taking another yolk thinned with half a teaspoon of cold water whisked well, then gradually whisking in the curdled sauce.

Making mayonnaise
http://bit.ly/xx315t

Try something different
Many ingredients can be used to vary mayonnaise, such as fresh herbs, garlic juice, Parmesan or blue cheese, red pepper purée and chopped sundried tomatoes. Lemon juice may be used in place of vinegar.

* For 8 portions

6 Andalusian sauce
(sauce andalouse)

vegetable fruits

Makes >	250 ml
mayonnaise	250 ml
tomato juice or ketchup	2 tbsp
red pepper, cut into julienne	1 tbsp

Mix the tomato juice and red pepper into the mayonnaise.

May be served with cold salads.

Key point

For Andalusian sauce, Thousand Island dressing, green sauce and other similar recipes, use a blender to achieve the desired texture and flavour.

7 Green sauce
(sauce verte)

leafy vegetables boiling

Portions >	8
spinach, tarragon, chervil, chives, watercress	50 g
mayonnaise	250 ml

1 Pick, wash, blanch and refresh the green leaves. Squeeze dry.
2 Pass through a very fine sieve. Mix with the mayonnaise.

May be served with cold salmon or salmon trout.

8 Remoulade sauce
(sauce remoulade)

vegetable fruits

energy	kcal	fat	sat fat	carb	sugar	protein	fibre	*
938 KJ	228 kcal	24.8 g	3.6 g	0.3 g	0.3 g	0.8 g	0.1 g	

Makes >	125 ml
mayonnaise	250 ml
capers	25 g
gherkins	50 g
anchovy essence	1 tsp
sprig of parsley, chopped	

1 Finely chop the gherkins and capers using a blender.
2 Combine the ingredients and mix thoroughly.

* Using gherkins

Note

This sauce may be served with fried fish. It can also be mixed with a fine julienne of celeriac to make an accompaniment to cold meats, terrines, etc.

9 Tomato chutney

vegetable fruits   simmering

Makes 〉	1 litre
tomatoes, peeled	1.5 kg
onions, finely chopped	450 g
brown sugar	300 g
malt vinegar	375 ml
mustard powder	1 ½ tsp
cayenne pepper	½ tsp
coarse salt	2 tsp
mild curry powder	1 tbsp

1 Peel and coarsely chop the tomatoes, then combine with the remaining ingredients in a large heavy-duty saucepan.
2 Stir over heat without boiling until the sugar dissolves. Simmer uncovered, stirring occasionally until the mixture thickens (about 1 ½ hours).
3 Place in hot, sterilised jars. Seal while hot.

Key point
Blend the ingredients to make a good chutney.

10 Beetroot relish

root vegetables   boiling, simmering

Makes 〉	1.75 litres
beetroots, cooked, peeled and chopped coarsely	1 kg
onions, finely chopped	800 g
caster sugar	225 g
coarse salt	1 tbsp
ground allspice	1 tsp
malt vinegar	500 ml
plain flour (optional)	1 tbsp

1 Mix the chopped beetroot and onion together, add the sugar, salt, allspice and 375 ml of the vinegar and put in a large saucepan. Bring to the boil and simmer for 30 minutes.
2 Mix the flour with the remaining vinegar, whisk together well. (Make sure it is smooth and does not contain any lumps.) Add to the beetroot mixture. Stir until all is well blended and thickens.
3 Place in hot sterilised jars. Seal while still hot.

Date and tamarind relish

fruit boiling, simmering

Makes >	625 ml
boiling water	500 ml
dried tamarind	75 g
olive oil	2 tsp
black mustard seeds	2 tsp
cumin seeds	2tsp
fresh dates, stoned and chopped	500 g
malt vinegar	60 ml

1 In a suitable bowl, pour the boiling water over the tamarind and allow to stand for 30 minutes.

2 Strain the liquid, press to extract all moisture, discard the tamarind stones.

3 Heat the oil in a suitable saucepan, cook the mustard seeds until they pop, add the cumin seeds, stir in the dates, tamarind liquid and vinegar, bring to the boil. Simmer for 5 minutes until almost dry.

4 Purée in a processor until smooth.

5 Place the hot relish into hot sterilised jars. Seal while hot.

12 Pickled red cabbage

leafy vegetables  boiling, pickling

energy	kcal	fat	sat fat	carb	sugar	protein	fibre	sodium
134 KJ	32 kcal	0.6 g	0.1 g	3.7 g	3.3 g	1.4 g	2.9 g	0.0 g

1 Remove the outer leaves of a medium-sized red cabbage and shred the rest finely.
2 Place in a deep bowl, sprinkle each layer with dry salt and leave for 24 hours.
3 Rinse and drain, cover with spiced vinegar (see below) and leave for a further 24 hours, mixing occasionally.
4 Pack and cover.

For the spiced vinegar

vinegar	1 litre
blade mace	5 g
allspice	5 g
cloves	5 g
stick cinnamon	5 g
peppercorns	6
root ginger (for hot pickle)	5 g

1 Tie the spices in muslin, place them in a covered pan with the vinegar and heat slowly to boiling point.
2 Remove from the heat and stand for 2 hours, then remove the bag.

13 Salad leaves

As these are eaten raw they may contain live, food-poisoning bacteria and must be thoroughly washed to remove any soil.

Lettuce (*laitue*) and iceberg lettuce

1 Trim off the root and remove the outside leaves.
2 Wash thoroughly and drain well.
3 The outer leaves can be pulled off and the hearts cut into quarters.

Cos lettuce (*laitue romaine*)

1 Trim off the root end and remove the outside leaves.
2 Wash thoroughly and drain well.
3 Cut into quarters.

Rocket

This is a small-leafed, sharp, peppery-tasting salad. Trim, wash well and drain.

Chicory (*endive belge*)

1 Trim off the root end.
2 Cut into 1 cm lengths, wash well and drain.

Curled chicory (*endive frisée*)

Thoroughly wash and trim off the stalk. Drain well.

Watercress (*cresson*)

Watercress, as the name suggests, is grown in water and, as there is always the danger that the water may have been polluted, it must be washed thoroughly in clean water.

Trim off the stalk ends, discard any discoloured leaves, thoroughly wash and drain.

Mustard and cress

1 Trim off the stalk ends of the cress.
2 Wash well and lift out of the water so as to leave the seed cases behind.
3 Drain well.

14 Mixed salad
(salade panachée)

A typical mixed salad would consist of lettuce, tomato, cucumber, watercress, radishes, etc. Almost any kind of salad vegetable can be used.

Neatly arrange in a salad bowl; offer a vinaigrette separately.

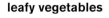

15 Green salad
(salade verte)

leafy vegetables

Any of the green salads – lettuce, cos lettuce, lamb's lettuce (also known as corn salad or mâche), curled chicory – or any combination of green salads may be used, and a few leaves of radicchio.

Neatly arrange in a salad bowl; serve with vinaigrette separately.

16 French salad
(salade française)

leafy vegetables, vegetable fruits

The usual ingredients are lettuce, tomato and cucumber, but these may be varied with other salad vegetables, in some cases with quarters of egg.

A vinaigrette made with French mustard (French dressing) should be offered.

17 Radishes
(radis)

1. Trim the green stems to about 2 cm long. Cut off the root end.
2. Wash well, drain. Cut into thin slices or serve whole. Dress neatly.

18 Cucumber

Portions ❭	4	10
cucumber	½	1 ¼
vinaigrette	1 tbsp	2 ½ tbsp

1. Peel the cucumber if desired.
2. Cut into thin slices and dress neatly.
3. Lightly dress with vinaigrette or serve separately.

Alternatively, cucumber may be sliced into 0.5 cm dice and bound with mayonnaise or yoghurt.

> **Note**
> Not to be served as a single hors d'oeuvre or main course.

> **Tip**
> To remove indigestible juices from the cucumber, slice and lightly sprinkle with salt. Allow the salt to draw out the water for approximately 1 hour, wash well under cold water and drain. This will make the cucumber limp.

Healthy eating tips
- All vegetable-based salads are a healthy way to start a meal.
- Add the minimum amount of salt.

19 Tomato
(tomate)

1. Wash the tomatoes. Remove the eyes, slice thinly or cut into segments.
2. Dress neatly.

20 Tomato salad
(salade de tomates)

vegetable fruits

energy	kcal	fat	sat fat	carb	sugar	protein	fibre	*
394 KJ	94 kcal	6.6 g	1.1 g	6.7 g	6.6 g	3.5 g	3.9 g	

Portions >	4	10
tomatoes	200 g	500g
lettuce	¼	½
vinaigrette	1 tbsp	2½ tbsp
onion or chives (optional), chopped	10 g	25 g
parsley or mixed fresh herbs, chopped		

1 Peel the tomatoes if required. Slice thinly. Arrange neatly on lettuce leaves.
2 Sprinkle with the vinaigrette, onion (blanched if required) and parsley.

Try something different
Alternate slices of tomato and mozzarella with a basic dressing.

* For 4 portions

21 Tomato and cucumber salad
(salade de tomates et concombres)

vegetable fruits

energy	kcal	fat	sat fat	carb	sugar	protein	fibre
112 KJ	27 kcal	2.0 g	0.3 g	1.9 g	1.8 g	0.5 g	0.6 g

Portions >	4	10
tomatoes	2	5
cucumber	½	1
vinaigrette	1 tbsp	2½ tbsp
parsley or mixed fresh herbs, chopped		

1 Alternate slices of tomato and cucumber.
2 Sprinkle with the vinaigrette and parsley.

Key point
Blanch the tomatoes so that you can remove the skins, which are hard to digest.

22 Beetroot salad
(salade de betterave)

root vegetables boiling

energy	kcal	fat	sat fat	carb	sugar	protein	fibre
134 KJ	32 kcal	2.0 g	0.3 g	3.2 g	3.1 g	0.7 g	0.9 g

Portions ›	4	10
cooked beetroot, peeled, neatly cut or sliced	200 g	500 g
onion or chive (optional), chopped	10 g	25 g
vinaigrette	1 tbsp	2½ tbsp
parsley, chopped		

1 Combine all the ingredients except the parsley, blanching the onion if required.
2 Dress neatly. Sprinkle with the chopped parsley.

Tips
- To cook the beetroot, blanch it and then simmer it.
- When handling beetroot, wear gloves to avoid staining the skin.

Try something different
Add 60–120 ml mayonnaise or natural yoghurt in place of vinaigrette (150–200 ml for 10 portions).

23 Melon

fruit

energy	kcal	fat	sat fat	carb	sugar	protein	fibre
82 KJ	20 kcal	0.0 g	0.0 g	4.7 g	4.7 g	0.6 g	0.9 g

Allow approximately half a honeydew or cantaloupe melon for four portions.

1 Cut the chilled melon in half, remove the seeds and peel. Cut it into thick slices.
2 Arrange overlapping slices on a suitable plate.

Note
Use caster sugar and ground ginger as accompaniments.

24 Salami and cooked or smoked sausages

pork

These sausages are usually prepared from pork by specialist butchers. Most countries have their own specialities, and a variety of them is exported. Mortadella, garlic sausage and zungenwurst are other examples of this type of sausage.

Slice the sausage thinly. Serve a single type or an assortment.

25 Foie gras

goose, offal  shallow frying

This is a ready-prepared delicacy made from goose liver.

Foie gras may be served in its original dish.

Alternatively, cut fresh foie gras into thick slices, lightly fry on both sides in butter or good-quality oil, and serve on a bed of salad leaves (lightly dressed with vinaigrette), accompanied by freshly toasted brioche or bread.

Tinned foie gras should be chilled thoroughly, removed from the tin and cut into 1 cm slices.

26 | Smoked salmon

energy	kcal	fat	sat fat	carb	sugar	protein	fibre
149 KJ	36 kcal	1.1 g	0.3 g	0.0 g	0.0 g	6.4 g	0.0 g

Allow 35–50 g per portion.

1 Before service, a side of smoked salmon must be carefully trimmed to remove the dry outside surface. Remove all bones; a pair of pliers is useful for this.
2 Carve the salmon on the slant, as thinly as possible.
3 Dress neatly, overlapping, on a plate or dish, decorated with sprigs of parsley. Accompaniments include brown bread and butter, and lemon.

> **Note**
> Other smoked fish served as hors d'oeuvres include halibut, eel, conger eel, trout, mackerel, herring (buckling), cod's roe and sprats.

Healthy eating tip
Oily fish (e.g. salmon, trout, mackerel, rollmops, sprats) are high in omega-3 fatty acids, which are beneficial for health.

27 | Oysters

energy	kcal	fat	sat fat	carb	sugar	protein	fibre	sodium
846 KJ	200 kcal	4.0 g	0.6 g	9.0 g	0.9 g	32.7 g	0.0 g	1.2 g

Portions ⟩	4
rock or native oysters	24
lemon	1
To accompany	
brown bread and butter	
Tabasco or chilli sauce	

1 Select only those oysters that are tightly shut and have a fresh smell (category A is best, which means the waters they have grown in are clean).
2 To open an oyster, only the point of the oyster knife is used. Hold the oyster with a thick oven cloth to protect your hand.
3 With the oyster in the palm of your hand, push the point of the knife about 1 cm deep into the 'hinge' between the 'lid' and the body of the oyster.

4 Once the lid has been penetrated, push down. The lid should pop open. Lift up the top shell, cutting the muscle attached to it.

5 Remove any splintered shell from the flesh and solid shell.

6 Return each oyster to its shell and serve on a bed of crushed ice with chilli sauce, brown bread and lemon.

> **Note**
> Make sure the oysters have been grown in or fished from clean waters. Take note of the famous rule only to use them when there is an 'r' in the month, i.e. not in the summer months, although rock oysters are available throughout the year.

When opening an oyster, hold it with a thick cloth

---

28 Coleslaw

leafy vegetables, root vegetables

energy	kcal	fat	sat fat	carb	sugar	protein	fibre	*
2514 KJ	599 kcal	59.0 g	8.8 g	11.7 g	11.4 g	5.9 g	7.2 g	

Portions ›	4	10
white or Chinese cabbage	200 g	500 g
carrot	50 g	125 g
onion (optional)	25 g	60 g
mayonnaise, natural yoghurt or fromage frais	125 ml	300 ml

1 Trim off the outside leaves of the cabbage.

2 Cut into quarters. Remove the centre stalk.

3 Wash the cabbage, shred finely and drain well.

4 Mix with a fine julienne of raw carrot and shredded raw onion. To lessen the harshness of raw onion, blanch and refresh.

5 Bind with mayonnaise, natural yoghurt or vinaigrette.

> **Key point**
> Cut the cabbage into fine chiffonade to give the coleslaw a good, even texture.

> **Healthy eating tip**
> Replace some or all of the mayonnaise with natural yoghurt and/or fromage frais.

* Using mayonnaise, for 4 portions

29 Celeriac remoulade

	energy 938 KJ	kcal 228 kcal	fat 24.0 g	sat fat 3.9 g	carb 2.0 g	sugar 1.6 g	protein 1.1 g	fibre 1.9 g

Portions ›	4	10
celeriac	200 g	500 g
lemon	½	1
English or continental mustard	1 level tsp	2½ level tsp
salt, pepper		
mayonnaise, natural yoghurt or fromage frais	125 ml	300 ml

1 Wash and peel the celeriac. Cut into fine julienne.
2 Combine with remoulade juice (lemon, mustard, seasoning) and the remainder of the ingredients.

Note
Used as an accompaniment to pâtés or terrines, either by itself or mixed with remoulade sauce (recipe 8).

Healthy eating tip
Use natural yoghurt rather than mayonnaise.

30 Tapenade

Portions ›	4
black olives, puréed or finely chopped	250 g
capers	45 g
anchovies, finely chopped	6 fillets
parsley, chopped (optional)	½ tsp
chives, chopped (optional)	½ tsp
tarragon, chopped (optional)	½ tsp
lemon, juice of (optional)	½
brandy (optional)	1 tbsp
garlic (optional)	
olive oil	4 tbsp
roast cumin and chopped red chilli, to garnish	

1 Mix all the ingredients together, adding the olive oil to make a paste.
2 Season, if required.
3 Garnish with a sprinkle of roast cumin and chopped red chilli.
4 Serve chilled.

Tapenade is a Provençale dish. Its name comes from the Provençale word for capers: *tapeno*. It is popular in the South of France, where it is generally eaten as an hors d'oeuvre, spread on toast.

Try something different
For a smoother tapenade, place garlic, lemon juice, capers and anchovies into a food processor and process until smooth. Add the olives and parsley, and sufficient oil to form a smooth paste.

31 French bean salad
(salade de haricots verts)

seeds and pods boiling

energy	kcal	fat	sat fat	carb	sugar	protein	fibre
125 KJ	30 kcal	1.9 g	0.3 g	2.5 g	1.2 g	0.9 g	2.0 g

Portions >	4	10
French beans, cooked	200 g	500 g
vinaigrette	1 tbsp	3 tbsp
salt, pepper		

Combine all the ingredients.

Key point

Cook the beans *al dente*, so that the salad will have a crunchy texture.

Healthy eating tip
Add salt sparingly.

32 Greek-style mushrooms
(champignons à la grecque)

fungi simmering

energy	kcal	fat	sat fat	carb	sugar	protein	fibre
587 KJ	142 kcal	15.2 g	2.2 g	0.4 g	0.3 g	1.0 g	0.6 g

Portions >	4	10
water	250 ml	625 ml
olive oil	60 ml	150 ml
lemon, juice of	1	1½
bay leaf	½	1
sprig of thyme		
peppercorns	6	18
coriander seeds	6	18
salt		
small white button mushrooms, cleaned	200 g	500 g

1 Combine all the ingredients except the mushrooms, to create a Greek-style cooking liquor.
2 Cook the mushrooms gently in the cooking liquor for 3–4 minutes.
3 Serve cold with the unstrained liquor.

Key point

Simmer the vegetables carefully so that they are correctly cooked and absorb the flavours.

33 Potato salad

(salade de pommes de terre)

energy	kcal	fat	sat fat	carb	sugar	protein	fibre	*
2013 KJ	479 kcal	34.9 g	5.1 g	40.0 g	1.3 g	4.0 g	2.6 g	

Portions ›	4	10
potatoes, cooked	200 g	500 g
vinaigrette	1 tbsp	2½ tbsp
onion or chive (optional), chopped	10 g	25 g
mayonnaise or natural yoghurt	125 ml	300 ml
salt, pepper		
parsley or mixed fresh herbs, chopped		

1 Cut the potatoes into 0.5 cm dice; sprinkle with vinaigrette.
2 Mix with the onion or chive, add the mayonnaise and correct the seasoning. (The onion may be blanched to reduce its harshness.)
3 Dress neatly and sprinkle with chopped parsley or mixed herbs.

This is not usually served as a single hors d'oeuvre or main course.

> **Key point**
> Mixing the potato, onion and mayonnaise gives a good flavour and texture, but be careful not to mix them too much or the potatoes will break up.

* Using mayonnaise, for 4 portions

Try something different
- Potato salad can also be made by dicing raw peeled or unpeeled potato, cooking them – preferably by steaming (to retain shape) – and mixing with vinaigrette while warm.
- Variations include the addition of two chopped hard-boiled eggs, or 100 g of peeled dessert apple mixed with lemon juice, or a small bunch of picked watercress leaves.
- Potatoes may be cooked with mint and allowed to cool with the mint.
- Cooked small new potatoes can be tossed whole in vinaigrette with chopped fresh herbs (e.g. mint, parsley, chives).

34 Waldorf salad

fruit, nuts, leafy vegetables

energy	kcal	fat	sat fat	carb	sugar	protein	fibre	sodium
1182 KJ	286 kcal	27.1 g	3.9 g	9.6 g	9.5 g	1.6 g	2.2 g	0.1 g

Portions ›	4
celery, diced *or*	2 sticks
celeriac, diced, grated or julienne	100 g
russet apples, medium, peeled or unpeeled	2
walnuts, shelled, peeled	25 g
mayonnaise	
lettuce or mixed leaves	

1 Dice celery or celeriac and crisp russet apples.
2 Mix with shelled and peeled walnuts, and bind with mayonnaise.
3 Dress on quarters or leaves of lettuce (may also be served in hollowed-out apples).

Key point

When mixing in the mayonnaise, add just enough to give the right texture and flavour.

Healthy eating tip

Try using some yoghurt in place of the mayonnaise, which will proportionally reduce the fat.

35 Vegetable salad/ Russian salad

(salade de légumes/salade russe)

root vegetables, seeds and pods 🍲 boiling

energy	kcal	fat	sat fat	carb	sugar	protein	fibre	*
1566 KJ	373 kcal	35.0 g	5.2 g	10.1 g	8.2 g	5.0 g	11.9 g	

Portions ❭	4	10
carrots	100 g	250 g
turnips	50 g	125 g
French beans	50 g	125 g
peas	50 g	125 g
vinaigrette	1 tbsp	2–3 tbsp
mayonnaise or natural yoghurt	125 ml	300 ml
salt, pepper		

1 Peel and wash the carrots and turnips, cut into 0.5 cm dice or batons.
2 Cook separately in salted water, refresh and drain well.
3 Top and tail the beans, and cut into 0.5 cm dice; cook, refresh and drain well.
4 Cook the peas, refresh and drain well.
5 Mix all the well-drained vegetables with vinaigrette and then mayonnaise.
6 Correct the seasoning. Dress neatly.

* Using mayonnaise, for 4 portions

Key point

Do not overcook the vegetables, and drain them well before adding the dressing – otherwise the salad will be too wet.

Healthy eating tips
● Try half mayonnaise and half natural yoghurt.
● Season with the minimum amount of salt.

36 Haricot bean salad
(salade de haricots blancs)

pulses 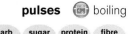 boiling

energy	kcal	fat	sat fat	carb	sugar	protein	fibre
278 KJ	66 kcal	2.1 g	0.4 g	9.0 g	0.7 g	3.3 g	3.1 g

Portions 〉	4	10
haricot beans, cooked	200 g	500 g
vinaigrette	1 tbsp	2½ tbsp
parsley, chopped		
onion, chopped and blanched if necessary	¼	½
chives (optional)	15 g	40 g
salt, pepper		

Combine all the ingredients.

> **Note**
> This recipe can be used for any type of dried bean (see page 367).

Healthy eating tip
Lightly dress with vinaigrette and add salt sparingly.

37 Three-bean salad

pulses  boiling

energy	kcal	fat	sat fat	carb	sugar	protein	fibre	*
1849 KJ	440 kcal	8.7 g	1.1 g	63.4 g	6.3 g	30.9 g	36.0 g	

Use 200 g (500 g for 10 portions) of three different dried beans (e.g. red kidney, black-eyed, flageolet). Proceed as for a haricot bean salad (recipe 36).

* For 4 portions

38 Lentil and goats' cheese salad

pulses, cheese, vegetable fruits simmering

energy	kcal	fat	sat fat	carb	sugar	protein	fibre
907 KJ	216 kcal	9.2 g	4.1 g	22.8 g	10.5 g	11.9 g	4.5 g

Portions >	4	10
puy lentils	100 g	250 g
bay leaf	1	3
spring onions, finely chopped	4	10
red pepper, finely chopped	1	3 tbsp
chopped parsley	1 tbsp	40 g
cherry tomatoes, sliced in half	400 g	1 kg
rocket leaves	200 g	500 g
goats' cheese, diced or crumbled	100 g	250 g
Dressing		
olive oil	1 tbsp	2½ tbsp
balsamic vinegar	1 tbsp	2½ tbsp
clear honey	2 tbsp	5 tbsp
garlic clove, crushed and chopped	1	3

1 Rinse the lentils and place in a saucepan. Add the bay leaf, cover with water, bring to the boil, simmer for 20–30 minutes until tender.
2 Drain and then place in a bowl. Add the spring onions, red pepper, parsley and cherry tomatoes, mix well.
3 For the dressing, whisk together in a bowl the oil, vinegar, honey and garlic.
4 Stir into the lentils. Serve on a bed of rocket, with the goats' cheese sprinkled over.

This dish provides a healthy, balanced starter.

39 Rice salad
(salade de riz)

rice, vegetable fruits, seeds and pods boiling

energy	kcal	fat	sat fat	carb	sugar	protein	fibre	*
906 KJ	216 kcal	6.9 g	1.1 g	34.6 g	3.3 g	5.9 g	8.3 g	

Portions ›	4	10
tomatoes	100 g	250 g
rice, cooked	100 g	250 g
peas, cooked	50 g	120 g
vinaigrette	1 tbsp	2½ tbsp
salt, pepper		

1 Skin and deseed the tomatoes; cut into 0.5 cm dice.
2 Mix with the rice and peas.
3 Add the vinaigrette and correct the seasoning.

* For 4 portions

Key point

Cook the rice so that it still has a bite, with the grains separate, not sticking together; it should not feel starchy in the mouth.

Healthy eating tips

- This dish is high in starchy carbohydrate and can be varied with different/additional vegetables, e.g. peppers.
- Lightly dress with vinaigrette and add salt sparingly.

40 Brown rice salad

rice, vegetable fruits, seeds and pods boiling

energy	kcal	fat	sat fat	carb	sugar	protein	fibre	sodium
1127 KJ	270 kcal	16.3 g	2.3 g	28.1 g	6.9 g	4.2 g	3.5 g	0.3 g

Portions ›	4	10
brown rice	100 g	250 g
salt		
boiling water	175 g	450 g
tomatoes	100 g	250 g
peas, cooked	50 g	125 g
haricots verts, cooked and finely sliced	25 g	60 kg
cucumber, finely chopped	5 cm	10 cm
spring onions, very finely chopped	3	5
red dessert apple, chopped but not peeled	1	2
walnuts, finely chopped	25 g	60 g
mixed peppers, de-seeded, cut into fine dice	25 g	60 g
vinaigrette	1 tbsp	2 ½ tbsp

1 Place the rice, with a sprinkle of salt, in a saucepan and cover with boiling water.
2 Bring the water back to the boil; stir once, put a lid on and simmer very gently for approximately 35–40 minutes, until all the liquid has been absorbed.
3 Empty the rice into a salad bowl, fluff it up with a fork and pour three-quarters of the vinaigrette over while it's still hot. Leave to cool.

4 While the rice is cooling, blanch the tomatoes, remove the skins and cut into quarters. Remove the seeds and cut in 0.5 cm dice.
5 Once the rice is cool, mix in the tomatoes and all the other ingredients, adding the remaining vinaigrette. Check the seasoning and keep in a cool place until needed.

41 Couscous salad with roasted vegetables and mixed herbs

grains roasting

energy	kcal	fat	sat fat	carb	sugar	protein	fibre
1248 KJ	300 kcal	12.5 g	1.7 g	42.2 g	8.6 g	6.6 g	3.8 g

Portions >	4	10
couscous	250 g	625 g
balsamic vinegar	1 tbsp	2½ tbsp
olive oil	3 tbsp	8 tbsp
lemon juice	¼ lemon	1 lemon
seasoning		
fresh mint, chopped	½ tsp	1 ¼ tsp
fresh coriander, chopped	½ tsp	1 ¼ tsp
fresh thyme, chopped	½ tsp	1 ¼ tsp
roasted vegetables (selection), finely chopped	100 g	250 g

1 Prepare the roasted vegetables. (Peppers, courgettes, onions, aubergines, mushrooms and garlic are all suitable.)
2 Place the couscous in a suitable bowl and gently pour over 300 ml of boiling water (750 ml for 10 portions).
3 Stir well, cover and leave to stand for 5 minutes.
4 Separate the grains with a fork.
5 Add the balsamic vinegar, olive oil, lemon juice and seasoning.
6 Mix well, stir in the chopped herbs.
7 Finish by adding the roasted vegetables.

8 Serve in a suitable bowl or use individual plates. For plated service, arrange the couscous neatly in the centre of the plate, arrange the roasted vegetables around, then garnish with fresh herbs.

Key point
When adding the vinegar and oil, add just enough to give the correct texture and flavour.

Healthy eating tips
● Use an unsaturated oil and lightly brush the vegetables when roasting.
● Use the minimum amount of salt.

42 Caesar salad

leafy vegetables, eggs   boiling, grilling, 🥣 shallow frying

energy	kcal	fat	sat fat	carb	sugar	protein	fibre *
1494 KJ	361 kcal	32.2 g	7.9 g	5.1 g	2.0 g	12.9 g	1.2 g

Portions ⟩	4	10
cos lettuce (medium size)	2	4
croutons, 2 cm square	16	40
eggs, fresh	2	4
Dressing		
garlic, finely chopped	1 tsp	2 tsp
anchovy fillets, mashed	4	8
lemon juice	1	2
virgin olive oil	150 ml	375 ml
white wine vinegar	1 tbsp	2 tbsp
salt, black mill pepper		
To serve		
Parmesan, freshly grated	75 g	150 g

1 Separate the lettuce leaves, wash, dry thoroughly and refrigerate.
2 Lightly grill or fry (in good fresh oil) the croutons on all sides.
3 Plunge the eggs into boiling water for 1 minute, remove and set aside.
4 Break the lettuce into serving-sized pieces and place into a salad bowl.
5 Mix the dressing, break the eggs, spoon out the contents, mix with a fork, add to the dressing and mix into the salad.
6 Mix in the cheese, scatter the croutons on top and serve.

Ingredients for Caesar salad

Key points
Because the eggs are only lightly cooked, they must be perfectly fresh, and the salad must be prepared and served immediately. In the interests of food safety, the eggs are sometimes hard boiled.
Alternatively, the salad may be garnished with hard-boiled gull's eggs.

Healthy eating tips
● No added salt is needed; anchovies and cheese are high in salt.
● Oven bake the croutons.
● Serve with fresh bread or rolls.

* Using toast for croutons

Practical Cookery 12th edition

43 Niçoise salad

vegetable fruits, potatoes, seeds and pods, oily fish boiling

energy	kcal	fat	sat fat	carb	sugar	protein	fibre	*
867 KJ	207 kcal	9.6 g	1.5 g	25.0 g	4.9 g	6.9 g	9.9 g	

Portions >	4	10
tomatoes	100 g	250 g
French beans, cooked	200 g	500 g
diced potatoes, cooked	100 g	250 g
salt, pepper		
vinaigrette	1 tbsp	2½ tbsp
anchovy fillets	10 g	25 g
capers	5 g	12 g
stoned olives	10 g	25 g

1 Peel the tomatoes, deseed and cut into neat petals.
2 Dress the beans, tomatoes and potatoes neatly.
3 Season with salt and pepper. Add the vinaigrette.
4 Decorate with anchovies, capers and olives.

Healthy eating tips
- Lightly dress with vinaigrette.
- The anchovies are high in salt, so no extra salt is necessary.

* For 4 portions

44 Avocado and bacon salad

vegetable fruits, bacon grilling

energy	kcal	fat	sat fat	carb	sugar	protein	fibre	sodium
1462 KJ	354 kcal	34.4 g	7.6 g	2.4 g	0.7 g	9.0 g	4.9 g	1.0 g

Portions ⟩	4	10
thin streaky bacon rashers, rind and excess fat trimmed	8	20
extra virgin olive oil	2 tbsp	5 tbsp
fresh lemon juice	1 tbsp	2½ tbsp
garlic, small clove, crushed finely	1	2½
salt and freshly ground black pepper		
ripe avocados, medium	2	5
snow pea sprouts, stems trimmed	50 g	125 g

1 Under a salamander, grill the bacon rashers until crisp. Transfer to a tray lined with kitchen paper and allow to cool.
2 Place the lemon juice and garlic in a mixing bowl and whisk in the olive oil. Season with salt and pepper.
3 Halve the avocados lengthways, remove the seeds and peel the skin. Place the avocados, cut side down, on a chopping board and cut in half lengthways, then crossways into slices 1 cm thick.
4 Layer the avocados, bacon and snow pea sprouts on serving plates, drizzling with the dressing between the layers. Serve immediately.

45 Cold salmon

oily fish boiling, poaching

energy	kcal	fat	sat fat	carb	sugar	protein	fibre	sodium *
2141 KJ	517 kcal	40.3 g	6.5 g	5.1 g	4.5 g	33.0 g	1.8 g	1.2 g

Salmon may be obtained in varying weights from 3.5–15 kg: 0.5 kg of uncleaned salmon yields 2–3 portions.

Size is an important consideration, depending on whether the salmon is to be cooked whole or cut into darnes. A salmon of any size may be cooked whole. When required for darnes, a medium-sized salmon is more suitable.

For the cooking liquid (court bouillon)

Portions 〉	4	10
water	1 litre	2.5 litres
salt	10 g	25 g
carrots, sliced	50 g	125 g
bay leaf	2–3	5–8
parsley stalks		
vinegar	60 ml	150 ml
peppercorns	6	15
onions, sliced	50 g	125 g
sprig of thyme		

1 Simmer all the ingredients for 30–40 minutes.
2 Pass through a strainer, use as required.

Cooking for service in darnes or portions

Portions 〉	8–10
salmon, cleaned	1.25 kg
court bouillon (see above)	1 litre
cucumber	½
large lettuce	1
tomatoes	200 g
mayonnaise (recipe 5) or	
green sauce (recipe 7)	250 ml

1 Cook the salmon in the court bouillon, either whole or cut into 4 or 8 darnes.
2 Allow to cool thoroughly in the cooking liquid to keep it moist. Divide a whole salmon into eight even portions; for darnes, remove centre bone and cut each darne in half, if required.
3 Except when whole, remove the centre bone, the skin and brown layer, and dress neatly on a flat dish.
4 Peel and slice the cucumber and neatly arrange a few slices on each portion.
5 Garnish with quarters of lettuce and quarters of tomatoes.
6 Serve the sauce or mayonnaise in a sauceboat separately.

Cooking and presenting salmon whole

1 Scrape off all scales, from tail to head, using the back of a knife.
2 Remove all gills and clean out the head.
3 Remove the intestines and clear the blood from the backbone.
4 Trim off all fins. Wash well.
5 Place in a salmon kettle, cover with cold court bouillon (see above).
6 Bring slowly to the boil, skim, then simmer very gently.
7 Allow the following approximate simmering times:
   - 3.5 kg – 15 minutes
   - 7 kg – 20 minutes
   - 10.5 kg – 25 minutes
   - 14 kg – 30 minutes.
8 Allow the cooked salmon to cool, then remove it from the liquid. Carefully remove the skin and the dark layer under the skin (which is cooked blood). The now bared salmon flesh should be perfectly smooth.
9 Make sure the salmon is well drained and place it on to the serving dish or board.
10 The salmon is now ready for decorating and garnishing. Keep this to the minimum and avoid over-covering the fish and the dish. Neatly overlapping thin slices of cucumber (the skin may be left on or removed), quartered tomatoes (which can be peeled and neatly cut), small pieces of hearts of lettuce can, if artistically set out, give a quick, neat-looking, appetising appearance. Remember, time is money and there is no justification for spending a lot of time cutting fiddly little pieces of many different items to form patterns that often look untidy.

> Note
> Always allow the salmon to remain in the court bouillon until cold.

* Served with mayonnaise

46 Fish salad
(salade de poisson)

white fish, eggs, leafy vegetables poaching

energy	kcal	fat	sat fat	carb	sugar	protein	fibre
978 KJ	233 kcal	13.5 g	3.0 g	1.5 g	1.4 g	26.4 g	1.3 g

Portions ›	4	10
cooked white fish, free from skin and bone	200 g	500 g
egg, hard-boiled	1	2–3
cucumber (optional)	50 g	125 g
lettuce	½	1
parsley or fennel, chopped		
salt, pepper		
vinaigrette	1 tbsp	2–3 tbsp

* For 4 portions

1 Flake the fish. Cut the egg and cucumber into 0.5 cm dice.
2 Finely shred the lettuce. Mix ingredients together, add the parsley.
3 Correct the seasoning. Mix with the vinaigrette.
4 May be decorated with lettuce, anchovies and capers.

Cod, haddock, plaice or lemon sole are all suitable.

> **Key point**
> Be careful not to overcook the fish.

Healthy eating tip
Use salt sparingly.

47 Sea bass ceviche

white fish curing

energy	kcal	fat	sat fat	carb	sugar	protein	fibre	sodium *
540 KJ	128 kcal	3.8 g	0.6 g	3.8 g	3.5 g	19.8 g	0.5 g	0.3 g

Portions 〉	4	10
sea bass fillet, skinless, free of bone	400 g	1 kg
large lime, juice only	1	2
yuzu juice	2 tbsp	5 tbsp
coriander leaves, finely chopped	1 tbsp	3 tbsp
shallots, finely chopped	2	5
ginger, shredded	1 tsp	2½ tsp
red chilli, deseeded, finely chopped	1	2
sugar	1 tsp	2 tsp
light pomace oil or vegetable oil	1 tsp	2½ tsp
rock salt, to serve		
crunchy raw salad of carrot, fennel and celeriac		

1 In a shallow, non-metallic tray, combine all the ingredients except the fish.
2 Slice the fish at a 45 degree angle, 5 mm thick.
3 Place the fish into the curing liquid. Refrigerate for 20 minutes until the edges of the fish turn white (do not leave too long as the fish will cure through and resemble rollmops).
4 To finish, lay the fish neatly on a plate with a little of the curing garnish and juice.
5 Season with a little sea salt and serve with crunchy salad.

Note
Yuzu is a citrus fruit grown in east Asia. The juice is available in bottles.

* Tangerine used in place of yuzu

48 Soused herring or mackerel

oily fish boiling, braising

energy	kcal	fat	sat fat	carb	sugar	protein	fibre
2419 KJ	576 kcal	44.5 g	9.4 g	3.0 g	3.0 g	41.0 g	1.1 g

*

Portions >	4	10
herrings or mackerel	2	5
salt, pepper		
button onions	25 g	60 g
carrots, peeled and fluted	25 g	60 g
bay leaf	½	1 ½
peppercorns	6	12
thyme, sprig	1	2
vinegar	60 ml	150 ml

Healthy eating tips
- Serve with plenty of salad vegetables and bread or toast (optional butter or spread).
- Keep the added salt to a minimum.

* For 4 portions

1. Clean, scale and fillet the fish.
2. Wash the fillets well and season with salt and pepper.
3. Roll up with the skin outside. Place in an earthenware dish.
4. Peel and wash the onion. Cut the onion and carrots into neat, thin rings.
5. Blanch for 2–3 minutes.
6. Add to the fish with the remainder of the ingredients.
7. Cover with greaseproof paper and cook in a moderate oven for 15–20 minutes.
8. Allow to cool, place in a dish with the onion and carrot.
9. Garnish with picked parsley, dill or chives.

49 Crab, lobster, shrimp or prawn cocktails

(cocktail de crabe, homard, crevettes, crevettes roses)

shellfish, leafy vegetables

energy	kcal	fat	sat fat	carb	sugar	protein	fibre
966 KJ	230 kcal	21.0 g	3.2 g	0.6 g	0.6g	9.6 g	0.3 g

Portions ❯	4	10
lettuce	½	1 ½
prepared shellfish	100–150 g	250–350 g
shellfish cocktail sauce (see below)	125 ml	300 ml

1. Wash, drain well and finely shred the lettuce, avoiding long strands. Place about 2 cm deep in cocktail glasses or dishes.
2. Add the prepared shellfish: crab (shredded white meat only); lobster (cut in 2 cm dice); shrimps (peeled and washed); prawns (peeled, washed and, if large, cut into two or three pieces).
3. Coat with sauce.
4. Decorate with an appropriate piece of the content, such as a prawn with the shell of the tail removed, on the edge of the glass of a prawn cocktail.

Shellfish cocktail sauce – method 1

Portions ❯	4	10
egg yolk, pasteurised	1	3
vinegar	1 tsp	2½ tsp
salt, pepper, mustard		
olive oil or sunflower oil	8 tbsp	12 tbsp
tomato juice or ketchup to taste		
Worcester sauce (optional)	2–3 drops	6–8 drops

1. Make the mayonnaise with the egg yolk, vinegar, seasonings and oil.
2. Combine with the tomato juice and Worcester sauce (if using).

Key points
Portion control is important so that this dish does not cost too much to produce.
The cocktail needs to be presented well.

Shellfish cocktail sauce – method 2

Portions ❯	4	10
lightly whipped cream or unsweetened non-dairy cream	5 tbsp	12 tbsp
tomato juice or ketchup to taste		
salt, pepper		
lemon juice	a few drops	a few drops

1. Mix all the ingredients together.

Tip
Fresh or tinned tomato juice, or diluted tomato ketchup, may be used for both the above methods, but the use of tinned tomato purée gives an unpleasant flavour.

Healthy eating tips
- Keep added salt to a minimum.
- Extend the high-fat mayonnaise/cream with low-fat yoghurt to proportionally reduce the fat content.

50 Potted shrimps

energy	kcal	fat	sat fat	carb	sugar	protein	fibre	sodium
3887 KJ	942 kcal	92.9 g	58.1 g	1.1 g	0.7 g	25.7 g	0.1 g	0.9 g

Portions ❯	4	10
butter	100 g	250 g
chives, chopped	2 tbsp	5 tbsp
cayenne pepper, to taste		
peeled brown shrimps	600 g	1.5 kg
clarified butter	150 ml	375 ml

1 Put the butter, chives and cayenne pepper in a medium-sized pan and leave to melt over a gentle heat.
2 Add the peeled shrimps and stir over the heat for a couple of minutes until they have heated through, but don't let the mixture boil.
3 Divide the shrimps and butter between 4 small ramekins. Level the tops and then leave them to set in the refrigerator.
4 Spoon over a thin layer of clarified butter and leave to set once more. Serve with plenty of brown toast or crusty brown bread.

Key points
- Do not let the mixture boil (step 2) – if it does, the shrimps will become tough.
- Remove from the fridge and allow to warm slightly before serving, to bring out the flavour.

This is a real seaside dish, full of flavour and eaten with plenty of brown bread and butter. Lobster or langoustine can be used, although timings will need to be adapted accordingly. The traditional seasoning for potted shrimps is ground mace.

51 Fruits de mer

shellfish boiling, steaming

energy	kcal	fat	sat fat	carb	sugar	protein	fibre	sodium
3440 KJ	828 kcal	56.5 g	8.7 g	6.8 g	3.7 g	65.6 g	0.9 g	2.3 g

Portions ❯	4	10		For the sauces	4	10
lobster, cooked	1	2		mayonnaise (recipe 5)	250 ml	625 ml
crab, cooked	1	2		garlic cloves, finely chopped	2	5
large prawns, cooked	12	30		tomato ketchup	2 tsp	5 tsp
winkles, raw	100 g	250 g		brandy	1 tbsp	2 tbsp
fresh clams	200 g	500 g		Tabasco sauce		
fresh cockles	200 g	500 g		red wine vinegar	100 ml	250 ml
mussels, live	200 g	500 g		shallots, finely chopped	2	5
langoustines, live	6	10		sprigs of parsley and lemon wedges, to garnish		
white wine	75 ml	200 ml				
parsley stalks	4	10		chorizo sausage, warm, to garnish (optional)		
shallots, roughly chopped	2	5				
salt						
oysters	12	30				

To prepare the seafood

1 Cut the lobster in half lengthways. Remove the stomach and give the claws a crack to break the shell.
2 Open the crab, remove the 'dead man's fingers' and cut the body into four. Give the claws a few cracks to break the shell – this will make getting the meat out at the table easier.
3 Put the prawns, winkles, clams, cockles, mussels and langoustines into a pan with the white wine, parsley stalks, shallots and salt. Bring to the boil, cover and steam for 4 minutes until the mussels, clams and cockles open. Remove from the water and put on a tray to cool.
4 Using an oyster knife, open the oysters.
5 Place a generous portion of crushed ice on a tray. Arrange the lobster, crab, langoustines, clams, mussels, cockles, winkles, prawns and oysters on the ice, garnishing with lemon and parsley.

Dead man's fingers are the crab's gills. You can see them inside the crab: they are grey and shaped like fingers.

To make the sauces

1 Divide the mayonnaise into thirds. Set one third to one side. Mix the chopped garlic into another third of the mayonnaise. To make seafood sauce, mix the tomato ketchup, the brandy and a dash of Tabasco into the remaining mayonnaise.
2 To make shallot vinegar, mix together the red wine vinegar and the shallots.

Serve the fruits de mer with the mayonnaise, aioli (garlic mayonnaise), seafood sauce, shallot vinegar, lemon wedges and Tabasco, and chorizo sausage if desired.

52 Dressed crab

energy	kcal	fat	sat fat	carb	sugar	protein	fibre	sodium
1974 KJ	474 kcal	28.6 g	4.4 g	0.8 g	0.7 g	53.1 g	0.7 g	1.2 g

Allow 200–300 g unprepared crab per portion.

1 Take a whole, cooked crab. Remove large claws and sever at the joints.
2 Remove the flexible pincer from the claw.
3 Crack or saw carefully and remove all flesh.
4 Remove flesh from two remaining joints with the handle of spoon.
5 Carefully remove the soft undershell.
6 Discard the gills (dead man's fingers) and the sac behind the eyes.
7 Scrape out all the inside of the shell and pass through a sieve.
8 Season with salt, pepper, Worcester sauce and a little mayonnaise sauce; thicken lightly with fresh white breadcrumbs.

9 Trim the shell by tapping carefully along the natural line.
10 Scrub the shell thoroughly and leave to dry.
11 Dress the brown meat down the centre of the shell.
12 Shred the white meat, taking care to remove any small pieces of shell.
13 Dress neatly on either side of the brown meat.
14 Decorate as desired, using any of the following: chopped parsley, hard-boiled white and yolk of egg, anchovies, capers, olives.
15 Serve the crab on a flat dish, garnish with lettuce leaves, quarters of tomato and the crab's legs.
16 Serve a vinaigrette or mayonnaise sauce separately.

53 Chicken salad

chicken poaching

energy	kcal	fat	sat fat	carb	sugar	protein	fibre	sodium
4752 KJ	1148 kcal	95.2 g	27.3 g	3.6 g	2.7 g	70.0 g	0.7 g	0.4 g

Portions ›	4	10
fresh chicken	1.5 kg	3.75 kg
black peppercorns	10	25
bay leaves	3	7
cumin seeds, ground	2 tsp	5 tsp
almonds, sliced	25 g	60 g
For the dressing		
Greek yoghurt	2 tbsp	5 tbsp
mayonnaise (recipe 5)	3 tbsp	7 tbsp
lemons, juice and zest	2	5
cucumber, peeled, diced	1	2½
fresh basil, picked and torn	25 g	60 g
To serve		
mixed salad leaves	100 g	250 g
vinaigrette	20 ml	50 ml

1 Place the chicken in a large saucepan and cover with water.

2 Add the peppercorns and bay leaves and bring to a gentle simmer. Poach gently for about 40 minutes and leave it to cool in the liquid.

3 Once cool, take the chicken out of the pan, remove the skin and shred the meat. Cover and place in a refrigerator.

4 Dry fry the cumin and almonds in a hot pan and leave to cool.

5 To make the dressing, mix the yoghurt, mayonnaise and lemon zest and juice in a large bowl.

6 Add the chicken, cucumber, cumin and almonds with the torn basil. Mix well and serve on a bed of the mixed salad leaves tossed lightly in vinaigrette.

54   Raised pork pie

pork, pastry   baking

energy	kcal	fat	sat fat	carb	sugar	protein	fibre	sodium
3005 KJ	721 kcal	47.7 g	19.3 g	49.2 g	1.7 g	26.7 g	2.7 g	1.2 g

Hot water paste

Portions ＞	4	10
strong plain flour	250 g	500 g
salt		
lard or margarine (alternatively use 100 g lard and 25 g butter or margarine)	125 g	300 g
water	125 ml	300 ml

1 Sift the flour and salt into a basin. Make a well in the centre.
2 Boil the fat with the water and pour immediately into the flour.
3 Mix with a wooden spoon until cool enough to handle.
4 Mix to a smooth paste and use while still warm.

Raised pork pie

Portions ＞	4	10
shoulder of pork, without bone	300 g	1 kg
bacon	100 g	250 g
allspice (or mixed spice) and chopped sage	½ tsp	1 ½ tsp
salt, pepper		
bread, soaked in milk	50 g	125 g
stock or water	2 tbsp	5 tbsp
In addition		
eggwash		
stock, hot	125 ml	375 ml
gelatine	5 g	12.5 g
picked watercress and salad to serve		

1 Cut the pork and bacon into small even pieces and combine with the rest of the main ingredients.
2 Keep one-quarter of the paste warm and covered.
3 Roll out the remaining three-quarters and carefully line a well-greased raised pie mould. Ensure that there is a thick rim of pastry.
4 Add the filling and press down firmly.
5 Roll out the remaining pastry for the lid, and eggwash the edges of the pie.
6 Add the lid, seal firmly, neaten the edges, cut off any surplus paste; decorate if desired.
7 Make a hole 1 cm in diameter in the centre of the pie; brush all over with eggwash.
8 Bake in a hot oven (230–250°C) for approximately 20 minutes.
9 Reduce the heat to moderate (150–200°C) and cook for 1 ½–2 hours in total.
10 If the pie colours too quickly, cover with greaseproof paper or foil. Remove from the oven and carefully remove tin. Eggwash the pie all over and return to the oven for a few minutes.
11 Remove from the oven and fill with approximately 125 ml of good hot stock in which 5 g of gelatine has been dissolved (see photo in recipe 55).
12 Serve when cold, garnished with picked watercress and offer a suitable salad.

55 Veal and ham pie

veal, pork  baking

energy	kcal	fat	sat fat	carb	sugar	protein	fibre
607 KJ	144 kcal	4.5 g	1.5 g	3.8 g	0.8 g	22.4 g	0.1 g

Portions ❭	4	10
ham or bacon	150 g	375 g
salt, pepper		
hard-boiled egg	1	2
lean veal (shoulder, leg or loin)	250 g	625 g
parsley and thyme	½ tsp	1 tsp
lemon, grated zest of	1	2
stock or water	2 tbsp	5 tbsp
bread, soaked in milk	50 g	125 g
hot water paste (see recipe 54)	125 ml	375 ml
gelatine	5 g	12.5 g

Proceed as for raised pork pie (recipe 54). Place the shelled egg in the centre of the mixture. Serve when cold, garnished with picked watercress and offer a suitable salad.

Partly fill the pie, then place eggs into the centre

Add the pastry lid and seal it firmly

Pour gelatine dissolved in stock into the pie after baking

56 Liver pâté
(pâté de foie)

offal shallow frying, baking

energy	kcal	fat	sat fat	carb	sugar	protein	fibre
896 KJ	213 kcal	19.1 g	8.5 g	0.7 g	0.1 g	9.8 g	0.0 g

Portions ❯	4	10
liver (chicken, pig, calf, lamb, etc.)	100 g	250 g
butter or oil	25 g	75 g
onion, chopped	10 g	25 g
clove garlic	1	2
sprigs of parsley, thyme, chervil		
fat pork	50 g	125 g
salt, pepper		
fatty bacon	25 g	60 g

1 Cut the liver into 2 cm pieces.
2 Toss quickly in the butter or oil in a frying pan over a fierce heat for a few seconds with the onion, garlic and herbs.
3 Allow to cool.
4 Pass, with the fat pork, twice through a mincer. Season.
5 Line an earthenware terrine with wafer-thin slices of fat bacon.
6 Place the mixture into the terrine. Cover with fatty bacon.
7 Stand in a tray half full of water and bring to simmering point.
8 Cook in a moderate oven for 1 hour. Use a temperature probe to check that the centre reaches 70°C.

9 Blast chill. When quite cold, cut into 0.5 cm slices and serve on lettuce leaves. Usually served accompanied with freshly made toast.

This is a home-made preparation often seen on the menu as *pâté maison*. This is a typical recipe.

Healthy eating tips
- Use an unsaturated oil (sunflower or olive). Lightly oil the pan and drain off any excess after the frying is complete.
- The bacon is high in salt so very little (or no) added salt is necessary.

57 Terrine of bacon, spinach and mushrooms

bacon, leafy vegetables, fungi  boiling, shallow frying

energy	kcal	fat	sat fat	carb	sugar	protein	fibre	*
1436 KJ	347 kcal	30.4 g	7.2 g	1.2 g	1.0 g	17.0 g	1.4 g	

	Portions 〉	12
collar of bacon		1 kg
carrot		1
onion clouté		1
bouquet garni		1
celery		2 sticks
peppercorns		8
fresh spinach		500 g
butter		50 g
mushrooms (preferably morels)		200 g

1. If necessary soak the bacon overnight. Drain.
2. Place the bacon in cold water, bring to the boil, add the carrot, onion, bouquet garni, celery and peppercorns.
3. Poach until tender.
4. Pick some large leaves of spinach to line the terrine, blanch the leaves, refresh and drain.
5. Lightly cook the rest of the spinach gently, refresh, drain and shred.
6. Alternatively shred the spinach raw, quickly cook in butter, drain and then blast chill.
7. Cook the mushrooms in a little butter, chill well, season.
8. When cool, remove the bacon from the cooking liquor, chop into small pieces.
9. Line the terrine with clingfilm, then the spinach leaves. Layer with bacon, mushrooms and spinach. Cover with spinach leaves and clingfilm. Refrigerate for 12 hours or overnight.
10. When ready, turn out, slice and serve on plates, with vinaigrette served separately.

Healthy eating tips
- Soaking the bacon overnight will remove some of the salt.
- Use only a little butter to cook the mushrooms.
- Use a minimum amount of salt to season the vinaigrette.
- Serve with warm bread rolls, butter optional.

* Using common mushrooms

Terrine of chicken and vegetables

chicken, root vegetables boiling, baking

energy	kcal	fat	sat fat	carb	sugar	protein	fibre
930 KJ	226 kcal	17.3 g	9.4 g	2.0 g	1.8 g	15.5 g	0.9 g

Portions ⟩	8–10
carrots, turnips and swedes, peeled and cut into 7 mm dice	50 g of each
broccoli, small florets	50 g
baby corn, cut into 7 mm rounds	50 g
French beans, cut into 7 mm lengths	50 g
chicken (white meat only), minced	400 g
egg whites	2
double cream	200 ml
salt, mill pepper	

1 Blanch all the vegetables individually in boiling salted water, ensuring that they remain firm. Refresh in cold water, and drain well.

2 Blend the chicken and egg whites in a food processor until smooth. Turn out into a large mixing bowl and gradually beat in the double cream.

3 Season with salt and mill pepper, and fold in the vegetables.

4 Line a lightly greased 1-litre terrine with clingfilm or foil.

5 Spoon the farce into the mould and overlap the clingfilm.

6 Cover with foil, put the lid on and cook in a bain-marie in a moderate oven for about 45 minutes. Use a temperature probe to check that the centre has reached 70°C.

7 When cooked, remove the lid and leave to cool overnight.

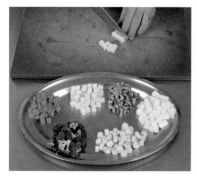

Cut the vegetables into neat dice, rounds and florets

Line the terrine with cling film and spoon in the mixture

Cover the mixture with cling film and press down gently

Healthy eating tips
- Keep the added salt to a minimum.
- Serve with plenty of salad vegetables and bread or toast (optional butter or spread).

59 Sandwiches

For speed of production, sandwiches are made in bands by cutting the bread rectangularly. When filled, the crusts are removed and the sandwiches cut into fingers.

Today, bakers will bake the bread to your specification and slice it ready for use. The specification may also include speciality breads such as tomato, basil, walnut and olive bread.

Sandwiches may also be cut into small cubes and a variety placed on a cocktail stick like a mini kebab.

Sandwiches may be made from every kind of bread, fresh or toasted, in a variety of shapes, and with an almost endless assortment of fillings. They may be garnished with potato or vegetable crisps and a little salad.

Toasted sandwiches

These are made by inserting a variety of savoury fillings between two slices of hot, freshly buttered toast (e.g. scrambled egg, bacon, fried egg, scrambled egg with chopped ham) or by inserting two slices of buttered bread with the required filling into a sandwich toaster.

Club sandwich

This is made by placing between two slices of hot buttered toast a filling of lettuce, grilled bacon, slices of hard-boiled egg, mayonnaise and slices of chicken.

Bookmaker sandwich

This is an underdone minute steak between two slices of hot buttered toast.

Double-decker and treble-decker sandwiches

Toasted and untoasted bread can be made into double-decker sandwiches, using three slices of bread with two separate fillings. Treble- and quadro-decker sandwiches may also be prepared. They may be served hot or cold.

Open sandwich or Scandinavian smorgasbord

These are prepared from a buttered slice of any bread, garnished with any type of meat, fish, eggs, vegetables, salads, etc. The varieties of open sandwich include the following:

- smoked salmon, lettuce, potted shrimps, slice of lemon
- cold sliced beef, sliced tomato, fans of gherkins
- shredded lettuce, sliced hard-boiled egg, mayonnaise, cucumber
- pickled herring, chopped gherkin, capers (sieved), hard-boiled egg.

Bookmaker sandwich

A selection of open sandwiches

60 Wraps

Wraps are fillings wrapped in tortillas (plain or flavoured – e.g. tomato, herbs).

A wide variety of fillings can be used – for example: chicken and roasted vegetables; beans and red pepper salad with guacamole (a well-flavoured avocado pulp).

Flat breads (e.g. pitta, ciabatta) can also be used with various fillings (e.g. chicken tikka).

61 Bagels

Bagels are ring, doughnut-shaped rolls of leavened bread that are boiled before being baked, giving them a shiny finish and a soft middle (see page 582).

They are traditionally filled with smoked salmon and cream cheese (a Jewish speciality). Other fillings can also be used.

Cut horizontally, bagels make a good base for open sandwiches.

62 Canapés

Canapés are offered, usually with drinks, before meals or at a drinks reception. They need to be small, attractive and well flavoured.

A wide variety of cold canapés can be offered. Just a few examples are presented here.

- Vichysoisse (see page 77) with potato foam.
- Aubergine and pine nut fritters with chilli jam.
- Chive pancake, red onion confit and crème fraîche roulade.
- Buckwheat blini with fromage blanc, smoked salmon and avruga caviar.
- Sashimi beef with wasabi and toasted sesame seeds on a croute.
- Rosemary shortbread with feta cheese, black olive and sun-roasted cherry tomato.
- Pumpernickel croute with salmon tartare.
- Lemon and saffron chicken bruschetta.
- Thai swordfish bonbon with samphire.

Some examples of hot canapés are as follows.

- Small Yorkshire puddings with a slice of beef topped with horseradish cream.
- Oyster beignets, garlic mayonnaise.
- Aubergine and goats' cheese tartlet.
- Monkfish spring rolls, remoulade sauce.
- Chicken and risotto croquettes.
- Small pizzas.
- Small pieces of chicken on skewers with bacon.
- Chicken satay with peanut sauce.
- Angels on horseback.
- Vegetable samosas (page 261).
- Latkes.

Dips for hot canapés:

- garlic mayonnaise
- yoghurt, cucumber and mint
- apricot chutney.

4 Eggs

This chapter is relevant to the following units:

- Prepare, cook and finish basic egg dishes (NVQ)
- Prepare and cook rice, pasta, grains and egg dishes (VRQ).

Types of egg

Almost all the eggs used for culinary purposes come from hens, but eggs from turkeys, geese, ducks, guinea fowl, quail and gulls are also edible and are often used for canapés.

Quails' eggs are used in a variety of ways: for example, as a garnish to many hot and cold dishes; as a starter or main course, such as a salad of assorted leaves with hot wild mushrooms and poached quail eggs, or tartlet of quail eggs on chopped mushrooms coated with hollandaise sauce.

Sizes

Hens' eggs are graded in four sizes: small, medium, large and very large, as shown in Table 4.1 below.

Table 4.1 Hens' egg sizes

Very large	73 g	Size 0
		Size 1
Large	63–73 g	Size 1
		Size 2
		Size 3
Medium	53–63 g	Size 3
		Size 4
		Size 5
Small	53 g and under	Size 5
		Size 6
		Size 7

Egg properties

Purchasing and quality points

The size of the eggs does not affect their quality, but it does affect their price. Eggs are tested for quality, then weighed and graded. When buying eggs the following points should be noted.

- The eggshell should be clean, well shaped, strong and slightly rough.
- When eggs are broken there should be a high proportion of thick white to thin white. If an egg is kept too long, the thick white gradually changes into thin white, and water passes from the white into the yolk.
- The yolk should be firm, round (not flattened) and of a good even colour. As eggs are kept the yolk loses strength and begins to flatten, water evaporates from the egg and is replaced by air.

Food value

Eggs are useful as a main dish as they provide the energy, fat, minerals and vitamins needed for growth and repair of the body. The fat in the egg yolk is high in saturated fat. The egg white is made up of protein and water.

Versatility

Fried, scrambled, poached and boiled eggs, and omelettes are mainly served at breakfast. A variety of dishes may be served for lunch, high tea, supper and snacks.

Storage

Store in a cool but not too dry place (1–4°C is ideal) where the humidity of the air and the amount of carbon dioxide present are controlled. Most eggs have date stamps and must not be used after that date.

Because eggshells are porous the eggs will absorb any strong odours; therefore, they should not be stored near strong-smelling foods such as onions, fish and cheese.

Pasteurised eggs are washed, sanitised and then broken into sterilised containers. After combining the yolks and whites they are strained, pasteurised – that is, heated, typically, to 63°C for 1 minute or a similar time/temperature combination – then rapidly cooled. Pasteurised egg whites and yolks are also available separately.

Food safety

- Eggs should be stored in a cool place, preferably under refrigeration. Eggs should be stored away from possible contaminants, such as raw meat, fish and strong-smelling foods.
- Stocks should be rotated: first in, first out.
- Hands should be washed before and after handling eggs.
- Cracked eggs should not be used.
- Preparation surfaces, utensils and containers should be cleaned regularly and always cleaned before and after handling eggs.
- Egg dishes should be consumed as soon as possible after preparation or, if not for immediate use, refrigerated.

Salmonella

Hens can pass salmonella bacteria into their eggs and thus cause food poisoning. To reduce this risk, pasteurised eggs may be used where appropriate (e.g. in omelettes, scrambled eggs, desserts).

1 Soft-boiled eggs in the shell
(oeufs à la coque)

eggs 🔄 boiling

energy	kcal	fat	sat fat	carb	sugar	protein	fibre	*
340KJ	81 kcal	6.0 g	1.9 g	0.0 g	0.0 g	6.8 g	0.0 g	

Allow 1 or 2 medium eggs per portion.

Method 1 (soft)

1 Place the eggs in cold water and bring to the boil.
2 Simmer for 2–2½ minutes, then remove from the water.
3 Serve at once in an egg cup.

Method 2 (medium soft)

1 Plunge the eggs in boiling water, then reboil.
2 Simmer for 4–5 minutes.
3 Serve at once in an egg cup.

* Using 1 egg per portion

2 Soft-boiled eggs out of the shell
(oeufs mollets)

eggs 🔄 boiling

energy	kcal	fat	sat fat	carb	sugar	protein	fibre	*
1052KJ	251 kcal	18.9 g	8.7 g	8.0 g	3.3 g	12.5 g	1.2 g	

Allow 1 or 2 medium eggs per portion.

1 Plunge the eggs into boiling water, then reboil.
2 Simmer for 4½–5 minutes. Refresh immediately.
3 Remove the shells carefully.
4 Reheat when required for 30 seconds in hot salted water.

* Using 1 egg per portion

Hard-boiled eggs (left) and soft-boiled eggs (right) – recipes 2 and 3

Boiling eggs
http://bit.ly/wglnMV

3 Hard-boiled eggs
(oeufs durs)

eggs boiling

energy	kcal	fat	sat fat	carb	sugar	protein	fibre *
753 KJ	181 kcal	13.5 g	3.8 g	0.0 g	0.0 g	15.0 g	0.0 g

Allow 1 or 2 eggs per portion.

1 Plunge the eggs into a pan of boiling water.
2 Reboil and simmer for 8–10 minutes.
3 Refresh until cold under running water.
4 Remove the shell carefully if required.

> **Key point**
> If high temperatures or a long cooking time are used to cook eggs, iron in the yolk and sulphur compounds in the white are released to form an unsightly blackish ring around the yolk. Stale eggs will also show a black ring round the yolk.

* For two eggs

4 Scotch eggs

eggs, meat deep frying

Portions ⟩	4	10
eggs	4	10
pork sausagemeat	275 g	700 g
fresh thyme leaves	1 tsp	2 tsp
fresh parsley, chopped	1 tsp	2 tsp
spring onion, very finely chopped	1	3
plain flour, seasoned	125 g	300 g
egg, beaten	1	2
breadcrumbs	250 g	625 g
salt and freshly ground black pepper		
vegetable oil for deep-frying		

Scotch eggs made with salmon, sausagemeat and colcannon

1 Place the eggs, still in their shells, in a pan of water.
2 Place over a high heat and bring to the boil, then reduce the heat to simmer for approximately 10 minutes.
3 Drain and refresh the eggs under cold running water, then peel.
4 Mix the sausagemeat with the thyme, parsley and spring onion in a bowl, season well with salt and freshly ground black pepper.
5 Divide the sausagemeat mixture into four and flatten each out on a clean surface into ovals about 12 cm long and 8 cm at the widest point.
6 Roll the boiled egg in the seasoned flour.

7 Place each egg onto a sausagemeat oval, then wrap the sausagemeat around the egg, making sure the coating is smooth and completely covers the egg.
8 Dip each meat-coated egg in the beaten egg, covering the entire surface area.
9 Roll in the breadcrumbs to coat completely.
10 Heat the oil in a deep heavy-bottomed pan, to 180°C.
11 Carefully place each Scotch egg into the hot oil and deep-fry for 6–8 minutes, until golden and crisp and the sausagemeat is completely cooked.
12 Carefully remove from the oil with a slotted spoon and drain on kitchen paper.
13 To serve, cut the egg in half and season slightly with rock salt. The Scotch eggs can be served hot, warm or cold.

Flatten out an oval of the sausagemeat mixture

Flour the egg and wrap the meat around it until it is completely covered

Dip in flour, then beaten egg

Roll the egg in the breadcrumbs

The egg should be completely coated in breadcrumbs, ready for frying

Try something different

- For a **vegetarian** version of the traditional pork Scotch egg, follow the same method as above, replacing the sausagemeat with 350 g of dry mashed potato.
- A **fish** version can be made. Follow the same method as above using 300 g fish mousse (this works best using salmon) instead of sausagemeat.

---

5 Fried eggs
(oeufs frits)

eggs · shallow frying

energy	kcal	fat	sat fat	carb	sugar	protein	fibre	*
536KJ	128 kcal	31.0 g	9.8 g	0.0 g	0.0 g	7.6 g	0.0 g	

Allow 1 or 2 eggs per portion.

1 Melt a little fat in a frying pan. Add the eggs.
2 Cook gently until lightly set. Serve on a plate or flat dish.

Key point

To prepare an excellent fried egg, it is essential to use a fresh high-quality egg, maintain a controlled low heat and use a high-quality fat (butter or oil, such as sunflower oil).

Food safety tip

Lightly cooked eggs do not reach high enough temperatures to kill all bacteria that may be present. Do not serve lightly cooked eggs to people in high-risk groups: very young children, elderly people, pregnant women or people who are ill.

* Fried in sunflower oil

6 Omelettes
(omelette nature)

eggs shallow frying

energy	kcal	fat	sat fat	carb	sugar	protein	fibre*
990KJ	236 kcal	20.2 g	9.1 g	0.0 g	0.0 g	13.6 g	0.0 g

Portions 〉	1
eggs	2–3
salt, pepper	
butter or oil	10 g

1 Break the eggs into a basin, season lightly with salt and pepper.
2 Beat well with a fork, or whisk until the yolks and whites are thoroughly combined and no streaks of white can be seen.
3 Heat the omelette pan; wipe thoroughly clean with a dry cloth.
4 Add the butter; heat until foaming but not brown.
5 Add the eggs and cook quickly, moving the mixture continuously with a fork or spatula until lightly set; remove from the heat.
6 Half fold the mixture over at right angles to the handle.
7 Tap the bottom of the pan to bring up the edge of the omelette.
8 With care, tilt the pan completely over so as to allow the omelette to fall into the centre of the dish or plate.
9 Neaten the shape if necessary and serve immediately.

Making an omelette
http://bit.ly/zWfvHq

Healthy eating tip
● Use salt sparingly and serve with plenty of starchy carbohydrate and vegetables or salad.

Whisk the eggs until the yolks and whites are combined

Move the mixture continuously while it cooks

Carefully tip the omelette out of the pan

* Using 2 eggs per portion. Using 3 eggs per portion, 1 portion provides: 1330 kJ/317 kcal energy; 26.2 g fat; 11.0 g sat fat; 0.0 g carb; 0.0 g sugar; 20.3 g protein; 0.0 g fibre.

Try something different
Variations to omelettes can easily be made by adding the ingredient that the guest or dish may require. For example:
● fine herbs (chopped parsley, chervil and chives)
● mushroom (cooked, sliced, wild or cultivated)
● cheese (25 g grated cheese added before folding)
● tomato (incision made down centre of cooked omelette, filled with hot tomato concassée; served with tomato sauce)
● bacon (grill and then julienne into small strips and fold in at the end).

7 Spanish omelette

eggs, vegetables, fruits  shallow frying

	energy 1726 KJ	kcal 416 kcal	fat 30.9 g	sat fat 11.2 g	carb 10.9 g	sugar 8.2 g	protein 24.6 g	fibre 2.5 g	sodium 0.8 g

Portions >	1
eggs	2–3
salt, pepper	
butter, or oil	10 g
tomato concassée	50 g
onions, cooked	100 g
red pepper, diced	25 g
parsley, chopped	

This omelette is cooked and served flat. Many other flat omelettes can be served with a variety of ingredients.

1 Make up an omelette following recipe 6, steps 1–6, but including the tomato, onion, red pepper and parsley with the eggs.

2 Sharply tap the pan on the stove to loosen the omelette and toss it over as for a pancake.

When the butter is foaming, add the egg mixture

The omelette is tipped out flat

8 Poached eggs
(oeufs pochés)

eggs poaching

energy 358KJ	kcal 85 kcal	fat 6.4 g	sat fat 2.0 g	carb 0.0 g	sugar 0.0 g	protein 6.8 g	fibre 0.0 g

High-quality fresh eggs should be used for poaching because they have a large amount of thick white and consequently less of a tendency to spread in the simmering water. Low-quality eggs are difficult to manage because the large quantity of thin white spreads in the simmering water.

A well-prepared poached egg has a firm, tender white surrounding the slightly thickened, unbroken yolk. The use of a little vinegar (an acid) helps to set the egg white, so preventing it from spreading; it also makes the white more tender and whiter. Too much malt vinegar will discolour and give the eggs a strong vinegar flavour; white vinegar may be used.

1 Carefully break the eggs one by one into a pan of vinegar water (approx. 15 per cent acidulation) and make sure the water is at a gentle boil.
2 Poach at just below boiling point until lightly set, for approximately 3–3½ minutes.
3 Remove carefully with a perforated spoon into a bowl of ice water.
4 Trim the white if necessary.
5 Reheat, when required, by placing into hot salted water for approximately ½–1 minute.
6 Remove carefully from the water using a perforated spoon.
7 Drain on a cloth and use as required. (The eggs can be refreshed and reheated for service.)

Place the egg into gently boiling, acidulated water

Poach until lightly set

Lift the egg out carefully on a slotted spoon

Healthy eating tip
● Serve with a thick slice of wholegrain bread or unbuttered toast.

Poaching eggs
http://bit.ly/zC1HWz

9 Eggs Benedict

eggs, bacon poaching

energy	kcal	fat	sat fat	carb	sugar	protein	fibre	sodium
3910 KJ	943 kcal	77.0 g	37.8 g	24.8 g	2.2 g	39.2 g	1.4 g	2.1 g

Portions ›	4	10
cooking medium (see note)		
large eggs	8	20
butter, unsalted	2 tbsp	5 tbsp
plain English muffins, split and toasted	4	10
smoked bacon or sweet cure bacon, cooked (optional)	12 slices	30 slices
hollandaise sauce (see page 57)	200 g	500 g

Key point

The cooking bath must be deep and must have a minimum of 15 per cent distilled or white wine vinegar added.

1 Bring the cooking medium to a slight simmer.
2 Crack an egg into a cup and carefully slide it into the hot poaching liquid. Quickly repeat with all the eggs.
3 Poach the eggs for 3 minutes, turning them occasionally with a spoon, until the whites are firm.
4 Using a slotted spoon, remove the eggs and transfer to a kitchen towel. Lightly dab the eggs with the towel to remove any excess water.
5 While the eggs are poaching, butter the muffins and place 2 halves on each plate.
6 Reheat the bacon and place on top of the muffins, then top with the drained eggs.
7 To finish, lightly spoon over a generous helping of warm hollandaise sauce and serve immediately, or serve the hollandaise separately.

10 Eggs in cocotte
(oeufs en cocotte)

eggs poaching

energy	kcal	fat	sat fat	carb	sugar	protein	fibre
534KJ	127 kcal	11.2 g	5.2 g	0.0 g	0.0 g	6.8 g	0.0 g

Portions ›	4	10
butter	25 g	60 g
eggs	4	10
salt, pepper		

Try something different

Variations include:

- half a minute before the cooking is completed, add 1 tsp of cream to each egg and complete the cooking
- when cooked, add 1 tsp of *jus-lié* to each egg
- place diced cooked chicken, mixed with cream, in the bottom of the cocottes; break the eggs on top of the chicken and cook
- as above, using tomato concassé in place of chicken.

1 Butter the appropriate number of egg cocottes or other small dishes.
2 Break an egg carefully into each and season.
3 Place the cocottes in a sauté pan containing 1 cm water.
4 Cover with a tight-fitting lid, place on a fierce heat so that the water boils rapidly.
5 Cook for 2–3 minutes until the eggs are lightly set, then serve.

11 Scrambled eggs
(oeufs brouillés)

energy	kcal	fat	sat fat	carb	sugar	protein	fibre	*
1105KJ	263 kcal	22.9 g	8.7 g	0.5 g	0.5 g	13.9 g	0.0 g	

Portions ›	4	10
eggs	6–8	15–20
milk (optional)	2 tbsp	5 tbsp
salt, pepper		
butter or oil	50 g	125 g

Scrambled eggs with smoked salmon

1 Break the eggs in a basin, add milk (if using), lightly season with salt and pepper and thoroughly mix with a whisk.
2 Melt the butter in a thick-bottomed pan, add the eggs and cook over a gentle heat, stirring continuously until the eggs are lightly cooked.
3 Remove from the heat and correct the seasoning. (A tablespoon of cream may also be added at this point.)
4 Serve in individual egg dishes.

Try something different
Scrambled eggs may be served with smoked salmon (as shown).

* Using hard margarine instead of butter

Key point
If scrambled eggs are cooked too quickly or for too long the protein will toughen, the eggs will discolour because of the iron and sulphur compounds being released, and syneresis (separation of water from the eggs) will occur. This means that they will be unpleasant to eat. The heat from the pan will continue to cook the eggs after it has been removed from the stove; therefore, the pan should be removed from the heat just before the eggs are cooked. Scrambled eggs can be served on a slice of freshly buttered toast with the crust removed.

Healthy eating tip
● Try to keep the butter used in cooking to a minimum and serve with unbuttered toast.
● Garnish with a grilled tomato.

12 Eggs *sur le plat*

eggs · baking

energy	kcal	fat	sat fat	carb	sugar	protein	fibre	sodium *
1473 KJ	357 kcal	32.9 g	6.6 g	0.0 g	0.0 g	15.0 g	0.0 g	0.2 g

Allow 1 or 2 eggs per portion.

1 Take a china *sur le plat* dish. Add a teaspoon of olive oil or butter. Heat it on the side of the stove, until it is moderately hot.
2 Break in 1 or 2 eggs. Allow them to set on the stove.
3 Transfer to the oven for 2–4 minutes to finish cooking.

> **Note**
> A *sur le plat* dish is a shallow porcelain dish used for cooking and serving eggs.

* For two eggs

Pasta, gnocchi and rice

This chapter is relevant to the following units:

- Prepare, cook and finish basic rice dishes (NVQ)
- Prepare, cook and finish basic pasta dishes (NVQ)
- Prepare and cook rice, pasta, grains and egg dishes (VRQ).

Pasta

Food value

Pasta is made from durum wheat, which has a 15 per cent protein content. This makes it a good alternative to rice and potatoes for vegetarians. Pasta also contains carbohydrates in the form of starch, which gives the body energy. Eating more pasta is in line with the recommendation to 'eat more starchy carbohydrates'.

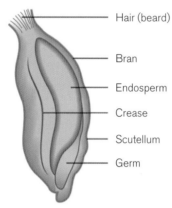

- Hair (beard)
- Bran
- Endosperm
- Crease
- Scutellum
- Germ

The structure of a grain of wheat

Storage

Dry pasta can be stored almost indefinitely, if kept in a tightly sealed package or a covered container in a cool, dry place, but you must observe the 'best before' date on the packaging.

Fresh egg pasta not for immediate use must be stored in a cool, dry place. If fresh egg pasta is to be stored, it should be allowed to dry, then kept in a clean, dry container or bowl in a cool, dry store.

If cooked pasta is not to be used immediately, drain and rinse thoroughly with cold water. If the pasta is left to sit in water, it will continue to absorb water and become mushy. When the pasta is cool, drain and toss lightly with salad oil to prevent it from sticking and drying out. Cover tightly and refrigerate or freeze. Refrigerate the pasta and sauce separately or the pasta will become soggy. To reheat, put pasta in a colander and immerse in rapidly boiling water just long enough to heat through. Do not allow the pasta to continue to cook. Pasta may also be reheated in a microwave.

Preparing pasta

For dried pasta: bring plenty of water (at least 3.8 litres for every 585 g of dry pasta) to a rapid boil. Add about 1 tbsp of salt per 4 litres of water, if desired. Add the pasta in small quantities to maintain the rapid boil. Stir frequently to prevent sticking. Do not cover the pan. Follow package directions for cooking time. Do not overcook. Pasta should be 'al dente' (meaning literally 'to the tooth' – tender, yet firm). It should be slightly resistant to the bite, but cooked through. Drain pasta to stop the cooking action. Do not rinse unless the recipe specifically says to do so. For salads, drain and rinse pasta with cold water.

For fresh egg pasta: this requires less cooking time than dried pasta. When cooking fresh pasta, some chefs add a few drops of olive oil in the water to prevent the pasta pieces from sticking together.

Cooking fresh and dried pasta http://bit.ly/wTU9K2

About dried pasta

There are an almost infinite number of types of pasta asciutta, especially if you include all the regional variations. Almost 90 per cent of the pasta eaten in Italy is dried, the remainder being home-made. A rule of thumb for cooking dried pasta and portion weights is 90–100 g per portion as a starter course and, if larger portions are required, increase accordingly. Traditionally, pasta was eaten as a starter, but now it is used much more as a main course or stand-alone dish.

Types of pasta, sauces and accompaniments

There are basically four types of pasta, each of which may be plain, or flavoured with spinach or tomato:
1   dried durum wheat pasta
2   egg pasta

3 semolina pasta

4 wholewheat pasta.

Examples of sauces to go with pasta include:

- tomato sauce
- cream, butter or béchamel-based
- rich meat sauce
- olive oil and garlic
- soft white or blue cheese
- pesto (see page 52).

Cheeses used in pasta cooking include the following:

- **Parmesan:** The most popular hard cheese for use with pasta, ideal for grating. The flavour is best when it is freshly grated. If bought ready-grated, or if it is grated and stored, the flavour deteriorates.
- **Pecorino:** A strong ewes' milk cheese, sometimes studded with peppercorns. Used for strongly flavoured dishes, it can be grated or thinly sliced.
- **Ricotta:** Creamy-white in colour, made from the discarded whey of other cheeses. It is widely used in fillings for pasta such as cannelloni and ravioli, and for sauces.
- **Mozzarella:** Traditionally made from the milk of the water buffalo. Mozzarella is pure white and creamy, with a mild but distinctive flavour, and usually round or pear-shaped. It will keep for only a few days in a container half-filled with milk and water.
- **Gorgonzola and dolcelatte:** Distinctive blue cheeses that can be used in sauces.

Ingredients for pasta dishes

A huge variety of ingredients may be used in pasta dishes. The list is almost endless, but includes:

- fish, e.g. smoked salmon, anchovies, tuna
- shellfish, e.g. shrimps, prawns, scallops, lobster, crab, cockles
- meat, e.g. smoked ham, sausage, salami, bacon, beef, chicken, duck
- offal, e.g. tongue, chicken livers
- herbs, e.g. parsley, rosemary, basil, tarragon, chives, marjoram
- spices, e.g. chillies, saffron, grated nutmeg

- vegetables, e.g. avocado, mushrooms, tomatoes, onions, fennel, courgettes, spring onions, peas, spinach, peppers, broad beans, broccoli
- nuts, e.g. pine nuts, walnuts, hazelnuts
- fruit, e.g. stoned olives, sultanas, lemon zest
- eggs
- capers
- cooked, dried beans
- Balsamic vinegar.

Stuffed pasta

Examples of stuffed pasta include the following:

- **Agnolini** are small half-moon shapes usually filled with ham and cheese or minced meat.
- **Cannelloni** are squares of pasta, poached, refreshed, dried and stuffed with a variety of fillings (e.g. ricotta cheese and spinach), rolled and finished with an appropriate sauce.
- **Cappelletti**, shaped like little hats, are usually filled as agnolini, and are available dried.
- **Ravioli** are usually square with serrated edges. A wide variety of fillings can be used (fish, meat, vegetarian, cheese, etc.).
- **Ravolini**, or 'little ravioli', are made half the size of ravioli.
- **Tortellini**, a slightly larger version of cappelletti, are also available in dried form.
- **Tortelloni** is a double-sized version of tortellini.

Pasta that is to be stuffed must be rolled as thinly as possible. The stuffing should be pleasant in taste and plentiful in quantity. The edges of the pasta must be thoroughly sealed otherwise the stuffing will seep out during poaching.

The list of possible stuffings is almost endless as every district in Italy has its own variations and, with thought and experimentation, many more can be produced. For examples, see recipe 9.

All stuffed pasta should be served in or coated with a suitable sauce and, depending on the type of recipe, may be finished 'au gratin' by sprinkling with freshly grated Parmesan and browning lightly under the salamander.

Summary: cooking pasta

- Always cook pasta in plenty of boiling salted water.
- Stir to the boil. Do not overcook.
- If not to be used immediately, refresh and reheat carefully in hot salted water when required. Drain well in a colander.
- With most pasta, freshly grated cheese (Parmesan) should be served separately.
- Allow 50 g dry weight as a first course; 100 g as a main course.
- When cooking fresh pasta add a little oil to the water to help prevent the pieces sticking together.

Noodles (oriental style)

Noodles are probably the world's oldest fast food; they are versatile and quick to cook. They may be steamed, boiled, pan-fried, stir-fried or deep-fried. A staple food in the Far East, their popularity is spreading rapidly in the West.

Noodles are high in starch (carbohydrate). They provide some protein, especially those made from hard wheat and beans. The addition of egg also increases noodles' protein content.

Examples of the nutritional content of some noodles are given in Table 5.1.

Table 5.1 Nutritional content of noodles

100 g dry weight	Calories	Carbohydrate	Protein	Fat	Sodium/salt
rice sticks	380	88%	6%	0	
rice vermicelli	363	85.5%	7.3%	0	
egg noodles	341	70%	11%	1.9%	0.8%
wheat noodles	308	60% + fibre 10%	12.5%	2%	0.8%
bean thread	320	65%	20%	0	
pasta	350	75%	11.5%	0.3%	

Source: Pat Chapman (1998) *Pat Chapman's Noodle Book*, Hodder & Stoughton Ltd

Rice

Rice is one of the world's most important crops: it is the main food crop for about half the world's population. A hot, wet atmosphere is required for the cultivation of rice, and it is grown chiefly in India, the Far East, South America, Italy and the southern states of the USA. In order to grow, it needs more water than any other cereal crop.

When it comes to cultivated rice, three primary species are grown. The first is *O. Sativa* and the second, *O. Glaberrima*. The first is found in Africa and, while it is the most widely used, it is not cultivated. It is

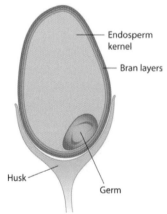

The structure of a grain of rice

Labels: Endosperm kernel, Bran layers, Husk, Germ

believed that this particular species was developed from other forms approximately 15 million years ago. The third species, *O. Rufipogon*, is grown in China, among other regions.

Rice varieties

There are around 250 different varieties of rice. The main ones are described below.

- **Long-grain:** a narrow, pointed grain that has had the full bran and most of the germ removed so that it is less fibrous than brown rice. Because of its firm structure, which helps to keep the grains separate when cooked, it is suitable for plain boiling and savoury dishes such as kedgeree and curry.
- **Brown grain:** any rice that has had the outer covering removed, but retains its bran and, as a result, is more nutritious and contains more fibre. It takes longer to cook than long-grain rice. The nutty

flavour of brown rice lends itself to some recipes, but does not substitute well in traditional dishes such as paella, risotto or puddings.

Many other types of rice are now available, which can add different colours and textures to dishes. Some of these are described below.

- **Short-grain:** a short, rounded grain with a soft texture, suitable for sweet dishes and risotto.
- **Arborio** is an Italian short-grain rice. It is used in risottos because it can absorb a good deal of cooking liquid without becoming too soft, and releases starch to slightly thicken the dish.
- **Basmati:** a narrow long-grain rice with a distinctive flavour, suitable for serving with Indian dishes.
- **Whole-grain rice:** the whole unprocessed grain of the rice.
- **Wild rice:** this is actually an aquatic grass, not a rice. See Chapter 9 for more information.
- **Red rice**: an unmilled, short-grain rice from the Camargue in France, with a brownish-red colour and a nutty flavour. It's slightly sticky when cooked, and is particularly good in salads.

Rice products include:
- **precooked instant rice:** parboiled, ready cooked and boil-in-the-bag rice are similar.
- **ground rice:** used for milk puddings
- **rice flour:** can be used for thickening cream soups. Because it's gluten free, it can't be used to make a yeasted loaf.
- **rice paper:** used for macaroons and nougat.
- **rice flakes** (brown and white): can be added to muesli or made into a milk pudding or porridge.

Storage

Uncooked rice can be stored on the shelf in a tightly sealed container. The shelf life of brown rice is shorter than that of white rice. The bran layers contain oil that can become rancid. Refrigerator storage is recommended for longer shelf life. Washing rice is not necessary; just measure and cook.

Once cooked, keep hot (above 65°C for no longer than two hours) or cool quickly (within 90 minutes) and keep cool, below 5°C. If this is not done, *Bacillus cereus* (a bacterium found in the soil) may multiply in the cooked rice. Cooked rice can be refrigerated for up to seven days (but it is not advisable for food safety reasons) or stored in the freezer for six months. Cooked rice always has the danger of contamination by *Bacillus cereus*. These bacteria can form protective spores that survive the cooking process. These spores may germinate, grow and produce a toxin, which may not be killed by reheating the rice.

Rice is a very useful and versatile carbohydrate. When added to dishes it helps to proportionally reduce the fat content.

Risotto

Recipe 20 in this chapter is an example of risotto.
- The whole process, not including heating the stock, should take 30 minutes.
- Arborio is the easiest rice to find.
- Vialone and carnaroli are other Italian types, and each has its adherents.
- Do not attempt to use pudding, patna or Japanese rice, despite their similar appearance to Italian rice.
- A perfect risotto is not a pile of stodgy rice on a plate, sitting like a glutinous mound, nor is it a soupy liquid mess lying flat on the plate. It should be just about moundable, fighting to hold its little peaks from collapsing back into the rest.
- All the liquid should be combined with the rice to give a creamy-type consistency. Finish with butter and cream.

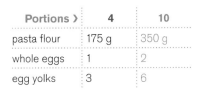

Fresh egg pasta dough (method 1)

energy	kcal	fat	sat fat	carb	sugar	protein	fibre
1672 KJ	400 kcal	17.2 g	9.4 g	50.0 g	10.2 g	11.8 g	4.0 g

Portions ⟩	4	10
pasta flour	175 g	350 g
whole eggs	1	2
egg yolks	3	6

1 Place all the ingredients into a food processor and mix quickly until a wet crumb mix appears; this should take no more than 30–45 seconds.
2 Tip the mix out on to a clean surface; this is where the working of the pasta begins. Lightly knead it.
3 The pasta dough may feel wet at this stage, however the working of the gluten will take the moisture back in to the dry mass, leaving a velvety-smooth finish that is malleable and easy to work; most of this process should be carried out using a pasta machine.
4 Rest the dough for 30 minutes and then it is ready to use.
5 For a classical noodle shape, roll out to a thin rectangle 45 x 15 cm. Cut into 0.5 cm strips. Leave to dry.

Combine the ingredients into a wet crumb mix

Work and roll out the pasta using a pasta machine

A pasta machine with an attachment can be used to cut noodles

Key points
- Do not knead the dough too much, or it will become tough.
- Let it rest before rolling it out.
- The best way to roll out pasta dough at the correct thickness is to use a pasta machine.

Making fresh pasta
http://bit.ly/xjvhHH

2 Fresh egg pasta dough (method 2)

pasta making dough

Potions ›	4	8
strong flour	200 g	400 g
salt		
eggs, medium, beaten	2	4
olive oil, as required	1 tbsp	approx. 1 tbsp

1 Sieve the flour and salt, shape into a well. Pour the beaten eggs into the well.
2 Gradually incorporate the flour and only add oil to adjust to required consistency. The amount of oil will vary according to the type of flour and the size of the eggs used.
3 Pull and knead the dough until it is of a smooth, elastic consistency.
4 Cover the dough with a dampened cloth and allow to rest in a cool place for 30 minutes.
5 Roll out the dough on a well-floured surface to a thickness of 0.5 mm, or use a pasta-rolling machine.
6 Trim the sides and cut the dough as required using a large knife.

Pour the beaten eggs into a well in the flour

Gradually incorporate the flour into the eggs

Pull and knead the dough until it is smooth and elastic

If using a pasta-rolling machine, divide the dough into three or four pieces. Pass each section by hand through the machine, turning the rollers with the other hand. Repeat this five or six times, adjusting the rollers each time to make the pasta thinner.

Try something different
- **Spinach:** add 40–50 g finely puréed, dry, cooked spinach to the dough.
- **Tomato:** add 1 tbsp of tomato purée to the dough.
- Other flavours used include **beetroot, saffron** and **black ink** from squid.
- **Wholewheat pasta:** use half wholewheat and half white flour.

3 Spaghetti with tomato sauce
(spaghetti alla pomodoro)

pasta, vegetable fruits 🔲 boiling

energy	kcal	fat	sat fat	carb	sugar	protein	fibre
1672 KJ	400 kcal	17.2 g	9.4 g	50.0 g	10.2 g	11.8 g	4.0 g *

Portions ❯	4	10
spaghetti	400 g	1 kg
butter (optional) or olive oil	25 g	60 g
tomato sauce (page 52)	250 ml	625 ml
salt, mill pepper		
fresh basil, to serve		
grated cheese, to serve		

1 Plunge the spaghetti into a saucepan containing boiling salted water. Allow to boil gently.
2 Stir occasionally with a wooden spoon. Cook for approximately 12–15 minutes, until *al dente*.
3 Drain well in a colander. Return to a clean, dry pan.
4 Mix in the butter and add the tomato sauce. Correct the seasoning.
5 Add 4–5 leaves of fresh basil torn into pieces with your fingers, and serve with grated cheese.

> **Key point**
> Cook pasta to an *al dente* texture.

Healthy eating tips
- Use very little or no salt as there is already plenty from the cheese.
- Reduce or omit the butter and serve with a large green salad.

Place the spaghetti into boiling water

Drain the cooked pasta

Add the sauce to the pasta

* Using hard margarine instead of butter

4 Spaghetti bolognaise
(spaghetti alla bolognese)

beef, pasta boiling, shallow frying

Portions ›	4	10
butter or oil	20 g	50g
onion, chopped	50 g	125 g
clove of garlic, chopped	1	2
lean minced beef or tail end fillet (see note), cut into 3 mm dice	400 g	1 kg
jus-lié	125 ml	300 ml
tomato purée	1 tbsp	2½ tbsp
marjoram or oregano	1/8 tsp	¼ tsp
mushrooms, diced	100 g	250 g
salt, mill pepper		
spaghetti	400 g	1 kg
grated cheese, to serve		

1 Place half the butter or oil in a sauteuse.
2 Add the chopped onion and garlic, and cook for 4–5 minutes without colour.
3 Add the beef and cook, colouring lightly.
4 Add the *jus-lié*, the tomato purée and the herbs.
5 Simmer until tender.
6 Add the mushrooms and simmer for 5 minutes. Correct the seasoning.
7 Meanwhile, cook the spaghetti in plenty of boiling salted water.
8 Allow to boil gently, stirring occasionally with a wooden spoon.
9 Cook for approximately 12–15 minutes. Drain well in a colander.
10 Return to a clean pan containing the rest of the butter or oil (optional).
11 Correct the seasoning.
12 Serve with the sauce in centre of the spaghetti.
13 Serve grated cheese separately.

Healthy eating tips
- Use an unsaturated oil (sunflower or olive). Lightly oil the pan and drain off any excess after the frying is complete. Skim the fat from the finished dish.
- Season with the minimum amount of salt.
- Try using more pasta and extending the sauce with tomatoes.
- Serve with a large green salad.

Try something different
There are many variations on bolognaise sauce, e.g. substitute lean beef with pork mince, or use a combination of both; add 50 g each of chopped carrot and celery; add 100 g chopped pancetta or bacon. The following is an example.

Alternative recipe for bolognaise sauce

Portions ›	4	10
olive oil	1 tbsp	2½ tbsp
beef mince and pork mince	270 g	700 g
onion, chopped	½	1
mushrooms, sliced	100 g	250 g
carrots, peeled and diced or cut as for paysanne	1	2
red wine	75 ml	180 ml
beef stock or meat stock, reduced	100 ml	250 ml
tomato purée	1 tbsp	2 tbsp
Tabasco sauce (optional)	½ tsp	1 tsp
salt and freshly ground black pepper, to taste		
fresh parsley, chopped	2 tbsp	5 tbsp
fresh chives, chopped, to garnish		

1 Heat the olive oil in a frying pan, over a medium heat.
2 Add the beef and pork mince and the chopped onion, and pan-fry for 4–6 minutes, stirring well, until the mince has browned and the onion has softened.
3 Add the mushrooms and carrots, and cook for a further minute, before adding the red wine, beef stock and tomato purée.
4 Add the Tabasco sauce and season to taste (optional).
5 Add the chopped parsley and cook for 2–4 minutes more, to allow the wine and stock to reduce a little.
6 When mixing the pasta into the sauce, first drain the water thoroughly from the pasta then place into the bolognaise sauce.
7 Toss well, to evenly coat, then spoon into a serving bowl.
8 Garnish with the chopped chives, to serve (optional).

5 Macaroni cheese

pasta, cheese boiling

energy	kcal	fat	sat fat	carb	sugar	protein	fibre *
7596 KJ	1808 kcal	116.6 g	64.2 g	136.6 g	26.6 g	60.0 g	6.8 g

Portions ›	4	10
macaroni	400 g	1 kg
butter or oil, optional	25 g	60 g
grated cheese	100 g	250 g
thin béchamel	500 ml	1.25 litres
diluted English or continental mustard	¼ tsp	1 tsp
salt, mill pepper		

1 Plunge the macaroni into a saucepan containing plenty of boiling salted water.
2 Allow to boil gently and stir occasionally with a wooden spoon.
3 Cook for approximately 15 minutes and drain well in a colander.
4 Return to a clean pan containing the butter.
5 Mix with half the cheese, and add the béchamel and mustard. Season.
6 Place in an earthenware dish and sprinkle with the remainder of the cheese.
7 Brown lightly under the salamander and serve.

Key point
Browning the macaroni well gives it a good flavour, texture and presentation.

* For 4 portions

Healthy eating tips

- Half the grated cheese could be replaced with a small amount of Parmesan (more flavour and less fat).
- Use semi-skimmed milk for the béchamel. No added salt is necessary.

Try something different

Variations include the addition of cooked, sliced mushrooms, diced ham, sweetcorn, tomato, and so on. Macaroni may also be prepared and served as for any of the spaghetti dishes.

6 Penne arrabiata

pasta, vegetable fruits shallow frying, boiling

energy	kcal	fat	sat fat	carb	sugar	protein	fibre
2263 KJ	539 kcal	24.1 g	4.4 g	65.7 g	10.2 g	19.3 g	2.8 g

Portions ⟩	4	10
onion, chopped	1	2½
extra virgin olive oil	6 tbsp	15 tbsp
medium hot chillies, finely chopped	2	5
cloves of garlic, chopped	1	2
basil leaves, shredded	5	12
tomato purée	1 tbsp	2½ tbsp
canned chopped plum tomatoes	600 g	1.5 kg
salt, to taste		
fresh/dried rigate penne pasta	400 g	1 kg
bacon lardons	100 g	250 g
Parmesan shavings, to serve		

1 Gently heat the olive oil in a frying pan. Add the onion, chilli and garlic and fry while stirring for one minute. Add the lardons and cook until golden.

2 Add the chopped tomatoes and tomato purée to the frying pan and simmer for 10–15 minutes, until the sauce has thickened a little. Season with salt to taste.

3 While the sauce is cooking, cook the pasta in large saucepan of boiling, salted water until *al dente* (fresh pasta will cook much more quickly than dried pasta). Drain the pasta and drizzle it with oil.

4 Add the basil to the sauce. Mix in the drained pasta.

5 Serve with shavings of Parmesan.

7 Spinach fettuccine with ham and creamy cheese

(fettucine verdi in salsa cremona)

pasta, leafy vegetables boiling

energy	kcal	fat	sat fat	carb	sugar	protein	fibre
3183 KJ	760 kcal	42.2 g	25.4 g	76.3 g	2.7 g	23.7 g	3.1 g

Portions ⟩	4	10
spinach fettuccine or other pasta	400 g	1 kg
cream cheese, mashed	200 g	500 g
single cream	2 tbsp	5 tbsp
Parmesan cheese, grated	50 g	125 g
salt, pepper		
butter, melted	50 g	
lean cooked ham, cut into thick julienne	100 g	250 g

1 Cook the fettuccine in plenty of boiling salted water.
2 Mix the cream cheese, cream, Parmesan, salt and pepper.
3 Drain the fettuccine and return to the pan.
4 Mix in the butter and cheese mixture. Add the ham. Toss and serve.

Healthy eating tips

- This sauce is high in fat and salt, so additional butter and salt is not necessary.
- For a lower-fat version, use a 'light' cream cheese.
- Serve with a large green salad.

Practical Cookery 12th edition

8 Tagliatelle carbonara

pasta, bacon boiling,  shallow frying

energy	kcal	fat	sat fat	carb	sugar	protein	fibre	sodium
2911 KJ	698 kcal	44.8 g	20.8 g	43.0 g	1.9 g	33.4 g	0.2 g	1.0 g

Portions ⟩	4	10
tagliatelle	400 g	1 kg
olive oil	1 tbsp	2½ tbsp
cloves of garlic, peeled and crushed	2	5
smoked bacon, diced	200 g	500 g
eggs	4	10
double or single cream	4 tbsp	150 ml
Parmesan cheese	4 tbsp	150 ml

1 Cook the tagliatelle in boiling salted water until *al dente*. Refresh and drain.
2 Heat the oil in a suitable pan. Fry the crushed garlic. Add the diced, smoked bacon.
3 Mix together the beaten eggs, cream and Parmesan. Season with black pepper.
4 Add the tagliatelle to the garlic and bacon. Add the eggs and cream, stirring until the eggs cook in the heat. Serve immediately.

9 Ravioli

energy	kcal	fat	sat fat	carb	sugar	protein	fibre
1027 KJ	249 kcal	9.4 g	1.4 g	38.9 g	0.8 g	4.8 g	1.6 g

To make the dough and form the ravioli

Portions ›	4	10
flour	200 g	500 g
salt		
olive oil	35 ml	150 ml
water	105 ml	250 ml

Fresh egg pasta dough (recipe 1 or 2) can also be used. If you have prepared the dough, start this recipe at step 3.

1 Sieve the flour and salt. Make a well. Add the liquid.
2 Knead to a smooth dough. Rest for at least 30 minutes in a cool place.
3 Roll out to a very thin oblong: 30 cm × 45 cm.
4 Cut in half and eggwash.
5 Place the stuffing in a piping bag with a large plain tube.
6 Pipe out the filling in small pieces, each about the size of a cherry, approximately 4 cm apart, on to one half of the paste.
7 Carefully cover with the other half of the paste and seal, taking care to avoid air pockets.
8 Mark each with the back of a plain cutter.

9 Cut in between each line of filling, down and across with a serrated pastry wheel, or use a plain, round pastry cutter.
10 Separate on a well-floured tray.
11 Poach in gently boiling salted water for approximately 10 minutes. Drain well.
12 Place in an earthenware serving dish.
13 Cover with 250 ml *jus-lié*, demi-glace or tomato sauce.
14 Sprinkle with 50 g grated cheese.
15 Brown under the salamander and serve.

These instructions make traditional, small ravioli. A more modern approach is to make larger ravioli – there will be more filling in each one. The modern presentation is shown here and in recipe 10.

Large ravioli are made individually

A pastry cutter is used to trim the edges neatly

Possible fillings

Here are some examples of stuffing for ravioli, tortellini and other pastas. Each recipe provides enough stuffing to use with 400 g pasta.

Chicken and ham

chicken, cooked, minced	200 g
ham, minced	100 g
butter	25 g
2 yolks or 1 egg	
cheese, grated	25 g
nutmeg, grated	pinch
salt and pepper	
fresh white breadcrumbs	25 g

Spinach and ricotta

dry spinach, cooked, puréed	200 g
ricotta cheese	200 g
butter	25 g
nutmeg	
salt and pepper	

Pork and veal

lean pork mince, cooked	200 g
lean veal mince, cooked	200 g
butter	25 g
cheese, grated	25 g
2 yolks or 1 egg	
fresh white breadcrumbs	25 g
salt and pepper	

Cheese

marjoram, chopped	pinch
ricotta cheese	150 g
Parmesan, grated	75 g
egg	1
nutmeg	
salt and pepper	

Meat and spinach

beef or pork mince, cooked	200 g
spinach, cooked	100 g
onion, chopped, cooked	50 g
oregano	
salt, pepper	

Fish and mushroom

fish, chopped, cooked	200 g
mushrooms, chopped, cooked	100 g
parsley, chopped	
anchovy paste	

10 Ravioli of squash and spinach with wild mushroom sauce

pasta, vegetable fruits, fungi

shallow frying, boiling

energy	kcal	fat	sat fat	carb	sugar	protein	fibre	sodium
2469 KJ	590 kcal	30.8 g	17.6 g	62.0 g	6.6 g	15.8 g	4.2 g	1.3 g

Portions ❯	4	10
Squash ravioli		
squash	500 g	1.25 kg
butter	100 g	250 g
salt	10 g	25 g
spinach	250 g	625 g
pasta dough (recipe 1 or 2)	400 g	1 kg
Wild mushroom sauce		
onions, finely sliced	50 g	125 g
button mushrooms, finely sliced	75 g	185 g
wild mushrooms, sliced	60 g	150 g
clove of garlic	½	1
bay leaf	1	2
sprig of thyme	1	2
butter	10 g	25 g
dried cep	5 g	12 g
Noilly Prat (dry vermouth)	75 g	185 g
vegetable stock	200 ml	500 ml
single cream	100 g	250 g
seasoning		

Ravioli

1 Peel the butternut squash, remove the seeds and chop the flesh roughly.
2 Cook the squash in the butter with the salt over a medium heat until soft.
3 Add the spinach and cook for a further minute.
4 Drain off the butter and chill the mixture until firm.
5 Once the mixture is firm, roll out and cut into 1 cm pieces.
6 Roll the pasta dough and make the ravioli to the required shape.
7 Place on a floured tray and reserve until required.

Sauce

1 Sweat down the onions, fresh mushrooms, garlic and aromats in the butter for 10 minutes.
2 Add the dried cep and sweat for a further 5 minutes.
3 Add the Noilly Prat and reduce completely.
4 Add the vegetable stock and reduce by three-quarters.
5 Add the cream and bring to the boil. Remove the thyme and bay leaf.
6 Blitz the sauce until smooth, season and reserve until required.

To serve

1 To serve the dish, blanch the ravioli in simmering, salted water for 3 minutes.
2 Heat the sauce gently in a pan. Drain the ravioli and add to the sauce.
3 Garnish with the squash (reheated in the oven).
4 Finish with chopped chives and serve as required.

11 Ricotta and spinach cannelloni with tomato and basil sauce

pasta, leafy vegetables boiling, baking

energy	kcal	fat	sat fat	carb	sugar	protein	fibre	sodium
1913 KJ	454 kcal	14.6 g	6.3 g	61.0 g	6.5 g	23.8 g	3.1 g	0.3 g

Portions ⟩	4	10
dried plain or spinach lasagne sheets	12	30
ricotta cheese	200 g	500 g
fresh spinach	350 g	850 g
tomato sauce (page 52)	200 ml	500 ml
basil, shredded	1 tbsp	2 tbsp
Parmesan cheese, grated	50 g	125 g

1 Pre-heat the oven to 190°C. Cook the lasagne sheets in a large pan of boiling salted water for the stated time as shown on the packaging. Refresh immediately in ice-cold water.

2 Pick the spinach to de-branch it. Blanch by plunging it into rapidly boiling water for 20 seconds before refreshing it in ice-cold water.

3 Strain the spinach and squeeze out the excess water, then chop roughly.

4 Beat the ricotta with a spoon until soft, stir in the spinach and season well with salt and pepper.

5 Using a piping bag, pipe the ricotta mixture down one side of each lasagne sheet and roll them up to form a filled tube. Cover and chill in a refrigerator.

6 Place the cannelloni into a lightly oiled baking dish.

7 Pour the sauce over the prepared cannelloni, and sprinkle with freshly sliced basil and the Parmesan.

8 Bake at 190°C for 20 minutes and serve.

De-branch the spinach

Stir the chopped spinach into the beaten ricotta

Pipe the ricotta mixture down one side of the lasagne sheet

Carefully lift the edge of the sheet with a knife, then roll the cannelloni by hand

12 Lasagne

pasta, beef boiling, shallow frying, baking

energy	kcal	fat	sat fat	carb	sugar	protein	fibre
2416 KJ	575 kcal	28.7 g	11.4 g	56.1 g	10.0 g	26.7 g	5.8 g

Portions ❯	4	10
lasagne pasta	200 g	500 g
oil	1 tbsp	3 tbsp
streaky bacon, thin strips of	50 g	125 g
onion, chopped	100 g	250 g
carrot, chopped	50 g	125 g
onions, finely sliced	50 g	125 g
celery, chopped	50 g	125 g
minced beef	200 g	500 g
tomato purée	2 tbsp	5 tbsp
jus-lié or demi-glace	375 ml	1 litre
clove of garlic	1	1½
salt, pepper		
marjoram	½ tsp	1½ tsp
mushrooms, sliced	100 g	250 g
béchamel sauce	250 ml	600 ml
Parmesan or Cheddar cheese, grated	25 g	125 g

1 This recipe can be made using 200 g of ready-bought lasagne or it can be prepared fresh using 200 g pasta dough. Wholemeal lasagne can be made using pasta dough made with 100 g wholemeal flour and 100 g strong flour.

2 Prepare the pasta dough and roll out to 1 mm thick.

3 Cut into 6 cm squares.

4 Allow to rest in a cool place and dry slightly on a cloth dusted with flour.

5 Whether using fresh or ready-bought lasagne, cook in gently simmering salted water for approximately 10 minutes.

6 Refresh in cold water, then drain on a cloth.

7 Gently heat the oil in a thick-bottomed pan, add the bacon and cook for 2–3 minutes.

8 Add the onion, carrot and celery, cover the pan with a lid and cook for 5 minutes.

9 Add the minced beef, increase the heat and stir until lightly brown.

10 Remove from the heat and mix in the tomato purée.

11 Return to the heat, mix in the jus-lié or demi-glace, stir to boil.

12 Add the garlic, salt, pepper and marjoram, and simmer for 15 minutes. Remove the garlic.

13 Mix in the mushrooms, reboil for 2 minutes, then remove from the heat.

14 Butter an ovenproof dish and cover the bottom with a layer of the meat sauce.

15 Add a layer of lasagne and cover with meat sauce.

16 Add another layer of lasagne and cover with the remainder of the meat sauce.

17 Cover with the béchamel.

18 Sprinkle with cheese, cover with a lid and place in a moderately hot oven at 190°C for approximately 20 minutes.

19 Remove the lid, cook for a further 15 minutes and serve in the cleaned ovenproof dish.

Brown the minced beef in a thick-bottomed pan

Place a layer of lasagne over a layer of meat sauce

Cover the final layer with béchamel

Fillings for lasagne can be varied in many ways. Tomato sauce may be used instead of *jus-lié*.

Healthy eating tips

- Use an unsaturated oil (sunflower or olive). Lightly oil the pan and drain off any excess after the frying is complete. Skim the fat from the finished meat sauce.
- Season with the minimum amount of salt.
- The fat content can be proportionally reduced by increasing the ratio of pasta to sauce and thinning the béchamel.

Try something different

Traditionally, pasta dishes are substantial in quantity but because they are so popular they are also sometimes requested as lighter dishes.

Obviously the portion size can be reduced but other variations can also be considered.

For example, freshly made pasta cut into 8–10 cm rounds or squares, rectangles or diamonds, lightly poached or steamed, well drained and placed on a light tasty mixture (e.g. a tablespoon of mousse of chicken, or fish or shellfish, well-cooked dried spinach flavoured with toasted pine nuts and grated nutmeg, duxelle mixture) using just the one piece of pasta on top or a piece top and bottom. A light sauce should be used (e.g. a measure of well-reduced chicken stock with a little skimmed milk, blitzed to a froth just before serving, pesto sauce, a drizzle of good-quality olive oil, or a light tomato sauce. The dish can be finished with a suitable garnish (e.g. lightly fried wild or cultivated sliced mushrooms).

13 Vegetarian lasagne

energy	kcal	fat	sat fat	carb	sugar	protein	fibre
2993 KJ	713 kcal	46.2 g	8.5 g	54.6 g	16.5 g	22.9 g	11.8 g

Portions ⟩	4	10
sheets of lasagne	10	30
sunflower oil	125 ml	300 ml
onions, finely chopped	100 g	250 g
cloves of garlic, chopped	2	5
mushrooms, sliced	200 g	500 g
seasoning		
medium-sized courgettes	2	5
oregano	3 g	9 g
tomatoes, skinned, deseeded and diced	200 g	500 g
tomato purée	2 tbsp	5 tbsp
broccoli (small florets)	300 g	750 g
carrots	100 g	250 g
pine kernels	25 g	60 g
béchamel	250 ml	625 ml
Parmesan cheese, grated	50 g	125 g
natural yoghurt	250 ml	625 ml

1 Cook the lasagne sheets in boiling salted water until *al dente*; refresh and drain.
2 Heat half the oil and sweat the onion and garlic.
3 Add the mushrooms and continue to cook without colour. Season.
4 Heat the remaining oil in a sauteuse, add the courgettes, cut into 1 cm dice and lightly fry; sprinkle with the oregano. Cook until crisp, add the tomato concassée and tomato purée.
5 Add the broccoli florets and carrots (cut into 0.5 cm dice), previously blanched and refreshed. Mix together with the pine kernels.
6 Make a cheese sauce using the béchamel and half the grated cheese; finish with the natural yoghurt.
7 Grease a suitable ovenproof dish well with the sunflower oil and place a layer of lasagne in the bottom.
8 Cover with a layer of mushrooms, then a layer of lasagne, then the broccoli and tomato mixture, then lasagne, then cheese sauce. Continue to do this, finishing with a layer of cheese sauce on the top.
9 Sprinkle with remaining grated Parmesan.
10 Bake in a preheated oven at 180°C for 20–25 minutes.

Healthy eating tips
- Try using a mixture of white and green lasagne.
- Use as little oil as possible to sweat the onion.
- Make the béchamel with semi-skimmed milk.
- No added salt is needed.

14 Gnocchi piemontaise (potato gnocchi)

potatoes 🍞 baking, 🍲 boiling

energy	kcal	fat	sat fat	carb	sugar	protein	fibre *
1045 KJ	248 kcal	9.7 g	4.7 g	35.2 g	2.1 g	7.2 g	2.1 g

Portions ⟩	4	10
potatoes	300 g	1 kg
flour, white or wholemeal	100 g	250 g
egg and egg yolk	1	2
butter	25 g	60 g
salt, pepper		
nutmeg, grated		
tomato sauce (page 52)	250 ml	625 ml
grated cheese, to serve		

1 Bake or boil the potatoes in their jackets.
2 Remove the skins and mash with a fork or pass through a sieve.
3 Mix with the flour, egg, butter and seasoning while hot.
4 Mould into balls the size of walnuts.
5 Dust well with flour and flatten slightly with a fork.

6 Poach in gently boiling water until they rise to the surface. Drain carefully.
7 Dress in a buttered earthenware dish, cover with tomato or any other pasta sauce.
8 Sprinkle with grated cheese, brown lightly under the salamander and serve.

Ingredients for gnocchi

Combine the mashed potato with the other ingredients while hot

Mould the mixture into balls, then flatten with a fork

Drop the gnocchi into gently boiling water and poach them

Healthy eating tip
No added salt is necessary.

* Using white flour

171

15 Parmesan gnocchi and tomato sauce

potatoes, vegetable fruits 🍞 baking, 🍲 boiling, 🍳 shallow frying

Portions ⟩	4	10
Parmesan gnocchi		
Desiree potatoes, cooked	350 g	875 g
Parmesan cheese	75 g	185 g
egg yolks	2	5
butter	10 g	25 g
seasoning		
pasta flour	125 g	300 g
Tomato sauce		
carrot	75 g	185 g
celery	20 g	50 g
butter	25 g	60 g
vegetable oil	25 g	60 g
clove of garlic	½	1
sprig of thyme	1	2
juniper berries	1	2
bay leaf	1	2
plum tomato	200 g	500 g
tomato purée	10 g	25 g
vegetable stock	500 ml	1.25 litres
cream	25 g	60 g
sherry vinegar, to taste		

Parmesan gnocchi

1 Place 4 large Desiree potatoes in an oven at 180°C for 1 hour.
2 Grate the Parmesan using a fine grater.
3 Discard the potato skins. Pass the cooked potato flesh through a drum sieve.
4 Add the Parmesan, egg yolks, butter and seasoning.
5 Mix until smooth, but do not over-work.
6 Incorporate the flour until all absorbed.
7 Wrap the dough in clingfilm and allow to rest for 30 minutes.
8 Roll and shape into 1 cm pieces.
9 Blanch the gnocchi in simmering water until they float.
10 Refresh the gnocchi and reserve until required.

Tomato sauce

1 Cut the carrot and celery into small pieces.
2 Heat the butter and oil in a pan, sweat down the carrot and celery with the garlic, thyme, juniper berries and bay leaf for 10 minutes.
3 Roughly chop the tomatoes and add to the pan with the tomato purée. Cook for 15 minutes.
4 Add the vegetable stock and reduce by half.
5 Add the cream and reduce by half.
6 Remove the bay leaf and thyme, add the sherry vinegar, then blitz until smooth.
7 Reserve until required.

To finish

1 Gently sauté the gnocchi in a little oil, and warm the sauce gently.
2 Combine the two together and finish with fresh herbs and shaved Parmesan.

16 Plain boiled rice

rice ⊞ boiling

energy	kcal	fat	sat fat	carb	sugar	protein	fibre
37 KJ	90 kcal	0.1 g	0.0 g	20.0 g	0.0 g	1.9 g	0.0 g

Portions >	4
rice (dry weight)	300 g

1 Pick and wash the long-grain rice. Add to plenty of boiling salted water.
2 Stir to the boil and simmer gently until tender (approx. 12–15 minutes).
3 Pour into a sieve and rinse well under cold running water, then boiling water. Drain and leave in sieve, placed over a bowl and covered with a cloth.
4 Place on a tray in the hotplate and keep hot.
5 Serve separately in a vegetable dish.

17 Steamed rice

rice 📟 steaming

energy	kcal	fat	sat fat	carb	sugar	protein	fibre
1277 KJ	305 kcal	1.4 g	0.0 g	63.7 g	0.0 g	7.1 g	0.0 g

Portions >	4
rice (dry weight)	300 g

1 Place the washed rice into a saucepan and add water until the water level is 2.5 cm above the rice.
2 Bring to the boil over a fierce heat and cook until most of the water has evaporated.
3 Turn the heat down as low as possible, cover the pan with a lid and allow the rice to complete cooking in the steam.
4 Once cooked, the rice should be allowed to stand in the covered steamer for 10 minutes.

18 Braised or pilaff rice
(riz pilaff)

energy	kcal	fat	sat fat	carb	sugar	protein	fibre	*
774 KJ	184 kcal	10.4 g	4.5 g	22.1 g	0.3 g	1.9 g	0.6 g	

Portions ›	4	10
butter or oil	50 g	125 g
onion, chopped	25 g	60 g
rice, long grain, white or brown	300 g	750 g
white stock (preferably chicken)	600 ml	1 litre
salt, mill pepper		
butter, to finish	50 g	125 g

1 Place the butter or oil into a small sauteuse. Add the onion.
2 Cook gently without colouring for 2–3 minutes. Add the rice.
3 Cook gently without colouring for 2–3 minutes.
4 Add twice the amount of stock to rice.
5 Season, cover with buttered paper, bring to the boil.
6 Place in a hot oven (230–250°C) for approximately 15 minutes, until cooked.
7 Remove immediately into a cool sauteuse.
8 Carefully mix in the additional butter with a two-pronged fork.
9 Correct the seasoning and serve.

Cook the rice gently without colouring

Add the stock

Cover with buttered paper, with a small hole at the centre

It is usual to use long-grain rice for pilaff because the grains are firm, and there is less likelihood of them breaking up and becoming mushy. During cooking, the long-grain rice absorbs more liquid, loses less starch and retains its shape as it swells; short or medium grains may split at the ends and become less distinct in outline.

Key point
Cook the rice for the exact time specified in the recipe. If it cooks for longer, it will be overcooked and the grains will not separate.

Try something different

Pilaff rice may also be infused with herbs and spices such as cardamom.

* Using white rice and hard margarine. Using brown rice and hard margarine, 1 portion provides: 769 kJ/183 kcal energy; 10.9 g fat; 4.6 g sat fat; 20.7 g carb; 0.7 g sugar; 1.9 g protein; 1.0 g fibre

Healthy eating tips

- Use an unsaturated oil (sunflower or olive). Lightly oil the pan and drain off any excess after the frying is complete.
- Keep the added salt to a minimum.

---

19 Braised rice with mushrooms
(riz pilaff aux champignons)

rice, fungi braising

Ingredients are as for braised rice (recipe 18) with the addition of 50–100 g of button mushrooms.

1 Place 25 g butter in a small sauteuse. Add the onion.
2 Cook gently without colour for 2–3 minutes.
3 Add the rice and well-washed, sliced mushrooms.
4 Complete as for braised rice (recipe 18) from step 4.

20 Risotto with Parmesan
(risotto con Parmigiano)

rice, cheese boiling, shallow frying

energy	kcal	fat	sat fat	carb	sugar	protein	fibre	salt
2598 KJ	621 kcal	36.2 g	14.1 g	49.9 g	4.2 g	23.0 g	0.3 g	1.4 g

This is the classic risotto. With the addition of saffron and bone marrow it becomes risotto Milanese.

Portions ❯	4	10
chicken stock	1.2 litres	3 litres
butter	80 g	200 g
onion, peeled and finely chopped	½	1
Arborio rice	240 g	600 g
Parmesan, freshly grated	75 g	180 g
salt, pepper		

1 Bring the stock to a simmer, next to where you will cook the risotto. Take a wide, heavy-bottomed pan or casserole, put half the butter in over a medium heat and melt.
2 Add the onion and sweat until it softens and becomes slightly translucent.
3 Add the rice and stir with a heat-resistant spatula until it is thoroughly coated in butter (about 2 minutes). Then take a soup ladle of hot stock and pour it into the rice.
4 Continue to cook and stir until this liquid addition is completely absorbed (about 3 minutes).
5 Repeat this procedure several times until the rice has swollen and is nearly tender. The rice should not be soft but neither should it be chalky. Taste and wait: if it is undercooked, it will leave a gritty, chalky residue in your mouth.
6 Normally the rice is ready in about 20 minutes after the first addition of stock
7 Off the heat, add the other half of the butter and half the Parmesan. Stir these in, season and cover. Leave to rest and swell a little more for 3 minutes. Serve immediately after this in soup plates, with more Parmesan offered separately.

Healthy eating tips
- For a healthy alternative to a risotto, use an unsaturated oil (sunflower or olive), instead of butter, to sweat the onion. Lightly oil the pan and drain off any excess after the frying is complete.
- Additional salt is not necessary.
- Serve with a large salad and tomato bread.

Key points
- Add the stock slowly, to give the rice time to absorb the liquid.
- Stir regularly during cooking.

Try something different
Risotto variations include:
- **saffron or Milanese-style** – soak ¼ teaspoon saffron in a little hot stock and mix into the risotto near the end of the cooking time
- **seafood** – add any one or a mixture of cooked mussels, shrimp, prawns, etc., just before the rice is cooked; also use half fish stock, half chicken stock
- **mushrooms**.

21 Indian-style rice (pilau)

rice, spices  shallow frying, stir frying, braising

energy	kcal	fat	sat fat	carb	sugar	protein	fibre
1315 KJ	315 kcal	5.8 g	3.3 g	60.0 g	0.0 g	5.9 g	0.0 g

Portions ⟩	4	10
basmati rice	300 g	750 g
water, boiling	570 ml	1425 ml
ghee	1 tbsp	2½ tbsp
bay leaves	2	5
cloves	5	12
green cardamom	5	12
cassia bark (5 cm piece)	1	2
fennel seeds	1 tsp	2½ tsp
cumin seeds	½ tsp	1 tsp
brown cardamom	1	2
star anise	1	2

1 Wash and drain the rice.
2 Heat the ghee in a large thick-based saucepan and stir fry the spices for 30 seconds.
3 Add the rice and very gently stir fry, not breaking the grain of the rice.
4 Add the boiling water and stir around.
5 Place a lid on top and turn down to the lowest heat.
6 Leave for 8 minutes – the water should have been completely absorbed.
7 Check the rice. If it is done, remove from the heat and gently fluff up with a fork.
8 If the rice is still brittle in the middle, replace the lid and leave for a further 2 minutes, adding a little more water if necessary.

6 Fish and shellfish

This chapter is relevant to the following units:

- Prepare fish for basic dishes (NVQ)
- Prepare shellfish for basic dishes (NVQ)
- Cook and finish basic fish dishes (NVQ)
- Cook and finish basic shellfish dishes (NVQ)
- Prepare and cook fish and shellfish (VRQ).

Fillets of fish Véronique http://bit.ly/yXmF4v	
Seafood in puff pastry (*bouchées de fruits de mer*) http://bit.ly/ylWbc3	
Tandoori prawns http://bit.ly/wVaFKr	

These online videos may be accessed from this chapter using the QR codes or web links (see page ix to find out how these work):	
Deep-frying fish	183
Filleting a round fish	185
Filleting a flat fish	186
Cutting a fillet of salmon into suprêmes	188
Cutting a fillet of fish into goujons	188
Making fish meunière	219

Fish

Origins

Fish are vertebrates (animals with a backbone) and are split into two primary groups: flat and round. From this they can be split again, into subgroups or secondary groups such as pelagic (oil-rich fish that swim midwater, such as mackerel and herring) and demersal (white fish that live at or near the bottom of the sea, such as cod, haddock, whiting and plaice).

Because of health considerations many people choose to eat fish in preference to meat, and consequently consumption of fish is and has been steadily increasing. This popularity has resulted in a far greater selection becoming available and, due to swift and efficient transport, well over 200 types of fish are on sale throughout the year.

Fish is plentiful in the UK because we are surrounded by water, although overfishing and pollution are having a detrimental effect on supplies of certain fish. Most catches are made off Iceland or Scotland, in the North Sea, Irish Sea and the English Channel. Salmon are caught in certain English and Scottish rivers, and are also extensively farmed. Frozen fish is imported from Scandinavia, Canada and Japan and other countries worldwide; Canada and Japan both export frozen salmon to Britain.

Unfortunately the supply of fish is not unlimited, due to overfishing, so it is now necessary to have fish farms (such as those for trout and salmon, turbot, bass and cod) to supplement natural sources. This is not the only problem: due to contamination by humans and industry, seas and rivers are becoming increasingly polluted, thus affecting both the supply and the suitability of fish – particularly shellfish – for human consumption.

Choosing and buying whole fish

These should have:
- clear, bright eyes, not sunken
- bright red gills
- no missing scales and scales should be firmly attached to the skin
- moist skin (fresh fish feels slightly slippery)
- shiny skin with bright natural colouring
- a stiff tail
- firm flesh
- a fresh sea smell and no trace of ammonia.

Choosing and buying fish fillets

These should be:
- neat and trim with firm flesh

- firm and closely packed together, not ragged or gaping
- a white translucent white colour if they are from a white fish, with no discoloration.

Choosing and buying smoked fish

These should have:
- a glossy appearance
- firm flesh and not sticky
- a pleasant, smoky smell.

Choosing and buying frozen fish

This should:
- be frozen hard with no signs of thawing
- be in packaging that is not damaged
- show no evidence of freezer burn (i.e. dull, white, dry patches).

Types or varieties

- **Oily fish** are round in shape (e.g. herring, mackerel, salmon, tuna, sardines).
- **White fish** are round (e.g. cod, whiting, hake) or flat (e.g. plaice, sole, turbot).
- **Shellfish (see page 191).**

Fresh fish is bought by the kilogram, by the number of fillets or whole fish of the weight that is required. For example, 30 kg of salmon could be ordered as 2 × 15 kg, 3 × 10 kg or 6 × 5 kg. Frozen fish can be purchased in 15 kg blocks.

Cooking

Fish is very economical to cook as it cooks quickly and thus can actually represent a fuel saving. When cooked, fish loses its translucent look and in most cases takes on an opaque white colour. It will also flake easily and has to be considered as a delicate product after preparation.

Fish easily becomes dry and loses its flavour if overcooked; for this reason, carefully considered methods of cookery need to be applied as certain fish will dry out too quickly before benefiting from the chosen cooking approach. Overcooked and dry fish is to be avoided as it will reduce the eating quality.

Storage

Spoilage is mainly caused by the actions of enzymes and bacteria. Enzymes are present in the gut of the living fish and help convert its food to tissue and energy. When the fish dies, these enzymes carry on working and help the bacteria in the digestive system to penetrate the belly wall and start breaking down the flesh itself. Bacteria exist on the skin and in the fish intestine. While the fish is alive, the normal defence mechanisms of the body prevent the bacteria from invading the flesh. Once the fish dies, however, the bacteria invade the flesh and start to break it down – the higher the temperature the faster the deterioration. Note that although these bacteria are harmless to humans, eating quality is reduced and the smell will deteriorate dramatically.

Fish, once caught, has a shelf life of 10 to 12 days if kept properly in a refrigerator at a temperature of between 0°C and 5°C. If the fish is delivered whole with the innards still in the fish, then gut and wash the cavity well before storage.

Once delivered, fresh fish should be used as soon as possible, but it can be stored overnight. Rinse, pat dry, cover with clingfilm and store towards the bottom of the refrigerator.

Ready-to-eat cooked fish, such as 'hot' smoked mackerel, prawns and crab, should be stored on shelves above other raw foodstuffs to avoid cross-contamination.

Food value

Fish is as useful a source of animal protein as meat. The oily fish (sardines, mackerel, herring, salmon, tuna) contain fat-soluble vitamins (A and D) in their flesh and omega-3 fatty acids (these are unsaturated fatty acids that are essential for health). It is recommended that we eat more oily fish.

The flesh of white fish does not contain any fat. Vitamins A and D are only present in the liver (e.g. cod liver or halibut liver oil).

The small bones in sardines, whitebait and tinned salmon provide the human body with calcium/phosphorus.

Owing to its fat content oily fish is not so digestible as white fish.

Preservation

Freezing

Fish is either frozen at sea or as soon as possible after reaching port. It should be thawed out before being cooked. Plaice, halibut, turbot, haddock, sole, cod, trout, salmon, herring, whiting, scampi, smoked haddock and kippers are available frozen, as well as a variety of shellfish.

Frozen fish should be checked for:
- no evidence of freezer burn
- undamaged packaging
- minimum fluid loss during thawing
- flesh that is still firm after thawing.

Frozen fish should be stored at −18°C to −20°C and thawed out overnight in a refrigerator. It should *not* be thawed out in water as this spoils the taste and texture of the fish, and valuable water-soluble nutrients are lost. Fish should not be re-frozen as this will impair its taste and texture.

When freezing a protein-based product, care should be taken with the speed at which the item freezes. The longer a product takes to freeze the larger and more angular the ice crystals become, and they invariably sever the protein strands allowing the liquid contained in them to flow out once it has been defrosted, leaving you with an inferior product. If, however, you freeze quickly the ice crystals are small (remember: quick = small); liquid loss will always be present, but if frozen quickly the loss will be less dramatic.

Canning

Canned fish are usually the oily type: sardines, salmon, anchovies, pilchards, tuna, herring and herring roe. They are canned in their own juice (as with salmon), brine, spring water, oil or tomato sauce.

Salting

In the UK, the salting of fish is usually accompanied by a smoking process.
- Cured herrings are packed in salt.
- Caviar – the slightly salted roe of the sturgeon – is sieved, tinned and refrigerated. Imitation caviar is also obtainable.

Pickling

Herrings pickled in vinegar are filleted, rolled and skewered, and known as rollmops.

Smoking

Fish that is to be smoked may be gutted or left whole. It is then soaked in a strong salt solution (brine) and in some cases a dye is added to improve colour. After this, it is drained, hung on racks in a kiln and exposed to smoke for five or six hours.

Smoked fish should be wrapped up well and kept separate from other fish to prevent the smell and dye penetrating other foods.

Cold smoking takes place at a temperature of no more than 33°C (this is to avoid cooking the flesh). Therefore, all cold-smoked fish is raw and is usually

cooked before being eaten, the exceptions being smoked salmon and cold-smoked trout.

Hot-smoked fish is cured at a temperature between 70°C and 80°C in order to cook the flesh, so does not require further cooking.

Choose fish with a pleasant smoky smell and a bright glossy surface. The flesh should be firm; sticky or soggy flesh means that the fish may have been of low quality or undersmoked.

> **Note**
> There is a high salt content in salted, pickled and smoked fish. Added salt is not necessary.

Cooking methods

The following are the main cooking methods used for fish.

En sous vide

Moisture from the flesh of fish can be lost very quickly while cooking by traditional methods. *Sous vide* is an ideal method; it helps eliminate this moisture loss and also isolates it, preventing absorption of outside flavours or liquids and thus offering a truer taste. The dish *escabeche* (cured fish) benefits very well from this method as it helps with the marinating process and distributes the liquor evenly around the fish.

Frying

Shallow-frying (recipes 25–31)
The fish should be seasoned and lightly coated with flour or crumb before frying, in order to protect it and seal in the flavour. Use a mixture of oil and butter when frying and turn the fish only once during cooking, to avoid it breaking up.

This method is suitable for small whole fish, cuts or fillets that are cooked in oil or fat in a frying pan. The fish are usually coated with flour but semolina, matzo meal, oatmeal or breadcrumbs may also be used. If the frying medium is to be butter, it must be clarified (see page 27) otherwise there is a risk that the fish may burn. Oil is the best medium, to which a little butter may be added for flavour.

Deep-frying *(recipes 19–24)*

The fish should be seasoned and coated before frying, usually with a batter or an egg and breadcrumb mixture. Use a suitable container and heat the oil to 190°C. Test the temperature before cooking the fish. Drain the fish on absorbent paper after cooking.

Deep-frying fish
http://bit.ly/
wSSk0e

This is suitable for small whole white fish, cuts and fillets. The fish must be coated to form a surface that prevents penetration of the cooking fat or oil into the fish. Coatings can be either:

- flour, egg and breadcrumbs
- milk and flour
- batter.

For further information, refer to the text on deep-frying on page 15 of Chapter 1.

Any white fish are suitable for deep-frying in batter, including cod, haddock, skate and rock salmon (a term used for catfish, coley, dog-fish and so on when cleaned and skinned). Depending on size the fish may be left whole, or may be portioned or filleted.

Stir-frying

This is a very fast and popular method of cooking. Use a wok or deep frying pan and a high cooking temperature. Food should be cut into thin strips and prepared before cooking begins. This method is very well suited to cooking firm-fleshed fish.

It is suitable for fish fillets cut into finger-sized pieces and quickly fried in hot oil. Finely cut ginger and vegetables (e.g. garlic, shallots, broccoli sprigs, mushrooms and beanshoots) may be added. Soy sauce is often used as a seasoning.

Grilling *(recipes 1–5)*

Grilling is cooking under radiant heat, and is a fast and convenient method suitable for fillets or small whole fish. When grilling whole fish cut through the thickest part of the fish to allow even cooking. Lightly oil and season fish or fillets and, to avoid breaking, do not turn more than once.

Poaching *(recipes 6–12)*

Poaching is cooking in a liquid just below boiling point. It is suitable for:

- whole fish (e.g. salmon, trout, bass)
- certain cuts on the bone (e.g. salmon, turbot, brill, halibut, cod, skate).

In either case, the prepared fish should be completely immersed in the cooking liquid, which can be either water, water and milk, fish stock (for white fish) or a court bouillon (water, vinegar, onion, carrot, thyme, bay leaf, parsley stalks and peppercorns) for oily fish. Most kinds of fish can be cooked in this way and should be poached gently for 5–8 minutes, depending on the thickness of the fish. Whole fish are covered with a cold liquid and brought to the boil then simmered *gently*. Cut fish are usually cooked in a *gently* simmering liquid. The resulting liquid is ideal for use in sauces and soups.

When poaching smoked fish, place in cold, unsalted water and bring to a slow simmer. This liquid will be salty and may not be suitable for reuse.

Roasting

Roasting is a word in common use nowadays and, particularly when describing a method of cookery in a menu, it is used quite loosely. It is not impossible to roast fish but a fishbone trivet should be used, primarily to prevent the fish frying in the oil or cooking medium and, second, to impart more flavour to the fish while cooking.

This method of cookery, when used with fish, should be quick and used only with thick cuts of fish such as cod, salmon, turbot, sea bass and monkfish. Depending on size, the fish may be roasted whole (e.g. sea bass).

The fish is more usually portioned, skin left on, and lightly seared in hot oil, skin side down in a pan, then roasted in a hot oven (230°C) skin side up. Finely sliced vegetables and sprigs of herbs can be added to the roasting tray and, when the fish is cooked and removed, the tray can be deglazed with a suitable wine (usually a dry white) and fish stock to form the basis of an accompanying sauce.

If the fish is skinned after it has been seared, a light crust of breadcrumbs mixed with a good oil, butter or margarine, lemon juice, fresh chopped herbs (e.g. parsley, tarragon, chervil, rosemary), a duxelle-based mixture or a light coating of creamed horseradish can be used.

The fish portions may be served with a sauce or salsa, or placed on a bed of creamed or flavoured mashed potato (page 430) with a compound butter sauce (page 27) and quarters of lemon. Examples of this method of cooking include roast cod on garlic mash and roast sea bass flavoured with fennel.

Steaming *(recipe 18)*

Small whole fish or fillets are good cooked in this way. Flavour can be added by using different cooking liquids, but usually the fish is seasoned. Place it in a steamer, cover it tightly and cook in the steam produced by simmering water for 10–15 minutes, depending on the thickness of the fish or the fillets. If a steamer is not available fish can be steamed between two plates above a pan of boiling water.

Any fish that can be poached or boiled may also be cooked by steaming. This method has a number of advantages.
- It is an easy method of cooking.
- Because it is quick, it conserves flavour, colour and nutrients.
- It is suitable for large-scale cookery.

Fish is prepared as for poaching. The liquor from the steamed fish should be strained off, reduced and incorporated into the sauce. Preparation can also include adding finely cut ingredients (e.g. ginger, spring onions, garlic, mushrooms and soft herbs), lemon juice and dry white wine to the fish on the steamer dish before cooking or served with the fish.

Baking *(recipes 13–18)*

Many fish (whole, portioned or filleted) may be oven-baked. To retain their natural moisture it is necessary to protect the fish from direct heat. There are various ways of preparing fish for baking:
- whole fish (scaled, gutted and washed)
- whole fish stuffed (e.g. a duxelle-based mixture, breadcrumbs, herbs)

- wrapped in pastry (puff or filo)
- completely covered with a thick coating of dampened sea salt
- portions of fish can be baked (e.g. cod, hake, haddock).

Then proceed as follows.
1. Place the prepared portions in a greased ovenproof dish, brush with oil and bake slowly, basting frequently. Add herbs (e.g. parsley, rosemary, thyme) and finely sliced vegetables (e.g. mushrooms, onions, shallots).
2. Depending on the size and shape of the fish, 100–150 g thick portions can be cut leaving the skin on (this helps to retain the natural moisture of the fish) and baked skin side up. The fish can then be served simply, e.g. on a bed of creamy or flavoured mashed potato (page 430) with a suitable sauce, such as compound butter (page 27) or a salsa (page 55).

Health, safety and hygiene

For information on maintaining a safe and secure working environment, a professional and hygienic appearance, clean food production areas, equipment and utensils, and food hygiene, please refer to Chapters 14 and 15. Additional food safety points relating to fish preparation and cookery are as follows.
- Store fresh fish in containers with ice (changed daily) in a refrigerator at a temperature of 1–2°C.
- To avoid the risk of cross-contamination, fish should be stored in a separate refrigerator away from other foods; cooked and raw fish must be kept separate.
- Frozen fish should be stored in a deep-freezer at −18°C. When required, frozen fish should be defrosted in a refrigerator. If the frozen food is removed from the freezer and left uncovered in the kitchen, there is a danger of contamination.
- Smoked fish should be kept in a refrigerator.
- Use the correct colour-coded boards for preparing raw fish, and different ones for cooked fish. Keep the boards clean using fresh disposable wiping cloths.
- Use equipment reserved for raw fish. If this is not possible, wash and sanitise equipment before and immediately after each use.
- Unhygienic equipment, utensils and preparation areas increase the risk of cross-contamination and danger to health.

- Fish offal and bones present a high risk of contamination and must not be mixed or stored with raw prepared fish.
- Wash equipment, knives and hands regularly using a bactericide detergent, or sanitising agent, to kill bacteria.
- Dispose of all wiping cloths immediately after use. Reused cloths may cause contamination.

Preparing fish

Unless otherwise stated, as a guide allow 110 g fish off the bone and 150 g on the bone for a portion. When ordering large fish, such as turbot, allow approximately 300 g of fish per portion including the bone and skin weight: a 3.5 kg fish will yield approximately 10 portions.

- All fish should be washed under running cold water before and after preparation.
- Whole fish are trimmed to remove the scales, fins and head using fish scissors and a knife. If the head is to be left on (as in the case of a salmon for the cold buffet), the gills and the eyes are removed.

Gutting and scaling

If the fish has to be gutted, the following procedure should be used.

- Cut from the vent to two-thirds along the fish.
- Draw out the intestines with the fingers or, in the case of a large fish, use the hook handle of a utensil such as a ladle.
- Ensure that the blood lying along the main bone is removed, then wash and drain thoroughly.
- If the fish is to be stuffed then it may be gutted by removing the innards through the gill slits, thus leaving the stomach skin intact, forming a pouch in which to put the stuffing. When this method is used, care must be taken to ensure that the inside of the fish is clear of all traces of blood.

Skinning and filleting

The following sequences demonstrate how to prepare and fillet a round or flat fish, and how to skin and prepare a whole Dover sole. These fish have already been gutted and cleaned.

When you fillet a fish, remove the first fillet by cutting along the backbone from head to tail. Then reverse the fish and remove the second fillet by cutting from tail to head.

Filleting a round fish (salmon)

Remove the head and clean thoroughly

Remove the first fillet by cutting along the backbone from head to tail. Keeping the knife close to the bone, remove the fillet

After both fillets have been removed, remove the rib cavity bones and trim the fish neatly

Boning a round fish (trout)

Remove the pin bones from the fillet

Filleting a round fish
http://bit.ly/wNRqo6

Filleting a flat fish (turbot)

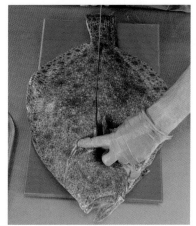

Using a filleting knife, make an incision from the head to tail. Cut around the gill and backbone

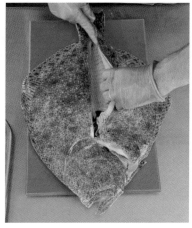

Remove the first fillet, holding the knife almost parallel to the work surface and keeping the knife close to the bone

Repeat for the second fillet

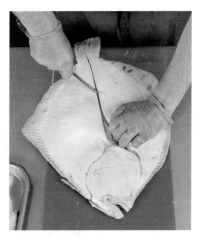

Turn the fish over and repeat, removing the last two fillets

Hold the fillet firmly at the tail end. Cut the flesh as close to the tail as possible, as far as the skin. Keep the knife parallel to the work surface, grip the skin firmly and move the knife from side to side to remove the skin

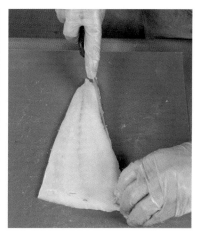

Trim the fillets neatly

Filleting a flat fish
http://bit.ly/wJKnim

Preparing a whole Dover sole

Score the skin just above the tail

Hold the tail firmly, then cut and scrape the skin until sufficient is lifted to be gripped

Pull the skin away from the tail to the head. Both the black and white skins may be removed in this way

Trim the tail and side fins with fish scissors

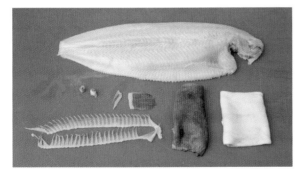

Remove the eyes. Clean and wash the fish thoroughly. The fish is shown here with all the parts that were removed

Cuts of fish

There are many different cuts of fish (as shown in the next photo).

- Fillets: cuts of fish free from bone (a round fish yields two, and a flat fish four fillets).
- Steaks: thick slices of fish on or off the bone.
- Darnes: steaks of round fish (salmon, cod).
- Tronçons: steaks of flat fish (turbot, halibut) on the bone.
- Suprêmes: prime cuts of fish without bone and skin (cut from fillets of salmon, turbot, brill, etc.).
- Goujons: filleted fish cut into strips approximately 8 × 0.5 cm.
- Paupiettes: fillets of fish (e.g. sole, plaice, whiting) spread with a stuffing and rolled.
- Plaited/*en tresse* – for example, sole fillets cut into three even pieces lengthwise to within 1 cm of the top, and neatly plaited.

Cuts of fish (clockwise from top left): darne, tronçon, fillet, paupiette, suprême, goujons

Cutting a fillet of salmon
into suprêmes
http://bit.ly/wt3MOt

Cutting a fillet of fish into
goujons
http://bit.ly/yoWESI

Fish types

Table 6.1 gives examples of the 200-plus fish types that are available. They are divided into oily and white varieties. The table also shows which methods of cookery are suitable for each fish.

Table 6.1 **Examples of fish types available, and suitable cooking methods**

	Baking	Boiling	Deep-frying	Grilling	Poaching	Roasting	Shallow-(pan) frying	Steaming	Stir-frying
Oily fish									
Barracuda				✓			✓		
Dorade (red sea bream)	✓			✓			✓		✓
Emperor bream	✓			✓			✓		
Herring				✓			✓		
Mackerel	✓			✓	✓		✓		
Marlin	✓			✓	✓		✓		
Red mullet	✓			✓		✓	✓		
Red snapper	✓			✓	✓		✓		
Salmon	✓	✓		✓	✓		✓	✓	✓
Sardines				✓			✓		
Trout	✓						✓		
Tuna				✓	✓		✓		✓
Whitebait			✓						
White fish									
Cod	✓	✓	✓	✓	✓	✓	✓	✓	
Coley		✓	✓						
Dover sole			✓	✓	✓				
Grouper				✓		✓	✓		
Haddock	✓		✓	✓					
Hake	✓			✓	✓				
Halibut	✓			✓	✓	✓	✓	✓	✓
Huss			✓	✓	✓		✓		
John Dory	✓				✓		✓		
Lemon sole	✓		✓				✓		
Monkfish	✓			✓		✓	✓		✓
Plaice	✓		✓	✓			✓		
Sea bass	✓			✓			✓	✓	
Shark	✓			✓		✓	✓	✓	✓
Skate wings		✓	✓		✓		✓		
Swordfish	✓			✓			✓		✓
Turbot	✓	✓	✓	✓	✓		✓		✓

Seasonality and availability of fish

Seasonality

The quality of fish can vary due to local climatic and environmental conditions. Generally, all fish spawn over a period of four to six weeks. During spawning, they use up a lot of their reserves of fat and protein in the production of eggs. This has the effect of making their flesh watery and soft. Fish in this condition are termed 'spent fish'. This takes anything between one and two months, depending on local environmental conditions.

Table 6.2 Seasonality of fish

	JAN	FEB	MAR	APR	MAY	JUN	JUL	AUG	SEP	OCT	NOV	DEC
Bream	●	●	●	●	◇	◇	◇	●	●	●	●	●
Brill	○	○	●	●	◇	●	●	●	●	●	●	●
Cod	○	○	◇	◇	●	●	●	●	●	●	●	●
Eel						●	●	●	●	●	●	○
Mullet (grey)	●	●	◇	◇	●	●	●	●	●	●	●	●
Gurnard	●	●	●	●	●	●	●	●	●	●	●	●
Haddock	○	○	●	●	●	●	●	●	○	○	○	○
Hake	○	●	◇	◇	◇	●	●	●	●	●	●	●
Halibut	○	○	○	●	◇	●	●	●	●	●	●	●
Herring	○	○	○	○	○	●	●	●	●	●	●	●
John Dory	●	●	●	●	●	○	○	○	●	●	●	●
Mackerel	●	●	●	●	●	●	○	○	●	●	●	●
Monkfish	●	●	●	●	●	●	●	●	●	●	●	●
Plaice	●	●	◇	●	●	●	●	●	●	●	●	●
Red mullet			●	●	●	○	○	○	○	○	●	●
Salmon (farmed)	●	●	●	●	●	●	●	●	●	●	●	●
Salmon (wild)				○	○	○	○	○				
Sardines	○	○	○	○	◇				○	○	○	○
Sea bass	●	●	●	◇	◇	○	○	○	○	○	○	○
Sea trout				●	○	○	○	◇	◇	◇	◇	
Skate	●	●			●	●	○	○	○	○	○	○
Squid	●								○	○	○	○
Sole (Dover)	◇	●	●						○	○	○	○
Sole (lemon)	○	○	○	○	○	○						
Trout				●	●	○	○	○	○	○		
Tuna	●	●	●	●	●	●	●	●	●	●	●	●
Turbot	○	○	●	◇	◇	◇	●	○	○	○	○	○
Whiting	●	●									●	●

Key:

Available

At best

Spawning and roeing – this can deprive the flesh of nutrients and will decrease the yield.

Availability

Naturally, prevailing weather conditions have an enormous bearing on fishing activities. The full range of species may not always be available during stormy weather, for instance.

Quality and food safety

To maintain the quality and food safety of fish and shellfish dishes it is advisable to check the internal temperature using a probe. It is recommended that all fish and shellfish should be cooked to an internal temperature of 62°C.

> **Note**
> Environmental Health Officers may require higher temperatures.

Some classic fish dishes

Recipes 8 and 9 (fish Dugléré and fish in white wine sauce) are from the classical repertoire. Although Dover sole fillets are used, any white fish fillets may be prepared and served by the same method. If shallots are used they must be *finely* chopped and sweated in a little butter before use.

The traditional way of making classic fish sauces is to strain off the cooking liquor (after the fish is cooked) and reduce it to a glaze (page 36). Remove the pan from the heat and gradually incorporate small pieces of butter. If the sauce is to be glazed, some lightly whipped double cream can be added.

Shellfish

Shellfish, such as lobsters and crabs, are all invertebrates (i.e. they do not possess an internal skeleton) and are split into two main groups: *molluscs* have either an external hinged double shell (e.g. scallops, mussels) or a single spiral shell (e.g. winkles, whelks), or have soft bodies with an internal shell (e.g. squid, octopus); *crustaceans* have tough outer shells that act like armour, and also have flexible joints to allow quick movement (e.g. crabs, lobsters).

Choosing and buying

Shellfish are prized for their tender, fine-textured flesh, which can be prepared in a variety of ways, but are prone to rapid spoilage. The reason for this is that they contain quantities of certain proteins, amino acids, which encourage bacterial growth.

To ensure freshness and best flavour it is preferable to choose live specimens and cook them yourself. This is often possible with the expansion of globalisation and air freight creating a healthy trade in live shellfish.

Bear in mind the following points when choosing shellfish:
- Shells should not be cracked or broken.
- Shells of mussels and oysters should be tightly shut; open shells that do not close when tapped sharply should be discarded.
- Lobsters, crabs and prawns should have a good colour and be heavy for their size.
- Lobsters and crabs should have all their limbs.

Table 6.3 Seasonality of shellfish

	JAN	FEB	MAR	APR	MAY	JUN	JUL	AUG	SEP	OCT	NOV	DEC
Crab (brown cock)	●	●	●	●	○	○	○	○	○	○	○	
Crab (spider)	○	○	○	○	●	●	●	●	●	●	○	○
Crab (brown hen)	●	●	○	●	○	○	○	●	●	●	●	●
Clams	●	●	●	○	○	○	○	○	○	○	○	○
Cockles	●	●	●	○	○	○	○	○	○	○	○	○
Crayfish (signal)				○	●	●	●	●	●	○		
Lobster	○	○	○	○	○	○	○	○	○	○	○	○
Langoustines			●	●	●	●	○	○	○			
Mussels	○	○	○	○	○				●	●	●	●
Oysters (rock)	●	●	●	●	○	○	○		●	●	●	●
Oysters (native)	○	○	○	○					●	●	●	●
Prawns						○	○	○	●	●	●	○
Scallops	○	○	○	○	○	○	●	●	●	●	●	○

Key:

Available	○
At best	●

Cooking

The flesh of fish and shellfish is different to meat and, as a consequence, their muscle make-up is very different too, making the connective tissue very fragile, the muscle fibres shorter and the fat content relatively low. Generally, care should be taken when cooking and shellfish should be cooked as little as possible, to the point that the protein in the muscle groups just coagulate. Beyond this point the flesh tends to dry out, leading to toughening and a dry texture. Shellfish are known for their dramatic colour change, from blue/grey to a vibrant orange colour. This is because they contain red and yellow pigments called carotenoids, bound to molecules of protein. The protein bonds obscure the yellow/red pigment and, once heat is applied, the bonds are broken and the vibrant pigmentation is revealed.

Storage

All shellfish will start to spoil as soon as they have been removed from their natural environment, therefore the longer shellfish are stored the more they will deteriorate due to the bacteria present (see the guidelines on choosing and buying, above). Best practice would be to cook immediately and store as for cooked fish. Shellfish can be blanched quickly to remove the shell and membrane (especially in lobsters), but they will still need to be stored as a raw product as they will require further cooking.

Bear in mind the following quality, purchasing and storage points:

- Whenever possible, all shellfish should be purchased live so as to ensure freshness.
- Shellfish should be kept in suitable containers, covered with damp seaweed or damp cloths, and stored in a cold room or refrigerator.
- Shellfish should be cooked as soon as possible after purchasing.

Shrimps and prawns

These are often bought cooked, either in the shells or peeled. Smell is the best guide to freshness. Shrimps and prawns can be used for garnishes, decorating fish dishes, cocktails, sauces, salads, hors d'oeuvres, omelettes, and snack and savoury dishes. They can also be used for a variety of hot dishes: stir-fries, risotto, curries, etc. Potted shrimps are also a popular dish. Freshly cooked prawns in their shells may also be served cold accompanied by a mayonnaise-based sauce, such as garlic mayonnaise. **King prawns** are a larger variety, which can also be used in any of the above ways.

Raw and cooked shrimps and prawns are prepared by having the head, carapace (upper shell), legs, tail section and the dark intestinal vein running down the back removed.

Scampi, crayfish and Dublin Bay prawns

Scampi, crayfish and Dublin Bay prawns are also known as Norway lobster or langoustine and are sold fresh, frozen, raw or cooked. Their tails are prepared like shrimps and they are used in a variety of ways: salads, rice dishes, stir-fries, deep-fried, poached and served with a number of different sauces. They are also used as garnishes to hot and cold fish dishes.

Freshwater crayfish are also known as écrevisse. These are small freshwater crustaceans with claws, found in lakes and lowland streams. They are prepared and cooked like shrimps and prawns, and used in many dishes, including soup. They are often used whole to garnish hot and cold fish dishes.

Remove the cord from each langoustine before cooking

Lobster

Purchasing points
Purchase alive, with both claws attached, to ensure freshness.
- Lobsters should be heavy in proportion to their size.
- The coral of the hen lobster is necessary to give the required colour for certain soups, sauces and lobster dishes.
- Hen lobsters are distinguished from cock lobsters by their broader tails.

Cooking
1 Wash then plunge the lobster/s into a pan of boiling salted water containing 60 ml vinegar to 1 litre water.
2 Cover with a lid, reboil, then allow to simmer for 15–20 minutes according to size.
3 Overcooking can cause the tail flesh to toughen and the claw meat to become hard and fibrous.
4 Allow to cool in the cooking liquid when possible.

Alternative approaches to killing lobsters
Entrepreneur Simon Buckhaven has created a device named the CrustaStun, which uses an electric current to stun and painlessly kill shellfish such as lobsters, crabs and langoustines.

The machine can knock a large crustacean unconscious in less than 0.3 seconds and kill it in five to ten. Crabs take four to five minutes to die in boiling water, while lobsters take three minutes.

Some believe the noise made by lobsters in the pan is evidence of them experiencing pain, although others insist it is caused by the release of gases under the shell. The lobster's tail also flaps around as it tries to escape and it dies only when its core temperature reaches 34°C.

This humane method of killing shellfish with an electric current is said to give a better flavour.

The CrustaStun comprises a stainless-steel box roughly the size of a microwave containing a tray with a wet sponge and an electrode.

The crustacean is placed in the box and when the lid is closed the wet sponge conducts the current, which electrocutes it.
Source: www.crustastun.com

Preparing a cooked lobster

Remove the claws and legs

Cut the lobster in half

Remove the meat from the cleaned lobster

Cleaning of cooked lobster

1 Remove the claws and the pincers from the claws.
2 Crack the claws and joints and remove the meat.
3 Cut the lobster in half by inserting the point of a large knife 2 cm above the tail on the natural central line.
4 Cut through the tail firmly.
5 Turn the lobster around and cut through the upper shell (carapace).
6 Remove the halves of the sac (which contains grit) from each half. This is situated at the top, near the head.
7 Using a small knife, remove the intestinal trace from the tail and wash if necessary.

Uses

Lobsters are served cold in cocktails, lobster mayonnaise, hors d'oeuvres, salads, sandwiches and in halves on cold buffets. They are used hot in soups, sauces, rice dishes, stir-fry dishes and in numerous ways served in the half shell with various sauces. They are also used to garnish fish dishes.

Crawfish

These are sometimes referred to as 'spiny lobsters', but unlike lobsters they have no claws and their meat is solely in the tail. Crawfish vary considerably in size from 1 to 3 kg; they are cooked as for lobsters and the tail meat can be used in any of the lobster recipes. Because of their impressive appearance crawfish dressed whole are sometimes used on special cold buffets. They are very expensive and are also available frozen.

Crab

Purchasing points

● Buy alive to ensure freshness.
● Ensure that both claws are attached.
● Crabs should be heavy in relation to size.

Cooking

1 Place the crabs in boiling salted water with a little vinegar added.
2 Reboil, then simmer for 15–30 minutes according to size. These times apply to crabs weighing from ½–2½ kg.
3 Allow the crabs to cool in the cooking liquor.

Uses

Crab meat can be used cold for hors d'oeuvres, cocktails, salads, sandwiches and dressed crab. Used hot, it can be covered with a suitable sauce and served with rice, in bouchées or pancakes, or made into crab fish cakes.

Cockles

Cockles are enclosed in small, attractive, cream-coloured shells. As they live in sand it is essential to purge them by washing well under running cold water and leaving them in cold salted water (changed frequently) until no traces of sand remain.

Cockles can be cooked either by steaming, boiling in unsalted water, on a preheated griddle, or as for any mussel recipe. They should be cooked only until the shells open.

They can be used in soups, sauces, salads, stir-fries and rice dishes, and as garnish for fish dishes.

Mussels

Mussels are extensively cultivated on wooden hurdles in the sea, producing tender, delicately flavoured plump fish. They are produced in Britain and imported from France, Holland and Belgium. French mussels are small, Dutch and Belgian mussels are plumper. The quality tends to vary from season to season.

Purchasing points

- The shells must be tightly closed, indicating the mussels are alive.
- They should be of a good size.
- There should not be an excessive number of barnacles attached.
- They should smell fresh.

Storage

Mussels should be kept in containers, covered with damp seaweed or cloths, and stored in a cold room or refrigerator.

Uses

Mussels can be used for soups, sauces and salads, and cooked in a wide variety of hot dishes.

Cooking

- Scrape the shells to remove any barnacles, etc. Remove the 'beards'. Wash well in several changes of water and drain in a colander.
- In a thick-bottomed pan with a tight-fitting lid, place 25 g chopped shallot or onion for each litre of mussels.

- Add the mussels, cover with a lid and cook on a fierce heat for 4–5 minutes until the shells open completely.
- Remove the mussels from the shells, checking carefully for sand, weed, etc.
- Retain the carefully strained liquid for the sauce.

Scallops

There are a number of varieties of scallop:
- great scallops are up to 15 cm in size
- bay scallops are up to 8 cm
- queen scallops, also known as queenies, are small, cockle-sized scallops.

Scallops are found on the seabed and are therefore dirty, so it is advisable to purchase them ready cleaned. If scallops are bought in their shells, the shells should be tightly shut, which indicates they are alive and fresh. The roe (orange in colour) should be bright and moist. Scallops in their shells should be covered with damp seaweed or cloths and kept in a cold room or refrigerator. To remove from the shells, place the shells on top of the stove or in an oven for a few seconds, when they will open and the flesh can then be removed with a knife. Scallops should then be well washed; remove the trail, leaving only the white scallop.

Cooking

Scallops should be only lightly cooked.
- Poach gently for 2–3 minutes in dry white wine with a little onion, carrot, thyme, bay leaf and parsley. Serve with a suitable sauce (e.g. white wine, mornay).
- Lightly fry on both sides for a few seconds in butter or oil in a very hot pan (if the scallops are very thick they can be cut in halves sideways) and serve with a suitable garnish (sliced wild or cultivated mushrooms, or a fine brunoise of vegetables and tomato) and a liquid that need not be thickened (white wine and fish stock, or cream- or butter-mounted sauce). Fried scallops can also be served hot on a plate of salad leaves.
- Deep-fry, either egg and crumbed or passed through a light batter and served with segments of lemon and a suitable sauce (e.g. tartare).

- Wrap in thin streaky bacon, place on skewers for grilling or barbecuing.

Whelks

The common whelk is familiar around the coast of Britain. It is actually a gastropod, which means it has a large, strong flat foot to move around on. Whelks are also equipped with a think siphon, which is used for breathing and feeling around for food.

British winkles

The main types of British winkle, which can be readily identified on rocky shores, are:
1 small periwinkle – approximately 4 mm
2 rough periwinkle – at least four different subspecies, with the largest reaching 30 mm
3 flat periwinkle.

Oysters

Oysters are bivalve molluscs found near the bottom of the sea in coastal areas. The upper shell (valve) is flattish and attached by an elastic ligament hinge to the lower, bowl-shaped shell. Oysters are high in protein and low in fat; they are rich in zinc and contain many other nutrients such as calcium, iron, copper, iodine, magnesium and selenium.

Size, shape and colour vary considerably. Native oysters are pricier and generally thought of as superior. Pacific or rock oysters tend to have a frillier shell and are smaller, with milder meat.

Purchasing points
- The shells should be clean, bright, tightly closed and unbroken.

Storage
Oysters should be stored at a low temperature and should smell briny fresh. Unopened live oysters can be kept in the fridge covered with wet cloths for two to three days; discard any that open. Do not store in an airtight container or under fresh water as this will cause them to die. Shucked oysters can be kept refrigerated in a sealed container for four to five days.

---

1 ## Grilled fillets of sole, plaice or haddock

white fish grilling

energy	kcal	fat	sat fat	carb	sugar	protein	fibre	sodium
802 KJ	191 kcal	7.8 g	1.0 g	3.9 g	0.1 g	26.6 g	0.2 g	0.1 g

1 Remove the black skin from sole and plaice. Wash the fillets and dry them well.
2 Pass through flour, shake off surplus and brush with oil.
3 Place on hot grill bars, a griddle or a greased baking sheet if grilling under a salamander. Brush occasionally with oil.
4 Turn the fish carefully and grill on both sides. Do not overcook.
5 Serve with lemon quarters and a suitable sauce (e.g. compound butter or salsa).

> **Key point**
> Oil the grill bars well, so that the fish does not stick.

2 Grilled tuna, rocket and fennel salad

oily fish grilling

energy	kcal	fat	sat fat	carb	sugar	protein	fibre	sodium
1619 KJ	388 kcal	24.3 g	4.3 g	4.2 g	3.7 g	38.4 g	4.5 g	0.6 g

Portions ⟩	4	10
For the fish		
tuna steaks (150 g, no skin or blood line)	4	10
lemon	1	2
olive oil	50 ml	125 ml
sea salt, fresh milled black pepper		
For the salad		
rocket salad, washed and picked	400 g	1 kg
fennel bulb	1	2
green beans, cooked and refreshed	200 g	500 g
baby spinach	100 g	250 g
coriander, picked	50 g	125 g
For the dressing		
Dijon mustard	1 tsp	3 tsp
cider vinegar	1 tsp	3 tsp
olive oil	3 tbsp	7 tbsp
sunflower oil	3 tbsp	7 tbsp
lemon juice	1 tsp	2 tsp
lime juice	1 tsp	2 tsp
seasoning		

For the salad

1 Ensure all the leaves are well washed and picked.
2 Cut the root and top off the fennel, leaving the main bulb.
3 On a mandolin, thinly slice the fennel. Place in cold water with plenty of ice (this will make the fennel very crisp and curly, giving the salad some height).
4 Place all the salad ingredients into a large bowl ready to dress with the dressing.
5 To dress, mix the salad and dressing well, check the seasoning and equally divide the salad between the four plates

For the dressing

1 Place the mustard and vinegar in a bowl, slowly whisk in the oil.
2 To finish, adjust the taste with the lemon juice, lime juice and seasoning.

For the tuna

1 Before you start to cook the tuna, ensure that the salad is dressed and on the serving plate.
2 Lightly brush the tuna steaks with the oil and season.
3 Ensure the grill is hot. Place two steaks on at a time (this is manageable as the tuna cooks very quickly).
4 Turn after 30 seconds and cook until the centre half of the tuna is still pink.
5 Remove and place on the salad. Repeat for the other two steaks. Serve with a wedge of lemon.

This recipe lends itself well to other fish such as salmon, sea bass, turbot, trout, hake or monkfish, as well as tuna.

3 Whole grilled mackerel with tomatoes, basil and shaved fennel

oily fish grilling, shallow frying

energy	kcal	fat	sat fat	carb	sugar	protein	fibre	sodium *
2067 KJ	497 kcal	39.4 g	7.8 g	3.9 g	3.8 g	32.4 g	2.2 g	0.2 g

Portions ❭	4	10
For the salad		
olive oil	50 ml	125 ml
baby plum tomatoes, cut in half	400 g	1 kg
fennel bulb, shaved on a mandolin	1	2
baby spinach	100 g	250 g
lemon, juice of	1	2
basil leaves, torn	6	15
For the mackerel		
medium mackerel, very fresh, head and guts removed	4	10
olive oil	50 ml	125 ml
freshly milled pepper		

For the salad

1 Heat the oil in a pan and add the tomatoes and fennel. Cook on a hot heat. Remove from the heat, stir in the spinach and allow it to wilt. Season with salt, pepper and a dash of lemon juice. Finish with basil leaves.

For the mackerel

1 Ensure that that the fish is clean. Score the flesh of each fish in the deepest part (near the head), about 3 mm into the fish but not through to the bone. (This scoring is called ciseler; it will help the fish to cook more evenly and can be used with most methods of cooking whole fish.)

2 Brush with the oil and place on a moderate grill. (Wrap the tail in foil to ensure that it doesn't burn.)

3 Turn the fish over to cook the other side, removing the foil. At this point, start making the salad.

4 Once the fish is cooked, dress the plates with the salad and lay the fish on top. Drizzle the pan juices over and around the fish and serve.

* Based on sardines instead of mackerel

4 Whole sole grilled with traditional accompaniments

white flat fish grilling

energy	kcal	fat	sat fat	carb	sugar	protein	fibre	sodium
3058 KJ	740 kcal	65.4 g	39.1 g	1.0 g	0.9 g	36.9 g	0.3 g	0.7 g

Portions ⟩	4	10
whole sole, white and black skin removed	4	10
butter for grilling	200 g	500 g
seasoning		
parsley butter	100 g	250 g
lemons, peeled and cut into wedges	1	3

This is a classic recipe using slip, Dover or lemon sole.
There is no need to modernise it.
Sole is a delicate fish: be careful not to overcook it.

1 Ensure the fish is clean of roe, scales and skin.
2 Place on a buttered grilling tray and rub soft butter into the flesh.
3 Season and place under the grill.
4 When the butter starts to brown slightly, remove from the grill and turn the fish over carefully using a roasting fork or a long pallet knife.
5 With a spoon, baste the flesh of the uncooked side and continue cooking. The tail end will cook faster than the head end, therefore the less hot area towards the front of the grill is where the tail should be cooked.
6 To check whether the fish is done, place your thumb just behind the gill area and you should feel the flesh ease away from the bone.
7 Finish with parsley butter and a wedge of lemon.

5 Sardines with tapenade

oily fish · grilling

	energy	kcal	fat	sat fat	carb	sugar	protein	fibre	sodium *
	3167 KJ	757 kcal	44.0 g	12.4 g	0.0 g	0.0 g	90.5 g	0.8 g	1.0 g

Portions ❯	4	10
sardines	8–12	20–30
For the tapenade		
kalamata olives	20	50
capers	1 tbsp	2½ tbsp
lemon juice	1 tsp	2½ tsp
olive oil	2 tsp	5 tsp
anchovy paste (optional)	½ tsp	1¼ tsp
freshly ground black pepper		

1 Finely chop the olives and capers. Add the lemon juice, olive oil, anchovy paste and black pepper. Mix well.

2 Allow 2–3 sardines per portion. Clean them, and grill them on both sides, either on an open flame grill or under the salamander.

3 When cooked, smear the tapenade on top. The tapenade can be heated slightly before spreading.

A little chopped basil and a crushed chopped clove of garlic may also be added to the tapenade.

* Using additional olives instead of capers

6 Poached salmon

oily fish · poaching

	energy	kcal	fat	sat fat	carb	sugar	protein	fibre	sodium
	1284 KJ	309 kcal	20.6 g	5.5 g	0.3 g	0.3 g	30.4 g	0.1 g	0.1 g

1 Place the prepared and washed darnes or tronçons of salmon in a simmering court bouillon for approximately 5 minutes.

2 Drain well and carefully remove centre bone and outer skin. Ensure that the fish is cleaned of any cooked blood.

3 Serve with a suitable sauce (e.g. hollandaise) or melted herb butter, and thinly sliced cucumber.

Depending on the size of the salmon, either a whole or half a darne would be served as a portion.

Cutting fish into darnes
http://bit.ly/w2ogem

7 Poached smoked haddock

white round fish  poaching

Portions >	4	10
smoked haddock fillets	400–600 g	1.2 kg
milk and water, mixed		

1 Cut fillets into even portions, place into a shallow pan and just cover with half milk and water.
2 Poach gently for a few minutes until cooked.
3 Drain well and serve.

This is a popular breakfast dish and is also served as a lunch and a snack dish. For example:
- When cooked, garnish with slices of peeled tomato or tomato concassé, lightly coat with cream, flash under the salamander and serve.
- Top with a poached egg.
- When cooked, lightly coat with Welsh rarebit mixture, brown under the salamander and garnish with peeled slices of tomato or tomato concassé.

8 Poached turbot, brill, halibut or cod (on the bone)

white fish  poaching

energy	kcal	fat	sat fat	carb	sugar	protein	fibre	sodium
1412 KJ	353 kcal	9.5 g	2.5 g	0.3 g	0.3 g	62.0 g	0.0 g	0.2 g

1 Place the prepared fish into a shallow pan of simmering, lightly salted water containing lemon juice. (The citric acid helps to make the flesh firm and white and gives a gentle flavour.)
2 Allow to poach gently. The cooking time depends on the thickness of the fish. Do not overcook.
3 Remove with a fish slice, remove skin, drain and serve.
4 Garnish with picked parsley and plain boiled potatoes, and serve with a suitable sauce (e.g. hollandaise, herb butter, shrimp or mushroom).

Place the fish into the gently simmering liquid

Allow the fish to poach

Lift out the fish and remove any black skin

9 Délice of flat white fish Dugléré

Portions ❯	4	10
fillets of flat white fish (e.g. sole, plaice)	400–600 g	1–1.5 kg
fish stock for poaching	approx. 200 ml	approx. 500 ml
For the sauce		
butter	25 g	60 g
shallots, finely chopped	20 g	50 g
fish stock	60 ml	150 ml
dry white wine	60 ml	150 ml
whipping cream	200 ml	500 ml
tomatoes, skinned and neatly diced (concassé)	2	5
butter, sliced and kept cold on ice	50 g	125 g
parsley, chopped finely	10 g	20 g

1 Skin the fish, trim and wash.
2 Fold the fillets neatly, ensuring the skinned side is facing inwards (délice).
3 Using a wide, shallow pan, poach the délice gently in fish stock for between 4 and 6 minutes (depending on the thickness of the fillet).
4 To make the sauce, sweat the finely chopped shallots with the butter in a saucepan, until translucent.
5 Add the fish stock and reduce by one third.
6 Add the dry white wine and reduce again by half.
7 Add the whipping cream and reduce by one third until the cream starts to thicken the sauce to a coating consistency.
8 Add the cold, sliced butter and ripple the sauce over the butter until the butter has emulsified into the sauce (monté). Check the seasoning and adjust accordingly. Do not allow the sauce to reboil as the butter will split and the sauce will become greasy.
9 Add the neatly cut tomato concassé and finely chopped parsley to the sauce.
10 To serve, drain the fish well and place neatly onto a plate.
11 Carefully coat each délice with the sauce and serve.

Fold each fillet into a délice

Sweat the finely chopped shallots

Coat each délice with sauce

10 **Fillets of fish with white wine sauce**

(filets de poisson vin blanc)

white flat fish poaching

energy	kcal	fat	sat fat	carb	sugar	protein	fibre
1421 KJ	342 kcal	24.0 g	12.8 g	5.8 g	0.9 g	25.9 g	0.2 g

Portions >	4	10
fillets of white fish (e.g. plaice, sole)	400–600 g	1–1.5 kg
butter, for dish and greaseproof paper		
shallots, finely chopped and sweated	10 g	25 g
fish stock	60 ml	150 ml
dry white wine	60 ml	150 ml
lemon, juice of	¼	½
fish velouté	250 ml	625 ml
butter	50 g	125 g
cream, lightly whipped	2 tbsp	5 tbsp

1 Skin and fillet the fish, trim and wash.
2 Butter and season an earthenware dish.
3 Sprinkle with the sweated chopped shallots and add the fillets of sole.
4 Season, add the fish stock, wine and lemon juice.
5 Cover with buttered greaseproof paper.
6 Poach in a moderate oven at 150–200°C for 7–10 minutes.
7 Drain the fish well; dress neatly on a flat dish or clean earthenware dish.
8 Bring the cooking liquor to the boil with the velouté.
9 Correct the seasoning and consistency, and pass through double muslin or a fine strainer.
10 Mix in the butter then, finally, add the cream.
11 Coat the fillets with the sauce. Garnish with a sprig of chervil or *fleurons* (puff paste crescents).

Key point

In this recipe, the shallots should be sweated before use; however, if they are very finely chopped, they could be added raw.

Healthy eating tips
- Keep the added salt to a minimum.
- Reduce the amount of butter and cream added to finish the sauce.
- Less sauce could be added, plus a large portion of potatoes and vegetables.

Try something different
Add to the fish before cooking:
- fish *bonne-femme* – 100 g thinly sliced white button mushrooms and chopped parsley
- fish *bréval* – as for *bonne-femme* plus 100 g diced, peeled and deseeded tomatoes.

Filleting a flat fish
http://bit.ly/wJKnim

11 Fillets of fish mornay
(filets de poisson mornay)

energy	kcal	fat	sat fat	carb	sugar	protein	fibre
1309 KJ	315 kcal	19.3 g	9.3 g	5.5 g	0.7 g	29.9 g	0.2 g

Portions ❯	4	10
white fish fillets	500–600 g	1.5 kg
butter, for dish and greaseproof paper		
fish stock	125 ml	300 ml
béchamel sauce	250 ml	625 ml
egg yolk or sabayon	1	3
grated cheese, preferably Gruyère or Parmesan	50 g	125 g
salt, Cayenne pepper		
butter	25 g	60 g
cream, lightly whipped	2 tbsp	5 tbsp

1 Prepare the fillets; place in a buttered, seasoned earthenware dish or shallow pan, such as a sauté pan.
2 Add the fish stock, cover with buttered paper.
3 Cook in a moderate oven at 150–200°C for approximately 5–10 minutes.
4 Drain the fish well, place in a clean earthenware or flat dish.
5 Bring the béchamel to the boil, add the reduced cooking liquor, whisk in the yolk and remove from the heat. Add the cheese and correct the consistency. Do not reboil, otherwise the egg will curdle.
6 Correct the seasoning and pass through a fine strainer.
7 Mix in the butter and cream, check the consistency.
8 Mask the fish with the sauce, sprinkle with grated cheese and gratinate under the salamander.

Healthy option: Served with less sauce, plus macaire potatoes and salad

Healthy eating tips
- Reduce the amount of butter and cream added to finish the sauce.
- Less sauce could be served, plus a large portion of potatoes and vegetables.

Try something different
Classical variations include:
- fillets of fish Walewska – place a slice of cooked lobster on each fish fillet before coating with the sauce; after the dish is browned decorate each fillet with a slice of truffle
- fillets of fish Florentine – proceed as for fillets mornay, placing the cooked fish on a bed of well-drained and heated dry leaf spinach.

12 Fish kedgeree
(cadgery de poisson)

white round fish, smoked fish poaching, braising

energy	kcal	fat	sat fat	carb	sugar	protein	fibre *
1974 KJ	472 kcal	28.2 g	15.3 g	29.3 g	4.7 g	25.7 g	1.2 g

Portions >	4	10
fish (usually smoked haddock or fresh salmon)	400 g	1 kg
milk for poaching	300 ml	1 litre
rice pilaff (see page 174)	200 g	500 g
eggs, hard-boiled	2	5
butter	50 g	125 g
salt, pepper		
chives, chopped	1 tsp	2 tsp
curry sauce, to serve	250 ml	625 ml

1 Poach the fish in milk. Remove all skin and bone. Flake the fish.
2 Cook the rice pilaff. Cut the eggs into dice.
3 Combine the eggs, fish and rice, and heat in the butter. Correct the seasoning and add the chives.
4 Serve hot with a sauceboat of curry sauce.

Remove the skin from the poached fish

Flake the fish

Dice the hard-boiled eggs

This dish is traditionally served for breakfast, lunch or supper. The fish used should be named on the menu (e.g. salmon kedgeree).

* Using smoked haddock

Healthy eating tips
● Reduce the amount of butter used to heat the rice, fish and eggs.
● Garnish with grilled tomatoes and serve with bread or toast.

white fish baking, roasting

energy	kcal	fat	sat fat	carb	sugar	protein	fibre	sodium
1659 KJ	400 kcal	29.9 g	4.3 g	4.3 g	2.5 g	28.6 g	2.1 g	0.4 g

Portions ❭	4	10
hake fillets (200 g, skin on, bones removed)	4	10
baby plum vine tomatoes	300 g	750 g
olive oil	100 ml	250 ml
garlic cloves, unpeeled	6	15
black olives, stoned	16	40

> **Tip**
> Kalamata olives are best – they have a subtle flavour.

1 Preheat the oven to 175°C.
2 Put the tomatoes in a small roasting pan, drizzle with the olive oil and add the garlic.
3 Roast for 15 minutes, then add the olives.

4 Move the mixture aside and add the hake fillets to the pan, skin side down.
5 Baste them with a little of the olive oil in the pan and bake for 8–10 minutes, depending on the thickness of the fillets, until just firm and flaking easily.
6 Remove the pan from the oven and squeeze the roasted garlic cloves out of their skins.
7 Gently mix them with the tomatoes and olives, trying not to break up the tomatoes too much.
8 Season the tomato mixture and spoon onto four plates. Place a piece of baked hake on top of each.
9 Serve with braised cabbage and mashed potato.

Cod, pollock or haddock may be used instead of hake.

14 Baked cod with a herb crust

white fish baking

energy	kcal	fat	sat fat	carb	sugar	protein	fibre	*
1882 KJ	452 kcal	30.8 g	18.7 g	12.7 g	0.8 g	31.7 g	0.4 g	

Portions ⟩	4	10
cod fillets, 100–150 g each	4	10
herb mustard		
fresh breadcrumbs	100 g	250 g
butter, margarine or oil	100 g	250 g
Cheddar cheese, grated	100 g	250 g
parsley, chopped	1 tsp	1 tbsp
salt, pepper		

Key point
Add a little bit of beaten egg to the breadcrumb mixture; this will help bind the mixture together.

Healthy eating tips
- Use a little sunflower oil when making the herb crust.
- Cheese is salty – no added salt is needed.
- Serve with a large portion of tomato or cucumber salsa and new potatoes.

* Using mustard powder (1 tsp) for herb mustard

1 Place the prepared, washed and dried fish on a greased baking tray or ovenproof dish.
2 Combine the ingredients for the herb crust (the mustard, breadcrumbs, butter, margarine or oil, cheese, parsley and seasoning) and press evenly over the fish.
3 Bake in the oven at 180°C for approx. 15–20 minutes until cooked and the crust is a light golden-brown.
4 Serve either with lemon quarters or a suitable salsa (page 55) or sauce, e.g. tomato or egg.

15 Cod boulangère

white fish 🗑 baking, 🥘 shallow frying

energy	kcal	fat	sat fat	carb	sugar	protein	fibre	sodium
2650 KJ	636 kcal	35.7 g	15.1 g	44.1 g	5.4 g	37.3 g	8.7 g	0.6 g

Portions ›	4	10
onion	1	2
oil	50 ml	125 ml
butter	100 g	250 g
sea salt, freshly-milled black pepper		
potatoes	750 g	2 kg
thyme		
lemon, zest and juice of	1	2
fish stock, hot	400 ml	1 litre
cod fillets (100 g, skinless, boneless)	4	10
fresh peas	300 g	750 g
chives, chopped		

1 Peel the onions and slice them approximately 3 mm thick.

2 Heat the oil in a thick-bottomed pan, place in the onions and cook slowly until a slight golden brown. (Do not fast-fry the onions – this is a caramelisation process to reveal their natural sugars.)

3 Meanwhile, preheat the oven to 190°C.

4 Grease a shallow baking tin with a little butter and season well with freshly-milled black pepper and sea salt.

5 Peel the potatoes and slice them finely (3 mm thick).

6 Once the onions are softened, arrange the potato and onion in alternate layers on the bottom of the baking dish, also adding the thyme throughout.

7 Mix the lemon juice and zest with the hot fish stock and pour over the potatoes and onion.

8 Randomly place knobs of butter over the top of the potatoes.

9 Cover the baking dish with foil and bake in the oven for 55 minutes.

10 While the potatoes are cooking, prepare the cod by cutting it into large bite-sized chunks and place in the fridge.

11 When the potatoes are cooked (check with the point of a knife), arrange the fish over the top of the potatoes, re-cover with the foil and cook for another 10 minutes.

12 Remove the foil and sprinkle over the peas, re-cover and place back in the oven for a further 3 minutes.

13 Remove from the oven, take off the foil, clean the outer rim of the dish if required, sprinkle with the chopped chives and serve.

16 Fish pie

fish, potatoes 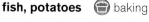 baking

energy	kcal	fat	sat fat	carb	sugar	protein	fibre
879 KJ	209 kcal	12.0 g	5.3 g	11.9 g	3.2 g	14.1 g	0.9 g

Portions ❭	4	10
béchamel (thin) (see page 41)	250 ml	625 ml
cooked fish (free from skin and bone)	200 g	500 g
mushrooms, cooked and diced	50 g	125 g
egg, hard-boiled and chopped	1	3
parsley, chopped		
salt, pepper		
potatoes, mashed or duchess	200 g	500 g
eggwash or milk, to finish		

1 Bring the béchamel to the boil.
2 Add the fish, mushrooms, egg and parsley. Correct the seasoning.
3 Place in a buttered pie dish.
4 Carefully spread or pipe the potato on top. Brush with eggwash or milk.
5 Brown in a hot oven or under the salamander and serve.

Healthy eating tips
● Keep the added salt to a minimum.
● This is a healthy main course dish, particularly when served with plenty of vegetables.

Heat the fish, mushrooms and egg in the béchamel

Pipe mashed potato over the top before baking

Try something different
Many variations can be made to this recipe with the addition of:
● prawns or shrimps
● herbs such as dill, tarragon or fennel
● raw fish poached in white wine, the cooking liquor strained off, double cream added in place of béchamel and reduced to a light consistency.

17 Salmon en papillote with crushed new potatoes

oily fish, potatoes baking, steaming

energy	kcal	fat	sat fat	carb	sugar	protein	fibre
3032 KJ	727 kcal	41.4 g	6.7 g	36.1 g	7.2 g	46.8 g	6.9 g

Portions ❯	4	10
For the salmon		
olive oil	2 tbsp	5 tbsp
cloves of garlic, thinly sliced	2	5
red chilli, deseeded, finely chopped	1	2
large shallots, thinly sliced	1	2
carrot, peeled and cut into thin matchsticks	1	2
sugar snap peas, halved lengthways	16	40
purple sprouting broccoli stems	8	20
flat-leaf parsley stems	2	5
suprêmes of salmon (200 g, skin on, pin boned)	4	10
rock salt		
white wine	200 ml	500 ml
For the potatoes		
new potatoes	20	50
olive oil	50 ml	125 ml
dill, finely chopped	1 tsp	2 tsp
sea salt, milled black pepper		

Cutting a fillet of salmon into suprêmes
http://bit.ly/wt3MOt

The term 'en papillotte' means butterfly and traditionally this method of cookery was all about the theatre at the restaurant table.

The ingredients are placed on a piece of parchment paper (today's greaseproof paper, or aluminium foil), shaped like a heart or a butterfly (both sides symmetrical). The edges of the paper are brushed with oil and crimped together, forming a waterproof seal. Once placed in the oven, the moisture from the ingredients inflates the parchment pouch like a pillow and cooks the dish in its own juices. This is then taken straight to the table and opened in front of the diner, allowing the aromas to escape, creating great theatre and sensory stimulation.

This method of cookery still has its place in the modern world of gastronomy. The parcel is likely to be opened in the kitchen and served on the plate, thus harnessing the natural cooking juices from the ingredients to create a light and clean-tasting dish.

1 Preheat one oven to 190°C and another to 220°C.
2 For timing purposes, start with the potatoes. Boil them until they are just cooked but not soft.
3 Mash roughly with the back of a fork and place on a lightly oiled baking tray. Sprinkle with the olive oil and black pepper. Put aside until the salmon is in the oven.
4 Cut two pieces of tin foil per portion, each measuring about 23 cm².
5 Place half of the foil squares on a work surface and drizzle with the olive oil.
6 Sprinkle over the garlic, chilli and shallots and arrange the vegetables and salmon suprêmes on top.
7 Season with the rock salt.

8 Place the remaining foil squares on top of the fish, lining up with the base foil.

9 Bring together the edges of the bottom foil with the top and fold together, then repeat to form a watertight seal (this is the essence of the cooking method – see above). Before making the last fold to seal each parcel, pour in 50 ml of white wine.

10 Place on a baking sheet and bake at 190°C for 10–12 minutes. Meanwhile, in the hotter oven, further cook the potatoes for 12 minutes until crisp and golden.

11 To serve, sprinkle the potatoes with the chopped dill and serve with the parcels of salmon.

---

18 Steamed fish with garlic, spring onions and ginger

 **white round fish** steaming

energy	kcal	fat	sat fat	carb	sugar	protein	fibre	*
468 KJ	112 kcal	3.5 g	0.7 g	1.2 g	0.4 g	18.7 g	0.1 g	

Portions ⟩	4	10
white fish fillets, e.g. cod, sole	400 g	1.5 kg
salt		
ginger, freshly chopped	1 tbsp	2½ tbsp
spring onions, finely chopped	2 tbsp	5 tbsp
light soy sauce	1 tbsp	2½ tbsp
cloves of garlic, peeled and thinly sliced	4	10
oil	1 tbsp	2½ tbsp

1 Wash and dry the fish well; rub *lightly* with salt on both sides.

2 Put the fish onto plates, scatter the ginger evenly on top.

3 Put the plates into the steamer, cover tightly and steam gently until just cooked (5–15 minutes, according to the thickness of the fish).

4 Remove the plates, sprinkle on the spring onions and soy sauce.

5 Brown the garlic slices in the hot oil and pour over the dish.

* Using 2 cloves of garlic

Key point

Garlic and ginger have intense flavours, so they must be chopped very finely.

Try something different

This is a Chinese recipe that can be adapted in many ways – for example, replace the spring onions and garlic and use thinly sliced mushrooms, diced tomato (skinned and deseeded), *finely* chopped shallots, lemon juice, white wine, chopped parsley, dill or chervil.

Healthy eating tips

- Steaming is a healthy way of cooking.
- Serve with a large portion of rice or noodles and stir-fried vegetables.

19 Frying batters
(pâtes à frire) **for fish**

🍳 **deep frying**

Recipe A

Portions ›	6–8	10
flour	200 g	500 g
salt		
yeast	10 g	25 g
water or milk	250 ml	625 ml

1 Sift the flour and salt into a basin.
2 Dissolve the yeast in a little of the water.
3 Make a well in the flour. Add the yeast and the liquid.
4 Gradually incorporate the flour and beat to a smooth mixture.
5 Allow to rest for at least 1 hour before using.

Batter mixed to the right consistency

Recipe B

Portions ›	6–8	10
flour	200 g	500 g
salt		
egg	1	2–3
water or milk	250 ml	625 ml
oil	2 tbsp	5 tbsp

1 Sift the flour and salt into a basin. Make a well. Add the egg and the liquid.
2 Gradually incorporate the flour and beat to a smooth mixture.
3 Mix in the oil. Allow to rest before using.

Recipe C

Portions ›	6–8	10
flour	200 g	500 g
salt		
water or milk	250 ml	625 ml
oil	2 tbsp	5 tbsp
egg whites, stiffly beaten	2	5

1 As for Recipe B, but fold in the egg whites just before using.

Other ingredients can be added to batter (e.g. chopped fresh herbs, grated ginger, garam masala, beer).

Practical Cookery 12th edition

20 Fried fish in batter

fish deep frying

energy	kcal	fat	sat fat	carb	sugar	protein	fibre
1736 KJ	415 kcal	14.0 g	1.8 g	41.6 g	3.5 g	33.2 g	2.1 g

1 Pass the prepared, washed and well-dried fish through flour, shake off the surplus and pass through the batter.
2 Place carefully away from you into the hot deep-fryer at 175°C until the fish turns a golden-brown. Remove and drain well.
3 Serve with either lemon quarters or tartare sauce.

Key point

Remove any excess batter before frying; too much batter will make the dish too heavy.

Deep-frying fish
http://bit.ly/
wSSk0e

Pass the prepared fish through the batter

Shake off any excess and then lower carefully into the fryer

21 Deep-fried fish coated with breadcrumbs

white flat fish deep frying

energy	kcal	fat	sat fat	carb	sugar	protein	fibre	sodium
1356 KJ	324 kcal	19.5 g	2.0 g	14.0 g	0.5 g	24.2 g	0.8 g	0.2 g

1 Pass the fillets through flour, beaten egg and fresh white breadcrumbs. (Pat the surfaces well to avoid loose crumbs falling into the fat, burning and spoiling both the fat and the fish.)
2 Deep-fry at 175°C, until the fish turns a golden-brown. Remove and drain well.
3 Serve with either lemon quarters or tartare sauce.

22 Goujons of plaice

white flat fish deep frying

energy	kcal	fat	sat fat	carb	sugar	protein	fibre	sodium
1094 KJ	261 kcal	13.8 g	0.0 g	13.8 g	0.0 g	21.3 g	0.6 g	0.3 g

1 Cut fillets of plaice into strips approx. 8 × 0.5 cm. Wash and dry well.
2 Pass through flour, beaten egg and fresh white breadcrumbs. Pat the surfaces well so that there are no loose crumbs which could fall into the fat and burn.
3 Deep-fry at 175°C, then drain well.
4 Serve with lemon quarters and a suitable sauce (e.g. tartare).

> **Key point**
> Keep the coating ingredients (flour, egg and breadcrumbs) separate. Shake off any excess flour and egg before dipping the fish into the breadcrumbs.
> Other fish, e.g. sole or salmon, may be used instead of plaice.

Cutting a fillet of fish into goujons
http://bit.ly/yoWESI

Pané the fish, passing it through flour, egg and breadcrumbs in turn

23 Fish cakes

fish deep frying

energy	kcal	fat	sat fat	carb	sugar	protein	fibre	*
1130 KJ	270 kcal	13.6 g	1.9 g	23.2 g	1.1 g	15.1 g	0.8 g	

Portions >	4	10
cooked fish (free from skin and bone)	200 g	500 g
potatoes, mashed	200 g	500 g
egg	1	3
salt, pepper		
flour	25 g	60 g
breadcrumbs	50 g	125 g

1 Combine the fish, potatoes and egg, and season.
2 Divide into 8 (or 20) pieces. Mould into balls.
3 Pass through a coating of flour, egg and breadcrumbs.
4 Flatten slightly and neaten with a palette knife.
5 Deep-fry in hot fat (185°C) for 2–3 minutes.

Combine the cooked fish and mashed potatoes

Mould the mixture into cakes

Fish cakes may be shallow-fried or deep-fried

Try something different

Other fish can be used – for example, cod, fresh haddock, salmon, crab.
- Optional extra seasonings are tomato ketchup, fresh chopped herbs (e.g. chervil, dill, parsley, tarragon, chives), anchovy essence, English or continental mustard.
- Coat lightly with flour and shallow-fry.
- Serve with a sauce (e.g. lemon butter, tartare, hollandaise, shrimp or tomato).
- Serve with a little dressed green salad.

Healthy eating tip

The fish cakes could be shallow-fried in a small amount of an unsaturated oil, then drained on kitchen paper.

* Using cod

fish shallow frying

energy	kcal	fat	sat fat	carb	sugar	protein	fibre
395 KJ	95 kcal	5.8 g	0.9 g	0.7 g	0.2 g	10.0 g	0.1 g

Portions ❭	4	10
salmon, filleted and skinned	100 g	250 g
cod, filleted and skinned	100 g	250 g
sesame oil	½ tsp	1 ¼ tsp
cloves of garlic	2	5
root ginger, grated	1 tbsp	2 ¼ tbsp
red chillies (small)	½	1
soy sauce	1 tsp	1 ½ tsp
lemon grass	12 g	30 g
salt	2 g	5 g
pepper	2 g	5 g
lime juice	10 ml (2 tsp)	25 ml (5 tsp)
sunflower oil for cooking	10 ml (2 tsp)	25 ml (5 tsp)

1 Pass all ingredients, except the oil for cooking, in a food processor, blend until bound together and smooth.

2 Turn out and divide into 12 small cakes for 4 portions, 30 for 10 portions. The cakes should be at least 2 cm thick.

3 Heat the oil in a suitable pan, place the fish cakes in, allowing approximately 3 minutes each side. Drain on kitchen paper after frying.

4 Serve immediately garnished with flat leaf parsley and Thai cucumber salad.

Healthy eating tips
● No added salt is needed.
● Serve with plenty of fragrant Thai rice and extra vegetables.

25 Shallow-fried fish

fish shallow frying

energy	kcal	fat	sat fat	carb	sugar	protein	fibre	sodium
1056 KJ	251 kcal	13.2 g	1.7 g	7.8 g	0.2 g	26.0 g	0.4 g	0.2 g

1 Prepare, clean, wash and dry the fish well.
2 Pass through flour and shake off all surplus. (If using non-stick pans it is not necessary to flour the fish.)
3 Heat the frying medium in a frying pan.
4 Shallow-fry on both sides (presentation side first), then serve.

> **Tip**
> Do not overcrowd the pan because this may cause the temperature of the fat to fall and this will affect the efficient cooking of the fish.

Pass the fish through seasoned flour

Place carefully into the pan, presentation side first

Turn the fish gently, once, during cooking

Try something different

- *À la meunière* (see recipe 27) – when cooked, mask with nut-brown butter, lemon juice and chopped parsley.
- As for meunière, with sliced almonds lightly browned in the butter.
- As for meunière, with picked shrimps and finely sliced button mushrooms heated in the butter.
- As for meunière, with a sprinkling of capers and segments of lemon or lime taken from peeled fruit (skin and pith removed).
- When cooked, sprinkle with a mixture of grated lemon zest, finely chopped garlic and chopped parsley – known as gremolata.

26 | Shallow-fried sole with shrimp and caper dressing

white flat fish, shellfish   shallow frying

energy	kcal	fat	sat fat	carb	sugar	protein	fibre	sodium
4655 KJ	1117 kcal	74.9 g	25.2 g	39.7 g	1.6 g	74.5 g	2.3 g	1.0 g

Portions >	4	10
lemon sole (350 g)	4	10
ground cumin, toasted	5 g	12 g
sea salt, freshly-milled black pepper		
plain flour	200 g	500 g
sunflower oil	100 ml	250 ml
lemon	1	2
For the dressing		
shrimps, cooked and peeled	200 g	500 g
small capers	75 g	200 g
butter, cut into small cubes	150 g	375 g
olive oil	50 ml	125 ml
parsley, chopped	2 tbsp	5 tbsp
lemon, juice of	1	2

1 Fillet the fish and trim the fillets to neaten them.
2 Mix the cumin, salt, pepper and flour together.
3 Before you start cooking the fish, make sure the other components of the dish are ready, as the sole will cook quickly.
4 Heat the oil in a non-stick pan large enough to cook one portion (4 fillets). Flour 4 fillets at a time by passing the sole through the flour well, ensuring that the whole fillet is coated in the flour.
5 Place the fillets into the hot oil, presentation side first, and cook until golden. Turn and cook for a further 10 seconds, remove and place on an oven tray (they will be flashed in the oven just before serving).
6 Repeat the process for the other 3 portions.
7 Add the dressing ingredients, except the parsley and lemon juice, to the pan, and heat until the butter foams and brings out the flavour of the capers.
8 Squeeze in the lemon juice and add the parsley.
9 Flash the sole in a moderate oven. Spoon the dressing over the sole to serve. Accompany with purple sprouting broccoli or green salad.

27 | Fish meunière

energy	kcal	fat	sat fat	carb	sugar	protein	fibre
1314 KJ	313 kcal	24.1 g	10.3 g	3.1 g	0.0 g	21.2 g	0.1 g

Many fish, whole or filleted, may be cooked by this method: for example, sole, sea bass, bream, fillets of plaice, trout, brill, cod, turbot, herring, scampi.

1 Prepare and clean the fish, wash and drain.
2 Pass through seasoned flour, shake off all surplus.
3 Shallow-fry on both sides, presentation side first, in hot clarified butter or oil.
4 Dress neatly on an oval flat dish or plate/plates.
5 Peel a lemon, removing the peel, white pith and pips.
6 Cut the lemon into slices and place some on each portion.
7 Squeeze some lemon juice on the fish.
8 Allow 10–25 g butter per portion and colour in a clean frying pan to the nut-brown stage (*beurre noisette*).
9 Pour over the fish.
10 Sprinkle with chopped parsley and serve.

Key point

When the butter has browned, try adding a squeeze of lemon juice or a splash of white wine for extra flavour.

Healthy eating tips

- Use a small amount of unsaturated oil to fry the fish.
- Use less *beurre noisette* per portion. Some customers will prefer the finished dish without the additional fat.

Making fish meunière
http://bit.ly/xzAnYO

Try something different

Variations include the following.

- **Fish meunière with almonds**: as for fish meunière, adding 10 g of almonds cut in short julienne or coarsely chopped into the meunière butter just before it begins to turn brown. This method is usually applied to trout.
- **Fish belle meunière**: as for fish meunière, with the addition of a grilled mushroom, a slice of peeled tomato and a soft herring roe (passed through flour and shallow-fried), all neatly dressed on each portion of fish.
- **Fish Doria**: as for fish meunière, with a sprinkling of small turned pieces of cucumber carefully cooked in 25 g of butter in a small covered pan, or blanched in boiling salted water.
- **Fish Grenobloise**: as for fish meunière, the peeled lemon being cut into segments, neatly dressed on the fish, with a few capers sprinkled over.
- **Fish Bretonne**: as for fish meunière, with a few picked shrimps and cooked sliced mushrooms sprinkled over the fish.

For each of these classical dishes, chefs may wish to add some chopped herbs for flavour; for example, add chopped dill to fish Doria.

Pan-fried fillets of sole with rocket and broad beans

white flat fish shallow frying

energy 2710 KJ	kcal 654 kcal	fat 54.2 g	sat fat 28.0 g	carb 5.1 g	sugar 1.4 g	protein 36.6 g	fibre 6.6 g	sodium 0.6 g

Portions ❯	4	10
sole fillets, trimmed	16	40
seasoning		
butter	200 g	500 g
broad beans, cooked and shelled	250 g	625 g
rocket, picked and washed	300 g	750 g
vinaigrette	50 ml	125 ml

1 Heat a little oil in a non-stick pan.
2 Place the fillets of sole on a tray and season on both sides.
3 Place the fish in the pan carefully (presentation side down).

4 Cook for 1 minute on a medium/high heat, and then carefully turn the fish, remove the pan from the heat and allow the residual heat to finish the cooking.
5 Place the sole fillets (4 per portion) on serving plates and keep warm.
6 Place the butter in the cooking pan, heat to the noisette stage, add the broad beans and cook for 30 seconds to 1 minute just to re-heat the beans.
7 Mask the fish with the noisette butter and the beans. Finish with a dressed rocket salad.

This is a very simple and quick dish. Any salad or greens, if they are quickly cooked or lightly dressed, can go with this dish.

29 | **Pan-fried skate with capers and *beurre noir***

white flat fish shallow frying

energy	kcal	fat	sat fat	carb	sugar	protein	fibre	sodium *
2395 KJ	579 kcal	51.9 g	24.7 g	0.8 g	0.8 g	27.1 g	1.2 g	1.0 g

Portions 〉	4	10
vegetable oil	50 ml	125 ml
seasoning		
skate, skinless fillets (approx. 160 g each)	4	10
butter	175 g	450 g
lemons, juice of	2	5
flat parsley, chopped	2 tbsp	5 tbsp
small capers	100 g	250 g

> **Key point**
> Because skate pass urine through their wings, if they are not super-fresh they will start to smell of ammonia after 3–4 days; this is a key indicator of their freshness.

1 Place a skillet or other suitable pan on the hottest part of the stove and an empty sauté pan to the side of the stove, achieving a moderate heat (this is for the *beurre noir*).

2 Ensure the skate wings are fresh, and free from ammonia aromas and skin.

3 Add the vegetable oil to the skillet and then the seasoned skate wings, cook with colour for 1–2 minutes and then carefully turn; at this point ease the skillet to a cooler point of the stove while the *beurre noir* cooks.

4 Place the butter in the pan and allow to foam (at this point remove the skate and place on the serving dish).

5 Add the lemon, parsley and capers to the *beurre noir*, stir well.

6 To finish, nap over the skate wing and serve.

* Using olives in place of capers

Nage of red mullet with baby leeks

white round fish, bulbs boiling, shallow frying

energy	kcal	fat	sat fat	carb	sugar	protein	fibre	sodium
2172 KJ	519 kcal	9.2 g	0.9 g	26.8 g	19.7 g	46.2 g	13.1 g	0.6 g

Portions ❭	4	10
mussels, cooked and out of shell	16	40
lemons, juice of	2	5
baby spinach	200 g	500 g
baby leeks	12	30
baby asparagus, spears of	12	30
green beans, pieces of	2 tbsp	5 tbsp
red mullet fillets (approx. 120 g each), pin bones and scales removed	4	10
Nage		
large onion	1	3
carrots, peeled	2	5
celery sticks	2	5
leeks	2	5
cloves of garlic	1	3
half white and half pink peppercorns	12	30
star anise	1	3
white wine	375 ml	950 ml
Noilly Prat	375 ml	950 ml
chervil	10 g	25 g
parsley	10 g	25 g
tarragon	10 g	25 g
chives, chopped	1 tbsp	3 tbsp

1 In a large pan place the onions, carrots, celery and leeks, which have been cut into 2 cm pieces.
2 Just cover the vegetables with water. Bring to the boil. Simmer for 4–5 minutes. Remove from the heat and add the rest of the ingredients.
3 Cover with clingfilm and allow to cool to room temperature. Place into a plastic container and store in the fridge overnight to develop flavour.
4 Pass through a fine sieve. Any surplus nage can be frozen for later use.
5 To finish, place 500 ml of the vegetable nage in a pan, add the mussels, a squeeze of lemon, spinach, baby leeks, asparagus and green beans.
6 Bring to the boil, check the seasoning and retain.
7 Heat a non-stick pan with a little vegetable oil. Season the mullet fillets and cook for 1 minute on each side (thickness dependent), starting with the skin side down.
8 Divide the vegetable garnish between the bowls. Place the red mullet on top of the vegetable garnish and, returning the pan the mullet was cooked in to the stove, pour in the nage.
9 When the nage has returned to the boil, spoon over the fish and garnish. Serve immediately.

Key point
This dish is open to many substitutions of fish and shellfish but one key point to remember is that the nage should not be allowed to overpower the main ingredients.

31 Barramundi with garlic, ginger and lemon butter and pak choi

white fish, leafy vegetables shallow frying, boiling

energy	kcal	fat	sat fat	carb	sugar	protein	fibre	sodium *
3174 KJ	766 kcal	62.2 g	19.7 g	7.9 g	6.9 g	44.3 g	6.8 g	0.3 g

Portions ⟩	4	10
olive oil	75 ml	200 ml
barramundi fillets (200 g, skin off)	4	10
small heads of pak choi	8	20
salted butter	100 g	250 g
garlic, small cloves, chopped	1	2
root ginger, cut in to 2–3 pieces/6–8 pieces	50 g	125 g
fresh lemon juice	3 tbsp	7 tbsp
seasoning		
fresh basil leaves, chopped	5	12

Barramundi can be used in any recipe calling for a white fish such as cod, bass or haddock, or red snapper.

1 Bring a pan of salted water to the boil.

2 Heat the oil in a non-stick frying pan.

3 Season the fish fillets and place in the hot oil. Cook for 2 minutes and then turn, removing the pan from the heat. Allow the residual heat to finish the cooking process.

4 Meanwhile, blanch the pak choi for 2 minutes in the boiling water, until vibrant green.

5 Remove the fish from the pan and keep it warm. Return the pan to the heat and add the butter, garlic and ginger. Cook for 2 minutes until the garlic is soft and the ginger has imparted its flavour. Remove the ginger and add the lemon and basil.

6 Mix well and add the cooked, drained pak choi. Ensure that all the flavours are incorporated well.

7 Serve the fish and pak choi with the dressing from the pan over the top.

* Using spring greens instead of pak choi

223

32 Mussels in white wine sauce
(moules marinière)

shellfish  boiling, steaming

energy	kcal	fat	sat fat	carb	sugar	protein	fibre	sodium
1900 KJ	452 kcal	14.3 g	5.3 g	18.1 g	0.9 g	61.4 g	0.6 g	1.5 g

Portions ❯	4	10
shallots, chopped	50 g	125 g
parsley, chopped	1 tbsp	2 tbsp
white wine	60 ml	150 ml
strong fish stock	200 ml	500 ml
mussels	2 kg	5 kg
butter	25 g	60 g
flour	25 g	60 g
seasoning		

Try something different

For an eastern influence why not add a little red chilli and replace the parsley with coriander?

1 Take a thick-bottomed pan and add the shallots, parsley, wine, fish stock and the cleaned mussels.
2 Cover with a tight-fitting lid and cook over a high heat until the shells open.
3 Drain off all the cooking liquor in a colander set over a clean bowl to retain the cooking juices.
4 Carefully check the mussels and discard any that have not opened.
5 Place in a dish and cover to keep warm.
6 Make a roux from the flour and butter; pour over the cooking liquor, ensuring it is free from sand and stirring continuously to avoid lumps.
7 Correct the seasoning and garnish with more chopped parsley.
8 Pour over the mussels and serve.

33 Lobster beignets with tomato chutney

shellfish, vegetable fruits boiling, deep frying

energy	kcal	fat	sat fat	carb	sugar	protein	fibre	sodium
1914 KJ	451 kcal	3.3 g	0.6 g	77.4 g	26.1 g	28.1 g	7.8 g	0.3 g

Portions ⟩	4	10
onion, peeled and chopped	1	2
tomatoes, peeled, seeded and diced as for concassé	1 kg	2.5 kg
red wine vinegar	70 ml	175 ml
sugar	50 g	125 g
coriander powder	1 tbsp	2 tbsp
paprika	1 tbsp	2 tbsp
cooked lobster tails	4	10
plain flour (plus a little extra for coating)	145 g	360 g
fecule (potato starch)	120 g	300 g
active dry yeast	1 tbsp	2½ tbsp
real ale or beer	300 ml	750 ml

For the chutney

1 In a large pot over a medium-low heat, warm 1 tablespoon of oil.
2 Add onion and cook, stirring occasionally, until tender, 5–10 minutes.
3 Add tomatoes, vinegar, sugar, coriander and paprika; bring to a simmer, stirring occasionally, until thickened, 45–55 minutes.
4 Remove from heat and allow to cool.

For the lobster beignets

1 Slice lobster meat crosswise into 0.5 cm-thick medallions; keep chilled.
2 Heat the oil in a deep fryer to 180°C.
3 In a bowl, combine the flour, starch, yeast and ½ teaspoon of salt; stir to mix. Stir in the beer to make the batter.
4 Coat a lobster medallion in a little flour and then in the batter. Deep-fry until crispy and golden, 2–3 minutes.
5 Fry 3 or 4 at a time (do not crowd the fryer). Drain well. Sprinkle beignets lightly with salt and serve hot with chutney.

This can be served as a quick, hot and spicy bar dish.

Crab cakes with chilli lime dipping sauce

shellfish shallow frying

energy	kcal	fat	sat fat	carb	sugar	protein	fibre
557 KJ	133 kcal	5.6 g	0.7 g	1.2 g	0.4 g	19.6 g	0.1 g

Makes 〉	30–40 cakes
Crab cakes	
crab meat	350 g
uncooked prawns, shelled and de-veined	650 g
red curry paste	1 tbsp
egg	1
spring onions, chopped	2
fresh coriander, finely chopped	2 tbsp
lemon grass, finely chopped	2 tsp
red Thai chilli, deseeded and chopped	1
vegetable oil	2 tbsp
Dipping sauce	
lime juice	2 tbsp
water	2 tbsp
fish sauce	2 tsp
kaffir lime leaf, chopped	1
red Thai chilli, deseeded and finely chopped	1

For the crab cakes

1 In a food processor, place the crab, prawns, curry paste, egg, spring onions, coriander, lemon grass and chilli. Combine all ingredients until mixed together.

2 Shape into small cakes. Chill.

3 Heat the oil in a shallow pan and fry the crab cakes on both sides until golden brown. Drain, place on a suitable dish with the dipping sauce (see below).

For the dipping sauce

1 Combine all ingredients in a suitable bowl.

2 Stir well.

> **Note**
> These crab cakes may be served as a hot canapé.

35 Crab cakes with rocket salad and lemon dressing

shellfish 🥘 shallow frying

energy	kcal	fat	sat fat	carb	sugar	protein	fibre
3002 KJ	719 kcal	43.9 g	10.5 g	41.9 g	4.4 g	41.4 g	4.1 g

Portions >	4	10
Crab cakes		
shallots, finely chopped	25 g	60 g
spring onions, finely chopped	4	10
fish/shellfish glaze	75 ml	185 ml
crab meat	400 g	1 kg
mayonnaise	75 g	185 g
lemons, juice of	1	3
plum tomatoes, skinned, cut into concassé	2	5
wholegrain mustard	1 tsp	3 tsp
seasoning		
fresh white breadcrumbs	200 g	500 g
eggs, beaten with 100 ml of milk	2	5
Salad and dressing		
vegetable oil	170 ml	425 ml
white wine vinegar	25 ml	60 ml
lemons, juice of	1	3
seasoning		
rocket, washed and picked	250 g	625 g
Reggiano Parmesan, shaved	100 g	250 g

For the crab cakes

1 Mix the shallots, spring onions and the fish glaze with the hand-picked crab meat.
2 Add the mayonnaise, lemon juice, tomato concassé and mustard, check and adjust the seasoning.
3 Allow to rest for 30 minutes in the refrigerator.
4 Scale into 80–90 g balls and shape into discs 1.5 cm high, place in the freezer for 30 minutes to harden.
5 When firm to the touch, coat in breadcrumbs using the flour, egg and breadcrumbs.
6 Allow to rest for a further 30 minutes.
7 Heat a little oil in a non-stick pan, carefully place the cakes in and cook on each side until golden brown.

For the salad and dressing

1 Combine the oil, vinegar and lemon juice together, check the seasoning.
2 Place the rocket and Parmesan in a large bowl and add a little dressing, just to coat.
3 Place this in the centre of each plate, top with the crab cakes and serve.

Any excess crab meat can be used up in this recipe – a quick, classic dish. The crab can be exchanged for salmon or most fresh fish trimmings.

> **Key point**
> Make sure that the crab mixture is divided into equal-sized cakes.

36 Prawns with chilli and garlic

shellfish  shallow frying

energy	kcal	fat	sat fat	carb	sugar	protein	fibre	sodium *
728 KJ	173 kcal	3.8 g	0.6 g	6.6 g	6.3 g	28.6 g	0.1 g	0.3 g

Portions ❯	4	10
clove of garlic, crushed	1	3
lime, juice of	1	2
lemon, juice of	½	1
mild red chillies, deseeded and finely chopped	2	5
olive oil	1 tbsp	3 tbsp
honey	1 tbsp	3 tbsp
extra large prawns, raw, shells on, heads removed	32	80
black pepper		
To serve		
salsa verde (see page 55)	100 ml	250 ml
garlic bread	4 slices	10 slices
green salad		

1 In a shallow dish, mix together the garlic, lime juice, lemon juice, chillies, olive oil and honey.

2 Make an incision (don't cut all the way through – leave the prawn intact) in the back of each prawn and remove the entrails. Wash and dry well.

3 Add the prawns to the oil/chilli mix, season with black pepper and marinate in the fridge for 30 minutes.

4 Meanwhile, prepare the green salad, salsa verde and garlic bread.

5 Remove the prawns from the marinade and heat a small amount of oil in a non-stick frying pan.

6 Place the prawns in the pan and cook until pink and cooked through, basting with any leftover marinade while cooking.

7 To serve, place warm garlic bread on plates and pile up the prawns on top, allowing the cooking juices to run into the bread. Drizzle with salsa verde and serve with a green salad.

* Excluding accompaniments

37 Scallops and bacon

scallops, bacon shallow frying

energy	kcal	fat	sat fat	carb	sugar	protein	fibre	sodium
1705 KJ	410 kcal	26.8 g	6.9 g	5.9 g	2.8 g	36.4 g	2.3 g	1.3 g

Portions ⟩	4	10
large scallops, shelled, roe and skirt removed, washed	12	30
pancetta bacon rashers (rind off)	12	30
olive oil	50 ml	125 ml
lemon	1	2
asparagus sticks, peeled, blanched for 1 minute and refreshed	16	40
seasoning		

1 Wrap the scallops in the pancetta, pin with a cocktail stick and season (be mindful that the pancetta is salty).

2 Heat the oil in a non-stick pan, place the scallops in and cook until golden-brown. Squeeze the lemon over the scallops and allow the juice to evaporate slightly.

3 Remove from the pan and retain with all the pan juices.

4 Return the pan to the heat and add the asparagus, cooking for a further 2 minutes.

5 To serve, divide the asparagus onto plates. Top with the scallops, pour over the pan juices and serve.

38 Lobster thermidor
(homard thermidor)

shellfish boiling, grilling

energy	kcal	fat	sat fat	carb	sugar	protein	fibre
1973 KJ	475 kcal	35.8 g	19.5 g	10.8 g	1.1 g	28.1 g	0.4 g

Portions >	4	10
lobsters, cooked	2	5
butter	25 g	60 g
shallots, finely chopped	12 g	30 g
dry white wine	60 ml	150 ml
English mustard, diluted	½ tsp	1 tsp
parsley, chopped		
mornay sauce (see page 42)	250 ml	750 ml
Parmesan cheese, grated	25 g	60 g
picked parsley, to garnish		

1 Remove the lobsters' claws and legs.
2 Carefully cut the lobsters in halves lengthwise. Remove the meat.
3 Discard the sac and remove the trail from the tail.
4 Wash the halves of shell and drain on a baking sheet.
5 Cut the lobster meat into thick escalopes.
6 Melt the butter in a sauteuse, add the chopped shallots and cook until tender, without colour.
7 Add the white wine to the shallots and allow to reduce to a quarter of its original volume.
8 Mix in the mustard and chopped parsley.

9 Add the lobster slices, season lightly with salt, mix carefully and allow to heat slowly for 2–3 minutes. If this part of the process is overdone the lobster will become tough and chewy.
10 Meanwhile, spoon a little of the warm mornay sauce into the bottom of each lobster half-shell.
11 Neatly add the warmed lobster pieces and the juice in which they were reheated. If there is an excess of liquid it should be reduced and incorporated into the mornay sauce.
12 Coat the half lobsters with the remaining mornay sauce, sprinkle with the Parmesan and place under a salamander until golden-brown. Serve garnished with picked parsley.

Ingredients for lobster thermidor

Open lobster halves

Prepare the shallot mixture

Spoon a little sauce into each shell

Healthy eating tips
- Use a small amount of unsaturated oil (olive or sunflower) instead of butter.
- Use little or no salt as the cheese will provide the necessary seasoning.

7 Meat and offal

This chapter is relevant to the following units:

- Prepare meat for basic dishes (NVQ)
- Prepare offal for basic dishes (NVQ)
- Cook and finish basic meat dishes (NVQ)
- Cook and finish basic offal dishes (NVQ)
- Prepare and cook meat and offal (VRQ).

The structure of meat

To cook meat properly it is important to understand its structure.

- Meat comprises fibres bound by connective tissue.
- Connective tissue (elastin) is yellow and collagen white.
- Yellow tissue needs to be removed.
- Small fibres are present in tender cuts and young animals.
- Coarser fibres are present in tougher cuts and older animals.
- Fat assists in providing flavour, and moistens meat in roasting and grilling.
- Tenderness, flavour and moistness are increased if meat is hung after slaughter and before being used.
- Storage times: beef up to 3 weeks; veal 1–3 weeks; lamb 10–15 days; pork 7–14 days.
- Hang and store meat between 0 and 1°C.

Meat varies considerably in its fat content. This is found round the outside of meat, in marbling (the white flecks of fat throughout the lean muscle) and inside the meat fibres. The visible fat (saturated) should be trimmed off as much as possible before cooking.

Full information on meat, including cattle, sheep and pigs, can be obtained at www.qmscotland.co.uk.

Origins

Butcher's meat today is largely a product of selective breeding and feeding techniques, whereby animals are reared carefully to reach high standards and meet specific needs: the present-day demand is for lean and tender meat – modern cattle, sheep and pigs are well-fleshed yet compact creatures compared to their forebears of a century ago.

Preservation of meat

Chilling: Meat that is chilled is kept at a temperature just above freezing point in a controlled atmosphere. Chilled meat cannot be kept in the usual type of cold room for more than a few days, although sufficient time must be allowed for the meat to hang, enabling it to become tender.

Freezing: Small carcasses, such as lamb and mutton, can be frozen; their quality is not affected by freezing. They can be kept frozen until required and then thawed out before being used. Some beef is frozen, but it is inferior in quality to chilled beef.

Canning: Large quantities of meat are canned; corned beef is an example with a very high protein content. Pork is used for tinned luncheon meat. Ham cuts are also available in cans.

Salting

Salting, especially of meat, is an ancient preservation technique. The salt draws out moisture and creates an environment inhospitable to bacteria. If salted in cold weather (so that the meat does not spoil while the salt has time to take effect), salted meat can last for years.

Today, salting is still used with bacon, before the meat is smoked, and hams. It is also used for beef products, e.g. dried beef, corned beef (see below) and pastrami, which are made by soaking beef in a 10 per cent salt water brine for several weeks.

Meat can be pickled in brine; this method of preservation may be applied to silverside, brisket and ox tongues.

Brining – the use of salt water – has replaced the dry salt cure, but the name 'corned beef' is still used, rather than 'brined' or 'pickled' beef. Commonly used spices that give corned beef its distinctive flavour are peppercorns and bay leaf. (Of course, the spices used may vary regionally.)

Health, safety and hygiene

For information on maintaining a safe and secure working environment, a professional and hygienic appearance, and clean food production areas, equipment and utensils, as well as food hygiene, please refer to Chapters 14 and 15. Additional food safety points to reduce the risk of cross-contamination are as follows.

- When preparing uncooked meat or poultry, and then cooked food, or changing from one type of meat or poultry to another, equipment, working areas and utensils must be thoroughly cleaned, or changed.
- If colour-coded boards are used, it is essential to always use the correct colour-coded boards for the preparation of foods, and different ones for cooked foods.
- Store uncooked meat and poultry on trays to prevent dripping, in separate refrigerators at a temperature of 1–4°C. If separate refrigerators are not available then store in separate areas within the one refrigerator, with the uncooked meat at the bottom and cooked meat above it.

- Clean all work surfaces with detergent and sanitiser to kill bacteria. This is particularly important when handling poultry and pork.

To maintain the quality and safety of meat and poultry dishes it is advisable to check internal temperatures by means of a probe. The recommended temperatures are shown in Table 71.

For your own safety, when using a boning knife, wear a safety apron for protection. If you are doing a great deal of boning, then consider protective gloves as well.

Table 7.1 Recommended internal cooking temperatures*

Beef	rare 52°C; medium 57°C; well done 62°C
Lamb	pink 57°C; well done 62°C
Pork	75°C
Veal	62°C
Turkey/chicken	77°C
Duck	pink 57°C; well done 62°C

* Environmental Health Officers may require higher temperatures

Choosing and buying meat

Meat is a natural and therefore not a uniform product, varying in quality from carcass to carcass, while flavour, texture and appearance are determined by the type of animal and the way it has been fed. There is no reason to think that flavour is obtained only in meat that possesses a proportion of fat, although fat does give a characteristic flavour to meat and helps to keep it moist during roasting. Neither is the colour of meat any guide to quality. Consumers are inclined to choose light-coloured meat – bright-red beef, for example – because they think that it will be fresher than an alternative dark-red piece. Freshly butchered beef is bright red because the pigment in the tissues, myoglobin, has been chemically affected by the oxygen in the air. After several hours, the colour changes to dark red or brown as the pigment is further oxidised to become metamyoglobin. The colour of fat can vary from almost pure white in lamb, to bright

yellow in beef. Colour depends on the feed, on the breed and, to a certain extent, on the time of year.

The most useful guide to tenderness and quality is a knowledge of the cuts of meat and their location on the carcass. The various cuts are described under their respective headings (see below), but in principle the leanest and tenderest cuts – the 'prime' cuts – come from the hindquarters. The 'coarse' cuts, or meat from the neck, legs and forequarters, those parts of the animal that have had plenty of muscular exercise and where fibres have become hardened, provide meat for braising and stewing. Many consider these cuts to have more flavour, although they require slow cooking to make them tender. The meat from young animals is generally more tender and, since tenderness is a prime factor, animals may be injected before slaughter with an enzyme, such as papin, which softens the fibres and muscles. This merely speeds up a natural and more satisfactory process: meat contains its own proteolytic enzymes, which gradually break down the protein cell walls as the carcass ages; that is why meat is hung from 10 to 20 days in controlled conditions of temperature and humidity before being offered for sale. Meat that is aged longer becomes more expensive as the cost of refrigeration is high and the meat itself shrinks because of evaporation and the trimming of the outside hardened edges.

Kosher and halal meat

Meat that is sold as kosher or halal must have been slaughtered according to the food laws of Judaism (kosher) or Islam (halal).

Kosher slaughter is done by a quick, deep stroke across the throat with a sharp blade. This causes unconsciousness within two seconds and is widely recognised as the most humane method of slaughter possible. The animal is bled completely, and the meat soaked in suet and water to remove any residual blood, because blood must not be consumed in a kosher diet.

Halal slaughter is done by cutting the throat or piercing the hollow of the throat, causing a quick death with the least pain possible. The blood is completely drained from the carcass. Halal slaughter is preceded by a prayer.

Cooking meat

Meat is an extremely versatile product that can be cooked in a multitude of ways, and matched with practically any vegetable, fruit and herb. The cut (shin, steak, brisket), the method of heating (roasting, braising, grilling), and the time and temperature all affect the way the meat will taste.

Raw meat is difficult to chew because the muscle fibre contains an elastic protein (collagen), which is softened only by mincing – as in steak tartare – or by cooking. When you cook meat, the protein gradually coagulates as the internal temperature increases. At 77°C coagulation is complete, the protein begins to harden and further cooking makes the meat tougher.

Meat bones are useful for giving flavour to soups and stocks, especially beef ones with plenty of marrow. Veal bones are gelatinous and help to enrich and thicken soups and sauces. Fat can be rendered down for frying, or used as an ingredient when suet or lard is called for.

Time and temperature in meat cookery

Since tenderness combined with flavour is the aim in meat cookery, much depends on the ratio of time and temperature. In principle, slow cooking retains the juices and produces a more tender result than does fast cooking at high temperatures. There are,

of course, occasions when high temperatures are essential: for instance, you need to grill a steak under a hot flame for a very limited time in order to obtain a crisp, brown surface and a pink, juicy interior – using a low temperature would not give you the desired result. But in potentially tough cuts, such as breast, or where there is a quantity of connective tissue (neck of lamb), a slow rate of cooking converts the tissues to gelatine and helps to make the meat more tender. Meat containing bone will take longer to cook because bone is a poor conductor of heat.

Tough or coarse cuts of meat should be cooked by braising, pot roasting or stewing. Marinating in a suitable marinade, such as wine and wine vinegar, helps to tenderise the meat and imparts an additional flavour. Searing meat in hot fat or in a hot oven before roasting or stewing helps to produce a crisp exterior by coagulating the protein but does not, as is widely supposed, seal in the juices. However, if the external temperature is too high and cooking prolonged, rapid evaporation and contraction of the meat will cause considerable loss of juices and fat. Salt sprinkled on meat before cooking will also hasten loss of moisture since salt is hygroscopic and absorbs water.

To take this one step further, when fibrous proteins are heated they contract and squeeze out the associated water. For example, when a steak is cooked the proteins contract, therefore squeezing out all the water/juices. If the heat is increased or continues, the steak will then become dry and, consequently, the eating quality will be impaired. Cuts of meat also contain elastin and collagen: elastin (the muscle group associated with tendons and arteries) is extremely stretchy and further cooking adds to its strength; collagen (the main muscle proteins, which amount to the highest proportion of mass in the muscle) is rather tough and chewy. Meat that has a higher proportion of both, usually from the major and highly worked muscle groups, would not be suitable for prime cooking (e.g. grilling or frying). However, these cuts of meat may be cooked for longer at the correct temperature (braising), dissolving the collagen as it is water soluble, forming gelatine and offering a tasty joint of meat.

Prime cuts, such as beef fillets, have little collagen in their make-up (approximately 3 per cent) and do not require long cooking to tenderise the joint. Although most chefs would adopt a high temperature for a short period on the prime cuts, this does not always yield a perfect result. Due to the lack of fat and collagen in such cuts of meat, high heat will render the muscle fibres dry and, consequently, the eating quality is impaired. A lower temperature and longer in the oven will produce a gradual heat, therefore there is less extreme coagulation in the tissues and less fluid will have been squeezed out in the process.

Sirloin of beef has more collagen than fillet (it is essentially a worked muscle group) and is generally cooked on a high heat, either roasted or pan-fried. Using a slow cooking method, you can render the sirloin extremely tender, full of moisture, with a roasted outer and the flavoursome roasted meat taste that is craved. An average sirloin joint for roasting can weigh from 2–5 kg whole off the bone. The method is to seal the meat on the outside, as you would normally, place into a pre-heated oven at 180°C, cook at 180°C for 10 minutes, then reduce the temperature to 64°C (the oven door will need to be open at this stage). Once the oven has come down to 64°C, close the door and cook for a further 1 hour 50 minutes. This will give you an extremely tender piece of sirloin.

The Maillard reaction

When meat cooks, flavour is developed. This happens when the meat proteins are heated with sugars to temperatures above 140°C and a series of chemical reactions occur, known as the Maillard reaction.

Always ensure that the outside of the meat is cooked at a high temperature (until it is a dark brown colour), in order to seal in and develop the flavour. Cook meats with little connective tissue for only a short time. Seal the outside so that it is browned and so that the inside does not become tough (e.g. by grilling, frying or roasting).

Meats with lots of connective tissue should be cooked for longer so that all the connective tissue denatures and the bundles of coagulated muscle proteins fall apart, rendering the meat tender (e.g. by stewing or braising) (Barham, 2000).

Other meat preparations

Forcemeat

This is a term given to numerous mixtures of meats (usually veal and pork); meat and poultry; poultry; game; fish; vegetables and bread.

Forcemeats range from a simple sausagemeat to the finer mixtures used in the making of hot mousses (ham, chicken, fish) and soufflés. Also included are mixtures of bread, vegetables and herbs, which alternatively are referred to as stuffings.

Forcemeats are used for galantines, raised pies, terrines, meatballs and a wide variety of other dishes.

Crepinettes

These are small sausages, usually made from a forcemeat of veal, lamb, pork or chicken encased either in caul or paper-thin slices of salt pork. Other ingredients are sometimes added (e.g. chopped mushrooms or truffle). Crepinettes are usually covered with melted butter or good-quality oil, coated with fresh white breadcrumbs and grilled, sautéed or cooked in the oven. Traditionally they are served with potato purée and a well-flavoured demi-glace-type sauce.

Lamb and mutton

Lamb is the meat from a sheep under a year old; above that age the animal is called a 'hogget' and its meat becomes mutton. The demand for lamb in preference to mutton is partly due to the fact that the lamb carcass provides smaller cuts of more tender meat. Mutton needs to be well ripened by long hanging before cooking and, as it is usually fatty, needs a good deal of trimming as well.

Lamb has a very thin, parchment-like covering on the carcass, known as the 'fell', which is usually left on roasts to help them maintain their shape during cooking. It should, however, be removed from chops. The flesh of a younger lamb is usually more tender. A good way to judge age is through weight – especially with legs of lamb – the highest quality weighs about 2.3 kg and never more than 4 kg. Smaller chops are also more tender and, therefore, more expensive.

Mutton fell out of favour for some years, but has become more popular, backed by the Mutton Renaissance campaign, which was supported by several well-known chefs and the Prince of Wales. Using mutton is good for food sustainability because the animals are not killed young, are larger than lambs and have a higher yield.

Quality points

- Good-quality lamb should have fine, white fat, with pink flesh where freshly cut; in mutton the flesh is a deeper colour.
- A good-quality animal should be compact and evenly fleshed.
- The lean flesh should be firm, of a pleasing dull-red colour and of a fine texture or grain.
- There should be an even distribution of surface fat, which should be hard, brittle and flaky in structure and a clear white colour.
- In a young animal the bones should be pink and porous, so that when cut a degree of blood is shown in their structure. As age progresses the bones become hard, dense and white, and inclined to splinter when chopped.

Portions and cuts

As a guide, when ordering allow approximately 100 g meat off the bone per portion, and 150 g on the bone per portion. It must be clearly understood, however, that the weights given can only be approximate. They must vary according to the quality of the meat and also according to the purpose for which the meat is being butchered. For example, a chef will often cut differently from a shop butcher (a chef frequently needs to consider the presentation of the particular joint, while the butcher is more often concerned with economical cutting). In the text that follows, simple orders of dissection are given for each carcass. In general, bones need to be removed only when preparing joints, so as to facilitate carving. The bones are used for stock and the excess fat can be rendered down for second-class dripping.

Joints of lamb, viewed from different angles

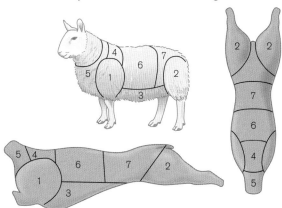

1	Shoulder	5	Scrag end
2	Leg	6	Best end/rack
3	Breast	7	Saddle
4	Middle neck		

Table 7.2 Joints, uses and weights

| Joint | Uses | Approx. weight (kg) | |
		Lamb	Mutton
whole carcass		16	25
shoulder (two)	roasting, stewing	3	4.5
leg (two)	roasting (mutton boiled)	3.5	5.5
breast (two)	roasting, stewing	1.5	2.5
middle neck	stewing	2	3
scrag end	stewing, broth	0.5	1
best end rack (two)	roasting, grilling, frying	2	3
saddle	roasting, grilling, frying	3.5	5.5
kidneys	grilling, sauté		
heart	braising		
liver	frying		
sweetbreads	braising, frying		
tongue	braising, boiling		

Table 7.3 Common cooking methods

Joint	Methods of cookery
Saddle	roast, pot roast (poêlé)
Loin	roast
Fillet	grill, fry
Loin chop	grill, fry, stew, braise
Chump chop	grill, fry, stew, braise
Kidney	grill, sauté

Order of dissection of a carcass

1 Remove the shoulders.
2 Remove the breasts.
3 Remove the middle neck and scrag.
4 Remove the legs.
5 Divide the saddle from the best end.

Preparing a shoulder

- **Boning:** remove the blade bone and upper arm bone, tie with string; the shoulder may be stuffed (see recipe 4) before tying.
- **Cutting for stews:** bone out, cut into even 25–50 g pieces.
- **For roasting:** remove the pelvic or aitchbone; clean and trim the knucklebone so as to leave approximately 3 cm of clean bone; trim off excess fat and tie with string if necessary.

Tying butcher's knots
http://bit.ly/y1VCTX

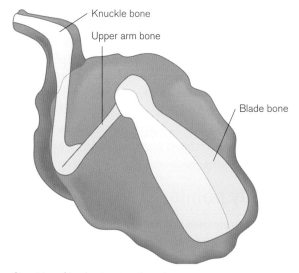

Knuckle bone
Upper arm bone
Blade bone

Shoulder of lamb, showing three bones

Preparing breasts of lamb

- Remove excess fat and skin.
- **For roasting:** bone, stuff and roll, tie with string.
- **For stewing:** cut into even 25–50 g pieces.

Preparing middle neck

- **Stewing:** remove excess fat, excess bone and gristle; cut into even 50 g pieces; this joint, when correctly butchered, can give good uncovered second-class cutlets.

Preparing scrag-end for stewing

- This can be chopped down the centre, the excess bone, fat and gristle removed, and cut into even 50 g pieces, or boned out and cut into pieces.

Preparing a saddle of lamb

- The saddle may be divided as follows: remove the skin, starting from head to tail and from breast to back; split down the centre of the backbone to produce two loins; each loin can be roasted whole, boned and stuffed, or cut into loin and chump chops.
- A full saddle is illustrated below.
- For large banquets it is sometimes found better to remove the chumps and use short saddles.
- Saddles may also be boned and stuffed.

Saddle of lamb

If the saddle is to be roasted:
- skin and remove the kidney
- trim the excess fat and sinew
- cut off the flaps leaving about 15 cm each side so as to meet in the middle under the saddle
- remove the aitch, or pelvic, bone
- score neatly and tie with string
- for presentation the tail may be left on, protected with foil and tied back
- the saddle can also be completely boned, stuffed and tied.

Left to right: rosette, valentine, noisette, Barnsley (double loin) chop

Preparing a loin of lamb

If the loin is to be roasted:
- skin, remove excess fat and sinew, remove the pelvic bone, tie with string.

If the loin is to be boned and stuffed:
- remove the skin, excess fat and sinew
- bone out
- replace the fillet, season and stuff if required, and tie with string.

Preparing lamb chops

- **Loin chops:** Skin the loin, remove the excess fat and sinew, then cut into chops approximately 100–150 g in weight. A first-class loin chop should have a piece of kidney skewered in the centre.
- **Double loin chop (Barnsley chop):** These are cut approximately 2 cm across a saddle on the bone. When trimmed they are secured with a skewer and may include a piece of kidney in the centre of each chop.
- **Chump chops:** These are cut from the chump end of the loin. Cut into approximately 150 g chops and trim where necessary.
- **Noisettes:** This is a cut from a boned-out loin. Cut slantwise into approximately 2 cm thick slices, bat out slightly, and trim into a cutlet shape.
- **Rosettes:** This is a cut from a boned-out loin approximately 2 cm thick. It is shaped round and tied with string.
- **Valentines:** These are cut from the boned loin, approximately 4 cm thick, and then cut in half but only two-thirds of the way through. They are then opened out in a heart shape (like a butterfly steak).

Lamb loin chops

Preparing a best end (rack) of lamb

Preparing best end of lamb for roasting

Remove the bark/skin, working from head to tail and from breast to back. Leave as much fat as possible on the joint

Mark or score the fat, 2 cm from the end of the bones

Score down the middle of the back of each bone, scoring the cartilage

Pull the skin fat and meat from the bone (to bring out the bone ends – this is an alternative to scraping them)

Remove the elastin as shown, then clean the sinew from between the rib bones

Trim the overall length of the bones to two and a half times the length of the nut of meat. Score the fat neatly to approx. 2 mm deep and tie the joint

To make the best end into cutlets, prepare as for roasting, excluding the scoring, and divide evenly between the bones. Alternatively, the cutlets can be cut from the best end and prepared separately.

A single cutlet consists of one bone, and a double cutlet two bones, so a six-bone best end yields six single or three double cutlets.

Lamb cutlets

Carving and serving roast lamb

Roast leg

Holding the bone, carve with a sharp knife at an angle of 45 degrees and take off each slice as it is cut. Continue in this manner along the joint, turning it from side to side as the slices get wider.

Shoulder

To obtain reasonable-sized slices of meat, carve the flesh side, not the skin side, of the joint. Having obtained the slices, carve round the bones. Due to the awkward shape of the bone structure, the shoulder may be boned out, rolled and tied before cooking to facilitate carving.

Roast saddle

● **Carving on the bone:** there are two usual ways of carving the saddle, one is by carving lengthways either side of the backbone, the other by making a deep cut lengthwise either side of the backbone and then slicing across each loin. It is usual to carve the saddle in thick slices.

- **Carving off the bone:** for economical kitchen carving it is often found best to bone the loins out whole, carve into slices, then re-form on the saddle bone.
- The fillets may be left on the saddle or removed; in either case they are carved and served with the rest of the meat.

Roast loin

- **On the bone:** proceed as for the saddle.

- **Boned-out:** cut in slices across the joint; when stuffed, the slices are cut slightly thicker.

Roast best end (rack)

Divide into cutlets by cutting between bones.

Service

All roast joints are served garnished with watercress and a sauceboat of roast gravy separately. When carved, serve a little gravy over the slices as well as a sauceboat of gravy. Mint sauce should be served with roast lamb and redcurrant jelly should be available. For roast mutton, redcurrant jelly and/or onion sauce should be served, with mint sauce available.

Beef

Quality points

- The lean meat should be bright red, with small flecks of white fat (marbled).
- The fat should be firm, brittle in texture, creamy-white in colour and odourless. Older animals and dairy breeds have fat that is usually a deeper yellow colour.

Butchery

A side of beef weighs approximately 180 kg. A whole side is divided between the wing ribs and the fore ribs. The fat around the kidney is called suet.

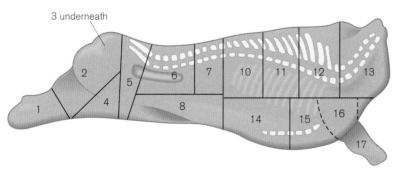

3 underneath

A side of beef

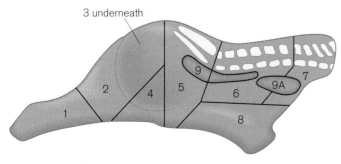

3 underneath

A hindquarter of beef in more detail

1	Shin	10	Fore rib
2	Topside	11	Middle rib
3	Silverside	12	Chuck rib
4	Thick flank	13	Sticking piece
5	Rump	14	Plate
6	Sirloin	15	Brisket
7	Wing ribs	16	Leg of mutton cut
8	Thin flank	17	Shank
9	Fillet		
9A	Fat and kidney		

Dissection of a hindquarter of beef

1 Remove the rump suet and kidney.
2 Remove the thin flank.
3 Divide the loin and rump from the leg (topside, silverside, thick flank and shin).
4 Remove the fillet.
5 Divide the rump from the sirloin.
6 Remove the wing ribs.
7 Remove the shin.
8 Bone out the aitchbone.
9 Divide the leg into the three remaining joints (silverside, topside and thick flank).

Table 7.4 Joints, uses and weights of the hindquarter

Joint	Uses	Approx. weight (kg)
shin	consommé, beef tea, stewing	7
topside	braising, stewing, second-class roasting	10
silverside	pickled in brine then boiled	14
thick flank	braising and stewing	12
rump	grilling and frying as steaks, braised in the piece	10
sirloin	roasting, grilling and frying in steaks	9
wing ribs	roasting, grilling and frying in steaks	5
thin flank	stewing, boiling, sausages	10
fillet	roasting, grilling and frying in steaks	3
fat (suet) and kidney	kidney: pies, puddings, braising; fat: rendered for deep-frying, basting	10

Preparing joints from a hindquarter of beef

- **Shin:** bone out, remove excess sinew; cut or chop as required.
- **Topside:** roasting – remove excess fat, cut into joints and tie with string; braising as for roasting; stewing – cut into dice or steaks as required.
- **Silverside:** remove the thigh bone; this joint is usually kept whole and pickled in brine prior to boning.
- **Thick flank:** as for topside.
- **Rump:** bone out; cut off the first outside slice for pies and puddings. Cut into approximately 1.5 cm

slices for steaks. The point steak – considered the tenderest – is cut from the pointed end of the slice.

Dissection of a forequarter of beef

1 Remove the shank.
2 Divide in half down the centre.
3 Take off the fore ribs.
4 Divide into joints.

Table 7.5 Joints, uses and weights of the forequarter

Joint	Uses	Approx. weight (kg)
fore rib	roasting and braising	8
middle rib	roasting and braising	10
chuck rib	stewing and braising	15
sticking piece	stewing and sausages	9
plate	stewing and sausages	10
brisket	pickled in brine and boiled, pressed beef	19
leg of mutton cut	braising and stewing	11
shank	consommé, beef tea	6

Cuts of beef

The cuts of beef vary considerably, from the very tender fillet steak to the tough brisket or the shin, and there is a greater variety of cuts in beef than for any other type of meat. While their names may vary, there are 14 primary cuts from a side of beef, each one composed of muscle, fat, bone and connective tissue. The least developed muscles, usually from the inner areas, can be roasted or grilled, while leaner and more sinewy meat is cut from the more highly developed external muscles. Exceptions are rib and loin cuts, which come from external but basically immobile muscles.

Knowing where the cuts come from helps to designate the cooking method.

- **Fillet** is taken from the back of the animal; this is the tenderest part, cut from the centre of the sirloin. It is usually cut into steaks and can be fried or grilled.
- **Sirloin** is either roasted as a joint or cut into boneless steaks, more tender than rump, but not as tender as fillet. Sirloin steaks are suitable for grilling or frying.

- **Rump** is a good-quality cut, though it is less tender than fillet or sirloin. It is suitable for roasting, grilling or frying.
- **Rib** is sold on the bone or unboned and rolled. It is suitable for roasting.
- **Topside** is a lean, tender cut from the hindquarters. It is suitable for braising or pot roasting.
- **Silverside** is taken from the hindquarters; this is a cut from the round. It can be pot roasted or used for traditional boiled beef.
- **Flank** is a boneless cut from the mid-to-hindquarters; suitable for braising or stewing.
- **Skirt** is a boneless, rather gristly cut. It is usually stewed or made into mince.
- **Brisket** is a cut from the fore end of the animal, below the shoulder. Quite a fatty joint, it is sold on or off the bone or salted. It is suitable for slow roasting.

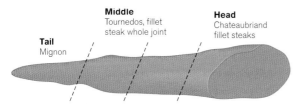

Cuts of fillet of beef

Fillet and loin of beef

Preparing cuts of beef

Sirloin

If the sirloin is to be roasted whole on the bone (*l'aloyau de boeuf*):
- Saw through the chine bone.
- Lift back the covering fat in one piece for approx. 10 cm.

- Trim off the sinew and replace the covering fat.
- Tie with string if necessary.
- Ensure that the fillet has been removed.

To roast the whole sirloin boned out:
- Remove the fillet and bone out the sirloin. Remove the sinew.
- Remove the excess fat and sinew from the boned side.
- This joint may be roasted open, or rolled and tied with string.

Sirloin may be cut into various steaks for grilling or frying:
- **Minute steaks:** cut into 1 cm slices, flatten with a cutlet bat dipped in water, making as thin as possible, then trim.
- **Sirloin steaks (*entrecôte*):** cut into 1 cm slices and trim (approx. weight 150 g).
- **Double sirloin steaks:** cut into 2 cm-thick slices and trim (approx. weight 250–300 g).
- **Porterhouse steaks** are cut including the bone from the rib end of the sirloin.
- **T-bone steaks** are cut from the rump end of the sirloin, including the bone and fillet.

T-bone steaks

Fillet

As a fillet of beef can vary from 2½–4½ kg it follows that there must be considerable variation in the number of steaks obtained from it. In this list of the different fillet steaks, it is assumed that a 3 kg fillet is used.

- **Chateaubriand:** double fillet steak 3–10 cm thick, 2–4 portions. Average weight 300 g–1 kg. Cut from the head of the fillet, trim off all the nerve and leave a little fat on the steak.

- **Fillet steaks:** approximately 4 steaks of 100–150 g each, 1.5–2 cm thick. These are trimmed as for chateaubriand.
- **Tournedos:** approximately 6–8 at 100 g each, 2–4 cm thick. Continue cutting down the fillet. Remove all the nerve and all the fat, and tie each tournedos with string.
- **Tail of fillet** is another possible cut. The tail of a 3 kg fillet will weigh approximately 0.5 kg. Remove all fat and sinew, and slice or mince as required. This cut is useful for dishes like stir fries that need small pieces of tender beef.

The whole fillet may be roasted or pot roasted (*poèlé*). Remove the head and tail of the fillet, leaving an even centre piece from which all the nerve and fat is removed. This may be larded by inserting pieces of fat bacon cut into long strips, with a larding needle.

Wing rib (côte de boeuf)

This joint usually consists of the last three rib bones, which, because of their curved shape, act as a natural trivet and because of its prime quality make it a first-class roasting joint, for hot or cold, particularly when it is to be carved in front of the customer.

To prepare, cut seven-eighths of the way through the spine or chine bone, remove the nerve, saw through the rib bones on the underside 5–10 cm from the end. Tie firmly with string. When the joint is cooked the chine bone is removed to facilitate carving.

Fore ribs and middle ribs from the forequarter are prepared in the same way as wing rib.

Other cuts

Thin flank from the hindquarter: trim off excessive fat and cut or roll as required.

Chuck ribs, sticking piece, brisket, plate, leg of mutton cut and **shank** are all cuts from the forequarter. Bone out, remove excess fat and sinew, and use as required.

Grilling beef

The following cuts may be grilled:
- rump steak
- point steak
- double fillet steak (chateaubriand)
- fillet steak
- tournedos
- porterhouse or T-bone steak
- sirloin steak (entrecôte)
- double sirloin steak
- minute steak
- rib eye steak.

All steaks may be lightly seasoned with salt and pepper, and brushed on both sides with oil. Place on hot, preheated and greased grill bars. Turn halfway through the cooking and brush occasionally with oil. Cook to the degree ordered by the customer.

Serve garnished with watercress and deep-fried potato, and offer a suitable sauce, such as compound butter or sauce béarnaise.

Barbecue cooking

1 **Choice of meat:** some fat is required for flavour, but not too much. Ensure size and thickness are uniform to allow even cooking. Suitable cuts include: T-bone steaks, rib steaks, double lamb chops and noisettes, well-trimmed pork cutlets and steaks.

2 **Seasoning:** add salt and pepper, brush lightly with oil before placing on the barbecue. Take care when using marinades, some may contain glucose, which burns easily. Try marinating with wine and herbs, avoid marinating oils, which may ignite and spoil the barbecue.

3 **Choice and preparation of barbecue:** gas is the preferred choice for temperature control. Allow time to preheat the barbecue: 30 minutes for gas, 1½ hours for charcoal. If cooking on charcoal always wait for the flames to go out and the embers to start glowing before commencing cooking.
   - Secure a layer of tin foil over the barbecue.
   - Wait until the grill bars are hot or the charcoal embers glow.
   - Remove tin foil and brush the grill bars with a firm, long-handled wire brush to remove any unwanted debris.

4 **Cooking:** place the seasoned and lightly oiled meat at a 45° angle on the barbecue and seal one side. Rotate through another 45° angle, allow to

cook, then turn the meat and repeat the process: this creates attractive markings on the meat. Control the temperature and do not let the meat burn or blacken unnecessarily. Only cook as much meat as required at one time; if left for too long it will dry out and become tough. Use a meat probe to ensure the desired internal temperature is reached (see above). 'Made up' items such as burgers and sausages must be cooked thoroughly to the centre.

5 Serve with fresh crisp vegetables or salads and traditional barbecue dips and sauces.

> Burgers and sausages should be cut open, checked and cooked for longer if necessary. Barbecued food may look well cooked when it isn't. Further advice is available at www.qmscotland.co.uk.

Testing whether beef is cooked

Roast joints

When using a temperature probe, insert it into the part of the joint that was thickest before the food was placed in the oven. The internal temperature reached should be as follows:

- rare meat – 55–60°C
- medium done – 66–71°C
- well done – 78–80°C.

To test without a temperature probe:

- Remove the joint from the oven and place on a plate or dish.

- Firmly press the surface of the meat so that some juice issues.
- Check the colour of the juice: *red* indicates the meat is underdone; *pink* indicates the meat is medium done; *clear* indicates that the meat is cooked through.

Grilled beef

The degrees of cooking for grilled meat are:

- very rare (or blue) – cooked over a fierce heat for a few seconds on each side
- rare – the cooked meat has a reddish tinge
- medium – the cooked meat is slightly pinkish
- well done – thoroughly cooked with no sign of pinkness.

When using a temperature probe, insert it into the part of the meat that was thickest before the food was placed under the grill. The internal temperature reached should be as follows:

- rare – 45–50°C
- medium – 55–60°C
- well done – 75–77°C.

You can also check how well done grilled meat is by using finger pressure. The springiness, or resilience, of the meat, and the amount of blood issuing from it, indicates the degree to which it is cooked. This calls for experience, but if the meat is placed on a plate and tested, then the more underdone the steak, the greater the springiness and the more blood will be shown on the plate.

Veal

Veal is obtained from good-quality carcasses weighing around 100 kg. This quality of veal is required for first-class cookery and is produced from calves slaughtered at between 12 and 24 weeks.

Veal is available all year round.

Quality points

- The flesh should be pale pink in colour and firm in structure – not soft or flabby.
- Cut surfaces should be slightly moist, not dry.

- Bones, in young animals, should be pinkish white, porous and with a degree of blood in their structure.
- The fat should be firm and pinkish white.
- The kidney should be firm and well covered with fat.

Where applicable, when offering veal on a menu, give the origin and breed of the veal. (For further information visit www.qmscotland.co.uk.)

The veal carcass

The average weight of English or Dutch milk-fed veal calves is 18 kg. The joints of veal are shown in the diagram and Table 7.6.

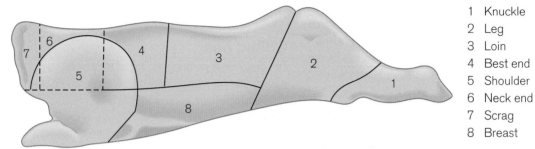

A side of veal

1 Knuckle
2 Leg
3 Loin
4 Best end
5 Shoulder
6 Neck end
7 Scrag
8 Breast

Table 7.6 Uses and weights of veal joints and offal

Joint	Uses	Approx. weight (kg)
knuckle	osso buco, sauté, stock	2
leg	roasting, braising, escalopes, sauté	5
loin	roasting, frying, grilling	3.5
best end	roasting, frying, grilling	3
shoulder	braising, stewing	5
neck end	stewing, sauté	2.5
scrag	stewing, stock	1.5
breast	stewing, roasting	2.5
kidneys	stewing (pies and puddings), sauté	–
liver	frying	–
sweetbreads	braising, frying	–
head	boiling, soup	4
brains	boiling, frying	–
bones	stock	–

The order of dissection for a veal carcass is as follows:

1 Remove the shoulders.
2 Remove the breast.
3 Take off the leg.
4 Divide the loin and best end from the scrag and neck end.
5 Divide the loin from the best end.

Table 7.7 Joints of the leg

Cuts	Weight	Proportion	Uses	Corresponding joint in beef
cushion or nut	2.75 kg	15%	escalopes, roasting, braising, sauté	topside
under cushion or under nut	3 kg	17%	escalopes, roasting, braising, sauté	silverside
thick flank	2.5 kg	14%	escalopes, roasting, braising, sauté	thick flank
knuckle (whole)	2.5 kg	14%	osso buco, sauté	
bones (thigh and aitch)	2.5 kg	14%	stock, jus-lié, sauces	
usable trimmings	2 kg	11%	pies, stewing	

Dissecting a leg of veal

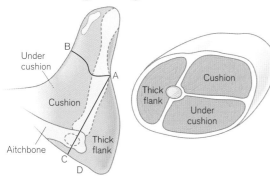

Dissection of a leg of veal

1 Remove the knuckle by dividing the knee joint (A) and cut through the meat away from the cushion line (A–B).
2 Remove the aitchbone (C) at thick end of the leg, separating it at the ball and socket joint.
3 Remove all the outside skin and fat, thus exposing the natural seams. It will now be seen that the thigh bone divides the meat into two-thirds and one-third (thick flank).
4 Stand the leg on the thick flank with point D uppermost. Divide the cushion from the under cushion, following the natural seam, using the hand and the point of a knife. Having reached the thigh bone, remove it completely.
5 When the boned leg falls open, the three joints can easily be seen joined only by membrane. Separate and trim the cushion, removing the loose flap of meat.
6 Trim the under cushion, removing the layer of thick gristle. Separate into three small joints through the natural seams. It will be seen that one of these will correspond with the round in silverside of beef.
7 Trim the thick flank by laying it on its round side and making a cut along the length about 2.5 cm deep. A seam is reached and the two trimmings can be removed.

The anticipated yield of escalopes from this size of leg would be 62.5 kg – that is, 55 kg x 100 g or 73 kg x 80 g.

Preparing joints and cuts of veal

Shin

- For stewing (on the bone) (*osso buco*): cut and saw into 2–4 cm thick slices through the knuckle.
- For sauté: bone out and trim, then cut into even 25 g pieces.

Leg

- For raising or roasting whole: remove the aitchbone, clean and trim 4 cm off the knuckle bone. Trim off the excess sinew.
- To braise or roast the nut: remove all the sinew; if there is insufficient fat on the joint then bard thinly and secure with string.
- Escalopes: remove all the sinew, cut into large 50–75 g slices against the grain and bat out thinly.
- For sauté: remove all the sinew and cut into 25 g pieces.

Veal escalopes

Loin and best end

- For roasting: bone out and trim the flap, roll out and secure with string. This joint may be stuffed before rolling.
- For frying: trim and cut into cutlets.

Shoulder

- For braising: bone out as for lamb; usually stuffed.
- For stewing: bone out, remove all the sinew and cut into 25 g pieces.

Neck end and scrag

For stewing or sauté: bone out and remove all the sinew; cut into approximately 25 g pieces.

Breast

- For stewing: as for neck end.
- For roasting: bone out, season, stuff and roll up, then tie with string.

Pork

The keeping quality of pork is less than that of other meat; therefore it must be handled, prepared and cooked with great care. Pork should always be well cooked, reaching at least 75°C in the centre.

Where applicable, name the origin and breed of the pork (e.g. Gloucester Old Spot, Tamworth) on the menu. For further information visit www.qmscotland.co.uk.

Quality points

- Lean flesh should be pale pink, firm and of a fine texture.
- The fat should be white, firm, smooth and not excessive.
- Bones should be small, fine and pinkish.
- The skin or rind should be smooth.

The pork carcass

The cuts of pork are shown below and their uses in Table 7.8.

Table 7.8 Cuts, uses and weights of pork

Joint	Uses	Approx. weight (kg)
leg	roasting, boiling	5
loin	roasting, frying, grilling	6
spare rib	roasting, pies	1.5
belly	pickling, boiling, stuffed, rolled and roasted	2
shoulder	roasting, sausages, pies	3
head (whole)	brawn	4
trotters	grilling, boiling	
kidneys	sauté, grilling	
liver	frying, pâté	

When 5–6 weeks old a piglet is known as a sucking or suckling pig. Its weight is then between 5 and 10 kg.

The order of dissection for a pig carcass is:

1 Remove the head.
2 Remove the trotters.
3 Remove the leg.
4 Remove the shoulder.
5 Remove the spare ribs.
6 Divide the loin from the belly.

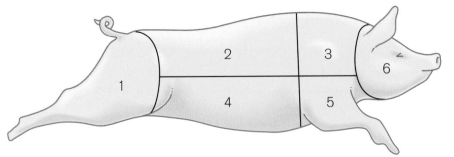

1 Leg
2 Loin
3 Spare rib
4 Belly
5 Shoulder
6 Head

Pig carcass dissection

Preparing joints and cuts of pork

Leg
- **For roasting:** remove the pelvic or aitchbone, trim and score the rind neatly – that is, with a sharp-pointed knife, make a series of 3 mm deep incisions approximately 2 cm apart all over the skin of the joint; trim and clean the knuckle bone.
- **For boiling:** it is usual to pickle the joint either by rubbing dry salt and saltpetre (potassium nitrate) into the meat or by soaking in a brine solution (see recipe 40); then remove the pelvic bone, trim and secure with string if necessary.

Loin
- **For roasting (on the bone):** saw down the chine bone in order to facilitate carving; trim the excess fat and sinew and score the rind in the direction that the joint will be carved; season and secure with string.
- **For roasting (boned out):** remove the fillets and bone out carefully; trim off the excess fat and sinew, score the rind and neaten the flap, season, replace the filet mignon, roll up and secure the string; this joint is sometimes stuffed.

Chops for grilling or frying:
- **Chops for grilling or frying:** remove the skin, excess fat and sinew, then cut and saw or chop through the loin in approximately 1 cm slices; remove the excess bone and trim neatly.

Spare rib
- **For roasting:** remove the excess fat, bone and sinew, and trim neatly.
- **For pies:** remove the excess fat and sinew, bone out and cut as required.

Belly
- Remove all the small rib bones, season with salt, pepper and chopped sage, roll and secure with string. This joint may be stuffed.

Shoulder
- **For roasting:** the shoulder is usually boned out, the excess fat and sinew removed, seasoned, scored and rolled with string; it may be stuffed and can also be divided into two smaller joints.
- **For sausages or pies:** skin, bone out and remove the excess fat and sinew; cut into even pieces or mince.

Boned leg of pork

Loin of pork

Pork chops

249

Bacon

Bacon is the cured flesh of a bacon-weight pig that is specifically reared for bacon – because its shape and size yield economic bacon joints. Bacon is cured either by dry salting and then smoking or by soaking in brine followed by smoking. Green bacon is brine-cured but not smoked; it has a milder flavour but does not keep for as long as smoked bacon.

Depending on the degree of salting during the curing process, bacon joints may or may not require soaking in cold water before being cooked.

Do not confuse ham with gammon.

Quality points

- There should be no sign of stickiness.
- There should be a pleasant smell.
- The rind should be thin, smooth and free from wrinkles.
- The fat should be white, smooth and not excessive in proportion to the lean meat.
- The lean meat should be a deep-pink colour and firm.

Preparing joints and cuts

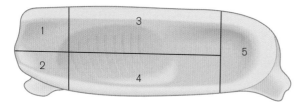

1 Collar
2 Hock
3 Back
4 Streaky
5 Gammon

Grilling cuts

Gammon

Cuts of bacon

Table 7.9 Cuts, uses and weights of bacon

Joint	Uses	Approx. weight (kg)
collar	boiling, grilling	4.5
hock	boiling, grilling	4.5
back	grilling, frying	9
streaky	grilling, frying	4.5
gammon	boiling, grilling, frying	7.5

Collar

- **For boiling:** remove bone (if any) and tie with string.
- **Rashers for grilling:** remove the rind, trim off the outside surface and cut into thin slices (rashers), across the joint.

Hock

Leave whole or bone out and secure with string. The hock is usually boiled.

Back and streaky bacon

- **Rashers for grilling:** remove all bones and rind, and cut into thin rashers.
- **Rashers or chops for frying:** remove the rind, trim off the outside surface, and cut into rashers or chops of the required thickness.

Gammon

Cut fairly thick slices from the middle of the gammon. Trim them and remove the rind. Slices of gammon are usually grilled or fried.

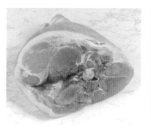

Gammon

Gammon steaks

Offal and other edible parts of the carcass

Offal is the name given to the edible parts taken from the inside of a carcass of meat: liver, kidneys, heart and sweetbreads. Tripe, brains, tongue, head and oxtail are also sometimes included under this term.

Fresh offal (unfrozen) should be purchased as required and can be refrigerated under hygienic conditions at a temperature of 1–4°C. Frozen offal must be kept in a deep freeze at −18°C or below, and defrosted in a refrigerator as required.

Liver

- **Calf's liver** is considered the best in terms of tenderness and flavour. It is also the most expensive.
- **Lamb's liver** is mild in flavour, light in colour and tender.
- **Sheep's liver**, being from an older animal, is firmer in substance, deeper in colour and has a stronger flavour.
- **Ox** or **beef liver** is the cheapest and, if taken from an older animal, can be coarse in texture and strong in flavour. It is usually braised.
- **Pig's liver** has a strong, full flavour and is used mainly for pâté recipes.

Quality points

- Liver should look fresh, moist and smooth, with a pleasant colour and no unpleasant smell.
- Liver should not be dry or contain an excessive number of tubes.

Liver is a good source of protein and iron, and also contains vitamins A and D. It is low in fat.

To prepare a liver:
- Remove the skin if possible.
- Remove the gristle and tubes.
- Cut into thin slices on the slant.

Kidneys

- **Lamb's kidneys** are light in colour, delicate in flavour and ideal for grilling and frying.

- **Sheep's kidneys** are darker in colour and stronger in flavour.
- **Calf's kidneys** are light in colour, delicate in flavour and used in a variety of dishes.
- **Ox kidney** is dark in colour, strong in flavour, and is either braised or used in pies and puddings (mixed with beef).
- **Pig's kidneys** are smooth, long and flat and have a strong flavour.

Quality points

- Suet – the saturated fat in which kidneys are encased – should be left on, otherwise the kidneys will dry out. The suet should be removed when kidneys are being prepared for cooking.
- Both suet and kidneys should be moist and have no unpleasant smell.

The nutritional value of kidney is similar to that of liver.

To prepare kidneys, skin them and remove the fat and gristle. Then cut as required:
- **For grilling:** split the kidney three-quarters of the way through, lengthwise. Cut out and discard the gristle. Skewer.
- **For sauté:** cut slantways. (A lamb's liver will yield 6–8 pieces.)
- **For calves' or pigs' kidneys**: cut down the middle lengthwise. Remove the sinew. Cut into thin slices or neat dice.

Veal kidneys

Hearts

- **Lamb's hearts** are small and light; they are normally served whole.
- **Sheep's hearts** are dark and solid; they can be dry and tough unless cooked carefully.
- **Ox** or **beef hearts** are dark coloured and solid, and tend to be dry and tough.
- **Calf's hearts**, coming from a younger animal, are lighter in colour and more tender.

Most hearts need slow braising to tenderise them.

Quality points

- Hearts should not be too fatty and should not contain too many tubes.
- When cut they should be moist, not sticky, and with no unpleasant smell.

Hearts are a good source of protein, which is needed for growth and repair of the body.

Before cooking, remove the arterial tubes and excess fat.

Sweetbreads

Sweetbreads are the pancreas gland (heart bread) and thymus gland (neck bread). The heart bread is round, plump and of better quality than the neck bread, which is long and uneven in shape. Calf's heart bread, considered the best, weighs up to 600 g, lamb's heart bread up to 100 g.

Quality points

- Heart and neck breads should be fleshy and of good size.
- They should be creamy-white in colour and have no unpleasant smell.

Sweetbreads are an easily digested source of protein, which makes them valuable for use in invalid diets.

To prepare sweetbreads:

- Soak in cold salted water for 2–3 hours to remove blood, which would darken the sweetbreads during cooking. Use several changes of water for calves' sweetbreads.
- Wash well, blanch, trim and refresh.

- For calves' sweetbreads, peel off the membrane and connective tissue.
- The sweetbreads can then be pressed between two trays with a weight on top, and refrigerated.

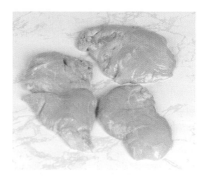

Veal sweetbreads

Tripe

Tripe is the stomach lining or white muscle of the ox, consisting of the rumen or paunch and the honeycomb tripe (considered the best); sheep tripe, darker in colour, is obtainable in some areas.

Tripe should be fresh, with no signs of stickiness or unpleasant smell.

Tripe contains protein, is low in fat and high in calcium.

To prepare tripe, wash it well and soak in cold water, then cut into even pieces. Boil or simmer until tender.

Brains

Calves' brains are those normally used. They must be fresh and have no unpleasant smell. They are a good source of protein with trace elements.

To prepare the brains:

- Using a chopper or saw, remove the top of the skull, making certain that the opening is large enough to remove the brain undamaged.
- Soak the brain in running cold water, then remove the membrane, or skin, and wash well to remove all blood.
- Keep in cold salted water until required.

Tongues

Ox, lamb and sheep tongues are those most used in cooking. Ox tongues are usually salted then soaked before being cooked. Lamb tongues are cooked fresh.

Quality points

- Tongues must be fresh and have no unpleasant smell.
- There should not be an excess of waste at the root end.

To prepare tongues for cooking:
- Remove the bone and gristle from the throat end.
- Soak in cold water for 2–4 hours. If salted, soak for 3–4 hours.

Heads

Sheep's heads can be used for stock and calves' heads for speciality dishes (e.g. calf's head vinaigrette).

Pigs' heads are usually boned and pressed by specialist pork butchers to make a cold meat called brawn.

Heads should be fresh, not sticky, well fleshed and free from any unpleasant smell.

To prepare a calf's head:
- Bone out by making a deep incision down the middle of the head to the nostrils.
- Follow the bone carefully and remove all the flesh in one piece.
- Lastly, remove the tongue.
- Wash the flesh well and keep covered in acidulated water.
- Wash off, blanch and refresh.
- Cut into 2–5 cm squares.
- Cut off the ears and trim the inside of the cheek.

Oxtail

Oxtails usually weigh 1.5–2 kg; they should be lean with not too much fat. There should be no sign of stickiness and no unpleasant smell.

To prepare the tail, cut between the natural joints, then trim off excess fat. The large pieces may be split in two.

Suet

Suet is the fat that surrounds the kidneys. Beef suet should be creamy-white, brittle and dry. Other meat fat should be fresh, not sticky, and with no unpleasant smell.

Bone marrow

Marrow is obtained from the bones of the leg of beef. It should be of good size, firm, creamy-white and odourless. Sliced, poached marrow may be used as a garnish for some meat dishes and savouries.

Bones

Bones must be fresh, not sticky, with no unpleasant smell and preferably meaty as they are used for stock, the foundation for so many preparations.

Pigs' trotters

To prepare trotters, boil in water for a few minutes, scrape with the back of a knife to remove the hairs, wash off in cold water and split in half.

Table 7.10 Uses of beef offal

Offal	Uses
tongue	pickled in brine, boiling, braising
heart	braising
liver	braising, frying
kidney	stewing, soup
sweetbread	braising, frying
tripe	boiling, braising
tail	braising, soup
suet	suet paste and stuffing, or rendered down for first-class dripping
bones	beef stocks

1 Grilled lamb cutlets
(côtelettes d'agneau grillées)

lamb  grilling, griddling

energy	kcal	fat	sat fat	carb	sugar	protein	fibre	sodium
1493 KJ	357 kcal	20.7 g	9.8 g	0.0 g	0.0 g	42.8 g	0.0 g	0.1 g

1 Season the cutlets lightly with salt and mill pepper.

2 Brush with oil or fat.

3 If the grill is heated from below, place the prepared cutlet on the greased, preheated bars. Cook for approximately 5 minutes, turn and complete the cooking.

4 If using a salamander, place the cutlets on a greased tray, cook for approximately 5 minutes, turn and complete the cooking.

5 Serve dressed, garnished with a deep-fried potato and watercress. A compound butter (e.g. parsley, herb or garlic) may also be served.

6 Each cutlet bone may be capped with a cutlet frill.

Healthy eating tip

When served with boiled new potatoes and boiled or steamed vegetables, the plate of food becomes more 'balanced'.

2 Mixed grill

energy	kcal	fat	sat fat	carb	sugar	protein	fibre	*
2050 KJ	488 kcal	40.8 g	19.3 g	0.0 g	0.0 g	30.4 g	0.0 g	

Portions ❯	4	10
sausages	4	10
lamb cutlets	4	10
kidneys	4	10
tomatoes	4	10
mushrooms	4	10
streaky bacon, rashers	4	10
deep-fried potato, to serve		
watercress, to serve		
parsley butter, to serve		

1 Grill in the order listed above.
2 Dress neatly on an oval flat dish or plates.
3 Garnish with deep-fried potato, watercress and a slice of compound butter on each kidney or offered separately.

These are the usually accepted items for a mixed grill, but there are many variations to this list (e.g. steaks, liver, a Welsh rarebit and fried egg).

Key point

The ingredients must be cooked in the order listed, so that they are all fully and evenly cooked at the end.

Healthy eating tip

Add only a small amount of compound butter and serve with plenty of potatoes and vegetables.

* 1 portion (2 cutlets). With deep-fried potatoes, parsley and watercress, 1 portion provides: 3050 kJ/726 kcal energy; 59.2 g fat; 26.6 g sat fat; 20.2 g carb; 2.5 g sugar; 29.5 g protein; 4.9 g fibre

3 Lamb kebabs
(shish kebab)

lamb grilling, griddling, marinating

energy	kcal	fat	sat fat	carb	sugar	protein	fibre	sodium
1544 KJ	372 kcal	25.1 g	9.9 g	7.2 g	5.9 g	29.6 g	2.0 g	0.1 g

The ideal cuts of lamb are the nut of the lean meat of the loin, best end or boned-out meat from a young shoulder of lamb.

1 Soak the skewers for an hour before using. Cut the meat into cubes and place them on skewers with squares of green pepper, tomato, onion and bay leaves in between.
2 Sprinkle with chopped thyme and cook over a hot grill.
3 Serve with pilaff rice, or with chickpeas and finely sliced raw onion.

Key point

The pieces of lamb and vegetables must be cut evenly so that they will cook evenly.

Kebabs, a dish of Turkish origin, are pieces of food impaled and cooked on skewers over a grill or barbecue. There are many variations and different flavours can be added by marinating the kebabs in oil, wine, vinegar or lemon juice with spices and herbs for 1–2 hours before cooking. Kebabs can be made using tender cuts, or mince of lamb and beef, pork, liver, kidney, bacon, ham, sausage and chicken, using either the meats individually or combining two or three. Vegetables and fruit can also be added (e.g. onion, apple, pineapple, peppers, tomatoes, aubergine). Kebabs can be made using vegetables exclusively (e.g. peppers, onion, aubergine, tomatoes).
Kebabs are usually served with a pilaff rice **(see** **page 174)**.

Try something different

Variations include:
- Miniature kebabs (one mouthful) can be made, impaled on cocktail sticks, grilled and served as canapés.
- Fish kebabs can be made using a firm fish, such as monkfish or tuna, and marinating in olive oil, lemon or lime juice, chopped fennel or dill, garlic and a dash of Tabasco or Worcester sauce.

Practical Cookery 12th edition

4 Grilled loin or chump chops, or noisettes of lamb

lamb grilling, griddling

energy	kcal	fat	sat fat	carb	sugar	protein	fibre	sodium
1338 KJ	320 kcal	16.1 g	7.4 g	0.0 g	0.0 g	43.8 g	0.0 g	0.1 g

1 Season the chops or noisettes lightly with salt and mill pepper.
2 Brush with oil and place on hot greased grill bars or place on a greased baking tray.
3 Cook quickly for the first 2–3 minutes on each side, in order to seal the pores of the meat.
4 Continue cooking steadily, allowing approximately 12–15 minutes in all.

A compound butter may also be served, and deep-fried potatoes.

Try something different
Variations include sprigs of rosemary or other herbs laid on the chops during the last few minutes of grilling to impart flavour.

5 Lamb satay

lamb  grilling, griddling

energy	kcal	fat	sat fat	carb	sugar	protein	fibre	sodium
1624 KJ	391 kcal	29.3 g	10.2 g	13.3 g	11.7 g	19.6 g	2.4 g	0.7 g

Makes ❯	10	20
lamb fillets or loin of lamb	250 g	500 g
clove of garlic, crushed and chopped	1	3
Thai fish sauce	1 tsp	2 tsp
sweet chilli sauce	1 tbsp	2 tbsp
fresh ginger, grated	1 tsp	2 tsp
lime juice	30 ml	60 ml
peanut butter (coarse)	1 tbsp	2 tbsp
ground cumin	½ tsp	1 tsp
ground turmeric	½ tsp	1 tsp
Sauce		
white vinegar	30 ml	62 ml
caster sugar	1 tbsp	2 tbsp
sweet chilli sauce	3 tsp	1 tbsp
unsalted, roasted peanuts, finely chopped	3 tsp	1 tbsp
fresh coriander leaves, finely chopped	3 tsp	1 tbsp

1 Prepare the lamb, cutting it into thin strips.

2 In a bowl place the garlic, sauces, ginger, lime juice, peanut butter and spices. Mix well.

3 Place the marinade over the lamb and put in refrigerator for 3 hours or overnight.

4 Meanwhile, prepare some bamboo skewers in water for about an hour to prevent scorching.

5 Thread the lamb onto the skewers. Grill the lamb skewers, turning once until cooked and nicely coloured.

6 Prepare the sauce. Place the vinegar and sugar in a small pan, stir until the sugar has dissolved. Bring to the boil, simmer for 2 minutes. Stir in the remaining ingredients.

7 Serve the lamb on a suitable platter on banana leaves (optional) with the sauce in a bowl in the centre.

6 Noisettes of lamb or fillet of lamb sauté

(noisettes d'agneau sautées)

lamb shallow frying, sauté

energy	kcal	fat	sat fat	carb	sugar	protein	fibre	sodium
1325 KJ	318 kcal	22.3 g	8.5 g	0.0 g	0.0 g	29.4 g	0.0 g	0.1 g

Allow two noisettes per portion.

1 Season and shallow-fry the lamb on both sides in a sauté pan.
2 Serve with the appropriate garnish (see below) and sauce. Unless specifically stated, a *jus-lié* or demi-glace should be served.

Suitable garnishes

- Tomatoes filled with jardinière of vegetables and château potatoes.
- Balls of cauliflower mornay and château potatoes.
- Artichoke bottoms filled with carrot balls and noisette potatoes.
- Artichoke bottoms filled with asparagus heads and noisette potatoes.
- Artichoke bottoms filled with peas and cocotte potatoes.

Fillet of lamb should be trimmed of fat and sinew before cooking.

Healthy eating tips
- Trim off as much fat as possible before cooking.
- Add starchy carbohydrate and vegetables to proportionally reduce the amount of fat.

7 Lamb rosettes with thyme and blueberries

lamb, fruit, herbs shallow frying, sauté

Portions ⟩	4	10
lamb rosettes	8	20
olive oil	2 tbsp	5 tbsp
red wine	250 ml	625 ml
fresh thyme	4 sprigs	10 sprigs
lamb stock	250 ml	625 ml
blueberries	200 g	500 g
salt, pepper		

1 Shallow-fry the rosettes in olive oil.
2 Deglaze the pan with wine, then add the thyme.
3 Add the lamb stock and reduce to a sauce consistency.
4 Add the blueberries, then season.
5 Serve the lamb with the blueberries and the sauce.

Risotto makes a suitable accompaniment.

8 Noisettes of lamb with baby ratatouille

lamb, vegetable fruits, bulbs shallow frying, sauté, tying

energy	kcal	fat	sat fat	carb	sugar	protein	fibre
1666 KJ	400 kcal	29.3 g	9.3 g	3.8 g	3.2 g	30.7 g	2.4 g

Portions ›	4	10
noisettes of lamb	8	20
baby ratatouille (see recipe on page 394 but cut the vegetables into 0.75 cm dice)	400 g	1 kg

1 Prepare the noisettes of lamb.
2 Shallow-fry the seasoned noisettes in vegetable oil on both sides until just pink.
3 Drain on kitchen paper. Serve on a bed of baby ratatouille.
4 Garnish with fresh basil or some fresh chopped mixed herbs, parsley, chervil, tarragon, etc.

9 Lamb valentine steaks with fresh pea hummus

lamb, seeds and pods  shallow frying, sauté, cold preparation

Portions ›	4	10
lamb steaks	8	20
olive oil	2 tbsp	5 tbsp
For the hummus		
peas	600 g	1.5 kg
cloves of garlic, crushed and chopped	4	10
ground cumin	1 tsp	2½ tsp
lemon juice	½ tsp	1 tsp
mint leaves, chopped	1 tsp	2 tsp
extra virgin olive oil	10 tbsp	25 tbsp
tahini paste	2 tbsp	5 tbsp

1 Prepare the valentine steaks.
2 To make the hummus, cook the peas in boiling salted water, drain well. Purée in a food processor with the garlic, cumin, lemon juice, mint, extra virgin olive oil and tahini paste.
3 Lightly season the valentines. Shallow-fry in olive oil or vegetable oil until golden brown and slightly pink.
4 Serve on individual plates on a bed of pea hummus, garnished with fresh mint. Alternatively, serve the steaks on plates with the pea hummus piped as a rosette, and a circle of lamb jus around.

10 Samosas

lamb, potatoes deep frying

energy	kcal	fat	sat fat	carb	sugar	protein	fibre	sodium *
2740 KJ	682 kcal	43.9 g	15.2 g	49.5 g	2.0 g	25.5 g	3.0 g	0.5 g

Samosa pastry

Makes ›	40–60 samosas	100–150 samosas
short pastry made from ghee fat and fairly strong flour (as the dough should be fairly elastic)	400 g	1 kg

1 Take a small piece of dough, roll into a ball 2 cm in diameter. Keep the rest of the dough covered with either a wet cloth, clingfilm or plastic, otherwise a skin will form on the dough.

2 Roll the ball into a circle about 9 cm round on a lightly floured surface. Cut the circle in half.

3 Moisten the straight edge with eggwash or water.

4 Shape the semicircle into a cone. Fill the cone with approximately 1½ tsp of filling, moisten the top edges with beaten egg white, flour paste or eggwash and press together well.

5 The samosas may be made in advance, covered with clingfilm or plastic, and refrigerated before being deep-fried.

6 Deep-fry at 180°C until golden brown; remove from fryer and drain well.

7 Serve on a suitable dish. Samosas can be garnished with coriander leaves and served with chutney.

> Samosas can also be made using filo pastry. Serve two per portion as a starter, or one as an accompaniment.

Filling 1: potato

Portions ›	4	10
potatoes, peeled	200 g	500 g
vegetable oil	1½ tsp	3¾ tsp
black mustard seeds	½ tsp	1¼ tsp
onions, finely chopped	50 g	125 g
fresh ginger, finely chopped	12 g	30 g
fennel seeds	1 tsp	2½ tsp
cumin seeds	¼ tsp	1 tsp
turmeric	¼ tsp	1 tsp
frozen peas	75 g	187 g
salt, to taste		
water	2½ tsp	6¼ tsp
fresh coriander, finely chopped	1 tsp	2½ tsp
garam masala	½ tsp	2½ tsp
pinch of cayenne pepper		

1 Cut the potatoes into 0.5 cm dice; cook in water until only just cooked.

2 Heat the oil in a suitable pan, add the mustard seeds and cook until they pop.

3 Add the onions and ginger. Fry for 7–8 minutes, stirring continuously until golden brown.

4 Stir in the fennel, cumin and turmeric, add the potatoes, peas, salt and water.

5 Reduce to a low heat, cover the pan and cook for 5 minutes.

6 Stir in the coriander; cook for a further 5 minutes.

7 Remove from the heat, stir in the garam masala and the cayenne seasoning.

8 Remove from the pan, place into a suitable bowl to cool before using.

Healthy eating tips
- Use the minimum amount of salt.
- Use a small amount of unsaturated oil to fry the mustard seeds and the onion.
- Skim any fat from the finished dish.

Filling 2: lamb

Portions ⟩	4	10
saffron	½ tsp	1¼ tsp
boiling water	2½ tsp	6¼ tsp
vegetable oil	3 tsp	7½ tsp
fresh ginger, finely chopped	12 g	30 g
cloves of garlic, crushed and chopped	2	5
onions, finely chopped	50 g	125 g
salt, to taste		
lean lamb, minced	400 g	1 kg
pinch of cayenne pepper		
garam masala	1 tsp	2½ tsp

1 Infuse the saffron in the boiling water; allow to stand for 10 minutes.
2 Heat the vegetable oil in a suitable pan. Add the ginger, garlic, onions and salt, stirring continuously. Fry for 7–8 minutes, until the onions are soft and golden brown.
3 Stir in the lamb, add the saffron with the water. Cook, stirring the lamb until it is cooked.
4 Add the cayenne and garam masala, reduce the heat and allow to cook gently for a further 10 minutes.
5 The mixture should be fairly tight with very little moisture.
6 Transfer to a bowl and allow to cool before using.

Prepare the pastry, filling and eggwash

Form the pastry into a semicircle and eggwash the straight edge

Shape the pastry into a cone

Fill the cone

Seal the top

Samosas before and after frying

* Using short pastry and lamb filling

Healthy eating tips
- No added salt is necessary.
- Use a small amount of unsaturated oil to fry the onions and lamb.
- Drain off the excess fat before adding the water.

11 Braised lamb chump chops

(chops d'agneau braisées)

energy	kcal	fat	sat fat	carb	sugar	protein	fibre
1452 KJ	349 kcal	23.4 g	10.8 g	9.4 g	3.8 g	25.8 g	1.2 g

Portions >	4	10
chump chops	4	10
salt, pepper		
onion, diced	100 g	250 g
carrot, diced	100 g	250 g
flour (white or wholemeal)	25 g	60 g
tomato purée	1 level tsp	2½ level tsp
brown stock	500 ml	1.25 litre
bouquet garni		
clove of garlic, optional	1	2
parsley, chopped		

1 Fry the seasoned chops in a sauté pan quickly on both sides in hot fat.
2 When turning the chops, add the mirepoix (onion and carrot).
3 Draw aside and drain off the surplus fat.
4 Add the flour and mix in, singe in the oven or on top of the stove. (Alternatively, use flour that has been browned in the oven.)
5 Add the tomato purée and the hot stock.
6 Stir with a wooden spoon until thoroughly mixed.
7 Add the bouquet garni and garlic, season, skim and allow to simmer; cover with a lid.
8 Cook (preferably in the oven), skimming off all fat and scum.
9 When cooked, transfer the chops to a clean pan.
10 Correct the seasoning and consistency of the sauce.
11 Skim off any fat and pass the sauce through a fine strainer over the chops.
12 Serve sprinkled with chopped parsley.

Lamb steaks cut from the chump end of the leg can also be cooked in this way.

Healthy eating tips
- Trim fat from the chops before frying.
- Use the minimum amount of salt.
- Lightly oil the pan with an unsaturated oil to fry the chops. Drain off any excess fat after the frying is complete.
- Serve with a large portion of vegetables.

Try something different
Variations include the following additions after the sauce has been strained:
- cooked pulse beans (e.g. haricot, butter, flageolet)
- cooked neatly cut vegetables (e.g. carrots, turnips, swede, green beans, peas).

12 Braised lamb shanks

Portions ❯	4	10
lamb shanks	4	10
olive oil for braising (to fill casserole about 1 cm deep)		
leeks, roughly chopped	1	2
celery sticks	2	5
carrots, roughly chopped	2	5
onions, roughly chopped	2	5
garlic head, broken into cloves (unpeeled)	1	2
bay leaf	1	3
thyme sprig	1	2
rosemary sprig	1	2
red wine	375 ml	1 litre
chicken stock	600 ml	1.5 litres

1 Take a casserole (or any oven-proof dish) and place on the hob over a high heat. Pour in the olive oil and, when hot, add the lamb shanks, turning occasionally until brown.

2 Once browned, remove the lamb from the pot and tip in the chopped leek, celery, carrot, onion and garlic cloves. Stir them all together and add the bay leaf, thyme and rosemary. These ingredients will all add flavour to the dish but won't be served at the end.

3 Once the vegetables are lightly browned, place the lamb back into the pot, allowing it to rest on top of the vegetables.

4 Pour in the red wine and chicken stock, and bring to the boil.

5 Cover the pot with a lid or kitchen foil, and place in the oven at 150°C to braise for 2 hours 30 minutes, or up to 5 hours depending on the amount of lamb you use. When the meat is cooked, the bone can easily be turned out of the meat (if you would like to present the lamb on the bone, only give it a small turn to check if the lamb is ready, as it will be difficult to re-insert the bone once removed).

6 Pass the cooking stock through a fine sieve and reduce to the correct consistency (coats the back of a spoon).

7 Serve the lamb shanks with the cooking juices poured over the top.

The lamb can be served with mashed potato and roast vegetables.

13 Hot pot of lamb or mutton

lamb, mutton shallow frying, braising

energy	kcal	fat	sat fat	carb	sugar	protein	fibre	*
1505 KJ	360 kcal	17.0 g	6.4 g	22.0 g	1.8 g	29.0 g	2.5 g	

Portions ⟩	4	10
stewing lamb (e.g. neck or shoulder)	500 g	1.25 kg
salt, pepper		
onions, thinly sliced	100 g	250 g
potatoes, thinly sliced	400 g	1.25 kg
brown stock	1 litre	2.5 litres
oil (optional)	25 g	60 g
parsley, chopped		

1 Trim the meat and cut into even pieces.
2 Place in a deep earthenware dish. Season with salt and pepper.
3 Lightly sauté the onions in the oil, if desired. Mix the onion and approx. three-quarters of the potatoes (thinly sliced) together.
4 Season and place on top of the meat; pour over stock to three-quarters of the way up the dish.
5 Neatly arrange an overlapping layer of the remaining potatoes on top, sliced about 2 mm thick.
6 Thoroughly clean the edges of the dish and place to cook in a hot oven at 230–250°C until lightly coloured.
7 Reduce the heat and continue cooking for approximately 1½–2 hours.
8 Press the potatoes down occasionally during cooking.

9 Serve with the potatoes brushed with butter or margarine and sprinkle with the chopped parsley.

Neck chops or neck fillet make a succulent dish.

Key point

When the dish is ready, the top layer of potatoes should be golden brown.

Try something different

Variations include:
- using leek in place of onion
- adding 200 g lambs' kidneys
- quickly frying off the meat and sweating the onions before putting in the pot
- adding 100–200 g sliced mushrooms
- adding a small tin of baked beans, or a layer of thickly sliced tomatoes before adding the potatoes
- using sausages in place of lamb.

Chop the lamb into even-sized pieces

Layer the potatoes over the lamb

Pour over the stock

* Using sunflower oil

14 Brown lamb or mutton stew
(navarin d'agneau)

lamb shallow frying, boiling, stewing

energy	kcal	fat	sat fat	carb	sugar	protein	fibre	*
1320 KJ	314 kcal	18.7 g	6.2 g	9.4 g	3.2 g	27.9 g	1.3 g	

Portions ⟩	4	10
stewing lamb	500 g	1.5 kg
oil	2 tbsp	5 tbsp
salt, pepper		
carrot, chopped	100 g	250 g
onion, chopped	100 g	250 g
clove of garlic (if desired)	1	3
flour (white or wholemeal)	25 g	60 g
tomato purée	1 level tbsp	2¼ level tbsp
brown stock (mutton stock or water)	500 g	1.25 litre
bouquet garni		
parsley, chopped, to serve		

Making brown lamb stew
http://bit.ly/y9YRJI

1 Trim the meat and cut into even pieces.
2 Partly fry off the seasoned meat in the oil, then add the carrot, onion and garlic, and continue frying.
3 Drain off the surplus fat, add the flour and mix.
4 Add the tomato purée and stir with a wooden spoon.
5 Add the stock and bouquet garni, bring to the boil, skim and cover with a lid.
6 Simmer gently until cooked (preferably in the oven) for approx. 1½–2 hours, until the lamb is tender.
7 When cooked, place the meat in a clean pan.
8 Correct the sauce and pass it on to the meat.
9 Serve sprinkled with chopped parsley. May also be served with cooked/glazed vegetables.

Fry the lamb, onions and carrots

Mix in the flour

Add the stock and bring to the boil

Healthy eating tips
- Trim off as much fat as possible before frying.
- Use the minimum amount of salt to season the meat.
- Serve with plenty of potatoes and vegetables.

Key points
- Make sure the oil is hot before placing the meat in the pan to brown quickly all over.
- Do not allow the meat to boil in the oil, because this will spoil the flavour and texture.

* Using sunflower oil

15 Irish stew

lamb, potatoes boiling, stewing

energy	kcal	fat	sat fat	carb	sugar	protein	fibre
1339 KJ	319 kcal	11.2 g	5.2 g	26.1 g	5.7 g	30.2 g	5.0 g

Portions ›	4	10
stewing lamb	500 g	1.5 kg
salt, pepper		
bouquet garni		
potatoes	400 g	1 kg
onions	100 g	250 g
celery	100 g	250 g
savoy cabbage	100 g	250 g
leeks	100 g	250 g
button onions	100 g	250 g
parsley, chopped		

1 Trim the meat and cut into even pieces. Blanch and refresh.
2 Place in a shallow saucepan, cover with water, bring to the boil, season with salt and skim. If tough meat is being used, allow ½–1 hour stewing time before adding any vegetables.
3 Add the bouquet garni. Turn the potatoes into barrel shapes.
4 Cut the potato trimmings, onions, celery, cabbage and leeks into small neat pieces and add to the meat; simmer for 30 minutes.
5 Add the button onions and simmer for a further 30 minutes.
6 Add the potatoes and simmer gently with a lid on the pan until cooked.
7 Correct the seasoning and skim off all fat.
8 Serve sprinkled with chopped parsley.

Key point
Keep the meat and vegetables covered with liquid during cooking, to keep the dish consistent and tasty.

Try something different
Alternatively, a more modern approach is to cook the meat for 1½–2 hours until almost tender, then add the vegetables and cook until all are tender. Optional accompaniments include Worcester sauce and/or pickled red cabbage.

Healthy eating tips
● Trim as much fat as possible from the stewing lamb.
● Use the minimum amount of salt.
● Serve with colourful seasonal vegetables to create a 'healthy' dish.

Ingredients for Irish stew

Boil the meat

Add the vegetables

16 Roast lamb or mutton

energy 1262 KJ	kcal 301 kcal	fat 20.2 g	sat fat 10.5 g	carb 0.0 g	sugar 0.0 g	protein 29.5 g	fibre 0.0 g	*

1 Season the joint lightly with salt and place on a trivet, or on bones, in a roasting tray.

2 Place a little vegetable oil or dripping on top and cook in a hot oven at 230–250°C.

3 Baste frequently. Reduce the heat to 180°C after 20 minutes.

4 Roast for approximately 20 minutes per 0.5 kilos, plus another 20 minutes.

5 To test if cooked, place on a tray and press firmly in order to see if the juices released contain any blood.

6 In general, all joints should be cooked through. If joints are required pink, reduce the cooking time by a quarter. For internal temperatures, see Table 7.1.

7 Allow to stand for approximately 10–15 minutes before carving; if this is not done the meat will tend to shrink and curl.

* Using leg of lamb, 1 portion (113 g lamb)

Allow approximately 150 g meat on the bone per portion (legs, shoulders, saddle or loin rump, best end and breast).
Where applicable, name the origin and breed of the lamb (e.g. Southdown, Shropshire) on the menu. For further information visit www.qmscotland.co.uk.

Healthy eating tips
- Use an unsaturated vegetable oil (e.g. sunflower).
- Make sure the fat is hot so that less will be absorbed during the roasting.
- The lamb will produce additional fat as it roasts.

Try something different
Variations include:
- several peeled cloves of garlic inserted into slashes cut in the flesh of joints before roasting
- a little rosemary sprinkled into boned joints before tying
- sprigs of rosemary placed on roasting joints halfway through cooking
- in small-scale cookery, vegetables (e.g. potatoes, parsnips, onions, carrots), left whole or cut into large pieces, can be roasted in with the meat
- slow cook – roast at 200°C for 30 minutes then reduce temperature to 150°C, basting frequently.

17 Roast leg of lamb with mint, lemon and cumin

lamb roasting

energy	kcal	fat	sat fat	carb	sugar	protein	fibre *
2192 KJ	524 kcal	39.1 g	13.7 g	0.3 g	0.3 g	29.7 g	0.0 g

Portions >	4	10
mint	25 g	60 g
lemons, juice of	2	5
cumin	2 tsp	5 tsp
olive oil	4 tbsp	10 tbsp
leg of lamb	3.5 kg	2 × 3.5 kg

1 Place the mint, lemon juice, cumin and olive oil in a food processor.
2 Rub the mixture into the lamb in a suitable roasting tray.
3 Roast the lamb in the normal way (see recipe 16).
4 Serve on a bed of boulangère potatoes or dauphinoise potatoes and a suitable green vegetable, e.g. leaf spinach with toasted pine nuts, or with a couscous salad.

Ingredients for roast leg of lamb with mint, lemon and cumin

Place the leg of lamb in a roasting tray and rub with the mint and lemon mixture

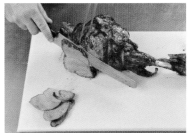

Carving a leg of lamb

Key point
Carefully blend the mint, lemon juice, cumin and olive oil to give maximum flavour.

* Using a 225 g portion of lamb

18 Roast saddle of lamb with rosemary mash

lamb, potatoes 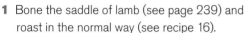 roasting, boiling, boning, tying

energy	kcal	fat	sat fat	carb	sugar	protein	fibre	sodium
3215 KJ	770 kcal	45.7 g	22.1 g	58.9 g	4.7 g	34.4 g	5.6 g	0.2 g

Portions ›	4	10
saddle of lamb, boned		
milk	250 ml	625 ml
rosemary	2 sprigs	5 sprigs
potato, mashed	1.3 kg	3.2 kg

1 Bone the saddle of lamb (see page 239) and roast in the normal way (see recipe 16).
2 Bring the milk to the boil with the rosemary. Remove from the heat, cover and leave to infuse for 10–15 minutes.
3 To make the rosemary mash, prepare a potato purée using the milk infused with rosemary.

19 Saddle of lamb with breadcrumbs and parsley

lamb  roasting, boning

energy	kcal	fat	sat fat	carb	sugar	protein	fibre	sodium
2242 KJ	361 kcal	46.0 g	22.4 g	4.9 g	0.2 g	27.1 g	0.3 g	0.2 g

1 Prepare the saddle of lamb by boning from the back and removing the bark.
2 Roast the saddle as usual (see recipe 16).
3 Ten minutes before cooking is completed, cover the fat surface of the meat with a mixture of 25–50 g of fresh white breadcrumbs mixed with plenty of chopped parsley, an egg and 25–50 g melted butter or margarine.
4 Return to the oven to complete the cooking, browning carefully.

Key points

Cook the lamb until it is pink. Carefully bind the breadcrumbs with herbs and beaten egg, so that they will hold together during cooking.

Try something different

Variations include:
- mixed fresh herbs used in addition to parsley
- adding finely chopped garlic
- chopped fresh herbs, shallots and mustard.

20 Slow-cooked shoulder of lamb with potatoes boulangère

lamb, potatoes roasting, boning, tying

energy	kcal	fat	sat fat	carb	sugar	protein	fibre	sodium
1815 KJ	437 kcal	30.8 g	14.5 g	2.2 g	0.3 g	27.6 g	0.4 g	0.6 g

Portions ›	4	10
boned shoulder of lamb, rolled and tied	1	3
olive oil	1 tbsp	3 tbsp
salt, pepper		
rosemary	6 sprigs	18 sprigs
thyme	6 sprigs	18 sprigs
garlic	4 cloves	10 cloves
mirepoix (carrots, onions, leeks)	400 g	1 kg
bay leaves	1	3
red wine or dry cider	250 ml	625 ml
brown stock	300 ml	750 ml

For instructions on how to prepare potatoes boulangère for baking, see page 444.

1 Rub the lamb with oil, and season with salt and pepper. Place in a suitable roasting tray and cook in an oven at 200°C for 15 minutes.

2 Remove from the oven and reduce the temperature to 140°C.

3 Add the remaining ingredients to the roasting tray.

4 Cook for 2 hours, basting every 20 minutes.

5 Remove the lamb from the roasting tray and return it to the oven on a rack. Place the potatoes boulangère directly below the lamb. Cook for ½ –1 hour, until the lamb is tender and sticky.

6 To finish the sauce, once the lamb is removed from the roasting tray, strain the cooking liquor and reduce it to the required consistency. Add a tablespoon of strained redcurrant jelly, mix well, correct seasoning, then strain.

21 Shepherd's pie

lamb, potatoes shallow frying, boiling, baking

energy	kcal	fat	sat fat	carb	sugar	protein	fibre	*
1744 KJ	415 kcal	25.3 g	9.1 g	22.1 g	2.5 g	26.3 g	1.6 g	

Portions ⟩	4	10
onions, chopped	100 g	250 g
oil	35 ml	100 ml
lamb or mutton (minced), cooked	400 g	1.25 kg
salt, pepper		
Worcester sauce	2–3 drops	5 drops
potato, cooked	400 g	1.25 kg
butter	25 g	60 g
milk or eggwash		
jus-lié or demi-glace	125–250 ml	300–600 ml

1 Cook the onion in the oil without colouring.
2 Add the cooked meat from which all fat and gristle has been removed.
3 Season and add Worcester sauce (sufficient to bind).
4 Bring to the boil; simmer for 10–15 minutes.
5 Place in an earthenware or pie dish.
6 Prepare the potatoes – mix with the butter, then mash and pipe, or arrange neatly on top.
7 Brush with the milk or eggwash.
8 Colour lightly under a salamander or in a hot oven.
9 Serve accompanied with a sauceboat of *jus-lié*.

When prepared with cooked beef, this dish is known as **cottage pie**.

Key points
- Pipe the potato carefully so that the meat is completely covered.
- When using reheated meats, care must be taken to heat thoroughly and quickly.

* Using sunflower oil, with hard margarine in topping

Healthy eating tips
- Use an oil rich in unsaturates (olive or sunflower) to lightly oil the pan.
- Drain off any excess fat after the lamb has been fried.
- Try replacing some of the meat with baked beans or lentils, and add tomatoes and/or mushrooms to the dish.
- When served with a large portion of green vegetables, a healthy balance is created.

Try something different
Variations include:
- adding 100–200 g sliced mushrooms
- adding a layer of thickly sliced tomatoes, then sprinkling with rosemary
- mixing a tin of baked beans in with the meat
- sprinkling with grated cheese before browning
- varying the flavour of the mince by adding herbs or spices
- varying the potato topping by mixing in grated cheese, chopped spring onions or herbs, or by using duchess potato mixture
- serving lightly sprinkled with garam masala and with grilled pitta bread.

22 Brine
(saumure)

boiling, curing

Makes >	2.5 litres
cold water	2.5 litres
saltpetre	15 g
salt	850 g
bay leaf	1
juniper berries	6
brown sugar	50 g
peppercorns	6

1 Boil all the ingredients together for 10 minutes, skimming frequently.
2 Strain into a china, wooden or earthenware container.
3 When the brine is cold, add the meat.
4 Immerse the meat for up to 10 days under refrigeration.

Ingredients for brine

Strain the liquid

Immerse the meat in the brine

23 Grilled beef

energy	kcal	fat	sat fat	carb	sugar	protein	fibre	*
706 KJ	168 kcal	6.0 g	2.7 g	0.0 g	0.0 g	28.6 g	0.0 g	

Approximate weight per portion: 110–175 g. (In many establishments these weights will be exceeded.)

The following cuts may be cooked in this way:

- rump steak
- point steak
- double fillet steak (*chateaubriand*)
- fillet steak
- tournedos
- porterhouse or T-bone steak
- sirloin steak (*entrecôte*)
- double sirloin steak
- minute steak
- rib eye steak.

1 Lightly season the steaks with salt and pepper, and brush on both sides with oil.
2 Place on hot, preheated and greased grill bars.
3 Turn halfway through the cooking and brush occasionally with oil. Cook to the degree ordered by the customer.

Serve garnished with watercress and deep-fried potato, and offer a suitable sauce, such as compound butter or sauce béarnaise.

* 1 portion (100 g cooked weight)

24 Hamburger, American style

beef grilling, griddling

energy	kcal	fat	sat fat	carb	sugar	protein	fibre	sodium
1868 KJ	450 kcal	32.4 g	13.9 g	0.0 g	0.0 g	39.4 g	0.0 g	0.2 g

Hamburgers – now more commonly known as burgers – were originally made using 200 g of minced beef per portion. The meat used should be pure beef with 20–25 per cent beef fat by weight. Less fat than this will result in a tough, dry hamburger. If more fat is used the hamburgers will be unpalatable, nutritionally undesirable and will shrink considerably during cooking.

1 Pass the meat through a mincer twice. This makes a more tender product.
2 Lightly mix the mince with any desired seasoning or ingredients. (Over-mixing will make the hamburger tough.)
3 Mould the mixture into patties. Mark the top with crossed lines using a palette knife.
4 Grill until cooked thoroughly to the centre. Do not prick the hamburgers while cooking, as the juices will seep out leaving a dry product.

Mini burgers (one mouthful) can be served as hot canapés at receptions.

Try something different
Variations in seasonings and ingredients can be added to the minced beef, but traditionally the sauces and garnishes offered are sufficient. These can include: ketchup, mustard, mayonnaise, chilli sauce, horseradish, cheese, raw onion rings, lettuce, avocado slices, bacon and various pickles and relishes; freshly fried chips and/or cut pieces of raw vegetables (e.g. carrot, celery, spring onions) can be added. The bun may be plain or seeded (sesame seeds). Alternative fillings can include:

- cheese – either on its own, or added to the beef
- egg – a freshly fried egg, or added to the beef
- chicken – a freshly grilled portion of chicken, either minced or in one piece
- fish – a freshly grilled portion of a whole fish (cod or haddock)
- vegetables – a selection of freshly grilled, or fried vegetables (e.g. onions, peppers, aubergines, mushrooms).

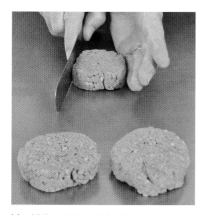

Mould the mixture into shape

Mark the top of each burger before grilling it

25 Tournedos

beef shallow frying, sauté

energy	kcal	fat	sat fat	carb	sugar	protein	fibre	sodium
1540 KJ	366 kcal	13.2 g	4.8 g	0.0 g	0.0 g	61.8 g	0.0 g	0.2 g

Tournedos are cut from the middle of a fillet of beef and are usually 100–150 g in weight.

1 Lightly season and shallow-fry on both sides in a sauté pan.
2 Serve with an appropriate garnish or sauce (see *Try something different*, below).

> Traditionally, tournedos are cooked underdone and served on a round croûte of bread fried in butter.

Healthy eating tips
- Use little or no salt to season the steaks.
- Fry in a small amount of an unsaturated oil and drain off all excess fat after frying.
- Serve with plenty of boiled new potatoes or a jacket potato and a selection of vegetables.

Try something different
Tournedos can be served with a variety of sauces, such as chasseur, red wine or mushroom, and numerous garnishes (e.g. diced cubed potatoes, wild or cultivated mushrooms). The photo shows **tournedos Rossini** – the tournedos are served with foie gras, Parma ham, girolles, truffle and a Madeira jelly.

Practical Cookery 12th edition

26 Beef stroganoff
(sauté de boeuf stroganoff)

beef  shallow frying, sauté

energy	kcal	fat	sat fat	carb	sugar	protein	fibre	*
1364 KJ	325 kcal	23.7 g	7.9 g	1.7 g	1.7 g	21.2 g	0.3 g	

Portions >	4	10
fillet of beef (tail end)	400 g	1.5 kg
butter or oil	50 g	125 g
salt, pepper		
shallots, finely chopped	25 g	60 g
dry white wine	125 ml	300 ml
cream	125 ml	300 ml
lemon, juice of	¼	½
parsley, chopped		

Healthy eating tips
- Use little or no salt to season the meat.
- Fry in a small amount of an unsaturated oil.
- Serve with a large portion of rice and a salad.

1 Cut the meat into strips approximately 1 cm × 5 cm.
2 Place the butter or oil in a sauteuse over a fierce heat.
3 Add the beef strips, lightly season with salt and pepper, and allow to cook rapidly for a few seconds. The beef should be brown but underdone.
4 Drain the beef into a colander. Pour the butter back into the pan.
5 Add the shallots, cover with a lid and allow to cook gently until tender.
6 Drain off the fat, add the wine and reduce to one-third.
7 Add the cream and reduce by a quarter.
8 Add the lemon juice and the beef strips; do not reboil. Correct the seasoning.
9 Serve lightly sprinkled with chopped parsley. Accompany with rice pilaff (see page 174).

* Using sunflower oil

Hamburg or Vienna steak
(bitok)

beef shallow frying

energy	kcal	fat	sat fat	carb	sugar	protein	fibre
681 KJ	162 kcal	6.7 g	1.9 g	12.7 g	1.0 g	13.8 g	1.0 g

Portions ❯	4	10
onion, finely chopped	25 g	60 g
butter or oil	10 g	25 g
lean minced beef	200 g	500 g
small egg	1	2–3
breadcrumbs	100 g	250 g
cold water or milk	2 tbsp approx.	60 ml approx.

Healthy eating tips

- Use a small amount of an unsaturated oil to cook the onion and to shallow-fry the meat.
- The minced beef will produce more fat, which should be drained off.
- Serve with plenty of starchy carbohydrate and vegetables.

1 Cook the onion in the fat without colour, then allow to cool.
2 Add to the rest of the ingredients and mix in well.
3 Divide into even pieces and, using a little flour, make into balls, flatten and shape round.
4 Shallow-fry in hot fat on both sides, reducing the heat after the first few minutes, making certain they are cooked right through.
5 Serve with a light sauce, such as piquant sauce (see page 40).

The 'steaks' may be garnished with French-fried onions and sometimes with a fried egg.

28 Carbonnade of beef
(carbonnade de boeuf)

beef shallow frying, braising

beef 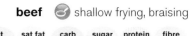 shallow frying, braising

energy	kcal	fat	sat fat	carb	sugar	protein	fibre
1037 KJ	247 kcal	9.1 g	1.8 g	14.0 g	8.1 g	24.7 g	1.1 g

Portions >	4	10
lean beef (topside)	400 g	1.25 kg
salt, pepper		
flour (white or wholemeal)	25 g	60 g
dripping or oil	25 g	60 g
onions, sliced	200 g	500 g
beer	250 ml	625 ml
caster sugar	10 g	25 g
tomato purée	25 g	60 g
brown stock		

1 Cut the meat into thin slices.
2 Season with salt and pepper and pass through the flour.
3 Quickly colour the meat on both sides in hot fat and place in a casserole.
4 Fry the onions to a light brown colour. Add to the meat.
5 Add the beer, sugar and tomato purée and sufficient brown stock to cover the meat.
6 Cover with a tight-fitting lid and simmer gently in a moderate oven at 150–200°C until the meat is tender (approx. 2 hours).
7 Skim, correct the seasoning and serve.

Slice the meat thinly

Pass each slice through the flour

Pour the liquid over the browned meat and onions

Healthy eating tips
- Trim off as much fat as possible before frying and drain off all surplus fat after frying.
- Use the minimum amount of salt to season the meat.
- Skim all fat from the finished sauce.
- Serve with plenty of potatoes and vegetables.

29 Boeuf bourguignonne

beef shallow frying, boiling, stewing, marinading

energy	kcal	fat	sat fat	carb	sugar	protein	fibre	sodium *
2838 KJ	681 kcal	33.3 g	9.1 g	20.1 g	7.2 g	44.9 g	8.0 g	0.9 g

Portions ❯	4	10
Beef		
beef shin, pre-soaked in red wine (see below) for 12 hours	600 g	1.5 kg
olive oil	50 ml	125 ml
bottle of inexpensive Bordeaux or other suitable red wine	1	2
onion	100 g	250 g
carrot	100 g	250 g
celery sticks	75 g	180 g
leek	100 g	250 g
cloves of garlic	2	5
fresh thyme, sprig	1	2
bay leaf	1	2
seasoning		
veal/brown stock to cover		
Garnish		
button onions, cooked	12 (150 g)	30 (300 g)
bacon lardons, cooked	150 g	300 g
button mushrooms, cooked	12 (150 g)	30 (300 g)
parsley, chopped	2 tsp	5 tsp
To finish		
mashed potato	300 g	750 g
washed, picked spinach	300 g	750 g
green beans, cooked	250 g	625 g

1 Preheat the oven to 180°C.

2 Trim the beef shin of all fat and sinew, and cut into 2.5 cm-thick rondelles.

3 Heat a little oil in a thick-bottomed pan and seal/brown the shin. Place in a large ovenproof dish.

4 Meanwhile, reduce the red wine by half.

5 Peel and trim the vegetables as appropriate, then add them to the pan that the beef has just come out of and gently brown the edges. Then place this, along with the garlic and herbs, in the ovenproof dish with the meat.

6 Add the reduced red wine to the casserole, then pour in enough stock to cover the meat and vegetables. Bring to the boil, then cook in the oven preheated to 180°C for 40 minutes; after that, turn the oven down to 90–95°C and cook for a further 4 hours until tender.

7 Remove from the oven and allow the meat to cool in the liquor. When cold, remove any fat. Reheat gently at the same temperature to serve.

8 Heat the garnish elements separately and sprinkle over each portion. Serve with a mound of mashed potato, wilted spinach and buttered green beans. Finish the whole dish with chopped parsley.

This is a classic dish. Other joints of beef can replace the beef shin: beef or veal cheek can be used, reducing the time for the veal, or modernise the dish by using the slow-cooked fillet preparation and serving the same garnish. If using chuck steak or topside beef, reduce the cooking time to 3 hours.

> **Key point**
> Shallow-fry the beef in hot oil to brown it all over, but do not let it boil in the oil. Then allow it to stew gently in the red wine.

* Including garnish and accompaniments

Marinate the beef

Gently brown the vegetables

Brown the meat

Pour in stock to cover the meat and vegetables

30 Braised beef
(boeuf braisé)

beef braising

energy	kcal	fat	sat fat	carb	sugar	protein	fibre *
1380 KJ	329 kcal	14.3 g	3.3 g	26.8 g	4.7 g	24.7 g	2.4 g

Portions ❯	4	10
lean beef (topside or thick flank)	400 g	1.25 kg
dripping or oil	25 g	60 g
onions, sliced and lightly fried	100 g	250 g
carrots, sliced and lightly fried	100 g	250 g
brown stock	500 ml	1.25 litres
salt, pepper		
bouquet garni		
tomato purée	25 g	60 g
demi-glace or *jus-lié*	250 ml	625 ml

Method 1

1 Trim and tie the joint securely.
2 Season and colour quickly on all sides in hot fat to seal the joint.
3 Place into a small braising pan (any pan with a tight-fitting lid that may be placed in the oven) or in a casserole.
4 Place the joint on the lightly fried, sliced vegetables.
5 Add the stock, which should come two-thirds of the way up the meat, and season lightly.
6 Add the bouquet garni and tomato purée and, if available, add a few mushroom trimmings.
7 Bring to the boil, skim and cover with a lid; cook in a moderate oven at 150–200°C.
8 After approximately 1½ hours' cooking, remove the meat.
9 Add the demi-glace or *jus-lié*, reboil, skim and strain.
10 Replace the meat; do not cover, but baste frequently and continue cooking for approx. 2–2½ hours in all. Braised beef should be well cooked (approx. 35 minutes per 0.5 kg plus 35 minutes). To test if cooked, pierce with a trussing needle, which should penetrate the meat easily and there should be no sign of blood.
11 Remove the joint and correct the colour, seasoning and consistency of the sauce.
12 To serve: remove the string and carve slices across the grain. Pour some of the sauce over the slices and serve the remainder of the sauce in a sauceboat.

Making braised beef
http://bit.ly/wGNSvn

Method 2

As for Method 1, but when the joint and vegetables are browned, sprinkle with 25 g (60 g for 10 portions) flour and singe in the oven; add the tomato purée, stock and bouquet garni; season and complete the recipe.

Suitable garnishes include spring vegetables or pasta. Red wine or *jus-lié* may be used in place of stock.

Trim the joint neatly

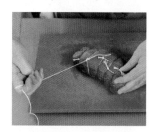

Tie the joint securely before braising it

Place the joint in the pan on a layer of vegetables

Healthy eating tips

- Trim off as much fat as possible before frying and drain off all surplus fat after frying.
- Use the minimum amount of salt.
- Skim all fat from the finished sauce.
- Serve with plenty of potatoes and vegetables.

* Using sunflower oil

Steak pudding

beef, pastry 🍲 steaming

energy	kcal	fat	sat fat	carb	sugar	protein	fibre
1369 KJ	326 kcal	17.3 g	7.8 g	20.6 g	1.0 g	23.0 g	1.1 g

Portions ›	4	10
suet paste	200 g	500 g
prepared stewing beef (chuck steak)	400 g	1.5 kg
Worcester sauce	1 tsp	3 tsp
parsley, chopped	1 tsp	2½ tsp
salt, pepper		
onion, chopped (optional)	50–100 g	200 g
water	125 ml approx.	300 ml approx.

1 Line a greased ½ litre basin with three-quarters of the suet paste and retain one-quarter for the top.
2 Mix all the other ingredients, except the water, together.
3 Place in the basin with the water to within 1 cm of the top.
4 Moisten the edge of the suet paste, cover with the top and seal firmly.

5 Cover with greased greaseproof paper and also, if possible, foil or a pudding cloth tied securely with string.
6 Cook in a steamer for at least 3½ hours.
7 Serve with the paper and cloth removed, clean the basin, place on a round flat dish and fasten a napkin round the basin.

Line the basin with suet paste

Fill the basin, then cover the top with paste

Make a foil cover for the basin, with a fold to allow it to expand (over an inner cover of paper)

Tie the cover over the basin securely

Extra gravy should be served separately. If the gravy in the pudding is to be thickened, the meat can be lightly floured.

Healthy eating tips
● Use little or no salt as the Worcester sauce contains salt.
● Trim off as much fat as possible from the raw stewing beef.
● Serve with plenty of potatoes and vegetables.

Try something different
Variations include:
● adding 50–100 g ox or sheep's kidneys cut in pieces with skin and gristle removed
● adding 50–100 g sliced or quartered mushrooms
● making the steak pudding with a cooked filling; in which case, simmer the meat until cooked in brown stock with onions, parsley, Worcester sauce and seasoning; cool quickly and proceed as above, steaming for 1–1½ hours.

32 Boiled silverside, carrots and dumplings

beef, pastry boiling

| | energy 1068 KJ | kcal 254 kcal | fat 10.17 g | sat fat 4.6 g | carb 15.5 g | sugar 5.5 g | protein 26.3 g | fibre 2.6 g |

Portions ⟩	4	10
silverside, pre-soaked in brine	400 g	1.25 kg
onions	200 g	500 g
carrots	200 g	500 g
suet paste	100 g	250 g

Key point

The beef is salted because this gives the desired flavour. The meat is usually salted before it is delivered to the kitchen.

Healthy eating tip

Adding carrots, onions, boiled potatoes and a green vegetable will give a healthy balance.

Try something different

- Herbs can be added to the dumplings.
- Boiled brisket and tongue can be served with the silverside.
- French-style boiled beef is prepared using unsalted thin flank or brisket with onions, carrots, leeks, celery, cabbage and a bouquet garni, all cooked and served together accompanied with pickled gherkins and coarse salt.

1 Soak the meat in cold water for 1–2 hours to remove excess brine.

2 Place in a saucepan and cover with cold water, bring to the boil, skim and simmer for 45 minutes.

3 Add the whole prepared onions and carrots and simmer until cooked.

4 Divide the suet paste into even pieces and lightly mould into balls (dumplings).

5 Add the dumplings and simmer for a further 15–20 minutes.

6 Serve by carving the meat across the grain, garnish with carrots, onions and dumplings, and moisten with a little of the cooking liquor.

A large joint of silverside is approximately 6 kg; for this size of joint, soak it overnight and allow 25 minutes cooking time per 0.5 kg plus 25 minutes.

33 Goulash

(goulash de boeuf)

beef, pastry, root vegetables shallow frying, boiling, stewing

energy	kcal	fat	sat fat	carb	sugar	protein	fibre
1625 KJ	389 kcal	20.4 g	6.0 g	26.1 g	3.9 g	26.9 g	1.7 g

Portions ＞	4	10
prepared stewing beef	400 g	1.25 kg
lard or oil	35 g	100 g
onions, chopped	100 g	250 g
flour	25 g	60 g
paprika	10–25 g	25–60 g
tomato purée	25 g	60 g
stock or water	750 ml approx.	2 litres approx.
turned potatoes or small new potatoes	8	20
choux paste (see page 479)	125 ml	300 ml

Healthy eating tips

- Trim off as much fat as possible before frying and drain all surplus fat after frying.
- Use the minimum amount of salt to season the meat.
- Serve with a large side salad.

1. Remove excess fat from the beef. Cut into 2 cm² pieces.
2. Season and fry in the hot fat until slightly coloured. Add the chopped onion.
3. Cover with a lid and sweat gently for 3 or 4 minutes.
4. Add the flour and paprika, and mix in with a wooden spoon.
5. Cook out in the oven or on top of the stove. Add the tomato purée, mix in.
6. Gradually add the stock, stir to the boil, skim, season and cover.
7. Allow to simmer, preferably in the oven, for approx. 1½–2 hours until the meat is tender.
8. Add the potatoes and check that they are covered with the sauce. (Add more stock if required.)
9. Re-cover with the lid and cook gently until the potatoes are cooked.
10. Skim, and correct the seasoning and consistency. A little cream or yoghurt may be added at the last moment.
11. Serve sprinkled with a few gnocchi made from choux paste, reheated in hot salted water or lightly tossed in butter or margarine.

34 Steak pie

beef, pastry stewing, baking

energy	kcal	fat	sat fat	carb	sugar	protein	fibre *
1442 KJ	346 kcal	22.2 g	2.9 g	13.6 g	1.8 g	24.3 g	0.4 g

Portions ❯	4	10
prepared stewing beef (chuck steak)	400 g	1.5 kg
oil or dripping	50 ml	125 ml
onion, chopped (optional)	100 g	250 g
Worcester sauce, few drops		
parsley, chopped	1 tsp	3 tsp
water, stock, red wine or dark beer	125 ml	300 ml
salt, pepper		
cornflour	10 g	25 g
short, puff or rough puff pastry (see pages 474, 476 and 478)	100 g	250 g

1 Cut the meat into 2 cm strips then cut into squares. Coat them in cornflour.
2 Heat the oil in a frying pan until smoking, add the meat and quickly brown on all sides.
3 Drain the meat off in a colander.
4 Lightly fry the onion.
5 Place the meat, onion, Worcester sauce, parsley and the liquid in a pan, season lightly with salt and pepper.
6 Bring to the boil, skim, then allow to simmer gently until the meat is tender.
7 Dilute the cornflour with a little water, stir into the simmering mixture, reboil and correct seasoning.
8 Place the mixture into a pie dish and allow to cool.
9 Cover with the pastry, eggwash and bake at 200°C for approximately 30–45 minutes.

Healthy eating tips
● Use little or no salt as the Worcester sauce contains salt.
● Fry in a small amount of an unsaturated oil and drain off all excess fat after frying.
● There will be less fat in the dish if short paste is used.
● Serve with boiled potatoes and plenty of vegetables.

Try something different
Variations include:
● adding 50–100 g ox or sheep's kidneys with skin and gristle removed and cut into neat pieces
● adding 50–100 g sliced or quartered mushrooms
● adding 1 heaped tsp tomato purée and some mixed herbs
● in place of cornflour, the meat can be tossed in flour before frying off
● in place of plain flour, 25–50 per cent wholemeal flour may be used in the pastry.

Dice the steak evenly

Coat the meat in cornflour before frying it

Cover the top with paste and trim off the excess

Press gently to ensure a seal between the paste and the dish

* Using puff pastry (McCance data)

Practical Cookery 12th edition

35 Cornish pasties

beef, pastry baking

energy	kcal	fat	sat fat	carb	sugar	protein	fibre
1217 KJ	290 kcal	16.2 g	6.0 g	29.3 g	1.2 g	8.7 g	1.8 g

Portions ›	4	10
raw beef, chuck or skirt, cut in thin pieces	100 g	250 g
short paste (see page 474)	200 g	500 g
potato (raw), finely diced	100 g	250 g
onion or leeks, chopped	50 g	125 g
swede (raw), finely diced (optional)	50 g	125 g
eggwash		

1 Lightly seal the meat in a little oil until brown. Allow to cool.
2 Roll out the short paste to 3 mm thick and cut into rounds 12 cm in diameter.
3 Mix the remaining ingredients together, moisten with a little water and place in the rounds in piles. Eggwash the edges.
4 Fold in half and seal; flute the edge and brush evenly with eggwash.
5 Cook in a moderate oven at 150–200°C for ½–1 hour.
6 Serve with a suitable sauce/gravy, or hot or cold as a snack.

> **Key point**
> The filling can be made from cooked meat that has been quickly chilled and held at 3°C.

Healthy eating tips
● Adding baked beans, tomatoes and/or mushrooms will 'dilute' the fat from the meat.
● Serve with a large portion of vegetables.

Try something different
Variations include:
● potato, onion or leek, and turnip or swede, fresh herbs
● bacon, hard-boiled eggs and leeks
● lamb, carrot and potato
● apples, cinnamon, cloves, brown sugar, cider
● puff pastry.

Ingredients for Cornish pasties

Place the filling on to the pastry

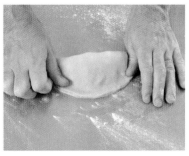
Fold the pastry over and seal the edge

Portions ›	10
piece wing rib of beef	1 × 2 kg
beef dripping	25 g
To serve	
Yorkshire puddings (recipe 37)	
roast gravy (see page 36)	
prepared English mustard	
horseradish sauce (see page 53)	

1 Preheat the oven to 195°C.
2 Place the dripping in a heavy roasting tray and heat on the stove top.
3 Place the beef in the tray and brown well on all sides.
4 Place in the oven at 195°C for 15 minutes, then turn down to 75°C for 2 hours.
5 Remove and allow to rest before carving.
6 Slice the beef and warm the Yorkshire puddings. Serve with the gravy, mustard and horseradish sauce.

The chine needs to be removed from the joint

Cut away the chine

Use a saw to finish removing the chine

Trim and clean the top bone

Remove the elastin

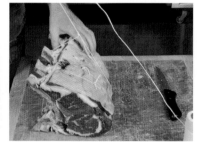

Tie the bone back – it will act as a trivet

Making roast beef
http://bit.ly/wEdAJJ

Brown the meat on all sides before roasting it

When carving, be aware of the location of the bone

Carve in slices

This dish would work well with most vegetables or potatoes. As an alternative, why not add slightly blanched root vegetables to the roasting tray when you start to cook the beef, remove when cooked, and reheat for service? The vegetables will get maximum flavour from the beef and juices.

37 Yorkshire pudding

 baking

Portions ❯	4	10
flour	85 g	215 g
eggs	2	5
milk	85 ml	215 ml
water	40 ml	100 ml
dripping or oil	20 g	50 g

> **Key point**
> The oven, and the oil, must be very hot before the mixture is placed into the pudding tray; if they are not hot enough, the puddings will not rise.

1 Place the flour and eggs into a mixing bowl and mix to a smooth paste.
2 Gradually add the milk and water, and place in the refrigerator for 1 hour. Preheat the oven to 190°C.
3 Heat the pudding trays in the oven with a little dripping or oil in each well.
4 Carefully ladle the mixture in, up to about two-thirds full.
5 Place in the oven and slowly close the door (if you have a glass-fronted door it will be easy to monitor progress; if not, after about 30 minutes check the puddings). The myth about opening the door during cooking has an element of truth in it – however, it is slamming and the speed at which the door is opened that have most effect, so have just a small, careful peek to check and see if they are ready.
6 For the last 10 minutes of cooking, invert the puddings (take out and turn upside down in the tray) to dry out the base.
7 Serve immediately.

Portions >	4	10
rolled brisket of beef	1 kg	2½ kg
button onions, peeled	16	40
carrots, peeled	4	10
small swede, cut into eighths	1	2
beef dripping	150 g	375 g
field mushrooms	8	20
good beef stock	500 ml	1.4 litres
bay leaf	1	2
thyme sprig	1	2
flour	20 g	50 g
butter	20 g	50 g
salt	15 g	30 g
freshly-milled black pepper		

1 Preheat the oven to 69°C.
2 Melt the dripping in a thick cooking pot. When it's hot, put in the meat, sear and brown it all over, then transfer it to a tray.
3 Lightly brown the onions, carrots, celery and swede, then remove and place on the tray with the meat.
4 Empty all the fat from the pot, then replace the brisket and arrange the vegetables and mushrooms around the meat.
5 Add the hot stock, bay leaf and thyme and half the salt and pepper.
6 Cover with foil and a tightly fitting lid and place on the stove. Bring to the boil and place in the oven for about 6 hours.
7 When ready, remove the meat and vegetables and place on a warmed serving dish. Bring the liquid to the boil, correct the seasoning if necessary and boil briskly until slightly reduced. Mix the butter and flour to a paste (beurre manié), then add this to the liquid and whisk until the sauce thickens.
8 Pour the sauce over the meat and serve.

39 | Slow-roast sirloin, lyonnaise onions and carrot purée

beef, bulbs, root vegetables  roasting

energy	kcal	fat	sat fat	carb	sugar	protein	fibre	sodium
2436 KJ	584 kcal	26.9 g	7.4 g	13.5 g	11.2 g	72.5 g	5.9 g	0.8 g

Portions ›	4	10
For the beef		
sirloin, outer skin removed, with fat tied back on	1.2 kg	3 kg
seasoning		1
oil	50 ml	125 ml
clove of garlic, sliced	1	2
thyme, sprig	1	2
bay leaf	1	2
For the lyonnaise onions		
onions	200 g	500 g
seasoning		
For the carrot purée		
medium-sized carrots	600 g	1.5 kg
star anise	1	2

For the beef

1 Preheat the oven to 180°C. Season the beef and heat the oil in the pan. Add the garlic, thyme, bay leaf and beef.

2 Place the beef in the oven for 15 minutes. Remove, then turn the oven down to 69°C. When the oven has reached this new temperature, return the beef to it for a further 1 hour 10 minutes.

3 While the beef is cooking, make the carrot purée and the Lyonnaise onions (see below) and keep warm.

For the Lyonnaise onions

1 Finely slice the onions and put them into a large induction pan while cold.

2 Put on medium heat and season.

3 When they are starting to colour, turn down and cook slowly for approx. 2 hours.

4 Cool and refrigerate.

For the carrot purée

1 Peel the carrots and juice just over half of them into a small pan (or use half as many, but add 100 ml/250 ml of carrot juice).

2 Cut the remaining carrots into equal slices of about 1 cm and place into the carrot juice.

3 Boil the carrots for 15–20 minutes, ensuring that you scrape down the sides of the pan.

4 For the last 8 minutes of cooking, before all the liquid has completely evaporated, drop in the star anise.

5 Pass, retaining the juice.

6 Remove the star anise pod(s) and blitz the purée for 7 minutes, adding the retained juice.

To finish

When the beef is cooked, remove from the oven and carve evenly. Place a portion of carrot purée and Lyonnaise onions on each plate. Top with the beef and pour over the *jus de viande* (meat juice); garnish with sprigs of chervil and serve.

Escalope of veal
(escalope de veau)

energy	kcal	fat	sat fat	carb	sugar	protein	fibre
2079 KJ	495 kcal	39.8 g	11.4 g	10.3 g	0.5 g	24.7 g	1.0 g

Portions ❯	4	10
nut or cushion of veal	400 g	1.25 kg
seasoned flour	25 g	60 g
egg	1	2
breadcrumbs	50 g	125 g
oil *for frying*	50 g	125 g
butter	50 g	125 g
beurre noisette (optional)	50 g	125 g
jus-lié (page 37)	60 ml	150 ml

1 Trim and remove all sinew from the veal.
2 Cut into four even slices and bat out thinly using a little water.
3 Flour, egg and crumb. Shake off surplus crumbs. Mark with a palette knife.
4 Place the escalopes into shallow hot fat and cook quickly for a few minutes on each side.
5 Dress on a serving dish or plate.
6 An optional finish is to pour over 50 g *beurre noisette* (nut-brown butter), and finish with a cordon of *jus-lié*.

Veal escalope Holstein

> **Key point**
> The escalopes need to be batted out thinly. Excess breadcrumbs must be shaken off before the escalopes are placed into the hot fat.

Healthy eating tips
- Use an unsaturated oil to fry the veal.
- Make sure the fat is hot so that less will be absorbed into the crumb.
- Drain the cooked escalope on kitchen paper.
- Use the minimum amount of salt.
- Serve with plenty of starchy carbohydrate and vegetables.

* Fried in sunflower oil, using butter to finish

Try something different
Variations include the following.
- **Escalope of veal Viennoise:** as for this recipe, but garnish the dish with chopped yolk and white of egg and chopped parsley; on top of each escalope place a slice of peeled lemon decorated with chopped egg yolk, egg white and parsley, an anchovy fillet and a stoned olive; finish with a little lemon juice and nut-brown butter.
- **Veal escalope Holstein:** prepare and cook the escalopes as for this recipe; add an egg fried in butter or oil, and place two neat fillets of anchovy criss-crossed on each egg; serve.
- **Escalope of veal with spaghetti and tomato sauce:** prepare escalopes as for this recipe, then garnish with spaghetti with tomato sauce (page 158), allowing 100 g spaghetti per portion.

41 Breadcrumbed veal escalope with ham and cheese

(escalope de veau cordon bleu)

veal  shallow frying

energy	kcal	fat	sat fat	carb	sugar	protein	fibre	*
2632 KJ	627 kcal	48.1 g	16.3 g	12.0 g	1.3 g	37.1 g	0.7 g	

Portions >	4	10
nut or cushion of veal	400 g	1.25 kg
cooked ham, slices	4	10
Gruyère cheese, slices	4	10
seasoned flour	25 g	60 g
egg	1	2
breadcrumbs	50 g	125 g
oil	50 g	125 g
butter (optional)	100 g	250 g
beurre noisette (optional)	50 g	125 g
jus-lié (page 37)	60 ml	150 ml

1 Trim and remove all sinew from the veal.
2 Cut into 8 even slices (20 for 10 portions) and bat out thinly using a little water.
3 Place a slice of ham and a slice of cheese onto 4 (10 for 10 portions) of the veal slices, cover with the remaining slices and press together firmly.
4 Flour, egg and crumb. Shake off all surplus crumbs. Mark on one side with a palette knife.
5 Place the escalopes marked side down into the hot oil (with butter if desired) and cook quickly for a few minutes on each side, until golden brown.
6 An optional finish is to serve coated with 50 g (125 g for 10 portions) nut-brown butter (*beurre noisette*) and a cordon of *jus-lié*.

Veal escalopes may be cooked plain (not crumbed), in which case they are only slightly batted out.

Healthy eating tips
● No added salt is needed as there is plenty in the ham and cheese.
● This is a high-fat dish, so serve with plenty of starchy carbohydrate and vegetables to 'dilute' the fat.

* Fried in sunflower oil, using butter to finish

Bat out the escalopes

Layer the veal, ham and cheese

Coat the escalope with breadcrumbs and mark on one side

42 Veal escalopes with Parma ham and mozzarella cheese

(involtini di vitello)

veal shallow frying, sauté

energy	kcal	fat	sat fat	carb	sugar	protein	fibre
1642 KJ	394 kcal	26.1 g	15.5 g	0.1 g	0.1 g	39.8 g	0.0 g

Portions ❯	4	10
small, thin veal escalopes (75 g)	8	20
flour		
Parma ham, thinly sliced	100 g	250 g
mozzarella cheese, thinly sliced	200 g	500 g
fresh leaves of sage	8	20
or		
dried sage	1 tsp	2½ tsp
salt, pepper		
butter or oil	50 g	125 g
Parmesan cheese, grated		

1 Sprinkle each slice of veal lightly with flour and flatten.
2 Place a slice of Parma ham on each escalope.
3 Add several slices of mozzarella cheese to each.
4 Add a sage leaf or a light sprinkling of dried sage.
5 Season, roll up each escalope, and secure with a toothpick or cocktail stick.
6 Melt the butter in a sauté pan, add the escalopes and brown on all sides.
7 Transfer the escalopes and butter to a suitably sized ovenproof dish.
8 Sprinkle generously with grated Parmesan cheese and bake in a moderately hot oven at 190°C for 10 minutes.
9 Clean the edges of the dish and serve.

Key point

Make sure the ham and cheese are well sealed within the escalope before cooking.

Healthy eating tips

- Use a small amount of oil to fry the escalopes, and drain the cooked escalopes on kitchen paper.
- No added salt is necessary as there is plenty of salt in the cheese.
- Serve with plenty of vegetables.

Layer the veal, ham and cheese, then roll them up

Transfer the fried escalopes to an ovenproof dish and sprinkle with cheese

43 Braised shin of veal
(osso buco)

veal braising

energy	kcal	fat	sat fat	carb	sugar	protein	fibre *
1748 KJ	416 kcal	28.6 g	7.8 g	9.3 g	4.1 g	28.5 g	1.9 g

Portions ❯	4	10
meaty knuckle of veal	1.5 kg	3.75 kg
salt, pepper		
flour	25 g	60 g
butter	50 g	125 g
oil	60 ml	150 ml
onion, finely chopped	50 g	125 g
small clove of garlic, finely chopped	1	2–3
carrot	50 g	125 g
leek	25 g	60 g
celery	25 g	60 g
dry white wine	60 ml	150 ml
white stock	60 ml	150 ml
tomato purée	25 g	60 g
bouquet garni	1	1
tomatoes, concassé	200 g	500 g
parsley and basil, chopped		
lemon or orange, grated zest and juice of	½	1

1 Prepare the veal knuckle by cutting and sawing through the bone in 5 cm-thick pieces.
2 Season the veal pieces with salt and pepper, and pass through flour on both sides.
3 Melt the butter and oil in a sauté pan.
4 Add the veal slices and cook on both sides, colouring slightly.
5 Add the finely chopped onion and garlic, cover with a lid and allow to sweat gently for 2–3 minutes.
6 Add the carrot, leek and celery cut in brunoise, cover with a lid and allow to sweat for 3–4 minutes. Pour off the fat.
7 Deglaze with the white wine and stock. Add the tomato purée.

8 Add the bouquet garni, replace the lid and allow the dish to simmer gently, preferably in an oven, for 1 hour.
9 Add the tomato concassé, correct the seasoning.
10 Replace the lid, return to the oven and allow to continue simmering until the meat is so tender that it can be pulled away from the bone easily with a fork.
11 Remove the bouquet garni, add the lemon juice, correct the seasoning and serve sprinkled with a mixture of chopped fresh basil, parsley, and grated orange and lemon zest (known as gremolata).

A risotto with saffron may be served separately. *Osso buco* is an Italian regional dish that has many variations.

> **Key point**
> At step 4, only colour the veal lightly.

Healthy eating tips
- Use the minimum amount of salt to season the meat and in the finished sauce.
- Lightly oil the pan with an unsaturated oil and drain off any excess after the frying is complete.
- Serve with a large portion of risotto.

* Using hard margarine and sunflower oil

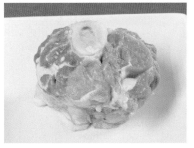
Raw shin of veal

Colour the meat

Combine all the ingredients for braising

44 Fricassée of veal
(fricassée de veau)

veal • stewing

energy	kcal	fat	sat fat	carb	sugar	protein	fibre *
992 KJ	236 kcal	13.6 g	7.5 g	5.3 g	0.4 g	23.3 g	0.2 g

Portions >	4	10
boned stewing veal (shoulder or breast)	400 g	1.25 kg
butter or oil	35 g	100 g
flour	25 g	60 g
white veal stock	500 ml	1.25 litres
salt, pepper		
egg yolk	1	2–3
cream	2–3 tbsp	5–7 tbsp
squeeze of lemon juice		
parsley, chopped, to finish		
heart-shaped croutons, to finish		

1 Trim the meat. Cut into even 25 g pieces.
2 Sweat the meat gently in the butter without colour in a sauté pan.
3 Mix in the flour and cook out without colour.
4 Allow to cool.
5 Gradually add boiling stock just to cover the meat, stir until smooth.
6 Season, bring to the boil, skim.
7 Cover and simmer gently on the stove until tender (approx. 1½–2 hours).
8 Pick out the meat into a clean pan. Correct the sauce.
9 Pass onto the meat and reboil. Mix the yolk and cream in a basin.
10 Add a little of the boiling sauce, mix in and pour back onto the meat, shaking the pan until thoroughly mixed; do not reboil. Add the lemon juice.

11 Serve, finished with chopped parsley and heart-shaped croutons fried in butter or oil.

Key points
- After adding the flour, cook carefully so that it does not colour.
- Add the liaison of yolks and cream carefully. Do not allow the sauce to boil after this, because it will curdle.

Healthy eating tips
- Add the minimum amount of salt.
- Brush the croutons with olive oil and bake them, or serve with sippets (small, thin pieces of toasted bread).
- A large serving of starchy carbohydrate and vegetables will help to proportionally reduce the fat content.

Ingredients for fricassée of veal

Cook the meat and flour

Add the stock and continue to cook

Try something different

A variation is to add mushrooms and button onions. Proceed as for this recipe but, after 1 hour's cooking, pick out the meat, strain the sauce back onto the meat and add 2 small button onions per portion. Simmer for 15 minutes, add 2 small white button mushrooms per portion, washed and peeled if necessary, then complete the cooking. Finish and serve as in this recipe. This is known as *fricassée de veau à l'ancienne*.

Add the liaison of egg yolk and cream

* Using butter

---

45 Pork escalopes

pork shallow frying

energy	kcal	fat	sat fat	carb	sugar	protein	fibre	sodium *
878 KJ	210 kcal	8.8 g	1.7 g	0.0 g	0.0 g	32.6 g	0.0 g	0.1 g

Pork escalopes are usually cut from the prime cuts of meat in the leg or loin, and can be dealt with in the same way as a leg of veal. They may be cut into 75–100 g slices, flattened with a meat bat, and used plain or crumbed and served with vegetables or pasta (noodles) with a suitable sauce (e.g. Madeira, or as for veal escalopes (recipes 40 and 41)).

> **Key point**
> Bat out the escalopes thinly.

* Plain, not crumbed

Pork escalopes with Calvados sauce

pork shallow frying, sauté

energy	kcal	fat	sat fat	carb	sugar	protein	fibre	*
1856 KJ	447 kcal	34.2 g	20.3 g	12.7 g	12.5 g	22.8 g	1.1 g	

Portions ⟩	4	10
crisp eating apples (e.g. russet)	2	5
cinnamon	¼ tsp	¾ tsp
lemon juice	1 tbsp	2½ tbsp
brown sugar	2 tsp	5 tsp
butter, melted	25 g	70 g
pork escalopes (see recipe 45)	4 × 100 g	10 × 100 g
butter or oil	50 g	125 g
shallots or onions, finely chopped	50 g	125 g
Calvados	30 ml	75 ml
double cream or natural yoghurt	125 ml	300 ml
salt, cayenne pepper		
basil, sage or rosemary, chopped		

1 Core and peel the apples.
2 Cut into 0.5 cm-thick rings and sprinkle with a little cinnamon and a few drops of lemon juice.
3 Place on a baking sheet, sprinkle with brown sugar and a little melted butter, and caramelise under the salamander or in the top of a hot oven.
4 Lightly sauté the escalopes on both sides in the butter.
5 Remove from the pan and keep warm.
6 Add the chopped shallots to the same pan, cover with a lid and cook gently without colouring (use a little more butter if necessary).
7 Strain off the fat, leaving the shallots in the pan, and deglaze with the Calvados.
8 Reduce by a half, add the cream or yoghurt, seasoning and herbs.
9 Reboil, correct the seasoning and consistency, and pass through a fine strainer onto the meat.
10 Garnish with slices of caramelised apple.

Special care must be taken not to overheat if using yoghurt, otherwise the sauce will curdle.

Healthy eating tips
- Use a little unsaturated oil to sauté the escalopes.
- Add the minimum amount of salt.
- Try using yoghurt stabilised with a little cornflour, or half cream and half yoghurt.

Variation
Calvados can be replaced with twice the amount of cider and reduced by three-quarters as an alternative. Add a crushed clove of garlic and 1 tablespoon of continental mustard (2–3 cloves and 2½ tablespoons for 10 portions).

* Using lean meat only, and double cream

47 Sweet and sour pork

energy	kcal	fat	sat fat	carb	sugar	protein	fibre	*
3067 KJ	730 kcal	43.9 g	9.2 g	69.7 g	54.7 g	13.4 g	1.6 g	

Portions >	4	10
loin of pork, boned	250 g	600 g
sugar	12 g	30 g
dry sherry	70 ml	180 ml
soy sauce	70 ml	180 ml
cornflour	50 g	125 g
vegetable oil, for frying	70 ml	180 ml
oil	2 tbsp	5 tbsp
clove of garlic, finely chopped	1	2
fresh root ginger, finely chopped	50 g	125 g
onion, chopped	75 g	180 g
green pepper, in 1 cm dice	1	2½
chillies, chopped	2	5
sweet and sour sauce (see below)	210 ml	500 ml
pineapple rings (fresh or canned)	1	3
spring onions	2	5

1 Cut the boned loin of pork into 2 cm pieces.
2 Marinate the pork for 30 minutes in the sugar, sherry and soy sauce.
3 Pass the pork through cornflour, pressing the cornflour in well.
4 Deep-fry the pork pieces in oil at 190°C until golden brown, then drain. Add the tablespoons of oil to a sauté pan.
5 Add the garlic and ginger, and fry until fragrant.
6 Add the onion, pepper and chillies, sauté for a few minutes.
7 Stir in the sweet and sour sauce (see below), bring to the boil.
8 Add the pineapple cut into small chunks, thicken slightly with diluted cornflour. Simmer for 2 minutes.
9 Deep-fry the pork again until crisp. Drain, mix into the vegetables and sauce or serve separately.
10 Serve garnished with rings of spring onions or button onions.

Key point
It is important to allow the pork enough time to marinate.

Sweet and sour sauce

Portions >	4	10
white vinegar	375 ml	1 litre
brown sugar	150 g	375 g
tomato ketchup	125 ml	300 ml
Worcester sauce	1 tbsp	2½ tbsp
seasoning		

1 Boil the vinegar and sugar in a suitable pan.
2 Add the tomato ketchup, Worcester sauce and seasoning.
3 Simmer for a few minutes then use as required. This sauce may also be lightly thickened with cornflour or another thickening agent.

Healthy eating tips
● Use hot sunflower oil to fry the pork and a small amount of an unsaturated oil to fry the vegetables.
● No added salt is needed, as the soy sauce is high in sodium.
● Serve with plenty of rice or noodles, and additional vegetables.

* Using sunflower oil

48 Stir-fried pork fillet

pork shallow frying, stir frying

energy	kcal	fat	sat fat	carb	sugar	protein	fibre
831 KJ	199 kcal	9.8 g	2.2 g	5.1 g	4.2 g	22.9 g	0.8 g

Portions ›	4	10
shallots, finely chopped	2	6
clove of garlic (optional), chopped	1	2
button mushrooms, sliced	200 g	400 g
olive oil		
pork fillet	400 g	2 kg
Chinese five-spice powder	1 pinch	2 pinches
soy sauce	1 tbsp	2 tbsp
clear honey	2 tsp	3 tsp
dry white wine	2 tbsp	5 tbsp
salt, pepper		

1 Gently fry the shallots, garlic and sliced mushrooms in a little oil in a frying pan or wok.
2 Add the pork cut into strips, stir well, increase the heat, season and add the Chinese five-spice powder; cook for 3–4 minutes then reduce the heat.
3 Add the soy sauce, honey and wine, and reduce for 2–3 minutes.
4 Correct the seasoning and serve.

Healthy eating tips
- No extra salt is needed, as soy sauce is added.
- Adding more vegetables and a large portion of rice or noodles can reduce the overall fat content.

49 Pork casserole with black pudding crust

pork casserole, braising

energy	kcal	fat	sat fat	carb	sugar	protein	fibre	sodium
3474 KJ	838 kcal	64.7 g	23.2 g	17.4 g	3.6 g	41.4 g	2.2 g	0.6 g

Portions ⟩	4	10
loin of pork, diced	750 g	2 kg
seasoned flour	25 g	60 g
oil	3 tbsp	7 tbsp
butter	25 g	60 g
onion, finely chopped	1	3
leek, finely shredded	1	3
clove of garlic, crushed and chopped	2	5
white wine or cider	150 ml	375 ml
brown stock	150 ml	375 ml
black pudding	200 g	500 g

1 Pass the pork through the seasoned flour.

2 Heat half the oil in a suitable casserole with the butter.

3 Quickly fry off the pork in batches, drain well and remove the meat.

4 Add the remaining oil to the pan, add the onion, leek and garlic. Sweat until slightly coloured.

5 Return the meat to the casserole, add the wine and stock. Bring to the boil. Place in the oven for approximately 1 hour at 190°C.

6 Slice the black pudding and place the slices on top of the casserole, overlapping slightly. Brush with oil and place back in the oven for approximately 25 minutes.

Sauerkraut, ham hocks and lentils

bacon, pulses, leafy vegetables   braising, pickling

Sauerkraut is made by a process of pickling called lacto-fermentation. The bacteria and yeasts needed for the fermentation process are found on the cabbage leaves. No additional bacteria are added for this reaction to take place.

The process begins by washing and finely slicing the white cabbage. The sliced cabbage is put into a large pot, a specific amount of salt is mixed in and it is mashed with a cabbage masher. This allows the cabbage juices to be extracted: it produces enough to cover the cabbage in liquid. It is important for the cabbage to be completely covered in liquid to keep air out – any cabbage exposed to air would spoil during the fermentation process.

Using salt in this way can extract the natural juices of many ingredients by breaking down the cell structure. In meat, this 'tightening action' concentrates on the myosin protein, and in vegetables it breaks down the cell wall structure – commonly done when preparing cauliflower for piccalilli or aubergine for ratatouille.

The cabbage, covered with its juices, is put into a large, covered, airtight container and allowed to ferment for 4 to 6 weeks. The bacteria and yeast begin the fermentation process. Over time, the lactic acid bacteria become active, converting the sugars in the cabbage into lactic acid. The sauerkraut is ready when the desired 'sourness' is obtained.

Sauerkraut can keep for several months if it is stored in an airtight container and stored at or below 13°C. Refrigeration is not essential, but it greatly increases the shelf life of the sauerkraut. Many commercial producers also use pasteurisation to further increase its shelf life.

1 Finely slice the cabbage. Mix with the salt and mash down, encouraging the cell structure to break down and extracting the natural liquid from the cabbage.

2 Ensure that the cabbage is completely covered with the liquid.

3 Place the cabbage in a covered container (not air sealed as the bacteria need air movement) for 4–6 weeks, until the cabbage takes on the natural sourness.

4 Store in an airtight jar for up to 6 months at 13°C, or place in the fridge if a longer shelf life is required.

Sauerkraut – modern interpretation

	Portions 〉	8–10
head of white cabbage (1 kg)		1
salt		10 g
streaky bacon, cut into lardons		300 g
oil		50 ml
butter		50 g
shallots, sliced		2
chicken stock		1 litre
Alsace-style wine		250 ml
juniper berries		5

If you can plan ahead, then this is a worthwhile recipe to make. It highlights some of the near-forgotten culinary techniques that are making a comeback at every level of gastronomy.

Below there are two methods for making sauerkraut: traditional and modern. Alternatively, use 600 g of ready-made sauerkraut for this ham hock recipe.

Sauerkraut – traditional method

	Portions 〉	8–10
head of white cabbage (1 kg)		1
salt		40 g

1 Shred the cabbage and place in a colander over a dish. Sprinkle with the salt and leave to extract the liquid for an hour.

2 Squeeze out the remaining liquid by hand, wash the cabbage and pat dry with kitchen towel.

3 Heat the oil and butter in a pan and add the bacon. Cook until the bacon is crisp and has released its fat into the pan.

4 Add the cabbage and cook until soft, without colour.

5 Add the juniper, and then deglaze with the wine and reduce until half the liquid has evaporated.

6 Add the chicken stock and reduce the heat until the cabbage mix is soft and has absorbed the liquid (you may have to regularly top up with a little water to aid the cooking).

For the ham hocks

Portions ›	8–10
ham hocks, about 1.3 kg	2
onion, quartered	1
carrots, quartered lengthways	2
sticks celery, cut into thirds crossways	2
fresh thyme, few sprigs	
bay leaf	

1 Before starting the cooking process, blanch the hocks to rinse away any impurities and excess salt.

2 Put the joints in a large saucepan, cover with cold water and bring to the boil.

3 Reduce the heat and simmer for 1 minute, then carefully move the pan to the sink and drain off the hot water.

4 Refresh the hams under cold running water for a minute or so, then tip out the water.

5 Put the blanched hams in the pan, and add the onions, carrots, celery sticks, thyme and bay leaf.

6 Pour in enough fresh cold water to cover and bring to a simmer.

7 The pan can now be covered with its lid and the hams cooked, keeping the liquor at a gentle simmer for 3 hours.

8 To check if hams are cooked, pull out the small bone close to the large one – it should be loose and come out easily.

9 Rest hams in the stock for 15–20 minutes.

10 Lift out the hams and set aside until cool enough to handle. Wrap in clingfilm to retain the moisture.

11 Retain 900 ml of the stock to cook the lentils.

For the lentils

Portions ›	8–10
puy lentils	250 g
butter	75 g
large onion, peeled and finely diced	1
large carrot, peeled and finely diced	1
celery stick, finely diced	1
fresh parsley, flat leaf or curly, coarsely chopped	1 heaped tbsp
stock from cooking the hams	900 ml

1 First blanch the lentils by plunging them into a pan of boiling water, then drain into a sieve and refresh under the cold tap.

2 Melt the butter in a medium saucepan. Add the diced onion, carrot and celery, cover the pan and cook without colouring for 5–6 minutes.

3 Tip in the blanched lentils, then pour in 900 ml strained stock from the hams.

4 Bring the lentils to a simmer and cook for about 30 minutes, until tender. Check occasionally and top up with more stock if needed.

5 About 10 minutes before the lentils are ready, strip off the skin and fat from the hams with a knife, then remove the meat from the bones and cut it into rough pieces or shred it with your fingers.

To finish

Warm the sauerkraut gently in a pan and place on a large serving plate. Scatter the shredded ham over the top. Add the chopped parsley to the lentils, season with a twist of pepper, then scatter the lentils over the dish. Serve with crusty sourdough bread.

51 Boiled bacon (hock, collar or gammon)

bacon boiling

energy	kcal	fat	sat fat	carb	sugar	protein	fibre
1543 KJ	367 kcal	30.5 g	12.2 g	0.0 g	0.0 g	23.1 g	0.0 g

1 Soak the bacon in cold water for 24 hours before cooking. Change the water.
2 Bring to the boil, skim and simmer gently (approx. 25 minutes per 0.5 kg, plus another 25 minutes). Allow to cool in the liquid.
3 Remove the rind and brown skin; carve.
4 Serve with a little of the cooking liquor.

Boiled bacon may be served with pease pudding and a suitable sauce such as parsley (see page 42). It may also be served cold, or used as an ingredient in other dishes.

* Using 113 g per portion

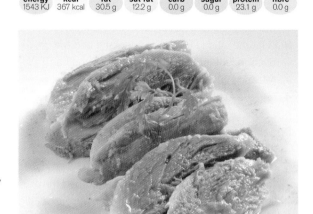

52 Roast leg of pork

pork roasting, boning, tying

energy	kcal	fat	sat fat	carb	sugar	protein	fibre	*
1357 KJ	323 kcal	22.4 g	8.9 g	0.0 g	0.0 g	30.4 g	0.0 g	

1 Prepare leg for roasting (see page XX).
2 Moisten with water, oil, cider, wine or butter and lard, then sprinkle with salt, rubbing it well into the cracks of the skin. This will make the crackling crisp.
3 Place on a trivet in a roasting tin with a little oil or dripping on top.
4 Start to cook in a hot oven at 230–250°C, basting frequently.
5 Gradually reduce the heat to 180–185°C, allowing approximately 25 minutes per 0.5 kg plus another 25 minutes. Pork must always be well cooked. If using a probe, the minimum temperature should be 75°C for 2 minutes.
6 When cooked, remove from the pan and prepare a roast gravy from the sediment (see page 36).
7 Remove the crackling and cut into even pieces for serving.
8 Serve the joint garnished with picked watercress and accompanied by roast gravy, sage and onion dressing and apple sauce. If to be carved, proceed as for roast lamb (see page 240).

* 113 g portion

Other joints can also be used for roasting (e.g. loin, shoulder and spare rib).

53 Sage and onion dressing for pork

bulbs, herbs shallow frying

Portions >	4	10
onion, chopped	50 g	125 g
pork dripping	50 g	125 g
white breadcrumbs	100 g	250 g
chopped parsley, pinch		
powdered sage, good pinch		
salt, pepper		

1 Cook the onion in the dripping without colour.
2 Combine all the ingredients. Dressing is usually served separately.

Modern practice is to refer to this as a dressing if served separately to the meat, but as stuffing if used to stuff the meat.

Healthy eating tips
- Use a small amount of unsaturated oil instead of dripping.
- Add the minimum amount of salt.

54 Roast pork belly with shallots and champ potatoes

pork, potatoes 🥘 roasting

energy	kcal	fat	sat fat	carb	sugar	protein	fibre	sodium
2680 KJ	645 kcal	50.5 g	18.3 g	0.0 g	0.0	47.8 g	0.0 g	0.2 g

Portions ›	4	10
pork belly	1.2 kg	3 kg
salt, pepper		
olive oil	1 tbsp	3 tbsp
shallots	20	50
butter	70 g	175 g
potatoes, peeled and chopped	1 kg	2.5 kg
spring onions, chopped	8	20
double cream	100 ml	250 ml

1 Place the pork on a rack in a roasting tray; season and oil. Roast in the oven for 10 minutes at 200°C and then for 3–3½ hours at 140°C.
2 Peel the shallots, fry gently in half the butter until caramelised. Keep warm.
3 Purée the potatoes.
4 Melt the remaining butter in a pan and sauté the spring onions until soft. Add the spring onions and the butter to the potato purée.
5 Add the cream and mix well.
6 Serve the pork with the caramelised shallots and potato.
7 Serve with a reduced brown stock flavoured with cider; alternatively, a red wine sauce may be served.

55 Slow roast pork belly

pork 🥘 roasting

energy	kcal	fat	sat fat	carb	sugar	protein	fibre
3216 KJ	774 kcal	60.6 g	21.9 g	0.0 g	0.0 g	57.3 g	0.0 g

Portions ›	4	10
pork belly	1.2 kg	3 kg

1 Pre-heat oven to 145°C.
2 Season the pork with salt and pepper.
3 Place on a rack in a large roasting tray, skin side up.
4 Roast for 4½–5 hours, then remove from the tray.
5 Pour off excess fat and make a gravy.
6 Carve into thick slices and serve with apple sauce, sage and onion dressing and a suitable potato and vegetable.

56 Spare ribs of pork in barbecue sauce

pork roasting

energy	kcal	fat	sat fat	carb	sugar	protein	fibre	*
6151 KJ	1465 kcal	12.6 g	37.3 g	20.3 g	17.1 g	63.5 g	0.3 g	

Portions ›	4	10
onion, finely chopped	100 g	250 g
clove of garlic, chopped	1	2
oil	60 ml	150 ml
vinegar	60 ml	150 ml
tomato purée	150 g	375 g
honey	60 ml	150 ml
brown stock	250 ml	625 ml
Worcester sauce	4 tbsp	10 tbsp
dry mustard	1 tsp	2 tsp
pinch thyme		
salt		
spare ribs of pork	2 kg	5 kg

1 Sweat the onion and garlic in the oil without colour.
2 Mix in the vinegar, tomato purée, honey, stock, Worcester sauce, mustard and thyme, and season with salt.
3 Allow the barbecue sauce to simmer for 10–15 minutes.
4 Place the prepared spare ribs fat side up on a trivet in a roasting tin.
5 Brush the spare ribs liberally with the barbecue sauce.
6 Place in a moderately hot oven: 180–200°C.
7 Cook for ¾–1 hour.
8 Baste generously with the barbecue sauce every 10–15 minutes.
9 The cooked spare ribs should be brown and crisp.
10 Cut the spare ribs into individual portions and serve.

* Using sunflower oil

Key point

Apply plenty of barbecue sauce before and during cooking, to give the ribs a good flavour.

Healthy eating tips

● Sweat the onion and garlic in a little unsaturated oil.
● No added salt is necessary as the Worcester sauce is salty.

57 Roasted joint of bacon

bacon roasting

energy	kcal	fat	sat fat	carb	sugar	protein	fibre
1021 KJ	245 kcal	14.8 g	4.9 g	0.0 g	0.0 g	28.0 g	0.0 g

1 Soak the joint in cold water for 24 hours.

2 Remove from the water. Dry well.

3 Place on a roasting tray and roast for
   approximately 25 minutes per 0.5 kg, plus another
   25 minutes.

4 Remove from the oven and allow to stand for
   5 minutes before carving.

5 Use the sediment to make roast gravy (see
   page 36), having checked for saltiness.

6 The joint may be cooked in foil and, for the last
   25–30 minutes, cooked out of the foil.

58 Calf's liver and bacon
(foie de veau au lard)

offal, bacon shallow frying, grilling, griddling

energy	kcal	fat	sat fat	carb	sugar	protein	fibre
998 KJ	238 kcal	13.4 g	5.0 g	2.8 g	2.7 g	26.9 g	1.1 g

Portions ❯	4	10
calf's liver	300 g	1 kg
flour		
oil, for frying	50 g	125 g
streaky bacon	50 g	125 g
jus-lié (page 37)	125 ml	300 ml

1 Skin the liver and remove the gristle.
2 Cut in slices on the slant.
3 Pass the slices of liver through flour. Shake off the excess flour.
4 Quickly fry on both sides in hot oil.
5 Remove the rind and bone from the bacon and grill on both sides.
6 Serve the liver and bacon with a cordon of *jus-lié* and a sauceboat of *jus-lié* separately.

Try something different

Lamb's liver may be cooked in the same way.
Variations include the following.
- Fry in butter and sprinkle with powdered sage or chopped fresh sage.
- Fry in butter, remove the liver, deglaze the pan with raspberry vinegar and powdered thyme.
- When cooked, sprinkle with chopped parsley and a few drops of lemon juice.
- Flour, egg and breadcrumb the liver before cooking.
- The liver may be lightly brushed with oil and grilled.

Key point

Liver dishes are often cooked so that the liver is still pink in the centre. It is safer to cook to a higher core temperature, especially if the dish is for anyone in a high-risk group (see Chapter 15).

Healthy eating tips
- Bacon is salty, so no added salt is needed.
- Use a little unsaturated oil to fry the liver, and drain off any excess fat.
- Serve with boiled new potatoes and a variety of vegetables.

59 Grilled lambs' kidneys
(rognons grillés)

offal grilling, griddling

energy	kcal	fat	sat fat	carb	sugar	protein	fibre
614 KJ	147 kcal	10.3 g	5.9 g	0.1 g	0.1 g	13.7 g	0.0 g

1 Season the prepared skewered kidneys (as for lamb kebabs, recipe 3).
2 Brush with melted butter or oil.
3 Place on preheated greased grill bars or on a greased baking tray.
4 Grill fairly quickly on both sides (approx. 5–10 minutes depending on size).
5 Serve with parsley butter, picked watercress and straw potatoes.

Healthy eating tips
- Use the minimum amount of salt.
- Serve with plenty of starchy carbohydrate and vegetables.

60 Devilled lambs' kidneys

offal shallow frying, sauté

Portions >	4	10
lambs' kidneys	8	20
olive oil	1 tbsp	2½ tbsp
salt, pepper		
amontillado sherry	62 ml	180 ml
white wine vinegar	1 tbsp	2½ tbsp
redcurrant jelly	1 tsp	2½ tsp
Worcester sauce	3 drops	7 drops
double cream	1 tbsp	2½ tbsp
English mustard	1 tsp	2½ tsp
mixed herbs, chopped		

1 Prepared the kidneys, cut in half, remove the white ducts and cut into quarters.
2 Heat the oil in the pan, season the kidneys. When cooked, remove.
3 Add the sherry to the pan. Bring to the boil. Add the vinegar and redcurrant jelly.
4 Add the Worcester sauce. Season.
5 Add the cream and mustard. Simmer and reduce to a sauce consistency.
6 Add the kidneys and warm through.
7 Serve on a bed of pilaff rice (see page 174), garnished with chopped herbs.

61 Shallow-fried lambs' sweetbreads

offal  shallow frying

energy	kcal	fat	sat fat	carb	sugar	protein	fibre	sodium *
1635 KJ	396 kcal	36.0 g	11.0 g	0.4 g	0.4 g	17.6 g	0.1 g	0.4 g

Portions ⟩	4	10
sweetbreads	8	20
oil	50 ml	125 ml
butter	50 g	125 g
lemon, juice of	1	3
parsley, chopped	½ tsp	1 tsp

1 Trim the sweetbreads, blanch for 30 seconds. Pass through seasoned flour.
2 Shallow-fry in oil for 2 minutes, turning.
3 Add butter to pan (*beurre noisette*), then add the lemon juice and chopped parsley.
4 Drain and serve.

* Using lambs' brains in place of sweetbreads

62 Braised calf's cheeks with vegetables

Portions >	4	10
salt, pepper		
calf's cheeks	800 g	2 kg
olive oil or vegetable oil	2 tbsp	5 tbsp
ground cumin	½ tsp	1¼ tsp
white peppercorns	½ tsp	1¼ tsp
cloves	4	10
celery, 5 mm dice	1 stick	2 sticks
bay leaves	2	5
cloves of garlic	8	20
leeks, finely shredded	1	2½
onions, chopped	1	2½
shallots, quartered	2	5
savoy cabbage, shredded	400 g	1 kg
dry white wine	500 ml	1.25 litres
cider	350 ml	875 ml
chopped chives	½ tsp	1 tsp

1 Season the cheeks.
2 Heat the oil in a suitable pan. Sear the cheeks on all sides. Remove and keep warm. Add to the pan the cumin, peppercorns, cloves, celery, bay leaves, garlic, leeks, onions and shallots. Cook until the vegetables start to brown.
3 Add the cabbage and cook until wilted and slightly brown.
4 Add half the white wine and three-quarters of the cider.
5 Return the cheeks to the pan. Cover and braise in the oven at 180°C for approx. 2½ hours until the meat is tender.

6 Remove the cheeks and vegetables from the juices. Set aside and keep warm.
7 Strain the juices and return to the pan. Then add the remaining wine and cider. Bring to the boil. Reduce to a sauce consistency.
8 Return the cheeks to the pan and simmer, basting with the sauce until it is syrupy and the meat is glazed.
9 To serve, place the vegetables on plates with the cheeks on top. Mask with the sauce and sprinkle with chopped chives.
10 Serve with polenta or couscous.

63 Braised oxtail
(ragoût de queue de boeuf)

beef, offal braising

energy	kcal	fat	sat fat	carb	sugar	protein	fibre
2481 KJ	595 kcal	38.0 g	12.0 g	12.3 g	4.7 g	51.6 g	1.4 g

Portions ›	4	10
oxtail	1 kg	2.5 kg
dripping or oil	50 g	125 g
onion	100 g	250 g
carrot	100 g	250 g
flour, browned in the oven	35 g	100 g
tomato purée	25 g	60 g
brown stock	1 litre	2.5 litres
bouquet garni		
clove of garlic	1	2
salt, pepper		
parsley, chopped		

1 Cut the oxtail into sections. Remove the excess fat.
2 Fry on all sides in hot fat.
3 Place in a braising pan or casserole.
4 Roughly cut the onion and carrot. Fry them, then add them to the braising pan.
5 Mix in the flour.
6 Add tomato purée, brown stock, bouquet garni and garlic, and season lightly.
7 Bring to the boil, then skim.
8 Cover with a lid and simmer in the oven until tender (approx. 3 hours).
9 Remove the meat from the sauce, place in a clean pan.
10 Correct the sauce, pass on to the meat and reboil.
11 Serve sprinkled with chopped parsley.

Brown the pieces of oxtail

Mix in the flour

This is usually garnished with glazed turned or neatly cut carrots and turnips, button onions, peas and diamonds of beans.
Oxtail must be very well cooked so that the meat comes away from the bone easily.

Healthy eating tips
- Keep added salt to a minimum.
- Fry in a small amount of an unsaturated oil and drain off all excess fat after frying.
- Serve with mashed potato and additional green vegetables.

Try something different
Haricot oxtail can be made using the same recipe with the addition of 100 g (250 g for 10 portions) cooked haricot beans, added approx. ½ hour before the oxtail has completed cooking.

This chapter is relevant to the following units:

- Prepare poultry for basic dishes (NVQ)
- Prepare game for basic dishes (NVQ)
- Cook and finish basic poultry dishes (NVQ)
- Cook and finish basic game dishes (NVQ)
- Prepare and cook poultry (VRQ).

Chicken vol-au-vent http://bit.ly/xrFVRm	
Fricassée of chicken http://bit.ly/xCozjz	
Duckling with orange sauce http://bit.ly/Arrg0Q	

These online videos may be accessed from this chapter using the QR codes or web links (see page ix to find out how these work):	
Cutting chicken for sauté	319
Preparing a duck	323

Poultry

The term 'poultry' in its general sense is applied to all domestic fowl bred for food, and includes turkeys, geese, ducks, fowls and pigeons.

Originally, fowl were classified according to size and feeding by specific names as shown in Table 8.1.

Table 8.1 Traditional classification of fowl

	Weight (kg)	Number of portions
single baby chicken (poussin)	0.3–0.5	1
double baby chicken (poussin)	0.5–0.75	2
small roasting chicken	0.75–1	3–4
medium roasting chicken	1–2	4–6
large roasting or boiling chicken	2–3	6–8
capon	3–4.5	8–12
old boiling fowl	2.5–4	

There is approximately 15–20 per cent bone in poultry. The different types of chicken are:

- Spring chickens: poussin 4–6 weeks old, used for roasting and grilling.
- Broiler chickens: 3–4 months old, used for roasting, grilling, casserole.
- Medium roasting chickens: fully grown, tender prime birds, used for roasting, grilling, sauté, casserole, suprêmes and pies.
- Large roasting or boiling chickens: used for roasting, boiling, casserole, galantine.
- Capons: specially bred, fattened cock birds used for roasting.
- Old hens: used for stocks and soups.

Food value

The flesh of poultry is more easily digested than that of butcher's meat. It contains protein and is therefore useful for building and repairing body tissues and providing heat and energy. The fat content is low and it contains a high percentage of unsaturated fatty acids.

Storage

Chilled birds should be stored between 1°C and 4°C. Oven-ready birds are eviscerated (gutted and cleaned) and should be stored in a refrigerator. Frozen birds must be kept in a deep freeze until required, but must be completely thawed, preferably in a refrigerator, before being cooked. This procedure is essential to reduce the risk of food poisoning: chickens are potential carriers of salmonella and campylobacter, and if birds are cooked from the frozen state there is a risk that the centre of the bird will not reach the required degree of heat to kill off these pathogens.

When using frozen poultry, check that:

- the packaging is undamaged
- there are no signs of freezer burns, which are indicated by white patches on the skin
- frozen birds are defrosted by moving them from the freezer to a refrigerator.

Quality points

- Plump breast, pliable breast bone and firm flesh.
- Skin white and unbroken. Broiler chickens have a faint bluish tint.
- Corn-fed are yellow. Free-range have more colour, a firmer texture and more flavour.
- Bresse chickens are specially bred in France and are highly regarded for their quality and flavour.
- Old birds have coarse scales, large spurs on the legs and long hairs on the skin.

Trussing

To truss a bird for roasting:

- Clean the legs by dipping in boiling water for a few seconds, then remove the scales with a cloth.

- Cut off the outside claws, leaving the centre ones; trim these to half their length.
- To facilitate carving, remove the wishbone.
- Place the bird on its back.
- Hold the legs back firmly.
- Insert a trussing needle through the bird, midway between the leg joints.

- Turn on to its side.
- Pierce the winglet, the skin of the neck, the skin of the carcass and the other winglet.
- Tie the ends of the string securely.
- Secure the legs by inserting the needle through the carcass and over the legs, taking care not to pierce the breast.

Trussing can also be done without a needle.

Trussing a bird for roasting or boiling

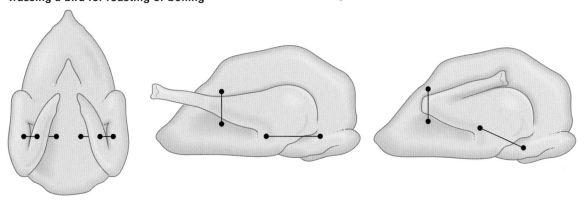

The black dots on the diagrams show where the trussing needle pierces the chicken

Trussing a turkey for roasting (without a needle)

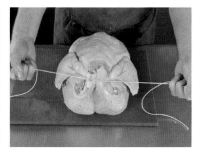

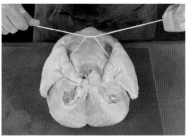

To truss for boiling or pot roasting:

- Proceed as for roasting.
- Cut the leg sinew just below the joint.
- Bend back the legs so that they lie parallel to the breast and secure when trussing, or insert the legs through incisions made in the skin at the rear end of the bird, and secure when trussing.

Cutting chicken

Chicken is cut into pieces as shown in the diagram.
The leg is cut into two parts: drumstick and thigh.

1 wing
2 breast
3 thigh
4 drumstick
5 winglet
6 carcass

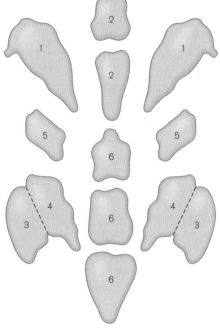

Cuts of chicken

Cutting chicken for sauté, fricassée, pies, etc.

Remove the winglets

Remove the legs from the carcass,
cutting around the oyster

Cut off the feet

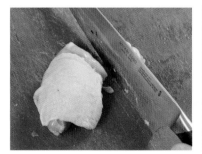

Separate the thigh from the drumstick

Trim the drumstick neatly

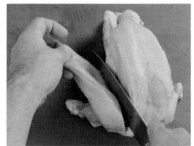

Remove each breast from the carcass

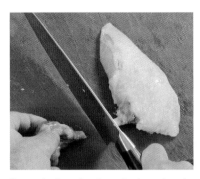

Separate the wing from the breast and trim it

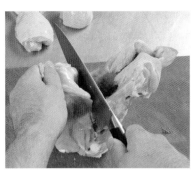

Cut into the cavity, splitting the carcass (this may be used for stock)

Cut each breast in half

Chicken cut for sauté, on the bone, clockwise from top left: thighs, wings, breast pieces, drumsticks and winglets

Cutting chicken for sauté
http://bit.ly/xBU6qv

To prepare chicken for grilling:
- Remove the wishbone.
- Cut off the claws at the first joint.
- Place the bird on its back.
- Insert a large knife through the neck end and out of the vent.
- Cut through the backbone and open out.
- Remove back and rib bones.

The chicken may then be grilled whole (spatchcock, see recipe 2) or cut into pieces.

Preparing a spatchcock chicken

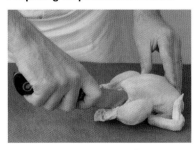

Insert the knife through the neck end

Remove the backbone

Spatchcock chicken ready for cooking

A suprême is the wing and half the breast of a chicken with the trimmed wing bone attached; the white meat of one chicken yields two suprêmes. To cut suprêmes, use a chicken weighing 1.25–1.5 kg. Removing the skin is optional.

Preparing chicken suprêmes

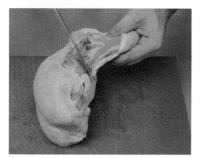

Cut off both the legs

Scrape the wing bone bare, adjoining the breasts. Cut off the winglets near the joints, leaving 1.5–2 cm of bare bone attached. Then remove the wishbone

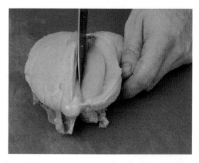

Cut the breasts close to the breastbone and follow the bone down to the wing joint

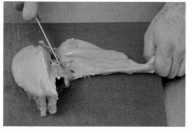

Cut through the joint. Pull the suprêmes off, using the knife to assist

To finish, lift the fillets from the suprêmes and remove the sinew from each. Make an incision lengthways, along the thick side of the suprêmes; open and place the fillets inside. Close, lightly flatten with a bat moistened with water, and trim if necessary

A ballotine is a boned, stuffed leg of bird. To prepare a ballotine for stuffing:

- Using a small, sharp knife, remove the thigh bone.
- Scrape the flesh off the bone of the drumstick towards the claw joint.
- Sever the drumstick bone leaving approximately 2–3 cm at the claw joint end.

Ballotines of chicken may be cooked and served using any of the recipes for chicken sauté presented in this chapter.

Stuffing and tying a ballotine

The scraped drumstick bone has been cut out

Fill the cavities in both the drumstick and thigh with a savoury stuffing

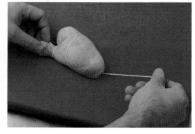

Neaten the shape and secure with string using a trussing needle

To cut up a cooked chicken (roasted or boiled):
- Remove the legs and cut in two (drumstick and thigh).
- Remove the wings.

- Separate the breast from the carcass and divide in two.
- Serve a drumstick with a wing and the thigh with the breast.

Turkey

Turkeys can vary in weight from 3.5 to 20 kg. They are trussed in the same way as chicken. The wishbone should always be removed before trussing in order to facilitate carving. The sinews should be drawn out of the legs. Allow 200 g per portion raw weight.

Stuffings may be rolled in foil, steamed or baked and thickly sliced. If a firmer stuffing is required, mix in one or two raw eggs before cooking.

Preparing a large turkey for roasting

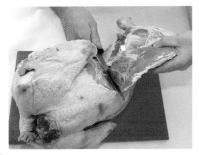

Remove the legs; cooking them separately will reduce the cooking time, and enable the legs and breast to cook more evenly

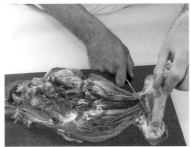

Remove the leg bones

Stuff and roll each leg if required

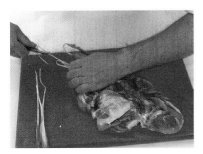

Tie the stuffed legs securely

Cut the remainder of the bird in half, again to reduce the cooking time

The two halves, ready for roasting, with one leg left whole and the other boned, stuffed and rolled

Preparing a chicken or turkey crown

Cut off the legs

Sever the leg at the joint with a sharp tap of the knife

Cut off the front of the bird, leaving the crown

A prepared crown: this is useful for roasting when only a few portions are required or the legs are not wanted

Tunnel boning a turkey or chicken

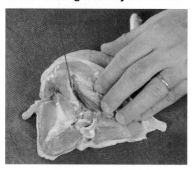

Cut around the exposed end of the bone

Scrape and cut, gently parting the flesh from the bone

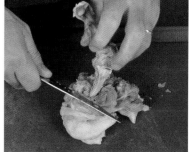

Push down the meat as it is freed, and lift the bone out

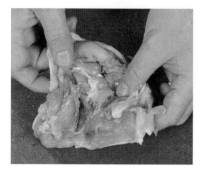

The de-boned leg

Quality points

- Large full breast with undamaged skin and no signs of stickiness.
- Legs smooth with supple feet and a short spur.
- As birds age, the legs turn scaly and the feet harden.

Ducks and geese

Approximate sizes are as follows:
- Duck: 3–4 kg.
- Goose: 6 kg.
- Duckling: 1.5–2 kg.
- Gosling: 3 kg.

Quality points

- Plump breasts.
- Webbed feet tear easily.

- Lower back bends easily.
- Feet and bill should be yellow.

Ducks and geese are prepared for roasting in the same way as chickens. The gizzard is not split but trimmed off with a knife.

Preparing a duck
http://bit.ly/z2rBxZ

Game

Game is the name given to certain wild birds and animals that are eaten. There are two types of game:

1 feathered
2 furred.

The word game is used, for culinary purposes, to describe animals or birds that are hunted for food, although many birds and animals categorised as game are now being bred domestically (e.g. squab (pigeon), duck, venison). Wild animals, because of their diet and general lifestyle, have more of certain enzymes in their tissues than poultry. These tissues break down or metabolise meat proteins; they become active about 24 hours after the animal has been killed, softening the meat, and making it gelatinous and more palatable, as well as giving the characteristic 'gamey' flavour. They also contain micro-organisms (anaerobes), which also help to break down the proteins.

Choosing and buying

The most important factor when buying game is to know its 'life age' and its 'hanging age', since this will determine the method of cookery to be used. Indications of age are by no means infallible, but there are some general guidelines when buying young birds – soft-textured feet, pliable breastbones – and young partridges have pointed flight feathers (the first large feather of the wing), while in older birds these feathers are more rounded. There are many other distinctive guidelines you can use when selecting game, however the grading of game is a specialised subject and best left to the experts.

The seasons for game are shown in Table 8.2.

Table 8.2 Seasonality of game

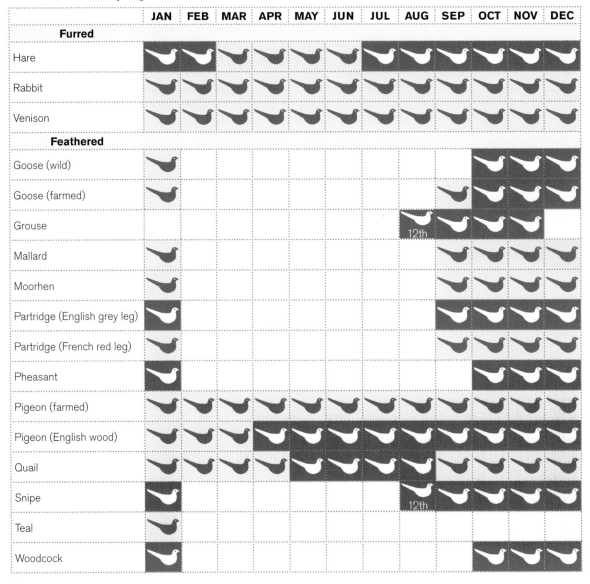

	JAN	FEB	MAR	APR	MAY	JUN	JUL	AUG	SEP	OCT	NOV	DEC
Furred												
Hare	At best	Available	Available	Available	Available	Available	At best	At best	At best	At best	At best	At best
Rabbit	Available	Available	Available	Available	Available	Available	Available	Available	Available	Available	Available	Available
Venison	Available	Available	Available	Available	Available	Available	Available	Available	Available	Available	Available	Available
Feathered												
Goose (wild)	Available									At best	At best	At best
Goose (farmed)	Available								Available	At best	At best	At best
Grouse								At best (12th)	At best	At best	At best	
Mallard	Available									At best	At best	At best
Moorhen	Available									At best	At best	At best
Partridge (English grey leg)	At best									At best	At best	At best
Partridge (French red leg)	Available									Available	Available	Available
Pheasant	At best									At best	At best	At best
Pigeon (farmed)	Available	Available	Available	Available	Available	Available	Available	Available	Available	Available	Available	Available
Pigeon (English wood)	Available	Available	Available	Available	At best	At best	At best	At best	Available	Available	Available	Available
Quail	At best	Available	Available	Available	Available		At best	At best	Available	Available	Available	Available
Snipe	At best							At best (12th)	At best	At best	At best	At best
Teal	At best											
Woodcock	At best									Available	Available	Available

Key:

Available	
At best	

Storage and hanging of game

Game bought from a main dealer will probably have been hung correctly. If, however, you require your game (or any other meat that benefits from hanging) to be hung specifically for you, speak to your butcher or game dealer. The general rules are to hang in a cool, dry, airy place, protected from flies to prevent maggot infestation. As a general rule you should hang the carcass until you detect the first whiff of tainting. In Britain, birds are usually hung from their heads, feet

Practical Cookery 12th edition

down, and rabbits and other game hung with their heads down.

However, there is no real need to hang game, due to the metabolic enzymes present, so if you object to the strong flavour hanging promotes, a short hanging period, or no hanging at all, may be preferable.

Current legislation does not allow a normal kitchen environment to hang or pluck game.

Game should be wrapped well and careful consideration given to its age; strict labelling is essential because, when in prime condition, the meat may have a slightly tainted smell, which may be difficult to discern from the smell that denotes the meat is past its best.

Drawing and washing

This is the process that is carried out when the bird is sold with all its entrails still inside. To remove, make a small lateral incision into the backside of the bird, then insert your forefinger and index finger, and roll them around the inner cavity of the bird, thus loosening the membrane that holds in the innards. When loose, remove from the wider backside and discard. Ensure that all the innards are removed, wash and dry well.

Cooking game

Game meat responds best to roasting. Young game birds in particular should be roasted and it is traditional to leave them unstuffed. Due to the low fat content of game, especially wild non-domestic varieties, added fat in the form of sliced streaky bacon, lardons and the like can be wrapped around the bird to help baste while cooking, thus retaining moisture. Older, tougher game or high-worked muscle groups, such as a haunch of venison, should be casseroled/stewed or made into pies or terrines. Marinating in oil, vinegar or wine with herbs and spices helps make tough meat more tender; it may also enhance the taste and it speeds up the action of the metabolic enzyme that breaks the game down.

As game birds are deficient in fat, a thin slice of fat bacon (bard) should be tied over the breast during cooking to prevent it from drying; this is also placed on the breast when serving.

The preparation techniques for poultry, such as stuffing ballotines, also apply to game birds.

Roast game birds are served with gravy; bread sauce and browned breadcrumbs (toasted or fried) are served separately.

Roast pheasant, partridge or grouse may also be served in the traditional manner: on a croûte of fried bread, garnished with thick round pieces of toasted French bread spread with game farce (recipe 29), game chips and picked watercress.

Game birds

Pigeon

As pigeons do not have gall bladders it is not necessary to remove the livers when they are drawn and cleaned.

Tender young pigeons less than 12 months old can be roasted, pot roasted, or split open and grilled and served (for example, with a Robert, charcutière or devilled sauce).

Young pigeons (squabs) can be cut in half, flattened slightly, seasoned, shallow-fried in butter, and cooked and finished as for sautés of chicken (e.g. chasseur, bordelaise).

Quail

Only plump birds with firm white fat should be selected. When prepared the entrails are drawn, but the heart and liver are retained inside the birds. They may be roasted, spit roasted, cooked 'en casserole' or poached in a rich, well-flavoured chicken or veal stock (or a combination of both).

Quails may also be boned out from the back and stuffed with a forcemeat.

Hare and rabbits

The rabbit is distinguished from the hare by its shorter ears, feet and body.

The ears of good-quality hare and rabbits should tear easily. With old hare, the lip is more pronounced than in young animals.

Venison

Venison is the meat of the red deer, fallow deer and roe deer. Of these three, the meat of the roe deer is considered to have the best and most delicate eating quality. The prime cuts are the legs, loins and best ends. The shoulder of young animals can be boned, rolled and roasted, but if in any doubt as to its tenderness, it should be cut up and used for stewed or braised dishes.

The main types available are:

- roe deer
- fallow deer
- red deer
- muntjac
- sika deer.

Venison is available from most catering butchers.

The cuts and joints of venison are shown in the diagram and Table 8.3.

Cuts and joints of venison

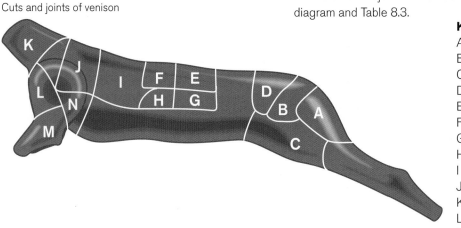

Key

A Silverside
B Rump
C Thick flank
D Topside
E Loin
F Best end
G Fillet
H Mignon
I Cutlets
J Chuck rib
K Neck
L Plate
M Shin
N Shoulder

Table 8.3 Cuts and joints of venison

Cut	Joints	Approx. weights	Uses
Haunch	Silverside	2 kg	Stewing, braising
	Topside	2 kg	Roasting, braising
	Thick flank	1.5 kg	Stewing
	Rump dice, escalopes	1.5 kg	Roasting, braising, frying
Saddle	Saddle	8 kg	
	Loin	1.4 kg	
	Noisettes	1 kg	Roasting, braising, frying
	Chops	1 kg	
	Filet mignon	0.5 kg	
Best end	Best end cutlets	1.5 kg	Frying, roasting, braising
Fillet	Fillet	1 kg	Escalopes, medallions, steaks
Shin	Shin	0.5 kg	Dice, mince, stewing
Neck	Neck	2 kg	Grilling, dice, mince, stewing
Shoulder	Shoulder	4 kg	Roasting/stewing, braising, dice, mince, burgers, sausages
	Chuck rib	2 kg	

Practical Cookery 12th edition

Food value

The nutritional value of venison is compared with other meats in Table 8.4. It is a good meat to use when planning healthier menus as it contains little fat. The fat in venison is mainly polyunsaturated and therefore lower in cholesterol.

Table 8.4 Nutritional information: venison and other meats

	Fat g/100 g	Protein g/100 g	Iron mg/100 g	Cholesterol mg/100 g
venison	1.6	22.2	3.3	29
chicken	2.1	22.3	0.7	90
beef	12.9	20.4	1.3	48
lamb	12.3	19.0	0.25	78
pork	2.2	21.7	0.8	64

Venison is a good source of protein as 100 g of venison supplies 68.5 per cent of the daily value for protein for only 179 calories and 1.4 g of saturated fat. It is also a source of iron, Vitamin B12 and other B vitamins.

Quality points

- The flesh should be dark red in colour.
- The flesh should be dry and firm.
- The carcass should have a good amount of flesh and a close grain texture.
- The flesh should be lean, with little fat.
- There should be no unpleasant smell.

After slaughter, carcasses should be hung well in a cool place for several days and, when cut into joints, are usually marinated before being cooked. Joints of venison should be well fleshed and a dark brownish-red colour.

Cooking and serving cutlets

Venison cutlets (cut from the best end) and chops (cut from the loin) are usually well trimmed and cooked by shallow-frying, provided that the meat is tender. If in doubt, they should be braised.

After they are cooked they should be removed from the pan, the fat poured off and the pan deglazed with stock, red wine, brandy, Madeira or sherry, which is then added to the accompanying sauce.

A spicy, peppery sauce is usually offered, which can be varied by the addition of any one or more extra ingredients (e.g. cream, yoghurt, redcurrant jelly, choice of cooked beetroot, sliced button or wild mushrooms, cooked pieces of chestnut, and so on).

Accompaniments can include, for example, a purée of a root vegetable (e.g. celeriac, turnip, swede, carrot, parsnip or any combination of these).

Cooking and serving steaks

Venison steaks, or escalopes, are cut from the boned-out nuts of meat from the loins, trimmed well and thinned slightly with a meat bat.

The escalopes can be quickly shallow-fried and finished as for cutlets and chops, and served with a variety of accompanying sauces and garnishes.

Cooking and serving haunch of venison

The haunch may be roasted or braised. It is popular served hot or cold.

Wild boar

For good quality, buy animals obtained from suppliers using as near as possible 100 per cent pure breeding stock wild boars that are free to roam and forage for food, rather than those that have been penned and fed.

Animals between 12 and 18 months old, weight 60–75 kg on the hoof, are best slaughtered in the late summer when their fat content is lower. The meat should be hung for 7 to 10 days before being used.

Young boar up to the age of six months are sufficiently tender for cooking in noisettes and cutlets, and joints for roasting. The prime cuts of older animals (e.g. leg, loin, best end) can be marinated and braised.

Boar's head is prepared by boning the head and stuffing it with a forcemeat to which strips of ox tongue, foie gras, truffles and pistachio nuts can be added. The head is tied securely in a cloth and simmered gently. When cooled it is completely coated and the tusks are re-inserted. Boar's head is a traditional Christmas cold buffet dish served with a spicy sauce (e.g. Cumberland).

1 Grilled chicken
(poulet grillé)

chicken grilling, griddling

energy	kcal	fat	sat fat	carb	sugar	protein	fibre
975 KJ	234 kcal	15.7 g	4.3 g	0.0 g	0.0 g	23.3 g	0.0 g
*

1 Season the chicken with salt and mill pepper, and prepare as for grilling (see page 319).
2 Brush with oil or melted butter or margarine, and place on preheated greased grill bars or on a barbecue or a flat baking tray under a salamander.
3 Brush frequently with melted fat during cooking; allow approximately 15–20 minutes each side.
4 Test if cooked by piercing the drumstick with a skewer or trussing needle; there should be no sign of blood issuing from the leg. The breast will take less time to cook than the drumstick.
5 Serve garnished with picked watercress and offer a suitable sauce separately.

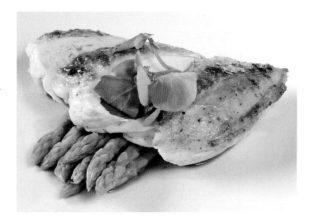

Season the chicken before cooking

Brush with oil while grilling or griddling

Grilled chicken is frequently served garnished with streaky bacon, tomatoes and mushrooms. The chicken may be marinated for 2–3 hours before grilling, in a mixture of oil, lemon juice, spices, herbs, freshly grated ginger, finely chopped garlic, salt and pepper. Chicken or turkey portions can also be grilled and marinated beforehand if wished (breasts or boned-out lightly battered thighs of chicken).

Healthy eating tips
- Use a minimum amount of salt and an unsaturated oil.
- Garnish with grilled tomatoes and mushrooms, and serve with Delmonico potatoes and green vegetables.

* Based on chicken with bone, wing and leg quarters

2 Chicken spatchcock
(poulet grillé à la crapaudine)

chicken  grilling, griddling

energy	kcal	fat	sat fat	carb	sugar	protein	fibre
1560 KJ	372 kcal	24.1 g	8.0 g	0.0 g	0.0 g	38.9 g	0.0 g

Portions ›	4	10
chicken, 1.25–1.5 kg	1	2½

1 Cut horizontally from below the point of the breast over the top of the legs down to the wing joints, without removing the breasts. Fold back the breasts.

2 Snap and reverse the backbone into the opposite direction so that the point of the breast now extends forward.

3 Flatten slightly. Remove any small bones.

4 Skewer the wings and legs in position.

5 Season with salt and mill pepper.

6 Brush with oil or melted butter.

7 Place on preheated grill bars or on a flat tray under a salamander.

8 Brush frequently with melted fat or oil during cooking and allow approximately 15–20 minutes on each side.

9 Test if cooked by piercing the drumstick with a needle or skewer – there should be no sign of blood.

10 Serve garnished with picked watercress and offer a suitable sauce separately (e.g. devilled sauce or a compound butter).

Healthy eating tips

- Use a minimum amount of salt to season the chicken.
- The fat content can be reduced if the skin is removed from the chicken.
- Use a small amount of an unsaturated oil to brush the chicken.
- Serve with a large portion of potatoes and vegetables.

3 Sauté of chicken
(poulet sauté)

chicken shallow frying, sauté

energy	kcal	fat	sat fat	carb	sugar	protein	fibre	*
1329 KJ	320 kcal	22.3 g	8.1 g	0.3 g	0.3 g	29.3 g	0.0 g	

Portions >	4	10
chicken, 1.25–1.5 kg	1	2½
butter or oil	50 g	125 g
salt, pepper		
jus-lié or demi-glace	250 ml	625 ml
parsley, chopped		

Cutting chicken for sauté
http://bit.ly/xBU6qv

1 Prepare the chicken for sauté (see page 318).
2 Place the butter or oil in a sauté pan on a fairly hot stove.
3 Season the pieces of chicken and place in the pan in the following order: drumsticks, thighs, wings, winglets and breast (thicker pieces first, as they take longer to cook).
4 Cook to a golden brown on both sides.
5 Cover with a lid and cook on the stove or in the oven until tender.
6 Remove the chicken pieces and dress neatly in an entrée dish.
7 Drain off all fat from the sauté pan.
8 Return to the heat, add the *jus-lié* or demi-glace and simmer for 3–4 minutes.
9 Correct the seasoning and skim.
10 Pass through a fine strainer on to the chicken.
11 Sprinkle with chopped parsley and serve.

* Based on average edible portion of roasted meat (100 g)

The leg meat takes longer to cook than the breast meat, which is why the drumsticks and thighs should be added first.
The cleaned chicken giblets may be used in the making of the sauce.

Healthy eating tips
- Use a minimum amount of salt to season the chicken.
- The fat content can be reduced if the skin is removed from the chicken.
- Use a little unsaturated oil to cook the chicken, and drain off all excess fat from the cooked chicken.
- Serve with a large portion of new potatoes and seasonal vegetables.

4 Chicken sauté chasseur
(poulet sauté chasseur)

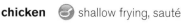

chicken · shallow frying, sauté

energy	kcal	fat	sat fat	carb	sugar	protein	fibre	*
2430 KJ	579 kcal	45.8 g	20.7 g	2.1 g	1.6 g	37.6 g	1.5 g	

Portions ⟩	4	10
butter or oil	50 g	125 g
salt, pepper		
chicken, 1.25–1.5 kg, cut for sauté	1	2½
shallots, chopped	10 g	25 g
button mushrooms, washed and sliced	100 g	250 g
dry white wine	3 tbsp	8 tbsp
jus-lié, demi-glace or reduced brown stock	250 ml	625 ml
tomato concassé	200 g	500 g
parsley and tarragon, chopped		

1 Place the butter or oil in a sauté pan on a fairly hot stove.
2 Season the pieces of chicken and place in the pan in the following order: drumsticks, thighs, wings and breast.
3 Cook to a golden brown on both sides.
4 Cover with a lid and cook on the stove or in the oven until the chicken is tender, there are no signs of blood and the thickest parts show 75°C on a probe. Dress neatly in a suitable dish.
5 Add the shallots to the sauté pan, rubbing them into the pan sediment to extract the flavour. Cover with a lid and cook on a gentle heat for 1–2 minutes.

6 Add the washed, sliced mushrooms and cover with a lid. Cook gently for 3–4 minutes, without colour. Drain off the fat.
7 Add the white wine and reduce by half. Add the *jus-lié*, demi-glace or reduced stock.
8 Add the tomatoes. Simmer for 5 minutes.
9 Correct the seasoning and pour over the chicken.
10 Sprinkle with chopped parsley and tarragon and serve.

Ballotines of chicken chasseur can be used for this recipe or lightly braised (as shown).

Key point
Add the soft herbs and tomatoes just before serving.

Healthy eating tips
- Use a minimum amount of salt to season the chicken.
- The fat content can be reduced if the skin is removed from the chicken.
- Use a little unsaturated oil to cook the chicken, and drain off all excess fat from the cooked chicken.
- Serve with a large portion of new potatoes and seasonal vegetables.

Place the chicken into the hot pan

Cook the shallots in the pan that was used for the chicken – they will pick up the sediment and flavour

* Using butter

Crumbed breast of chicken with asparagus

(suprême de volaille aux pointes d'asperges)

chicken, stems and shoots shallow frying

energy	kcal	fat	sat fat	carb	sugar	protein	fibre
1831 KJ	439 kcal	26.4 g	8.9 g	15.7 g	1.5 g	35.5 g	1.3 g

Portions ⟩	4	10
suprêmes of chicken (page 320)	4 x 125 g	10 x 125 g
egg	1	2
breadcrumbs (white or wholemeal)	50 g	125 g
butter	100 g	250 g
jus-lié	60 ml	150 ml
asparagus	200 g	500 g

1 Pané the chicken suprêmes. Shake off all surplus crumbs.
2 Neaten and mark on one side with a palette knife.
3 Heat half of the butter in a sauté pan.
4 Gently fry the suprêmes to a golden brown on both sides (6–8 minutes). Use a probe to check that the centre has reached 75°C.
5 Dress the suprêmes on a flat dish and keep warm.
6 Mask the suprêmes with the remaining butter cooked to the nut-brown stage *(beurre noisette)*.
7 Surround the suprêmes with a cordon of *jus-lié*.
8 Garnish each suprême with a neat bundle of asparagus points (previously cooked, refreshed and reheated with a little butter).

Healthy eating tips
- Use a minimum amount of salt.
- Remove the skin from the suprêmes and fry in a little unsaturated vegetable oil. Drain on kitchen paper.
- Try omitting the additional cooked butter.
- Serve with plenty of boiled new potatoes and vegetables.

6 Suprême of chicken in a cream sauce

chicken  shallow frying

(suprême de volailles à la crème)

Portions ›	4	10
suprême of chicken	4	10
butter or oil	50 g	125 g
flour (optional)	25 g	60 g
dry sherry or white wine	30 ml	75 ml
double cream	125 ml	300 ml
salt, cayenne pepper		
fresh parsley, chervil and tarragon, chopped, to garnish		

1 Heat the butter or oil in a suitable pan (sauté pan).
2 Lightly flour and season the suprêmes. Gently cook on both sides for approximately 7–9 minutes without colour. Check that the suprêmes are cooked to the centre: insert a small, sharp knife into the thickest part to check that the juices run clear, or check that the temperature has reached 75°C.

3 Once cooked, remove the suprêmes and keep warm.
4 Drain off the fat from the pan.
5 Deglaze with the sherry or white wine.
6 Add the cream, bring to the boil, and correct the seasoning.
7 Allow to reduce slightly, then strain through a fine strainer.
8 Plate the suprêmes on individual plates, mask with the sauce and garnish with chopped fresh herbs.

Try something different
- An alternative method for the sauce is to use half the amount of cream, and an equal amount of chicken velouté (see page 43).
- The sauce may be garnished with a small dice of cooked peppers (yellow, red and green) or with sliced mushrooms and peppers.

7 Paella

(savoury rice with chicken, fish, vegetables and spices)

chicken, shellfish, rice boiling, braising

energy	kcal	fat	sat fat	carb	sugar	protein	fibre
3383 KJ	804 kcal	31.0 g	6.2 g	48.8 g	3.8 g	85.7 g	1.3 g	*

Portions ›	4	10
lobster, cooked	400 g	1 kg
squid	200 g	500 g
gambas (Mediterranean prawns), cooked	400 g	1 kg
mussels	400 g	1 kg
white stock	1 litre	2.5 litres
pinch of saffron		
onion, finely chopped	50 g	125 g
clove of garlic, finely chopped	1	2–3
red pepper, diced	50 g	125 g
green pepper, diced	50 g	125 g
roasting chicken, cut for sauté	1.5 kg	3.75 kg
olive oil	60 ml	150 ml
short-grain rice	200 g	500 g
thyme bay leaf seasoning		
tomatoes, skinned, deseeded, diced	200 g	500 g
lemon wedges, to finish		

1 Prepare the lobster: cut it in half, remove the claws and legs, discard the sac and trail. Remove the meat from the claws and cut the tail into 3–4 pieces, leaving the meat in the shell.
2 Clean the squid, pull the body and head apart. Extract the transparent 'pen' from the body. Rinse well, pulling off the thin purple membrane on the outside. Remove the ink sac. Cut the body into rings and the tentacles into 1 cm lengths.
3 Prepare the gambas by shelling the body.
4 Boil the mussels in water or white stock until the shells open. Shell the mussels and retain the cooking liquid.
5 Boil the white stock and mussel liquor together, infused with saffron. Simmer for 5–10 minutes.
6 Sweat the finely chopped onion in a suitable pan, without colour. Add the garlic and the peppers.

7 Sauté the chicken in olive oil until cooked and golden brown, then drain.
8 Add the rice to the onions and garlic and sweat for 2 minutes.
9 Add about 200 ml white stock and mussel liquor.
10 Add the thyme, bay leaf and seasoning. Bring to the boil, then cover with lightly oiled greaseproof paper and lid. Cook for 5–8 minutes, in a moderately hot oven at 180°C.
11 Add the squid and cook for another 5 minutes.
12 Add the tomatoes, chicken and lobster pieces, mussels and gambas. Stir gently, cover with a lid and reheat the rice in the oven.
13 Correct the consistency of the rice if necessary by adding more stock, so that it looks sufficiently moist without being too wet. Correct the seasoning.
14 When all is reheated and cooked, place in a suitable serving dish, decorate with 4 (10) gambas and 4 (10) mussels halved and shelled. Finish with wedges of lemon.

* Using edible chicken meat

For a traditional paella, a raw lobster may be used, which should be prepared as follows. Remove the legs and claws and crack the claws. Cut the lobster in half crosswise, between the tail and the carapace. Cut the carapace in two lengthwise. Discard the sac. Cut across the tail in thick slices through the shell. Remove the trail, wash the lobster pieces and cook with the rice.

Healthy eating tips

- To reduce the fat, skin the chicken and use a little unsaturated oil to sweat the onions and fry the chicken.
- No added salt is necessary.
- Serve with a large green salad.

8 Chicken palak
(chicken fried with spinach and spices)

chicken, leafy vegetables shallow frying, stewing

energy	kcal	fat	sat fat	carb	sugar	protein	fibre	*
1575 KJ	378 kcal	21.9 g	9.5 g	4.4 g	3.5 g	41.3 g	1.9 g	

Portions >	4	10
chicken, 1.5 kg, cut for sauté	1	2
ghee, butter or oil	50 g	125 g
onion, finely chopped	50 g	125 g
clove of garlic, crushed and chopped	1	2–3
fresh ginger, chopped	25 g	60 g
green chilli, chopped	1	2
ground cumin	1 tsp	2½ tsp
ground coriander	1 tsp	2½ tsp
spinach, washed and finely chopped	250 g	625 g
tomatoes, skinned, deseeded, diced	200 g	500 g
chicken stock	250 ml	625 ml

1 Gently fry the chicken in the fat until golden brown.
2 Remove the chicken; fry the onion and garlic until lightly browned. Add the spices and sweat for 3 minutes.
3 Stir in the spinach, add the tomatoes and season. Add the chicken pieces.
4 Add the chicken stock, bring to the boil.

5 Cover with a lid and cook in a moderate oven at 180°C for 30 minutes or until the chicken is tender. Stir occasionally, adding more stock if necessary.
6 Serve in a suitable dish with rice, chapatis (see page 587) and dhal.

Healthy eating tips

- Skin the chicken and fry in a small amount of unsaturated oil.
- Skim excess fat from the finished dish.
- Serve with plenty of rice, dhal, chapatis and a vegetable dish.

* Estimated edible meat used; butter used

9 Deep-fried chicken

chicken deep frying

energy	kcal	fat	sat fat	carb	sugar	protein	fibre
1754 KJ	421 kcal	28.6 g	6.1 g	14.5 g	0.4 g	27.2 g	0.5 g

1 Cut the chicken as for sauté. It is advisable to remove the bones from chicken that will be deep-fried.

2 Coat with flour, egg and crumbs (pané), or pass them through a light batter (see page 212) to which herbs can be added.

3 Deep-fry in hot fat (approx. 170–180°C) until golden brown and cooked through – about 5 minutes. When the chicken is cooked, a probe in the thickest part will read 75°C+, and the juices will run clear when the chicken is pierced.

For suprêmes, make an incision, stuff with a compound butter, flour, egg and crumb, and deep-fry as in Chicken Kiev (recipe 10).

Healthy eating tip

The fat content can be reduced if the skin is removed from the chicken.

336

Practical Cookery 12th edition

10 Chicken Kiev

chicken 🙂 deep frying

energy	kcal	fat	sat fat	carb	sugar	protein	fibre	sodium
2094 KJ	500 kcal	26.1 g	14.4 g	24.4 g	0.9 g	43.4 g	1.0 g	0.5 g

Portions ⟩	4	10
suprêmes of chicken	4 x 150 g	10 x 150 g
butter	100 g	250 g
seasoned flour	25 g	65 g
eggs	2	5
breadcrumbs	100 g	250 g

1. Make an incision along the thick sides of the suprêmes. Insert 25 g cold butter into each. Season.
2. Pass through seasoned flour, eggwash and crumbs, ensuring complete coverage. Eggwash and crumb twice if necessary.
3. Deep-fry until completely cooked. When the chicken is cooked, a probe in the thickest part will read 75°C+, and the juices will run clear when the chicken is pierced. Drain and serve.

Carefully make an incision in the top of the suprême

Stuff with softened butter

Dip the chicken in flour, egg and then coat with breadcrumbs

Key point

The butter must be pushed well into the suprême, and the incision must be sealed, or the butter will leak out during cooking.

Try something different

Additional ingredients may be added to the butter before insertion:
- chopped garlic and parsley
- fine herbs such as tarragon or chives
- liver paté.

11 Braised chicken leg forestière

chicken, fungi braising

energy	kcal	fat	sat fat	carb	sugar	protein	fibre	sodium
1878 KJ	448 kcal	15.9 g	3.9 g	16.9 g	8.7 g	49.9 g	3.6 g	1.0 g

Portions ⟩	4	10
chicken legs	4	10
olive oil	2 tbsp	5 tbsp
onions, sliced fairly thickly	2	5
clove of garlic, crushed	1	2
smoked bacon, thickly sliced rashers cut into lardons	3	8
whole button or small chestnut mushrooms (if larger, cut in half)	100 g	250 g
oyster mushrooms, sliced in half	100 g	250 g
plain flour	1½ tbsp	4½ tbsp
tomato purée	1 tbsp	2½ tbsp
red wine	250 ml	625 ml
brown chicken stock	400 ml	1 litre
tomatoes, blanched, peeled, concassé	3	7½
fresh tarragon and parsley, chopped	15 g	35 g

These quantities give a suitable quantity for a moderate portion, served during a three-course meal. For a hearty portion, allow 2 chicken legs.

1 Season the chicken with salt and pepper. Heat the olive oil in a lidded sauté pan or shallow casserole. Pan-fry the chicken over a medium-high heat, turning, until golden on both sides.

2 Remove from the pan and keep to one side. You will need about 2 tablespoons of fat left in the pan to cook the onions, so if the legs have released a lot of fat, drain off the excess.

3 Add the onions and fry for 2–3 minutes before adding the bacon, garlic and mushrooms to the pan. Continue to stir until they have a little colour and the mushrooms are beginning to soften.

4 Sprinkle over the flour and stir until the flour has lightly browned.

5 Stir in the tomato purée and then gradually add the red wine and chicken stock, stirring until the liquid has fully mixed into the flour and purée paste.

6 Return the chicken to the pan and bring to a simmer. Place a lid on the pan and continue to cook, allowing the sauce to just simmer for about 1 hour, or until the meat is completely tender.

7 To finish, remove the chicken legs, place onto a plate or tray and keep in a warm place, e.g. the side of the stove. Skim the sauce of any further excess fat and adjust the consistency of the sauce as necessary.

8 Adjust the seasoning before adding the tomatoes.

9 Place the chicken legs back into the sauce and scatter over the chopped herbs before serving.

Practical Cookery 12th edition

12 Steamed ballotine of chicken with fines herbes stuffing and red wine jus

chicken, herbs 🏠 steaming

energy	kcal	fat	sat fat	carb	sugar	protein	fibre	sodium
1626 KJ	390 kcal	24.9 g	8.5 g	1.8 g	0.9 g	33.4 g	0.5 g	1.1 g

Portions >	4	10
chicken legs	4	10
Forcemeat		
minced chicken	120 g	300 g
parsley	1 tsp	3 tsp
tarragon	1 tsp	3 tsp
chives	1 tsp	3 tsp
chervil	1 tsp	3 tsp
salt and pepper		
Red wine jus		
shallots, sliced	75 g	150 g
butter	25 g	50 g
garlic	5 g	10 g
red wine	175 ml	350 ml
chicken stock	175 ml	350 ml
veal or beef jus	125 ml	250 ml
bay leaves	1	2
thyme, sprigs	½	1

1 Mix all of the herbs with the minced chicken. Season the mix and divide evenly between the chicken legs.
2 Remove the thighbone and the knuckle joint from the chicken legs.
3 Season the leg and then stuff with the forcemeat and roll the leg into a neat cylinder. Either tie the leg in place or roll tightly in clingfilm, and tie off the ends.
4 Steam the legs for 30–45 minutes or until the core temperature reaches 84°C.
5 Allow the chicken legs to rest so they will stay in shape.
6 When the chicken legs have rested and cooled slightly, remove the string or clingfilm and dry them.
7 Heat a sauté pan with oil and butter, add the chicken legs and brown the skin. Slice and serve with the sauce.

For the red wine jus
1 Caramelise the shallots in the butter until golden, adding the garlic at the end.
2 Strain off any excess butter, deglaze the pan with the red wine and reduce by half.
3 Add the chicken stock and veal jus and reduce to a sauce consistency, adding the aromats for the last 5 minutes.
4 Pass through muslin cloth and serve over the sliced ballotines.

Try something different
Instead of the traditional chicken legs, ballotines can be made using:
● chicken suprêmes, batted out, stuffed and rolled
● chicken breasts: make an incision in the thicker part and fill this with forcemeat.
These ballotines are cooked in the same way.

13 Chicken à la king
(emincé de volaille à la king)

chicken shallow frying, poaching

energy	kcal	fat	sat fat	carb	sugar	protein	fibre
1226 KJ	292 kcal	16.7 g	7.8 g	3.2 g	0.8 g	30.4 g	0.9 g

Portions ❯	4	10
button mushrooms	100 g	250 g
butter or oil	25 g	60 g
red pepper, skinned	50 g	125 g
chicken, boiled or steamed	400 g	1.25 kg
sherry	30 ml	75 ml
chicken velouté	125 ml	300 ml
cream or non-dairy cream	30 ml	75 ml

1. Wash, peel and slice the mushrooms.
2. Cook them without colour in the butter or oil.
3. If using raw pepper, discard the seeds, cut the pepper into dice and cook with the mushrooms.
4. Cut the chicken into small, neat slices.
5. Add the chicken to the mushrooms and pepper.
6. Drain off the fat. Add the sherry.
7. Add the velouté and bring to the boil.
8. Finish with the cream and correct the seasoning.
9. Place in a serving dish and decorate with small strips of cooked pepper.

> **Key point**
> Use a velouté with a good chicken flavour, to create the best sauce.

Slice the mushrooms and dice the red pepper

Neatly slice the cooked chicken

Add the velouté during cooking

1 or 2 egg yolks may be used to form a liaison with the cream, mixed into the boiling mixture at the last possible moment and immediately removed from the heat. Chicken à la king may be served in a border of golden-brown duchess potato, or a pilaff of rice (see page 174) may be offered as an accompaniment. It is suitable for a hot buffet dish.

Healthy eating tips
- Use the minimum amount of salt.
- Remove the skin from the cooked chicken.
- Try reducing or omitting the cream used to finish the sauce.
- Serve with plenty of rice and vegetables or salad.

* Using butter or hard margarine

14 Poached suprême of chicken with Madeira and mushroom café cream sauce

chicken, fungi  poaching, shallow frying, sauté

energy	kcal	fat	sat fat	carb	sugar	protein	fibre
2126 KJ	512 kcal	37.3 g	22.4 g	2.5 g	2.2 g	38.2 g	0.8 g

Portions ›	4	10
chicken suprêmes	4	10
butter	40 g	100 g
shallots, finely chopped	40 g	100 g
button mushrooms, sliced	160 g	400 g
Madeira wine	2 tbsp	5 tbsp
brown chicken stock	250 ml	625 ml
double cream	200 ml	500 ml

1 Sauté the shallots and mushrooms in butter until golden brown.
2 Divide the mushroom and shallots into equal piles in a shallow pan – place each of the trimmed chicken suprêmes onto one pile.
3 Add the Madeira and bring to the boil.
4 Add the reduced chicken stock. Bring to the boil. Cover with buttered greaseproof paper.
5 Place the chicken in a oven, pre-heated to 170°C, and cook for 12 minutes or until the core temperature reaches 75°C. (In the suprême with the wing bone, ensure that the meat near the bone reaches 82°C.)
6 When cooked, remove the chicken from the pan and set aside.
7 Leave the mushrooms in the pan for the sauce. Reduce the cooking liquor until it begins to thicken naturally.
8 Add the cream and reduce to a sauce consistency.
9 Season and serve with the chicken suprêmes.

The café cream sauce of Madeira wine, chicken stock and double cream is also known as café au lait.

15 Confit chicken leg with leeks and artichokes

chicken, bulbs confit, braising

energy	kcal	fat	sat fat	carb	sugar	protein	fibre	sodium
3622 KJ	875 kcal	75.9 g	26.1 g	7.4 g	3.6 g	43.3 g	2.6 g	0.8 g

Portions ›	4	10
confit oil	1 litre	2.5 litres
garlic, cloves	4	10
bay leaf	1	3
thyme, sprig		
chicken legs	4 x 200 g	10 x 200 g
vegetable oil	50 ml	125 ml
globe artichokes, prepared, cooked and cut into quarters	4	10
whole leeks, blanched	2	5
brown chicken stock	250 ml	625 ml
butter	50 g	125 g
chives, chopped	1 tbsp	3 tbsp
seasoning		

> Confit oil is 50/50 olive oil and vegetable oil infused with herbs, garlic, whole spice or any specific flavour you wish to impart into the oil; then, through slow cooking in the oil, the foodstuff picks up the flavour.

1 Gently heat the confit oil, add the garlic, bay and thyme.

2 Put the chicken legs in the oil and place on a medium to low heat, ensuring the legs are covered.

3 Cook gently for 3–3½ hours.

4 To test if the legs are cooked, squeeze the flesh on the thigh bone and it should just fall away.

5 When cooked, remove the legs carefully and place on a draining tray.

6 Heat the vegetable oil in a medium sauté pan, add the artichokes and leeks, colour slightly and then add the brown chicken stock.

7 Reduce the heat to a simmer and cook for 4–5 minutes; meanwhile place the confit leg on a baking tray and place in a pre-heated oven at 210°C; remove when the skin is golden brown (approx. 5 minutes), taking care as the meat is delicate.

8 Place the chicken in a serving dish or on a plate, check the leeks and artichokes are cooked through, and bring the stock to a rapid boil, working in the butter to form an emulsion.

9 Add the chopped chives to the sauce and nap over the chicken leg.

After cooking in oil, squeeze the thigh to determine whether it is done

Remove from the oven once the chicken is golden brown

Add the butter to the stock to form an emulsion

> This dish utilises the less popular chicken legs; this is not only very cost-effective but has great depth of flavour due to the work the muscle group has done.

16 Chicken in red wine
(coq au vin)

chicken stewing

energy	kcal	fat	sat fat	carb	sugar	protein	fibre	*
4794 KJ	1141 kcal	95.7 g	32.9 g	16.6 g	2.3 g	49.0 g	1.7 g	

Portions ⟩	4	10
roasting chicken, 1.5 kg	1	2–3
lardons	50 g	125 g
small chipolatas	4	10
button mushrooms	50 g	125 g
butter	50 g	125 g
sunflower oil	3 tbsp	7 tbsp
small button onions	12	30
red wine	500 ml	900 ml
For the beurre manié		
butter	25 g	60 g
flour	10 g	25 g

1 Cut the chicken as for sauté (see page 318). Blanch the lardons.
2 If the chipolatas are large divide into two.
3 Wash and cut the mushrooms into quarters.
4 Sauté the lardons, mushrooms and chipolatas in a mixture of butter and oil. Remove when cooked.
5 Lightly season the pieces of chicken and place in the pan in the correct order (see recipe 3) with the button onions. Sauté until almost cooked.
6 Place in a casserole with the mushrooms and lardons.
7 Drain off the fat from the sauté pan. Deglaze with the red wine and stock; bring to the boil.
8 Transfer the liquid to the casserole (just covering the chicken); cover with a lid and finish cooking.
9 Remove the chicken and onions, place into a clean pan.
10 Lightly thicken the liquor with a beurre manié of butter and flour by whisking small pieces of it slowly into the simmering liquid.
11 Pass the sauce over the chicken and onions, add the mushrooms, chipolatas and lardons. Correct the seasoning and reheat.

Sauté the other ingredients before the chicken

Sauté the chicken pieces and onion in the same pan

Add a beurre manié

* Using sunflower oil and hard margarine

energy	kcal	fat	sat fat	carb	sugar	protein	fibre	*
3357 KJ	799 kcal	62.6 g	25.1 g	16.4 g	1.9 g	43.3 g	1.8 g	

Portions ❯	4	10
chicken, 1.25–1.5 kg	1	2–3
salt, pepper		
streaky bacon	100 g	250 g
button mushrooms, washed and sliced	100 g	250 g
onion, chopped	1	2½
chicken stock	250 ml	625 ml
chopped parsley, pinch		
hard-boiled egg, chopped	1	2
puff pastry (page 476)	200 g	500 g

1 Cut the chicken as for sauté (see page 318) or bone out completely and cut into pieces 4 cm × 1 cm.
2 Season lightly with salt and pepper.
3 Wrap each piece in very thin streaky bacon. Place in a pie dish.
4 Add the washed, sliced mushrooms and remainder of the ingredients, except the pastry.
5 Add sufficient cold stock to barely cover the chicken.
6 Cover with puff pastry and allow to rest in a refrigerator.

7 Eggwash and bake at 200°C for approximately 30 minutes, until the paste has set and the juice is simmering.
8 Reduce heat to 160–180°C and continue cooking for 1 hour.

Healthy eating tips
- Add little or no salt – the bacon is salty.
- Remove the skin from the chicken.
- Serve with plenty of starchy carbohydrate and a large mixed salad.

Wrap the chicken pieces in bacon

Pour stock over the pie filling

Eggwash the edge of the pie dish and lay the pastry over

* Using hard margarine in the pastry

Press down gently at the edges to form a seal

Trim off the excess and then crimp the edges with your fingers

18 Tandoori chicken

chicken tandoori cooking

energy	kcal	fat	sat fat	carb	sugar	protein	fibre	*
1436 KJ	342 kcal	14.1 g	4.6 g	10.1 g	8.6 g	44.6 g	0.3 g	

Portions ⟩	4	10
chicken, cut as for sauté (page 318)	1.25–1.5 kg	3–4 kg
salt	1 tsp	2½ tsp
lemon, juice of	1	2½
plain yoghurt	300 ml	800 ml
small onion, chopped	1	3
clove of garlic, peeled	1	3
ginger, piece of, peeled and quartered	5 cm	12 cm
fresh hot green chilli, sliced	½	1
garam masala	2 tsp	5 tsp
ground cumin	1 tsp	2½ tsp
red and yellow colouring, few drops each		

1 Cut slits bone-deep in the chicken pieces.
2 Sprinkle the salt and lemon juice on both sides of the pieces, lightly rubbing into the slits; leave for 20 minutes.
3 Combine the remaining ingredients in a blender or food processor.
4 Brush the marinade on the chicken pieces on both sides, ensuring it goes into the slits. Cover and refrigerate for 6–24 hours.
5 Preheat the oven to the maximum temperature.

6 Shake off as much of the marinade as possible from the chicken pieces; place on skewers and bake for 15–20 minutes or until cooked.
7 Serve with red onion rings and lime or lemon wedges.

Key point

If cooking in a tandoori oven, make sure the chicken is secure on the skewer, so that it cannot slip off during cooking.

Healthy eating tips
● Skin the chicken and reduce the salt by half.
● Serve with rice and vegetables.

* Estimated edible meat used; vegetable oil used

19 Roast chicken with dressing

(poulet rôti à l'anglaise)

chicken roasting

energy	kcal	fat	sat fat	carb	sugar	protein	fibre
1363 KJ	327 kcal	20.4 g	3.7 g	6.7 g	0.7 g	29.5 g	0.3g	*

Portions 〉	4 (per chicken)
chicken, 1.25–1.5 kg	1
onion, chopped	25 g
salt, pepper	
oil or butter	100 g
chopped parsley, pinch	
powdered thyme, pinch	
breadcrumbs (white or wholemeal)	50 g
liver from the chicken, raw, chopped (optional)	

Key point

Arrange the chicken to cook sitting on one leg, then the other leg and then with the breast upright, so that the whole bird cooks evenly.

Healthy eating tips

- Use a little unsaturated oil to cook the onion.
- Keep the added salt to a minimum.
- Serve with plenty of potatoes and vegetables.

* Based on average edible portion of roasted meat (100 g)

1 Lightly season the chicken inside and out with salt.
2 Place on its side in a roasting tin.
3 Cover with 50 g of oil or butter.
4 Place in a hot oven for approx. 20–25 minutes, then turn on to the other leg.
5 Cook for approx. a further 20–25 minutes. Baste frequently.
6 To test whether the chicken is fully cooked, pierce it with a fork between the drumstick and thigh, and hold it over a plate. The juice issuing from the chicken should not show any sign of blood. If using a temperature probe, insert in the thickest part of the leg; it should read 77°C. Place the cooked chicken breast side down to retain all the cooking juices.
7 To make the dressing, gently cook the onion in 50 g of oil or butter without colour.
8 Add the seasoning, herbs and breadcrumbs.
9 Mix in the liver.
10 Correct the seasoning and bake or steam the dressing separately, for approx. 20 minutes, until thoroughly cooked.

20 Turkey escalopes

turkey  shallow frying

energy	kcal	fat	sat fat	carb	sugar	protein	fibre	sodium *
1712 KJ	414 kcal	37.0 g	14.0 g	5.9 g	0.2 g	14.8 g	0.3 g	0.1 g

1 100 g slices cut from boned-out turkey breast can be: lightly floured and gently cooked on both sides in butter or oil with a minimum of colour; or floured, egged and crumbed, and shallow-fried.

2 Serve with a suitable sauce and/or garnish (e.g. pan-fried turkey escalope cooked with oyster mushrooms and finished with white wine and cream).

> **Key point**
> The oil or fat must be hot enough before the escalopes are placed in the pan. If it is too cool, the breadcrumbs will absorb the fat and the dish will be greasy.

* Floured and cooked in butter

21 Roast turkey
(dinde rôti)

energy	kcal	fat	sat fat	carb	sugar	protein	fibre	*
836 KJ	200 kcal	11.75 g	4.0 g	0.0 g	0.0 g	29.0 g	0.0g	

Portions ❯	4	10
turkey	5 kg	12 kg
fat bacon	100 g	250 g
brown stock	375 ml	1 litre
bread sauce, to serve		
Chestnut stuffing (dressing)		
chestnuts	200 g	500 g
sausagemeat	600 g	1.5 kg
onion, chopped	50 g	125 g
Parsley and thyme stuffing (dressing)		
onion, chopped	50 g	125 g
oil or butter	100 g	250 g
salt, pepper		
breadcrumbs (white or wholemeal)	100 g	250 g
powdered thyme, pinch		
chopped parsley, pinch		
turkey liver (raw), chopped		

For the chestnut stuffing

1 Slit the chestnuts on both sides using a small knife.
2 Boil the chestnuts in water for 5–10 minutes.
3 Drain and remove the outer and inner skins while warm.
4 Cook the chestnuts in a little stock for 5 minutes.
5 When cold, dice and mix into the sausagemeat and cooked onion.

For the parsley and thyme stuffing

1 Cook the onion in oil or butter without colour.
2 Remove from the heat, and add the seasoning, crumbs and herbs.
3 Mix in the raw chopped liver (optional) from the bird.

Roasting the turkey and finishing the accompaniments

1 Truss the bird firmly (removing the wishbone first).
2 Season with salt and pepper.
3 Cover the breast with fat bacon.
4 Place the bird in a roasting tray on its side and coat with 200 g dripping or oil.
5 Roast in a moderate oven at 180–185°C.
6 Allow to cook on both legs; complete the cooking with the breast upright for the last 30 minutes.
7 Baste frequently and allow 15–20 minutes per 0.5 kg. If using a temperature probe, insert in the thickest part of the leg for a reading of 77°C.
8 Bake the two stuffings separately in greased trays until well cooked to 77°C.
9 Prepare the gravy from the sediment and the brown stock. Correct the seasoning and remove the fat.
10 Remove the string and serve with the stuffings, roast gravy, bread sauce and/or hot cranberry sauce.
11 The turkey may be garnished with chipolata sausages and bacon rolls.

* No accompaniments, 200 g raw with skin and bone. With stuffing, roast gravy and bread sauce, 1 portion (200 g raw, with skin and bone) provides: 1589 kJ/380 kcal energy; 24.0 g fat; 8.4 g sat fat; 8.6 g carb; 1.6 g sugar; 34.0 g protein; 0.9 g fibre

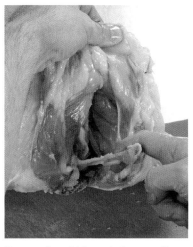

Remove the wishbone before roasting

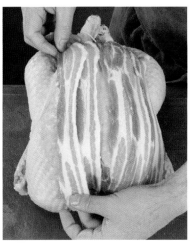

Bard the turkey with rashers of bacon

Key points

- Arrange the turkey to cook sitting on one leg, then the other leg and then with the breast upright, so that the whole bird cooks evenly.
- When the turkey is cooked, to facilitate carving, remove and de-bone the legs. For ease of carving, before cooking turkeys may be completely boned and the tough sinew removed from each leg.
- The breasts and the legs can both be stuffed, rolled and tied prior to roasting.

22 Duck breast steaks with cherries

duck, fruit 🍳 shallow frying

energy	kcal	fat	sat fat	carb	sugar	protein	fibre	sodium
1432 KJ	341 kcal	15.3 g	3.8 g	21.5 g	21.5 g	30.3 g	0.9 g	0.2 g

Portions ❯	4	10
duck breasts, skinned and scored	4	10
extra virgin olive oil	2 tbsp	5 tbsp
cherries	300 g	750 g
raspberry vinegar	4 tbsp	10 tbsp
bramble jelly or redcurrant jelly	4 tbsp	10 tbsp

1 Season and shallow-fry the duck breasts in the olive oil, skin side down, and finish in the oven at 200°C if required.

2 Meanwhile, place the cherries, vinegar and jelly in a pan and heat gently until the jelly has melted. Simmer and remove from the heat.

3 Stir in 2 tbsp of the extra virgin olive oil for 4 portions and 5 tbsp for 10 portions.

4 Carve the breasts into slices and serve on top of the sauce with a garnish of delicate vegetables, e.g. button mushrooms, baby carrots, mange tout or asparagus.

Confit duck leg with red cabbage and green beans

Portions ›	4	10
confit oil	1 litre	2.5 litres
cloves of garlic	4	10
bay leaf	1	3
sprig of thyme	1	2
duck legs	4 x 200 g	10 x 200 g
butter	50 g	125 g
green beans, cooked and trimmed	300 g	750 g
braised red cabbage	250 g	625 g
seasoning		

1 Gently heat the confit oil, add the garlic, bay leaf and thyme.
2 Put the duck legs in the oil and place on a medium to low heat, ensuring the legs are covered.
3 Cook gently for 4–4½ hours.
4 To test if the legs are cooked, squeeze the flesh on the thigh bone and it should just fall away.
5 When cooked, remove the legs carefully and place on a draining tray.

6 When drained, put the confit leg on a baking tray and place in a pre-heated oven at 210°C; remove when the skin is golden brown (approx. 9–10 minutes), taking care as the meat is delicate.
7 Heat the butter in a medium sauté pan and reheat the green beans.
8 Place the braised cabbage in a small pan and reheat slowly.
9 Place the duck leg in a serving dish or plate along with the red cabbage and green beans.

Confit oil is 50/50 olive oil and vegetable oil, infused with herbs, garlic, whole spice or any specific flavour you wish to impart into the oil; then, through slow cooking in the oil, the foodstuff picks up the flavour.

Key points
● Control the temperature carefully as the duck legs cook, to obtain the right texture and flavour.
● Confit duck legs can be prepared up to three or four days in advance. Remove them carefully from the fat they are stored in, clean off any excess fat and place directly into the oven. This is a great time-saver in a busy service.

24 Cassoulet of duck

 duck, pulses stewing

energy	kcal	fat	sat fat	carb	sugar	protein	fibre	sodium *
5124 KJ	1220 kcal	52.4 g	20.2 g	116.9 g	16.8 g	69.9 g	38.2 g	2.9 g

Portions ❯	4	10
dried white haricot beans	600 g	1.5 kg
duck fat	2 tbsp	5 tbsp
streaky bacon lardons	200 g	500 g
small duck or pork sausages	4	10
onions	2	5
cloves of garlic, sliced	6	15
juniper berries, crushed	12	30
thyme leaves	1 tbsp	2 tbsp
bay leaves	2	5
tomato purée	2 tbsp	5 tbsp
white wine	200 ml	500 ml
duck stock or dark chicken stock	1 litre	2.5 litres
confit duck legs (see recipe 23)	4	10
white breadcrumbs	4 tbsp	10 tbsp
parsley, chopped	1 tbsp	2 tbsp
sea salt and freshly-ground black pepper		

1 Soak the dried beans in water for 24 hours.
2 Melt the duck fat in a large saucepan or casserole dish and fry the bacon until golden brown. Remove from the pan and set aside.
3 Add the sausages to the pan and cook until golden. Remove from the pan and set aside.
4 Cut the onions in half and slice thinly.
5 Add the onions to the pan with the garlic, juniper berries, thyme and bay leaves, and fry over a gentle heat for about 10 minutes, or until the onions become translucent.
6 Stir in the tomato purée and cook for 3–4 minutes.
7 Add the white wine and cook until reduced by half.

8 Add the duck stock and the beans. Bring to the boil and cook for about 20 minutes.
9 Return the bacon and sausages to the pan and cook for a further 20 minutes.
10 Add the confit duck legs and cook for 20 minutes.
11 Season with salt and freshly ground black pepper.
12 To serve, spoon a generous portion of haricot beans, a leg of duck, sausage, some of the streaky bacon and a little of the juice into an individual earthenware dish.
13 Spread breadcrumbs over the top.
14 Brown under the salamander until the crumbs are golden, sprinkle with parsley and serve.

* Using cranberries in place of juniper berries

25 Roast duck or duckling
(canard ou caneton rôti)

duck roasting

energy	kcal	fat	sat fat	carb	sugar	protein	fibre	*
3083 KJ	734 kcal	60.5 g	16.9 g	8.2 g	7.8 g	40.0 g	1.4g	

Portions ⟩	4	10
duck	1	2–3
salt		
oil		
brown stock	0.25 litres	600 ml
salt, pepper		
watercress, bunch	1	2
apple sauce (page 53)	125 ml	300 ml

1 Lightly season the duck inside and out with salt.
2 Truss and brush lightly with oil.
3 Place on its side in a roasting tin, with a few drops of water.
4 Place in a hot oven for 20–25 minutes.
5 Turn onto the other side.
6 Cook for a further 20–25 minutes. Baste frequently.
7 To test if cooked, pierce with a fork between the drumstick and thigh and hold over a plate. The juice issuing from the duck should not show any signs of blood. If using a probe, the temperature should be 62°C. If the duck is required pink, the temperature could be 57°C, although never for a customer in a high-risk group.
8 Prepare the roast gravy with the stock and the sediment in the roasting tray. Correct the seasoning, remove the surface fat.
9 Serve garnished with picked watercress.
10 Accompany with a sauceboat of hot apple sauce, a sauceboat of gravy, and game chips. Also serve sage and onion dressing (recipe 26).

* With apple sauce and watercress

Key points

- Arrange the duck to cook sitting on one leg, then the other leg and then with the breast upright, so that the whole bird cooks evenly.
- The temperatures in this recipe reflect industry standards for cooking duck. An environmental health officer may advise higher temperatures of 75–80°C. You must use these higher temperatures for high-risk groups (see Chapter 14).

Healthy eating tips

- Use the minimum amount of salt to season the duck and the roast gravy.
- Take care to remove all the fat from the roasting tray before making the gravy.
- This dish is high in fat and should be served with plenty of boiled new potatoes and a variety of vegetables.

Preparing a duck
http://bit.ly/z2rBxZ

26 Sage and onion dressing for duck

bulbs, herbs shallow frying, baking

Portions ›	4	10
onion, chopped	100 g	250 g
duck fat or butter	100 g	250 g
powdered sage	¼ tsp	½ tsp
parsley, chopped	¼ tsp	½ tsp
salt, pepper		
white or wholemeal breadcrumbs	100 g	250 g
duck liver (optional), chopped	50 g	125 g

1 Gently cook the onion in the fat without colour. Add the chopped liver (if required) and fry until cooked.
2 Add the herbs and seasoning. Mix in the crumbs. Form into thick sausage shapes, in foil.
3 Place in a tray and finish in a hot oven at 180°C for approx. 5–10 mins. Check with a probe that the centre has reached 75°C.
4 Serve separately with roast duck.

27 Cranberry and orange dressing for duck

fruit boiling

energy	kcal	fat	sat fat	carb	sugar	protein	fibre
398 KJ	93 kcal	0.2 g	0.0 g	22.7 g	22.7 g	1.3 g	4.2g

Portions ›	4	10
cranberries	400 g	1 kg
granulated sugar	50 g	125 g
red wine	125 ml	250 ml
red wine vinegar	2 tbsp	5 tbsp
orange, zest and juice	2	4

1 Place the cranberries in a suitable saucepan with the rest of the ingredients.
2 Bring to the boil and simmer gently for approx. 1 hour, stirring from time to time.
3 Remove from the heat and leave to cool. Use as required.

The dressing may also be liquidised if a smooth texture is required.

28 Roast goose

goose roasting

energy	kcal	fat	sat fat	carb	sugar	protein	fibre
9541 KJ	2305 kcal	210.5 g	60.0 g	0.0 g	0.0 g	103.1 g	0.0 g

1 The average weight of a goose is 5–6 kg. Clean and truss the goose like a chicken (see page XX).
2 Roast the goose using the procedure for roasting a duck (recipe 25), with the oven at 200–230°C. After 20 minutes, turn it down to 180°C. Allow 15–20 minutes per 0.5 kg.

Food safety

The goose must reach a temperature of 75°C.

29 Game farce

game, offal shallow frying, baking

Portions ⟩	4	10
butter	50 g	125 g
game livers	100 g	250 g
onion, chopped	25 g	60 g
thyme, sprig		
bay leaf	1	2–3
salt, pepper		

1 Heat half the butter in a frying pan.
2 Quickly toss the seasoned livers, onion and herbs in the butter, browning well but keeping underdone. Pass through a sieve or mincer.
3 Mix in the remaining butter. Correct the seasoning.
4 Place in an oven-proof dish and oven cook in a bain marie (a roasting tray half-filled with water) at 180°C for 25 minutes. Check with a probe that the centre has reached 75°C.

Food safety

Traditionally, the livers were kept underdone, but this is not advisable in a modern kitchen due to the risk of food poisoning, particularly campylobacter.

30 Pot au feu of pigeon

game stewing

energy	kcal	fat	sat fat	carb	sugar	protein	fibre
1545 KJ	367 kcal	11.2 g	3.44 g	11.12 g	9.98 g	56.2 g	4.79g

Portions ⟩	4	10
squabs, legs removed	6 (approx. 2 kg)	10 (approx. 3.5 kg)
carrot, peeled and cut into 4 laterally	1	3
celery stick, cut into 4	1	3
baby turnips	8	20
medium turnips, peeled and blanched	2	4
leek, washed, cut in rounds	1	3
small shallots, peeled and left whole	8	20
smoked streaky bacon, rind removed	100 g	250 g
chicken/game stock	400 ml	1 litre
bouquet garni with 4 black peppercorns and 1 clove of garlic	1	3
salt		

This is a social dish, designed to be placed in the middle of the table and served with warm, crusty bread, mashed potato or buttered new potatoes.

1 Place the squab legs in a large casserole and arrange the vegetables tightly in one layer with the legs, add the bacon, then cover with the stock to about 4 cm above the ingredients (you may need to top this up with water).

2 Add the muslin-wrapped bouquet garni. Season with salt and bring to a gentle boil.

3 Skim off any impurities, cover with a lid (leaving a small gap), and simmer gently for 50 minutes.

4 Skim off any fat or impurities, then add the squab breasts and cook for a further 12 minutes.

Arrange the squab legs and vegetables in the pan

Cover with stock

Add the breasts later, as they need less time to cook

* Chicken was used for the saturated fat analysis

31 Roast partridge

game roasting

energy	kcal	fat	sat fat	carb	sugar	protein	fibre
2495 KJ	596 kcal	26.7 g	7.6 g	0.3 g	0.1 g	88.5 g	0.0 g

Portions ›	4	10
grey-legged partridges (approx. 400 g each), oven-ready, with livers	4	10
unsalted butter	20 g	50 g
groundnut oil or vegetable oil	20 g	50 g
salt		
freshly ground pepper		
roasting juices from veal, pork or beef	70 ml	175 ml
water	50 ml	125 ml

1 Shorten the wings and sear the partridges under a flame to remove the feather stubs. Remove any trace of gall from the liver. Wash briefly, pat dry and reserve.

2 In a roasting tray sear the wing bones and the partridges in butter and oil for 2 minutes on each side and 2 minutes on the breast (6 minutes in total) until they are brown.

3 Season with salt and pepper, and roast in the preheated oven for 5–6 minutes, according to the size of the partridges.

4 Remove from the oven and place the partridges on a cooling wire breast-side down, cover loosely with aluminium foil and allow to rest.

5 In the same roasting tray, fry the livers in the remaining butter and oil until well done, and reserve. Spoon out the excess fat and add the roasting juices and water to the winglets, bring to the boil then simmer for 5 minutes.

6 Taste and season with salt and pepper, then strain through a fine sieve.

7 Serve with roasted seasonal vegetables (e.g. roast parsnips, carrots and braised cabbage). Suggested accompaniments: bread sauce, roast gravy, watercress and game chips. The partridge livers may be puréed and served on croutes of toasted bread as another accompaniment.

> Simply-roasted partridge is a great autumnal and winter base for most accompaniments: braised cabbage, roast carrots, parsnips, and so on.

32 Traditional-contemporary roast grouse

game roasting

energy	kcal	fat	sat fat	carb	sugar	protein	fibre	*
3932 KJ	943 kcal	24.7 g	7.1 g	63.8 g	9.5 g	107.4 g	5.6 g	

Portions ›	4	10
Grouse		
young grouse (approx. 750 g each), wings removed	4	10
hearts and livers from the grouse		
sage leaves	4	10
butter	20 g	50 g
salt and pepper		
Stock		
oil	30 ml	80 ml
grouse wings		
giblets		
large onion	1	2
celery stick	1	3
carrot	1	3
red wine	250 ml	625 ml
water		
thyme, sprig of		
bay leaf	1	3
Toast		
small slices of bread	16	40
duck fat		
To serve		
bread sauce (see page 51)		
watercress, bunches	1	2
game chips		

1 Trim the wings from the young grouse, draw and reserve the livers, hearts and giblets. Season birds liberally inside and out, and put the livers and hearts back in with a sage leaf and a knob of butter. Pre-heat the oven to 210°C.

2 Brown the wings and the remaining giblets with the diced onion, celery and carrot. Deglaze pan with red wine, cover with water and simmer for 30 minutes with the thyme and bay leaf. Strain and reserve.

3 Meanwhile, fry the bread in duck fat. Make bread sauce and pick through watercress.

4 Seal the birds in a little hot oil until golden. Then place the birds in the oven and roast. Cook until a probe inserted between the leg and the cavity reads 75°C, or until the juices run clear.

5 Remove from the pan and leave the birds to rest for 10 minutes.

6 Put the roasting tray over a flame, add a splash of brandy and the stock, and allow to bubble down to a thin gravy.

7 A traditional way to serve grouse is to scoop out the livers and hearts, mash these up and serve on the toast. Stick a bunch of the watercress into the grouse's cavity and put the bird and toast onto a plate with some bread sauce and game chips. Pour a little of the gravy over each bird and serve remaining gravy separately. Alternatively, serve with apple sauce.

Good-quality grouse that has not been over-hung is essential for this dish. The meat will already have a strong pungent flavour embedded in it from the birds' diet of heather.

* Including accompaniments

Pot-roasted quail with roast carrots and mashed potato

energy	kcal	fat	sat fat	carb	sugar	protein	fibre
2839 KJ	680 kcal	41.89 g	16.61 g	9.99 g	2.47 g	66.1 g	1.15g

*

Portions ❯	4	10
quails (approx. 75 g each)	12	30
pancetta, thinly sliced	12 (approx. 250 g)	30 (approx. 625 g)
fresh sage leaves	12	30
vegetable oil	15 ml	50 ml
butter	20 g	50 g
salt and freshly-ground pepper		
carrots, peeled and cut into quarters	3 (100 g)	8 (250 g)
oil	30 ml	80 ml
dry white wine	125 ml	310 ml
red wine	125 ml	310 ml
brown stock	250 ml	625 ml
unsalted butter	50 g	125 g
mashed potato, portions	4 (200 g)	10 (500 g)
chives, chopped	1 tsp	2 tsp

1 Wash the quails thoroughly inside and out, then place them in a large colander to drain for at least 20 minutes; pat the quail dry.

2 Stuff the cavity of each bird with 1 slice of pancetta and 1 sage leaf.

3 Put the oil in a large thick-bottomed roasting pan on high heat. When the fat is hot, add all the quails in a single layer and cook until browned on one side, gradually turning them, and continue cooking until they are evenly browned all over.

4 Lightly sprinkle the quails with salt and pepper, then add the carrots and cook for a couple of minutes until a slight colour appears.

5 Add the wine and brown stock then turn the birds once, let the wine bubble for about 1 minute, then lower the heat to moderate and partially cover the pan. Cook the quails until the meat feels very tender when poked with a fork and comes away from the bone (approx. 35 minutes).

6 Check from time to time that there are sufficient juices in the pan to keep the birds from sticking; if this does occur, add 1 to 2 tbsp of water at a time. When the quail are done, transfer them to a warmed tray and reserve.

7 Turn up the heat and reduce the cooking juices to a glaze – enough to coat all the birds, scraping the bottom of the pan with a spoon to loosen any cooking residues.

8 Add the butter and whisk in to form an emulsion; at this point, if the sauce splits or is too thick, add a little water and re-boil.

9 Remove the carrots from the pan and place neatly on the plate with the mashed potato.

10 Pass the juices, then pour them over the quail, sprinkle with chopped chives and serve immediately.

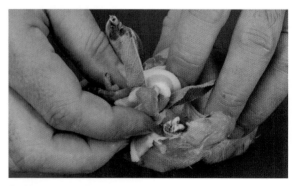

Stuff the cavity of the quail

* Partridge was used for the saturated fat analysis. Streaky bacon was used instead of pancetta

34 Braised baron of rabbit with olives and tomatoes

energy	kcal	fat	sat fat	carb	sugar	protein	fibre
2365 KJ	568 kcal	40.98 g	8.42 g	5.47 g	4.75 g	44.6g	0.87g

Portions ›	4	10
farm-raised rabbit barons (approx. 750–800 g each), including bones and trim for gravy	2	5
carrot	1	3
onion	1	3
celery stick	1	3
olive oil	90 ml	225 ml
balsamic vinegar	15 ml	40 ml
caster sugar	10 g	25 g
dry white wine	750 ml	2 litres
butter, to brown the meat	125 g	300 g
basil leaves	12	30
black olives ('Mediterranean influence')	32	80
pieces sun-dried tomato	8	20
salt and pepper		

1 Well ahead of time, prepare the rabbits; cut the rabbits across at the point where the ribs end, and chop the forequarters into small pieces.
2 Cut the vegetables into a mirepoix.
3 In a large saucepan, brown the bones and mirepoix in 2 tbsp/5 tbsp of the olive oil.
4 Add the vinegar and sugar, and toss to coat. Cook until light brown.
5 Pour over almost all the white wine, reserving about 150 ml/375 ml for deglazing the roasting pan later. Boil hard to reduce until the liquid has a syrupy consistency.
6 Just cover with cold water, return to the boil and skim.
7 Simmer for 1½ hours.
8 Pass the resulting stock into a bowl, wash out the saucepan and return the stock to it.
9 Bring back to the boil, skim again and, once more, return to a slow simmer until reduced by half. Reserve.
10 Cut the rabbit legs into two (thigh and drumstick), and the rack into two.

11 In a large saucepan, brown the meat cuts in foaming butter; when golden brown, add the finished stock and cook for a further 1½ hours (approx.).
12 When cooked, pass the sauce through a fine strainer, bring to the boil and reduce by half.
13 While reducing, put the rabbit into a casserole/serving dish, julienne the basil and remove the stones from the olives.
14 When the sauce is reduced by half, add the tomatoes, olives and basil. Correct the seasoning, pour over the rabbit and serve.

A baron is the rear end of the rabbit – the rack and the two hind legs.

Try something different
The 'Mediterranean influence' can be omitted, substituted with a British theme – woodland mushrooms, parsnips – and served with braised cabbage.

35 German-style saddle of hare

game roasting, marinating

energy	kcal	fat	sat fat	carb	sugar	protein	fibre
3561 KJ	859 kcal	60.6 g	14.3 g	9.4 g	7.1 g	47.3 g	3.6 g

Portions >	4	10
For the marinade		
carrot, finely sliced	200 g	450 g
onion, finely sliced	200 g	450 g
celery, finely sliced	100 g	225 g
garlic, cloves	2	4
parsley stalks	25 g	50 g
sprig of thyme		
bay leaf	½	1
cloves	2	4
peppercorns	12	30
red wine	500 ml	1.25 litres
wine vinegar	125 ml	325 ml
oil	125 ml	325 ml
For the hare		
saddles of hare	2–4	5–10
salt, pepper		
cream	125 ml	310 ml
lemon juice		

1 Season the hare with salt and pepper, and place into a suitable container (e.g. stainless steel or china).
2 Cover with the marinade ingredients.
3 Refrigerate, turning the joints over frequently, for approx. 24 hours.
4 Remove the saddles from the marinade and dry thoroughly.
5 Remove the vegetables from the marinade and place into a roasting tray. Place the saddles on top of the vegetables and roast in the oven at 180°C.
6 When the saddle is three-quarters cooked, remove the vegetables.
7 Add the cream to the roasting tray and continue cooking. Baste the meat frequently with the cream. Keep the meat pink.

8 Remove the saddles from the tray. Separate the meat from the bone and slice each side into 4 pieces.
9 Add a few drops of lemon juice to the cooking liquor, correct the seasoning and consistency, and pass through a fine strainer. Serve the sauce with the saddles.

Suitable accompaniments include: braised chestnuts, or chestnut purée, or Brussels sprouts with chestnuts; purée of celeriac, or celeriac or parsnips, or celeriac and onion; buttered noodles.

The saddle is a joint cut from the back of the hare, usually in a similar way to a short saddle of lamb – that is, a pair of uncut loins. All skin and sinew must be removed and the joint trimmed before use. If desired, the joint may be larded with pork fat.
A saddle of hare yields 1 or 2 portions, depending on size. It is not essential to marinade the saddle if obtained from a young hare, but if there is any doubt as to its tenderness, or if it is to be kept for a few days, then the joint should be marinated, as in this recipe.

Try something different
- After the saddle is removed, the roasting tray can be deglazed with brandy, whiskey or gin.
- Sliced mushrooms (cultivated or wild) can be added to the sauce.

Vegetables, pulses and grains

This chapter is relevant to the following units:

- Prepare vegetables for basic dishes (NVQ)
- Cook and finish basic vegetable dishes (NVQ)
- Prepare, cook and finish basic pulse dishes (NVQ)
- Prepare, cook and finish basic grain dishes (NVQ)
- Prepare and cook fruit and vegetables (VRQ)
- Prepare and cook rice, pasta, grains and egg dishes (VRQ).

Vegetables

Vegetable is a culinary term that generally refers to the edible part of a plant. The definition is traditional rather than scientific and is somewhat arbitrary and subjective. All parts of herbaceous plants eaten as food by humans, whole or in part, are normally considered vegetables. Mushrooms, though belonging to the biological kingdom fungi, are also commonly considered vegetables. In general, vegetables are thought of as being savoury, not sweet, although there are many exceptions; in most countries, they are associated with poultry, meat or fish as part of a meal or as an ingredient. Nuts, grains, herbs, spices and culinary fruits (see below) are not normally considered vegetables. Some vegetables are botanically classed as fruits: tomatoes are berries, and avocados are drupes, but both are commonly used as vegetables because they are not sweet.

Since 'vegetable' is not a botanical term, there is no contradiction in referring to a plant part as a fruit while also being considered a vegetable. Given this general rule of thumb, vegetables can also include leaves (lettuce), stems (asparagus), roots (carrots), flowers (broccoli), bulbs (garlic), seeds (peas and beans) and botanical fruits such as cucumbers, squash, pumpkins and capsicums. Botanically, fruits are reproductive organs (ripened ovaries containing one or many seeds), while vegetables are vegetative organs that sustain the plant.

Fresh vegetables are important foods both from an economic and nutritional point of view. Vegetables are an important part of our diet, therefore it is essential to pay attention to quality, purchasing, storage and efficient preparation and cooking if the nutritional content of vegetables is to be conserved. (Potatoes are discussed separately in Chapter 10.)

Nutritional value

Vegetables are eaten in a variety of ways as part of main meals and as snacks. The nutrient content of different types varies considerably. With the exception of pulses, vegetables provide little protein or fat. Vegetables contain water-soluble vitamins like Vitamin B and Vitamin C, fat-soluble vitamins including Vitamin A and Vitamin D, as well as carbohydrates and minerals. Root vegetables contain starch or sugar for energy, a small but valuable amount of protein, some mineral salts and vitamins. They are also useful sources of cellulose and water. Green vegetables are rich in mineral salts and vitamins, particularly Vitamin C and carotene. The greener the leaf, the larger the quantity of vitamins present. The chief mineral salts are calcium and iron.

Purchasing and selection

The purchasing of vegetables is affected by:
- the perishable nature of the products
- varying availability owing to seasonal fluctuations, and supply and demand
- the effects of preservation (e.g. freezing, drying, canning vegetables).

The high perishability of vegetables causes problems not encountered in other markets. Fresh vegetables are living organisms and will lose quality quickly if not properly stored and handled. Automation in harvesting and packaging speeds the handling process and helps retain quality.

The EU vegetable quality grading system is:
- **Extra class:** produce of the highest quality
- **Class 1:** produce of good quality
- **Class 2:** produce of reasonably good quality
- **Class 3:** produce of low market quality.

Quality points

Root vegetables must be:
- clean, free from soil
- firm, not soft or spongy
- sound
- free from blemishes
- of an even size
- of an even shape.

Green vegetables must be absolutely fresh and have leaves that are bright in colour, crisp and not wilted. In addition:

- cabbage and Brussels sprouts should be compact and firm
- cauliflowers should have closely grown flowers, a firm white head and not too much stalk or too many outer leaves
- peas and beans should be crisp and of medium size; pea pods should be full and beans not stringy
- blanched stems must be firm, white, crisp and free from soil.

Storage

Many root and non-root vegetables that grow underground can be stored over winter in a root cellar or other similarly cool, dark and dry place, to prevent the growth of mould, greening and sprouting. Care should be taken in understanding the properties and vulnerabilities of the particular roots to be stored. These vegetables can last through to early spring and be almost as nutritious as when fresh.

During storage, leafy vegetables lose moisture and Vitamin C degrades rapidly. They should be stored for as short a time as possible in a cool place in a container, such as a plastic bag or a sealed plastic container.

Key points for storage

- Store all vegetables in a cool, dry, well-ventilated room at an even temperature of 4–8°C, which will help to minimise spoilage. Check vegetables daily and discard any that are unsound.
- Remove root vegetables from their sacks and store in bins or racks.
- Store green vegetables on well-ventilated racks.
- Store salad vegetables in a cool place and leave in their containers.
- Store frozen vegetables at −18°C or below. Keep a check on use-by dates, damaged packages and any signs of freezer burn.
- The fresher the vegetables the better the flavour, so ideally they should not be stored at all. However, as in many cases storage is necessary, then it should be for the shortest time possible.
- Green vegetables lose Vitamin C quickly if they are bruised, damaged, stored for too long, prepared too early or overcooked.

Health, safety and hygiene

For information on maintaining a safe and secure working environment, a professional and hygienic appearance, and clean food production areas, equipment and utensils, as well as food hygiene, please refer to Chapters 14 and 15. Additional food safety points are as follows.

- If vegetables are stored at the incorrect temperature micro-organisms may develop.
- If vegetables are stored in damp conditions moulds may develop.
- To prevent bacteria from raw vegetables passing on to cooked vegetables, store them in separate areas.
- Thaw out frozen vegetables correctly (if not cooking from frozen) and *never* refreeze them once they have thawed out.

Preparing and cooking vegetables

Approximate times only are given in the recipes in this chapter for the cooking of vegetables, as quality, age, freshness and size all affect the length of cooking time required. Young, freshly picked vegetables will need to be cooked for a shorter time than vegetables that have been allowed to grow older and that may have been stored after picking.

As a general rule, all root vegetables (with the exception of new potatoes) are started off by cooking in cold salted water. Those vegetables that grow above the ground are started in boiling salted water; this is so that they may be cooked as quickly as possible for the minimum period of time so that maximum flavour, food value and colour are retained. (See also 'Blanching', below.)

All vegetables cooked by boiling may also be cooked by steaming. The vegetables are prepared in exactly the same way as for boiling, placed into steamer trays, lightly seasoned with salt and steamed under pressure for the minimum period of time in order to conserve maximum food value and retain colour. High-speed steam cookers are ideal for this purpose and also because of the speed of cooking they offer; batch cooking (cooking in small quantities

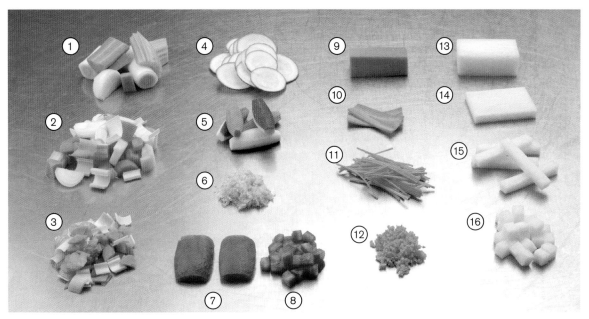

Cuts of vegetables

1	Large mirepoix	6	Finely diced onion	10	Carrot strips
2	Small mirepoix	7	Tomato petals	11	Julienne
3	Paysanne	8	Tomato concassé	12	Brunoise
4	Sliced courgette		(gros brunoise)	13	Large block of mooli
5	Turned vegetables	9	Carrot block	14	Flat block

15 Jardinière
16 Macédoine

throughout the service) can be practised instead of cooking large quantities prior to service, refreshing and reheating.

Many vegetables are cooked from raw by the stir-fry method, a quick and nutritious method of cooking.

Blanching

Delicate vegetables – particularly green vegetables – can be blanched in salted boiling water and then refreshed in ice-cold water to arrest the cooking process. The main reason for this is because, between the temperatures of 66°C and 77°C, chlorophyll is unstable. Chlorophyll is the green pigment in any plant that photosynthesises. For this reason it is important to get through this temperature zone as quickly as possible.

Cuts of vegetables

The size and shape to which the vegetables are cut may vary according to their type and use.

Cutting vegetables into gros brunoise
http://bit.ly/ySdUEu

To cut short **julienne** (strips):

- Cut the vegetables into 2 cm lengths.
- Cut the lengths into thin slices.
- Cut the slices into thin strips.

Double the length gives a long julienne, used for garnishing (e.g. salads, meats, fish, poultry dishes).

To cut **brunoise** (small dice):

- Cut the vegetables into convenient-sized lengths.
- Cut the lengths into 2 mm slices.
- Cut the slices into 2 mm strips.
- Cut the strips into 2 mm squares.

To cut **macédoine** (0.5 cm dice):

- Cut the vegetables into convenient lengths.
- Cut the lengths into 0.5 cm slices.
- Cut the slices into 0.5 cm strips.
- Cut the strips into 0.5 cm cubes.

Cutting vegetables
into macédoine
http://bit.ly/A0oPrD

To cut **jardinière** (batons):

- Cut the vegetables into 1.5 cm lengths.
- Cut the lengths into 3 mm slices.
- Cut the slices into batons (3 mm x 3 mm x 18 mm).

There are at least four accepted methods of cutting **paysanne**. In order to cut economically, the shape of the vegetables should dictate which method to choose. All are cut thinly. The shapes are:

- 1 cm sided triangles
- 1 cm sided squares
- 1 cm diameter rounds
- 1 cm diameter rough-sided rounds.

Cutting vegetables
into paysanne
http://bit.ly/yR3COz

Concassé means roughly chopped. Skinned and deseeded tomatoes are roughly chopped for many food preparations (see recipe 56). The term is also used to refer to skinned and deseeded tomatoes that are cut into neat strips or cubes and used as a garnish.

Pulses

Pulses are defined as annual leguminous crops, yielding from 1 to 12 grains or seeds of variable size, shape and colour within a pod.

The term 'pulse' is reserved for crops harvested solely for the dry grain. This therefore excludes green beans and green peas, which are considered vegetable crops. Also excluded are crops that are grown mainly for oil extraction (oilseeds such as soybeans and peanuts), and crops that are used exclusively for sowing (e.g. clovers, alfalfa).

Pulses are one of the most versatile commodities. They can be used extensively in a wide range of dishes. Imaginative and experimental use of different herbs, spices, flavourings and vegetables can give individual variation to the pulse recipes.

Food value

Pulses are important food crops due to their high protein and essential amino acid content. They are

20–25 per cent protein, which is double that found in wheat and three times that found in rice.

All pulses, except for soya beans, are very similar in nutritional content. They are rich in protein, carbohydrate and fibre, and low in fat, which is mostly of the unsaturated kind. They are also important sources of some B vitamins, and contain iron. Fresh pulses contain Vitamin C, but this declines after harvesting and virtually all is lost from dried pulses.

Storage

One advantage of dried pulses is that they store very well for long periods if kept in a dry, airtight container away from the light. However, it is best to eat them as fresh as possible. Pulses toughen on storage and older ones will take longer to cook.

- Store fresh pulses in a refrigerator at a temperature below 5°C.

- Store frozen pulses in a freezer at a temperature below −18°C.
- Store dried pulses in clean airtight containers off the floor in the dry store.
- Unpack tinned pulses and check that the tins are sound and undamaged.

Cooking

Allow about 55 g of dried pulses per person. Once soaked and cooked the pulses will at least double in weight.

Most dried pulses need soaking for several hours before they can be cooked; exceptions are all lentils, green and yellow split peas, black-eyed and mung beans.

Soaking times vary from 4–12 hours. It is usually most convenient to soak pulses overnight. Amply cover the pulses with cold water (they will expand gradually.) Leave in a cold place; if leaving overnight, store in the refrigerator at a temperature below 5°C.

Always discard the soaking water, rinse and cook in fresh water without any salt, which toughens the skins and makes for longer cooking. Changing the water will also help to reduce the flatulence some people suffer when eating pulses; also reputed to help is the addition of a pinch of aniseed, caraway, dill or fennel seeds.

After soaking, salt should *not* be added before or during the cooking as this causes the pulses to toughen. Salt, however, may be added if required towards the end of the cookery process.

Soya beans should be soaked for at least 12 hours, drained and rinsed then covered with fresh water and brought to the boil. Soya beans should be boiled for the first hour of cooking. They can then be simmered for the remaining 2–3 hours that it takes to cook them.

When preparing pulses and lentils, cook them in sparkling bottled water. The sparkling motion helps ensure even cooking through momentum; the reason for using bottled water over tap water is the reduced calcium. Especially in hard-water areas there is a lot of calcium. Calcium actually blocks the pores of pulses, causing beans to 'boil in their jackets', then the jacket bursts and the pulses are undesirable. Bottled water allows the fluid to pass through the tiny pores and cook evenly, perfectly.

Health, safety and hygiene

For information on health and safety and food hygiene, please refer to Chapters 14 and 15. Additional food safety points for pulses are as follows.

- Always check pulses for food pests (e.g. flour moths) and any foreign matter (stones, etc.).
- When storing cooked pulses, keep them covered and in a refrigerator at a temperature below 5°C.
- To prevent risk of cross-contamination, store cooked pulses away from any raw foods.

It is not safe to eat raw or undercooked kidney and soya beans.

Types of pulses

Beans

- **Aduki:** small, round, deep red, shiny, nutty and sweet (the flavour used in oriental confectionery).
- **Black:** glistening black skins, creamy flesh.
- **Black-eyed:** small white beans with a savoury, creamy flavour, and with a black 'scar' where they were joined to the pod. Used a lot in American and African cooking, they are the essential ingredient in the traditional southern-style dish 'Hoppin John' – a mixture of black-eyed beans, bacon and white rice traditionally eaten on New Year's Day.
- **Broad:** also known as fava beans, strongly flavoured.
- **Borlotti:** Italian beans with a mild bittersweet flavour; they're used in regional stews and often mixed with rice, and are particularly good in soups such as minestrone and *pasta e fagioli*.
- **Butter:** also known as lima beans, available large or small.
- **Cannellini:** Italian haricot, slightly larger than the English.
- **Dutch brown:** light brown in colour.
- **Flageolet:** pale green, kidney-shaped with a delicate flavour.
- **Ful mesdames:** also known as Egyptian brown beans; small, brown and knobbly, known as the field bean in the UK.
- **Haricot:** white, smooth and oval; used for baked beans.

- **Mung:** small, olive green in colour, good flavour, available split, whole and skinless. Widely used sprouted for their shoots.
- **Pinto:** the original ingredient of Mexican refried beans; an orange-pink bean with rust-coloured specks that grows freely across Latin America and throughout the American south-west; the bean is creamy-white in colour with a fluffy texture when cooked, and is good in soups, salads and rich stews.
- **Red kidney:** normally dark red-brown, this kidney-shaped bean holds its shape and colour and is therefore great in mixed bean salads and stews, including the traditional chilli con carne. Dried kidney beans need to be cooked carefully – soak for at least 8 hours; after soaking, drain and rinse them, discarding the soaking water; put them into a pan with cold water to cover and bring to the boil – the beans must be boiled for 10 minutes to destroy toxins; after this, simmer until cooked (approximately 45–60 minutes). The beans should have an even, creamy texture throughout – if the centre is still hard and white, they require longer cooking.
- **Soissons:** finest haricot beans.
- **Soy:** soybeans are very high in nutrients, especially protein, and they contain all the essential amino acids. They are processed into many forms: soy flour, TVP (meat substitute), tofu (curd), oils, margarine, soy milk and soy sauce.

Peas
- **Blue:** also known as marrowfat peas; pleasant flavour, floury texture, retain shape when cooked.
- **Chickpeas:** shaped like hazelnuts, they have a tasty nutty flavour when cooked. Chickpeas are used all over the world in dishes such as the Indian *kabli chana* or Spanish *caldo gallego*. Chickpeas are a key ingredient of hummus – a traditional Greek dip of cooked chickpeas, tahini, oil and garlic. They can be bought and soaked from dried, but canned chickpeas do just as well for most recipes.
- **Split green:** a sweeter variety than the blue pea; cook to a purée easily.
- **Split yellow:** cook to a purée easily.

Both yellow and green split peas are used for vegetable purées and soups.

Lentils
Lentils, varying in size and colour, can form a nutritious basis for a meal. Larger brown or green lentils retain their shape during cooking and are particularly good in soups. Red and yellow lentils cook down well, can be puréed and are used a great deal in Indian cooking, such as in a spicy dhal. Tiny green puy lentils have a distinctive flavour and also keep their shape and colour when cooked.
- **Orange:** several types, which vary in size and shade and may be sold whole or split.
- **Green or continental:** retain shape after cooking, available in small or large varieties.
- **Yellow:** of Asian origin, often used as a dhal accompaniment to curry dishes.
- **Red:** purée easily, used for soups and stews, etc.
- **Indian brown:** red lentils from which the seed coat has not been removed; they purée easily.
- **Puy:** dark French lentils, varied in size, retain their shape when cooked and are considered the best of their type.
- **Dhal:** the Hindi word for dried peas and beans.

Grains

Cereal crops, or grains, are mostly grasses cultivated for their edible grains or seeds. Cereal grains are grown in greater quantities and provide more energy worldwide than any other type of crop; they are therefore known as 'staple crops'.

Food value

Grains are a rich source of carbohydrate. They supply most of their food energy as starch. They are also a significant source of protein. Whole grains are good sources of dietary fibre, essential fatty acids and other important nutrients. Rice, for example, is eaten as cooked entire grains (although rice flour is also produced). Oats are rolled, ground or cut into bits (steel-cut oats) and cooked into porridge (see below). Most other cereal grains are ground into flour or meal. During this process the outer layers of bran and germ are lost.

Storage

Cereals are best stored in airtight containers in a cool, dark, dry place. Whole grains can be stored for up to two years; flaked or cracked grains and flours should be used within two to three months of purchase.

Types of grain

Barley

Barley grows in a wider variety of climatic conditions than any other cereal. Usually found in the shops as **whole** or **pot barley** (or **polished pearl barley**), you can also buy **barley flakes** or **kernels**. It can be cooked on its own (one part grain to three parts water for 45–60 minutes) as an alternative to rice, pasta or potatoes, or added to stews. Malt extract is made from sprouted barley grains.

Barley must have its fibrous hull removed before it is eaten (hulled barley). Hulled barley still has its bran and germ and is considered a whole grain, making it a popular health food. Pearl barley is hulled barley that has been processed further to remove the bran.

Buckwheat

When roasted, the seeds of buckwheat are dark reddish-brown. It can be cooked (one part grain to two parts water for 6 minutes, leave to stand for 6 minutes) and served like rice, or it can be added to stews and casseroles. **Buckwheat flour** can be added to cakes, muffins and pancakes, where it imparts a distinctive flavour. Soba noodles, made from buckwheat, are an essential ingredient in Japanese cooking. Buckwheat is gluten free.

Corn/maize

Fresh corn – available in the form of sweetcorn and corn on the cob – is eaten as a vegetable. The dried grain is most often eaten as cornflakes or popcorn.

The flour made from corn (**cornmeal**) is used to make Italian **polenta**, and can be added to soup, pancakes and muffins. Cook polenta (one part grain to three parts water) for 15–20 minutes, stirring carefully to avoid lumps. Use it like mashed potato: it's quite bland, so try stirring in tasty ingredients like Gorgonzola, Parmesan and fresh herbs, or press it when cold, cut into slices, brush with garlicky olive oil, and grill. You can also get ready-made polenta.

Tortillas are made from maize meal, as are quite a lot of snack foods.

Don't confuse cornmeal with **refined corn starch/flour**, used for thickening. Corn is gluten free.

Millet

The millets are a group of small-seeded species of cereal crops or grains widely grown around the world for food and fodder.

The main millet varieties are:

- pearl millet
- foxtail millet
- proso millet, also known as common millet, broom corn millet, hog millet or white millet
- finger millet.

Coeliac patients can replace certain cereal grains in their diets by consuming millets in various forms, including breakfast cereals.

In western India, millet flour (called 'bajari' in Marathi) has been commonly used with 'jowar' (sorghum) flour for hundreds of years to make the local staple flatbread, 'bhakri'.

Millet can often be used in place of buckwheat, rice or quinoa.

The protein content in millet is very close to that of wheat; both provide about 11 per cent protein by weight. Millets are rich in B vitamins, especially niacin, B6 and folacin, calcium, iron, potassium, magnesium and zinc. Millets contain no gluten, so they cannot rise to make bread. When combined with wheat or xanthan gum (for those who have coeliac disease), though, they can be used to make raised bread. Alone, they are suited to flatbread.

As none of the millets is closely related to wheat, they are appropriate foods for those with coeliac disease, as mentioned above, or other forms of allergies/intolerances of wheat.

Millet is an alternative to rice but the tiny grains need to be cracked before they will absorb water easily. Before boiling, sauté them with a little vegetable oil for 2–3 minutes until some are seen to crack, then add water carefully (one part grain to three parts water). Bring to the boil and simmer for 15–20 minutes until fluffy.

Millet flakes can be made into porridge or added to muesli. **Millet flour** is available, sometimes also made into pasta.

Oats

There are various grades of **oatmeal**, **rolled oats** or **jumbo oat flakes**. All forms can be used to make porridge, combined with ground nuts to make a nut roast, or added to stews. Oatmeal is low in gluten so can't be used to make a loaf, but can be mixed with wheat flour to add flavour and texture to bread, muffins and pancakes. Oatmeal contains some oils and can become rancid, so watch the best-before date.

Oatmeal is created by grinding oats into a coarse powder; various grades are available depending on the thoroughness of the grinding (including coarse, pinhead and fine). The main uses of oats are:

- as an ingredient in baking
- in the manufacture of bannocks or oatcakes
- as a stuffing for poultry
- as a coating for some cheeses
- as an ingredient of black pudding
- for making traditional porridge (or 'porage').

Rice

For information about rice, and recipes, see Chapter 5.

Wild rice

Not, in fact, a rice, but an aquatic grass! Difficulty in harvesting makes it expensive, but the colour (a purplish black) and its subtly nutty flavour make it a good base for a special dish or rice salad, and it can be economically mixed with other rices (but may need pre-cooking as it takes 45–50 minutes to cook, using one part grain to three parts water).

Rye

Rye is the only cereal (apart from wheat and barley) that has enough gluten to make a yeasted loaf. However, with less gluten than wheat, **rye flour** makes a denser, richer-flavoured bread. It's more usual to mix rye flour with wheat flour.

Rye grains should be cooked using one part grain to three parts water for 45–60 minutes. **Kibbled rye** is often added to granary-type loaves. Rye grains can be added to stews, and **rye flakes** are good in muesli.

Spelt

Originating in the Middle East, spelt is closely related to common wheat and has been popular for decades in eastern Europe. It has an intense nutty, wheaty flavour. The flour is excellent for breadmaking and spelt pasta is becoming more widely available.

Wheat

This is the most familiar cereal in Britain today, used for bread, cakes, biscuits, pastry, breakfast cereals and pasta.

- **Wheat grains** can be eaten whole (cook one part grain to three parts water for 40–60 minutes) and have a satisfying, chewy texture.
- **Cracked** or **kibbled wheat** is the dried whole grains cut by steel blades.
- **Bulgar wheat** is parboiled before cracking, has a light texture and only needs rehydrating by soaking in boiling water or stock.
- **Semolina** is a grainy yellow flour ground from durum or hard wheat, and is the main ingredient of dried Italian pasta.
- **Couscous** is made from semolina grains that have been rolled, dampened and coated with finer wheat flour. Soak in two parts of water/stock to rehydrate; traditionally, it is steamed after soaking.
- **Strong wheat flour** (with a high gluten content) is required for yeasted breadmaking.
- **Plain flour** is used for general cooking including cakes and shortcrust pastry.
- **Wheat flakes** are used for porridge, muesli and flapjacks.

Quinoa

Quinoa is an ancient crop that fed the South American Aztec Indians for thousands of years, and has recently been cultivated in Britain. It's a seed that is high in protein, making it useful for vegetarians.

The small, round grains look similar to millet, but are pale brown in colour. The taste is mild, and the texture firm and slightly chewy. It can be cooked like millet and absorbs twice its volume in liquid. Cook for 15 minutes (one part grain to three parts water); it's ready when all the grains have turned from white to transparent, and the spiral-like germ has separated. Use in place of more common cereals or pasta, or in risottos, pilaff and vegetable stuffings. It may be used in place of rice and is served in salads and some stuffings.

The vegetarian diet

According to the Vegetarian Society, vegetarians who eat milk products and eggs often enjoy excellent health. Vegetarian diets are consistent with dietary guidelines and can meet recommended dietary allowances for nutrients. You can get enough protein from a vegetarian diet as long as the variety of foods and the amounts consumed are adequate. Meat, fish and poultry are major contributors of iron, zinc and B vitamins in most diets, and vegetarians need to pay special attention to getting sufficient amounts of these nutrients.

Here's a quick summary from the Vegetarian Society of what vegetarians need to eat every day:

- 4 or 5 servings of fruit and vegetables
- 3 or 4 servings of cereals/grains or potatoes
- 2 or 3 servings of pulses, nuts and seeds
- 2 servings of milk, cheese, eggs or soya products (e.g. tofu)
- a small amount of vegetable oil, margarine or butter
- some yeast extract that has been fortified with Vitamin B12.

Vegetarian cheese

Cheese made using non-animal rennet is now widely available, so look out for the words 'suitable for vegetarians' on the packet, or if buying from a cheese-monger ask if it is suitable.

Unfortunately, there is no such thing as vegetarian Parmesan, so recipes that use Parmesan are not, strictly speaking, truly vegetarian. If Parmesan is being used to garnish a finished dish, offer it separately if you can so that diners can choose for themselves whether or not they wish to add it.

There are now some branded vegetarian substitutes for Parmesan, such as Bookhams. They are very similar to Parmesan in appearance and flavour. Vegetarian Cheddar is another substitute.

Meat substitutes

Tofu

Tofu is a product of the soya bean and is generally available in two forms: silken tofu, made from lightly pressed soya bean curd; firm tofu, which is more heavily pressed. Soft or regular tofu has a texture somewhere between the two.

Textured vegetable protein (TVP)

This is a meat substitute manufactured from protein derived from wheat, oats, cottonseed, soybean and other sources. The main source of TVP is the soybean; this is due to its high protein content.

TVP is used chiefly as a meat extender, varying from 10 to 60 per cent replacement of fresh meat. Some caterers on very tight budgets make use of it, but its main use is in food manufacturing.

By partially replacing the meat in certain dishes – such as casseroles, stews, pies, pasties, sausage rolls, hamburgers, meat loaf and pâté – it is possible to reduce costs, meet nutritional targets and serve food that is acceptable in appearance.

Soya protein can also be useful in making vegetarian dishes.

Myco-protein

A meat substitute such as Quorn is produced from a plant that is a distant relative of the mushroom. This myco-protein contains protein and fibre, and is the result of a fermentation process similar to the way yoghurt is made. It may be used as an alternative to chicken or beef or in vegetarian dishes.

Quorn is a low-fat, high-protein food that can be used in a variety of dishes (e.g. oriental stir-fry). Quorn does not shrink during preparation and cooking. Quorn mince or pieces can be substituted for chicken or minced meats. Its mild savoury flavour means that it complements the herbs and spices in a recipe and it is able to absorb flavour. Frozen Quorn may be cooked straight from the freezer or may be defrosted overnight in the refrigerator. Once thawed, it must be stored in the refrigerator and used within 24 hours.

1 Globe artichokes
(artichauts en branche)

brassicas boiling

energy	kcal	fat	sat fat	carb	sugar	protein	fibre	*
32 KJ	8 kcal	0.0 g	0.0 g	1.4 g	1.4 g	0.6 g	0.0 g	

1 Allow 1 artichoke per portion.
2 Cut off the stems close to the leaves.
3 Cut off about 2 cm across the tops of the leaves.
4 Trim the remainder of the leaves with scissors or a small knife.
5 Place a slice of lemon at the bottom of each artichoke.
6 Secure with string.
7 Simmer in gently boiling, lightly salted water (to which a little ascorbic acid – one Vitamin C tablet – may be added) until the bottom is tender (20–30 minutes).
8 Refresh under running water until cold.
9 Remove the centre of the artichoke carefully.
10 Scrape away all the furry inside (the choke) and leave clean.
11 Replace the centre, upside down.
12 Reheat by placing in a pan of boiling salted water for 3–4 minutes.
13 Drain and serve accompanied by a suitable sauce.

Artichokes may also be served cold with vinaigrette sauce. Do not cook artichokes in an iron or aluminium pan because these metals cause a chemical reaction that will discolour them.

* Not including sauce

2 Artichoke bottoms
(fonds d'artichauts)

brassicas boiling

1 Cut off the stalk and pull out all the underneath leaves.
2 With a large knife, cut through the artichoke leaving only 1.5 cm at the bottom of the vegetable.
3 With a small, sharp knife, while holding the artichoke upside down, peel carefully, removing all the leaf and any green part, keeping the bottom as smooth as possible. If necessary, smooth with a peeler.
4 Rub immediately with lemon and keep in lemon water or ascorbic acid solution.
5 Using a spoon or the thumb, remove the centre furry part, which is called the choke. The choke is sometimes removed after cooking.
6 Artichoke bottoms should always be cooked in a blanc (see next page).

Pull out the stalk of the artichoke

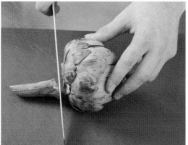

Alternatively, cut the stalk off

Pull off the leaves at the bottom

Peel the artichoke

Remove the choke

Artichoke bases may be served as a vegetable; they are sometimes filled with another vegetable (e.g. peas, spinach). When they are served ungarnished they are usually cut into quarters.

Blanc (version 1)

Portions ›	4	10
flour	10 g	20 g
cold water	0.5 litres	1 litre
salt, to taste		
lemon, juice of	½	1

1 Mix the flour and water together.
2 Add the salt and lemon juice. Pass through a strainer.
3 Place in a pan, bring to the boil, stirring continuously.

Blanc (version 2)

Portions ›	4	10
water	0.5 litres	1.25 litres
Vitamin C (ascorbic acid) tablets	2	5
oil	30 ml	75 ml
salt		

1 Combine the ingredients.

Healthy eating tip
Use the minimum amount of salt.

---

3 Purée of Jerusalem artichokes

(topinambours en purée)

tubers boiling

energy	kcal	fat	sat fat	carb	sugar	protein	fibre
502 KJ	108 kcal	5.3 g	3.3 g	16.0 g	2.5 g	2.5 g	7.0 g

Portions ›	4	10
Jerusalem artichokes	600 g	1.5 kg
salt, pepper		
butter	25 g	60 g

1 Wash, peel and rewash the artichokes.
2 Cut in pieces if necessary. Barely cover with water; add a little salt.
3 Simmer gently until tender. Drain well.
4 Pass through a sieve or mouli or liquidise.
5 Return to the pan, reheat and mix in the butter; correct the seasoning and serve.

125 ml (300 ml for 10 portions) cream or natural yoghurt may be mixed in before serving.

Healthy eating tip
Use the minimum amount of salt.

4 Jerusalem artichokes in cream sauce

tubers boiling

(topinambours à la crème)

energy	kcal	fat	sat fat	carb	sugar	protein	fibre	sodium
641 KJ	141 kcal	5.6 g	2.1 g	21.4 g	5.1 g	4.9 g	7.1 g	0.5 g

1 Wash and peel the artichokes, then rewash. Cut to an even size.
2 Barely cover with water, add a little salt and simmer until tender; do not overcook.
3 Drain well and add 250 ml (600 ml for 10 portions) cream sauce.

Cream sauce may be made using cream, fromage frais, skimmed milk and natural yoghurt, added to béchamel sauce until it has the consistency of double cream.

Healthy eating tips
● Use the minimum amount of salt.
● Try replacing half the cream sauce with natural yoghurt.

5 Asparagus points or tips
(pointes d'asperges)

1 Using the back of a small knife, carefully remove the tips of the leaves.
2 Scrape the stem, either with the blade of a small knife or a peeler.
3 Wash well. Tie into bundles of about 12 heads.
4 Cut off the excess stem.
5 Cook in lightly salted boiling water for approximately 5–8 minutes.
6 Test if cooked by gently pressing the green part of the stem, which should be tender; do not overcook.
7 Lift carefully out of the water. Remove the string, drain well and serve.

Microwaved asparagus

As the flavour of asparagus is mild and can be leached out very easily through the cooking medium, a method of cookery that ensures that no flavour is lost in the cooking process is microwaving.

1 Place a piece of clingfilm over a plate that will fit in the microwave and, more importantly, is microwave safe. Spread the clingfilm with a little oil and salt.
2 Evenly place the asparagus on the plate in a single layer.
3 Cover the plate and asparagus with another piece of clingfilm, and microwave for 30-second stints until the asparagus is tender; serve immediately.

The benefit of this method is that it retains flavour and colour, and it can be cooked in minutes, as opposed to batch cooking, which will, invariably, cause the asparagus to lose flavour and colour the longer it is stored.

If larger-scale cooking is required, the more traditional method, boiling in lightly salted water, should be used: cooking, say, 100 portions of asparagus in the microwave should be avoided for obvious reasons!

Young thin asparagus, 50 pieces to the bundle, is known as sprew or sprue. It is prepared in the same way as asparagus except that, when it is very thin, the removal of the leaf tips is dispensed with. It may be served as a vegetable, perhaps brushed with butter.
Asparagus tips are also used in numerous garnishes for soups, egg dishes, fish, meat and poultry dishes, cold dishes, salad, and so on.

6 Asparagus wrapped in puff pastry with Gruyère

stems, cheese baking

energy	kcal	fat	sat fat	carb	sugar	protein	fibre
2017 KJ	485 kcal	37.7 g	15.0 g	23.4 g	2.5 g	15.9 g	0.8 g

Portions ⟩	4	10
Gruyère cheese	175 g	400 g
Parmesan, freshly grated	3 tbsp	7 tbsp
crème fraiche	250 ml	625 ml
puff pastry (page 476)	350 g	875 g
eggwash or milk, for brushing		
asparagus, freshly cooked	350 g	875 g
salt, pepper		
watercress, for garnish		

1 Cut the Gruyère cheese into 1 cm dice. In a suitable bowl, mix the Parmesan cheese and crème fraiche; season.
2 Roll out the puff pastry to approximately 0.25 cm thick and cut into squares approximately 18 cm x 18 cm.
3 Brush the edges with eggwash or milk.
4 Divide the crème fraiche, putting equal amounts onto the centre of each square. Lay the asparagus on top. Place the diced Gruyère cheese firmly between the asparagus.
5 Fold the opposite corners of each square to meet in the centre, like an envelope. Firmly pinch the seams together to seal them. Make a small hole in the centre of each one to allow the steam to escape. Place on a lightly greased baking sheet.
6 Allow to relax for 20 minutes in the refrigerator. Brush with eggwash or milk, sprinkle with Parmesan.
7 Bake in a hot oven at 200°C for approximately 20–25 minutes until golden brown.
8 Serve garnished with watercress.

Key point
Make sure the pastry parcels are well sealed so that the mixture does not escape during cooking.

Healthy eating tip
The puff pastry and cheese make this dish high in fat. Serve with plenty of starchy carbohydrate to dilute it.

7 Stuffed aubergine
(aubergine farcie)

vegetable fruits deep frying

energy	kcal	fat	sat fat	carb	sugar	protein	fibre	sodium
557 KJ	134 kcal	12.2 g	1.5 g	4.3 g	3.8 g	2.4 g	4.5 g	0.7 g

Portions ❯	4	10
aubergines	2	5
shallots, chopped	10 g	25 g
oil or fat, to fry		
mushrooms	100 g	250 g
parsley, chopped		
tomato concassé	100 g	250 g
salt, pepper		
demi-glace or *jus-lié*	125 ml	300 ml

1 Cut the aubergines in two lengthwise.
2 With the point of a small knife, make a cut round the halves approximately 0.5 cm from the edge, then make several cuts 0.5 cm deep in the centre.
3 Deep-fry in hot fat at 185°C for 2–3 minutes; drain well.
4 Scoop out the centre pulp and chop it finely.
5 Cook the shallots in a little oil or fat without colouring.
6 Add the well-washed mushrooms. Cook gently for a few minutes.
7 Mix in the pulp, parsley and tomato; season. Replace in the aubergine skins.
8 Sprinkle with breadcrumbs and melted butter. Brown under the salamander.
9 Serve with a cordon of demi-glace or *jus-lié*.

8 Fried aubergine
(aubergine frite)

vegetable fruits deep frying

energy	kcal	fat	sat fat	carb	sugar	protein	fibre
994 KJ	225 kcal	20.0 g	3.8 g	10.1 g	5.9 g	1.9 g	5.2 g

1 Allow half an aubergine per portion.
2 Remove alternate strips of the dark skin with a peeler.
3 Cut into 0.5 cm slices on the slant.
4 Pass through seasoned flour or milk and flour.
5 Shake off all surplus flour.
6 Deep-fry in hot fat at 185°C. Drain well and serve.

Aubergines may also be shallow-fried, grilled or griddled.

9 Broad beans
(fèves)

seeds and pods boiling

energy	kcal	fat	sat fat	carb	sugar	protein	fibre	*
344 KJ	81 kcal	0.6 g	0.1 g	5.0 g	0.4 g	7.9 g	6.5 g	

0.5 kg will yield about 2 portions.

1 Shell the beans and cook in boiling salted water for 10–15 minutes until tender. Do not overcook.
2 If the inner shells are tough, remove before serving.

Key point
The modern technique is to take the beans out of their pod and outer skin before serving – this reveals the bright green, tender beans.

Try something different
Variations include:
● brushing with butter
● brushing with butter then sprinkling with chopped parsley
● binding with ½ litre cream sauce or fresh cream.

* 100 g portion

Remove the inner shells of broad beans

10 French beans
(haricots verts)

seeds and pods boiling, steaming

energy 646 KJ	kcal 154 kcal	fat 2.9 g	sat fat 0.5 g	carb 28.5 g	sugar 2.1 g	protein 5.1 g	fibre 5.9 g

0.5 kg will yield 3–4 portions.

1. Top and tail the beans, carefully and economically.
2. Using a large sharp knife cut the beans into strips 5 cm x 3 mm.
3. Wash.
4. Cook in lightly salted boiling water, or steam, for 5–10 minutes, until tender.
5. Do not overcook. Drain well and serve.

Try something different
Variations include:
- brushing the beans with butter
- gently tossing the cooked beans in butter over heat without colour
- adding to 400 g cooked French beans, 50 g shallow-fried onions
- combining 400 g cooked French beans with 100 g cooked flageolet beans.

Boiling vegetables
http://bit.ly/w817Pb

11 Runner beans

seeds and pods boiling, steaming

energy 80 KJ	kcal 19 kcal	fat 0.2 g	sat fat 0.0 g	carb 2.7 g	sugar 1.3 g	protein 1.9 g	fibre 3.4 g

1. Wash the beans and string them with a small knife, then cut them into thin strips approximately 4–6 cm long.
2. Cook in boiling lightly salted water, or steam, for approx. 10 minutes.
3. Drain well and serve. Do not overcook.

12 Beetroot
(betterave)

root vegetables boiling, steaming

energy	kcal	fat	sat fat	carb	sugar	protein	fibre
92 KJ	22 kcal	0.0 g	0.0 g	5.0 g	5.0 g	0.9 g	1.3 g

1 Select medium-sized or small beetroots, carefully twist off the green leaves (do not cut).
2 Wash well in cold water, cover with water and simmer gently until the skin is easily removed by rubbing between the fingers.

Do not cut or prick with a knife as the beetroots will 'bleed' and turn pale.

Try something different
Beetroot may also be cooked in a steamer, or baked. It may be served hot:
● in cream sauce
● coated in herb-flavoured oil (see page 57)
● coated in butter and marmalade.

Peel the cooked beetroot, wearing gloves to avoid staining your skin

Cut into neat dice

13 Goats' cheese and beetroot tarts, with salad of watercress

cheese, root vegetables 🍲 baking, 🍳 shallow frying

energy	kcal	fat	sat fat	carb	sugar	protein	fibre	salt
2377 KJ	568 kcal	37.7 g	9.0 g	43.6 g	7.5 g	18.6 g	1.8 g	1.7 g

Portions ›	4	10
puff pastry	400 g	1 kg
shallots	150 g	375 g
beetroot, cooked	200 g	500 g
goats' cheese	200 g	500 g
watercress, bunch	1	2

1 Roll the puff pastry to a thickness of 3 mm.
2 Chill the rolled puff pastry for 10 minutes.
3 Finely slice the shallots and sweat down without colour.
4 Cut the puff pastry into 4 discs approximately 150 mm in diameter or into rectangles plus strips to build up the sides.
5 Chill the pastry for 10 minutes.
6 Dice the cooked beetroot into pieces 10 mm x 10 mm.
7 To make the tarts, place the shallots on the pastry discs.

8 Cook at 180°C for 12 minutes.
9 Once cooked, remove from the oven and top with the diced beetroot and crumbled goats' cheese.
10 To finish the dish, place the tarts on plates and finish with picked watercress and vinaigrette.

14 Broccoli

brassicas 🍲 boiling

energy	kcal	fat	sat fat	carb	sugar	protein	fibre
76 KJ	18 kcal	0.0 g	0.0 g	1.6 g	1.5 g	3.1 g	4.1 g

Cook in lightly salted water, or steam.

Broccoli is usually broken down into florets and, as such, requires very little cooking: once brought to the boil, 1–2 minutes should be sufficient. This leaves the broccoli slightly crisp.

Green and purple broccoli, because of their size, need less cooking time than cauliflower.

Tenderstem broccoli is increasingly popular. It has long, slim, evenly sized stems and small flower heads, so it cooks quickly. The distinctive flavour is similar to asparagus. Green and purple varieties are available, and, because of the uniform shape, they can be presented very attractively.

15 Cabbage
(chou vert)

leafy vegetables 🔘 boiling, 🔘 steaming

energy	kcal	fat	sat fat	carb	sugar	protein	fibre
38 KJ	9 kcal	0.0 g	0.0 g	1.1 g	1.1 g	1.3 g	2.5 g

0.5 kg will serve 3–4 portions; 1.25 kg will serve 8–10 portions.

1 Cut the cabbage in quarters.
2 Remove the centre stalk and outside leaves.
3 Shred and wash well.
4 Place into boiling, lightly salted, water.
5 Boil steadily or steam until cooked (approx. 5–10 minutes, according to age and type). Do not overcook.
6 Drain immediately in a colander and serve.

Overcooking will lessen the vitamin content and also spoil the colour. This applies to cooking any green vegetable.

Cooked cabbage presented wrapped in a cabbage leaf

16 Spring greens
(choux de printemps)

leafy vegetables 🔘 boiling

0.5 kg will serve 3–4 portions; 1.25 kg will serve 8–10 portions.

Prepare and cook as for cabbage (recipe 15), for 10–15 minutes according to age and type. Do not overcook.

17 Braised red cabbage
(choux à la flamande)

energy	kcal	fat	sat fat	carb	sugar	protein	fibre
754 KJ	180 kcal	15.2 g	8.4 g	7.8 g	7.7 g	3.4 g	3.2 g

Portions ❯	4	10
red cabbage	400 g	1 kg
salt, pepper		
butter	50 g	125 g
cooking apples	100 g	250 g
caster sugar	10 g	25 g
vinegar or red wine	125 ml	300 ml
bacon trimmings (optional)	50 g	125 g

1 Quarter, trim and shred the cabbage. Wash well and drain.
2 Season lightly with salt and pepper.
3 Place in a well-buttered casserole or pan suitable for placing in the oven (not aluminium or iron, because these metals will cause a chemical reaction that will discolour the cabbage).
4 Add the peeled and cored apples. Cut into 1 cm dice and sugar.
5 Add the vinegar and bacon (if using), cover with a buttered paper and lid.
6 Cook in a moderate oven at 150–200°C for approximately 1½ hours.
7 Remove the bacon (if used) and serve.

Other optional flavourings include 50 g sultanas, grated zest of one orange, pinch of ground cinnamon.

Healthy eating tip
The fat and salt content will be reduced by omitting the bacon.

Strain off most of the liquid after braising

18 Buttered carrots
(carottes au beurre)

root vegetables boiling

energy	kcal	fat	sat fat	carb	sugar	protein	fibre
297 KJ	71 kcal	5.1 g	3.3 g	5.8 g	5.8 g	0.7 g	2.8 g

Portions ›	4	10
carrots	400 g	1 kg
salt, pepper		
sugar		
butter	25 g	60 g
parsley, chopped		

1 Peel and wash the carrots.
2 Cut into neat even pieces, turned barrel shapes, or batons.
3 Place in a pan with a little salt, a pinch of sugar and butter. Barely cover with water.
4 Cover with a buttered paper and allow to boil steadily in order to evaporate all the water.
5 When the water has completely evaporated check that the carrots are cooked; if not, add a little more water and continue cooking. Do not overcook.
6 Toss the carrots over a fierce heat for 1–2 minutes in order to give them a glaze.
7 Serve sprinkled with chopped parsley.

Healthy eating tip
Use the minimum amount of salt.

19 Purée of carrots
(purée de carottes)

root vegetables boiling

energy	kcal	fat	sat fat	carb	sugar	protein	fibre
410 KJ	99 kcal	5.6 g	3.4 g	11.9 g	11.1 g	0.9 g	3.6 g

Portions ›	4	10
carrots	600 g	1.5 kg
salt, pepper		
butter	25 g	60 g

1 Wash, peel and rewash the carrots. Cut into pieces.
2 Barely cover with water, add a little salt. Simmer gently or steam until tender.
3 Drain well. Pass through a sieve or mouli.
4 Return to the pan, reheat and mix in the butter, correct the seasoning, and serve.

Healthy eating tip
Use the minimum amount of salt.

20 Carrots in cream sauce
(carottes à la crème)

root vegetables boiling, steaming

energy	kcal	fat	sat fat	carb	sugar	protein	fibre	*
511 KJ	123 kcal	8.2 g	4.6 g	11.5 g	7.8 g	1.4 g	2.5 g	

Portions >	4	10
carrots	400 g	1 kg
salt, pepper		
butter	25 g	60 g
parsley, chopped		
cream sauce	100 ml	250 ml

1 Prepare and cook carrots as for buttered carrots (recipe 18).
2 Mix with the sauce, correct the seasoning and serve.

* Using a cream sauce based on béchamel with single cream added 40:10

Healthy eating tips
- Use the minimum amount of salt.
- Try replacing half the cream sauce with natural yoghurt.
- The cream sauce may be made with wholemeal flour, skimmed milk and natural yoghurt.

21 Cauliflower
(chou-fleur nature)

brassicas boiling, steaming

energy	kcal	fat	sat fat	carb	sugar	protein	fibre	*
142 KJ	34 kcal	0.9 g	0.2 g	3.0 g	2.5 g	3.6 g	1.8 g	

1 Allow 1 medium-sized cauliflower for 4 portions. Trim the stem and remove the outer leaves.
2 Hollow out the stem with a peeler or cut into florets. Wash.
3 Cook in lightly salted boiling water, or steam, for approx. 10–15 minutes. Do not overcook (if cut into florets, cook for only 3–5 minutes).
4 Drain well and serve cut into 4 even portions.

Try something different
- **Cauliflower** may be served with 250 ml of cream sauce, 100 g of melted butter or 125 ml of hollandaise sauce. Serve the sauce in a sauceboat.
- **Buttered cauliflower** is brushed with 25–50 g melted butter before serving and can be sprinkled with chopped parsley.
- **Fried cauliflower**: cut the cooked cauliflower into 4 portions, and lightly colour on all sides in 25–50 g butter.

Multiply the above quantities by 2.5 for 10 portions.

* Using no additions

Boiling vegetables
http://bit.ly/w817Pb

22 Cauliflower au gratin
(chou-fleur mornay)

brassicas boiling, grilling

energy	kcal	fat	sat fat	carb	sugar	protein	fibre
632 KJ	150 kcal	10.4 g	3.9 g	8.6 g	3.8 g	6.3 g	2.0 g

1 Cook a medium-sized cauliflower (see recipe 21). Cut the cooked cauliflower into four.
2 Reheat in a pan of hot salted water (*chauffant*), or reheat in butter in a suitable pan.
3 Place in vegetable dish or on a greased tray.
4 Coat with 250 ml of mornay sauce (see page 42).
5 Sprinkle with grated cheese.
6 Brown under the salamander and serve.

Healthy eating tip
No additional salt is needed as cheese is added.

23 Celeriac

root vegetables boiling

energy	kcal	fat	sat fat	carb	sugar	protein	fibre *
264 KJ	65 kcal	5.5 g	3.3 g	2.3 g	1.8 g	1.2 g	3.7 g

Celeriac, or celery root, makes an excellent soup and is a versatile vegetable that can be prepared and served raw as an hors d'oeuvre or as a hot vegetable using any of the carrot recipes (recipes 18–20).

* Using butter

24 Purée of celeriac, turnips, swedes or parsnips

root vegetables boiling, steaming

energy	kcal	fat	sat fat	carb	sugar	protein	fibre *
395 KJ	95 kcal	5.9 g	3.3 g	9.2 g	6.4 g	1.8 g	4.7 g

Portions >	4	10
celeriac, turnips, swedes or parsnips	600 g	1.5 kg
salt, pepper		
butter	25 g	60 g

1 Wash, peel and rewash the vegetables. Cut into pieces if necessary.
2 Barely cover with water; add a little salt.
3 Simmer gently until tender, or steam. Drain well.
4 Pass through a sieve or mouli, or use a food processor.
5 Return to the pan, reheat and mix in the butter, correct the seasoning and serve.

Try something different
Combination vegetable purée can include, for example, swede and carrot, parsnip and potato.

* Using mixed vegetables and 25 g butter

25 Buttered celeriac, turnips or swedes

root vegetables boiling

energy	kcal	fat	sat fat	carb	sugar	protein	fibre
253 KJ	60 kcal	5.4 g	3.3 g	2.5 g	2.5 g	0.7 g	1.9 g

Portions ⟩	4	10
celeriac, turnips or swedes	400 g	1 kg
salt, sugar		
butter	25 g	60 g
parsley, chopped		

1 Peel and wash the vegetables.
2 Cut into neat pieces or turn barrel shaped.
3 Place in a pan with a little salt, a pinch of sugar and the butter. Barely cover with water.
4 Cover with a buttered paper and allow to boil steadily in order to evaporate all the water.
5 When the water has completely evaporated, check that the vegetables are cooked; if not, add a little more water and continue cooking. Do not overcook.

6 Toss the vegetables over a fierce heat for 1–2 minutes to glaze.
7 Drain well, and serve sprinkled with chopped parsley.

26 Braised chicory
(endive au jus)

stems braising

energy	kcal	fat	sat fat	carb	sugar	protein	fibre
476 KJ	114 kcal	6.3 g	3.7 g	17.8 g	13.5 g	1.1 g	1.8 g

Portions ⟩	4	10
fish or chicken stock	200 ml	500 ml
chicory heads	8	20
fresh lemon juice	3 tbsp	8 tbsp
caster sugar	3 tbsp	8 tbsp
sea salt, freshly-ground black pepper		
butter	25 g	60 g

1 Have the stock ready and set aside.
2 Trim the chicory of any bruised outside leaves, then trim the ends and use a small, sharp knife to remove the bitter core at the base of each head.
3 Bring a pan of water to the boil and add the lemon juice, 1 tbsp of the sugar, and salt to taste. Blanch the chicory for 8–10 minutes and drain well.

4 Drain all the liquid from the chicory. In a large frying pan, heat the butter and brown the chicory on all sides. Deglaze with a little stock and simmer for a few minutes, basting the chicory at all times.
5 Arrange the heads in a single layer on a platter, sprinkle with the remaining sugar, and season with salt and pepper.

27 Shallow-fried chicory
(endive meunière)

energy	kcal	fat	sat fat	carb	sugar	protein	fibre	*
484 KJ	118 kcal	12.0 g	7.3 g	4.8 g	1.3 g	0.9 g	1.5 g	

1 Trim the stem, remove any discoloured leaves, wash.
2 Cook as for braised chicory (recipe 26).
3 Drain, shallow-fry in a little butter and colour lightly on both sides.
4 Serve with 10 g per portion nut-brown butter, lemon juice and chopped parsley.

* Using 37.5 g butter

28 Braised fennel with black olives and cardamom

stems braising

energy	kcal	fat	sat fat	carb	sugar	protein	fibre	sodium
531 KJ	128 kcal	6.9 g	0.9 g	3.3 g	2.6 g	1.7 g	4.2 g	0.6 g

Portions >	4	10
fennel bulbs, medium	2	5
olive or vegetable oil	2 tbsp	5 tbsp
cloves of garlic, crushed or chopped	1	2
black olives, stoned and halved	8	20
cardamom pods	2	5
thyme, sprigs	1	2
chicken stock	300 ml	750 ml
white wine	300 ml	750 ml
seasoning		

1 Prepare the fennel: remove any tough outer leaves and cut into quarters vertically.
2 Heat the oil in a suitable pan, add the fennel, and sweat without colour for 5–10 minutes.
3 Add the garlic, olives, cardamom and thyme. Add the stock and white wine, and season. Bring to the boil.
4 Cover with a lid and braise in an oven at 180–200°C for approx. 1 hour, until tender.
5 When cooked, remove.

Braised fennel may be served with a variety of meat and fish dishes. It may be coated with a cream, cheese, red wine or Madeira sauce.

Try something different
● The fennel may also be blanched for 2 minutes in boiling water, and refreshed before sweating.
● Cinnamon or mixed spice may be used in place of cardamom.

29 Braised leeks with garlic and olives

Portions 〉	4	10
leeks, large	4	10
cloves of garlic, crushed and chopped	4	10
chicken stock	250 ml	625 ml
thyme, sprigs	1	2
bay leaves	1	2
white wine	125 ml	300 ml
green olives, quartered	50 g	125 g
butter	50 g	125 g

1 Trim the leeks and discard any withered leaves.
2 Cut the leeks in half lengthways, but keeping them attached at the root. Wash well.
3 Melt the butter in a suitable pan. Sweat the garlic.
4 Blanch the leeks in boiling water for 2 minutes, then refresh.

5 Place the leeks in the pan; add all other ingredients except the olives. The chicken stock should almost cover the leeks. Season.
6 Bring to the boil and cover.
7 Place in a moderate oven at 180°C for approx. 20 minutes.
8 When cooked, remove the thyme and bay leaf, and add the olives.
9 Serve as a vegetable or as a garnish to accompany roast meats, fish or pasta.

After blanching the leeks it may be necessary to fold them in half before braising.

Try something different
- Leeks may also be boiled in salted water for approx. 10–15 minutes.
- Leeks may be served with a cream sauce, parsley sauce or a cheese sauce.
- Coat the leeks with a red wine sauce, sometimes garnished with mushrooms.

30 Kohlrabi

stems boiling

energy	kcal	fat	sat fat	carb	sugar	protein	fibre
77 KJ	18 kcal	0.2 g	0.0 g	3.1 g	3.0 g	1.2 g	1.9 g

Kohlrabi is a stem that swells to a turnip shape above the ground. When grown under glass it is pale green in colour; when grown outdoors it is purplish.

Select kohlrabi with tops that are green, young and fresh. If the globes are too large they may be woody and tough.

1 Trim off the stems and leaves – these may be used for soups.
2 Peel thickly at the root end and thinly at the top end. Wash.
3 Cut into even-sized pieces. Young kohlrabi can be cooked whole.
4 Simmer in well-flavoured stock until tender.

Uses and variations
- Kohlrabi may be served with cream sauce.
- It may be baked and stuffed.
- It can be added to casseroles and stews.

31 Marrow
(courge)

vegetable fruits boiling, steaming

energy	kcal	fat	sat fat	carb	sugar	protein	fibre
44 KJ	11 kcal	0.0 g	0.0 g	2.1 g	2.0 g	0.6 g	0.9 g

1 Peel the marrow with a peeler or small knife.
2 Cut in half lengthwise.
3 Remove the seeds with a spoon.
4 Cut into even pieces, approximately 5 cm square.
5 Cook in lightly salted boiling water, or steam, for 10–15 minutes. Do not overcook.
6 Drain well and serve.

All the variations for cauliflower (recipes 21–22) may be used with marrow.

32 Marrow provençale
(courge provençale)

vegetable fruits  stewing, braising

energy	kcal	fat	sat fat	carb	sugar	protein	fibre
524 KJ	126 kcal	10.6 g	6.5 g	6.4 g	5.7 g	1.8 g	1.4 g

Portions ❯	4	10
marrow	400 g	1 kg
onion, chopped	50 g	125 g
clove of garlic, chopped	1	2–3
oil or butter	50 g	125 g
salt, pepper		
tomato concassé	400 g	1 kg
parsley, chopped		

1 Lightly peel the marrow, remove the seeds and cut into 2 cm dice.
2 Cook the onion and garlic in the oil in a pan for 2–3 minutes without colour.
3 Add the marrow, season lightly with salt and pepper.
4 Add the tomato concassé.
5 Cover with a lid, cook gently in the oven or on the side of the stove for 1 hour or until tender.
6 Sprinkle with chopped parsley and serve.

Baby marrows may be served similarly, but reduce the cooking time to 5–10 minutes.

Healthy eating tips
● Use a little unsaturated oil to cook the onion.
● Use the minimum amount of salt.

33 Shallow-fried courgettes
(courgettes sautées)

vegetable fruits  shallow frying

energy	kcal	fat	sat fat	carb	sugar	protein	fibre	*
456 KJ	111 kcal	10.7 g	6.6 g	1.9 g	1.8 g	1.9 g	0.9 g	

1 Wash. Top and tail, and cut into round slices 3–6 cm thick.
2 Gently fry in hot oil or butter for 2 or 3 minutes, drain and serve.

* Using butter

34 Deep-fried courgettes
(courgettes frites)

vegetable fruits  deep frying

energy	kcal	fat	sat fat	carb	sugar	protein	fibre	*
481 KJ	111 kcal	11.4 g	1.4 g	1.8 g	1.7 g	1.8 g	0.9 g	

1 Wash. Top and tail, and cut into round slices 3–6 cm thick.

2 Pass through flour, or milk and flour, or batter, and deep-fry in hot fat at 185°C. Drain well and serve.

> **Key point**
> Make sure the oil is very hot before adding the courgette. Fry it quickly and drain it before serving.

* Using vegetable oil

35 Fettuccini of courgette with chopped basil and balsamic vinegar

vegetable fruits  shallow frying, sauté

energy	kcal	fat	sat fat	carb	sugar	protein	fibre	sodium
745 KJ	181 kcal	17.9 g	2.6 g	1.9 g	1.8 g	1.8 g	1.2 g	0.0 g

Portions ❯	4	10
courgettes, large	2	5
olive oil	50 ml	125 ml
olive oil, to finish	20 ml	125 ml
balsamic vinegar, to finish	20 ml	50 ml
basil leaves, shredded	2	5

1 Slice the courgettes finely lengthwise, using a mandolin (Japanese slicer).

2 Heat the olive oil in a suitable pan. Sauté the courgette slices quickly without colour for 35 seconds.

3 Place on suitable plates. Drizzle with olive oil and balsamic vinegar, and top with shredded basil leaves.

> This may be served as a vegetarian starter or as a garnish for fish and meat dishes.

36 | Ratatouille

vegetable fruits, bulbs shallow frying, stewing

energy	kcal	fat	sat fat	carb	sugar	protein	fibre
579 KJ	138 kcal	12.6 g	1.7 g	5.2 g	4.6 g	1.3 g	2.4 g

Portions ⟩	4	10
baby marrow (courgette)	200 g	500 g
aubergines	200 g	500 g
tomatoes	200 g	500 g
oil	50 ml	125 ml
onions, finely sliced	50 g	125 g
clove of garlic, peeled and chopped	1	2
red peppers, diced	50 g	125 g
green peppers, diced	50 g	125 g
salt, pepper		
parsley, chopped	1 tsp	2–3 tsp

1 Trim off both ends of the marrow and aubergines.
2 Remove the skin using a peeler.
3 Cut into 3 mm slices or 1 cm dice.
4 Concassé the tomatoes (peel, remove seeds, roughly chop).
5 Place the oil in a thick-bottomed pan and add the onions.
6 Cover with a lid and allow to cook gently for 5–7 minutes without colour.
7 Add the garlic, marrow and aubergine slices, and the peppers.
8 Season lightly with salt and mill pepper.
9 Allow to cook gently for 4–5 minutes, toss occasionally and keep covered.
10 Add the tomato and continue cooking for 20–30 minutes or until tender.
11 Mix in the parsley, correct the seasoning and serve.

Ingredients for ratatouille

Add the tomato to the vegetables during cooking (step 10)

Key point

The vegetables need to be cut evenly so that they will cook evenly; it also improves the texture of the dish. The skins are sometimes left on courgettes and aubergines, which gives extra colour.

Healthy eating tips

● Use a little unsaturated oil to cook the onions.
● Use the minimum amount of salt.

37 Ratatouille pancakes with a cheese sauce

vegetable fruits, bulbs shallow frying, stewing

energy	kcal	fat	sat fat	carb	sugar	protein	fibre
2398 KJ	571 kcal	35.8 g	6.5 g	46.1 g	19.0 g	19.6 g	6.5 g

Portions ›	4	10
ratatouille (recipe 36)		
Pancake batter		
flour	100 g	250 g
skimmed milk	250 ml	625 ml
egg	1	2–3
pinch of salt		
sunflower margarine, melted	10 g	25 g
Cheese sauce		
skimmed milk	500 ml	1.25 litres
sunflower oil	50 g	125 g
flour	50 g	125 g
onion, studded with clove	1	2–3
Parmesan, grated	25 g	60 g
egg yolk	1	2–3
seasoning		

1 Prepare and make the pancakes (one per portion).
2 Prepare the ratatouille and cheese sauce.
3 Season with salt and cayenne pepper.
4 Fill the pancakes with the ratatouille, roll up and serve on individual plates or on a service dish, coated with cheese sauce and sprinkled with grated Parmesan. Finish by gratinating under the salamander.

38 | Courgette flowers

flower heads, fish steaming, deep frying

energy	kcal	fat	sat fat	carb	sugar	protein	fibre	sodium
810 KJ	193 kcal	6.6 g	1.2 g	27.4 g	2.2 g	7.5 g	1.5 g	0.0 g

Portions >	4	10
flowering courgettes	4	10
fish mousse (or other mousse, e.g. chicken, veal)	100 g	250 g
corn oil		
plain flour for dusting		
batter		

1 Gently break off the flowers from the courgettes, ensuring they stay intact.
2 Carefully snap out and discard the stigma from the flowers.
3 Place the fish mousse in a bowl, season lightly and mix.
4 Once the mousse is ready, place into a disposable piping bag.
5 Gently open the courgette flowers a little and pipe in the mousse until the flower is half full.
6 Twist the ends of the petals to seal in the mousse.
7 Place the filled flowers in a steamer or steaming basket over a pan of boiling water.
8 Steam for 2–3 minutes, then carefully immerse into a bowl of iced water to stop the cooking.
9 Remove from the water, pat dry and store in an airtight container in the fridge for up to 2 hours.
10 Heat the oil for deep-frying to 180°C.
11 Roll the filled courgette flowers in plain flour; shake off the excess.
12 Dip them into some batter, then place them all into the fryer for 1 minute until golden brown.
13 Drain briefly on some kitchen paper and serve.

Courgettes with flowers

39 Grilled mushrooms
(champignons grillés)

fungi grilling

energy	kcal	fat	sat fat	carb	sugar	protein	fibre *
499 KJ	119 kcal	12.8 g	1.7 g	0.0 g	0.0 g	0.9 g	1.3 g

Portions >	4	10
grilling mushrooms (flat mushrooms)	200 g	500 g
salt, pepper		
butter, margarine or oil	50 g	125 g

1 Peel the mushrooms, remove the stalks; wash and drain well.
2 Place on a tray and season lightly with salt and pepper.
3 Brush with melted fat or oil and grill on both sides for 3–4 minutes. Serve with picked parsley.

* Using sunflower oil

Healthy eating tip
Use the minimum amount of salt.

40 Stuffed mushrooms
(champignons farcis)

fungi grilling

energy	kcal	fat	sat fat	carb	sugar	protein	fibre *
577 KJ	137 kcal	13.1 g	1.8 g	3.2 g	0.3 g	1.9 g	2.1 g

Portions >	4	10
grilling mushrooms	300 g	1 kg
shallots, chopped	10 g	25 g
butter, margarine or oil	50 g	125 g
breadcrumbs	25 g	60 g

1 Peel the mushrooms, remove stalks and wash well.
2 Retain 8 or 12 of the best mushrooms. Finely chop the remainder with the well-washed peelings and stalks.
3 Cook the shallots, without colour, in a little fat.
4 Add the chopped mushrooms and cook for 3–4 minutes (duxelle).
5 Grill the mushrooms as in recipe 39.
6 Place the duxelle in the centre of each mushroom.
7 Sprinkle with a few breadcrumbs and some melted butter.
8 Reheat in the oven or under the salamander; serve.

* Using sunflower oil

Healthy eating tip
Use a little unsaturated oil to cook the shallots.

Try something different
Mushrooms may be stuffed with ratatouille, a meat forcemeat, creamed spinach or a vegetable purée.

energy	kcal	fat	sat fat	carb	sugar	protein	fibre	sodium
722 KJ	173 kcal	10.4 g	1.1 g	16.3 g	14.3 g	5.3 g	8.2 g	0.3 g

Portions ⟩	4	10
okra, small	450 g	1.25 kg
vegetable oil	2 tbsp	5 tbsp
cumin seeds	2 tsp	5 tsp
onions, finely chopped	110 g	250 g
mild curry paste	1 tbsp	2½ tbsp
tomatoes, medium, skinned, deseeded, finely chopped	3	8
fresh coriander, chopped	1 tbsp	2½ tbsp
red pepper, diced	½	1½
green pepper, diced	½	1½
fresh red chillies, finely sliced	2	5
brown sugar	1 tbsp	2½
salt, to taste		

1 Very carefully and lightly wash the okra. Pat dry and leave intact.

2 Heat the oil in a wok to a medium heat, add the cumin seeds and fry for 30 seconds.

3 Add the onion and curry paste and stir-fry for 5 minutes.

4 Add the tomato, coriander, peppers, chillies and sugar and continue to stir-fry for 5 minutes.

5 While stir-frying, trim the okra to remove the tops and tails.

6 Add the trimmed okra to the other ingredients and gently stir-fry until cooked through (approximately 3–4 minutes).

7 Season and serve.

42 Fried onions

(oignons sautées ou oignons lyonnaise)

bulbs  shallow frying, sauté

energy	kcal	fat	sat fat	carb	sugar	protein	fibre *
681 KJ	162 kcal	12.9 g	2.4 g	10.4 g	10.4 g	1.8 g	2.6 g

0.5 kg of onions will yield approximately 2 portions.

1 Peel and wash the onions, cut in halves, slice finely.
2 Cook slowly in 25–50 g oil in a frying pan, turning frequently until tender and browned; season lightly with salt.

Healthy eating tips
- Use a little unsaturated oil to cook the onion.
- Use the minimum amount of salt.

* Using peanut oil

43 French-fried onions

(oignons frites à la française)

bulbs  deep frying

energy	kcal	fat	sat fat	carb	sugar	protein	fibre *
661 KJ	159 kcal	11.7 g	1.6 g	12.3 g	3.5 g	2.0 g	1.0 g

0.5 kg of onions will yield approximately 2 portions.

1 Peel and wash the onions.
2 Cut into 2 mm slices, against the grain. Separate into rings.
3 Pass through milk and seasoned flour.
4 Shake off the surplus. Deep-fry in hot fat at 185°C.
5 Drain well on kitchen paper, season lightly with salt and serve.

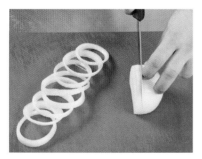

Slice the onions thinly

Pass each piece through milk and then flour

Healthy eating tips
- Make sure the oil is hot so that less is absorbed into the onions.
- Drain on kitchen paper.
- Use the minimum amount of salt.

* Using 50 g onions, to give 83.5 g finished weight

44 Caramelised button onions

bulbs shallow frying, sauté

energy	kcal	fat	sat fat	carb	sugar	protein	fibre	sodium
713 KJ	171 kcal	10.8 g	6.5 g	18.4 g	16.7 g	1.2 g	1.2 g	0.5 g

Portions ›	4	10
butter or vegetable oil	50 g	125 g
button onions	250 g	700 g
water or brown stock	100 ml	250 ml
sugar	50 g	125 g

1 Place the butter or oil in a shallow pan.
2 Fry the button onions quickly to a light golden brown colour.
3 Barely cover with water or brown stock. Add the sugar. Cook the button onions until they are tender and the liquid has reduced with the sugar to a light caramel glaze. Carefully coat the onions with the glaze.

Key point
The important thing is to reduce the stock and sugar until they form a light caramel syrup.
Serve a smaller portion if using the onions as a garnish.

45 Parsnips
(panais)

root vegetables boiling, steaming, roasting

energy	kcal	fat	sat fat	carb	sugar	protein	fibre
235 KJ	56 kcal	0.0 g	0.0 g	13.5 g	2.7 g	1.3 g	2.5 g

1 Wash well. Peel the parsnips and re-wash well.
2 Cut into quarters lengthwise, remove the centre root if tough.
3 Cut into neat pieces and cook in lightly salted water until tender, or steam.
4 Drain and serve with melted butter or in a cream sauce.

Roasting
Parsnips may be roasted in the oven in a little fat (as shown here) or in with a joint, and can be cooked and prepared as a purée.

Key point
For great roast parsnips, blanch them for 2 minutes, drain, then roast in hot olive oil.

46 Peas French-style
(petit pois à la française)

seeds and pods boiling

energy	kcal	fat	sat fat	carb	sugar	protein	fibre
515 KJ	123 kcal	5.6 g	3.4 g	12.9 g	5.8 g	5.9 g	5.7 g

Portions >	4	10
peas (in the pod, or frozen)	1 kg	2.5 kg
spring or button onions	12	40
lettuce, small	1	2–3
butter	25 g	60 g
salt		
caster sugar	½ tsp	1 tsp
flour	5 g	12 g

1 Shell and wash the peas (if in pods) and place in a sauteuse.
2 Peel and wash the onions, shred the lettuce and add to the peas with half the butter, a little salt and the sugar.
3 Barely cover with water. Cover with a lid and cook steadily, preferably in the oven, until tender.
4 Correct the seasoning.
5 Mix the remaining butter with the flour, making a *beurre manié*, and place it into the boiling peas in small pieces until thoroughly mixed; serve.

When using frozen peas, allow the onions to almost cook before adding the peas.

Shell the peas and discard the pods

Place the prepared ingredients into the sauteuse

Add a *beurre manié* at the end of the cooking time

47 Mangetout

seeds and pods boiling

Boiling vegetables
http://bit.ly/w817Pb

0.5 kg of mangetout will yield 4–6 portions.

1 Top and tail, wash and drain.
2 Cook in boiling salted water for 2–3 minutes, until slightly crisp.
3 Serve whole, brushed with butter.

48 Salsify
(salsifi)

root vegetables boiling, deep frying

energy	kcal	fat	sat fat	carb	sugar	protein	fibre
76 KJ	18 kcal	0.0 g	0.0 g	2.8 g	2.8 g	1.9 g	0.0 g

½ kg will yield 2–3 portions.

1 Wash, peel and rewash the salsify.
2 Cut into 5 cm lengths.
3 Cook in a blanc (see below). Do not overcook.
4 Salsify may then be served brushed with melted butter, or coated in mornay sauce (see page 42), sprinkled with grated cheese and browned under a salamander. It may also be passed through batter and deep-fried.

To make the blanc

Portions ›	4	10
flour	10 g	20 g
cold water	0.5 litres	1 litre
salt, to taste		
lemon, juice of	½	1

1 Mix the flour and water together.
2 Add the salt and lemon juice. Pass through a strainer.
3 Place in a pan, bring to the boil, stirring continuously.

An alternative recipe for a blanc using ascorbic acid (Vitamin C) tablets is included in recipe 2.

49 Stuffed peppers
(piment farci)

vegetable fruits braising

energy	kcal	fat	sat fat	carb	sugar	protein	fibre
1291 KJ	308 kcal	11.4 g	6.7 g	48.8 g	5.3 g	5.4 g	3.1 g

Portions ⟩	4	10
red peppers, medium-sized	4	10
carrots, sliced	50 g	125 g
onions, sliced	50 g	125 g
bouquet garni		
white stock	0.5 litres	1.25 litres
salt, pepper		
Pilaff		
rice (long grain)	200 g	500 g
salt, pepper		
onion, chopped	50 g	125 g
butter	50 g	125 g

1 Place the peppers on a tray in the oven or under the salamander for a few minutes, or deep-fry in hot oil at 180°C, until the skin blisters.
2 Remove the skin and stalk carefully, and empty out all the seeds.
3 Stuff with a well-seasoned pilaff of rice (ingredients as listed above), which may be varied by the addition of mushrooms, tomatoes, ham, etc.
4 Replace the stem.
5 Place the peppers on the sliced carrot and onion in a pan suitable for the oven; add the bouquet garni, stock and seasoning. Cover with a buttered paper and lid.
6 Cook in a moderate oven at 180–200°C for 1 hour or until tender.
7 Serve garnished with picked parsley, basil or other herbs.

Healthy eating tips
- This dish is low in fat if the peppers are placed in the oven or under the salamander, not deep-fried, and the butter/oil is kept to a minimum.
- Add little or no salt.
- If extra vegetables are added to the rice, and a vegetable stock used, this dish can be a useful vegetarian starter.

Briefly heat the peppers and then peel them

Cut off the top and empty out the seeds

Fill the pepper and then replace the stem

50 Leaf spinach
(epinards en branches)

leafy vegetables boiling

energy	kcal	fat	sat fat	carb	sugar	protein	fibre	*
512 KJ	123 kcal	10.8 g	6.6 g	1.4 g	1.2 g	5.2 g	6.3 g	

0.5 kg will yield 2 portions.

1 Remove the stems and discard them.
2 Wash the leaves very carefully in plenty of water, several times if necessary.
3 Cook in lightly salted boiling water for 3–5 minutes; do not overcook.
4 Refresh under cold water, squeeze dry into a ball.
5 When required for service, either reheat and serve plain or place into a pan containing 25–50 g butter, loosen with a fork and reheat quickly without colouring.

* Using 25 g butter per 0.5 kg

51 Spinach purée
(epinards en purée)

leafy vegetables boiling

energy	kcal	fat	sat fat	carb	sugar	protein	fibre	*
588 KJ	143 kcal	11.9 g	6.7 g	3.3 g	3.1 g	5.7 g	4.2 g	

0.5 kg will yield 2 portions.

1 Remove the stems and discard them.
2 Wash the leaves very carefully in plenty of water, several times if necessary.
3 Wilt for 2–3 minutes, taking care not to overcook.
4 Place on a tray and allow to cool.
5 Pass through a sieve or mouli, or use a food processor.
6 Reheat in 25–50 g butter, mix with a kitchen spoon, correct the seasoning and serve.

Try something different

- Creamed spinach purée can be made by mixing in 30 ml cream and 60 ml béchamel or natural yoghurt before serving. Serve with a border of cream. An addition would be 1 cm triangle-shaped croutons fried in butter.
- Spinach may also be served with toasted pine kernels or finely chopped garlic.

* Using 25 g butter per 0.5 kg

52 Brussels sprouts
(choux de bruxelles)

leafy vegetables boiling, steaming

energy	kcal	fat	sat fat	carb	sugar	protein	fibre
82 KJ	20 kcal	0.0 g	0.0 g	1.9 g	1.8 g	3.1 g	3.2 g

0.5 kg will serve 3–4 portions; 1.25 kg will serve 8–10 portions.

1 Using a small knife trim the stems and cut a cross 2 mm deep; remove any discoloured leaves. Wash well.
2 Cook in boiling lightly salted water, or steam, for 5–10 minutes according to size. Do not overcook.
3 Drain well in a colander and serve.

Variations

Brussels sprouts with butter are cooked and served as outlined here, but brushed with 25–50 g melted butter (60–125 g for 10 portions).
For Brussels sprouts with chestnuts, to every 400 g sprouts add 100 g cooked peeled chestnuts.

53 Roast butternut squash

vegetable fruits roasting

1 Peel the squash and cut it into thick, even pieces.
2 Place on a lightly oiled roasting tray and roast for approximately 20–25 minutes in a hot oven, until the flesh is soft and golden brown.

54 Roast squash or pumpkin with cinnamon and ginger

vegetable fruits  roasting

energy	kcal	fat	sat fat	carb	sugar	protein	fibre	sodium
519 KJ	125 kcal	11.0 g	4.2 g	6.0 g	5.3 g	1.1 g	1.7 g	0.0 g

Portions >	4	10
butternut squash or pumpkin	500 g	1.25 kg
butter or margarine	25 g	60 g
olive oil	2 tbsp	5 tbsp
ground cinnamon	½ tsp	1 tsp
ginger, peeled and freshly chopped	½ tsp	1 tsp
caster sugar	10 g	25 g
lemon, juice of	½	1

1 Peel the squash, cut it in half and remove the seeds.
2 Cut the squash into 1.5 cm dice or into small wedges.
3 Place the butter into a suitable roasting pan and heat gently. Add the olive oil, ginger and cinnamon.
4 Add the squash gently and stir until the squash is coated in the spice mixture. Season and add the sugar.

5 Place in an oven at 200°C until tender and golden brown.
6 When cooked, sprinkle with lemon juice.

Variations
Garlic may be added to the spice mixture, and mixed spice may be used in place of cinnamon.

Peel and halve the squash, then remove the seeds

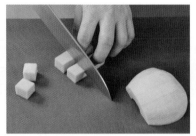
Cut the squash into even pieces

Stir the squash pieces into the warm butter and spices before roasting

55 Corn on the cob
(maïs)

vegetable fruits boiling

energy	kcal	fat	sat fat	carb	sugar	protein	fibre
646 KJ	154 kcal	2.9 g	0.5 g	28.5 g	2.1 g	5.1 g	5.9 g

Allow 1 cob per portion.

1 Remove the leaves and 'silks' (fibres). Trim the stem.
2 Cook in lightly salted boiling water for 10–20 minutes or until the corn is tender. Do not overcook.
3 Serve with a sauceboat of melted butter.

Creamed sweetcorn can be made by removing the corn from the cooked cobs, draining well and binding lightly with cream (fresh or non-dairy), béchamel sauce or yoghurt.

56 Tomato concassé
(tomate concassé)

vegetable fruits boiling, shallow frying, sauté

Portions ❯	4	10
tomatoes	400 g	1.25 kg
shallots or onions, chopped	25 g	60 g
butter or oil	25 g	60 g
salt, pepper		

This is a cooked preparation that is usually included in the normal *mise-en-place* of a kitchen as it is used in a great number of dishes.
Uncooked tomato concassé, with the tomato cut into neat cubes or strips, is often used as a garnish.

1 Plunge the tomatoes into boiling water for 5–10 seconds – the riper the tomatoes, the less time is required. Refresh immediately.
2 Remove the skins, cut in quarters and remove all the seeds.
3 Roughly chop the flesh of the tomatoes.
4 Meanwhile, cook the chopped onion or shallots without colour in the butter or oil.
5 Add the tomatoes and season lightly.
6 Simmer gently on the side of the stove until the moisture is evaporated.

Cut each tomato into quarters

Remove the seeds from each petal

Roughly chop the tomatoes

57 Stuffed tomatoes
(tomates farcies)

vegetable fruits boiling, baking

energy	kcal	fat	sat fat	carb	sugar	protein	fibre
430 KJ	102 kcal	5.9 g	3.5 g	10.6 g	5.7 g	2.5 g	2.2 g

	Portions ❯	4	10
tomatoes, medium-sized		8	20
Duxelle			
shallots, chopped		10 g	25 g
butter or oil		25 g	60 g
mushrooms		150 g	375 g
salt, pepper			
clove of garlic, crushed (optional)		1	2–3
breadcrumbs (white or wholemeal)		25 g	60 g
parsley, chopped			

1. Wash the tomatoes, remove the eyes.
2. Remove the top quarter of each tomato with a sharp knife.
3. Carefully empty out the seeds without damaging the flesh.
4. Place on a greased baking tray.
5. Cook the shallots in a little butter or oil without colour.
6. Add the washed chopped mushrooms; season with salt and pepper; add the garlic if using. Cook for 2–3 minutes.
7. Add a little of the strained tomato juice, the breadcrumbs and the parsley; mix to a piping consistency. Correct the seasoning. At this stage, several additions may be made (e.g. chopped ham, cooked rice).
8. Place the mixture in a piping bag with a large star tube and pipe into the tomato shells. Replace the tops.
9. Brush with oil, season lightly with salt and pepper.
10. Cook in a moderate oven at 180–200°C for 4–5 minutes.
11. Serve garnished with picked parsley or fresh basil or rosemary.

Healthy eating tips
- Use a small amount of an unsaturated oil to cook the shallots and brush over the stuffed tomatoes.
- Add the minimum amount of salt.
- Adding cooked rice to the stuffing will increase the amount of starchy carbohydrate.

Cut out the eye of the tomato

Slice off the top and remove the seeds from inside

Pipe in the filling and then replace the top

58 Mixed vegetables
(macédoine or jardinière de légumes)

root vegetables · boiling

energy	kcal	fat	sat fat	carb	sugar	protein	fibre
58 KJ	14 kcal	0.1 g	0.0 g	2.5 g	1.7 g	1.0 g	2.1 g

Portions ›	4	10
carrots	100 g	250 g
turnips	50 g	125 g
salt		
French beans	50 g	125 g
peas	50 g	125 g

1 Peel and wash the carrots and turnips; cut into 0.5 cm dice (macédoine) or batons (jardinière); cook separately in lightly salted water, do not overcook. Refresh.
2 Top and tail the beans; cut into 0.5 cm dice, cook and refresh, do not overcook.
3 Cook the peas and refresh.
4 Mix the vegetables and, when required, reheat in hot salted water.
5 Drain well, serve brushed with melted butter.

Cutting vegetables into macédoine
http://bit.ly/AOoPrD

Roasted vegetables

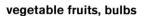

energy	kcal	fat	sat fat	carb	sugar	protein	fibre
343 KJ	82 kcal	3.6 g	0.6 g	10.0 g	8.6 g	3.0 g	3.8 g

Portions >	4	10
red onions, small	1	3
red peppers	1	3
yellow peppers	1	3
courgettes	2	5
aubergines	1	3
cloves of garlic, coarsely chopped	1–2	2–4
olive oil	1 tbsp	2½ tbsp
balsamic vinegar	1 tbsp	2½ tbsp
sea salt		
black mill pepper		
fresh rosemary fresh basil } roughly chopped		

1 Peel the vegetables. Cut the onion into 8 pieces. Cut the peppers into halves, deseed and cut each into approximately 4–6 even pieces. Cut the courgettes into 2 cm x 1 cm batons. Cut the aubergine into 2 cm x 1 cm batons.

2 Place all the vegetables (and the garlic) into a suitable roasting dish, sprinkle with the olive oil and balsamic vinegar.

3 Season lightly with sea salt and pepper.

4 Sprinkle with rosemary and basil.

5 Place in a preheated oven at 180°C for approx. 15 minutes.

6 Serve immediately.

These vegetables may also be chilled and served with a salad as a starter.

Healthy eating tip

Lightly brush the vegetables with the olive oil and add the minimum amount of salt.

60 Chinese-style stir-fried vegetables

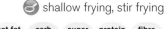 shallow frying, stir frying

energy	kcal	fat	sat fat	carb	sugar	protein	fibre
1429 KJ	340 kcal	31.9 g	4.2 g	9.1 g	4.2 g	4.7 g	4.5 g

Portions ⟩	4	10
beansprouts	100 g	250 g
button mushrooms	100 g	250 g
carrots	100 g	250 g
celery	100 g	250 g
cauliflower	100 g	250 g
broccoli	100 g	250 g
French beans	50 g	125 g
red peppers	50 g	125 g
green peppers	50 g	125 g
baby sweetcorn	50 g	125 g
sunflower oil	50 ml	125 ml
root ginger, grated	5 g	12 g
soy sauce	60 ml	150 ml
ground white or mill pepper, to season		

1 Wash the beansprouts; wash and slice the mushrooms. Peel the carrots and cut into large batons. Trim the celery and cut into large batons. Wash the cauliflower and broccoli, and cut into florets. Top and tail the French beans and cut in halves. Wash and slice the peppers. Trim the baby sweetcorn as necessary. The green vegetables may be quickly blanched and refreshed to retain their colour.

2 Heat the sunflower oil in a wok or frying pan and add all the vegetables. Fry and continuously stir for approximately 3 minutes.

3 Add the grated ginger, cook for 1 minute. Add the soy sauce, stir well.

4 Correct the seasoning, serve immediately.

Healthy eating tips
- No additional salt is needed; there is plenty of flavour from the soy sauce, ginger and pepper.
- Use a smaller amount of sunflower oil.
- Serve with a large portion of rice or noodles.

61 Vegetable curry with rice pilaff

mixed vegetables, rice stewing, braising

energy	kcal	fat	sat fat	carb	sugar	protein	fibre
1814 KJ	432 kcal	35.5 g	7.4 g	23.5 g	16.3 g	6.4 g	6.7 g

Portions >	4	10
mixed vegetables (e.g. cauliflower, broccoli, peppers, carrots, courgettes, mushrooms, aubergines)	600 g	1.5 kg
butter or oil	100 g	250 g
onions, chopped finely	150 g	375 g
garam masala	25 g	60 g
creamed coconut (or 50 g/125 g desiccated coconut)	25 g	60 g
curry sauce made using vegetable stock (page 50)	500 ml	1.5 litre
rice pilaff (page 174)	100 g	250 g
flaked almonds, roasted	50 g	125 g

1 Prepare the vegetables: cut the cauliflower and broccoli into small florets, blanch and refresh; cut the peppers in half, remove the seeds, cut into 1 cm dice; cut the carrots into large dice, blanch and refresh; and the courgettes into 1 cm dice; leave the mushrooms whole; cut the aubergines into 1 cm dice.

2 Heat the butter or oil and sweat the onion.

3 Add the garam masala; sweat for approx. 2 minutes and add the coconut.

4 Add all the vegetables; sweat together for approx. 5 minutes.

5 Add the curry sauce, bring to the boil and gently simmer until all the vegetables are cooked but crunchy in texture.

6 Make the rice pilaff according to the recipe on page 174. Add the roasted flaked almonds after cooking.

7 Serve the curry in a suitable dish with the rice pilaff, poppadoms and a curry tray with mango chutney.

Healthy eating tips
- Use a small amount of an unsaturated oil to sweat the onions.
- No added salt is necessary if the stock used contains yeast extract.

62 Vegetable biryani

mixed vegetables, rice braising

energy 2014 KJ	kcal 482 kcal	fat 7.3 g	sat fat 0.9 g	carb 91.3 g	sugar 9.9 g	protein 12.2 g	fibre 4.6 g

Portions ⟩	4	10
basmati rice	400 g	1.25 kg
oil	2 tbsp	5 tbsp
cinnamon stick	½	1
cardamom pods	4	10
cloves	4	10
onions, sliced	100 g	250 g
clove of garlic	1	2–3
green chilli, finely chopped	1	2–3
root ginger, grated	1 tbsp	2–3 tbsp
mixed vegetables (e.g. carrots, celery, broccoli, cauliflower, French beans)	600 g	1.5 kg
tomatoes, blanched, deseeded and chopped, or canned plum tomatoes	400 g	1.25 kg
tomato purée	25 g	60 g
salt, pepper		
coriander leaves, chopped		

1 Wash, soak and drain the rice.
2 Partly cook the rice in boiling salted water for 3 minutes. Refresh and drain well.
3 Heat the oil in a suitably sized pan. Add the crushed cinnamon, cardamom and cloves, and sweat for 2 minutes.
4 Add the sliced onions, garlic, chilli and ginger. Continue to sweat until soft.
5 Prepare the vegetables: cut the carrots and celery into batons, the cauliflower and broccoli into florets and the French beans into 2.5 cm lengths.
6 Add the vegetables to the pan, and fry for 2–3 minutes.
7 Add the tomatoes and tomato purée. Season.
8 Make sure there is sufficient moisture in the pan to cook the vegetables; usually a little water needs to be added. Ideally, though, the vegetables should cook in their own juices, combined with the tomatoes.

9 When the vegetables are partly cooked, layer them in a casserole or suitable pan with the rice. (Make sure that there is sufficient liquid to cook the rice.)
10 Cover the casserole, finish cooking in a moderate oven at 180°C for about 20 minutes, or until the rice is tender.
11 Sprinkle with chopped coriander leaves and serve.

A biryani is usually served with a side dish of vegetable curry.

Healthy eating tips
● Keep added salt to a minimum.
● Use a little unsaturated oil to sweat the spices, onions and vegetables.

63 Tempura

energy	kcal	fat	sat fat	carb	sugar	protein	fibre
3397 KJ	815 kcal	55.9 g	7.4 g	67.4 g	5.3 g	14.8 g	5.0 g

Portions ❯	4	10
vegetable oil	500 ml	1.25 litres
courgettes, sliced	2	5
sweet potato, scrubbed and sliced	1	2 large
green pepper, seeds removed and cut into strips	1	2
shiitake mushroom, stalks removed and halved if large	4	10
onion, sliced as half moons	1	2
parsley sprigs, to garnish	4	10
Batter (NB all ingredients must be stored in the fridge until just before mixing)		
egg yolk	1	2
ice-cold water	200 ml	600 ml
plain flour, sifted	100 g	250 g
Tentsuyu dipping sauce (optional)		
dashi stock	200 ml	600 ml
mirin	3 tbsp	8 tbsp
soy sauce	3 tbsp	8 tbsp
ginger, grated	½ tsp	1 tsp

1 To prevent splattering during the frying, make sure to dry all deep-fry ingredients thoroughly first with a kitchen towel.

2 For the batter, beat the egg yolk lightly and mix with the ice-cold water.

3 Add half the flour to the egg and water mixture. Give the mixture a few strokes. Add the rest of the flour all at once. Stroke the mixture a few times with chopsticks or a fork until the ingredients are loosely combined. The batter should be very lumpy. If over-mixed, tempura will be oily and heavy.

4 Heat the oil to 160°C.

5 Dip the vegetables into plain flour and then into the batter, a few pieces at a time. Fry until just crisp and golden (about 1½ minutes).

6 Drain the cooked vegetables on kitchen towel.

7 Serve immediately with a pinch of salt, garnished with parsley sprigs and lemon wedges, dry-roasted salt or with Tentsuyu dipping sauce in a small bowl with grated ginger. This dish can also be served with an accompaniment of grated white radish.

8 To make the Tentsuyu sauce (if required), combine the ingredients in a small saucepan; heat it through and leave to one side.

Any vegetables with a firm texture may be used for tempura.

Use sparkling water to make tempura batter

Cut a variety of vegetables into even pieces

Dip each piece into the batter and then deep-fry it

415

64 Bean goulash

pulses stewing, shallow frying, boiling

energy	kcal	fat	sat fat	carb	sugar	protein	fibre
1728 KJ	411 kcal	17.9 g	2.7 g	50.0 g	7.3 g	17.3 g	18.5 g

Portions ❯	4	10
red kidney or haricot beans, dried	200 g	500 g
sunflower oil	60 ml	150 ml
onion, finely chopped	50 g	125 g
clove of garlic, crushed	1	2–3
paprika	25 g	60 g
red peppers	2	5
green pepper	1	2–3
yellow pepper	1	2–3
button mushrooms, sliced	200 g	500 g
tomato purée	50 g	125 g
vegetable stock	750 ml	2 litre
bouquet garni		
seasoning		
small turned potatoes, cooked	8	20
parsley, chopped, to serve		

1. Soak the beans for 24 hours in cold water. Drain, place into a saucepan. Cover with cold water, boil for at least 10 minutes and then simmer until tender.
2. Heat the oil in a sauté pan, sweat the onion and garlic without colour for 2–3 minutes; add the paprika and sweat for a further 2–3 minutes.
3. Add the peppers (cut in halves, with seeds removed and cut into 1 cm dice). Add the button mushrooms; sweat for a further 2 minutes.
4. Add the tomato purée, vegetable stock and bouquet garni. Bring to the boil and simmer until the pepper and mushrooms are cooked.
5. Remove the bouquet garni. Add the drained cooked beans, correct the seasoning and stir.
6. Garnish with potatoes (or gnocchi) and chopped parsley.
7. Serve wholegrain pilaff or wholemeal noodles separately.

Healthy eating tips
- Use less sunflower oil to sweat the onions.
- Add a pinch of salt.
- Serve with rice or noodles and a green salad or mixed vegetables.

65   Mexican bean pot

pulses   boiling,   stewing

energy	kcal	fat	sat fat	carb	sugar	protein	fibre
672 KJ	161 kcal	1.2 g	0.2 g	27.0 g	4.6 g	12.3 g	14.0 g

Portions ⟩	4	10
red kidney or haricot beans, dried	300 g	1 kg
onions, finely chopped	100 g	250 g
carrots, sliced	100 g	250 g
tomato, skinned, deseeded and diced	200 g	500 g
cloves of garlic, crushed and chopped	2	5
paprika	10 g	25 g
dried marjoram	3 g	9 g
fresh chilli, small, finely chopped	1	2–3
red pepper, small, finely diced	1	2–3
yeast extract	5 g	12 g
chives, chopped		
seasoning		

1 Soak the beans in cold water for 24 hours. Drain. Place into a saucepan, cover with cold water, boil for at least 10 minutes and then simmer gently.
2 When three-quarters cooked, add all the other ingredients except the chopped chives.
3 Continue to simmer until all is completely cooked.
4 Serve sprinkled with chopped chives.

Healthy eating tips

● No added salt is needed; there is plenty in the yeast extract.
● Serve with a selection of colourful vegetables.

meat substitutes deep frying

energy	kcal	fat	sat fat	carb	sugar	protein	fibre	*
543 KJ	131 kcal	8.9 g	0.0 g	1.0 g	0.5 g	11.8 g	0.0 g	

Portions 〉	4	10
firm tofu, cut into cubes	200 g	500 g
coating (see step 1)		
ginger	1 cm	2 cm
herbs		

Healthy eating tips

- Use an unsaturated oil to fry the tofu.
- Make sure the oil is hot so that less is absorbed.
- Alternatively, try dry-frying the tofu.

* Data for a 50 g portion

1 Coat the tofu cubes with any of the following: flour, egg and breadcrumbs; milk and flour; cornstarch; arrowroot.
2 Deep-fry the tofu at 180°C, until golden brown. Drain.
3 Serve garnished with freshly grated ginger and julienne of herbs.
4 Serve with a tomato sauce flavoured with coriander.

67 Crisp polenta and roasted Mediterranean vegetables

grains, vegetable fruits boiling, roasting

energy	kcal	fat	sat fat	carb	sugar	protein	fibre	sodium
3267 KJ	790 kcal	71.4 g	18.9 g	28.6 g	14.0 g	10.1 g	6.6 g	0.1 g

Portions ⟩	4	10
Polenta		
water	200 ml	500 ml
butter	30 g	75 g
polenta flour	65 g	160 g
Parmesan, grated	25 g	60 g
egg yolks	1	2
crème fraiche	110 g	275 g
seasoning		
Roasted vegetables		
red peppers	2	5
yellow peppers	2	5
courgettes	2	5
red onions	2	5
vegetable oil	200 ml	500 ml
seasoning		
clove of garlic	1	3
thyme, sprigs	2	5

To make the polenta

1 Bring the water and the butter to the boil.
2 Season the water well and whisk in the polenta flour.
3 Continue to whisk until very thick.
4 Remove from the heat and add the Parmesan, egg yolk and crème fraiche.
5 Whisk until all incorporated; check the seasoning.
6 Set in a lined tray.
7 Once set, cut using a round cutter or cut into squares.
8 Reserve until required.

Key point

Line the tray with clingfilm and silicone paper before pouring in the polenta – this will stop it from sticking to the tray when it sets.

To make the roasted vegetables

1 Roughly chop the vegetables into large chunks. Ensure the seeds are removed from the peppers.
2 Toss the cut vegetables in the oil and season well.
3 Place the vegetables in an oven with the aromats for 30 minutes at 180°C.
4 Remove from the oven and drain. Reserve until required.

To serve

1 To serve the dish, shallow-fry the polenta in a non-stick pan until golden on both sides.
2 Warm the roasted vegetables and place them in the middle of the plate. Place the polenta on top.
3 Finish with rocket salad and balsamic dressing.

Polenta and lentil cakes with roasted vegetables and cucumber and yoghurt sauce

grains, pulses 🫓 shallow frying, 🍳 roasting

energy	kcal	fat	sat fat	carb	sugar	protein	fibre
1898 KJ	452 kcal	15.2 g	4.1 g	55.6 g	7.9 g	25.2 g	4.3 g

Portions ›	4	10
puy lentils	250 g	625 g
vegetable stock	250 ml	625 ml
fine polenta	75 g	187 g
Parmesan cheese, grated	25 g	62 g
egg, beaten	1	3
leeks, finely chopped and blanched	75 g	187 g
clove of garlic, crushed and finely chopped	1	3
seasoning		
olive oil	3 tbsp	8 tbsp
Sauce		
cucumber	250 g	625 g
natural yoghurt	250 ml	625 ml
mint, chopped	¼ tsp	1 ¼ tsp
chives, chopped	1 tsp	2½ tsp

1 Wash the lentils and cook in salted water for about 25 minutes until tender but still firm. Drain well, refresh and drain again. Dry on a suitable cloth.

2 Bring the vegetable stock to the boil, add the polenta and cook gently, stirring until thickened.

3 Add the Parmesan and beaten egg; season.

4 Mix in the lentils, polenta, leeks and garlic.

5 Correct the seasoning; cool and shape into 4 (or 10) round cakes.

6 Place in the fridge and chill well for at least 1 hour.

7 Heat the olive oil in a suitable pan, gently fry the cakes for about 3–4 minutes on each side until heated through and well browned.

8 To make the sauce, liquidise the peeled cucumber with the yoghurt, finish with chopped mint and chives.

9 To serve, place a small amount of the sauce onto a plate and place the cakes on top. Garnish the plate with freshly roasted vegetables.

Healthy eating tips

- No additional salt is needed.
- Use less olive oil to fry the cakes, and drain on kitchen paper.
- Brush the vegetables with a little unsaturated oil when roasting.

69 Couscous with meat and vegetables

grains, lamb   boiling, steaming, stewing

energy	kcal	fat	sat fat	carb	sugar	protein	fibre	*
2146 KJ	515 kcal	28.5 g	12.6 g	42.2 g	14.7 g	25.3 g	2.8 g	

Portions ⟩	4	10
couscous	200 g	500 g
lean stewing lamb	400 g	1 kg
stewing beef *or* chicken, cut for sauté	200 g	500 g
olive oil	2 tbsp	5 tbsp
onion, finely chopped	50 g	125 g
clove of garlic, crushed and chopped	1	2–3
celery	100 g	250 g
leek	100 g	250 g
carrot	100 g	250 g
chickpeas	25 g	60 g
seasoning ground ginger (optional)	¼ tsp	½ tsp
saffron (optional)	¼ tsp	½ tsp
raisins	50 g	125 g
courgettes	100 g	250 g
tomatoes, skinned, deseeded, diced	50 g	125 g
parsley, chopped		
tomato purée	50 g	125 g
cayenne pepper		
paprika	½ tsp	1 tsp
butter	50 g	125 g

Healthy eating tips

- No additional salt is needed.
- Add only a small amount of fat to the couscous before adding the meat and vegetables.
- The fat content will be reduced if skinned chicken is used or less lamb/beef and more vegetables.

* Using butter

1 Soak the couscous in warm water for 10 minutes.
2 Fry the meat in the oil until browned and sealed. Remove quickly; fry the onions and garlic.
3 Drain, place the meat, onions and garlic into a saucepan.
4 Add the celery, leeks and carrots cut into 1 cm dice. Add the chickpeas, cover with water, season.
5 Add the ginger and saffron. Bring to the boil and simmer for about 1 hour.
6 Drain the couscous, place in the top part of the couscousier and steam for 30 minutes. Alternatively, place the couscous in a metal colander lined with muslin. Fit into the top of the saucepan, making sure that the liquid from the stew does not touch the steamer as the couscous will become lumpy. Stir occasionally.
7 Add to the stew the raisins and courgettes, the tomato, chopped parsley and tomato purée. Cook for a further 30 minutes.
8 Remove approx. 250 ml (625 ml) sauce from the stew and stir in the cayenne pepper, enough to make it strong and fiery. Finish with paprika.
9 To serve, pile the couscous into a suitable serving dish, preferably earthenware, add knobs of butter and work into the grains with a fork.
10 Carefully arrange the meat and vegetables over the couscous and pour the broth over. Serve the hot peppery sauce separately.
11 Alternatively, the couscous, meat and vegetables, the broth and the peppery sauce can be served in separate bowls.

A pre-cooked couscous is also available.

70 Cheese soufflé
(soufflé au fromage)

cheese 🍰 baking

energy	kcal	fat	sat fat	carb	sugar	protein	fibre
3223 KJ	767 kcal	60.2 g	28.2 g	17.6 g	6.1 g	39.7 g	0.5 g

Portions ❯	4	10
butter or margarine	25 g	60 g
flour	15 g	50 g
milk	125 ml	300 ml
egg yolks	3	8
salt, cayenne pepper		
cheese, grated	50 g	125 g
egg whites	4	10

1 Melt the butter in a thick-based pan.
2 Add the flour and mix with a kitchen spoon.
3 Cook out for a few seconds without colouring.
4 Gradually add the cold milk and mix to a smooth sauce.
5 Simmer for a few minutes.
6 Add 1 egg yolk, mix in quickly; immediately remove from the heat.
7 When cool, add the remaining yolks. Season with salt and cayenne.
8 Add the cheese.
9 Place the egg whites and a pinch of salt (a pinch of egg white powder will help strengthen the whites) in a scrupulously clean bowl and whisk until stiff.
10 Add one-eighth of the whites to the mixture and mix well.
11 Gently fold in the remaining seven-eighths of the mixture, mix as lightly as possible. Place into a buttered soufflé case.
12 Cook in a hot oven at 220°C for 25–30 minutes.
13 Remove from the oven, place on a round flat dish and serve immediately.

Healthy eating tips
● Use sunflower margarine and semi-skimmed milk to make the sauce.
● No added salt is needed as the cheese has salt in it.

* Using hard margarine

71 Cheese fritters
(beignets au fromage)

cheese  deep frying

energy	kcal	fat	sat fat	carb	sugar	protein	fibre
1409 KJ	340 kcal	28.4 g	11.2 g	11.8 g	0.4 g	9.9 g	0.5 g

Portions ⟩	4	10
water	125 ml	300 ml
butter	50 g	150 g
flour, white or wholemeal	60 g	200 g
eggs, medium	2	5
Parmesan cheese, grated	50 g	125 g
salt, cayenne		

1 Bring the water and butter to the boil in a thick-based pan. Remove from the heat.
2 Add the flour, mix with a kitchen spoon.
3 Return to a gentle heat and mix well until the mixture leaves the sides of the pan. Remove from the heat. Allow to cool slightly.
4 Gradually add the eggs, beating well. Add the cheese and seasoning.
5 Using a spoon, scoop out the mixture in pieces the size of a walnut; place into deep hot fat at 185°C.
6 Allow to cook, with the minimum of handling, for about 10 minutes.
7 Drain and serve sprinkled with grated Parmesan.

Healthy eating tips
● Use sunflower margarine for the fritters.
● No extra salt is needed as the cheese has salt in it.
● Fry in hot sunflower oil and drain on kitchen paper.

10 Potatoes

This chapter is relevant to the following units:

- Prepare vegetables for basic dishes (NVQ)
- Cook and finish basic vegetable dishes (NVQ)
- Prepare and cook fruit and vegetables (VRQ).

What are potatoes?

Potatoes are tubers. A tuber is a fleshy, food-storing swelling at the tip of an underground stem, also called a stolon. Potatoes have white, brown, purple or red skin, and white or golden flesh.

Several varieties of potato are grown in Britain and are available according to the season. They have differing characteristics and some are more suitable for certain methods of cooking than others (see Table 10.1 and the variety chart on page 428).

Cooking potatoes

This section describes what happens to the potato while cooking in three common styles.

Baking

For good baked potatoes, long slow cooking is best. The skin becomes very crisp and turns darker because the starch just below the skin converts to sugar, which browns in heat. Cut a slit in the potato as soon as it comes out of the oven so the interior doesn't steam, which makes for a heavier consistency.

Mashed potatoes

Mashed potatoes can be made from many varieties of potato; some of these are mentioned in Table 10.1 and another is Maris Bintje (season dependent). The starch in the potatoes absorbs water and swells during the cooking process. Then, when the potato is mashed or riced, the cells break open, releasing more starch, which makes the potatoes creamy and smooth.

If you boil potatoes for mashing, return them to the hot pan after draining and shake it over a medium heat for 2–3 minutes to dry the potatoes.

Whatever the cooking method, add butter when you begin mashing. The butter coats the cells and the starch so they absorb less liquid, making the potatoes less gluey and fluffier.

The slower the mash is cooked, the better for the starch as it has more structure in the final mixing process, allowing the potato to hold in more fat/liquid than if cooked by the more traditional quicker method.

> **A quick tip for mashed potatoes**
> Bring the potatoes up to the boil from cold, as normal, and boil for 2–3 minutes. Remove and rinse in cold water, then repeat the process of boiling from cold and turn the heat down, not even to a simmer. This will obviously take longer but will reduce the water absorption rate dramatically due to the starch wall created by the first process.

Roasting

Roast potatoes are simply cut into chunks, or neatly shaped/turned, and parboiled slowly until just cooked on the inside. Drain and toss in a liberal amount of olive oil and seasoning, then roast at a high temperature (220°C) for 15 minutes. Turn the temperature down to 180°C and baste every 5 minutes to ensure a crisp coat all over. Once cooked, serve immediately, as prolonged holding will cause the inside to steam, making the outside soft and leathery.

Purchasing, selection and storage

Purchasing

Inspect and select your potatoes before buying or on delivery. Choose firm, smooth ones. Avoid excessively wrinkled, withered, cracked potatoes, and do not buy those that have a lot of sprouts or green areas.

Selection

The careful selection of potatoes to suit the job in hand is essential, as the variety chosen (see Table 10.1) will be reflected in the end product.

Table 10.1 Recommended cooking methods

Potato variety	Methods of cookery
Cara	boil, bake, chip, wedge
Charlotte	boil, salad use
Desiree	boil, roast, bake, chip, mash, wedge
Golden Wonder	boil, roast, crisps
King Edward	boil, bake, roast, mash, chip
Maris Piper	boil, roast, bake, chip
Pink Fir Apple	boil, salad use
Premiere	boil
Record	crisps
Romano	boil, bake, roast, mash
Saxon	boil, bake, chip
Wilja	boil, bake, chip, mash

Cooked potatoes may have different textures, depending on whether they are 'waxy' or 'floury' varieties. This is due to changes that happen to the potato cells during cooking. 'Waxy' potatoes are translucent and may have a moist and pasty feel. 'Floury' potatoes are brighter and granular in appearance, leaving a drier feel. These differences influence the performance of the potato when cooked in different ways (e.g. boiling versus roasting).

During cooking, as noted above, the starch in the potato starts to absorb water and swells in size. Potatoes need to be cooked for sufficient time to gelatinise the starch, or they will look and taste undercooked.

Floury potatoes

A type rather than a variety, floury potatoes are especially popular in the UK. They are suitable for baking, mashing and chipping as they have a soft, dry texture when cooked. They are not suitable for boiling, however, because they tend to disintegrate. Popular varieties of floury potato include King Edward and Maris Piper.

Floury potatoes

Waxy potatoes

Waxy potatoes are more solid than floury potatoes and hold their shape when boiled, but do not mash well. They are particularly suitable for baked and layered potato dishes such as boulangère potatoes. Popular varieties include Cara and Charlotte.

Waxy potatoes

Storage

You can store potatoes for several months without affecting their quality; they should be stored at a constant temperature (3°C). If it is not possible to store them in this way, buying fresh potatoes regularly is best practice. There are three essential rules to bear in mind when storing potatoes: 'dry, dark and cool'. You should avoid light as this will cause sprouting and eventually the greening effect that contains mild toxins; if you have inadvertently purchased potatoes with this green tinge, remove the green bits and the rest of the potato is then fine to use.

The storage of the potato is perhaps the most important aspect of its life – the closer the temperature is to freezing point, the quicker the potato starch coverts to sugar, producing a sweet flesh, but a loss of structure and, often, discoloration.

Yield

- 0.5 kg of old potatoes will yield approximately 3 portions.
- 0.5 kg of new potatoes will yield approximately 4 portions.
- 1.5 kg of old potatoes will yield approximately 10 portions.
- 1.25 kg of new potatoes will yield approximately 10 portions.

Ready-prepared potatoes

Potatoes are obtainable in many convenience forms: peeled, turned, cut into various shapes for frying, or scooped into balls (*Parisienne*) or olive shaped.

- Chips are available fresh, frozen, chilled or vacuum packed.
- Frozen potatoes are available as croquettes, hash browns, sauté and roast.
- Mashed potato powder is also available.

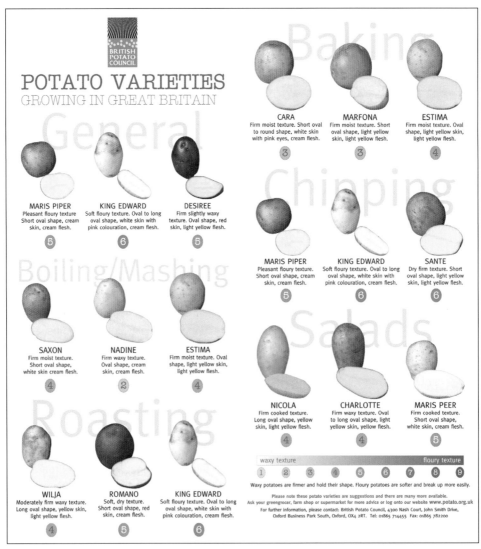

Source: British Potato Council

Food value

Potatoes are a good source of Vitamin C, although this can be lost when they are stored, soaked in water or cooked for too long. They also contain iron, calcium, thiamin, nicotine acid, protein and fibre.

---

1 ### Plain boiled potatoes
(pommes natures)

potatoes boiling

energy	kcal	fat	sat fat	carb	sugar	protein	fibre	*
487 KJ	116 kcal	0.1 g	0.0 g	28.6 g	0.6 g	2.0 g	1.5 g	

1 Wash, peel and rewash the potatoes.
2 Cut or turn into even-sized pieces allowing 2–3 pieces per portion.
3 Cook carefully in lightly salted water for approximately 20 minutes.
4 Drain well and serve.

* Using old potatoes

---

2 ### Parsley potatoes
(pommes persillées)

potatoes boiling

energy	kcal	fat	sat fat	carb	sugar	protein	fibre	*
798 KJ	190 kcal	8.3 g	5.2 g	28.6 g	0.6 g	2.1 g	1.5 g	

1 Wash, peel and rewash the potatoes.
2 Cut or turn into even-sized pieces allowing 2–3 pieces per portion.
3 Cook carefully in lightly salted water for approximately 20 minutes.
4 Drain well. Brush with melted butter and sprinkle with chopped parsley.

* Using 10 g butter per portion, old potatoes

3 Mashed potatoes
(pommes purées)

potatoes  boiling

	energy 763 KJ	kcal 182 kcal	fat 7.1 g	sat fat 4.4 g	carb 29.0 g	sugar 1.1 g	protein 2.4 g	fibre 1.5 g	*

Portions >	4	10
floury potatoes	0.5 kg	1.25 kg
butter	25 g	60 g
milk, warm	30 ml	80 ml

1 Wash, peel and rewash the potatoes. Cut to an even size.
2 Cook in lightly salted water, or steam.
3 Drain off the water, cover and return to a low heat to dry out the potatoes.
4 Pass through a medium sieve or a ricer.
5 Return the potatoes to a clean pan.
6 Add the butter and mix in with a wooden spoon.
7 Gradually add warm milk, stirring continuously until a smooth creamy consistency is reached.
8 Correct the seasoning and serve.

Pass the cooked potato through a sieve   Add milk to the potatoes and combine

Key point
Drain the potatoes as soon as they are cooked. If they are left standing in water, they will become too wet and spoil the texture of the dish.

Healthy eating tips
- Add a minimum amount of salt.
- Add a little olive oil in place of the butter, and use semi-skimmed milk.

Try something different
Variations of mashed potatoes can be achieved by:
- dressing in a serving dish and surrounding with a cordon of fresh cream
- placing in a serving dish, sprinkling with grated cheese and melted butter, and browning under a salamander
- adding 50 g diced cooked lean ham, 25 g diced red pepper and chopped parsley
- adding lightly sweated chopped spring onions
- using a good-quality olive oil in place of butter
- adding a little garlic juice (use a garlic press)
- adding a little fresh chopped rosemary or chives
- mixing with equal quantities of parsnip
- adding a little freshly grated horseradish or horseradish cream.

* Using old potatoes, butter and whole milk

4 Duchess potatoes
(pommes duchesse)

potatoes 🍲 boiling, 🧁 baking

energy	kcal	fat	sat fat	carb	sugar	protein	fibre	*
819 KJ	195 kcal	8.2 g	3.3 g	28.6 g	0.6 g	3.5 g	1.5 g	

Portions ⟩	4	10
floury potatoes	600 g	1.5 kg
egg yolks	1	3
butter	25 g	60 g
salt, pepper		

1 Wash, peel and rewash the potatoes. Cut to an even size.
2 Cook in lightly salted water.
3 Drain off the water, cover and return to a low heat to dry out the potatoes.
4 Pass through a medium sieve or a special potato masher or mouli.
5 Place the potatoes in a clean pan.
6 Add the egg yolks and stir in vigorously with a kitchen spoon.

7 Mix in the butter. Correct the seasoning.
8 Place in a piping bag with a large star tube and pipe out into neat spirals, about 2 cm in diameter and 5 cm tall, on to a lightly greased baking sheet.
9 Place in a hot oven at 230°C for 2–3 minutes in order to firm the edges slightly.
10 Remove from the oven and brush with eggwash.
11 Brown lightly in a hot oven or under the salamander.

Add egg yolks to the mashed potato

Pipe the potato into neat spirals, ready for baking

* Using old potatoes, whole milk, hard margarine

Key point
At step 3, it is important to return the drained potatoes to the heat, so that they are as dry as possible.

Making duchess potatoes
http://bit.ly/zZhyQy

5 New potatoes
(pommes nouvelles)

potatoes boiling

energy	kcal	fat	sat fat	carb	sugar	protein	fibre
383 KJ	91 kcal	0.1 g	0.0 g	22.0 g	0.8 g	1.9 g	2.4 g

Method 1

1 Wash the potatoes, and boil or steam in their jackets until cooked.
2 Cool slightly, peel while warm and place in a pan of cold water.
3 When required for service add a little salt and a bunch of mint to the potatoes; heat through slowly.
4 Drain well, serve brushed with melted butter and sprinkled with chopped mint, or decorate with blanched, refreshed mint leaves.

Method 2

1 Scrape the potatoes and wash well.
2 Place in a pan of lightly salted boiling water with a bunch of mint and boil gently until cooked (about 20 minutes). Serve as above.

The starch cells of new potatoes are immature; to help break down these cells new potatoes are cooked in water that is already boiling.

Turned new Pink Fir potatoes

6 Steamed potatoes in their jackets
(pommes vapeur)

potatoes steaming

energy	kcal	fat	sat fat	carb	sugar	protein	fibre	sodium
424 KJ	150 kcal	0.3 g	0.0 g	23.1 g	0.8 g	2.7 g	2.3 g	0.1 g

Choose the most suitable varieties for steaming: Saxon, Nadine, Estima, Maris Piper or Desiree. Steaming retains more flavour than boiling.

Always choose evenly sized potatoes so that they will cook in the same amount of time.

If the potato is going to be cooked further, e.g. sauté, it is best to leave the skin on during steaming. The skin will protect the flesh of the potato from the steam.

1 Wash the potatoes well.
2 Place the potatoes into a steamer tray, sprinkle with salt and steam until tender.
3 When steaming new potatoes, add some sprigs of mint.
4 Drain before serving or peeling for sauté.

<table>
<tr><td>**7**</td></tr>
</table>

Sauté potatoes
(pommes sautées)

potatoes ⊕ boiling, ⊚ shallow frying, sauté

energy	kcal	fat	sat fat	carb	sugar	protein	fibre	*
1249 KJ	297 kcal	11.4 g	1.3 g	46.8 g	0.4 g	4.9 g	1.7 g	

1 Select medium even-sized potatoes. Scrub well.
2 Plain boil or cook in the steamer. Cool slightly and peel.
3 Cut into 3 mm slices.
4 Toss in hot shallow oil in a frying pan until lightly coloured; season lightly with salt.
5 Serve sprinkled with chopped parsley.

Maris Piper or Cara potatoes are good varieties for this dish.

Healthy eating tips

● Use a little hot sunflower oil to sauté the potatoes.
● Add little or no salt; the customer can add more if required.

* Using old potatoes and sunflower oil

8 Sauté potatoes with onions
(pommes lyonnaise)

potatoes ⊕ boiling, ⊚ shallow frying, sauté

energy	kcal	fat	sat fat	carb	sugar	protein	fibre	sodium
1098 KJ	261 kcal	9.4 g	1.1 g	41.5 g	6.4 g	5.4 g	5.3 g	0.3 g

1 Allow 0.25 kg onion to 0.5 kg potatoes.
2 Shallow-fry the onions slowly in 25–50 g oil, turning frequently, until tender and nicely browned; season lightly with salt.
3 Prepare sauté potatoes as for recipe 7.
4 Combine the two and toss together.
5 Serve as for sauté potatoes.

Cut the potatoes into 3 mm slices

Finely slice the onions

Sauté the potatoes and onions together

9 New rissolée potatoes
(pommes nouvelles rissolées)

potatoes  shallow frying

energy	kcal	fat	sat fat	carb	sugar	protein	fibre
610 KJ	145 kcal	6.1 g	1.1 g	22.0 g	0.8 g	1.9 g	2.4 g

1 Boil or steam new potatoes, then drain them.

2 Fry to a golden brown in oil or butter, or a combination of both.

10 Parmentier potatoes
(pommes parmentier)

potatoes  shallow frying

energy	kcal	fat	sat fat	carb	sugar	protein	fibre	*
1819 KJ	433 kcal	33.5 g	6.3 g	32.8 g	0.7 g	2.3 g	1.7 g	

0.5 kg will yield 2–3 portions.

1 Select medium to large potatoes.

2 Wash, peel and rewash.

3 Trim on 3 sides and cut into 1 cm slices.

4 Cut the slices into 1 cm strips.

5 Cut the strips into 1 cm dice.

6 Wash well and dry in a cloth.

7 Cook in hot shallow oil in a frying pan until golden brown.

8 Drain, season lightly and serve sprinkled with chopped parsley (optional).

* Using peanut oil

Practical Cookery 12th edition

11 Swiss potato cakes
(rösti)

potatoes 🔘 shallow frying

energy	kcal	fat	sat fat	carb	sugar	protein	fibre	*
700 KJ	168 kcal	10.5 g	6.5 g	17.3 g	0.7 g	2.2 g	1.3 g	

Portions ⟩	4	10
potatoes, unpeeled	400 g	1 kg
oil or butter	50 g	125 g
salt, pepper		

1 Parboil in salted water (or steam) for approx. 5 minutes.
2 Cool, then shred into large flakes on a grater.
3 Heat the oil or butter in a frying pan.
4 Add the potatoes, and season lightly with salt and pepper.
5 Press the potato together and cook on both sides until brown and crisp.

Shred the parboiled potatoes on a grater

Press into shape in the frying pan

Turn out carefully after cooking

The potato can be made in a 4-portion cake or in individual rounds.

Healthy eating tips
- Lightly oil a well-seasoned pan with sunflower oil to fry the rösti.
- Use the minimum amount of salt.

Try something different
- These potato cakes may also be made from raw potatoes.
- Add sweated chopped onion.
- Add sweated lardons of bacon.
- Use 2 parts of grated potato to 1 part grated apple.

* Using butter

12 Noisette potatoes
(pommes noisettes)

potatoes shallow frying, roasting

energy	kcal	fat	sat fat	carb	sugar	protein	fibre	sodium
839 KJ	200 kcal	5.9 g	0.7 g	34.4 g	1.2 g	4.2 g	3.5 g	0.0 g

0.5 kg will yield 2 portions.

1 Wash, peel and rewash the potatoes.
2 Scoop out balls with a noisette spoon. Blanch the balls in boiling water.
3 Cook in a little oil in a sauté pan or frying pan. Colour on top of the stove and finish cooking in the oven at 230–250°C.

13 Cocotte potatoes
(pommes cocotte)

potatoes shallow frying

energy	kcal	fat	sat fat	carb	sugar	protein	fibre	sodium
839 KJ	200 kcal	5.9 g	0.7 g	34.4 g	1.2 g	4.2 g	3.5 g	0.0 g

1 Proceed as for château potatoes (recipe 17), but with the potatoes a quarter the size.
2 Cook in a sauté pan or frying pan.

14 Fried or chipped potatoes
(pommes frites)

potatoes deep frying

energy	kcal	fat	sat fat	carb	sugar	protein	fibre *
1541 KJ	367 kcal	15.8 g	2.8 g	54.1 g	0.0 g	5.5 g	1.5 g

1 Prepare and wash the potatoes.

2 Cut into slices approx. 1 cm thick and 5 cm long.

3 Cut the slices into strips approx. 5 cm x 1 cm x 1 cm. There is no need to trim the ends as this is a characterful chip.

4 Wash well and dry in a cloth.

5 Blanch in water just below boiling point for 8 minutes.

6 Remove, drain and allow to dry naturally.

7 Cook in a frying basket in oil at 160°C for 6 minutes.

8 Remove, drain and place on kitchen paper on trays until required. (At this point, the chips can be frozen for later use if required.)

9 When required for service, place in a frying pan and cook in hot fat (185°C) until crisp and golden.

10 Drain well, season lightly with sea salt and serve.

Cut the potatoes into slices and then strips

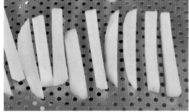

Partially cook by steaming or boiling

Deep fry and then drain the chips

Because chips are so popular, the following advice from the Potato Marketing Board is useful.

- Cook chips in small quantities; this will allow the oil to regain its temperature more quickly; chips will then cook faster and absorb less fat.
- Do not let the temperature of the oil exceed 199°C as this will accelerate the fat breakdown.
- Use oils high in polyunsaturates for a healthier chip.
- Ideally use a separate fryer for chips and ensure that it has the capacity to raise the fat temperature rapidly to the correct degree when frying chilled or frozen chips.
- Although the majority of chipped potatoes are purchased frozen, the Potato Marketing Board recommends the following potatoes for those who prefer to make their own chips: Maris Piper, Cara, Desiree.

Healthy eating tips

- Chipped potatoes may be blanched in oil twice, first at 140°C, followed by a re-blanch at 160°C until lightly coloured.
- For healthy eating, blanch in a steamer until just cooked, drain and dry well – final temperature 165°C. The chips will absorb less oil when they are fried for service.

* Using old potatoes and peanut oil

15 Croquette potatoes
(pommes croquettes)

potatoes boiling, deep frying

energy	kcal	fat	sat fat	carb	sugar	protein	fibre	*
1699 KJ	405 kcal	25.4 g	6.6 g	40.8 g	1.1 g	6.0 g	2.2 g	

1 Use a duchess mixture (see recipe 4) moulded into cylinder shapes 5 cm x 2 cm.

2 Pass through flour, eggwash and breadcrumbs.

3 Reshape with a palette knife and deep-fry in hot deep oil (185°C) in a trying basket.

4 When the potatoes are a golden colour, drain well and serve.

Healthy eating tips

● Add the minimum amount of salt.

● Use peanut or sunflower oil to fry the croquettes.

Mould the potato mixture into long cylinders

Cut into shorter pieces

Roll each croquette in flour, eggwash and breadcrumbs

Reshape the croquettes and then deep fry them

* Using hard margarine and frying in peanut oil

16 Roast potatoes

(pommes rôties)

potatoes  roasting

energy	kcal	fat	sat fat	carb	sugar	protein	fibre	*
956 KJ	228 kcal	7.0 g	1.1 g	39.6 g	0.9 g	4.1 g	1.5 g	

1 Wash, peel and rewash the potatoes.
2 Cut into even-sized pieces (allow 3–4 pieces per portion).
3 Heat a good measure of oil or dripping in a roasting tray.
4 Add the well-dried potatoes and lightly brown on all sides.
5 Season lightly with salt and cook for about 1 hour in a hot oven at 230–250°C.
6 Turn the potatoes over after 30 minutes.
7 Cook to a golden brown. Drain and serve.

Roast potatoes can be part-boiled for 10 minutes, refreshed and well dried before roasting. This will cut down on the cooking time and can also give a crisper potato.

Healthy eating tips
- Brush the potatoes with peanut or sunflower oil, with only a little in the roasting tray.
- Drain off all the fat when cooked.

* Using old potatoes and peanut oil for 1 portion (125 g raw potato)

17 Château potatoes

(pommes château)

potatoes  boiling,  roasting

energy	kcal	fat	sat fat	carb	sugar	protein	fibre	sodium
839 KJ	200 kcal	5.9 g	0.7 g	34.4 g	1.2 g	4.2 g	3.5 g	0.0 g

1 Select small, even-sized potatoes and wash them.
2 Turn the potatoes into barrel-shaped pieces about the same size as fondant potatoes (recipe 21).
3 Place in a saucepan of boiling water for 2–3 minutes, then refresh immediately. Drain in a colander.
4 Finish as for roast potatoes. Use a non-stick tray, lightly oiled greaseproof paper or non-stick mat for the roasting.

18 Baked jacket potatoes
(pommes au four)

potatoes baking

energy	kcal	fat	sat fat	carb	sugar	protein	fibre	*
401 KJ	94 kcal	0.2 g	0.0 g	21.8 g	0.9 g	2.7 g	1.6 g	

1 Select good-sized potatoes; allow 1 potato per portion.
2 Scrub well, make a 2 mm-deep incision round the potato.
3 Place the potato, on a small mound of ground (sea) salt to help keep the base dry, on a tray in a hot oven at 230–250°C for about 1 hour. Turn the potatoes over after 30 minutes.
4 Test by holding the potato in a cloth and squeezing gently; if cooked it should feel soft.

Key points
- Lightly scoring the potatoes will help to make sure that they cook evenly.
- If the potatoes are being cooked in a microwave, you must prick the skins first.

* Using medium potato, 180 g analysis given per potato

Healthy eating tips
- Potatoes can be baked without sea salt.
- Fillings based on vegetables with little or no cheese or meat make a healthy snack meal.

Try something different
Variations include the following.
- Split and filled with any of the following: grated cheese, minced beef or chicken, baked beans, chilli con carne, cream cheese and chives, mushrooms, bacon, ratatouille, prawns in mayonnaise, coleslaw, and so on.
- The cooked potatoes can also be cut in halves lengthwise, the potato spooned out from the skins, seasoned, mashed with butter, returned to the skins, sprinkled with grated cheese and reheated in an oven or under the grill.

19 Macaire potatoes (potato cakes)
(pommes Macaire)

potatoes baking, shallow frying

energy	kcal	fat	sat fat	carb	sugar	protein	fibre	*
4392 KJ	1047 kcal	65.7 g	14.7 g	109.8 g	2.7 g	11.4 g	10.8 g	

0.5 kg will yield 2–3 portions.

1 Prepare and cook as for baked jacket potatoes (recipe 18).
2 Cut in halves, remove the centre with a spoon, and place in a basin.
3 Add 25 g butter per 0.5 kg, a little salt and milled pepper.
4 Mash and mix as lightly as possible with a fork.
5 Using a little flour, mould into a roll, then divide into pieces, allowing one or two per portion.
6 Mould into 2 cm round cakes. Quadrille with the back of a palette knife. Flour lightly.
7 Shallow-fry on both sides in very hot oil and serve.

Place the potatoes on a baking tray with salt

Once baked, cut in half and scoop out the centre

Mould the potato into cakes

Key point

Make sure the potato mixture is firm enough to be shaped, and fry the cakes in very hot oil, or they will lose their shape.

Try something different

Additions to potato cakes can include:
- chopped parsley, fresh herbs or chives, or duxelle
- cooked chopped onion
- grated cheese.

* Using hard margarine and sunflower oil

20 Byron potatoes
(pommes Byron)

potatoes baking, shallow frying,  grilling

energy	kcal	fat	sat fat	carb	sugar	protein	fibre	*
2099 KJ	505 kcal	39.0 g	18.7 g	33.4 g	1.8 g	7.1 g	2.4 g	

1 Prepare and cook as for Macaire potatoes (recipe 19).

2 Using the back of a dessertspoon make a shallow impression on each potato cake.

3 Carefully sprinkle the centres with grated cheese. Make sure no cheese is on the edge of the potato cake.

4 Cover the cheese with cream.

5 Brown lightly under the salamander and serve.

This is a classical variation on Macaire potatoes.

* Using 1 tbsp each of cheese and double cream per person, analysis given per potato

21 Potatoes with bacon and onions
(pommes au lard)

potatoes, bacon shallow frying, braising

energy	kcal	fat	sat fat	carb	sugar	protein	fibre	*
836 KJ	199 kcal	10.1 g	3.8 g	22.2 g	1.8 g	6.4 g	2.5 g	

Portions >	4	10
potatoes, peeled	400 g	1.25 kg
streaky bacon (lardons)	100 g	250 g
button onions	100 g	250 g
white stock	250 ml	600 ml
salt, pepper		
parsley, chopped		

1 Cut the potatoes into 1 cm dice.

2 Cut the bacon into 0.5 cm lardons; lightly fry in a little fat together with the onions and brown lightly.

3 Add the potatoes, half cover with stock, season lightly with salt and pepper. Cover with a lid and cook steadily in the oven at 230–250°C for approximately 30 minutes.

4 Correct the seasoning, serve in a vegetable dish, sprinkled with chopped parsley.

* Using old potatoes

Healthy eating tips

● Dry-fry the bacon in a well-seasoned pan and drain off any excess fat.

● Add little or no salt.

22 Fondant potatoes
(pommes fondantes)

potatoes roasting, braising

energy	kcal	fat	sat fat	carb	sugar	protein	fibre *
956 KJ	228 kcal	7.0 g	2.1 g	39.6 g	0.9 g	4.1 g	1.5 g

1 Select small or even-sized medium potatoes.

2 Wash, peel and rewash.

3 Turn into 8-sided barrel shapes, allowing 2–3 per portion, about 5 cm long, end diameter 1.5 cm, centre diameter 2.5 cm.

4 Brush with melted butter or oil.

5 Place in a pan suitable for the oven.

6 Half cover with white stock, season lightly with salt and pepper.

7 Cook in a hot oven at 230–250°C, brushing the potatoes frequently with melted butter or oil.

8 When cooked, the stock should be completely absorbed by the potatoes.

9 Brush with melted butter or oil and serve.

Making fondant potatoes
http://bit.ly/yWfGg1

Turn the potatoes into barrel shapes

Place in a pan, half covered with stock, to cook

Key point

To give the potatoes a good glaze, use a high-quality stock and baste during cooking.

Try something different

The potatoes may be cut into shapes using cutters, e.g. round, square, oval. Fondant potatoes can be lightly sprinkled with:

● thyme, rosemary or oregano (or this can be added to the stock)

● grated cheese (Gruyère and Parmesan or Cheddar).

Try using chicken stock in place of white stock.

Healthy eating tips

● Use a little unsaturated oil to brush over the potatoes before and after cooking.

● No added salt is needed; rely on the stock for flavour.

* Using old potatoes and hard margarine for 1 portion (125 g raw potato)

23 Savoury potatoes
(pommes boulangères)

potatoes braising

energy	kcal	fat	sat fat	carb	sugar	protein	fibre
595 KJ	142 kcal	5.3 g	2.2 g	22.3 g	1.8 g	2.8 g	2.4 g *

Portions ⟩	4	10
potatoes	400 g	1.25 kg
onions	100 g	250 g
salt, pepper		
white stock	125 ml	350 ml
butter or oil	25–50 g	60–100 g
parsley, chopped		

1 Cut the potatoes into 2 mm slices on a mandolin. Set aside the best slices to use for the top.
2 Peel, halve and finely slice the onions.
3 Mix the onions and potatoes together and season lightly with pepper and salt.
4 Place in a well-buttered shallow earthenware dish or roasting tin.
5 Barely cover with stock.
6 Neatly arrange overlapping slices of potato on top.
7 Brush lightly with oil.
8 Place in a hot oven at 230–250°C for 20 minutes until lightly coloured.
9 Reduce the heat to 175–180°C and allow to cook steadily, pressing down firmly from time to time with a flat-bottomed pan.
10 When ready all the stock should be cooked into the potato. Allow 1½ hours cooking time in all.
11 Serve sprinkled with chopped parsley. If cooked in an earthenware dish, clean the edges of the dish with a cloth dipped in salt, and serve in the dish.

* Using 25 g hard margarine. Using 50 g hard margarine: 787 kJ/187 kcal energy; 10.3 g fat; 4.4 g sat fat; 22.3 g carb; 1.8 g sugar; 2.8 g protein; 2.4 g fibre

Leeks can be used in place of onions for variety. This potato can be cooked under a joint of lamb, shoulder or leg. Place an oven rack with the meat on above the potatoes for the final 1½ hours of cooking. The juices from the meat will baste the potatoes as it cooks, then serve the lamb on top of the potato if the style of the restaurant dictates.

Healthy eating tips
● Use an unsaturated oil.
● Add the minimum amount of salt; the stock provides flavour.
● This dish can be used to accompany fattier meat dishes and will help to dilute the fat.

24 Potatoes cooked in milk with cheese

(gratin dauphinoise)

potatoes 🍲 baking

Portions >	4	10
potatoes, peeled	500 g	1.25 kg
milk	225 ml	550 ml
cream	250 ml	600 ml
egg yolk	1	3
cloves of garlic	1	3
salt, pepper		
grated cheese, preferably Gruyère	50 g	125 g

1 Slice the peeled potatoes 3 mm thick.
2 Heat the milk and cream with the garlic.
3 Add the sliced potatoes to the milk and cream. Season and place in an ovenproof dish.
4 Sprinkle with grated cheese and cook in the oven at 170°C until the potatoes are cooked and golden brown.

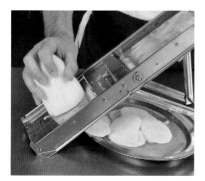

Peel and slice the potatoes

Add the potatoes to the warm milk and stir in an egg yolk, off the heat

Layer the potatoes in an oven-proof dish

25 Delmonico potatoes
(pommes Delmonico)

potatoes  boiling, grilling

energy	kcal	fat	sat fat	carb	sugar	protein	fibre	*
900 KJ	214 kcal	6.3 g	3.7 g	37.5 g	2.7 g	4.4 g	2.0 g	

1 Wash, peel and rewash the potatoes.
2 Cut into 6 mm dice.
3 Barely cover with milk, season lightly with salt and pepper and allow to cook on the stove for 30–40 minutes.
4 Place in an earthenware dish, sprinkle with breadcrumbs and melted butter, brown in the oven or under the salamander and serve.

Dice the potatoes

Place in a dish, barely covered with milk, to cook

After cooking, sprinkle with breadcrumbs and gratinate

* Using old potatoes and whole milk

Pastry

11

This chapter is relevant to the following units:

- Prepare, cook and finish basic hot and cold desserts (NVQ)
- Cook and finish simple bread and dough products (NVQ)
- Prepare, cook and finish basic bread and dough products (NVQ)
- Prepare, cook and finish basic cakes, sponges and scones (NVQ)
- Prepare, cook and finish basic pastry products (NVQ)
- Prepare and cook desserts and puddings (VRQ)
- Prepare and cook bakery products (VRQ).

54	Vanilla soufflé (*soufflé à la vanille*)	512
55	Mango soufflé	513
56	Lemon curd soufflé (flourless)	514
57	Baked Alaska (*omelette soufflé surprise*)	515

Cold desserts

58	Fresh fruit salad (*salade de fruits*)	516
59	Tropical fruit plate	516
60	Poached fruits or fruit compote (*compote de fruits*)	517
61	Cream caramel (*crème caramel*)	518
62	Crème brûlée	519
63	Zabaglione (sabayon with Marsala)	520
64	Fruit mousse	520
65	Bavarois (often referred to as a mousse)	521
66	Chocolate mousse	522
67	Vanilla panna cotta served on a fruit compote	523
68	Fruit fool	524
69	Meringue (*meringue*)	525
70	Vacherin with strawberries and cream (*vacherin aux fraises*)	526
71	Black Forest vacherin	527
72	Lime soufflé frappe	528
73	Trifle	529
74	Lime and mascarpone cheesecake	530
75	Baked blueberry cheesecake	531

Iced desserts

76	Vanilla ice cream (*glace vanille*)	532
77	Lemon curd ice cream	533
78	Peach Melba (*pêche Melba*)	533
79	Pear belle Hélène (*poire belle Hélène*)	534
80	Apple sorbet	534
81	Raspberry parfait	535

Short pastry goods

82	*Quiche lorraine* (cheese and ham savoury flan)	536
83	Fruit pies	537
84	Treacle tart	538

Sweet pastry goods

85	Flan cases	538
86	Egg custard tart	539
87	Fruit tart/flan	540
88	Fruit tartlets or barquettes	540
89	Apple flan (*flan aux pommes*)	541
90	Lemon tart (*tarte au citron*)	542
91	Lemon meringue pie	543
92	Pear and almond tart	544
93	Pecan pie	545

94	Bakewell tart	546
95	Mince pies	547

Puff pastry goods

96	Puff pastry cases (*bouchées, vol-au-vents*)	548
97	Cheese straws (*paillettes au fromage*)	549
98	Sausage rolls	549
99	Gâteau pithiviers	550
100	Palmiers	551
101	Pear jalousie	551
102	Puff pastry slice (*mille-feuilles*)	552
103	Fruit slice (*bande aux fruits*)	553
104	Cream horns	554
105	Eccles cakes	555
106	Apple turnovers (*chausson aux pommes*)	555

Choux pastry goods

107	Cream buns (*choux à la crème*)	556
108	Profiteroles and chocolate sauce (*profiteroles au chocolat*)	556
109	Chocolate éclairs (*éclairs au chocolat*)	557
110	Paris-Brest	558
111	Choux paste fritters (*beignets soufflés*)	559

Cakes

112	Victoria sandwich	560
113	Genoise sponge (*génoise*)	561
114	Fresh cream and strawberry gateau	562
115	Chocolate Genoise sponge (*génoise au chocolat*)	562
116	Chocolate gâteau	563
117	Coffee gâteau (*gâteau moka*)	564
118	Roulade sponge	565
119	Swiss roll	566
120	Small cakes	567
121	Scones	568
122	Rock cakes	569
123	Madeleines	570
124	Rich fruit cake	570
125	Banana bread	572

Breads

126	Seeded bread rolls	573
127	Wheatmeal bread	574
128	Parmesan rolls	575
129	Red onion and sage rolls	575
130	Onion and walnut bread	576
131	Sun-dried tomato bread	577
132	Olive bread	578
133	Rye bread	580

Pastry work

In addition to being one of the most important sections of the kitchen, pastry work can also be particularly enjoyable and rewarding. Although it is called 'pastry work', it actually includes making breads, desserts, sweets, and much more, not just goods made from pastry. Bakery products are explored later in the chapter with the initial focus and attention placed on desserts and puddings, of which there is a great variety.

There is a range of pastes, all vital components of pastry work. Each type of paste is included in this chapter, along with several recipes that use it. Remember that pastry goods, such as lemon tart, tarte tatin and profiteroles, are often served as desserts.

Ingredients for pastry work

This section provides information about the most commonly utilised ingredients and commodities used in the production of pastry and bakery items.

The principal ingredients of pastry products are flour, fat, sugar, raising agents, eggs and cream. An analysis of each of these key ingredients and their importance in the production of pastry products is outlined below.

Flour

Flour is probably the most common commodity in daily use. It forms the foundation of bread, pastry and cakes and is one of the most important ingredients in patisserie, if not the most important.

There are a great variety of high-quality flours made from cereals, nuts or legumes, such as chestnut flour and cornflour. They have been used in patisserie, baking, dessert cuisine and savoury cuisine in all countries throughout history. The most commonly used and versatile flour, particularly in Western cuisine, is wheat flour.

The composition of wheat flour

Wheat flour is composed of starch, gluten, sugar, fats, water and minerals.

- Starch is the main component.
- Gluten is also a significant element. Elastic and impermeable (water resistant), it is the gluten that makes wheat flour the most common flour used in bread making.
- The quantity of sugar in wheat is very small but it plays a very important role in fermentation.
- Wheat contains a maximum of only 16 per cent water, but its presence is important.
- The mineral matter (ash), which is found mainly in the husk of the wheat grain and not in the kernel, determines the purity and quality of the flour.

From the ear to the final product, flour, wheat goes through several distinct processes. These are carried out in modern industrial plants, where wheat is subjected to the various treatments and phases necessary for the production of different types of flour.

These arrive in perfect condition at our workplaces and are made into items like sponge cakes, yeast dough, puff pastries, biscuits, pastries and much more.

What you need to know about flour

- Flour is a particularly delicate living material, and it must be used and stored carefully. It must always be in the best condition, which is why storing large quantities is not recommended.
- It must be kept in an environment which is a clean, organised, disinfected and aerated storeroom.
- It must never be stored in warm and humid places.

The production of flour

White flour is made up almost entirely of the part of the wheat grain known as the endosperm, which contains starch and protein. When flour is mixed with water it is converted into a sticky dough. This characteristic is due to the gluten, which becomes sticky when moistened. The relative proportion of starch and gluten varies in different wheats, and those with a low percentage of gluten (soft flour) are not suitable for bread making. For this reason, wheat is blended.

In milling, the whole grain is broken up, the parts separated, sifted, blended and ground into flour. Some of the outer coating of bran is removed, as is the wheatgerm, which contains oil and is therefore likely to become rancid and spoil the flour. For this reason wholemeal flour should not be stored for more than 14 days.

Types of flour

- White flour contains 72–85 per cent of the whole grain (the endosperm only).
- Wholemeal flour contains 100 per cent of the whole grain.
- Wheatmeal flour contains 85–95 per cent of the whole grain.
- High-ratio or patent flour contains 40 per cent of the whole grain.
- Self-raising flour is white flour with baking powder (usually bicarbonate of soda and tartaric acid added to it).

- Semolina is granulated hard flour prepared from the central part of the wheat grain. White or wholemeal semolina is available.

Fats

Pastry goods may be made with various types of fat, either a single named fat or a combination. Examples of fats are:

- butter
- margarine
- shortening
- lard.

Butter

Butter brings smoothness, perfumes and aromas, as well as impeccable textures, to pastry items. It is a point of reference for good gastronomy.

Butter is an emulsion – the perfect symbiosis of water and fat. It is composed of a minimum of 82 per cent fat, a maximum of 16 per cent water and 2 per cent dry extracts.

Here are some important facts about butter:

- It is a very delicate ingredient that can quickly spoil if a series of basic rules are not followed in its use.
- It absorbs odours very easily, so it should be kept well covered and should always be stored far from anything that produces strong odours.
- When kept at 15°C, butter is stable and retains all its properties: finesse, aroma and creaminess.
- It should not be kept for long periods of time, as it is always better to work with fresh butter.
- Good-quality butter has a stable texture, pleasing taste, fresh odour, homogenous (even) colour and, most important, it melts perfectly in the mouth.
- It softens products such as cookies and petit fours, and helps to keep sponge cakes soft.
- Butter enhances flavour – as in brioches, for example.
- The melting point of butter is between 30°C and 35°C, approximately.

Margarine

Margarine is often made from a blend of oils that have been hardened or hydrogenated (with the addition of hydrogen gas). Margarine may contain up to 10 per cent butterfat.

Cake margarine is again a blend of oils, hydrogenated, to which is added an emulsifying agent that helps combine water and fat. Cake margarine may contain up to 10 per cent butterfat.

Pastry margarine is used for puff pastry. It is a hard plastic or waxy fat that is suitable for layering.

Shortening

Shortening is the term for some other fats used in pastry making. It is made from oils and is 100 per cent fat. Examples of shortening include hydrogenated lard and rendered pork fat.

Sugar

Sugar (or sucrose) is extracted from sugar beet or sugar cane. The juice is crystallised by a complicated manufacturing process. It is then refined and sieved into several grades, such as granulated, caster or icing sugars.

Syrup and treacle are produced during the production of sugar.

Loaf or cube sugar is obtained by pressing the crystals together while they are slightly wet, drying them in blocks, and then cutting the blocks into squares.

Fondant is a cooked mixture of sugar and glucose which, when heated, is coloured and flavoured, and used for decorating cakes, buns, gâteaux and petits fours. Fondant is generally bought ready made.

Inverted sugar

When sucrose is broken down with water, in a chemical process called hydrolysis, it separates into the two types of sugar that make it: fructose and glucose. Sugar that has been treated in this way is called inverted sugar and is, after sucrose, one of the most commonly used sugars in the catering profession, thanks to its sweetening properties.

Inverted sugar is used because:

- It improves the aroma of products.
- It improves the texture of doughs.
- It prevents the dehydration of frozen products.

- It reduces or stops crystallisation in ice cream making, improves smoothness and lowers its freezing point.

Glucose

Glucose takes on various forms:
- the characteristics of a viscous syrup, called crystal glucose
- its natural state, in fruit and honey
- a dehydrated white paste (used mainly in the commercial food industry, but also used in catering).

Glucose syrup:
- is a transparent, viscous paste
- prevents the crystallisation of boiled sugars, jams and preserves
- delays the drying of a product
- aids consistency and creaminess in ice cream and the fillings of chocolate bonbons
- prevents the crystallisation of ice cream.

Honey

Honey, a sweet syrup that bees make with the nectar extracted from flowers, is without doubt the oldest known sugar. A light golden-brown thick syrup, it is 30 per cent sweeter than sucrose.

Honey lowers the freezing point of ice cream. It can also be used like inverted sugar, but it is important to take into account that honey, unlike inverted sugar, will give flavour to the preparation. Also, it is inadequate for preparations that require long storage, since honey re-crystallises after some time.

Isomalt

Isomalt is a sweetener that has been used by the food manufacturing industry for many years in the production of confectionery (sweets and gums). It has properties distinct from those of the sweeteners already mentioned. It is produced through the hydrolysis of sugar, followed by hydrogenation (the addition of hydrogen). Produced through these industrial processes, this sugar is perfect for candy and chewing gum production but it is now being used far more widely in the professional kitchen.

One of its most notable characteristics is that it can melt without the addition of water or another liquid.

This is a very interesting property for making artistic decorations in caramel. Its appearance is like that of confectioners' sugar: a glossy powder. Its sweetening strength is half that of sucrose and it is much less soluble than sugar, which means that it melts less easily in the mouth.

Isomalt's main claim in gastronomy over the past few years has been as a replacement for normal sugar or sucrose when making sugar decorations, blown sugar, pulled sugar or spun sugar. Isomalt is not affected by air humidity, so sugar pieces will keep for longer.

Raising agents

A raising agent is added to a cake or bread mixture to give lightness to the product, because they produce gases, which expand when heated. The gases produced are air, carbon dioxide or water vapour. These gases are introduced before baking or are produced by substances added to the mixture before baking. When the product is cooked, the gases expand. These gases are trapped in the gluten of the wheat flour. On further heating and cooking, the product, because of the pressure of the gluten, rises and sets.

Baking powder

Chemical raising agents cause a reaction between certain acidic and alkaline compounds, which produce carbon dioxide. The alkaline component is almost always sodium bicarbonate or sodium acid carbonate, commonly known as baking soda. It is ideal because it is cheap to produce, easily purified, non-toxic and naturally tasteless. Potassium bicarbonate is available for those on low-sodium diets, but this compound tends to absorb moisture and react prematurely, and gives off a bitter flavour.

Baking powder may be used without the addition of acid if the dough or batter is already acidic enough to react with it to produce carbon dioxide. Yoghurt and sour milk contain lactic acid, and often are used in place of water or milk in such products as scones, for example. Sour milk can also be added along with the baking soda as a separate 'natural' component of the leavening.

Baking powder contains baking soda and an acid in the form of salt crystals that dissolve in water. Ground dry starch is also added to prevent premature reactions in humid air by absorbing moisture and to dilute the powder.

Most baking powders are 'double acting' – that is, they produce an initial set of gas bubbles when the powder is mixed into the batter and then a second set during the baking process. The first and smaller reaction is necessary to form many small gas bubbles in the batter or dough; the second is necessary to expand these bubbles to form the final light texture. This second reaction must happen late enough in the baking for the surrounding materials to have set, preventing the bubbles from escaping and the product from collapsing.

Baking powder is made from alkali (bicarbonate of soda) plus acid (cream of tartar – potassium hydrogen tartrate). Commercial baking powders differ mainly in their proportions of the acid salts. Cream of tartar is not normally used due to its high cost, so calcium phosphate and glucono-delta-lactose are now commonly used in its place.

Water vapour

Water vapour is produced during the baking process, from the liquid content used in the mixing. Water vapour has approximately 1600 times the original volume of the water. The raising power is slower than that of a gas. This method is used in the production of choux pastry, puff pastry, rough puff and flaky pastry as well as batter products.

Using raising agents

- Always buy a reliable brand of baking powder.
- Store in a dry place in an airtight container.
- Do not store for long periods of time, as the baking powder loses some of its residual carbon dioxide over time and therefore will not be as effective.
- Check the recipe carefully, making sure that the correct preparation for the type of mixture is used; otherwise, under- or over-rising may result.
- Sieve the raising agent with the flour and/or dry ingredients to give an even mix and thus an even reaction.

- Distribute moisture evenly into the mixture to ensure even action of the raising agent.
- If a large proportion of raising agent has been added to a mixture, and is not to be cooked immediately, keep it in a cool place to avoid too much reaction before baking.

Too much raising agent causes:
- an over-risen product that may collapse, giving a sunken effect
- a coarse texture
- poor colour and flavour
- fruit to sink to the bottom of the cake
- a bitter taste.

Insufficient raising agent causes:
- a lack of volume
- insufficient lift
- a close texture
- shrinkage.

Eggs

Eggs are an important and versatile ingredient in pastry work. Hens' eggs are graded in four sizes – small, medium, large, and very large. For the recipes in this chapter, use medium-sized eggs (approximately 50 g), unless otherwise stated.

Eggs are used in pastry work because of their binding, emulsifying and coating properties. Eggs add both protein and fat, thus improving nutritional value and flavour.

The use of eggs in desserts is discussed in more detail later in this chapter (see page 458).

Milk

Full-cream, skimmed or semi-skimmed milk can be used for the desserts in this chapter.

Milk is a basic and fundamental element in pastry work, and often forms a substantial part of the diet, particularly in the western world. It is composed of water, sugar and fat (whole cow's milk has a minimum fat content of 3.5 per cent but milk is also available with some or all of the fat removed). It is essential in an infinite number of products, from creams, ice creams, yeast doughs, mousses and custards to certain ganaches, cookies, tuiles and muffins. A yeast dough will change considerably in texture, taste and colour if made with milk instead of water.

Milk has a slightly sweet taste and little odour. Two distinct processes are used to conserve it:

- **Pasteurisation** – the milk is heated to between 73°C and 85° for a few seconds, then cooled quickly to 4°C.
- **Sterilisation (UHT)** – the milk is heated to between 140°C and 150°C for 2 seconds, then cooled quickly.

Milk is homogenised to disperse the fat evenly, since the fat has a tendency to rise to the surface (see 'Cream', below).

Here are some useful facts about milk.

- Pasteurised milk has a better taste and aroma than UHT milk.
- Milk is a useful for developing flavour in sauces and creams, due to its lactic fermentation.
- Milk contributes to colour as well as the development of texture and aroma in doughs.
- Because of its lactic ferments, it helps in the maturation of doughs and creams.
- There are other types of milk, such as sheep's milk, that are very interesting to use in many desserts and patisserie products.
- Milk is much more fragile than cream. In recipes, adding it in certain proportions is advisable for a much more subtle and delicate final product.

Cream

Cream is used in many recipes because of its great versatility and capabilities.

Cream is the concentrated milk fat that is skimmed off the top of the milk. A film forms on the surface because of the difference in density between fat and liquid. This process is speeded up mechanically in manufacturing by heating and using centrifuges.

Cream should contain at least 18 per cent butterfat. Cream for whipping must contain more than 30 per cent butterfat. Commercially frozen cream is available

in pre-weighed slabs. Types, packaging, storage and uses of cream are listed in Table 11.1.

Whipping and double cream may be whipped to make them lighter and to increase volume. Cream will whip more easily if it is kept refrigerated. Indeed, all cream products must be kept in the refrigerator for food safety reasons. They should be handled with care and, as they will absorb odour, they should never be stored near onions or other strong-smelling foods.

As with milk, there are two main methods for conserving cream:

- **Pasteurisation** – the cream is heated to between 85°C and 90°C for a few seconds and then cooled quickly; this cream retains all its flavour properties.
- **Sterilisation (UHT)** – this consists of heating the cream to between 140°C and 150°C for 2 seconds; cream treated this way loses some of its flavour properties, but it keeps for longer.

Always use pasteurised cream when possible, for example, in the restaurant when specialities are made for immediate consumption, such as 'ephemeral', patisserie (dessert cuisine) with a short life, e.g. a chocolate bonbon or a soufflé that will be consumed immediately.

Here are some useful facts about cream.

- Cream whips with the addition of air, thanks to its fat content. This retains air bubbles formed during beating.
- Understand how to use fresh cream; remember that it is easily over-whipped.
- Cream adds texture.
- All cream, once boiled and cooled, can be whipped again with no problem.
- Once cream is boiled and mixed or infused with other ingredients to add flavour, it will whip again if first left to cool; when preparing a chocolate Chantilly, for example.
- To whip cream well, it must be cold (around 4°C).
- Cream can be infused with other flavours when it is hot or cold. The flavour of cream will develop if left to infuse prior to preparation.

Table 11.1 Types of cream

Type of cream	Legal minimum fat	Processing and packaging	Storage	Characteristics and uses
Half cream	12%	Homogenised; may be pasteurised or ultra-heat treated		Does not whip; used for pouring; suitable for low-fat diets
Cream (single cream)	18%	Homogenised; pasteurised by heating to 79.5°C for 15 seconds, then cooling to 4.5°C; packaged in bottles and cartons, sealed with foil caps; may be available in bulk		A pouring cream suitable for coffee, cereals, soup or fruit; added to cooked dishes and sauces; does not whip
Whipping cream	35%	Not homogenised; pasteurised and packaged like single cream	2–3 days	Ideal for whipping; suitable for piping, cake and dessert decoration; used in ice cream, cake and pastry fillings
Double cream	48%	Slightly homogenised; pasteurised and packaged like single cream		A rich pouring cream; will whip; floats on coffee or soup
'Thick' double cream	48%	Heavily homogenised; pasteurised and packaged like single cream; usually only sold in domestic quantities		A rich, spoonable cream; cannot be poured
Clotted cream	55%	Heated to 82°C then cooled for about 4½ hours; the cream crust is then skimmed off; packed in cartons, usually by hand; may be available in bulk		Very thick; has its own special flavour and colour; used with scones, fruit and fruit pies
Ultra-heat treated (UHT) cream	12% (half), 18% (single) or 35% (whipping)	Homogenised; heated to 132°C for 1 second, then cooled immediately; aseptically packaged in polythene and foil-lined containers; available in catering-size packs	6 weeks if unopened; does not need refrigeration; usually date stamped	UHT half or single cream is a pouring cream; UHT cream with 35% fat can be whipped

Convenience products

Convenience mixes, such as short pastry, sponge mixes and choux pastry mixes, are now becoming increasingly used in a variety of establishments. These products have improved enormously over the last few years. Using such products gives the chef the opportunity to save on time and labour; and with skill, imagination and creativity, the finished products are not impaired.

Not surprisingly many caterers, including some luxury establishments, have turned to using frozen puff pastry. It is now available in ready rolled 30 cm squares, thereby avoiding the possibility of uneven thickness and the waste that can occur when rolling out yourself. The large food manufacturers dominate the frozen puff pastry market.

Manufactured puff pastry is available in three types, defined often by their fat content. The cheapest is made with the white hydrogenated fat, which gives the product a pale colour and a waxy taste. Puff pastry made with bakery margarine has a better colour and, often, a better flavour. The best-quality puff pastry is that which is made with all butter, giving a richer texture, colour and flavour.

Pastry bought in blocks is cheaper than pre-rolled separate sheets, but has to be rolled evenly to give an even bake. The sizes of sheets do vary with manufacturers and all are interleaved with greaseproof paper. Ready rolled and shaped pie tops are also available.

Filo pastry and *feuille de brick* are further examples of convenient pastry products. They are available in frozen sheets of various sizes. No rolling out is required and once thawed, they can be used as required and moulded if necessary.

As well as convenience pastry mixes, there is also a whole range of frozen products suitable to serve as sweets and afternoon tea pastries. These include fruit pies, flans, gâteaux and charlottes. The vast majority are ready to serve once defrosted, but very often they do require a little more decorative finish. The availability of such products gives the caterer the advantage of further labour cost reductions, while permitting the chef to concentrate on other areas of the menu.

Storage and food safety

- Store all goods according to the Food Hygiene Regulations 2006.
- Handle all equipment carefully to avoid cross-contamination.
- Take special care when using cream, and ensure that products containing cream are stored under refrigerated conditions.
- All piping bags must be sterilised after each use (or use disposable bags).

- Always make sure that storage containers are kept clean and returned ready for re-use. On their return they should be hygienically washed and stored.

Points to remember

When handling ingredients for pastry work:
- Check all weighing scales for accuracy.
- Follow recipes carefully.
- Check all storage temperatures are correct.
- Always work in a clean, tidy and organised way; clean all equipment after use.
- Always store ingredients correctly: for example, eggs should be stored in a refrigerator, flour in a bin with a tight-fitting lid, sugar and other dry ingredients in closed storage containers.
- Keep all small moulds clean and dry to prevent rusting.

Techniques in pastry work

Adding fat to flour

Fats act as a shortening agent. The fat has the effect of shortening the gluten strands, which are easily broken when eaten, making the texture of the product more crumbly. However, the development of gluten in puff pastry is very important as long strands are needed to trap the expanding gases, and this is what makes the paste rise.

Fat can be added to flour by:
- **Rubbing in** by machine or by hand: e.g. short pastry.
  - Fat is better to work with if it is cold when rubbing in. It will be much easier to produce a fine crumb.
- **Creaming** by machine or by hand: e.g. sweet pastry.
  - Fat is better to work with if it is 'plastic' (i.e. at room temperature). This will make it easier to cream.
  - Always cream the fat and sugar well, before adding the liquid.
- **The flour batter method:** e.g. slab cakes.
- **Lamination:** e.g. puff pastry.
- **Boiling:** e.g. choux pastry.

Blending

Blending means mixing all the ingredients carefully by weight.

Handling pastry

Techniques used to work pastry include:
- **Folding:** for example, folding puff pastry to create its layers as in a vol-au-vent or gâteau pithivier.
- **Kneading:** using your hands to work dough or puff pastry in the first stage of making.
- **Relaxing:** keeping pastry covered with a damp cloth, clingfilm or plastic covering to prevent a skin forming on the surface. A period of resting allows the gluten in the pastry to relax and lose some of its resistance to rolling. It will also help to prevent the pastry from shrinking during the cooking process.
- **Shaping** refers to producing flans, tartlets, barquettes and other such goods with pastry. Shaping also refers to crimping with the back of a small knife or using the thumb technique.

- **Docking:** this is piercing raw pastry with small holes to prevent it from rising during baking, as when cooking tartlets blind (without a filling).

Rolling

- Roll the pastry on a lightly floured surface; turn the pastry to prevent it sticking. Keep the rolling pin lightly floured and free from the pastry.
- Always roll with care, treating the pastry lightly – never apply too much pressure.
- Always apply even pressure when using a rolling pin.

Cutting

- Always cut with a sharp, damp knife.
- When using cutters, always flour them before use by dipping in flour. This will give a sharp, neat cut.
- When using a lattice cutter, use only on firm pastry; if the pastry is too soft, you will have difficulty lifting the lattice.

Glazing

A glaze is something that gives a product a smooth, shiny surface. Examples of glazes used for pastry dishes are as follows.

- A hot clear gel produced from a pectin source obtainable commercially for finishing flans and tartlets; always use while still hot. A cold gel is exactly the same except that it is used cold. The gel keeps a sheen on the goods and keeps out all oxygen, which might otherwise cause discoloration.
- Apricot glaze, produced from apricot jam, acts in the same way as hot gels.
- Eggwash, applied prior to baking, produces a rich glaze during the cooking process.
- Icing sugar dusted on the surface of the product caramelises in the oven or under the grill.
- Fondant gives a rich sugar glaze, which may be flavoured and/or coloured.
- Water icing gives a transparent glaze, which may also be flavoured and/or coloured.

Finishing and presentation

It is essential that all products are finished according to the recipe requirements. Finishing and presentation is often a key stage in the process, as failure at this point can affect sales. The way goods are presented is an important part of the sales technique. Each product of the same type must be of the same shape, size, colour and finish. The decoration should be attractive, delicate and in keeping with the product range. All piping should be neat, clean and tidy.

Some methods of finishing and presentation are as follows.

- **Dusting:** a light sprinkling of icing sugar on a product using a fine sugar dredger or sieve.
- **Piping:** using fresh cream, chocolate or fondant.
- **Filling:** with fruit, cream, pastry cream, etc. Never overfill as this will often given the product a clumsy appearance.

Piping fresh cream

- The piping of fresh cream is a skill; like all other skills it takes practice to become proficient. The finished item should look attractive, simple, clean and tidy, with neat piping.
- All re-usable piping bags should be sterilised after each use, as these may well be a source of contamination; alternatively use a disposable piping bag.
- Make sure that all the equipment you need for piping is hygienically cleaned before and after use to avoid cross-contamination.

Other considerations when preparing pastry items

- Ensure all cooked products are cooled before finishing.
- Always plan your time carefully.
- Understand why pastry products must be rested or relaxed and docked. This will prevent excessive shrinkage in the oven, and docking will allow the air to escape through the product, preventing any unevenness.
- Use silicone paper for baking in preference to greaseproof.

Ingredients commonly used in desserts

Two important ingredients in many desserts are eggs and, perhaps surprisingly, salt, both of which are discussed below. Milk and cream are also common ingredients.

Salt

Salt (chemical name 'sodium chloride') is one of the most important ingredients. It is well known that salt is a necessary part of the human diet, present in small or large proportions in many natural foods. Salt considerably enhances all preparations, whether they be sweet or savoury. We generally associate it with seasoning foods to improve or enhance their flavour, but it is also necessary in the making of many sweet dishes.

It is a good idea to add a pinch of salt to all sweet preparations, nougats, chocolate bonbons and cakes to intensify flavours. Salt also softens sugar and butter, activates the taste buds and enhances all aromas.

What you need to know about salt

- Salt gives us the possibility of many combinations. At times, these may seem normal (like a terrine of *foie gras* and coarse salt), others surprising (like praline with coarse salt).
- The addition of salt enhances the flavour of foods when its quantity is well adjusted; but if added it in greater quantity than we are used to, it produces a very interesting, completely unknown result. Care needs to be taken when adding salt. There is a fine line between the enhancement of food with salt and spoiling it by adding too much salt.
- Excessive salt can cause high blood pressure, which could lead to a stroke and heart attacks, so it should be used in moderation. For this reason, many chefs are looking for ways to reduce the amount of salt they use in their products and dishes.

Eggs

Eggs are one of the principal ingredients in cooking, and essential for many desserts. Their great versatility and extraordinary properties as a thickener, emulsifier and stabiliser make their presence important in various creations in patisserie: sauces, creams, sponge cakes, custards and ice creams. Although it is not often the main ingredient, the egg plays specific and determining roles in terms of texture, taste and aroma. It is fundamental in products such as brioches, *crème anglaise*, sponge cakes and *crème pâtissière*. The extent to which eggs are used (or not) makes an enormous difference to the quality of the product.

A good custard cannot be made without eggs, as they cause the required coagulation and give it the desired consistency and finesse.

Eggs are also an important ingredient in ice cream, where their yolks act as an emulsifier, due to the lecithin they contain, which aids the emulsion of fats.

Eggs are used for several reasons:
- They act as a texture agent in, for example, crème patisserie and ice creams.
- They intensify the aroma of pastries like brioche.
- They enhance flavours.
- They give volume to whisked sponges and batters.
- They strengthen the structure of products such as sponge cakes.
- They act as a thickening agent, e.g. in crème anglaise.
- They act as an emulsifier in products such as mayonnaise and ice cream.

Quality and nutritional value

Important facts about eggs:
- A fresh egg (in shell) should have a small, shallow air pocket inside it.
- The yolk of fresh egg should be bulbous, firm and bright.
- The fresher the egg, the more viscous (thick and not runny) the egg white.
- Eggs should be stored away from strong odours as their shells are porous and smells are easily absorbed.
- In a whole 60 g egg, the yolk weighs about 20 g, the white 30 g and the shell 10 g.

Egg yolk is high in saturated fat. The yolk is a good source of protein and also contains vitamins and iron.

The egg white is made up of protein (albumen) and water. The egg yolk also contains lecithin, which acts as an emulsifier in dishes such as mayonnaise – it helps to keep the ingredients mixed, so that the oils and water do not separate.

Working with egg whites

- If egg white is not going to be cooked to a temperature of 70°C, there is a risk of salmonella food poisoning: use pasteurised egg whites.
- Egg white is available chilled, frozen or dried.
- Equipment must be thoroughly clean and free from any traces of fat, as this prevents the whites from whipping; fat or grease prevents the albumen strands from bonding and trapping the air bubbles.
- Take care that there are no traces of yolk in the white, as yolk contains fat.

- A little acid (cream of tartar or lemon juice) strengthens the egg white, extends the foam and produces more meringue. The acid also has the effect of stabilising the meringue.
- If the foam is over-whipped, the albumen strands, which hold the water molecules with the sugar suspended on the outside of the bubble, are overstretched. The water and sugar make contact and the sugar dissolves, making the meringue heavy and wet. This can sometimes be rescued by further whisking until it foams up, but very often you will find that you may have to discard the mixture and start again.

Beaten egg white forms a foam that is used for aerating sweets and many other desserts, including meringues (see recipe 69). It is advisable to use Italian meringue in desserts that are not going to be cooked, such as bavarois.

Egg custard-based desserts

The essential ingredients for an egg custard are eggs and milk. For desserts, this mixture may be sweetened with sugar.

Cream is often added to egg custard desserts to enrich them and to improve the feel in the mouth (mouth-feel) of the final product.

Egg custard mixture provides the chef with a versatile basic set of ingredients that covers a wide range of sweets. Often the mixture is referred to as crème renversée. Some examples of sweets produced using this mixture are:

- crème caramel
- bread and butter pudding
- diplomat pudding
- cabinet pudding
- queen of puddings
- baked egg custard.

Savoury egg custard is used to make:

- quiches
- tartlets
- flans.

When a starch such as flour is added to the ingredients for an egg custard mix, this changes the characteristic of the end product, as per crème patisserie, for example.

Pastry cream (also known as confectioner's custard or *crème pâtissiere*) is a filling used for many sweets, gâteaux, flans and tartlets, and as a basis for soufflé mixes.

Sauce/crème anglaise is used as a base for some ice creams. It is also used in its own right as a sauce to accompany a range of sweets.

Basic egg custard sets by coagulation of the egg protein. Egg white coagulates at approximately 60°C, egg yolk at 70°C. Whites and yolks mixed together will coagulate at 66°C. If the egg protein is overheated or overcooked, it will shrink and water will be lost from the mixture, causing undesirable bubbles in the custard. This loss of water is called syneresis, commonly referred to as scrambling or curdling. This will occur at temperatures higher than 85°C. Therefore, a sauce anglaise should be ideally cooked between 70°C and 85°C. The sauce will become thicker as it becomes closer to 85°C but is at risk or curdling (syneresis) beyond this temperature.

Traditional custard made from custard powder

Custard powder is used to make custard sauce. It is made from vanilla-flavoured cornflour with yellow colouring added, which is a substitute for eggs. The fat content can be reduced by making it with semi-skimmed milk rather than full-fat milk.

Points to remember when making egg custards

- Always work in a clean and tidy way, complying with food hygiene regulations.
- Prevent cross-contamination by not allowing any foreign substances to come into contact with the mixture.
- Always heat the egg yolks or eggs to at least 70°C, or use pasteurised egg yolks or eggs.
- Follow the recipe carefully.
- Ensure that all heating and cooling temperatures are followed.
- Always store the end product carefully at the right temperature.
- Check all weighing scales are accurate.
- Check all raw materials for correct use-by dates.
- Always wash your hands when handling fresh eggs or dairy products and other pastry ingredients.
- Never use cream to decorate a product that is still warm.
- Always remember to follow the Food Hygiene Regulations 2006.
- Check the temperature of refrigerators and freezers to ensure that they comply with the current regulations.

Ice creams and sorbets

Ice cream

Traditional ice cream is made from a basic egg custard sauce (sauce anglaise). The sauce is cooled and mixed with fresh cream. It is then frozen by a rotating machine where the water content forms ice crystals.

Ice cream should be served at around −13°C; this is the correct eating temperature, as it is too hard if it is any colder and too soft if it is any warmer. Long-term storage should be at between −18°C and −20°C.

The traditional method of making ice cream uses only egg yolks, sugar and milk/cream in the form of a sauce anglaise base. Modern approaches to making ice cream use stabilisers (see page 462) and different sugars as well as egg whites. This can help to reduce the fat content and the sometimes high wastage of egg whites that might otherwise occur in the pastry section.

The ice cream regulations

The Dairy Products (Hygiene) Regulations 1995 apply to the handling of milk-based ice cream and the Ice Cream Heat Treatment Regulations 1959 and 1963 apply to non-milk-based ice cream in any catering business or shop premises. The production process must also take into consideration the Food Hygiene Regulations of 2006.

The regulations state that:

- Ice cream must be obtained from a mixture which has been heated to any of the temperatures in Table 11.2 for the times specified.
- The mix must be reduced to a temperature of not more than 7.2°C within 1½ hours. This temperature must not be exceeded until freezing begins.
- If the temperature of ice cream rises (above −2.2°C) it cannot be sold/used until it has been heated again as described above.
- A complete cold mix which is reconstituted with water does not need to be pasteurised first to comply with these regulations.
- A complete cold mix reconstituted with water must be kept below −2.2°C once it has been frozen.

Table 11.2

Temperature	Time (not less than)
65.5°C	30 minutes
71.1°C	10 minutes
79.4°C	15 seconds

Ice cream needs this treatment to kill harmful bacteria. Freezing without the correct heat treatment does not kill bacteria; it allows them to remain dormant. The storage temperature for ice cream should not exceed −20°C ideally, although standard freezers operate between −18°C and −22°C.

The rules for sterilised ice cream are the same except that:

- The temperature for the heat treatment must not be less than 149.9°C for at least 2 seconds.
- If the sterilised mix is kept in unopened, sterile and air-tight containers, there no requirement to refrigerate the mixture before it is frozen.
- In the case of non-milk-based products, the temperature of opened containers must not exceed 7.2°C, except where food mixtures are added that have a pH of 4.5 or less to make water ice or similar products and the combined product is frozen within 1 hour of combination.

Any ice cream sold must comply with the following compositional standards.

- It must contain not less than 5 per cent fat and not less than 2.5 per cent milk protein (not necessary in natural proportions).
- It must conform to the Dairy Product Regulations 1995.

For further information contact the Ice Cream Alliance (see www.ice-cream.org).

The ice cream making process

1 **Weighing:** ingredients should be weighed precisely in order to ensure the best results and, what is more difficult, regularity and consistency.
2 **Pasteurisation:** this is a vital stage in making ice cream. Its primary function is to minimise bacterial contamination by heating the mixture of ingredients to between 70°C and 85°C, then quickly cooling it to 4°C. (The higher temperature is advised for normal kitchen production.)
3 **Homogenisation:** high pressure is applied to cause the explosion of fats, which makes ice cream more homogenous, creamier, smoother and much lighter. It is not usually done for homemade ice cream.
4 **Ripening:** this basic but optional stage refines flavour, further develops aromas and improves texture. This occurs during a rest period (4–24 hours), which gives the stabilisers and proteins time to act, improving the overall structure of the ice cream. This has the same effect on a *crème anglaise*, which is much better the day after it is made than it is on the same day.
5 **Churning:** here, the mixture is frozen while at the same time air is incorporated. The ice cream is removed from the machine at about −10°C to −13°C.

The main components of ice cream

- **Sucrose** (common sugar) not only sweetens ice cream, but also gives it body. An ice cream that contains only sucrose has a higher freezing point than ice cream made with other types of sugar.
- The optimum sugar percentage of ice cream is between 15 and 20 per cent.
- Ice cream that contains **dextrose** (another type of sugar) has a lower freezing point, and better taste and texture.
- As much as 50 per cent of the sucrose can be substituted with other sweeteners, but the recommended amount is 25 per cent.
- **Glucose** (another type of sugar) improves smoothness and prevents the crystallisation of sucrose.
- The quantity of glucose used should be between 25 and 30 per cent of the sucrose by weight.
- **Atomised glucose** (glucose powder) is more water absorbent, so helps to reduce the formation of ice crystals.
- The quantity of dextrose used should be between 6 and 25 per cent of the substituted sucrose (by weight).
- **Inverted sugar** is a paste or liquid obtained from heating sucrose with water and an acid (e.g. lemon juice). Using inverted sugar in ice cream lowers the freezing point.

- Inverted sugar also improves the texture of ice cream and delays crystallisation.
- The quantity of inverted sugar used should be a maximum of 33 per cent of the sucrose by weight. It is very efficient at sweetening and gives the ice cream a low freezing point.
- **Honey** has very similar properties as those of inverted sugar.
- The purpose of **cream** in ice cream is to improve creaminess and taste.
- **Egg yolks** act as stabilisers for ice cream due to the lecithin they contain – they help to prevent the fats and water in the ice cream from separating.
- Egg yolks improve the texture and viscosity of ice cream.
- The purpose of stabilisers (e.g. gum Arabic, gelatine, pectin) is to prevent crystal formation by absorbing the water contained in ice cream and making a stable gel.
- The quantity of stabilisers in ice cream should be between 3 g and 5 g per kg of mix, with a maximum of 10 g.
- Stabilisers promote air absorption, making products lighter to eat and also less costly to produce, as air makes the product go further.

What you need to know about ice cream

- Hygienic conditions are essential while making ice cream – personal hygiene and high levels of cleanliness in the equipment and the kitchen environment must be maintained.
- An excess of stabilisers in ice cream will make it sticky.
- Stabilisers should always be mixed with sugar before adding, to avoid lumps.
- Stabilisers should be added at 45°C, which is when they begin to act.
- Cold stabilisers have no effect on the mixture, so the temperature must be raised to 85°C.
- Ice cream can 'ripen' for flavour for 4–24 hours. This helps to improve its properties.
- Ice cream should be cooled quickly to 4°C, because micro-organisms reproduce rapidly, particularly between 20°C and 55°C.

Sorbets

Sorbets belong to the ice cream family; they are a mixture of water, sucrose, atomised glucose, stabiliser, fruit juice, fruit pulp and, sometimes, liqueurs.

- Sorbet is generally more refreshing and easier to digest than ice cream.
- Fruit for sorbets must always be of a high quality and perfectly ripe.
- The percentage of fruit used in sorbet varies according to the type of fruit, its acidity and the properties desired.
- The percentage of sugar will depend on the type of fruit used.
- The minimum sugar content in sorbet is about 13 per cent.
- As far as ripening is concerned, the syrup can be left to rest for 4–24 hours but never mixed with the fruit because its acidity would damage the stabiliser.
- Stabiliser is added in the same way as for ice cream.
- Sorbets are not to be confused with granitas, which are semi-solid.

Stabilisers

Gelling substances, thickeners and emulsifiers are all stabilisers. They are products we use regularly, each with its own specific function; but their main purpose is to retain water to make a gel. The case of ice cream is the most obvious, in which they are used to prevent ice crystal formation. They are also used to stabilise the emulsion, increase the viscosity of the mix and give a smoother product that is more resistant to melting. There are many stabilising substances, both natural and artificial.

Edible gelatine

Edible gelatine is extracted from animals' bones (e.g. pork and veal) and, more recently, fish skin. Sold in sheets of 2 g, it is easy to precisely control the amount used and to manipulate it. Gelatine sheets must be soaked in plenty of cold water, then squeezed out before use.

Gelatine sheets melt at 40°C and should be melted in a little of the liquid from the recipe before adding it to the base preparation.

Pectin

Pectin is another commonly used gelling substance because of its great absorption capacity. It comes from citrus peel (orange, lemon, etc.), though all fruits contain some pectin in their peel.

It is a good idea always to mix pectin with sugar before adding it to the rest of the ingredients.

Agar-agar

Agar-agar is a gelatinous marine algae found in Asia. It is sold in whole or powdered form and has a great absorption capacity. It dissolves very easily and, in addition to gelling, adds elasticity and resists heat (this is classified as a non-reversible gel).

Other stabilisers

- **Carob gum**, which comes from the seeds of the carob tree, makes sorbets creamier and improves heat resistance.
- **Guar gum** and **carrageenan** are, like agar-agar, extracted from marine algae and are some of many other existing gelling substances available, but they are used less often.

Fruit

Fruit is used as an ingredient in many desserts.

Quality and purchasing

Fresh fruit should be:
- whole and fresh looking (for maximum flavour the fruit must be ripe but not overripe)
- firm, according to type and variety
- clean, and free from traces of pesticides and fungicides
- free from external moisture
- free from any unpleasant foreign smell or taste
- free from pests or disease
- sufficiently mature; it must be capable of being handled and travelling without being damaged
- free from any defects characteristic of the variety in shape, size and colour
- free of bruising and any other damage.

Soft fruits deteriorate quickly, especially if they are not sound. Take care to see that they are not damaged or overripe when purchased. Soft fruits should look fresh; there should be no signs of wilting, shrinking or mould. The colour of certain soft fruits is an indication of their ripeness (e.g. strawberries or dessert gooseberries).

Food value

Fruit is rich in antioxidant minerals and vitamins. Antioxidants protect cells from damage by oxygen, which may lead to heart disease and cancer. The current recommendation is to eat at least five portions of fruit and vegetables each day.

Storage

Hard fruits, such as apples, should be left in boxes and kept in a cool store. Soft fruits, such as raspberries and strawberries, should be left in their punnets or baskets in a cold room. Stone fruits, such as apricots and plumbs, are best placed in trays so that any damaged fruit can be seen and discarded. Peaches and citrus fruits are left in their delivery trays or boxes. Bananas should not be stored in too cold a place because their skins will turn black.

Healthy eating and desserts

Desserts and puddings remain popular with the consumer, but there is now a demand for products with reduced fat and sugar content, as many people are keen to eat healthily. Chefs will continue to respond to this demand by modifying recipes to reduce the fat and sugar content; they may also use alternative ingredients, such as low-calorie sweeteners where possible and unsaturated fats. Although salt is an essential part of our diet, too much of it can be unhealthy (see page xx), and this is something else that chefs should take into consideration.

Dough products

This section focuses on the other work of the pastry area: preparing and cooking bakery products.

The principal ingredients in bread and dough products are wheat flour and yeast. Bread and bread products form the basis of our diet and are staple products in our society. We eat bread at breakfast, lunch and dinner, as slices, bread rolls, croissants, French sticks, etc. Bread is also used as an ingredient for many other dishes, either as slices for sandwiches, toast or fried bread or as breadcrumbs.

Dough consists of strong flour, water, salt and yeast, which are kneaded together to the required consistency at a suitable temperature. It is then allowed to prove (to rise and increase in size), when the yeast produces carbon dioxide and water, which aerates the dough. When baked it produces a light digestible product with flavour and colour.

Salted dough is more manageable than unsalted dough. Salt is usually added a few moments before the end of the kneading, since its function is to help expand the dough's volume (and to enhance the flavour).

Flour-based products provide a variety of energy, vitamins and minerals. Wholemeal bread products also provide fibre, an essential part of a healthy diet.

Understanding fermentation

For dough to become leavened bread (bread that has risen, rather than flat bread) it must go through a fermentation process. This is brought about by the action of yeast, a living micro-organism rich in protein and Vitamin B. The yeast reacts with enzymes in the dough, which convert sugar into alcohol, producing the characteristic flavour of bread. The action also produces carbon dioxide, which makes the bread rise.

Yeast requires ideal conditions for growth. These are:

- **warmth:** a good temperature for dough production is 22–30°C
- **moisture:** the liquid should be added at approximately 37°C
- **food:** this is obtained from the starch in the flour
- **time:** this is needed to allow the yeast to grow.

Dried yeast has been dehydrated and must be creamed with a little water before use. It will keep for several months in its dry state. Some types of dried yeast can be used straight from the packet.

Yeast will not survive in a high concentration of sugar or salt, and its growth will slow down in a very rich dough with a high fat and egg content.

When mixing yeast in water or milk, make sure that the liquid is at the correct temperature (37°C), and disperse the yeast in the liquid. (As a living organism cannot be dissolved, the word 'disperse' is used.)

Why does dough ferment?

The occurrence of dough fermenting is extraordinary. However, as it is so frequent in the profession, rarely is much attention paid to exactly how it happens. It is very interesting to know why doughs ferment and what the effects are on the end product. In order to understand why yeast dough rises, it is important to note that the main ingredients of natural leavening are water, air and, most importantly, sugar, which is transformed into carbon dioxide and alcohol and causes the leavening. This carbon dioxide forms bubbles inside the dough and makes it rise. Fermentation is a transformation undergone by organic matter (sugars).

Working with dough

- Yeast should be removed from the refrigerator and used at room temperature.
- Check that all ingredients are weighed carefully.
- Work in a clean and tidy manner to avoid cross-contamination.
- Check all temperatures carefully.
- All wholemeal doughs absorb more water than white doughs. The volume of water absorbed by flour also varies according to the strength (protein and bran content).
- When using machines, check that they are in good working order.
- Always remember the health and safety rules when using machinery.
- Divide the dough with a dough divider, hard scraper or hydraulic cutting machine.
- Check the divided dough pieces for weight. When weighing, remember that doughs lose up to 12.5 per cent of their water during baking.
- Keep the flour, bowl and liquid warm.
- Remember to knock the dough back (re-knead it) carefully once proved, as this will expel the gas and allow the yeast to be dispersed properly, coming back into direct contact with the dough.
- Proving allows the dough to ferment; the second prove is essential for giving dough products the necessary volume and a good flavour.
- Time and temperature are crucial when cooking dough products.
- When using frozen dough products, always follow the manufacturer's instructions.
- Contamination can occur if doughs are defrosted incorrectly.

Types of dough

Enriched doughs

The basic bread dough of wheat flour, yeast and water may be enriched with fat, sugar, eggs, milk and numerous other added ingredients. Some examples of enriched doughs are:

- **buns**
- **savarin:** a rich yeast dough used for savarins, babas and marignans
- **brioche:** a rich yeast dough with a high butter (fat) content.

Laminated doughs

Croissants and Danish pastries are enriched doughs to which the fat is added by layering or lamination. This makes them softer to eat because the fat in the dough insulates the water molecules, keeping the moisture level higher during baking.

Danish pastries may be filled with fruit, frangipane, apple, custard, cherries and many other ingredients.

Speciality doughs

- **Blinis:** a type of savoury pancake traditionally made from buckwheat flour.
- **Naan bread:** a leavened Indian bread traditionally cooked in a tandoor (oven).
- **Pitta bread:** Middle Eastern and Greek unleavened bread.
- **Chapatti:** Indian unleavened bread made from a fine ground wholemeal flour, known as 'atta'.

Storage of cooked dough products

Crusty rolls and bread are affected by changes in storage conditions; they are softened by a damp environment and humid conditions, so should be stored in a dry environment to keep them crusty.

Store dough products in clean, air-tight containers at room temperature or in a freezer for longer periods. Do not store in a refrigerator unless you want the bread to stale quickly for use as breadcrumbs. Staling will also occur quickly in products that contain a lot of fat and milk. Many commercial dough products contain anti-staling agents.

Convenience dough products

There are many different types of convenience dough product on the market.

- dry bread mixes: just add water
- fresh and frozen pre-proved dough products: rolls; croissants; Danish pastries; French breads
- bake-off products that are ready for baking. These can be bought either frozen or fresh, or in modified atmosphere-packaged forms. This process removes most of the oxygen around the product to slow down spoilage. Such products have to be kept refrigerated. They include garlic bread, rolls and Danish pastries. Vacuum-packed part-baked dough can be stored without refrigeration.

Possible reasons for faults in yeast doughs

If your dough has a close texture this may be because:
- it was insufficiently proved
- it was insufficiently kneaded
- it contains insufficient yeast
- the oven was too hot
- too much water was added
- too little water was added.

If your dough has an uneven texture this may be because:
- it was insufficiently kneaded
- it was over-proved
- the oven was too cool.

If your dough has a coarse texture this may be because:
- it was over-proved, uncovered
- it was insufficiently kneaded
- too much water was added
- too much salt was added.

If your dough is wrinkled this may be because it was over-proved.

If your dough is sour this may be because:
- the yeast was stale
- too much yeast was used.

If the crust is broken this may be because the dough was under-proved at the second stage.

If there are white spots on crust this may be because the dough was not covered before second proving.

Breads

It is customary today for restaurants to offer a range of different flavoured breads. Internationally there is a wide variety available; different nations and regions have their own speciality breads. Bread plays an important part in many religious festivals, especially Christian and Jewish.

Bulk fermentation

The traditional bread-making process is known as the bulk fermentation process. This was used by many bakers before the introduction of high-speed mixing and dough conditioners, which both eliminate the need for bulk fermentation time. However, this traditional method produces a fine flavour due to the fermentation which is evident in the final product.

Bulk fermentation time (BFT) is the term is used to describe the length of time that the dough is allowed to ferment in bulk. BFT is measured from the end of the mixing method to the beginning of the scaling (weighing) process. The length of BFT can be from 1 to 6 hours and is related to the level of salt and yeast in the recipe, as well as the dough temperature.

It is important during the bulk fermentation process that ideal conditions are adhered to:
- The dough must be kept covered to prevent the surface of the dough developing a skin.
- The appropriate temperature must be maintained and monitored to control the rate of fermentation.

Cakes, sponges and biscuits

Making cakes

There are three basic methods of making cake mixtures, also known as cake batters. The working temperature of cake batter should be 21°C.

The sugar batter method

For the sugar batter method, the fat (cake margarine, butter or shortening) is blended in a machine with caster sugar. This is the basic or principal stage; usually the other ingredients are then added in the order shown in the diagram below.

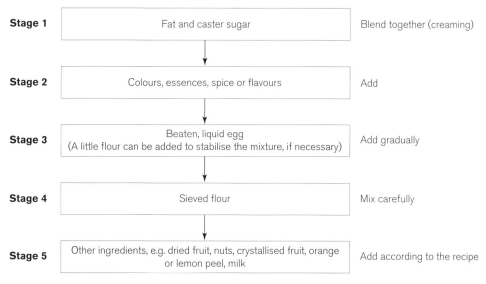

Stage 1	Fat and caster sugar	Blend together (creaming)
Stage 2	Colours, essences, spice or flavours	Add
Stage 3	Beaten, liquid egg (A little flour can be added to stabilise the mixture, if necessary)	Add gradually
Stage 4	Sieved flour	Mix carefully
Stage 5	Other ingredients, e.g. dried fruit, nuts, crystallised fruit, orange or lemon peel, milk	Add according to the recipe

The sugar batter method

The flour batter method

For the flour batter method, the eggs and sugar are whisked to a half sponge; this is the basic or principal stage, which aims to foam the two ingredients together until half the maximum volume is achieved. Other ingredients are added as shown in the diagram below.

A type of product called a humectant, which helps the product to stay moist, may be added (e.g. glycerine); if so, add this at stage 2.

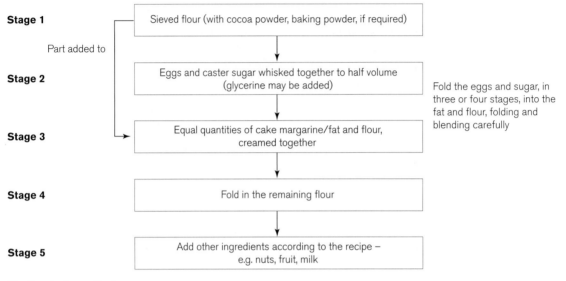

The flour batter method

....

The blending method

The blending method is used for high-ratio cake mixtures. It uses high-ratio flour specially produced so that it will absorb more liquid. It also uses a high-ratio fat, made from oil to which a quantity of emulsifying agent has been added, enabling the fat to take up a greater quantity of liquid.

High-ratio cakes contain more liquid and sugar, resulting in a fine stable crumb, extended shelf life, good eating and excellent freezing qualities.The principal or basic stage is the mixing of the fat and flour to a crumbling texture. It is essential that each stage of the batter is blended into the next to produce a smooth batter, free from lumps. When using mixing machines, it is important to remember to:

- blend on a slow speed
- beat on a medium speed, using a paddle attachment.

When blending, always clear the mix from the bottom of the bowl to ensure that any first- or second-stage batter does not remain in the bowl.

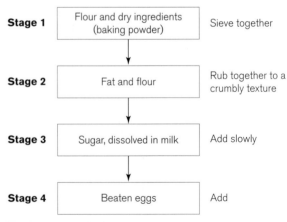

The blending method

Baking powder in cakes

Baking powder may be made from one part sodium bicarbonate to two parts cream of tartar. In commercial baking the powdered cream of tartar may be replaced by another acid product, such as acidulated calcium phosphate.

When used under the right conditions, with the addition of liquid and heat, it produces carbon dioxide gas. As the acid has a delayed action, only a small amount of gas is given off when the liquid is added, and the majority is released when the mixture is heated. Therefore, when cakes are mixed they do not lose the property of the baking powder if they are not cooked right away.

Possible reasons for faults in cakes

If your cake has an uneven texture, this may be because:
- the fat was insufficiently rubbed in
- there was too little liquid
- there was too much liquid.

If your cake has a close texture, this may be because:
- there was too much fat
- your hands were too hot when rubbing in
- the fat to flour ratio was incorrect.

If your cake is dry, this may be because:
- there was too little liquid
- the oven was too hot.

If your cake has a bad shape, this may be because:
- there was too much liquid
- the oven was too cool
- there was too much baking powder.

If the fruit in the cake has sunk, this may be because:
- the fruit was wet
- there was too much liquid
- the oven was too cool.

If the cake has cracked, this may be because:
- there was too little liquid
- there was too much baking powder.

Batters and whisked sponges

Batters and sponges allow the production of a large assortment of desserts and cakes. Basically, they are a mix of eggs, sugar, flour and the air incorporated when these are beaten. Certain other raw materials can be combined – for example, almonds, hazelnuts, walnuts, chocolate, butter, fruit, ginger, anise, coffee and vanilla.

Sponge mixtures are produced from a foam of eggs and sugar. The eggs may be whole eggs or separated. Examples of sponge products include gâteaux, sponge fingers and sponge cakes.

The egg white traps the air bubbles. When eggs and sugar are whisked together, they thicken until maximum volume is reached; then flour is carefully folded in by a method known as cutting in. This is the most difficult operation, as the flour must not be allowed to sink to the bottom of the bowl, otherwise it becomes lumpy and difficult to clear. However, the mixture must not be stirred too much as this will disturb the aeration and cause the air to escape, resulting in a much heavier sponge. If butter, margarine or oil is added, it is important that this is added at about 36°C, otherwise overheating will cause the fat or oil to act on the flour and create lumps, which are difficult, often impossible, to get rid of.

Stabilisers are often added to sponges to prevent them from collapsing. The most common are ethylmethyl cellulose and glycerol monostearate; these are added to the eggs and sugar at the beginning of the mixing.

Making sponge cakes
- You should never add flour or ground dry ingredients to a batter until the end because they impede the air absorption in the first beating stage.
- When making sponge cakes, always sift the dry ingredients (flour, cocoa powder, ground nuts, etc.) to avoid clumping.
- Mix in the flour as quickly and delicately as possible, because a rough addition of dry ingredients acts like a weight on the primary batter and can remove part of the air already absorbed.

- Flours used in sponge cakes are low in gluten content. In certain sponge cakes, a portion of the flour can be left out and substituted with cornstarch. This yields a softer and more aerated batter.
- The eggs used in sponge cake batters should be fresh and at room temperature so that they take in air faster.
- Adding separately beaten egg whites produces a lighter and fluffier sponge cake.
- Once sponge cake batters are beaten and poured into moulds or baking trays, they should be baked as soon as possible. Delays will cause the batter to lose volume.

There are several methods of making sponge cake:
- **Foaming method** – whisking eggs and sugar together to the ribbon stage; folding in/cutting flour.
- **Melting method** – as with foaming, but adding melted butter, margarine or oil to the mixture at the final stage. The fat content enriches the sponge, improves the flavour, texture and crumb structure, and will extend shelf life.
- **Boiling method** – sponges made by this method have a stable crumb texture that is easier to handle and crumbles less when cut than the standard basic sponge containing fat (known as Genoese sponge). This method will produce a sponge that is suitable for dipping in fondant. The stages are shown in the diagram below.
- **Blending method** – this is used for high-ratio sponges, which follow the same principles as high-ratio cakes. As with cakes, high-ratio goods produce a fine, stable crumb, an even texture, excellent shelf life and good freezing qualities.
- **Creaming method** – this is the traditional method and is still used today for Victoria sandwich and light fruitcakes. The fat and sugar are creamed together, then beaten egg is added and, finally, the sieved flour is added with the other dry ingredients as desired.
- **Separate yolk and white method** – this method is used for sponge fingers (recipe 153).

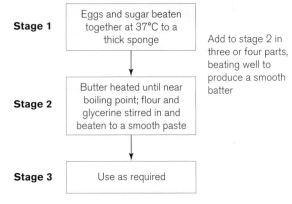

The boiling method

Possible reasons for faults in sponges

If your sponge has a close texture, this may be because:
- it was not beaten enough
- there was too much flour
- the oven was too cool or too hot.

If your sponge has a 'holey' texture, this may be because:
- the flour was insufficiently folded in
- the tin was unevenly filled.

If the sponge has a cracked crust, this may be because the oven was too hot.

If the sponge is sunken, this may be because:
- the oven was too hot
- the tin was removed during cooking.

White spots on the surface may indicate that it was not beaten enough.

Possible reasons for faults in Genoise sponges

If the sponge has a close texture, this may be because:
- the eggs and sugar were overheated
- the eggs and sugar were under-beaten
- there was too much flour
- the flour was insufficiently folded in
- the oven was too hot.

If the sponge is sunken, this may be because:
- there was too much sugar
- the oven was too hot
- the tin was removed during cooking.

If the sponge is heavy, this may be because:
- the butter was too hot
- the butter was insufficiently mixed in
- the flour was over-mixed.

The introduction of steam or moisture

Because they become too dry while baking due to oven temperature producing a dry atmosphere, some cakes require the injection of steam. Combination ovens are ideally suited for this purpose. The steam delays the formation of the crust until the cake batter has become fully aerated and the proteins have set. Alternatively, add a tray of water to the oven while baking. If the oven is too hot the cake crust will form early and the cake batter will rise into a peak.

Points to remember when baking cakes and sponges

- Check all ingredients carefully.
- Make sure scales are accurate; weigh all ingredients carefully.
- Check ovens are at the right temperature and that the shelves are in the correct position.
- Check that all work surfaces and equipment are clean.
- Check that all other equipment required, such as cooling wires, is within easy reach.
- Always sieve flour to remove lumps and any foreign material.
- Make sure that eggs and fats are at room temperature.
- Check dried fruits carefully; wash, drain and dry if necessary.
- Always follow the recipe carefully.
- Always scrape down the sides of the mixing bowl when creaming mixtures.
- Always seek help if you are unsure, or lack understanding.

- Try to fill the oven space when baking by planning production carefully; this saves time, labour and money.
- Never guess quantities. Time and temperature are important factors; they too should not be guessed.
- The shape and size of goods will determine the cooking time and temperature: the wider and deeper the cake, the longer and more slowly it will need to cook.
- Where cakes contain a high proportion of sugar in the recipe, this will caramelise the surface quickly before the centre is cooked. Therefore cover the cake with sheets of silicone or wetted greaseproof and continue to cook.
- When cake tops are sprinkled with almonds or sugar, the baking temperature needs to be lowered slightly to prevent over-colouring of the cake crust.
- When glycerine, glucose and invert sugar, honey or treacle is added to cake mixtures, the oven temperature should be lowered as these colour at a lower temperature than sugar.
- Always work in a clean and hygienic way; remember the hygiene and safety rules, in particular the Food Hygiene Regulations 2006.
- All cakes and sponges benefit from being allowed to cool in their tins as this makes handling easier. If sponges need to be cooled quickly, place a wire rack over the top of the tin and invert, then remove the lining paper and cool on a wire rack.

Biscuits

Biscuits and cookies may be produced by the following methods:
- rubbing in
- flour batter
- foaming
- blending
- sugar batter.

Rubbing in

Rubbing in is probably the best-known method and is used to produce some of the most famous types of biscuits, such as shortbread. The method is exactly the same as that for producing short pastry.

- Rub the fat into the flour, by hand or by machine. Dissolve the liquid and the sugar and mix into the flour to produce a smooth biscuit paste.
- Do not overwork the paste when mixing to combine. The consequence of overworking the paste at this stage is that the gluten in the flour will strengthen and result in the tightening of the paste. If this happens the paste will become very difficult to roll and is likely to shrink during the baking process.

Foaming

This is where a foam is produced from egg whites, egg yolks or both. Sponge fingers are an example of a two-foam mixture. Meringue is an example of a single-foam mixture using egg whites.

Great care must be taken not to over-mix the product.

The sugar batter method

Fat and sugar are mixed together to produce a light aerated cream. Beaten egg is added gradually. The dry ingredients are then carefully folded in.

Cat's tongues (*langues de chat*) and sablé biscuits are made in this way.

The flour batter method

Half the sieved flour is creamed with the fat. The eggs and sugar are beaten together before they are added to the fat and flour mixture. Finally, the remainder of the flour is folded in, together with any other dry ingredients.

Cookies are made using this method.

The blending method

In several biscuit recipes, the method requires the blending of all the ingredients together to produce a smooth paste. This method is used to make almond biscuits using a basic commercial mixture.

Convenience cake, biscuit and sponge mixes

There is now a vast range of prepared mixes and frozen goods available on the market. Premixes enable the caterer to calculate costs more effectively, reduce labour costs (with less demand for highly skilled labour) and limit the range of stock items to be held.

Every year, more and more convenience products are introduced onto the market by food manufacturers. The caterer should be encouraged to investigate these products, and to experiment in order to assess their quality.

Decorating and finishing for presentation

Fillings

Cakes, sponges and biscuits may be filled or sandwiched together with a variety of different types of filling. Some examples are presented below.
- Creams:
  - buttercream (plain), flavoured and/or coloured
  - pastry cream, flavoured and/or coloured
  - whipped cream
  - clotted cream.
- Fruit:
  - fresh fruit purée
  - jams
  - fruit mousses
  - preserves
  - fruit gels.
- Pastes and spreads:
  - chocolate
  - praline
  - nut
  - curds.

Spreading and coating

This is where smaller cakes and gâteaux are covered top and sides with any of the following:
- fresh whipped cream
- fondant
- chocolate
- royal icing
- buttercream
- water icing
- meringue (French, Italian or Swiss)
- commercially manufactured preparations.

Piping

Piping is a skill that takes practice. There are many different types of piping bag and tube available. The following may be used for piping:

- royal icing
- meringue
- chocolate
- boiled sugar
- fondant
- fresh cream.

Dusting, dredging and sprinkling

These techniques are used to give products a final design or glaze during cooking, using sugar. Light dusting is usually performed with icing sugar or Neige Décor, an icing sugar product resistant to humidity but used in the same way, using a very fine sieve.

- **Dusting:** a light dusting, giving an even finish.
- **Dredging:** heavier dusting with sugar.
- **Sprinkling:** a very light sprinkle of sugar.

Caster or granulated white sugar, demerara, Barbados or dark brown sugar can also be used, particularly if the product is returned to the oven for glazing, or glazed under the salamander or using a blow torch.

Other decorative media

Remember that decorating is an art form and there is a range of equipment and materials available to assist you in this work. Some examples of decorative media are as follows.

- Glacé and crystallised fruits:
  - cherries
  - lemons
  - oranges
  - pineapple
  - figs.
- Crystallised flowers:
  - rose petals
  - violets
  - mimosa
  - lilac.
- Crystallised stems such as angelica.
- Nuts:
  - almonds (nibbed, flaked)
  - coconut (fresh slices, desiccated)
  - hazelnuts
  - brazil nuts
  - pistachio.
- Chocolate:
  - rolls
  - vermicelli
  - lakes
  - piping chocolate
  - chips.

Piped biscuit pastes

Piped biscuits can be used for decoration. For example:

- piped sablé paste (recipe 158)
- cats' tongues (recipe 155)
- almond biscuits (recipe 159).

1 Short paste
(pâte à foncer)

flour making pastry

energy	kcal	fat	sat fat	carb	sugar	protein	fibre	*
6269 kJ	1493 kcal	92.6 g	38.0 g	155.5 g	3.1 g	18.9 g	7.2 g	

Short paste (recipe 1), rough puff paste (recipe 4) and sugar paste (recipe 2)

Portions ⟩	5–8	10–16
flour (soft)	200 g	500 g
salt	pinch	large pinch
lard or vegetable fat	50 g	125 g
butter or margarine	50 g	125 g
water	2–3 tbsp	5–8 tbsp

1 Sieve the flour and salt.
2 Cut the fat into small pieces. Rub it in to the flour to achieve a sandy texture.
3 Make a well in the centre.
4 Add sufficient water to make a fairly firm paste.
5 Handle as little and as lightly as possible.

> **Key point**
> The amount of water used varies according to:
> - the type of flour (a very fine soft flour is more absorbent)
> - the degree of heat (e.g. prolonged contact with hot hands, and warm weather conditions).

Try something different
- For wholemeal short pastry use half to three-quarters wholemeal flour in place of white flour.
- Short pastry is used in fruit pies, Cornish pasties, etc.
- Short pastry for sweet dishes such as baked jam roll may be made with self-raising flour.

* Using ½ lard, ½ hard margarine (5–8 portions)

Possible reasons for faults in short pastry
- Hard:
  - too much water
  - too little fat
  - fat rubbed in insufficiently
  - too much handling and rolling
  - over-baking.
- Soft-crumbly:
  - too little water
  - too much fat.
- Blistered:
  - too little water
  - water added unevenly
  - fat not rubbed in evenly.
- Soggy:
  - too much water
  - too cool an oven
  - baked for insufficient time.
- Shrunken:
  - too much handling and rolling
  - pastry stretched whilst handling.

Making short pastry
http://bit.ly/zZFyPn

2 | Sugar paste
(pâte à sucre)

energy	kcal	fat	sat fat	carb	sugar	protein	fibre	*
7864 kJ	1872 kcal	109.8 g	46.4 g	208.0 g	55.6 g	25.7 g	7.2 g	

Portions ❯	5–8	10–16
sugar	50 g	125 g
butter	125 g	300 g
egg	1	2–3
flour (soft)	200 g	500 g
salt	pinch	large pinch

Method 1 – traditional French sugar paste (creaming)

1 Taking care not to over-soften, cream the butter and sugar.
2 Add the egg, and mix for a few seconds.
3 Gradually incorporate the sieved flour and salt. Mix lightly until smooth.
4 Allow to rest in a cool place before using.

Measure out the sugar and cut the butter into small chunks

Cream the butter and sugar together

Add the egg

Incorporate the flour and salt

Press into a tray and leave to chill

The paste will need to be rolled out before use in any recipe

Method 2 – sweet lining paste (rubbing in)

1 Sieve the flour and salt. Lightly rub in the butter to achieve a sandy texture.
2 Make a well in the centre. Add the sugar and beaten egg.
3 Mix the sugar and egg until dissolved.
4 Gradually incorporate the flour and butter, and lightly mix to a smooth paste. Allow to rest before using.

Sugar pastry is used for flans, fruit tartlets, and so on.
50 per cent, 70 per cent or 100 per cent wholemeal flour may be used; the butter may be reduced from 125 to 100 g.

* 5–8 portions using hard margarine

3 Puff paste
(feuilletage)

Portions 〉	5–8	10–16
flour (strong)	200 g	500 g
salt		
pastry margarine or butter	200 g	500 g
water, ice-cold	125 ml	300 ml
lemon juice or ascorbic or tartaric acid	a few drops	a few drops

1 Sieve the flour and salt
2 Rub in one-quarter of the butter or margarine.
3 Make a well in the centre.
4 Add the water and lemon juice or acid (to make the gluten more elastic), and knead well into a smooth dough in the shape of a ball.
5 Relax the dough in a cool place for 30 minutes.
6 Cut a cross halfway through the dough and pull out the corners to form a star shape.
7 Roll out the points of the star square, leaving the centre thick.

8 Knead the remaining butter or margarine to the same texture as the dough. This is most important; if the fat is too soft it will melt and ooze out, if too hard it will break through the paste when being rolled.
9 Place the butter or margarine on the centre square, which is four times thicker than the flaps.
10 Fold over the flaps.
11 Roll out to 30 cm × 15 cm, cover with a cloth or plastic and rest for 5–10 minutes in a cool place.
12 Roll out to 60 cm × 20 cm, fold both the ends to the centre, fold in half again to form a square. This is one double turn.
13 Allow to rest in a cool place for 20 minutes.
14 Half-turn the paste to the right or the left.
15 Give one more double turn; allow to rest for 20 minutes.
16 Give two more double turns, allowing to rest between each.
17 Allow to rest before using.

Rub one-quarter of the butter into the flour

Mix in the water and lemon juice

Knead into a smooth dough

Roll the dough out into a cross shape

Knead the remaining butter in a plastic bag, then place it on the centre of the dough

Fold over each flap

The folded dough forms a parcel

Roll out in a rectangle, then fold the ends to the middle

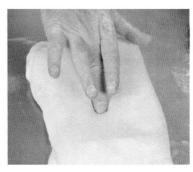

When resting the turned and folded dough, leave a finger mark to show the number of turns completed

---

Key point

Care must be taken when rolling out the paste to keep the ends and sides square.

The lightness of the puff pastry is mainly due to the air that is trapped when folding the pastry during preparation. The addition of lemon juice (acid) is to strengthen the gluten in the flour, thus helping to make a stronger dough so that there is less likelihood of the fat oozing out; 3 g (7.5 g for 10 portions) ascorbic or tartaric acid may be used in place of lemon juice.

The rise is caused by the fat separating layers of paste and air during rolling. When heat is applied by the oven, steam is produced causing the layers to rise and give the characteristic flaky formation.

4 Rough puff paste

flour making pastry

energy	kcal	fat	sat fat	carb	sugar	protein	fibre	*
7464 kJ	1777 kcal	124.3 g	53.2 g	150.8 g	3.0 g	23.2 g	0.0g	

Portions ›	5–8	10–16
flour (strong)	200 g	500 g
salt		
butter or pastry margarine	150 g	375 g
water, ice-cold	125 ml	300 ml
lemon juice, ascorbic or tartaric acid	squeeze	large squeeze

Each time you leave the paste to rest, gently make finger indentations, one for each turn you have given the paste. This will help you to keep track.

1 Sieve the flour and salt (50 per cent wholemeal flour may be used).
2 Cut the fat into 10 g pieces and lightly mix them into the flour without rubbing in.
3 Make a well in the centre.
4 Add the liquid and mix to a fairly stiff dough.
5 Turn on to a floured table and roll into an oblong strip, about 30 cm × 10 cm, keeping the sides square.
6 Give one double turn as for puff pastry.
7 Allow to rest in a cool place, covered with cloth or plastic for 30 minutes.
8 Give three more double turns, resting between each. Allow to rest before using.

Make a well in the centre of the flour and butter, and add the liquid

Mix to a fairly stiff dough

Roll out and fold the ends to the middle

Keep rolling, folding and turning

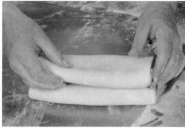

The finished paste, ready to rest and then use

Making rough puff pastry
http://bit.ly/yZjB8u

* Using hard margarine (5–8 portions)

5 Choux paste
(pâte à choux)

flour boiling, making pastry

energy	kcal	fat	sat fat	carb	sugar	protein	fibre
6248 kJ	1488 kcal	106.6 g	43.3 g	99.3 g	4.1 g	38.9 g	4.5 g *

Portions ⟩	5–8	10–16
water	250 ml	625 ml
sugar	pinch	large pinch
salt	pinch	large pinch
butter, margarine or oil	100 g	250 g
flour (strong)	125 g	300 g
eggs	4	10

1 Bring the water, sugar, salt and fat to the boil in a saucepan. Remove from heat.
2 Add the sieved flour and mix in with a kitchen spoon (50 per cent, 70 per cent or 100 per cent wholemeal flour may be used).
3 Return to a moderate heat and stir continuously until the mixture leaves the sides of the pan.
4 Remove from the heat and allow to cool.
5 Gradually add the beaten eggs, beating well. Do not add all the eggs at once – check the consistency as you go. The mixture may not take all the egg. It should just flow back when moved in one direction.

Possible reasons for faults in choux paste

- Greasy and heavy:
  - basic mixture over-cooked.
- Soft, not aerated:
  - flour insufficiently cooked
  - eggs insufficiently beaten in the mixture
  - oven too cool
  - under-baked.

Making choux pastry
http://bit.ly/ArP7MJ

Choux paste is used for éclairs, cream buns and profiteroles.

Cut the butter into cubes and then melt them

Add the flour

When the mixture is ready, it will start to come away from the sides

Add egg until the mixture is the right consistency: it should drop from a spoon under its own weight

Pipe the paste into the shape required: these rings can be used for Paris-Brest (recipe 110)

A selection of shapes in raw choux paste

* Using hard margarine (5–8 portions)

6 Suet paste

flour making pastry

energy	kcal	fat	sat fat	carb	sugar	protein	fibre	*
6402 kJ	1524 kcal	89.3 g	40.6 g	171.3 g	3.0 g	19.3 g	7.2 g	

Portions >	5–8	10
flour (soft) or self-raising flour	200 g	500 g
baking powder	10 g	25 g
salt	pinch	large pinch
prepared beef or vegetarian suet	100 g	250 g
water	125 ml	300 ml

1 Sieve the flour, baking powder and salt.
2 Mix in the suet. Make a well. Add the water.
3 Mix lightly to a fairly stiff paste.

Suet paste is used for steamed fruit puddings, steamed jam rolls, steamed meat puddings and dumplings. Vegetarian suet is also available.

Possible reasons for faults in suet paste

● If the paste is heavy and soggy, it may be that the cooking temperature was too low.
● If the paste is tough, it may have been handled too much or over-cooked.

* 5–8 portions

7 Chantilly cream

cream

Makes approx. >	500 ml
whipping cream	500 ml
caster sugar	100 g
vanilla arome	a few drops

1 Place all ingredients in a bowl. Whisk over ice until the mixture will form soft peaks. If using a mechanical mixer, stand and watch until the mixture is ready – do not leave it unattended.
2 Cover and place in the fridge immediately.

8 Pastry cream
(crème pâtissière)

cream boiling

Pastry cream, *crème diplomat* and *crème chiboust*

Makes approx. ❯	1 litre
milk	1 litre
vanilla pod (can be replaced with a few drops of vanilla arome)	1
eggs	4
caster sugar	200 g
flour (strong)	100 g
custard powder	30 g

Try something different

- *Crème chiboust:* when the pastry cream mixture has cooled slightly, fold in an equal quantity of Italian meringue (recipe 13).
- *Crème diplomat*: when the pastry cream is chilled, fold in an equal quantity of whipped double cream.
- Additional flavourings can also be added to pastry cream, *crème chiboust* or *crème diplomat*.

1 Split open the vanilla pod and scrape out the seeds. Place pod and seeds in a heavy stainless steel pan, add the milk and place on the heat.

2 Whisk the eggs and sugar together.

3 Sieve the flour and custard powder onto paper and then add to the eggs. Whisk them all together to form a liaison.

4 When the milk has boiled, pour about one-third into the egg mixture and whisk in.

5 Bring the rest of the milk back to the boil, then pour in the liaison. Whisk hard until the mixture comes back to the boil again.

6 Simmer gently for 5 minutes.

7 Pour into a sterilised tray and stand on a wire rack. Stir occasionally to help the mixture cool quickly.

8 When cold, store in a plastic container in the fridge. Use within 3 days.

9 Buttercream

Makes ❯	350 g
icing sugar	150 g
butter	200 g

1 Sieve the icing sugar.
2 Cream the butter and icing sugar until light and creamy.
3 Flavour and colour as required.

Try something different
Variations include:
- **rum buttercream:** add rum to flavour and blend in
- **chocolate buttercream:** add melted chocolate, sweetened or unsweetened according to taste.

10 Boiled buttercream

eggs boiling

Makes ❯	750 ml
eggs	2
icing sugar	50 g
granulated sugar or cube sugar	300 g
water	100 g
glucose	50 g
unsalted butter	400 g

1 Beat the eggs and icing sugar until at ribbon stage (sponge).
2 Boil the granulated or cube sugar with water and glucose to 118°C.
3 Gradually add the sugar at 118°C to the eggs and icing sugar at ribbon stage, whisk continuously and allow to cool to 26°C.
4 Gradually add the unsalted butter while continuing to whisk until a smooth cream is obtained.

Try something different
Buttercream may be flavoured with numerous flavours and combinations of flavours:
- chocolate and rum
- whisky and orange
- strawberry and vanilla
- lemon and lime
- apricot and passionfruit
- brandy and praline
- coffee and hazelnut.

Whisk the eggs

Add the boiling sugar and water

Add the butter

11 # Frangipane
(almond cream)

nuts

Makes >	300 g
butter	100 g
caster sugar	100 g
eggs	2
ground almonds	100 g
flour	10 g

1 Cream the butter and sugar.
2 Gradually beat in the eggs.
3 Mix in the almonds and flour (mix lightly).
4 Use as required.

Cut the butter into small pieces and add to the sugar

Cream the butter and sugar together

Beat in the eggs (before adding the flour)

12 Ganache

	Makes ›	750 g
Version 1		
double cream		300 ml
couverture, cut into small pieces		350 g
unsalted butter		85 g
spirit or liqueur		20 ml
	Makes ›	1 kg
Version 2		
double cream		300 ml
vanilla pod		½
couverture, cut into small pieces		600 g
unsalted butter		120 g

1 Boil the cream (and the vanilla for version 2) in a heavy saucepan.
2 Pour the cream over the couverture. Whisk with a fine whisk until the chocolate has melted.
3 Whisk in the butter (and the liqueur for version 1).
4 Stir over ice until the mixture has the required consistency.

13 Italian meringue

Makes ›	250 g	625 g
granulated or cube sugar	200 g	500 g
water	60 ml	140 ml
cream of tartar	pinch	large pinch
egg whites	4	10

1 Boil the sugar, water and cream of tartar to hard-ball stage 121°C.
2 Beat the egg whites to full peak and, while stiff, beating slowly, pour on the boiling sugar. Use as required.

Making Italian meringue
http://bit.ly/AE5Ug9

Boil the sugar

Combine with the beaten egg whites

The mixture will stand up in stiff peaks when it is ready

---

14 Apple purée
(marmalade de pomme)

fruit

Makes ⟩	400 g	1 kg
cooking apples	400 g	1 kg
butter	10 g	25 g
sugar	50 g	125 g

1 Peel, core and slice the apples.
2 Place the butter in a thick-bottomed pan; heat until melted.
3 Add the apples and sugar, cover with a lid and cook gently until soft.
4 Drain off any excess liquid and pass through a sieve or liquidise.

---

15 Stock syrup

sugar boiling

Makes ⟩	500 ml	1.25 litres
water	500 ml	1.25 litres
granulated sugar	150 g	375 g
glucose	50 g	125 g

1 Boil the water, sugar and glucose together.
2 Strain and cool.

Glucose helps to prevent crystallising.

16 Sabayon sauce

(sauce sabayon)

eggs

energy	kcal	fat	sat fat	carb	sugar	protein	fibre
454 kJ	108 kcal	3.4 g	1.0 g	13.3 g	13.3 g	1.8 g	0.0 g	*

Portions ›	8
egg yolks, pasteurised	4–6
caster or unrefined sugar	100 g
dry white wine	250 ml

1 Whisk the egg yolks and sugar in a 1-litre pan or basin until white.
2 Dilute with the wine.
3 Place the pan or basin in a bain-marie of boiling water.
4 Whisk the mixture continuously until it increases to four times its bulk and is firm and frothy.

* Using 5 egg yolks

Sauce sabayon may be offered as an accompaniment to any suitable hot sweet (e.g. soufflé pudding or soufflés).

Try something different

A *sauce sabayon* may also be made using milk in place of wine, which can be flavoured according to taste (e.g. vanilla, nutmeg, cinnamon).

17 Fresh egg custard sauce

(sauce à l'anglaise)

eggs   boiling

energy	kcal	fat	sat fat	carb	sugar	protein	fibre
1666 kJ	397 kcal	21.7 g	9.9 g	38.0 g	38.0 g	14.7 g	0.0 g	*

Portions ›	4	10
egg yolks, pasteurised	2	5
caster or unrefined sugar	25 g	60 g
vanilla essence or vanilla pod	2–3 drops	5–7 drops
milk, whole or skimmed, boiled	250 ml	625 ml

1 Mix the yolks, sugar and essence in a basin.
2 Whisk on the boiled milk and return to a thick-bottomed pan.
3 Place on a low heat and stir with a wooden spoon until it coats the back of the spoon. Do not allow to boil or the eggs will scramble.
4 Put through a fine sieve into a bowl. Set on ice to arrest the cooking.

If using skimmed milk, double the number of egg yolks in order to achieve the right consistency.

Try something different

Other flavours may be used in place of vanilla. For example:

- coffee
- curaçao
- chocolate
- Cointreau
- rum
- Tia Maria
- brandy
- whisky
- ground cinnamon
- kirsch
- orange flower water.

* Using whole milk; four portions

Making egg custard sauce
http://bit.ly/Ap8pHF

Practical Cookery 12th edition

18 Custard sauce

milk  boiling

energy	kcal	fat	sat fat	carb	sugar	protein	fibre	*
1245 kJ	296 kcal	9.6 g	6.0 g	47.2 g	38.0 g	8.3 g	0.3 g	

Portions ›	4	10
custard powder	10 g	25 g
milk, whole or semi-skimmed	250 ml	600 ml
caster or unrefined sugar	25 g	65 g

1 Dilute the custard powder with a little of the milk.
2 Boil the remainder of the milk.
3 Pour a little of the boiled milk on to the diluted custard powder.
4 Return to the saucepan.
5 Stir to the boil and mix in the sugar.

* Using whole milk

19 Fruit coulis

fruit  boiling

Makes ›	1 litre
fruit purée	1 litre
caster sugar	500 g

1 Warm the purée.
2 Boil the sugar with a little water to soft-ball stage (121°C).
3 Pour the soft-ball sugar into the warm fruit purée while whisking vigorously.
4 This will then be ready to store or serve with a variety of cold desserts.

The reason the soft-ball stage needs to be achieved when the sugar is mixed with the purée is that this stabilises the fruit and prevents separation once the coulis has been put onto the plate.

Apricot coulis

20 Apricot sauce
(sauce abricot)

boiling

energy	kcal	fat	sat fat	carb	sugar	protein	fibre
595 kJ	139 kcal	0.0 g	0.0 g	37.0 g	34.7 g	0.2 g	0.0 g

Portions ⟩	4	10
apricot jam	200 g	500 g
water	100 ml	220 ml
lemon juice	2–3 drops	½ tsp
cornflour	10 g	25 g

1 Boil the jam, water and lemon juice together.
2 Adjust the consistency with a little cornflour (or arrowroot) diluted with water.
3 Reboil until clear and pass through a conical strainer.

21 Strawberry sauce

fruit

energy	kcal	fat	sat fat	carb	sugar	protein	fibre
350 kJ	83 kcal	0.0 g	0.0 g	16.5 g	16.5 g	0.3 g	0.4 g

Portions ⟩	4	10
strawberry purée	200 g	500 g
water	60 ml	150 ml
caster sugar	50 g	125 g

1 Mix all the ingredients together and strain.

Alternative fruit purées that can be used are peach, apricot, mango, pawpaw, strawberry and raspberry. For peach sauce, for example, proceed as for strawberry sauce, substituting peach purée for strawberry purée.

22 Melba sauce
(sauce Melba)

boiling

energy	kcal	fat	sat fat	carb	sugar	protein	fibre
558 kJ	131 kcal	0.0 g	0.0 g	34.7 g	34.7 g	0.2 g	0.0 g

Portions ⟩	4	10
raspberry jam	200 g	500 g
water	125 ml	300 ml

1 Boil ingredients together and pass through a conical strainer.

Raspberry coulis (see recipe 19) can also be used as Melba sauce.

23 Orange, lemon or lime sauce

fruit boiling

energy	kcal	fat	sat fat	carb	sugar	protein	fibre *
306 kJ	72 kcal	0.1 g	0.0 g	18.5 g	16.2 g	0.4 g	0.6 g

Portions ›	4	10
sugar, caster or unrefined	50 g	125 g
water	250 ml	750 ml
cornflour or arrowroot	10 g	25 g
oranges, lemons or limes	1–2	4–5

1 Boil the sugar and water.
2 Add the cornflour (or arrowroot) diluted with water, stirring continuously.
3 Reboil until clear, strain.
4 Add blanched julienne of orange zest and the strained orange juice.

A little curaçao or Cointreau may be added for additional flavour.

* Using oranges and cornflour

24 Chocolate sauce
(sauce chocolat)

cream, chocolate boiling

Method 1

Portions ›	4	10
double cream	150 ml	375 ml
butter	25 g	60 g
milk or plain chocolate pieces	180 g	420 g

1 Place butter and cream in a saucepan and gently bring to a simmer.
2 Add the chocolate and stir well until the chocolate has melted and the sauce is smooth.

Method 2

Portions ›	4	10
caster sugar	40 g	100 g
water	120 ml	220 ml
dark chocolate (75% cocoa solids)	160 g	300 g
unsalted butter	25 g	75 g
single cream	80 ml	200 ml

1 Dissolve the sugar in the water over a low heat.
2 Remove from the heat. Stir in the chocolate and butter.
3 When everything has melted, stir in the cream and gently bring to the boil.

Butterscotch sauce

cream boiling

Portions >	4	10
double cream	250 ml	625 ml
butter	62 g	155 g
Demerara sugar	100 g	250 g

1 Boil the cream, then whisk in the butter and sugar, and simmer for 3 minutes.

26 **Caramel sauce**

cream boiling

Portions >	8
caster sugar	100 g
water	80 ml
double cream	500 ml
egg yolks, lightly beaten (optional)	2

1 In a large saucepan, dissolve the sugar with the water over a low heat and bring to boiling point.

2 Wash down the inside of the pan with a pastry brush dipped in cold water to prevent crystals from forming.

3 Cook until the sugar turns to a deep amber colour. Immediately turn off the heat and whisk in the cream.

4 Set the pan back over a high heat and stir the sauce with the whisk. Let it bubble for 2 minutes, then turn off the heat.

5 You can now strain the sauce and use it when cooled, or, for a richer, smoother sauce, pour a little caramel onto the egg yolks, then return the mixture to the pan and heat to 80°C, taking care that it does not boil.

6 Pass the sauce through a conical strainer and keep in a cool place, stirring occasionally to prevent a skin from forming.

27 Syrup sauce

🍳 boiling

Portions ⟩	8
golden syrup	200 g
water	125 ml
grated zest and juice of lime or orange	1
cornflour or arrowroot	10 g

1 Bring the syrup, water and lemon juice to the boil and thicken with diluted cornflour (or arrowroot).

2 Boil for a few minutes and strain.

This is a traditional sauce served with the classic British golden syrup pudding. It is also used with steamed puddings or chilled and served over ice cream.

The sauce may be flavoured with white rum or whisky.

28 Rum or brandy cream or butter

butter, cream

To make rum/brandy cream, use whipped, sweetened cream and flavour it with rum or brandy.

To make rum/brandy butter, cream equal quantities of butter and sieved icing sugar together and add rum or brandy to taste.

29 Apricot glaze

🍳 boiling

Makes ⟩	150 ml
apricot jam	100 g
water	50 ml

1 Prepare by boiling apricot jam with a little water.

2 Pass through a strainer. Glaze should be used hot.

A flan jelly (commercial pectin glaze) may be used as an alternative to apricot glaze. This is usually a clear glaze to which food colour may be added.

30 Water icing, glacé icing

1 Take 400 g of icing sugar and start to add 60 ml (4 tbsp) of warm water; add the water until the icing is thick enough to coat the back of a spoon.
2 If necessary, add more water or icing sugar to adjust the consistency.

Try something different
Water may be replaced with other liquids to add flavour to the icing – for example, orange juice, mango juice, lemon juice, apple juice, lime juice, grape juice, passionfruit juice – or use a combination of juices with Cointreau, kirsch, Grand Marnier, rum, Calvados, etc.

31 Royal icing

Makes ›	400 g
icing sugar	400 g
whites of egg, pasteurised	3
lemon, juice of	1
glycerine	2 tsp

1 Mix well together in a basin the sieved icing sugar and the whites of egg, with a wooden spoon.
2 Add a few drops of lemon juice and glycerine and beat until stiff.

400g is enough to cover a small 18 cm cake.

Modern practice is to use egg white substitute or dried egg whites. Always follow the manufacturer's instructions for quantities.

32 Marzipan (almond paste)

nuts boiling

Makes ›	400 g
water	250 ml
caster sugar	1 kg
ground almonds	400 g
yolks	3
almond essence	2–3 drops

1 Place the water and sugar in a pan and boil. Skim as necessary.
2 When the sugar reaches 116°C, draw aside and mix in the ground almonds; then add the yolks and essence and mix in quickly to avoid scrambling.
3 Knead well until smooth.

400g is enough to cover a small 18 cm cake.

33 Praline

nuts baking

Makes >	875 g
flaked almonds, hazelnuts and pecans (any combination)	375 g
granulated sugar	500 g

1 Place the nuts on a baking sheet and toast until evenly coloured.

2 Place the sugar in a large, heavy stainless steel saucepan. Set the pan over a low heat and allow the sugar to caramelise. Do not over-stir, but do not allow the sugar to burn.

3 When the sugar is evenly coloured and reaches a temperature of 170°C, remove from the heat and stir in the nuts.

4 Immediately deposit the mixture on a silpat mat (non-stick baking mat). Place another mat over the top and roll as thin as possible.

5 Allow to go completely cold. Break up and store in an airtight container.

Toast the nuts

Place the sugar in a dry pan to make the caramel

Add the nuts to the caramelised sugar

Protect the praline with a sheet of paper while rolling it out

Roll as thin as possible

34 Pancakes with lemon or orange

(crêpes au citron ou à l'orange)

flour, eggs, fruit shallow frying

energy	kcal	fat	sat fat	carb	sugar	protein	fibre	*
1275 kJ	304 kcal	16.2 g	4.8 g	35.5 g	16.4 g	6.1 g	0.9 g	

Portions ›	4	10
flour, white or wholemeal	100 g	250 g
salt	pinch	large pinch
egg	1	2–3
milk, whole, semi-skimmed or skimmed	250 ml	625 ml
melted butter, margarine or oil	10 g	25 g
oil for frying		
sugar, caster or unrefined	50 g	125 g
lemon/orange quarters, to serve		

When making a batch of pancakes it is best to keep them all flat, one on top of the other, on a plate. Sprinkle sugar between each or place circles of silicone paper between the pancakes. Fold them all when ready for service, sprinkle again with sugar and dress neatly overlapping on a serving dish or hot plates.

1 Sieve the flour and salt into a bowl, make a well in the centre.
2 Add the egg and milk, gradually incorporating the flour from the sides, whisk to a smooth batter.
3 Mix in the melted butter.
4 Heat the pancake pan, clean thoroughly.
5 Add a little oil; heat until smoking.
6 Add enough mixture to just cover the bottom of the pan thinly.
7 Cook for a few seconds until lightly coloured.
8 Turn and cook on the other side. Turn on to a plate.
9 Sprinkle with sugar. Fold in half then in half again.
10 Garnish with quarters of lemon or orange free from pips. Serve very hot, two pancakes per portion.

* Using white flour, whole milk, hard margarine and peanut oil

35 Pancakes with apples
(crêpes normande)

flour, eggs, fruit shallow frying

energy	kcal	fat	sat fat	carb	sugar	protein	fibre
1178 KJ	280 kcal	8.2 g	2.9 g	47.7 g	28.7 g	6.6 g	2.8 g

Portions ›	4	10
cooked apple, thinly sliced	150 g	375 g
flour, white or wholemeal	100 g	250 g
salt	pinch	large pinch
egg	1	2–3
milk, whole, semi-skimmed or skimmed	250 ml	625 ml
melted butter, margarine or oil	10 g	25 g
oil for frying		
caster sugar to serve		

1 Place a little cooked apple in a pan, add the pancake mixture and cook on both sides.
2 Turn out, sprinkle with caster sugar and roll up or fold.

36 Baked apples
(pommes bonne femme)

fruit baking

energy	kcal	fat	sat fat	carb	sugar	protein	fibre	*
663 kJ	156 kcal	5.1 g	2.2 g	29.7 g	29.5 g	0.4 g	2.7 g	

Portions ›	4	10
cooking apples, medium-sized	4	10
sugar, white or unrefined	50 g	125 g
cloves	4	10
butter	20 g	50 g
water	60 ml	150 ml

1 Peel and core the apples and make an incision 2 mm deep round the centre of each.
2 Place in a roasting tray or ovenproof dish.
3 Fill the centre with sugar and add a clove to each.
4 Place 5 g butter on each. Add the water.
5 Bake in a moderate oven at 200–220°C for 15–20 minutes.
6 Turn the apples over carefully.
7 Return to the oven until cooked, about 40 minutes in all.
8 Serve with a little cooking liquor and custard, cream or ice cream.

* Using hard margarine

Cooking apples require careful temperature control. Some varieties will turn into purée very quickly. Check carefully at step 5: some apples, baked without the skin, may be fully cooked by this point – in this case, skip steps 6 and 7. To protect the peeled apple, wrap it in lightly oiled greaseproof paper or silicone before putting it in the oven.

Variations
Traditional baked apples are cooked with the skin on.
For stuffed baked apple, fill the centre with washed sultanas, raisins or chopped dates, or a combination of these.

Apple charlotte
(charlotte aux pommes)

fruit baking

energy	kcal	fat	sat fat	carb	sugar	protein	fibre	*
2163 kJ	515 kcal	22.3 g	9.3 g	74.5 g	23.4 g	9.4 g	6.1 g	

Portions >	4	10
stale bread	400 g	1.25 kg
butter	100 g	250 g
cooking apples	400 g	1.25 kg
sugar, caster or unrefined	50–75 g	125–150 g
breadcrumbs or cake crumbs	35 g	85 g

1 Use either one charlotte mould or four dariole moulds.
2 Cut the bread into 3 mm slices and remove the crusts.
3 Cut a round the size of the mould bottom, dip into melted butter on one side and place in the mould fat side down.
4 Cut fingers of bread 2–4 cm wide, and fit, overlapping well, to the sides of the mould after dipping each one in melted fat. Take care not to leave any gaps.

* Using hard margarine

5 Peel, core and wash the apples, cut into thick slices and three-parts cook in a little butter and sugar (a little cinnamon or a clove may be added), and add the breadcrumbs.
6 Fill the centre of the mould with the apple.
7 Cut round pieces of bread to seal the apple in.
8 Bake at 220°C for 30–40 minutes. Remove from the mould.
9 Suitable accompaniments are apricot (recipe 20) or custard (recipe 18) sauce. The apple charlotte shown here is served with ice cream and decorated with bubble sugar.

38 Apple fritters
(beignets aux pommes)

fruit deep frying

energy	kcal	fat	sat fat	carb	sugar	protein	fibre	*
1034 kJ	246 kcal	10.2 g	1.9 g	38.9 g	25.0 g	2.1 g	3.0 g	

Portions ⟩	4	10
cooking apples	400 g	1 kg
flour, as needed		
frying batter (page 212, method A, omitting the salt)	150 g	375 g
apricot sauce	125 ml	300 ml

1 Peel and core the apples and cut into 0.5 cm rings or into regular pieces.
2 Pass through flour, shake off the surplus.
3 Dip into the frying batter.
4 Lift out with the fingers, into fairly hot deep fat: 185°C.
5 Cook for about 5 minutes on each side.
6 Drain well on kitchen paper, dust with icing sugar and glaze under the salamander.
7 Serve with hot apricot sauce (recipe 20).

* Fried in peanut oil

Left to right: apple, fig and banana fritters

39 Banana fritters
(beignets aux bananes)

fruit deep frying

energy	kcal	fat	sat fat	carb	sugar	protein	fibre
1405 kJ	333 kcal	11.5 g	1.4 g	57.9 g	41.7 g	3.0 g	1.6 g

Portions ⟩	4	10
bananas, large	2	5
frying batter (page 212, method A, omitting the salt)	150 g	375 g
apricot sauce (recipe 20)	125 ml	300 ml

1 Peel and cut the bananas in half lengthwise, then in half across.
2 Cook and serve as for apple fritters (recipe 38).

Bananas may be dipped in hot pastry cream flavoured with rum, allowed to cool on an oiled tray, before passing through flour and dipping in the frying batter.

40 Griottines clafoutis

fruit baking

energy	kcal	fat	sat fat	carb	sugar	protein	fibre
790 KJ	187 kcal	4.3 g	1.5 g	28.8 g	21.4 g	6.7 g	1.3 g

Portions ❯	4	10
griottines (cherries)	28 (approx.)	70 (approx.)
neige-decor or icing sugar		
For the batter		
eggs	2	5
caster sugar	40 g	100 g
milk	175 ml	450 ml
kirsch, from the griottines (optional)	1 tsp	3 tsp
flour	40 g	100 g

To make the batter

1 In a large bowl, beat the eggs and sugar together until well dissolved. Add the milk and kirsch.
2 Sieve in the flour, mix well, then strain the batter through a sieve and set aside.

To make the clafoutis

1 Place the griottines liberally into flat dishes (sur le plat dishes, approx. 10 cm). Cover with the batter.
2 Bake at 200°C for approx. 15 minutes, until the batter has risen and set.
3 Serve warm, dusted with neige-decor.

41 Rice pudding

rice, milk  boiling

energy	kcal	fat	sat fat	carb	sugar	protein	fibre
644 KJ	153 kcal	2.7 g	1.7 g	28.6 g	18.7 g	5.2 g	0.0 g

Portions ❯	4	10
rice, short or whole grain	50 g	125 g
sugar, caster or unrefined	50 g	125 g
milk, whole, semi-skimmed or skimmed	0.5 litres	1.25 litres
butter or margarine	10 g	25 g
vanilla essence	2–3 drops	6–8 drops
grated nutmeg		

1 Boil the milk in a thick-based pan.
2 Add the washed rice, stir to the boil.
3 Simmer gently, stirring frequently until the rice is cooked, tender and has absorbed most of the liquid. Whole grain rice will take longer than white rice.
4 Mix in the sugar, flavouring and butter (at this stage an egg yolk may also be added). A vanilla pod can be used in place of essence.
5 Pour into a pie dish or individual dishes. Serve with diced poached apple and reduced syrup.

Candied fruit and chopped nuts may be added for variety.

rice, milk baking

energy	kcal	fat	sat fat	carb	sugar	protein	fibre
1006 kJ	239 kcal	7.0 g	3.9 g	40.7 g	19.0 g	5.8 g	0.6 g

Portions ❭	4	10
rice, short or whole grain	50 g	125 g
sugar, caster or unrefined	50 g	125 g
milk, whole, semi-skimmed or skimmed	0.5 litres	1.25 litres
butter or margarine	10 g	25 g
vanilla essence	2–3 drops	6–8 drops
grated nutmeg		

* Using whole milk and hard margarine

1 Wash the rice, place in a pie dish or individual dishes.
2 Add the sugar and milk, mix well.
3 Add the butter, essence and nutmeg.
4 Place on a baking sheet; clean the rim of the pie dish.
5 Bake at 180–200°C, until the milk starts simmering.
6 Reduce the heat and allow the pudding to cook slowly, allowing 1½–2 hours in all (less time for individual dishes).

The pudding may be garnished with nuts, as shown.

43 Bread and butter pudding

eggs baking

energy	kcal	fat	sat fat	carb	sugar	protein	fibre	*
1093 kJ	260 kcal	11.6 g	5.9 g	30.4 g	23.4 g	10.6 g	1.0 g	

Portions >	4	10
sultanas	50 g	100 g
slices of white or wholemeal bread, spread with butter or margarine	2	5
eggs	3	7
sugar, caster or unrefined	50 g	125 g
vanilla essence or a vanilla pod	2–3 drops	5 drops
milk, whole, semi-skimmed or skimmed	0.5 litres	1.25 litres

1 Wash the sultanas and place in a pie dish or individual dishes.
2 Remove the crusts from the bread and cut each slice into four triangles; neatly arrange overlapping in the pie dish.
3 Prepare an egg custard: whisk the eggs, sugar and vanilla essence together. Warm the milk and pour it on to the eggs, whisking continuously.
4 Pass through a fine strainer on to the bread, dust lightly with sugar.
5 Stand in a roasting tray half full of water and cook slowly in a moderate oven at 160°C for 45 minutes to 1 hour.
6 Clean the edges of the pie dish and serve.

Making bread and butter pudding
http://bit.ly/x01Z8F

- For a crisp crust finish, sprinkle with icing sugar and brown well under the salamander.
- Traditional bread and butter pudding is made in a pie dish and is of soft consistency. To prepare individual plated portions in the contemporary fashion (served outside the pie dish) requires either more egg or bread, which gives a firmer consistency.

Healthy eating tips
- Try using half wholemeal and half white bread.
- Adding more dried fruit would reduce the need for so much sugar.

Try something different
- Before cooking, add either freshly grated nutmeg or orange zest, or a combination of both
- Use fruit loaf, brioche or panettone in place of bread
- Chocolate bread and butter pudding – add 25 g chocolate powder to the egg custard mix
- Add soft, well-drained poached (or tinned) fruit (e.g. peaches, pears) to the bottom of the dish.

* Using white bread and butter

44 Sticky toffee pudding

 boiling, baking

energy	kcal	fat	sat fat	carb	sugar	protein	fibre
4104 kJ	980 kcal	60.4 g	36.7 g	106.7 g	78.9 g	9.1 g	1.8 g

Portions ❭	4	10
Medjool dates, stoned and chopped	150 g	375 g
water	250 ml	625 ml
bicarbonate of soda	1 tsp	2½ tsp
unsalted butter	50 g	125 g
caster sugar	150 g	375 g
eggs	2	5
self-raising flour	150 g	375 g
vanilla essence	1 tsp	2½ tsp

1 For 4 portions, grease a baking tin approx. 28 cm × 18 cm in size (32 cm × 22 cm for 10 portions). (The alternative approach is to use individual pudding or dariole moulds.)

2 Boil the dates in the water for approx. 5 minutes until soft, then add the bicarbonate of soda.

3 Cream the butter and sugar together until combined, gradually beat in the eggs.

4 Mix in the dates, flour and vanilla essence, stir well.

5 Form into the greased baking tin and bake in a pre-heated oven 180°C for approx. 30–40 minutes, until firm to the touch.

6 Carefully portion the sponge (or remove from the individual moulds).

45 Cabinet pudding
(pouding cabinet)

baking

Portions >	4	10
plain sponge cake	100 g	250 g
zest of unwaxed lemons, grated	1	2
currants and sultanas	25 g	60 g
milk, whole or skimmed	0.5 litres	1.25 litres
eggs	3–4	8–10
caster or unrefined sugar	50 g	125 g
vanilla essence or a vanilla pod	2–3 drops (1 pod)	7 drops (2 pods)

Try something different
Diplomat pudding is made as for cabinet pudding, but served cold with either redcurrant, raspberry, apricot or vanilla sauce.

1 Cut the cake into 0.5 cm dice.
2 Mix with the lemon zest and fruits (which can be soaked in rum).
3 Place in a greased, sugared charlotte mould or 4 dariole moulds. Do not fill more than halfway.
4 Warm the milk and whisk on to the eggs, sugar and essence (or vanilla pod).
5 Strain into a jug, then pour into the moulds.
6 Place in a roasting tin, half full of water; allow to stand for 5–10 minutes.
7 Cook in a moderate oven at 150–160°C for 30–45 minutes.
8 Leave to set for a few minutes before turning out.
9 Serve a fresh egg custard (recipe 17) or hot apricot sauce (recipe 20) separately.

Soufflé pudding
(pouding soufflé)

eggs boiling, baking

energy	kcal	fat	sat fat	carb	sugar	protein	fibre	*
510 kJ	122 kcal	7.6 g	3.2 g	5.9 g	4.8 g	0.2 g	0.0 g	

Portions ⟩	6	10
milk, whole or skimmed	185 ml	375 ml
flour, white or wholemeal	25 g	50 g
butter or margarine	25 g	50 g
caster or unrefined sugar	25 g	50 g
eggs, separated	3	6

Orange or lemon soufflé pudding is made by flavouring the basic mixture with the grated zest of an orange or lemon and a little appropriate sauce. Use the juice in the accompanying sauce.

* Using white flour and hard margarine

1 Boil the milk in a sauteuse.
2 Combine the flour, butter and sugar.
3 Whisk into the milk and reboil.
4 Remove from heat, add the egg yolks one at a time, whisking continuously.
5 Stiffly beat the whites and carefully fold into the mixture.
6 Three-quarters fill buttered and sugared dariole moulds.
7 Place in a roasting tin, half full of water.
8 Bring to the boil and place in a hot oven at 230–250°C for 12–15 minutes.
9 Turn out on to a flat dish and serve with a suitable hot sauce, such as custard or sabayon sauce.

47 Chocolate fondant

energy	kcal	fat	sat fat	carb	sugar	protein	fibre
2830 kJ	675 kcal	46.8 g	29.6 g	55.9 g	40.9 g	11 g	0.6 g

Portions ❯	4	10
couverture chocolate	150 g	375 g
unsalted butter	125 g	312 g
eggs	3	7
yolks	2	5
caster sugar	75 g	182 g
flour	75 g	182 g
white chocolate pieces (optional)		

1 Lightly grease and flour individual dariole moulds or a ring mould.
2 Carefully melt the chocolate and butter in a suitable bowl, either in a microwave or over a pan of hot water (bain-marie).
3 In a separate bowl, whisk the eggs, egg yolks and caster sugar until aerated to ribbon stage. Pour into the chocolate and butter mix, then whisk together.
4 Add the flour, then mix until smooth.
5 Pour into the moulds. Place white chocolate pieces at the centre to give a two-tone effect. Bake in the oven at 200°C for 8 minutes.
6 Remove from the oven, leave for 2 minutes before turning out onto suitable plates.
7 Serve with a suitable ice cream (e.g. vanilla, pistachio, almond or Baileys).

Melt the chocolate and butter in small pieces

Fold the melted chocolate into the egg mixture

Add the dry ingredients

To make the centre, add white chocolate pieces on a base of the chocolate mixture

Pipe in more of the chocolate mixture until the mould is full

48 Apple crumble tartlets

Portions ›	4	10
sweet paste (recipe 2)	175 g	435 g
eating apples, e.g. Reinette or Granny Smith, cored and thinly sliced	2	5
For the filling		
soured cream	200 ml	500 ml
caster sugar	25 g	62 g
plain flour	30 g	75 g
egg	1	3
vanilla extract		
For the crumble		
unsalted butter, melted	25 g	62 g
plain flour	30 g	75 g
walnuts, chopped	25 g	62 g
brown sugar	25 g	62 g
ground cinnamon	a good pinch	
salt		
icing sugar, to garnish		

1 Line individual ramekins with sweet paste.
2 Fill each of the lined ramekins with the finely sliced apple. To make the filling, whisk the soured cream, caster sugar, flour and egg together. Pass through a fine sieve and flavour with vanilla extract.
3 Cover the apple with the filling mixture and bake at 190°C for 10 minutes.
4 To make the crumble topping, combine the walnuts, flour, brown sugar, cinnamon and a small pinch of salt. Mix with the melted butter to form a crumb.
5 Sprinkle the crumble on top of each ramekin and bake for a further 10 minutes.
6 Leave to cool slightly and then turn out onto individual plates.
7 Dust with icing sugar. Serve with warm crème anglaise. An alternative garnish would be fresh raspberries and raspberry coulis.

49 Tatin of apple
(tarte tatin)

fruit, pastry 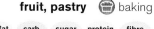 baking

energy	kcal	fat	sat fat	carb	sugar	protein	fibre
1299 KJ	308 kcal	12.6 g	7.2 g	50.2 g	43.6 g	1.8 g	5.2 g

Portions ⟩	10
caster sugar	200 g
glucose	10 g
water	100 ml
unsalted butter, diced	100 g
Granny Smith's apples, peeled and cored	7
lemon, juice of	½
puff pastry (recipe 3)	175 g

Individual tatin of apple (a modern presentation)

1 Cook the sugar, glucose and water in a thick-bottomed pan (bear in mind that the tatin will be cooked in this so it must be ovenproof) until it reaches a pale, amber colour, which is pre-caramel.
2 Remove from the heat and add the diced butter.
3 While the butter is melting, cut the apples into quarters, lightly sprinkle with lemon juice and place on top of the caramel/butter.
4 Place in the oven for 25 minutes until the apples are half-cooked and starting to caramelise.
5 Meanwhile, roll out the puff pastry, 3–4 mm thick, and slightly larger than the diameter of the pan.
6 Cover the apples with the pastry and bake for a further 15–20 minutes, until the pastry is golden.
7 Remove from the oven and leave to cool slightly before turning out.
8 Serve with vanilla ice cream or crème fraîche.

Cook the sugar, water and glucose to pre-caramel

Add the diced butter, and then the apple pieces

Lay the pastry over the top once the apples are half-cooked

Tuck in the edges

Turn out the tart carefully

This is a delicious dessert in which the taste of caramel is combined with the flavour of the fruit, finished with a crisp pastry base; it was the creation of the Tatin sisters in the nineteenth century. Having been made famous by the Tatin sisters, the dish was first served at Maxim's in Paris, as a house speciality. It is still served there to this day.

eggs, flour steaming

energy	kcal	fat	sat fat	carb	sugar	protein	fibre	*
1295 kJ	309 kcal	16.3 g	9.4 g	37.8 g	18.1 g	5.2 g	0.8 g	

Portions ⟩	6	12
butter or margarine	100 g	200 g
caster or soft brown sugar	100 g	200 g
eggs, beaten	2	4
flour, white or wholemeal	150 g	300 g
baking powder	10 g	20 g
milk	few drops	several drops

1 Cream the butter or margarine and sugar in a bowl until fluffy and almost white.
2 Gradually add the beaten eggs, mixing vigorously.
3 Sieve the flour and baking powder.
4 Gradually incorporate into the mixture as lightly as possible, keeping to a dropping consistency by the addition of the milk.
5 Place in a greased pudding basin or individual moulds (45 minutes' cooking time).
6 Cover securely with greased greaseproof paper, silicone or aluminium foil. Steam for 1–1½ hours.

Try something different

Variations include the following (double the quantities for 12 portions).

- **Vanilla sponge pudding** (shown here): add a few drops of vanilla essence to the basic mixture and serve with a vanilla-flavoured sauce.
- **Chocolate sponge pudding:** add 25 g chocolate or cocoa powder in place of 25 g flour (that is 125 g flour, 25 g chocolate to basic recipe); serve with a chocolate sauce (recipe 24).
- **Lemon sponge pudding:** add the grated zest of one or two lemons, and a few drops of lemon essence to basic recipe; serve with a lemon (recipe 23) or vanilla sauce.
- **Orange sponge pudding:** proceed as for lemon pudding, but using oranges in place of lemons; serve with an orange (recipe 23) or vanilla sauce.
- **Cherry sponge pudding:** add 100 g chopped or quartered glacé cherries to basic recipe; serve with a custard (recipe 18) or almond sauce.
- **Sultana/currant/raisin sponge pudding:** add 100 g of washed, well-dried fruit to basic recipe; serve with custard sauce (recipe 18).

* Using butter

51 Golden syrup pudding

eggs, flour steaming

energy	kcal	fat	sat fat	carb	sugar	protein	fibre
1315 kJ	313 kcal	13.0 g	5.9 g	47.8 g	26.6 g	4.3 g	0.9 g

Portions >	6	12
flour	150 g	300 g
salt	pinch	large pinch
baking powder	10 g	20 g
or self-raising flour *instead of the flour, salt and baking powder*	150 g	300 g
suet, chopped	75 g	150 g
caster or unrefined sugar	50 g	100 g
lemon, zest of	1	2
egg, beaten	1	2
milk, whole or skimmed	125 ml	250 ml
golden syrup	125 ml	250 ml

1 Sieve the flour, salt and baking powder (or replace the flour and baking powder with self-raising flour) into a bowl.
2 Mix the suet, sugar and zest.
3 Mix to a medium dough, with the beaten egg and milk.
4 Pour the syrup in a well-greased basin or individual moulds (1 hour cooking time). Place the pudding mixture on top.
5 Cover securely; steam for 1½ –2 hours.
6 Serve with a sauceboat of warm syrup containing the lemon juice, or with sauce anglaise or ice cream.

To make a **treacle pudding**, use a light treacle in place of the golden syrup.
Vegetarian suet is available.

eggs, flour, fruit steaming

energy	kcal	fat	sat fat	carb	sugar	protein	fibre
1930 KJ	453 kcal	15.0 g	6.4 g	71.7 g	56.3 g	5.8 g	2.0 g

	Portions ›	8–10 (1-litre basin)
sultanas		100 g
raisins		100 g
currants		100 g
mixed chopped candied peel		25 g
barley wine		70 ml
Guinness (stout)		70 ml
rum		2 tbsp
self-raising flour		50 g
mixed spice		1 tsp
ground nutmeg		¼ tsp
cinnamon		1 tsp
breadcrumbs, fresh, white or brown		100 g
suet, shredded		100 g
soft dark brown sugar		200 g
ground almonds		25 g
cooking apples, peeled and chopped		75 g
orange, grated zest of		½
lemon, grated zest of		½
eggs		2

1 Place all the dried fruit and candied peel in a mixing bowl; soak overnight with the barley wine, Guinness and rum.

2 Sift the flour with the mixed spice, nutmeg and cinnamon.

3 Add breadcrumbs, suet and sugar to the flour.

4 Drain the fruit from the alcohol. Add to the flour along with the almonds, apple and grated zest.

5 In a separate basin, beat the eggs with the alcohol.

6 Add the dried fruit to the flour, mix thoroughly.

7 Pack into a lightly greased basin (1 litre). Cover with a sheet of silicone and aluminium foil. Secure well.

8 Steam for 8 hours at normal atmospheric pressure.

9 Remove from steamer and allow to cool, remove foil and silicone, replace with fresh. Secure well.

10 Allow to mature for at least 2 months. Reheat by steaming for a further 2 hours.

11 Serve with rum and brandy sauce.

53 Steamed fruit puddings

fruit, pastry steaming

energy	kcal	fat	sat fat	carb	sugar	protein	fibre	*
967 kJ	230 kcal	7.4 g	3.4 g	41.5 g	27.1 g	1.9 g	3.0 g	

Portions ❯	6
suet paste (recipe 6)	200 g
fruit	0.75–1 kg
sugar	100 g
water	2 tbsp

Steamed fruit puddings can be made with apple, apple and blackberry, rhubarb, rhubarb and apple, and so on.

* Using apple

1 Grease a basin or individual moulds.
2 Line, using three-quarters of the paste.
3 Add prepared and washed fruit and the sugar. (Add 1–2 cloves in an apple pudding.)
4 Add water. Moisten the edge of the paste.
5 Cover with the remaining quarter of the pastry. Seal firmly.
6 Cover with greased greaseproof paper, a pudding cloth or foil.
7 Steam for about 1½ hours (large basin) or 40 minutes (individual moulds). Serve with custard.

54 Vanilla soufflé
(soufflé à la vanille)

milk, eggs boiling, baking

	energy 757 kJ	kcal 180 kcal	fat 9.1 g	sat fat 3.5 g	carb 16.6 g	sugar 14.6 g	protein 9.1 g	fibre 0.1 g

Portions >	4	10
butter	10 g	25 g
caster sugar, for soufflé mould	50 g	125 g
milk	125 ml	300 ml
natural vanilla or pod		
eggs, separated	4	10
flour	10 g	25 g
caster sugar	50 g	125 g
icing sugar, to serve		

1 Lightly coat the inside of a soufflé mould/dish with fresh butter.
2 Coat the butter in the soufflé mould with caster sugar as needed, tap out surplus.
3 Boil the milk and vanilla in a thick-bottomed pan.
4 Mix half the egg yolks, the flour and sugar to a smooth consistency in a bowl.
5 Add the boiling milk to the mixture, stir vigorously until completely mixed.
6 Return this mixture to a clean thick-bottomed pan and stir continuously with a wooden spoon over a gentle heat until the mixture thickens, then remove from heat.
7 Allow to cool slightly. Add the remaining egg yolks and mix thoroughly.
8 Stiffly whip the egg whites and carefully fold into the mixture, which should be just warm. (An extra egg white can be added for extra lightness.)

9 Place the mixture into the prepared case(s) and level it off with a palette knife – do not allow it to come above the level of the soufflé case.
10 Place on a baking sheet and cook in a moderately hot oven – approx. 200–230°C – until the soufflé is well risen and firm to the touch – approx. 15–20 minutes. (For individual soufflés, reduce time by 5 minutes.)
11 Remove carefully from oven, dredge with icing sugar and serve at once. A hot soufflé must not be allowed to stand or it may sink.

A pinch of egg white powder can be added when whisking the whites, to strengthen them and assist in the aeration process.

Prepare the mould

Mix half the egg yolks into the flour

Fold the mixture

Thumb the edge

55 Mango soufflé

fruit, milk, eggs boiling, baking

energy	kcal	fat	sat fat	carb	sugar	protein	fibre
1116 KJ	264 kcal	6.8 g	2.1 g	45.0 g	34.6 g	8.5 g	4.8 g

Portions ⟩	4	10
milk	100 ml	250 ml
mango purée	150 ml	375 ml
egg yolks	4	10
caster sugar for liaison	60 g	150 g
cornflour for liaison	15 g	45 g
egg whites	4	10
lemon juice	a few drops	a few drops
caster sugar	30 g	75 g
cornflour	5 g	12 g
mango compote (see below)		

1 Bring the milk and mango purée to the boil.
2 Make the liaison by whisking the egg yolks with 60 g of caster sugar. Sieve in 15 g of cornflour and continue whisking until smooth.
3 Add one-third of the boiling liquid to the liaison.
4 Bring the rest of the liquid back to the boil. Whisk the liaison into it, then continue whisking until it returns to the boil. Simmer for 2–3 minutes. Cover and cool.

5 Whisk the egg whites, lemon juice, 30 g of sugar and 5 g of cornflour together to the consistency of shaving foam. (For 10 portions, adjust the quantities as shown in the table.) Fold this into the cooled mango pastry cream mixture.
6 Place a spoonful of mango compote into the bottom of each prepared soufflé mould. Pour in the mixture and level it off with a palette knife.
7 Bake at 200°C for approximately 12 minutes.
8 Remove carefully from the oven, dredge with icing sugar and serve immediately.

To make mango compote

Portions ⟩	4	10
mango	1	2
stock syrup (recipe 15)	100–125 ml	200–250 ml

1 Remove the skin and stone from the mango. Cut it into small, neat dice.
2 Pour hot stock syrup over the mango dice. Leave to cool.

56 Lemon curd soufflé (flourless)

milk, eggs boiling,  baking

energy	kcal	fat	sat fat	carb	sugar	protein	fibre
1179 kJ	280 kcal	13.3 g	5.7 g	31.7 g	30.4 g	10.1 g	0.1 g

Portions ❭	4	10
eggs	4	9
caster sugar	75 g	187 g
lemon, zest and juice	2	5
cream of tartar	pinch	large pinch
egg white powder	pinch	large pinch
icing sugar, to serve		
Lemon curd		
lemons, juice of	2	5
eggs	1	2
caster sugar	37 g	100 g
butter, unsalted	25 g	60 g
cornflour	6 g	15 g

1 Lightly grease the individual soufflé dishes with butter or margarine, and lightly dust with caster sugar.

2 Prepare the lemon curd by whisking the eggs with the caster sugar over a bain-marie of hot water, add the lemon juice, butter cut into small pieces and the cornflour. Whisk well until the mixture thickens.

3 Divide the lemon curd into the soufflé dishes.

4 Separate the egg whites and egg yolks. Mix the yolks with the caster sugar, the lemon zest and juice. Whisk well to thoroughly incorporate.

5 Carefully whisk the egg whites to soft peaks with a pinch of cream of tartar and egg white powder to strengthen.

6 Carefully fold the whites into the yolk and lemon mixture. Do not over-mix.

7 Divide the mixture into the soufflé dishes.

8 Place on a baking sheet and cook in a pre-heated oven (170°C) for approx. 12–16 minutes. Remove, dust with icing sugar and serve immediately.

57 Baked Alaska

(omelette soufflé surprise)

eggs baking

energy	kcal	fat	sat fat	carb	sugar	protein	fibre
2190 kJ	521 kcal	16.4 g	7.3 g	91.3 g	81.2 g	7.7 g	0.6 g

Portions >	4	10
sponge cake, sliced	100 g	250 g
fruit syrup or stock syrup	60 ml	150 ml
vanilla ice cream or parfait	4 scoops	10 scoops
egg whites, pasteurised	4	10
caster sugar	200 g	500 g

1 Neatly arrange the pieces of sponge cake on a tray.
2 Sprinkle the sponge cake with a little fruit syrup.
3 Place a flattened scoop of vanilla ice cream on each piece of sponge. Alternatively, mould a ball of parfait – this will be more stable than ice cream.
4 Surround the ice cream or parfait with sponge to conceal it (optional). Place in the freezer to prevent this from melting.
5 Meanwhile, stiffly whip the egg whites and fold in the sugar.
6 Use half the meringue and completely cover the ice cream and sponge. Neaten with a palette knife.
7 Place the remainder of the meringue into a piping bag with a large tube (plain or star) and decorate over.
8 Place into a hot oven at 230–250°C and colour a golden brown or brown with a blowtorch. Serve immediately.

Try something different
- The fruit syrup for soaking the sponge may be flavoured with rum, sherry, brandy, whisky, Tia Maria, curaçao or any other suitable liqueur.
- **Baked Alaska with peaches:** proceed as for the basic recipe, adding a little maraschino to the fruit syrup and using raspberry ice cream instead of vanilla; cover the ice cream with four halves of peaches.
- **Baked Alaska with pears:** proceed as for the basic recipe, adding a little kirsch to the fruit syrup and adding halves of poached pears to the ice cream.

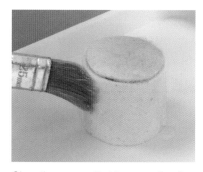
Glaze the sponge that is concealing the ice cream centre

Pipe meringue to cover

Pipe swirls of meringue to decorate

58 Fresh fruit salad
(salade de fruits)

fruit

energy	kcal	fat	sat fat	carb	sugar	protein	fibre
493 kJ	117 kcal	0.0 g	0.0 g	30.3 g	29.5 g	0.9 g	3.0 g

Portions 〉	4	10
orange	1	2–3
dessert apple	1	2–3
dessert pear	1	2–3
cherries	50 g	125 g
grapes	50 g	125 g
banana	1	2–3
Stock syrup		
caster sugar	50 g	125 g
water	125 ml	375 ml
lemon, juice of	½	1

1 For the syrup, boil the sugar with the water. Place just enough to coat all the fruit in a bowl.
2 Allow to cool, add the lemon juice.
3 Peel and cut the orange into segments.
4 Quarter the apple and pear, remove the core, peel and cut each quarter into two or three slices, place in the bowl of syrup and mix with the orange.
5 Stone the cherries, leave whole.
6 Cut the grapes in half, peel if required, and remove the pips.
7 Mix carefully and place in a glass bowl in the refrigerator to chill.
8 Just before serving, peel and slice the banana and mix in.

Try something different
- Any of the following fruits may be used: dessert apples, pears, pineapple, oranges, grapes, melon, strawberries, peaches, raspberries, apricots, bananas, cherries, kiwi fruit, plums, mangoes, pawpaws and lychees. Allow about 150 g unprepared fruit per portion. All fruit must be ripe.
- Kirsch, Cointreau or Grand Marnier may be added to the syrup.
- A fruit juice (e.g. apple, orange, grape or passion fruit) can be used instead of syrup.

59 Tropical fruit plate

fruit

energy	kcal	fat	sat fat	carb	sugar	protein	fibre
405 KJ	95 kcal	0.4 g	0.1 g	23.0 g	18.7 g	1.2 g	4.5 g

An assortment of fully ripe fruits, e.g. pineapple, papaya, mango (see photos), peeled, deseeded, cut into pieces and neatly dressed on a plate.

An optional accompaniment could be yoghurt, vanilla ice cream, crème fraiche, fresh or clotted cream.

60 Poached fruits or fruit compote

(compote de fruits)

fruit  boiling, ⬛ poaching

energy	kcal	fat	sat fat	carb	sugar	protein	fibre	*
531 kJ	126 kcal	0.0 g	0.0 g	33.5 g	33.5 g	0.2 g	2.2 g	

Portions ›	4	10
stock syrup (recipe 15)	250 ml	625 ml
fruit	400 g	1 kg
sugar	100 g	250 g
lemon, juice of	½	1

Apples, pears

1 Boil the water and sugar.
2 Quarter the fruit, remove the core and peel.
3 Place in a shallow pan in sugar syrup.
4 Add a few drops of lemon juice.
5 Cover with greaseproof paper or aluminium foil.
6 Allow to simmer slowly, preferably in the oven, cool and serve.

Soft fruits (raspberries, strawberries)

1 Pick and wash the fruit. Place in a glass bowl.
2 Pour on the hot syrup. Allow to cool and serve.

Stone fruits (plums, damsons, greengages, cherries)

1 Wash the fruit, barely cover with sugar syrup and cover with greaseproof paper or a lid.
2 Cook gently in a moderate oven until tender.

Rhubarb

1 Trim off the stalk and leaf and wash. Cut into 5 cm lengths and cook as above, adding extra sugar if necessary. A little ground ginger may also be added.

Gooseberries, blackcurrants, redcurrants

1 Top and tail the gooseberries, wash and cook as for stone fruit, adding extra sugar if necessary.
2 The currants should be carefully removed from the stalks, washed and cooked as for stone fruits.

Dried fruits (prunes, apricots, apples, pears)

1 Dried fruits should be washed and soaked in cold water overnight.
2 Gently cook in the liquor with sufficient sugar to taste.

* Using pears

Poached rhubarb and pears

Try something different

● A piece of cinnamon stick and a few slices of lemon may be added to the prunes or pears, one or two cloves to the dried or fresh apples.
● Any compote may be flavoured with lavender and/or mint.

Healthy eating tips

● Use fruit juice instead of stock syrup.
● If dried fruits are used, no added sugar is needed.

61 Cream caramel
(crème caramel)

milk, eggs, sugar boiling, baking

energy	kcal	fat	sat fat	carb	sugar	protein	fibre
868 kJ	207 kcal	7.2 g	3.3 g	30.2 g	30.2 g	7.3 g	0.0 g

*

A cream caramel decorated with poached kumquats

Portions >	4–6	10–12
Caramel		
sugar, granulated or cube	100 g	200 g
water	125 ml	250 ml
Cream		
milk, whole or skimmed	0.5 litres	1 litre
eggs	4	8
sugar, caster or unrefined	50 g	100 g
vanilla essence or a vanilla pod	3–4 drops	6–8 drops

Cream caramels may be served with whipped cream or a fruit sauce such as passion fruit, and accompanied by a sweet biscuit (e.g. shortbread, palmiers).
Adding a squeeze of lemon juice to the caramel will invert the sugar, thus preventing recrystallisation.

* Using whole milk

1 Prepare the caramel by placing three-quarters of the water in a thick-based pan, adding the sugar and allowing to boil gently, without shaking or stirring the pan.
2 When the sugar has cooked to a golden-brown caramel colour, add the remaining quarter of the water, reboil until the sugar and water mix, then pour into the bottom of dariole moulds.
3 Prepare the cream by warming the milk and whisking on to the beaten eggs, sugar and essence (or vanilla pod).
4 Strain and pour into the prepared moulds.
5 Place in a roasting tin half full of water.
6 Cook in a moderate oven at 150–160°C for 30–40 minutes.
7 When thoroughly cold, loosen the edges of the cream caramel with the fingers, shake firmly to loosen and turn out on to a flat dish or plates.
8 Pour any caramel remaining in the mould around the creams.

62 *Crème brûlée*

milk, eggs, cream, sugar baking

energy	kcal	fat	sat fat	carb	sugar	protein	fibre
1154 kJ	278 kcal	21.9 g	12.1 g	14.8 g	14.8 g	6.2 g	0.0 g

Portions ❯	4	10
milk	125 ml	300 ml
double cream	125 ml	300 ml
natural vanilla essence or pod	3–4 drops	7–10 drops
eggs	2	5
egg yolk	1	2–3
caster sugar	25 g	60 g
Demerara sugar		

1 Warm the milk, cream and vanilla essence in a pan.
2 Mix the eggs, egg yolk and caster sugar in a basin and add the warm milk. Stir well and pass through a fine strainer.
3 Pour the cream into individual dishes and place them into a tray half-filled with warm water.
4 Place in the oven at approx. 160°C for about 30–40 minutes, until set.
5 Sprinkle the tops with Demerara sugar and glaze under the salamander or by blowtorch to a golden brown.
6 Clean the dishes and serve.

Try something different
Sliced strawberries, raspberries or other fruits (e.g. peaches, apricots) may be placed in the bottom of the dish before adding the cream mixture, or placed on top after the creams are caramelised.

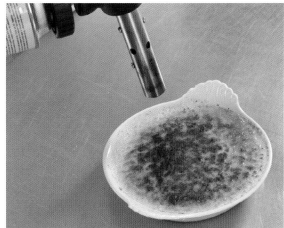

Use a blowtorch carefully to glaze the top

63 Zabaglione
(sabayon with Marsala)

energy	kcal	fat	sat fat	carb	sugar	protein	fibre
746 kJ	177 kcal	5.5 g	1.6 g	27.4 g	27.4 g	2.9 g	0.0 g

Portions ›	4	10
egg yolks, pasteurised	8	20
caster or unrefined sugar	200 g	500 g
Marsala	150 ml	375 ml

This is a traditional Italian dessert, which is sometimes prepared in the restaurant in a special zabaglione pan.

Try something different
Use sherry, whisky or brandy instead of Marsala.

1 Whisk the egg yolks and sugar in a bowl until almost white.
2 Mix in the Marsala.
3 Place the bowl and contents in a bain-marie of warm water.
4 Whisk the mixture continuously until it increases to four times its bulk and is firm and frothy.
5 Pour the mixture into glass goblets.
6 Accompany with a suitable biscuit (e.g. sponge fingers).

64 Fruit mousse

fruit, eggs  boiling

energy	kcal	fat	sat fat	carb	sugar	protein	fibre
660 KJ	158 kcal	10.2 g	6.3 g	13.7 g	11.8 g	2.4 g	0.8 g

Portions ›	4	10
fruit purée (e.g. raspberry, mango or passion fruit)	100 g	250 g
egg whites, pasteurised	2 (50 g)	5 (125 g)
caster sugar	40 g	120 g
gelatine sheets (bronze)	2	5
semi-whipped cream	50 ml	250 ml
desired liquor	2 tsp	1 tbsp

1 Bring the fruit purée to just under boiling point.
2 Whip the egg whites to a snow, add the sugar and combine (this offers a softer, less dense meringue finish and homogenises into a mousse).
3 Slowly add the softened gelatine to the warmed warm purée.
4 Add all the ingredients and pour into the desired moulds.
5 To serve, unmould on to suitable plates, garnish with fresh fruit and a suitable coulis.

Passion fruit mousse

65 Bavarois
(often referred to as a mousse)

fruit, eggs  boiling

energy	kcal	fat	sat fat	carb	sugar	protein	fibre	*
970 kJ	231 kcal	18.2 g	10.9 g	11.8 g	11.8 g	5.8 g	0.0 g	

	Portions ❯	6–8
gelatine		10 g
eggs, pasteurised, separated		2
caster sugar		50 g
milk, whole, semi-skimmed or skimmed		250 ml
whipping or double cream or non-dairy cream		125 ml

1 If using leaf gelatine, soak in cold water.
2 Cream the yolks and sugar in a bowl until almost white.
3 Whisk in the milk, which has been brought to the boil; mix well.
4 Clean the milk saucepan, which should be a thick-based one, and return the mixture to it.
5 Return to a low heat and stir continuously with a kitchen spoon until the mixture coats the back of the spoon. The mixture must not boil.
6 Remove from the heat; add the gelatine and stir until dissolved.
7 Pass through a fine strainer into a clean bowl, leave in a cool place, stirring occasionally until almost at setting point.
8 Fold in the lightly beaten cream.
9 Fold in the stiffly beaten whites.
10 Pour the mixture into a mould or individual moulds (which may be very lightly greased with almond oil).
11 Allow to set in the refrigerator.
12 Shake and turn out on to a flat dish or plates.

Bavarois may be decorated with sweetened, flavoured whipped cream (crème Chantilly, recipe 7).
It is advisable to use pasteurised egg yolks and whites.

Healthy eating tip
Use semi-skimmed milk and whipping cream to reduce the overall fat content.

* Using whole milk and whipping cream

Flavours for bavarois
- **Raspberry or strawberry bavarois:** when the custard is almost cool, add 200 g of picked, washed and sieved raspberries or strawberries. Decorate with whole fruit and whipped cream.
- **Chocolate bavarois:** dissolve 50 g chocolate couverture in the milk. Decorate with whipped cream and grated chocolate.
- **Coffee bavarois:** proceed as for a basic bavarois, with the addition of coffee essence to taste.
- **Orange bavarois:** add grated zest and juice of 2 oranges and 1 or 2 drops orange colour to the mixture, and increase the gelatine by 2 leaves. Decorate with blanched, fine julienne of orange zest, orange segments and whipped cream.
- **Lemon or lime bavarois:** as orange bavarois, using lemons or limes in place of oranges.
- **Vanilla bavarois:** add a vanilla pod or a few drops of vanilla essence to the milk. Decorate with vanilla-flavoured sweetened cream (crème Chantilly).

Chocolate mousse on a sponge base; the mousse on the left is finished with a chocolate glaze (a commercial product)

Portions >	8	16
egg yolks, pasteurised	80 ml	160 ml
stock syrup at 30° Baume	125 ml	250 ml
bitter couverture	250 g	500 g
leaf gelatine	2	4
whipping cream, whipped	500 ml	1 litre

1 Boil the syrup.
2 Place the yolks into the bowl of a food mixer. Pour over the boiling syrup and whisk until thick. Remove from the machine.
3 Add all the couverture at once, and fold it in quickly.
4 Drain the soaked gelatine, melt it and fold it into the chocolate sabayon mixture.
5 Add all the whipped cream at once, and fold it in carefully.
6 Place the mixture into prepared moulds. Refrigerate or freeze immediately.

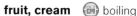

67 Vanilla panna cotta served on a fruit compote

fruit, cream boiling

energy	kcal	fat	sat fat	carb	sugar	protein	fibre *
1565 kJ	378 kcal	34.0 g	21.1 g	16.1 g	16.1 g	2.9 g	1.5 g

Portions >	6	12
milk	125 ml	250 ml
double cream	375 ml	750 ml
aniseeds	2	5
vanilla pod	½	1
leaf gelatine (soaked)	2 leaves	5 leaves
caster sugar	50 g	125 g
Fruit compote		
apricot purée	75 g	200 g
vanilla pod	½	1
peach	1	2
kiwi fruit	1	2
strawberries	75 g	150 g
blueberries	75 g	150 g
raspberries	50 g	125 g

Healthy eating tip

This dish will contribute to the recommended five portions of fruit and vegetables per day.

1 Prepare the fruit compote by boiling the apricot purée and infusing with vanilla pod. Remove pod, allow purée to cool.

2 Finely dice the peach and the kiwi and quarter the strawberries. Mix, then add blueberries and raspberries.

3 Bind the fruit with the apricot purée. A little stock syrup (recipe 15) may be required to keep the fruit free flowing.

4 For the panna cotta, boil the milk and cream, add aniseeds, infuse with the vanilla pod, remove after infusion.

5 Heat again and add the soaked gelatine and caster sugar. Strain through a fine strainer.

6 Place in a bowl set over ice and stir until it thickens slightly; this will allow the vanilla seeds to suspend throughout the mix instead of sinking to the bottom.

7 Fill individual dariole moulds.

8 Place the fruit compote on individual fruit plates, turn out the panna cotta, place on top of the compote, finish with a tuile biscuit.

* Using blackcurrants for blueberries

68 Fruit fool

energy 942 kJ	kcal 222 kcal	fat 2.6 g	sat fat 1.6 g	carb 50.3 g	sugar 44.5 g	protein 2.4 g	fibre 1.6 g	*

Method 1

Portions ›	4	10
fruit (apple, gooseberry, rhubarb, etc.)	400 g	1 kg
water	60 ml	150 ml
granulated or unrefined sugar	100 g	250 g
cornflour	25 g	60 g
milk, whole or skimmed	250 ml	625 ml
caster or unrefined sugar	25 g	60 g

1 Cook the fruit in water and granulated sugar, to a purée. Pass through a sieve.
2 Dilute the cornflour in a little of the milk, add the caster sugar.
3 Boil the remainder of the milk.
4 Pour on the diluted cornflour, stir well.
5 Return to the pan on a low heat and stir to the boil.
6 Mix with the fruit purée. The quantity of mixture should not be less than 0.5 litres.
7 Pour into 4 (or 10) glass coupes or suitable dishes and allow to set.
8 Decorate with whipped sweetened cream. The colour may need to be adjusted slightly with food colour.

Method 2

Portions ›	4	10
fruit in purée (raspberries, strawberries, etc.)	400 g	1 kg
caster sugar	100 g	250 g
fresh whipped cream	250 ml	625 ml

1 Mix the ingredients and serve in coupes.

Healthy eating tip
In methods 2 and 3 the fat content may be reduced by using equal quantities of cream and natural Greek-style yoghurt.

* Method 1 (using whole milk, apples). Method 2 (using strawberries): 1540 kJ/370 kcal energy; 25.3 g fat; 15.8 g sat fat; 35.7 g carb; 35.7 g sugar; 2.0 g protein; 1.2 g fibre. Method 3 (using raspberries and double cream): 1606 kJ/385 kcal energy; 25.2 g fat; 15.6 g sat fat; 40.0 g carb; 31.9 g sugar; 2.0 g protein; 2.7 g fibre

Method 3

Portions ›	4	10
cornflour	35 g	85 g
water	375 ml	900 ml
sugar	100 g	250 g
fruit in purée (raspberries, strawberries, etc.)	400 g	1.25 kg
cream	185 ml	500 ml

1 Dilute the cornflour in a little of the water.
2 Boil the remainder of the water with the sugar and prepared fruit until soft.
3 Pass through a fine sieve.
4 Return to a clean pan and reboil.
5 Stir in the diluted cornflour and reboil. Allow to cool.
6 Lightly whisk the cream and fold into the mixture.
7 Serve as for method 1.

Practical Cookery 12th edition

69 Meringue
(meringue)

eggs, sugar 🍳 baking

energy	kcal	fat	sat fat	carb	sugar	protein	fibre
3491 kJ	831 kcal	0.0 g	0.0 g	210.0 g	210.0 g	10.8 g	0.0 g

Portions ❯	4	10
egg whites, pasteurised	4	10
caster sugar	200 g	500 g

1 Whip the egg whites stiffly.
2 Sprinkle on the sugar and carefully mix in.
3 Place in a piping bag with a large plain tube and pipe onto silicone paper on a baking sheet.
4 Bake in the slowest oven possible or in a hot plate (110°C). The aim is to dry out the meringues without any colour whatsoever; it is likely to take 3–5 hours, depending on size.

Unfilled meringues and vacherins

Piping meringues

Whipping egg whites

The reason egg whites increase in volume when whipped is because they contain so much protein (11 per cent). The protein forms tiny filaments, which stretch on beating, incorporate air in minute bubbles then set to form a fairly stable puffed-up structure expanding to seven times its bulk. To gain maximum efficiency when whipping egg whites, the following points should be observed.

● Because of possible weakness in the egg white protein, it is advisable to strengthen it by adding a pinch of cream of tartar and a pinch of dried egg white powder. If all dried egg white powder is used no additions are necessary.
● Eggs should be fresh.
● When separating yolks from whites no speck of egg yolk must be allowed to remain in the white; egg yolk contains fat, the presence of which can prevent the white being correctly whipped.
● The bowl and whisk must be scrupulously clean, dry and free from any grease.
● When egg whites are whipped, the addition of a little sugar (15 g to 4 egg whites) will assist the efficient beating and reduce the chances of over-beating.

Vacherin with strawberries and cream

(vacherin aux fraises)

eggs, sugar, fruit ⬛ baking

energy	kcal	fat	sat fat	carb	sugar	protein	fibre	*
1436 kJ	341 kcal	12.6 g	7.9 g	56.3 g	56.3 g	3.9 g	0.6 g	

Portions ⟩	4	10
egg whites	4	10
caster sugar	200 g	500 g
strawberries, picked and washed)	100–300 g	250–750 g
cream (whipped and sweetened) or non-dairy cream	125 ml	300 ml

A vacherin is traditionally a round meringue shell piped into a suitable shape so that the centre may be filled with sufficient fruit (such as strawberries, stoned cherries, peaches and apricots) and whipped cream to form a rich sweet. The vacherin may be prepared in one-, two- or four-portion sizes, or larger.
Modern versions may be piped oval or square.

Try something different

- Melba sauce (recipe 22) or a concentrated strawberry coulis may be used to coat the strawberries before decorating with cream.
- Raspberries can be used instead of strawberries.

* Using 280 g strawberries and whipped cream

1 Stiffly whip the egg whites. (Refer to the notes in recipe 69 for more guidance.)
2 Carefully fold in the sugar.
3 Place the mixture into a piping bag with a 1 cm plain tube.
4 Pipe onto silicone paper on a baking sheet.
5 Start from the centre and pipe round in a circular fashion to form a base 16 cm then pipe around the edge 2–3 cm high.
6 Bake in a cool oven at 100°C until the meringue case is completely dry. Do not allow to colour.
7 Allow the meringue case to cool then remove from the paper.
8 Spread a thin layer of cream on the base. Add the strawberries.
9 Decorate with the remainder of the cream.

Healthy eating tip

Try 'diluting' the fat in the cream with some low fat fromage frais.

71 Black Forest vacherin

chocolate, eggs, sugar 🍽 baking

energy	kcal	fat	sat fat	carb	sugar	protein	fibre	*
2751 KJ	657 kcal	34.2 g	18.3 g	79.5 g	71.4 g	7.3 g	2.5 g	

Portions ›	6	12
egg whites, pasteurised	125 ml	250 ml
caster sugar	250 g	500 g
lemon juice	½ tsp	5 ml
vanilla essence	drop	drop
cornflour, sieved	15 g	30 g
cocoa powder, sieved	25 g	50 g
small discs of chocolate sponge	6	12
Kirsch syrup or Kirsch	50 ml	100 ml
cherries (fresh, tinned or griottines)	30–36	60–72
pastry cream (see recipe 8)	100 ml	200 ml
Kirsch	10 ml	20 ml
leaf gelatine, soaked	1	2
couverture, melted	100 g	200 g approx.
double cream, whipped	200 ml	400 ml
chocolate shavings		
icing sugar		
cocoa powder (to dust)		

1 Whisk the egg white and one-quarter of the sugar until firm. Continue to whisk while streaming in half of the sugar.
2 Add the lemon juice and vanilla. Fold in the cornflour and cocoa powder, and the remaining quarter of the sugar.
3 Pipe this vacherin mixture into 12 rounds, 80 mm in diameter. Bake at 150°C for approx. 1 hour.
4 Place a sponge disc on each vacherin. Moisten the sponge with Kirsch syrup and place 5 or 6 cherries on top.

5 Beat the pastry cream. Dissolve the gelatine in the warm Kirsch and then beat it into the pastry cream.
6 Beat in the melted couverture to taste. Fold in the cream.
7 Pipe the chocolate mixture onto the prepared bases in a spiral.
8 Cover with chocolate shavings. Dust with icing sugar first, then cocoa powder.

* Using single cream in place of pastry cream

72 Lime soufflé frappe

eggs, fruit, cream boiling

energy 2734 KJ	kcal 655 kcal	fat 40.8 g	sat fat 20.7 g	carb 66.9 g	sugar 61.2 g	protein 9.2 g	fibre 0.8 g	sodium 0.2 g

Portions >	10	15
couverture	150 g	200 g
sponge, thin slices, cut into rounds	10	15
stock syrup, flavoured with lime	100 ml	150 ml
For the Swiss meringue		
egg whites	190 ml	300 ml
caster sugar	230 ml	340 ml
For the sabayon		
whipping cream	600 ml	900 ml
lime zest, finely grated and blanched, and juice	8	12
egg yolks	10	15
caster sugar	170 g	250 g
leaf gelatine, soaked in iced water	9½	14
To decorate		
confit of lime segments		
moulded chocolate		

1 Use individual stainless steel ring moulds. Cut a strip of acetate, 8 cm wide, to fit inside each ring. Cut a 6 cm strip to fit inside the first, spread it with tempered couverture and place inside the first strip, in the mould.

2 Place a round of sponge in the base of each mould and moisten with lime syrup.

3 Make up the Swiss meringue.

4 Whisk the cream until it is three-quarters whipped, then chill.

5 Whisk together the egg yolks, sugar and blanched lime zest. Boil the juice and pour it over the mixture to make the sabayon. Whisk over a bain-marie until it reaches 75°C, then continue whisking away from the heat until it is cold.

6 Drain and melt the gelatine. Fold it into the sabayon.

7 Fold in the Swiss meringue, and then the chilled whipped cream.

8 Fill the prepared moulds. Level the tops and chill until set.

9 To serve, carefully remove the mould, peel away the acetate, plate and decorate.

73 Trifle

cream 🍴 boiling

| | energy 2280 kJ | kcal 543 kcal | fat 29.1 g | sat fat 17.1 g | carb 66.2 g | sugar 51.3 g | protein 8.2 g | fibre 1.9 g | * |

Portions ⟩	6–8
sponge (made with 3 eggs)	1
jam	25 g
tinned fruit (pears, peaches, pineapple)	300–400 g
sherry (optional)	
Custard	
custard powder	35 g
milk, whole or skimmed	375 ml
caster sugar	50 g
cream (¾ whipped) or non-dairy cream	125 ml
whipped sweetened cream or non-dairy cream	250 ml
fresh fruit and/or glacé fruit, to garnish	50 g

1 Cut the sponge in half, sideways, and spread with jam.
2 Place in a glass bowl or individual dishes and soak with fruit syrup drained from the tinned fruit; a few drops of sherry may be added.
3 Cut the fruit into small pieces and add to the sponge.
4 Dilute the custard powder in a basin with some of the milk, add the sugar.
5 Boil the remainder of the milk, pour a little on the custard powder, mix well, return to the saucepan and over a low heat and stir to the boil. Allow to cool, stirring occasionally to prevent a skin forming; fold in the three-quarters whipped cream.
6 Pour on to the sponge. Leave to cool.
7 Decorate with the whipped cream and fruit.

A Genoise sponge is suitable – see recipe 113, but scale down the quantities.

Try something different
● Other flavourings or liqueurs may be used in place of sherry (e.g. whisky, rum, brandy, Tia Maria).
● For raspberry or strawberry trifle use fully ripe fresh fruit in place of tinned, and decorate with fresh fruit in place of angelica and glacé cherries.
● A fresh egg custard may be used with fresh egg yolks (see recipe 86).

* Using whole milk and whipping cream

Lime and mascarpone cheesecake

energy	kcal	fat	sat fat	carb	sugar	protein	fibre	sodium *
2624 KJ	633 kcal	54.0 g	32.3 g	31.5 g	24.3 g	7.1 g	0.0 g	0.3 g

Makes ›	1 (12 portions)
ginger biscuits	200 g
butter, melted	200 g
egg yolks, pasteurised	125 g
caster sugar	75 g
cream cheese	250 g
mascarpone	250 g
gelatine, softened in cold water	15 g
limes, juice and grated zest of	2
semi-whipped cream	275 ml
white chocolate, melted	225 g

1 Blitz the biscuits in a food processor. Mix in the melted butter. Line a cake ring or rectangular mould with this mixture and chill until required.

2 Make a sabayon by whisking the egg yolks and sugar together over a pan of simmering water.

3 Stir the cream cheese and mascarpone into the sabayon until soft.

4 Meanwhile, warm the gelatine in the lime juice, and pass through a fine chinois. Also whip the cream.

5 Pour the gelatine and melted white chocolate into the cheese mixture.

6 Remove from the food mixer and fold in the whipped cream with a spatula. Finally, whisk in the lime zest.

7 Pour over the prepared base. Chill for 4 hours. Cut into neat individual portions and decorate.

* Using additional cream cheese in place of mascarpone

75 Baked blueberry cheesecake

cheese, fruit baking

energy	kcal	fat	sat fat	carb	sugar	protein	fibre	sodium
1791 KJ	431 kcal	33.5 g	19.5 g	28.0 g	19.7 g	6.4 g	0.4 g	0.3 g

Makes >	1 (8–12 portions)
digestive biscuits	150 g
butter, melted	50 g
full-fat cream cheese	350 g
caster sugar	150 g
eggs	4
lemon, zest and juice of	1
vanilla essence	5 ml
blueberries	125
soured cream	350 ml

1 Blitz the biscuits in a food processor. Stir in the melted butter. Press the mixture into the bottom of a lightly greased cake tin with a removable collar.

2 Whisk together the cheese, sugar, eggs, vanilla and lemon zest and juice, until smooth.

3 Stir in the blueberries, then pour over the biscuit base.

4 Bake at 160°C for approx. 30 minutes.

5 Remove from the oven and leave to cool slightly for 10–15 minutes.

6 Spread soured cream over the top and return to the oven for 10 minutes.

7 Remove and allow to cool and set. Chill.

76 Vanilla ice cream
(glace vanille)

eggs, milk 🌡 boiling

energy	kcal	fat	sat fat	carb	sugar	protein	fibre	*
616 kJ	147 kcal	8.1 g	4.2 g	15.8 g	15.8 g	3.5 g	0.0 g	

Portions ⟩	8–10
egg yolks	4
caster or unrefined sugar	100 g
milk, whole or skimmed	375 ml
vanilla pod or essence	
cream or non-dairy cream	125 ml

1 Whisk the yolks and sugar in a bowl until almost white.
2 Boil the milk with the vanilla pod or essence in a thick-based pan.
3 Whisk on to the eggs and sugar; mix well.
4 Return to the cleaned saucepan, place on a low heat.
5 Stir continuously with a wooden spoon until the mixture coats the back of the spoon.
6 Pass through a fine strainer into a bowl.
7 Freeze in an ice cream machine, gradually adding the cream.

Whisk boiling milk into the egg yolks and sugar

Return the mixture to the hot pan used for the milk

Test the consistency on the back of a spoon

Pass through a fine strainer into a cold pot

The mixture will cool down; if it was left in the hot pan it would continue to cook

Gradually add cream to the mixture in the ice cream machine

Try something different

- **Coffee ice cream:** add coffee essence, to taste, to the custard after it is cooked.
- **Chocolate ice cream:** add 50–100 g of chopped couverture to the milk before boiling.
- **Strawberry ice cream:** add 125 ml of strawberry pulp in place of 125 ml of milk. The pulp is added after the custard is cooked.
- **Rum and raisin ice cream:** soak 50 g raisins in 2 tbsp rum for 3–4 hours. Add to mixture before freezing.

* Using whole milk and single cream

77 Lemon curd ice cream

	energy	kcal	fat	sat fat	carb	sugar	protein	fibre	sodium *
	5421 KJ	1294 kcal	62.6 g	36.3 g	173.5 g	117.0 g	19.4 g	0.0 g	0.4 g

Portions >	6–8
lemon curd	250 g
crème fraiche	125 g
Greek yoghurt	250 g

1 Mix all ingredients together.
2 Churn in ice cream machine.

* Values for the entire recipe

78 Peach Melba
(pêche Melba)

fruit

	energy	kcal	fat	sat fat	carb	sugar	protein	fibre
	607 kJ	145 kcal	2.6 g	1.3 g	30.5 g	30.2 g	1.6 g	1.3 g

Portions >	4	10
peaches	2	5
vanilla ice cream	125 ml	300 ml
Melba sauce (recipe 22) or raspberry coulis	125 ml	300 ml

1 Poach the peaches. Allow to cool, then peel, halve and remove the stones.
2 Dress the fruit on a ball of the ice cream in an ice cream coupe, or in a tuile basket.
3 Finish with the sauce. The traditional presentation is to coat the peach in Melba sauce or coulis, and decorate with whipped cream. In this picture, the peach is garnished with crushed fresh pistachios and covered with a caramel cage; the basket is then placed carefully onto a base of coulis.

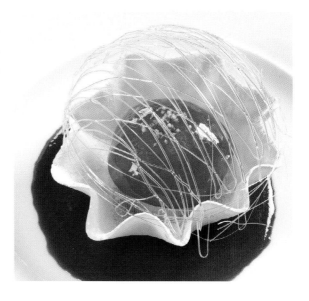

79 Pear belle Hélène
(poire belle Hélène)

fruit — poaching

energy	kcal	fat	sat fat	carb	sugar	protein	fibre	sodium
1888 KJ	453 kcal	29.7 g	18.2 g	44.5 g	43.6 g	4.5 g	5.3 g	0.0 g

Pear belle Hélène consists of a poached pear with vanilla ice cream (recipe 76) and chocolate sauce (recipe 24).

For the traditional presentation, serve the pear on top of the ice cream in a coupe. Decorate with whipped cream and serve a sauceboat of hot chocolate sauce separately.

For a modern presentation, coat the poached pear with chocolate sauce. Dress on a plate with the ice cream, more sauce and a tuile.

80 Apple sorbet

fruit, sugar — boiling

energy	kcal	fat	sat fat	carb	sugar	protein	fibre
673 KJ	158 kcal	0.1 g	0.0 g	41.5 g	38.7 g	0.4 g	2.4 g

	Portions ❯	8–10
Granny Smith apples, washed and cored		4
lemon, juice of		1
water		400 ml
sugar		200 g
glucose		50 g

1. Cut the apples into 1 cm pieces and place into lemon juice.
2. Bring the water, sugar and glucose to the boil, then allow to cool.
3. Pour the water over the apples. Blitz in a food processor.
4. Pass through a conical strainer, then churn in an ice cream machine.

Fruits of the forest and apple sorbets

Try something different
Fruits of the forest sorbet: use a mixture of forest fruits instead of apples.

81 Raspberry parfait

fruit, eggs

energy	kcal	fat	sat fat	carb	sugar	protein	fibre
981 KJ	234 kcal	10.7 g	5.6 g	31.3 g	30.2 g	4.7 g	0.5 g

Portions ⟩	6–8
egg yolks, pasteurised	80 g
caster sugar	60 g
gelatine, soaked	1 ½ leaves
raspberry liqueur	10 ml
lemon juice	10 ml
raspberry purée	120 g
whipped cream	150 ml
Italian meringue	
egg whites	200 g
water	80 ml
glucose	20 g
caster sugar	150 g

1 Make up the Italian meringue (see recipe 13).
2 Combine the egg yolks and caster sugar in a stainless steel bowl. Whisk over a bain-marie to make a sabayon.
3 Drain the gelatine and dissolve it in the liqueur and lemon juice.
4 Fold the gelatine mixture into the sabayon, then fold in the raspberry purée.
5 Fold in half the Italian meringue, then fold in the whipped cream.
6 Place into prepared moulds and freeze.
7 Once set, remove from the moulds.
8 In this presentation, the parfait has been set on a sponge disc. It is served with a raspberry coulis and fresh and dried raspberry garnishes.

82 *Quiche lorraine*
(cheese and ham savoury flan)

pastry, cheese, pork baking

energy	kcal	fat	sat fat	carb	sugar	protein	fibre
2955 kJ	704 kcal	48.4 g	22.6 g	38.1 g	6.5 g	31.6 g	1.8 g

Portions >	4	10
short pastry (recipe 1) or puff pastry (recipe 3)	100 g	250 g
ham, chopped	50 g	125 g
cheese, grated	25 g	60 g
egg	1	2
milk	125 ml	300 ml
cayenne, salt		

Try something different
- The filling can be varied by using lightly fried lardons of bacon (in place of the ham), chopped cooked onions and chopped parsley.
- A variety of savoury flans can be made by using imagination and experimenting with different combinations of food (e.g. Stilton and onion; salmon and cucumber; sliced sausage and tomato).

1 Lightly grease a flan ring or 4 (or 10) good-size barquette or tartlet moulds. Line thinly with pastry.
2 Prick the bottoms of the paste 2 or 3 times with a fork.
3 Cook in a hot oven at 230–250°C for 3–4 minutes or until the pastry is lightly set.
4 Remove from the oven; press the pastry down if it has tended to rise.
5 Add the chopped ham and grated cheese.
6 Mix the egg, milk, salt and cayenne thoroughly. Strain into the flan ring or moulds.
7 Return to the oven at 200–230°C and bake gently for 15–20 minutes or until nicely browned and set.

To make one large quiche, use a 12 cm flan ring.

83 Fruit pies

energy	kcal	fat	sat fat	carb	sugar	protein	fibre
6808 kJ	1621 kcal	65.0 g	26.6 g	260.0 g	144.1 g	15.3 g	15.0 g

*

Portions >	4–6	10–15
fruit (see note)	400 g	1.5 kg
sugar	100 g	250 g
water	2 tbsp	5 tbsp
Short pastry		
flour (soft)	100 g	250 g
butter or margarine	25 g	60 g
lard or vegetable fat	25 g	60 g
water to mix		

1 Prepare the fruit, wash it and place it in a bowl.
2 Add the sugar and water. (Place a clove in an apple pie.)
3 Make the pastry using the ingredients listed above, and allow it to relax. Roll out half of it to approximately 0.5 cm thick, to the shape of the flan ring.
4 Line the prepared flan ring with pastry, ensuring that the paste slightly overlaps the edge of the ring.
5 Place the prepared fruit into the pastry base.
6 Roll out the remaining paste. Carefully lay it over the flan ring, without stretching it, to join the edges of the pastry lining. Firmly seal the rim of the pie. Cut off any surplus pastry. (This can be used to create a lattice design on the pie – see photo.)
7 Brush with milk and sprinkle with caster sugar.
8 Place the pie on a baking sheet and bake in a hot oven at 220°C for about 10 minutes.

9 Reduce the heat or transfer to a cooler part of the oven and continue cooking for a further 30 minutes. If the pastry colours too quickly, cover it with a sheet of paper.
10 Clean the pie dish, and serve with a sauceboat of custard (250 ml), cream or ice cream.

Preparation of fruit for pies

The pie may be filled with a single fruit or a combination such as blackberry and apple or damson and apple.

- **Apples:** peeled, quartered, cored, washed, cut in slices.
- **Cherries:** stalks removed, washed.
- **Blackberries:** stalks removed, washed.
- **Gooseberries:** stalks and tails removed, washed.
- **Damsons:** picked and washed.
- **Rhubarb:** leaves and root removed, tough strings removed, cut into 2 cm pieces, washed.

* Using white flour and apple (4–6 portions). Using 50 per cent wholemeal flour and apple (4–6 portions): 6709 kJ/1598 kcal; 65.6 g fat; 26.7 g sat fat; 251.1 g carb; 144.5 g sugar; 17.8 g protein; 18.8 g fibre

84 Treacle tart

pastry baking

energy	kcal	fat	sat fat	carb	sugar	protein	fibre
1100 kJ	262 kcal	10.7 g	5.8 g	41.1 g	20.3 g	2.8 g	0.8 g

Portions ⟩	4	10
Short paste		
flour	100 g	250 g
lard, margarine or vegetable fat	25 g	60 g
butter or margarine	25 g	60 g
salt	pinch	large pinch
water, to mix		
Filling		
treacle	100 g	250 g
water	1 tbsp	2½ tbsp
lemon juice	3–4 drops	8–10 drops
fresh white bread or cake crumbs	15 g	50 g

1 Make pastry as in recipe 1. Allow to rest in refrigerator.
2 Roll out on a lightly floured surface until 2 mm thick.
3 Line an 18 cm flan ring, placed on a baking sheet.
4 Warm the treacle, water and lemon juice; add the crumbs.

5 Spoon into the pastry base and bake at 170°C for about 20 minutes.

Try something different
Any pastry debris can be rolled and cut into 0.5 cm strips and used to decorate the top of the tart before baking.
Treacle tarts can also be made in individual moulds.
For a traditional treacle tart, line an ovenproof plate with pastry. Spread the treacle filling over the pastry and bake as in the recipe.

85 Flan cases

pastry

1 Allow 25 g flour per portion and prepare sugar pastry as per recipe 2.
2 Grease the flan ring and baking sheet.
3 Roll out the pastry 2 cm larger than the flan ring. The pastry may be rolled between greaseproof or silicone paper.
4 Place the flan ring on the baking sheet.
5 Carefully place the pastry on the flan ring, by rolling it loosely over the rolling pin, picking up and unrolling it over the flan ring.
6 Press the pastry into shape without stretching it, being careful to exclude any air.
7 Allow a 0.5 cm ridge of pastry on top of the flan ring.
8 Cut off the surplus paste by rolling the rolling pin firmly across the top of the flan ring.
9 Mould the edge with thumb and forefinger. Decorate (a) with pastry tweezers or (b) with thumbs and forefingers, squeezing the pastry neatly to form a corrugated pattern.

Lining a flan
http://bit.ly/xrFgiv

86 Egg custard tart

Makes ›	1 (10–12 portions)
Pastry	
flour (soft)	500 g
salt	pinch
lemon, zest of	1
butter	250 g
icing sugar	120 g
eggs	2
Egg custard filling	
egg yolks	9
caster sugar	75 g
whipping cream, gently warmed and infused with 2 sticks of cinnamon	500 ml
nutmeg, freshly grated	

1 To make the pastry, rub together the flour, salt, lemon zest and butter until the mixture resembles breadcrumbs.

2 Add the sugar. Beat the eggs and then add them slowly, mixing until the pastry forms a ball. Wrap tightly in clingfilm and refrigerate.

3 Roll out the pastry on a lightly floured surface, to 2 mm thickness. Use it to line a 22 cm flan ring, placed on a baking sheet.

4 Line the pastry with greaseproof paper and fill with baking beans. Bake blind in a preheated oven at 175°C, for about 10 minutes or until the pastry is turning golden brown. Remove the paper and beans, and allow to cool. Turn the oven down to 130°C.

5 To make the custard filling, whisk together the egg yolks and sugar. Add the cream and mix well.

6 Pass the mixture through a fine sieve into a saucepan. Heat to blood temperature.

7 Fill the pastry case with the custard to 5 mm below the top. Place it carefully into the middle of the oven and bake for 30–40 minutes or until the custard appears to be set but not too firm.

8 Remove from the oven and cover liberally with grated nutmeg. Allow to cool to room temperature.

87 Fruit tart/flan

pastry, fruit baking

Portions ›	4	10
sugar paste (recipe 2)	100 g	250 g
fruit	200 g	500 g
glaze	2 tbsp	5 tbsp

1 Make the sweet paste and pastry cream.
2 Roll the pastry out to 3 mm thick. Line a flan ring and bake it blind (see recipe 85).
3 Allow the pastry case to cool. Transfer it to a serving plate and half fill it with pastry cream.
4 Arrange the prepared fruit neatly in the flan case.
5 Apply the glaze neatly and carefully. Cut into slices to serve.

Use a glaze suitable for the fruit chosen; for example, with a strawberry tart, use a red glaze.

88 Fruit tartlets or barquettes

pastry, fruit baking

energy	kcal	fat	sat fat	carb	sugar	protein	fibre	sodium
690 KJ	165 kcal	8.7 g	2.7 g	21.1 g	6.3 g	2.0 g	1.2 g	0.1 g

Allow one large or two small tartlets per person.

1 Roll out sugar pastry 3 mm thick.
2 Cut out rounds with a fluted cutter and place them neatly in greased tartlet moulds. If soft fruit (e.g. strawberries, raspberries) will be used, the pastry should be cooked blind first.
3 After baking and filling (or filling and baking), glaze the top.

Certain fruits (e.g. strawberries, raspberries) are sometimes served in boat-shaped moulds (barquettes). The preparation is the same as for tartlets. Tartlets and barquettes should be glazed and served allowing one large or two small per portion.

89 Apple flan
(flan aux pommes)

pastry, fruit baking

energy	kcal	fat	sat fat	carb	sugar	protein	fibre
1428 kJ	340 kcal	13.8 g	5.8 g	53.8 g	36 g	3.5 g	2.9 g

Portions 〉	4	10
sugar paste (recipe 2)	100 g	250 g
cooking apples	400 g	1 kg
sugar	50 g	125 g
apricot glaze (recipe 29)	2 tbsp	6 tbsp

1 Line a flan ring with sugar paste. Pierce the bottom several times with a fork.
2 Keep the best-shaped apple and make the remainder into a purée.
3 When cool, place in the flan case.

4 Peel, quarter and wash the selected apple.
5 Cut into neat thin slices and lay carefully on the apple purée, overlapping each slice. Ensure that each slice points to the centre of the flan then no difficulty should be encountered in joining the pattern up neatly.
6 Sprinkle a little sugar on the apple slices and bake the flan at 200–220°C for 30–40 minutes.
7 When the flan is almost cooked, remove the flan ring carefully, return to the oven to complete the cooking. Mask with hot apricot glaze or flan jelly.

90 Lemon tart
(tarte au citron)

pastry, fruit  baking

energy	kcal	fat	sat fat	carb	sugar	protein	fibre
1878 kJ	450 kcal	28.0 g	15.2 g	42.7 g	36.1 g	9.4 g	0.3 g

Portions >	8
sugar paste (recipe 2)	150 g
lemons	juice of 3, zest from 4
eggs	8
caster sugar	300 g
double cream	250 ml

1 Prepare 150 g of sugar paste, adding the zest of 1 lemon to the mix.
2 Line a 16 cm flan ring with the paste.
3 Bake blind for approx. 15 minutes.
4 Prepare the filling: mix the eggs and sugar together until smooth, add the cream, lemon juice and zest. Whisk well.
5 Seal the pastry, so that the filling will not leak out. Pour the filling into the flan case, bake for 30–40 minutes at 150°C until just set. (Take care when almost cooked as overcooking will cause the filling to rise and possibly crack.)

6 Remove from oven and allow to cool. Remove the flan ring when cold.
7 Dust with icing sugar and glaze under the grill or use a blowtorch. Portion and serve.

The mixture will fill one 16 cm × 4 cm or two 16 cm × 2 cm flan rings. If using two flan rings, double the amount of pastry and reduce the baking time when the filling is added.

> **Key point**
> If possible, make the filling one day in advance. The flavour will develop as the mixture matures.

Try something different
Limes may be used in place of lemons. If so, use the zest and juice of 5 limes or use a mix of lemons and limes.
If you can obtain them, use 7 duck eggs instead of 8 hen's eggs. This will make the filling more stable and reduce the risk of cracking.

91 Lemon meringue pie

pastry, fruit, eggs baking

energy	kcal	fat	sat fat	carb	sugar	protein	fibre
12138 KJ	2895 kcal	147.4 g	84.8 g	379.4 g	305.0 g	36.4 g	4.2 g

	Makes ›	2 × 20 cm
sweet paste flan cases (recipe 85)		2
granulated sugar		450 g
lemon zest, grated		2
fresh lemon juice		240 ml
eggs, large		8
large egg yolks		2
unsalted butter, cut into small pieces		350 g
For the meringue		
egg whites		6
caster sugar		600 g

1 Place the sugar into a bowl and grate the zest of lemon into it, rubbing together.

2 Strain the lemon juice into a non-reactive pan. Add the eggs, egg yolks, butter and zested sugar. Whisk to combine.

3 Place over a medium heat and whisk continuously for 3–5 minutes, until the mixture begins to thicken.

4 At the first sign of boiling, remove from the heat. Strain into a bowl and cool before filling the pastry cases.

5 Make the meringue (see recipe 69). Pipe it on top of the filled pie.

6 Colour in a hot oven at 220°C.

pastry, fruit baking

energy	kcal	fat	sat fat	carb	sugar	protein	fibre	sodium
1663 KJ	400 kcal	29.8 g	13.4 g	30.9 g	16.9 g	3.9 g	3.0 g	0.1 g

	Portions ›	8
sweet paste (recipe 2)		250 g
apricot jam		25 g
almond cream (recipe 11)		350 g
poached pears		4
apricot glaze		
flaked almonds		
icing sugar		

1 Line a buttered 20 cm flan ring with sweet paste. Trim and dock.

2 Using the back of a spoon, spread a little apricot jam over the base.

3 Pipe in almond cream until the flan case is two-thirds full.

4 Dry the poached pears. Cut them in half and remove the cores and string.

5 Score across the pears and arrange on top of the flan.

6 Bake in the oven at 200°C for 25–30 minutes.

7 Allow to cool, then brush with apricot glaze.

8 Sprinkle flaked almonds around the edge and dust with icing sugar.

93 Pecan pie

energy	kcal	fat	sat fat	carb	sugar	protein	fibre
1898 KJ	455 kcal	30.6 g	6.4 g	39.4 g	29.7 g	6.6 g	2.3 g

Makes ⟩	1 × 20 cm (12 portions)
sweet or lining paste	250 g
eggs	4
light brown sugar	185 g
golden syrup	85 g
salt	2 g
vanilla extract	2.5 ml
whisky	30 ml
unsalted butter, melted	42 g
pecan nuts	285 g
apricot glaze	
chocolate for piping	

1 Make up the paste (see recipe 2 for instructions) and place a 20 cm flan ring on a baking tray. Line it with the paste and bake the flan case blind.
2 Whisk the eggs a little, to break them up.
3 Mix in the sugar, syrup, salt, vanilla and whisky.
4 Stir in the butter and pecan nuts.
5 Dock the flan case. Pour the pecan mixture into the case.
6 Bake at 180°C for approx. 30 minutes, until firm.
7 Allow to cool completely. Brush with apricot glaze. Remove from the flan ring and decorate if desired.

pastry, nuts baking

energy	kcal	fat	sat fat	carb	sugar	protein	fibre	*
2105 kJ	501 kcal	28.8 g	11.0 g	57.5 g	33.7 g	6.7 g	2.2 g	

Portions 〉	8
sugar paste (using 227 g flour) (recipe 2)	200 g
raspberry jam	50 g
eggwash	
apricot glaze	50 g
icing sugar	35 g
frangipane (recipe 11)	300 g
butter or margarine	100 g
ground almonds	50 g
eggs	2
caster sugar	100 g
flour	50 g
almond essence	

1 Line a flan ring using three-quarters of the paste, 2 mm thick.
2 Pierce the bottom with a fork.
3 Spread with jam and then the frangipane.
4 Roll the remaining paste, cut into neat 0.5 cm strips and arrange neatly criss-crossed on the frangipane (optional); trim off surplus paste. Brush the strips of paste with eggwash.
5 Bake in a moderately hot oven at 200–220°C for 30–40 minutes. Brush with hot apricot glaze.
6 When cooled brush over with very thin water icing.

* Using hard margarine

95 Mince pies

pastry, fruit baking

energy	kcal	fat	sat fat	carb	sugar	protein	fibre	sodium *
2009 KJ	479 kcal	23.4 g	0.0 g	66.6 g	32.0 g	4.6 g	2.8 g	0.3 g

Makes >	12
sweet paste (recipe 2)	200 g
mincemeat (see below, or ready-made)	200 g
eggwash	
icing sugar	

1 Roll out the pastry 3 mm thick.
2 Cut half the pastry into fluted rounds 6 cm in diameter.
3 Place on a greased, dampened baking sheet.
4 Moisten the edges. Place a little mincemeat in the centre of each.
5 Cut the remainder of the pastry into fluted rounds, 8 cm in diameter.
6 Cover the mincemeat with pastry and seal the edges. Brush with eggwash.
7 Bake at 200°C for about 20 minutes.
8 Sprinkle with icing sugar and serve warm. Accompany with a suitable sauce (e.g. custard, brandy sauce, brandy cream).

Short or puff pastry may also be used. Various toppings can also be added, such as crumble mixture or flaked almonds and an apricot glaze.

To make the mincemeat

suet, chopped	100 g
mixed peel, chopped	100 g
currants	100 g
sultanas	100 g
raisins	100 g
apples, chopped	100 g
Barbados sugar	100 g
mixed spice	5 g
lemon, grated zest and juice of	1
orange, grated zest and juice of	1
rum	60 ml
brandy	60 ml

1 Mix the ingredients together.
2 Seal in jars and use as required.

* For two pies

Puff pastry cases
(bouchées, vol-au-vents)

Makes ›	12 bouchées/ 6 vol-au-vents
puff pastry (recipe 3)	200 g

1 Roll out the pastry approximately 0.5 cm thick.
2 Cut out with a round, fluted 5 cm cutter.
3 Place on a greased, dampened baking sheet; eggwash.
4 Dip a plain 4 cm diameter cutter into hot fat or oil and make an incision 3 mm deep in the centre of each.
5 Allow to rest in a cool place.
6 Bake at 220°C for about 20 minutes.
7 When cool, remove the caps or lids carefully and remove any soft pastry from inside the cases.

Bouchées are filled with a variety of savoury fillings and are served hot or cold. They may also be filled with cream and jam or lemon curd as a pastry.

Large bouchées are known as vol-au-vents. They may be produced in one-, two-, four- or six-portion sizes; a single-sized vol-au-vent would be approximately twice the size of a bouchée.

When preparing one- and two-portion sized vol-au-vents, the method for bouchées may be followed. When preparing larger-sized vol-au-vents, it is advisable to have two layers of puff pastry each 0.5 cm thick, sealed together with eggwash. One layer should be a plain round, and the other of the same diameter with a circle cut out of the centre.

97 Cheese straws
(paillettes au fromage)

pastry, cheese baking

energy	kcal	fat	sat fat	carb	sugar	protein	fibre
2562 kJ	610 kcal	48.1 g	24.1 g	28.7 g	0.6 g	17.4 g	1.4 g

Portions ›	4	10
puff paste (recipe 3) or rough puff paste (recipe 4)	100 g	250 g
cheese, grated	50 g	125 g
cayenne		

1 Roll out the pastry to 60 cm × 15 cm.
2 Sprinkle with the cheese and cayenne.
3 Give a single turn – that is, fold the paste one-third the way over so that it covers the first fold.
4 Roll out to 3 mm thick.
5 Cut out 4 circles 4 cm in diameter.
6 Remove the centre with a smaller cutter leaving a circle 0.5 cm wide.
7 Cut the remaining paste into strips 8 cm × 0.5 cm.
8 Twist each once or twice.
9 Place on a lightly greased baking sheet.
10 Bake in a hot oven at 230–250°C for 10 minutes or until a golden brown.
11 To serve, place a bundle of straws into each circle.

50 per cent white and 50 per cent wholemeal flour can be used for the pastry.

98 Sausage rolls

pastry, pork baking

energy	kcal	fat	sat fat	carb	sugar	protein	fibre
799 kJ	190 kcal	15.9 g	5.8 g	7.9 g	0.2 g	4.3 g	0.4 g

Makes ›	12 rolls
puff pastry (recipe 3)	200 g
sausagemeat	400 g
eggwash	

1 Roll out the pastry 3 mm thick into a strip 10 cm wide.
2 Make the sausagemeat into a roll 2 cm in diameter.
3 Place on the pastry. Moisten the edges of the pastry.
4 Fold over and seal. Cut into 8 cm lengths.
5 Mark the edge with the back of a knife. Brush with eggwash.
6 Place on to a greased, dampened baking sheet.
7 Bake at 200–220°C for about 20 minutes.

pastry baking

energy	kcal	fat	sat fat	carb	sugar	protein	fibre
928 kJ	222 kcal	15.6 g	3.8 g	18.5 g	8.9 g	3.8 g	0.5 g

Portions ›	8–10	20
puff pastry (recipe 3)	200 g	500 g
apricot jam	1 tbsp	3 tbsp
frangipane (recipe 11)	150 g	450 g

1 Roll out one-third of the pastry into a 20 cm round, 2 mm thick; moisten the edges and place on a greased, dampened baking sheet; spread the centre with jam.

2 Prepare the frangipane as per recipe 11, by creaming the margarine and sugar in a bowl, gradually adding the beaten eggs, and folding in the flour and almonds.

3 Spread on the frangipane, leaving a 2 cm border round the edge.

4 Roll out the remaining two-thirds of the pastry and cut into a slightly larger round.

5 Place neatly on top, seal and decorate the edge.

6 Using a sharp-pointed knife, make curved cuts 2 mm deep, radiating from the centre to about 2 cm from the edge. Brush with eggwash.

7 Bake at 220°C for 25–30 minutes.

8 Sprinkle with icing sugar and return to a very hot oven to glaze.

Roll out the base and add the filling

Cover the top and trim the edge to shape

Mark the top with curved lines

100 Palmiers

1 Roll out puff pastry (recipe 3), 2 mm thick, into a square.
2 Sprinkle liberally with caster sugar on both sides and roll into the pastry.
3 Fold into three from each end so as to meet in the middle; brush with eggwash and fold in two.
4 Cut into strips approximately 2 cm thick; dip one side in caster sugar.
5 Place on a greased baking sheet, sugared side down, leaving a space of at least 2 cm between each.
6 Bake in a very hot oven for about 10 minutes.
7 Turn with a palette knife, cook on the other side until brown and the sugar is caramelised.

Puff pastry trimmings are suitable for these.
Palmiers may be made in all sizes. Two joined together with a little whipped cream may be served as a pastry, small ones for petits fours. They may be sandwiched together with soft fruit, whipped cream and/or ice cream and served as a sweet.

101 Pear jalousie

energy	kcal	fat	sat fat	carb	sugar	protein	fibre
1178 kJ	282 kcal	17.8 g	5.1 g	27.2 g	17.5 g	3.8 g	0.8 g

	Portions ›	8–10
puff pastry (recipe 3)		200 g
frangipane (recipe 11)		200 g
pears, poached (or tinned)		

1 Roll out one-third of the pastry 3 mm thick into a strip 25 cm × 10 cm and place on a greased, dampened baking sheet.
2 Pierce with a docker. Moisten the edges.
3 Pipe on the frangipane, leaving 2 cm free all the way round. Place the pears on top.
4 Roll out the remaining two-thirds of the pastry to the same size.
5 Cut the dough with a trellis cutter to make a lattice.
6 Carefully open out this strip and neatly place onto the first strip.

7 Trim off any excess. Neaten and decorate the edge. Brush with eggwash.
8 Bake at 220°C for 25–30 minutes.
9 Sprinkle with icing sugar and return to a very hot oven to glaze.

102 Puff pastry slice
(mille-feuilles)

pastry 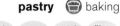 baking

energy	kcal	fat	sat fat	carb	sugar	protein	fibre
1158 kJ	369 kcal	10.9 g	1.3 g	67.7 g	52.3 g	4.9 g	0.1 g

Makes ⟩	6–8
puff pastry (recipe 3)	200 g
pastry cream (recipe 8)	250 ml
apricot jam	100 g
fondant or water icing	200 g

1 Roll out the pastry 2 mm thick into an even-sided square.
2 Roll up carefully on a rolling pin and unroll onto a greased, dampened baking sheet.
3 Using two forks, pierce as many holes as possible in the paste.
4 Cut in half with a large knife then cut each half in two to form four even-sized rectangles.
5 Bake in a hot oven at 220°C for 15–20 minutes; turn the strips over after 10 minutes. Allow to cool.
6 Keep the best strip for the top. Spread pastry cream on one strip.
7 Place another strip on top and spread with jam.
8 Place the third strip on top and spread with pastry cream.
9 Place the last strip on top, flat side up.
10 Press down firmly with a flat tray.
11 Decorate by feather-icing as follows:
   ● Warm the fondant to 37°C and correct the consistency with sugar syrup if necessary.
   ● Separate a little fondant into two colours (if required) and place in paper cornets.
   ● Pour the fondant over the mille-feuilles in an even coat.
   ● Immediately pipe on one of the colours lengthwise in strips 1 cm apart.
   ● Quickly pipe on the second colour (if required) between each line of the first.
   ● With the back of a small knife, wiping after each stroke, mark down the slice at 2 cm intervals.
   ● Quickly turn the slice around and repeat in the same direction with strokes in between the previous ones.
12 Allow to set and trim the edges neatly.
13 Cut into even portions with a sharp thin-bladed knife; dip into hot water and wipe clean after each cut.

Try something different
● Instead of coloured fondant, baker's chocolate or tempered couverture may be used for marbling. Whipped fresh cream may be used as an alternative to pastry cream.
● A variety of soft fruits may be incorporated in the layers, such as raspberries, strawberries, canned well-drained pears, peaches or apricots, kiwi fruit or caramelised poached apple slices.
● The pastry cream or whipped cream may also be flavoured with a liqueur if so desired, such as curaçao, Grand Marnier or Cointreau.

Pipe cream between layers of pastry

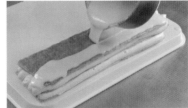

Ice the top with fondant

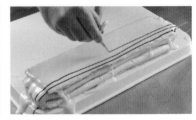

Decorate with chocolate

103 Fruit slice
(bande aux fruits)

energy	kcal	fat	sat fat	carb	sugar	protein	fibre
767 kJ	183 kcal	7.8 g	3.4 g	28.6 g	21.3 g	1.3 g	1.6 g

Portions ⟩	8–10
puff pastry (recipe 3)	200 g
fruit (see note)	400 g
pastry cream	250 ml approx.
appropriate glaze	2 tbsp

Fruit slices may be prepared from any fruit suitable for flans/tarts.

Try something different
Alternative methods are:
- to use short or sweet pastry for the base and puff pastry for the two side strips
- to use sweet pastry in a slice mould.

1 Roll out the pastry 2 mm thick in a strip 12 cm wide.
2 Place on a greased, dampened baking sheet.
3 Moisten two edges with eggwash; lay two 1.5 cm-wide strips along each edge.
4 Seal firmly and mark with the back of a knife. Prick the bottom of the slice.
5 Then, depending on the fruit used, either put the fruit (such as apple) on the slice and cook together, or cook the slice blind and afterwards place the pastry cream and fruit (such as soft red fruits) on the pastry. Glaze and serve as for flans.

104 Cream horns

pastry, cream baking

energy	kcal	fat	sat fat	carb	sugar	protein	fibre	*
735 kJ	176 kcal	14.9 g	8.6 g	9.8 g	6.3 g	1.2 g	0.2 g	

Makes ⟩	16
puff pastry (recipe 3)	200 g
eggwash	
icing sugar, to sprinkle	
jam	50 g
caster sugar	50 g
vanilla essence	few drops
cream	500 ml

Try something different

Cream horns may also be partially filled with pastry cream, to which various flavourings or fruit may be added. For example:

- praline
- chocolate
- coffee
- lemon
- raspberries
- strawberries
- mango
- orange segments.

* Using whipping cream

1 Roll out the pastry 2 mm thick, 30 cm long.
2 Cut into 1.5 cm-wide strips. Moisten on one side.
3 Wind carefully round lightly greased cream horn moulds, starting at the point and carefully overlapping each round slightly.
4 Brush with eggwash on one side and place on a greased baking sheet.
5 Bake at 220°C for about 20 minutes.
6 Sprinkle with icing sugar and return to a hot oven for a few seconds to glaze.
7 Remove carefully from the moulds and allow to cool.
8 Place a little jam in the bottom of each.
9 Add the sugar and essence to the cream and whip stiffly.
10 Place in a piping bag with a star tube and pipe a neat rose into each horn.

105 Eccles cakes

pastry, fruit baking

energy	kcal	fat	sat fat	carb	sugar	protein	fibre
691 kJ	164 kcal	8.6 g	3.7 g	22.1 g	17.3 g	1.1 g	1.4 g

Makes ⟩	12
puff pastry (recipe 3) or rough puff pastry (recipe 4)	200 g
egg white, to brush	
caster sugar, to coat	
Filling	
butter or margarine	50 g
raisins	50 g
Demerara sugar	50 g
currants	200 g
mixed spice (optional)	pinch

1 Roll out the pastry 2 mm thick.
2 Cut into rounds 10–12 cm diameter. Damp the edges.
3 Mix together all the ingredients for the filling and place a tbsp of the mixture in the centre of each round.

4 Fold the edges over to the centre and completely seal in the mixture.
5 Brush the top with egg white and dip into caster sugar.
6 Place on a greased baking sheet.
7 Cut two or three incisions with a knife so as to show the filling.
8 Bake at 220°C for 15–20 minutes.

106 Apple turnovers
(chausson aux pommes)

pastry, fruit baking

energy	kcal	fat	sat fat	carb	sugar	protein	fibre	sodium
353 KJ	84 kcal	4.4 g	2.0 g	10.4 g	4.4 g	1.5 g	0.1 g	0.0 g

Makes ⟩	12
puff pastry (recipe 3)	200 g
dry, sweetened apple purée	100 g
egg white, to brush	
caster sugar, to coat	

1 Roll out the pastry 2 mm thick.
2 Cut into 8 cm diameter rounds.
3 Roll out slightly oval, 12 × 10 cm.
4 Moisten the edges, place a little apple purée in the centre of each.
5 Fold over and seal firmly.
6 Brush with egg white and dip in caster sugar.
7 Place sugar side up on a dampened baking sheet.
8 Bake in hot oven, 220°C for 15–20 minutes.

Other types of fruit may be included in the turnovers, such as apple and mango, apple and blackberry, apple and passion fruit, and apple, pear and cinnamon.

107 Cream buns

(choux à la crème)

pastry, cream 🧁 baking

energy	kcal	fat	sat fat	carb	sugar	protein	fibre	sodium
752 KJ	182 kcal	16.4 g	8.5 g	6.7 g	3.6 g	2.2 g	0.2 g	0.0 g

Makes ⟩	8
choux paste (recipe 5)	125 ml
chopped almonds and/or nib sugar	25 g
whipped cream	250 ml
icing sugar, to serve	

1 Place the choux paste into a piping bag with a 1 cm plain tube.
2 Pipe out on to a lightly greased, dampened baking sheet into pieces the size of a walnut.
3 Eggwash the tops. 'Fork' each one (dip the fork in eggwash and lightly press down the top of each bun).
4 Sprinkle each with chopped almonds and/or nib sugar.
5 Bake at 200–220°C for about 30 minutes.
6 Allow to cool. Make a hole in the base of each bun.
7 Fill with sweetened, vanilla-flavoured whipped cream using a piping bag and small tube.
8 Sprinkle with icing sugar and serve.

108 Profiteroles and chocolate sauce

(profiteroles au chocolat)

pastry, chocolate 🧁 baking

energy	kcal	fat	sat fat	carb	sugar	protein	fibre
919 kJ	219 kcal	16.2 g	9.7 g	16.4 g	12.8 g	2.9 g	0.2 g

Portions ⟩	8
choux paste (recipe 5)	125 ml
chocolate sauce (recipe 24)	250 ml
whipped, sweetened, vanilla-flavoured cream	250 ml
icing sugar, to serve	

1 Line a baking sheet with greaseproof paper. Spoon the choux paste into a piping bag with a plain nozzle (approx. 1.5 cm diameter). Pipe a small blob of the paste under each corner of the paper to keep it in place.
2 Pipe walnut-sized balls of paste onto the sheet, spaced well apart. Level the peaked tops with the tip of a wet finger.

3 Bake for 18–20 minutes at 200°C, until well risen and golden brown. Remove from the oven, transfer to a wire rack and allow to cool completely.
4 Make a hole in each and fill with cream.
5 Dredge with icing sugar and serve with a sauceboat of cold chocolate sauce, or coat the profiteroles with the sauce.

Try something different
Alternatively, coffee sauce may be served and the profiteroles filled with non-dairy cream. Profiteroles may also be filled with chocolate-, coffee- or rum-flavoured pastry cream.

---

109 Chocolate éclairs
(éclairs au chocolat)

pastry, chocolate baking

energy	kcal	fat	sat fat	carb	sugar	protein	fibre
516 kJ	123 kcal	9.5 g	5.7 g	8.8 g	7.3 g	1.1 g	0.1 g

Makes >	12
choux paste (recipe 5)	125 ml
whipped cream	250 ml
fondant	100 g
chocolate couverture	25 g

1 Place the choux paste into a piping bag with a 1 cm plain tube.
2 Pipe into 8 cm lengths onto a lightly greased, dampened baking sheet.
3 Bake at 200–220°C for about 30 minutes.
4 Allow to cool. Slit down one side, with a sharp knife: this allows steam to escape and helps the éclairs to cool.
5 Fill with sweetened, vanilla-flavoured whipped cream, using a piping bag and small tube. The continental fashion is to fill with pastry cream.
6 Warm the fondant, add the finely cut chocolate, allow to melt slowly, adjust the consistency with a little sugar and water syrup if necessary. Do not overheat or the fondant will lose its shine.
7 Glaze the éclairs by dipping them in the fondant; remove the surplus with the finger. Allow to set.

Chocolate and coffee éclairs

Traditionally, chocolate éclairs were filled with chocolate pastry cream.

Try something different
- **Coffee éclairs** (*éclairs au café*): add a few drops of coffee essence to the fondant instead of chocolate; coffee éclairs may also be filled with pastry cream (recipe 8) flavoured with coffee.

Pierce the éclair

Pipe in the filling

Dip the éclair in fondant; wipe the edges to give a neat finish

pastry, nuts baking

energy 3180 KJ	kcal 761 kcal	fat 47.4 g	sat fat 14.7 g	carb 74.1 g	sugar 69.9 g	protein 14.1 g	fibre 0.2 g	*

Makes >	8
choux paste (recipe 5)	
crème diplomat (see recipe 8)	800 ml
flaked almonds	50 g
For the praline	
flaked almonds, hazelnuts and pecans (any combination)	375 g
granulated sugar	500 g

To make the praline

1 Place the nuts on a baking sheet and toast until evenly coloured.
2 Place the sugar in a large, heavy, stainless steel saucepan. Set the pan over a low heat and allow the sugar to caramelise. Do not over-stir, but do not allow the sugar to burn.
3 When the sugar is evenly coloured and reaches a temperature of 170°C, remove from the heat and stir in the nuts.
4 Immediately deposit the mixture on a silpat mat. Place another mat over the top and roll as thin as possible.
5 Allow to go completely cold. Break up and store in an airtight container.

For the Paris-Brest

1 Pipe choux paste (recipe 5) into rings and sprinkle with flaked almonds. Bake at 200–220°C for 35 minutes.
2 Slice each ring in half, allowing the steam to escape, and leave to cool. Fill with a mixture of crème diplomat (see recipe 8) and praline.

* Using single cream in place of crème diplomat

111 Choux paste fritters
(beignets soufflés)

energy	kcal	fat	sat fat	carb	sugar	protein	fibre
344 kJ	82 kcal	3.9 g	1.3 g	11.5 g	8.8 g	0.9 g	0.2 g

Portions ›	8
choux paste (recipe 5)	125 ml
icing sugar or caster sugar, to serve	
apricot sauce (recipe 20), to serve	125 ml

1 Using two spoons, shape the paste into pieces the size of a walnut. Place on sheets of silicone paper.
2 Lower the pieces into a moderately hot deep fat at 170–180°C. Allow to cook gently for 10–15 minutes.
3 Drain well, sprinkle liberally with icing sugar.
4 Serve with a sauceboat of hot apricot sauce (recipe 20).

Shape the fritter with two spoons

Lower the fritters into hot oil on a strip of paper

Lift them out with a spider

112 Victoria sandwich

eggs, flour   baking

energy	kcal	fat	sat fat	carb	sugar	protein	fibre	*
6866 kJ	1635 kcal	94.3 g	39.3 g	184.7 g	106.6 g	23.3 g	3.6 g	

Makes ⟩	single sponge	double sponge
butter	100 g	250 g
caster sugar	100 g	250 g
eggs	2	5
flour (soft)	100 g	250 g
baking powder	5 g	12 g

1 Cream the fat and sugar until soft and fluffy.
2 Gradually add the beaten eggs.
3 Lightly fold in the sieved flour, and baking powder.
4 Divide into two 18 cm greased sponge tins.
5 Bake at 190–200°C for 12–15 minutes.
6 Turn out on to a wire rack to cool.
7 Spread one half with jam, place the other half on top.
8 Dust with icing sugar.

* Using hard margarine

Blend the sugar and butter together

Place the mixture into greased cake tins

Flatten the top before baking

113 Genoise sponge
(génoise)

eggs, flour 🥧 baking

energy	kcal	fat	sat fat	carb	sugar	protein	fibre	*
5978 kJ	1423 kcal	65.8 g	25.6 g	182.8 g	106.6 g	36.5 g	3.6 g	

Makes ❯	single sponge	double sponge
eggs	4	10
caster sugar	100 g	250 g
flour (soft)	100 g	250 g
butter or oil	50 g	125 g

1 Whisk the eggs and sugar with a balloon whisk in a bowl over a pan of hot water.
2 Continue until the mixture is light and creamy, and has doubled in bulk.
3 Remove from the heat and whisk until cold and thick (ribbon stage). Fold in the flour very gently.
4 Take a small amount of the mixture and combine it with the melted butter. Then return this to the rest of the mixture and fold through.
5 Place in a greased, floured Genoise mould.
6 Bake in a moderately hot oven, at 200–220°C, for about 30 minutes.

A thinly sliced Genoise filled with cream and dusted with icing sugar

Making a Genoise
http://bit.ly/ABYLlu

Whisk the eggs and sugar together over boiling water

Carry on whisking as the mixture warms up

When the mixture is ready, it will form ribbons and you can draw a figure eight with it

Fold in the flour gently

Add part of the flour mixture to the butter

Bake the mixture in greased cake tins

* Using hard margarine (4 portions)

114 Fresh cream and strawberry gateau

fruit, cream

energy	kcal	fat	sat fat	carb	sugar	protein	fibre	*
1975 KJ	473 kcal	28.4 g	11.1 g	53.0 g	39.7 g	4.5 g	0.9 g	

Makes ⟩	1
Genoise sponge (recipe 113) made with vanilla	1
stock syrup (recipe 15)	100 ml
raspberry jam	50 ml
whipping or double cream	500 ml
icing sugar	75 g
strawberries, sliced	1 punnet

1 Carefully slice the sponge cake into three equal discs. Brush each with syrup.
2 Slowly whip the cream with the icing sugar to achieve the correct consistency.
3 Place the first piece of sponge on a cake board. Soak with syrup. Spread with a layer of jam, then a layer of cream. Arrange or scatter sliced strawberries on top.
4 Place the next piece of sponge on top. Repeat the layers of syrup, cream and strawberries. Top with additional cream.

5 Place the final piece of sponge on top.
6 Coat the top and sides with cream. Chill.
7 Comb scrape the sides of the gateau. Pipe 12 rosettes on top, and decorate.

* Based on 60 g of sponge per portion

115 Chocolate Genoise sponge
(génoise au chocolat)

eggs, flour baking

Makes ⟩	2 × 16 cm sponges
eggs	8
caster sugar	225 g
flour	175 g
cocoa powder	50 g
butter, melted	65 g

1 Whisk the eggs and sugar together to form a sabayon.
2 Slowly fold in the flour and cocoa powder.
3 Take a small amount of the mixture and combine it with the melted butter. Then return this to the rest of the mixture and fold through.
4 Place in a lined mould and bake at 180°C for 15–20 minutes.

A chocolate Genoise, sliced, ready for filling

Make sure you have prepared all the equipment before you start.

116 Chocolate gâteau

chocolate

energy	kcal	fat	sat fat	carb	sugar	protein	fibre	*
20113 kJ	4789 kcal	260.9 g	148.7 g	606.0 g	533.2 g	41.6 g	4.8 g	

Makes ›	single gâteau	double gâteau
chocolate Genoise sponge (recipe 115)	made with 4 eggs	made with 10 eggs
stock syrup (recipe 15), as required		
chocolate glaze (see below or ready made)	100 g	250 g
Chocolate buttercream		
unsalted butter	100 g	250 g
icing sugar	75 g	190 g
block chocolate (melted in a basin in a bain-marie)	25 g	60 g

1 Cut the Genoise into three slices crosswise.
2 Prepare the buttercream as for recipe 9, and mix in the melted chocolate.
3 Lightly moisten each slice of Genoise with stock syrup, which may be flavoured with kirsch, rum, etc.
4 Lightly spread each slice of Genoise with buttercream and sandwich together.
5 Coat the sides and top with glaze, then decorate.

To make the chocolate glaze

double cream	375 ml
water	350 ml
caster sugar	450 g
cocoa powder	150 g
leaf gelatine, soaked in cold water	8½ leaves (20 g)

1 Place the cream, water, sugar and cocoa powder in a heavy-bottomed saucepan. Bring to the boil slowly. Simmer for 2–3 minutes, then remove from the heat.
2 Drain the soaked gelatine and add it to the mixture. Stir until the gelatine has dissolved.
3 Pass, then stir over ice to cool.
4 Pour into a plastic container and press clingfilm directly onto the surface.

Try something different
Make twice as much buttercream, and use it to lightly coat the sides and top of the gateau, instead of a glaze. Cover the sides with chocolate vermicelli or flakes.

* Using hard margarine and butter, and buttercream (4 portions)

117 Coffee gâteau
(gâteau moka)

energy	kcal	fat	sat fat	carb	sugar	protein	fibre
4046 kJ	963 kcal	65.5 g	36.0 g	86.0 g	66.2 g	13.1 g	1.7 g

Makes ›	single gâteau	double gâteau
chocolate Genoise sponge (recipe 115)	made with 4 eggs	made with 10 eggs
stock syrup (recipe 15), as required		
fondant, flavoured with coffee	150 g	375 g
toasted, flaked or nibbed almonds (optional for decoration)	50 g	125 g
Coffee buttercream		
unsalted butter	100 g	250 g
icing sugar	75 g	190 g
coffee essence	1–2 drops	3–4 drops

1 Cut the Genoise into three slices crosswise.
2 Prepare the buttercream as for recipe 9, and flavour with coffee essence.
3 Lightly moisten each slice of Genoise with stock syrup, which may be flavoured with Tia Maria, brandy, etc.
4 Lightly spread each slice with buttercream and sandwich together.
5 Cover the top and sides with the coffee fondant.
6 Decorate. Possible decorations include flaked almonds, coffee beans and chocolate. The traditional decoration includes the word 'MOKA' piped in buttercream.

Try something different
Make twice as much buttercream and use it to lightly coat the sides and top of the gateau, instead of fondant.

118 Roulade sponge

eggs, flour 🍴 baking

Portions 〉	6	24
whole eggs	6 (225 ml)	16 (900 ml)
egg yolks	1	5
caster sugar	125 g	510 g
soft flour	85 g	340 g

1. Whisk the eggs, yolks and sugar by hand over boiling water until warm.
2. Whisk on a food mixer until the ribbon stage.
3. Sieve the flour onto paper.
4. Preheat the oven to 220°C.
5. Fold the flour into the egg mixture as quickly and lightly as possible (ask someone else to help).
6. Divide the mixture between two prepared baking sheets, as quickly as possible. Spread evenly.
7. Bake for 4–5 minutes.
8. Cool completely.
9. Cut the sheets in half. Wrap individually in clingfilm before stacking.
10. Store in the freezer, making sure they are not bent or squashed.

Roulade sponge should not be crisp: you should be able to bend it

Try something different

To make a **chocolate roulade sponge**, replace the flour with a mixture of 85 g cornflour, 85 g cocoa powder and 225 g soft flour.

119 Swiss roll

eggs, flour baking

energy	kcal	fat	sat fat	carb	sugar	protein	fibre
4445 kJ	1058 kcal	25.3 g	8.0 g	182.7 g	106.5 g	36.5 g	3.6 g

*

Portions ›	4–6	10–12
Method 1		
eggs	4	10
caster sugar	100 g	250 g
flour (soft)	100 g	250 g
jam, as required		
Method 2		
eggs	250 ml	625 ml
caster sugar	175 g	425 g
flour (soft)	125 g	300 g
jam, as required		

1 Whisk the eggs and sugar with a balloon whisk in a bowl over a pan of hot water, using the ingredients specified for either method 1 or 2.

2 Continue until the mixture is light, creamy and double in bulk.

3 Remove from the heat and whisk until cold and thick (ribbon stage).

4 Fold in the flour very gently.

5 Grease a Swiss roll tin and line with greased greaseproof or silicone paper.

6 Pour in the mixture and bake at 220°C for about 6 minutes.

7 Turn out on to a sheet of paper sprinkled with additional caster sugar.

8 Remove the paper from the Swiss roll, spread with warm jam.

9 Roll into a fairly tight roll, leaving the paper on the outside for a few minutes.

10 Remove the paper and allow to cool on a wire rack.

* 4 portions

120 Small cakes

eggs, flour 🍞 baking

energy	kcal	fat	sat fat	carb	sugar	protein	fibre	*
947 kJ	225 kcal	11.6 g	4.8 g	28.8 g	13.4 g	3.3 g	0.7 g	

Makes ›	20
flour (soft) or self-raising	200 g
baking powder (with plain flour)	1 level tsp
salt (optional)	pinch
margarine or butter	125 g
caster sugar	125 g
eggs	2–3

Method 1: rubbing in

1 Sieve the flour, baking powder and salt (if using).
2 Rub in the butter or margarine to achieve a sandy texture. Add the sugar.
3 Gradually add the well-beaten eggs and mix as lightly as possible until combined.

Method 2: creaming

1 Cream the margarine and sugar in a bowl until soft and fluffy.
2 Slowly add the well-beaten eggs, mixing continuously and beating really well between each addition.
3 Lightly mix in the sieved flour, baking powder and salt (if using).

In both cases the consistency should be a light dropping one and, if necessary, it may be adjusted with the addition of a few drops of milk.
This is a great base for a cupcake.

Try something different

● **Cherry cakes:** add 50 g glacé cherries cut in quarters and 3–4 drops vanilla essence to the basic mixture (method 2) and divide into 8–12 lightly greased cake tins or paper cases. Bake in a hot oven at 220°C for 15–20 minutes.
● **Coconut cakes:** in place of 50 g flour, use 50 g desiccated coconut and 3–4 drops vanilla essence to the basic mixture (method 2) and cook as for cherry cakes.
● **Queen cakes:** to the basic mixture (method 2) add 100 g washed and dried mixed fruit and cook as for cherry cakes.

* Using hard margarine

121 Scones

eggs, flour baking

energy	kcal	fat	sat fat	carb	sugar	protein	fibre
678 kJ	162 kcal	5.8 g	2.5 g	26.3 g	7.5 g	2.7 g	1.0 g

Makes >	8	20
self-raising flour	200 g	500 g
baking powder	5 g	12 g
salt	pinch	large pinch
butter or margarine	50 g	125 g
caster sugar	50 g	125 g
milk or water	95 ml	250 ml

Try something different

- Add 50 g (125 g for 20 scones) washed and dried sultanas to the scone mixture for fruit scones; 50 per cent wholemeal flour may be used.
- Add other flavours to the mixture: try coconut or dried cranberries.
- For precisely formed scones, roll out the dough to approx. 2 cm thick and cut scones with a 4–5 cm cutter.

* Using hard margarine

1 Sieve the flour, baking powder and salt.
2 Rub in the fat to achieve a sandy texture. Make a well in the centre.
3 Dissolve the sugar in the liquid.
4 Gradually incorporate the flour; mix lightly.
5 Roll out two rounds, 1 cm thick. Place on a greased baking sheet.
6 Cut a cross halfway through the rounds with a large knife.
7 Milkwash and bake at 200°C for 15–20 minutes.

The comparatively small amount of fat, rapid mixing to a soft dough, quick and light handling are essentials to produce a light scone.

122 Rock cakes

eggs, flour baking

energy	kcal	fat	sat fat	carb	sugar	protein	fibre	*
913 kJ	217 kcal	8.7 g	3.6 g	33.6 g	14.3 g	3.4 g	1.3 g	

Makes ⟩	16
medium flour (50% soft and 50% strong flour)	500 g
baking powder	30 g
salt	3 g
caster sugar	125 g
egg	60 g
butter	120 g
currants	90 g
citrus peel	30 g
milk	180 g
eggwash	

1 Sieve the flour, baking powder and salt through a fine sieve.
2 Dissolve the sugar in the liquid egg.
3 Rub the butter into the flour to form a crumb mix.
4 Add the currants and peel.
5 Blend in the milk to achieve a smooth mix.
6 Divide the mixture into small portions, approx. 70 g each, and place evenly onto a baking tray.
7 Eggwash and sprinkle with caster sugar.
8 Bake for 15–20 minutes at 210°C, until light golden brown.

Try something different
Add a small pinch of mixed spice.

* Using hard margarine

123 Madeleines

eggs, flour 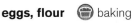 baking

Portions 〉	45 (585 g)
caster sugar	125 g
eggs	3
vanilla pod, seeds from	1
flour	150 g
baking powder	1 tsp
beurre noisette	125 g

1 Whisk the sugar, eggs and vanilla seeds to a hot sabayon.
2 Fold in the flour and the baking powder.
3 Fold in the *beurre noisette* and chill for up to 2 hours.
4 Pipe into well-buttered madeleine moulds and bake in a moderate oven.
5 Turn out and allow to cool.

124 Rich fruit cake

eggs, flour, fruit baking

energy	kcal	fat	sat fat	carb	sugar	protein	fibre	sodium
2367 KJ	563 kcal	24.8 g	11.3 g	81.9 g	69.4 g	8.8 g	2.8 g	0.6 g

1 Cream the butter or margarine and sugar until light and fluffy.
2 Gradually beat in the eggs, creaming continuously.
3 Add the glycerine.
4 Sift the flour, nutmeg, mixed spice and cinnamon. Add the ground almonds and salt, mix well.
5 Carefully fold in the flour, nutmeg, mixed spice, cinnamon, ground almonds and salt into the eggs and sugar.
6 Fold in the dried fruit, mixed peel, glacé cherries and lemon rind.
7 Place the mixture into a prepared cake tin lined with silicone. The outside of the tin should also be well protected with paper. Bake at the required temperature for the required time.
8 To test, insert a needle into the centre of the cake; when cooked, it should come out clean and free of uncooked mixture.

9 Remove from the oven and allow to cool.
10 Wrap in tin foil and allow to mature for 2–3 weeks before coating with marzipan and icing.

Cake size ⟩	16 cm dia, 8 cm deep	21 cm dia, 8 cm deep	26 cm dia, 8 cm deep	31 cm dia, 8 cm deep
butter or margarine	150 g	200 g	300 g	550 g
caster or soft brown sugar	150 g	200 g	300 g	550 g
eggs	4	6	8	10
glycerine	2 tsp	3 tsp	1 tbsp	2 tbsp
flour (soft)	125 g	175 g	275 g	500 g
nutmeg	¾ tsp	1 tsp	1¼ tsp	2 tsp
mixed spice	¾ tsp	1 tsp	1¼ tsp	2 tsp
cinnamon	¾ tsp	1 tsp	1¼ tsp	2 tsp
ground almonds	75 g	100 g	125 g	200 g
salt	6 g	8 g	10 g	12 g
currants	150 g	200 g	300 g	550 g
sultanas	150 g	200 g	300 g	550 g
raisins	125 g	150 g	225 g	400 g
mixed peel	75 g	100 g	125 g	200 g
glacé cherries	75 g	100 g	125 g	200 g
lemon, grated rind of	½	½	1	2
oven temperature	150°C	150°C	130°C	110°C
time (approx.)	3 hours	3½ hours	4½ hours	6–7 hours

The dried fruit may be soaked in brandy for 12 hours.
Allow 3 tbsp of brandy for a 16 cm diameter cake; 4
tbsp for 21 cm diameter; 5 tbsp for 26 cm diameter, etc.
Alternatively, instead of soaking the fruit before baking,
the brandy may be poured over the cake once it leaves the
oven after baking.

125 Banana bread

eggs, flour, fruit  baking

energy	kcal	fat	sat fat	carb	sugar	protein	fibre	sodium *
1421 KJ	338 kcal	13.6 g	2.4 g	52.7 g	36.3 g	4.4 g	2.0 g	0.1 g

Makes ›	1 cake	3 cakes
ripe bananas	150 g	460 g
vegetable oil	30 ml	110 ml
butter, melted	50 g	140 g
caster sugar	150 g	460 g
eggs	1	4
flour (soft)	155 g	460 g
baking powder	7 g	20 g
salt	pinch	2 g

1 Beat the bananas, oil and butter together at a medium speed with the paddle attachment in a food mixer.
2 Add sugar and eggs and mix until smooth.
3 Add the dry ingredients and mix well.
4 Place mixture into 3 well-greased or silicone-lined tins (7.5 cm deep × 17.5 cm long × 10 cm wide).
5 Bake at 170°C in a medium fan oven for 35 minutes and then check if cooked by inserting a skewer into the cake mixture. If the skewer comes out clean, the banana bread is done.
6 Allow to cool.

* For a 200 g slice

126 Seeded bread rolls

yeast, flour baking

Makes ›	8	16
flour (strong)	1 kg	2 kg
yeast	30 g	60 g
water at 37°C	600 ml	1175 ml
salt	20 g	40 g
caster sugar	10 g	20 g
sunflower oil	50 g	100 g
seeds (e.g. poppy, sunflower, sesame, fennel, caraway)		

1 Sieve the flour onto paper.
2 Dissolve the yeast in half the water.
3 Dissolve the salt, sugar and oil in the rest of the water.
4 Add both liquids to the flour at once.
5 Mix on speed number 1 for 5 minutes, or mix and then knead by hand for 10 minutes, to a smooth dough.
6 Cover with clingfilm and leave for 1 hour.

7 Knock back the dough. Divide it into 8 or 16 pieces. Keep it covered at all times.
8 Shape the pieces of dough. Place on a silicon-covered baking sheet, in neatly spaced, staggered rows.
9 Prove until the rolls double in size.
10 Eggwash carefully and scatter seeds over the top. Bake at 220°C for 8–10 minutes with steam.

127 Wheatmeal bread

yeast, flour baking

energy	kcal	fat	sat fat	carb	sugar	protein	fibre
6893 KJ	1628 kcal	32.5 g	16.7 g	302.3 g	62.6 g	50.5 g	40.0 g

Loaves >	2
unsalted butter or oil	60 g
honey	3 tbsp
water, lukewarm	500 ml
fresh yeast	25 g
or	
dried yeast	18 g
salt	1 tbsp
flour, unbleached strong white	125 g
flour, stoneground wholemeal	625 g

1 Melt the butter in a saucepan.
2 Mix together 1 tbsp of honey and 4 tbsp of the water in a bowl.
3 Disperse the yeast into the honey mixture.
4 In a basin, place the melted butter, remaining honey and water, the yeast mixture and salt.
5 Add the white flour and half the wholemeal flour. Mix well.
6 Add the remaining wholemeal flour gradually, mixing well between each addition.
7 The dough should pull away from the side of the bowl and form a ball. The resulting dough should be soft and slightly sticky.
8 Turn out onto a floured work surface. Sprinkle with white flour, knead well.
9 Brush a clean bowl with melted butter or oil. Place in the dough, cover with a damp cloth and allow to prove in a warm place. This will take approximately 1–1½ hours.
10 Knock back and further knead the dough. Cover again and rest for 10–15 minutes.
11 Divide the dough into two equal pieces.
12 Form each piece of dough into a cottage loaf or place in a suitable loaf tin.
13 Allow to prove in a warm place for approx. 45 minutes.
14 Place in a preheated oven, 220°C and bake until well browned (approx. 40–45 minutes).
15 When baked, the bread should sound hollow and the sides should feel crisp when pressed.
16 Cool on a wire rack.

Try something different

Alternatively, the bread may be divided into 50 g rolls, brushed with eggwash and baked at 200°C for approx. 10 minutes.

Healthy eating tip

Only a little salt is necessary to 'control' the yeast. Many customers will prefer less salty bread.

128 Parmesan rolls

yeast, flour, cheese baking

energy	kcal	fat	sat fat	carb	sugar	protein	fibre	sodium
2169 KJ	512 kcal	9.9 g	2.2 g	94.3 g	1.8 g	17.5 g	5.2 g	1.0 g

1 Make a basic bread dough (follow recipe 126 but omit the seeds). After kneading it, cover with a tea towel and leave to rest and prove for 30 minutes.
2 Using a rolling pin, pin out the dough to a thickness of approx. 3 cm. Brush with a little water.
3 Pass finely grated Parmesan (50 g for 8 rolls) through a coarse sieve onto the dough.
4 Cut the dough into evenly sized pieces, each about 40 g.
5 Place each piece of dough onto a baking sheet with a silpat mat or non-stick parchment. Place in the prover and leave until they have doubled in size.
6 Bake in a preheated oven at 220°C for approx. 10 minutes. Cool on a wire rack.

Try something different
Try adding white or black poppy seeds, sesame seeds or old bay seasoning to the dough.

129 Red onion and sage rolls

yeast, flour baking

energy	kcal	fat	sat fat	carb	sugar	protein	fibre	sodium
759 KJ	181 kcal	9.2 g	1.7 g	21.7 g	2.8 g	4.2 g	1.2 g	1.0 g

Makes >	8	16
red onion	½	1
dried sage	¼ tsp	½ tsp
bread roll dough (see recipe 126 but omit the seeds)		
oil	1 tbsp	2 tbsp

1 Finely dice the red onion. Sweat it, then leave to cool.
2 Chop the sage and add it to the onion.
3 Pin out bread dough in a rectangle. Spread the onion and sage mixture over seven-eighths of the dough. Eggwash the exposed edge.
4 Roll the dough as you would for a Swiss roll, and seal the edge.

5 Cut into 50 g slices.
6 Place the slices on a prepared baking sheet and eggwash. Bake in a preheated oven at 220°C for approx. 10 minutes. Cool on a wire rack.

130 Onion and walnut bread

yeast, flour, nuts 🍳 baking, 🍳 shallow frying, sauté

energy	kcal	fat	sat fat	carb	sugar	protein	fibre	sodium
11271 KJ	2673 kcal	85.7 g	13.8 g	417.2 g	41.7 g	85.2 g	27.5 g	4.2 g

Loaves >	1
milk	425 ml
fresh yeast	12 g
vegetable oil	30 ml
salt	10 g (2 tsp)
bread flour	500 g
onion, large, finely chopped	1
oil for greasing	
pepper	
walnut pieces, lightly toasted	50 g
eggwash	

1 Warm 60 ml (4 tbsp) of milk to 37°C.
2 Disperse the yeast into the milk.
3 Place the dispersed yeast, remaining milk, half the oil and salt into a large bowl.
4 Stir in half of the flour and mix well with your hand.
5 Gradually add the remaining flour, mixing well after each addition. Mix well until a smooth elastic dough is obtained. Adjust the consistency by adding more flour if necessary. The dough should be soft and slightly sticky.
6 Turn the dough out onto a floured work surface, knead well. Keep kneading until very smooth and elastic. This will take approx. 5–7 minutes.
7 Brush a large bowl with oil. Place the dough into the bowl, turn over so that it is covered with oil.
8 Cover with a damp cloth and allow to prove until double in size, approx. 1–1½ hours.
9 Heat the remaining oil in a frying pan. Sauté the finely chopped onion in the butter, season with salt and pepper. Sauté until lightly coloured. Allow to cool.
10 When proved, turn the dough out on to a lightly floured table and knock back for approx. 20 seconds, cover and allow to rest for approx. 5 minutes.

11 Knead the onion and walnuts into the dough. Cover and allow to rest for a further 5 minutes.
12 Mould the dough into a ball and form a flattened round loaf approx. 18–25 cm in diameter.
13 Place ring on to a lightly greased baking sheet. Cover and allow to prove to double in size for approx. 45 minutes, preferably in a prover.
14 Brush with eggwash lightly. Using kitchen scissors, snip the top of the ring in a zig-zag fashion.
15 Bake in a preheated oven at 200°C for 45–50 minutes.
16 When baked and golden brown place bread on a wire rack and allow to cool. If tapped, it should sound hollow and the sides should be crisp.

Healthy eating tip

Only a little salt is necessary to 'control' the yeast. Many customers will prefer less salty bread.

131 Sun-dried tomato bread

energy	kcal	fat	sat fat	carb	sugar	protein	fibre	sodium
10192 KJ	2414 kcal	70.8 g	12.8 g	401.8 g	29.6 g	67.4 g	20.7 g	5.0 g

Loaves ›	2 × 450 g
sun-dried tomatoes, chopped	100 g
water	300 ml
bread flour	500 g
salt	10 g
skimmed milk powder	12.5 g
shortening (white vegetable fat)	12.5 g
yeast (fresh)	20 g
sugar	12 g

1 Soak the sun-dried tomatoes in boiling water for 30 minutes.
2 Sieve the flour, salt and skimmed milk powder.
3 Add the shortening and rub through the dry ingredients.
4 Disperse the yeast into warm water, approx. 37°C. Add and dissolve the sugar. Add to the above ingredients.

5 Mix until a smooth dough is formed. Check for any extremes in consistency and adjust as necessary until a smooth elastic dough is formed.
6 Cover the dough, keep warm and allow to prove.
7 After approx. 30–40 minutes, knock back the dough and mix in the chopped sun-dried tomatoes (well drained).
8 Mould and prove again for another 30 minutes (covered).
9 Divide the dough into two and mould round.
10 Rest for 10 minutes. Keep covered.
11 Re-mould into long loaf shapes and place on baking trays.
12 Prove at 38–40°C in humid conditions, preferably in a prover.
13 Cut 3 or 4 slashes in the top of each loaf. Bake at 225°C for 25–30 minutes.
14 After baking, remove the bread from the trays immediately and place on a cooling wire.

energy	kcal	fat	sat fat	carb	sugar	protein	fibre	sodium
5174 KJ	1229 kcal	44.2 g	6.5 g	188.3 g	3.5 g	30.9 g	15.9 g	5.2 g

Loaves ⟩	6
olive ferment	540 g
black olives, chopped	320 g
yeast	15 g
olive oil	150 ml
water	850 ml
no. 4 flour (strong Canadian wheat flour)	1.5 kg
salt	30 g
Maldon salt	

1 Place all the ingredients (three-quarters of the oil), except the flour and salt, into a large bowl. Mix the ingredients by hand.

2 Sprinkle the flour on top, then the salt, and stir to a slack dough, working in six turns of the bowl. Fold the edge into the centre and add a little more olive oil. Leave for 20 minutes.

3 Fold with the same method. The dough should resemble the shape of a doughnut with a dip in the centre.

4 Add a little more olive oil and leave in a warm place for 20 minutes.

5 Fold again and leave in a warm place for 20 minutes.

6 Divide the dough into approx. five 550 g balls.

7 Roll into slipper shapes divided by supported greaseproof paper.

8 Spray with water. Wrap with clingfilm and prove in the fridge overnight.

9 Remove from the fridge, unwrap and spray with water.

10 Place in a prover for approx. 30 minutes.

11 Remove, then spray again, removing greaseproof paper from the sides of the bread.

12 Divide onto oven board. Sprinkle with Maldon salt and dust with flour.

13 Cook at 230°C steaming 5 pulses for 4 minutes with the vent closed.

Make up the ferment

Ferment ready for use

Start mixing in the ingredients, tearing up the ferment

Continue mixing in the ingredients and working the dough

Fold the dough at 20-minute intervals

Divide and roll into loaves

133 Rye bread

yeast, flour baking

energy	kcal	fat	sat fat	carb	sugar	protein	fibre	sodium
7174 KJ	1690 kcal	24.7 g	2.9 g	331.8 g	12.5 g	46.7 g	46.2 g	6.0 g

Loaves ›	1
fresh yeast (or dried yeast may be used)	15 g
water	60 ml (4 tbsp)
black treacle	15 ml (1 tbsp)
vegetable oil	15 ml (1 tbsp)
caraway seeds (optional)	15 g
salt	15 g
lager	250 ml
rye flour	250 g
unbleached bread flour	175 g
polenta	
eggwash	

1 Disperse the yeast in the warm water (at approx. 37°C).

2 In a basin mix the black treacle, oil, two-thirds of the caraway seeds (if required) and the salt. Add the lager. Add the yeast and mix in the sieved rye flour. Mix well.

3 Gradually add the bread flour. Continue to add the flour until the dough is formed and it is soft and slightly sticky.

4 Turn the dough onto a lightly floured surface and knead well.

5 Knead the dough until it is smooth and elastic.

6 Place the kneaded dough into a suitable bowl that has been brushed with oil.

7 Cover with a damp cloth and allow the dough to prove in a warm place until it is double in size. This will take about 1½–2 hours.

8 Turn the dough onto a lightly floured work surface, knock back the dough to original size. Cover and allow to rest for approx. 5–10 minutes.

9 Shape the dough into an oval approx. 25 cm long.

10 Place onto a baking sheet lightly sprinkled with polenta.

11 Allow the dough to prove in a warm place, preferably in a prover, until double in size (approx. 45 minutes to 1 hour).

12 Lightly brush the loaf with eggwash, sprinkle with the remaining caraway seeds (if required).

13 Using a small, sharp knife, make three diagonal slashes, approximately 5 mm deep into the top of the loaf.

14 Place in a pre-heated oven at 190°C and bake for approx. 50–55 minutes.

15 When cooked, the bread should sound hollow when tapped and the sides should feel crisp.

16 Allow to cool.

Healthy eating tip

Only a little salt is necessary to 'control' the yeast. Many customers will prefer less salty bread.

134 Soda bread

flour baking

energy	kcal	fat	sat fat	carb	sugar	protein	fibre	sodium
8341 KJ	1970 kcal	39.8 g	20.9 g	357.8 g	18.5 g	67.9 g	20.9 g	3.6 g

Loaves ›	2
flour, wholemeal	250 g
flour (strong)	250 g
bicarbonate of soda	1 tsp
salt	1 tsp
buttermilk	200 g
water, warm	60 ml
butter, melted	25 g

1 Sift the flours, salt and bicarbonate of soda into a bowl.

2 Make a well and add the buttermilk, warm water and melted butter.

3 Work the dough for about 5 minutes.

4 Mould into 2 round loaves and mark the top with a cross.

5 Bake at 200°C for about 25 minutes. When the bread is ready, it should make a hollow sound when tapped.

135 Bagels

yeast, flour  poaching, baking

energy	kcal	fat	sat fat	carb	sugar	protein	fibre	sodium
670 KJ	158 kcal	2.1 g	0.5 g	32.7 g	5.0 g	6.2 g	1.6 g	0.8 g

	Makes ⟩	12
water		125 ml
milk		250 ml
fresh yeast		12 g
or		
dried yeast		10 g
caster sugar		2 tbsp
bread flour		450 g
salt		15 g (3 tsp)
eggwash		
poppy seeds		1 tbsp
sea salt		10 g (2 tsp)

1 Warm the water and milk to 37°C, disperse the yeast in the water, add 1 tbsp of sugar, cover and leave to stand in a warm place for approx.10 minutes.

2 Add the sifted flour and salt gradually, mixing into a firm dough. Add a little more flour, or some water, if necessary, to form a smooth and elastic dough.

3 Turn dough onto a floured surface. Knead well until dough is smooth and elastic. Place dough into a well-greased bowl, cover and leave to stand in a warm place or in a prover for 1 hour or until the dough has doubled in size.

4 Turn dough out onto a floured surface, knead until smooth. Divide into 12, knead each into a ball. Make a hole in the centre of each.

5 Rotate each ball of dough with the finger until the hole is one-third of the size of the bagel.

6 Place bagels on a greased baking sheet approx. 3 cm apart. Cover and stand in a warm place or prover until double in size.

7 Drop bagels individually into a pan of boiling water. Do not allow them to touch. Turn bagels after 1 minute, simmer for a further 1 minute. Remove, drain well and place on greased baking sheet.

8 Brush each with eggwash, sprinkle with poppy seeds and sea salt. Bake in an oven at 200°C for about 20 minutes. Remove, cool on a wire rack.

- Bagels are now very popular and are usually filled with a variety of fillings (e.g. smoked salmon and cream cheese) and served as a snack.
- The dough can be flavoured with herbs, cinnamon or sultanas.

Use a rolling pin to make a hole in the centre of each bagel

Poach the bagels in water

Eggwash the bagels and sprinkle with seeds before baking

Practical Cookery 12th edition

136 Cholla bread

yeast, flour baking

energy	kcal	fat	sat fat	carb	sugar	protein	fibre	sodium
4876 KJ	1154 kcal	30.1 g	16.1 g	198.1 g	13.1 g	35.0 g	10.3 g	1.2 g

Loaves >	2
butter or margarine	56 g
flour (strong)	500 g
caster sugar	18 g
salt	1 tsp
egg	63 g
fresh yeast	25 g

1 Rub the butter or margarine into the sieved flour in a suitable basin.
2 Mix the sugar, salt and egg together.
3 Disperse the yeast in the water.
4 Add all these ingredients to the sieved flour and mix well to develop the dough. Cover with a damp cloth or plastic and allow to ferment for about 45 minutes.

5 Divide into 125–150 g strands and begin to plait as follows:

4–strand plait	5–strand plait
2 over 3	2 over 3
4 over 2	5 over 2
1 over 3	1 over 3

6 After moulding, place on a lightly greased baking sheet and eggwash lightly.
7 Prove in a little steam until double in size. Eggwash again lightly and decorate with maw seeds (poppy seeds).
8 Bake in a hot oven, at 220°C for 25–30 minutes.

137 Focaccia

yeast, flour baking

energy	kcal	fat	sat fat	carb	sugar	protein	fibre	sodium
12915 KJ	3052 kcal	78.7 g	11.5 g	553.6 g	14.7 g	66.7 g	30.0 g	5.6 g

Loaves ⟩	1
fresh yeast	20 g
sugar	1 tsp
lukewarm water (about 37°C)	230 ml
extra virgin olive oil, plus extra to drizzle on the bread	70 g
salt	1½ tsp
strong white flour	725 g
coarse salt	
picked rosemary	

1 Mix the yeast and sugar in half of the lukewarm water in a bowl until foamy. In another bowl, add the remaining water, the olive oil, and the salt.

2 Pour in the yeast mixture.

3 Blend in the flour, a quarter at a time, until the dough comes together. Knead on a floured board for 10 minutes, adding flour as needed to make it smooth and elastic. Put the dough in an oiled bowl, turn to coat well, and cover with a towel.

4 Let rise in a warm draught-free place for 1 hour, until doubled in size.

5 Knock back the dough, knead it for a further 5 minutes, and gently roll it out in to a large disc or sheet to approx. 2 cm thick.

6 Let rise for 15 minutes, covered. Oil your fingers and make impressions with them in the dough, 3 cm apart. Let prove for 1 hour.

7 Preheat the oven to 210°C. Drizzle the dough with olive oil and sprinkle with coarse salt and picked rosemary.

8 Bake for 15–20 minutes in a very hot oven at 200°C, until golden brown. Sprinkle with additional oil if desired. Serve warm.

Try something different

Instead of rosemary and coarse salt, other flavours may be used. The other focaccia shown here are made with black olives and anchovies.

138 Pizza

energy	kcal	fat	sat fat	carb	sugar	protein	fibre	*
3956 kJ	941 kcal	46.3 g	13 g	114.4 g	20.1 g	23.6 g	8.4 g	

	Makes ⟩ 2 × 18 cm
flour, strong white	200 g
pinch of salt	
margarine	12 g
yeast	5 g
water or milk at 24°C	125 ml
caster sugar	5 g
onions, finely chopped	100 g
cloves of garlic, crushed	2
sunflower oil	60 ml
plum tomatoes, canned	200 g
tomato purée	100 g
oregano	3 g
basil	3 g
sugar	10 g
cornflour	10 g
mozzarella cheese	100 g

Pizza with mozzarella and fresh basil

1 Sieve the flour and the salt. Rub in the margarine.
2 Disperse the yeast in the warm milk or water; add the caster sugar. Add this mixture to the flour.
3 Mix well, knead to a smooth dough, place in a basin covered with a damp cloth and allow to prove until doubled in size.
4 Knock back, divide into two and roll out into two 18 cm discs. Place on a lightly greased baking sheet.
5 Sweat the finely chopped onions and garlic in the oil until cooked.
6 Add the roughly chopped tomatoes, tomato purée, oregano, basil and sugar. Bring to the boil, simmer for 5 minutes, blend and pass.
7 Take the discs of pizza dough and spread a ladle of tomato sauce (*passata*) on each one.
8 Sprinkle with grated mozzarella cheese or lay slices of cheese on top.
9 Bake in a moderately hot oven at 240°C, for about 5 minutes.

The pizza dough may also be made into rectangles so that it can be sliced into fingers for buffet work.

Pizza is a traditional dish originating from southern Italy. In simple terms it is a flat bread dough that can be topped with a wide variety of ingredients and baked quickly. The only rule is not to add wet ingredients, such as tomatoes, which are too juicy, otherwise the pizza will become soggy. Traditionally, pizzas are baked in a wood-fired brick oven, but they can be baked in any type of hot oven for 5–10 minutes depending on the ingredients. The recipe given here is a typical one.

Try something different
Oregano is sprinkled on most pizzas before baking.
This is a basic recipe and many variations exist, some have the addition of olives, artichoke bottoms, prawns, mortadella sausage, garlic sausage or anchovy fillets. Other combinations include:
- mozzarella cheese, anchovies, capers and garlic
- mozzarella cheese, tomato and oregano
- ham, mushrooms, egg and parmesan cheese
- prawns, tuna, capers and garlic
- ham, mushrooms and olives.

* Using 100 per cent strong white flour

yeast, flour baking, tandoori

energy	kcal	fat	sat fat	carb	sugar	protein	fibre
1619 kJ	386 kcal	20.5 g	12.0 g	48.3 g	5.0 g	10.1 g	1.8 g	*

Portions ›	6
flour (strong)	350 g
caster sugar	1 ½ tsp
salt	1 tsp
baking powder	½ tsp
fresh yeast	15 g
warm milk (38°C)	150 ml
unsweetened plain yoghurt	150 ml
butter	100 g
poppy seeds	2 tbsp

This recipe comes from Punjab and goes well with tandoori meat dishes as well as vindaloos. Traditionally, naans are baked in clay ovens.
They must be eaten fresh and hot, and served immediately.

Healthy eating tips
- Cook the bread without added fat.
- Naan bread is a useful accompaniment for fattier meat dishes.

* With clarified butter – using ghee

1 Sift the flour into a suitable bowl and add the sugar, salt and baking powder.
2 Dissolve the yeast in the milk and stir in the yoghurt. Mix thoroughly with the flour to form a dough.
3 Knead the dough until it is smooth. Cover with a clean cloth and leave to rise in a warm place for about 4 hours.
4 Divide the risen dough into 12 equal portions and roll into balls, on a lightly floured surface.
5 Flatten the balls into oblong shapes, using both hands and slapping the naan from one hand to the other.
6 Cook the naan bread on the sides of the tandoori oven or on a lightly greased griddle or heavy-bottomed frying pan.
7 Cook the naan on one side only. Brush the raw side with clarified butter and poppy seeds, turn over, cook the other side or brown under a salamander.

140 Chapatis

flour shallow frying

energy	kcal	fat	sat fat	carb	sugar	protein	fibre
1066 kJ	254 kcal	12.1 g	1.4 g	32.0 g	1.1 g	6.4 g	4.5 g

Portions ›	4	10
flour, wholewheat	200 g	500 g
pinch of salt		
water	125 ml	213 ml

1 Sieve the flour and salt, add the water and knead to a firm dough.
2 Knead on a floured table until smooth and elastic.
3 Cover with a damp cloth or polythene and allow to relax for 30–40 minutes.
4 Divide into 8 pieces (20 pieces for 10 portions), flatten each and roll into a circle 12–15 cm in diameter.
5 Heat a frying pan (*tawa*) with no oil, add the chapati and cook as for a pancake. Traditionally, chapatis are allowed to puff by placing them over an open flame.
6 Serve immediately.

Chapatis are cooked on a tawa or frying pan. They are made fresh for each meal, and are dipped into sauces and used to scoop up food.

Healthy eating tips
● Use the minimum amount of salt.
● Dry-fry the chapatis.
● Chapatis are a useful accompaniment for fattier meat dishes.

Equipment and ingredients for chapatis, including chapati flour from a specialist supplier, and a traditional rolling board

Knead the dough into a ball

Divide the dough into evenly sized pieces

Roll out the dough

Fry the chapatis one at a time; this traditional pan is called a *tawa*

With care, place the chapati over the gas burner until it puffs up; use tongs to handle the chapati

141 Bun dough

yeast, flour

energy	kcal	fat	sat fat	carb	sugar	protein	fibre *
656 kJ	157 kcal	6.4 g	2.7 g	22.6 g	4.0 g	3.6 g	1.2 g

Makes >	8 buns	20 buns
flour (strong)	200 g	500 g
yeast	5 g	12 g
milk and water	60 ml (approx.)	300 ml (approx.)
egg	1	2–3
butter or margarine	50 g	125 g
caster sugar	25 g	60 g

1 Sieve the flour into a bowl and warm.
2 Cream the yeast in a basin with a little of the liquid.
3 Make a well in the centre of the flour.
4 Add the dispersed yeast, sprinkle with a little flour, cover with a cloth, leave in a warm place until the yeast ferments (bubbles).
5 Add the beaten egg, butter or margarine, sugar and remainder of the liquid. Knead well to form a soft, slack dough, knead until smooth and free from stickiness.
6 Keep covered and allow to prove in a warm place. Use as required.

Sift the flour

Rub in the yeast

Rub in the fat

Make a well in the flour, and pour in the beaten egg

Pour in the liquid

Fold the ingredients together

Knead the dough

Before and after proving: the same amount of dough is twice the size after it has been left to prove

* Using hard margarine, 1 portion (2 buns)

142 Bun wash

sugar	100 g
water or milk	125 ml

1 Boil ingredients together until the consistency of a thick syrup.
2 Use as required.

143 Bath buns

yeast, flour, fruit baking

energy	kcal	fat	sat fat	carb	sugar	protein	fibre	sodium
827 KJ	196 kcal	6.5 g	3.6 g	31.9 g	13.4 g	4.5 g	1.4 g	0.1 g

Recipes 143 to 145: Chelsea buns, hot cross buns and Bath buns

1 Add to basic bun dough (recipe 141), 50 g washed and dried fruit (e.g. currants and sultanas), 25 g chopped mixed peel and 25 g sugar nibs.
2 Pull off into 8 rough-shaped pieces.
3 Sprinkle with a little broken loaf sugar or nibs.

4 Place on a lightly greased baking sheet. Cover with a cloth and allow to prove.
5 Bake in a hot oven at 220°C for 15–20 minutes.
6 Brush liberally with bun wash (recipe 142) as soon as cooked.

144 Chelsea buns

yeast, flour, fruit baking

energy	kcal	fat	sat fat	carb	sugar	protein	fibre	sodium
922 KJ	219 kcal	9.6 g	5.6 g	30.7 g	12.2 g	4.5 g	1.4 g	0.1 g

1 Take the basic bun dough (recipe 141) and roll out into a rectangle 30 cm x 10 cm.
2 Brush with melted margarine or butter.
3 Sprinkle liberally with caster sugar.
4 Sprinkle with 25 g currants, 25 g sultanas and 25 g chopped peel.
5 Roll up like a Swiss roll, brush with melted margarine or butter.
6 Cut into 8 slices across the roll, 3 cm wide.
7 Place on a greased baking tray with deep sides. Cover and allow to prove.
8 Bake in a hot oven at 220°C for 15–20 minutes.
9 Brush liberally with bun wash (recipe 142) immediately after baking.

Combine the fruit and spices

Sprinkle the fruit over the rolled dough

Roll up the dough as if you were making a Swiss roll

Cut the roll into slices to make the buns

145 Hot cross buns

yeast, flour, fruit 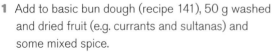 baking

energy	kcal	fat	sat fat	carb	sugar	protein	fibre	sodium
744 KJ	177 kcal	6.7 g	3.6 g	26.8 g	8.3 g	4.6 g	1.2 g	0.1 g

1 Add to basic bun dough (recipe 141), 50 g washed and dried fruit (e.g. currants and sultanas) and some mixed spice.
2 Mould into 8 round buns. Make a cross on top of each bun with the back of a knife, or make a slack mixture of flour and water and pipe on crosses using a greaseproof paper cornet.
3 Place on a lightly greased baking sheet. Cover with a cloth and allow to prove.
4 Bake in a hot oven at 220°C for 15–20 minutes.
5 Brush liberally with bun wash (recipe 142) as soon as cooked.

Practical Cookery 12th edition

146 Fruit buns

yeast, flour, fruit baking

energy	kcal	fat	sat fat	carb	sugar	protein	fibre *
728 kJ	173 kcal	6.5 g	2.7 g	26.9 g	8.0 g	3.7 g	1.7 g

1 Add 50 g washed, dried fruit (e.g. currants, sultanas) and a little mixed spice to the basic bun mixture (recipe 141).
2 Mould into 8 round balls.
3 Place on a lightly greased baking sheet.
4 Cover with a cloth, allow to prove.
5 Bake in hot oven at 220°C for 15–20 minutes.
6 Brush liberally with bun wash (recipe 142) as soon as cooked.

* Using hard margarine

147 Swiss buns

yeast, flour baking

energy	kcal	fat	sat fat	carb	sugar	protein	fibre	sodium
697 KJ	165 kcal	5.6 g	3.4 g	27.0 g	8.4 g	3.4 g	1.0 g	0.0 g

1 Divide basic bun dough (recipe 141) into 8 pieces.
2 Mould into balls, then into 10 cm lengths.
3 Place on a greased baking sheet, cover with a cloth.
4 Allow to prove.
5 Bake at 220°C, for 15–20 minutes.
6 When cool, glaze with fondant or water icing.

148 Doughnuts

yeast, flour deep frying

energy	kcal	fat	sat fat	carb	sugar	protein	fibre *
918 kJ	218 kcal	13.3 g	4.0 g	22.6 g	4.0 g	3.6 g	1.2 g

1 Take the basic bun dough (recipe 141) and divide into 8 pieces.
2 Mould into balls. Press a floured thumb into each. Add a little jam in each hole. Mould carefully to seal the hole. (For ring doughnuts, press your thumb right through each one and rotate to form a hole in the centre.)
4 Cover and allow to prove on a well-floured tray.
5 Deep-fry in moderately hot fat, 175°C, for 12–15 minutes.

6 Lift out of the fat, drain and roll in a tray containing caster sugar mixed with a little cinnamon.

* Using hard margarine and peanut oil

149 Savarin dough

yeast, flour 🧁 baking, 🍲 boiling

energy	kcal	fat	sat fat	carb	sugar	protein	fibre	*
700 kJ	167 kcal	7.4 g	3.9 g	21.5 g	2.5 g	4.9 g	0.8 g	

Portions ›	8	20
flour (strong)	200 g	500 g
yeast	5 g	12 g
milk	125 ml	300 ml
eggs	2	5
butter, softened	50 g	125 g
sugar	10 g	25 g
salt	pinch	large pinch

1 Sieve the flour in a bowl and warm.
2 Cream the yeast with a little of the warm milk in a basin.
3 Make a well in the centre of the flour and add the dissolved yeast. Mix some of the flour into the liquid, to feed the yeast.
4 Sprinkle with a little of the flour from the sides, cover with a cloth and leave in a warm place until it ferments.
5 Add the remainder of the warm milk and the beaten eggs, and mix to a smooth elastic dough, very soft compared to a normal dough. Allow to prove.
6 Replace in the bowl, add the butter in small pieces, cover with a cloth and allow to prove in a warm place.
7 Add the sugar and salt, mix well until absorbed.
8 Pipe into a greased savarin mould so that it is half full, and prove.
9 Bake in a hot oven at 220°C for about 30 minutes.
10 Turn out when cooked, cool slightly.
11 Soak carefully in hot syrup (see below).
12 Brush over with apricot glaze (recipe 29).

Syrup for savarin, baba and marignans

Makes enough for ›	4 babas	10 babas
sugar	100 g	250 g
bay leaf	1	2–3
lemon, rind and juice of	1	2–3
water	250 ml	600 ml
coriander seeds	2–3	6–7
cinnamon stick, small	½	1–1½

1 Boil all the ingredients together and strain. The mixture needs to be at 22° Baumé.
2 Use as required.

Cream the yeast in milk to make a ferment

Add the dissolved yeast to the flour, and sprinkle a little flour over it

The mixture after fermentation

Practical Cookery 12th edition

Add warm milk and beaten egg

The dough after proving

Add the butter

After proving, add sugar and salt and pipe the mixture into moulds

After proving for the final time

* 'Using syrup, 1 portion of complete savarin provides: 967 kJ/229 kcal energy; 7.4 g fat; 3.9 g sat fat; 38.2 g carb; 19.1 g sugar; 5.0 g protein; 0.8 g fibre

---

150 Savarin with fruit
(savarin aux fruits)

yeast, flour, fruit 🍞 baking

energy	kcal	fat	sat fat	carb	sugar	protein	fibre
1224 kJ	292 kcal	13.5 g	7.7 g	39.1 g	20.6 g	5.9 g	1.0 g

1. Prepare the basic savarin mixture (recipe 149).
2. Prove and cook for about 30 minutes in a large greased savarin mould or individual moulds.
3. Turn out when cooked. Cool slightly.
4. Soak carefully in hot syrup (see recipe 149).
5. Sprinkle liberally with rum (optional). Brush all over with apricot glaze.
6. Fill the centre with fruit salad.

151 Marignans Chantilly

yeast, flour, cream   baking

energy	kcal	fat	sat fat	carb	sugar	protein	fibre
1202 kJ	286 kcal	13.4 g	7.7 g	38.0 g	19.5 g	5.8 g	0.8 g

1 Marignans are prepared from a basic savarin mixture (recipe 149) and cooked in barquette moulds.
2 After the marignans have been soaked, carefully make a deep incision along one side.
3 Decorate generously with whipped, sweetened vanilla-flavoured cream.
4 Brush with apricot glaze.

152 Blueberry baba

yeast, flour, fruit baking

1 Prepare individual savarins using savarin dough (recipe 149).
2 For the filling, use crème diplomat (recipe 8) flavoured with Kirsch. Fold blueberries into the filling.

153 Sponge fingers
(biscuits à la cuillère)

energy	kcal	fat	sat fat	carb	sugar	protein	fibre
145 kJ	34 kcal	0.9 g	0.2 g	5.7 g	3.3 g	1.3 g	0.1 g

	Makes ›	32
eggs		4
caster sugar		100 g
flour (soft)		100 g
icing sugar, to sprinkle		

1 Cream the egg yolks and sugar in a bowl until creamy and almost white.
2 Whip the egg whites stiffly.
3 Add a little of the whites to the mixture and cut in.
4 Gradually add the sieved flour and remainder of the whites alternately, mixing as lightly as possible.
5 Place in a piping bag with 1 cm plain tube and pipe in 8 cm lengths onto baking sheets lined with greaseproof or silicone paper.
6 Sprinkle liberally with icing sugar. Rest for 5 minutes, repeat, then bake.
7 Bake in a moderate hot oven at 200–220°C for about 10 minutes.

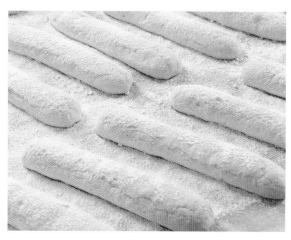

8 Remove from the oven, lift the paper on which the biscuits are piped and place upside down on the table.
9 Sprinkle liberally with water. This will assist the removal of the biscuits from the paper. (No water is needed if using silicone paper.)

Whisk the egg yolks and sugar until creamy

Whip the egg whites until they are stiff

Add some egg whites to the sugar mixture

Mix lightly and pour back into the egg white container

Add sieved flour

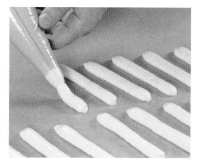

Pipe out in finger shapes

154 Tuiles

Makes ›	15–20
butter	100 g
icing sugar	100 g
flour	100 g
egg whites	2

1 Mix all ingredients; allow to rest for 1 hour.
2 Spread to the required shape and size.
3 Bake at approx. 200–210°C.
4 While hot, mould the biscuits to the required shape and leave to cool.

155 Cats' tongues
(langues de chat)

flour baking

energy 676 KJ	kcal 161 kcal	fat 8.3 g	sat fat 5.2 g	carb 20.7 g	sugar 13.2 g	protein 2.1 g	fibre 0.4 g	sodium * 0.1 g

Makes ›	Approx. 40
icing sugar	125 g
butter	100 g
vanilla essence	3–4 drops
egg whites	3–4
flour (soft)	100 g

1 Lightly cream the sugar and butter, add the vanilla essence.
2 Add the egg whites one by one, continually mixing and being careful not to allow the mixture to curdle.
3 Gently fold in the sifted flour and mix lightly.
4 Pipe on to a lightly greased baking sheet using a 3 mm plain tube, 2½ cm apart.
5 Bake at 230–250°C, for a few minutes.
6 The outside edges should be light brown and the centres yellow.
7 When cooked, remove on to a cooling rack using a palette knife.

* For four biscuits

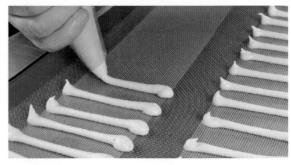

Pipe cats' tongues into their distinctive shape, thicker at the ends

Practical Cookery 12th edition

156 Cigarette paste cornets
(cornets)

flour  baking

Makes ›	Approx. 30
icing sugar	125 g
butter, melted	100 g
vanilla essence	3–4 drops
egg whites	3–4
flour (soft)	100 g

1 Proceed as for steps 1–3 of recipe 155 (cats' tongues).
2 Using a plain tube, pipe out the mixture onto a lightly greased baking sheet into bulbs, spaced well apart. Place a template over each bulb and spread it with a palette knife.
3 Bake at 150°C, until evenly coloured.
4 Remove the tray from the oven. Turn the cornets over but keep them on the hot tray.
5 Work quickly while the cornets are hot and twist them into a cornet shape using the point of a cream horn mould. (For a tight cornet shape it will be found best to set the pieces tightly inside the cream horn moulds and leave them until set.) If the cornets set hard before you have shaped them all, warm them in the oven until they become flexible.

Place a mould around the bulb of biscuit mixture

Spread the mixture out thinly

After baking, quickly twist the cornet around a mould

157 Brandy snaps

Makes approx. ⟩	20
flour (strong)	225 g
ground ginger	10 g
golden syrup	225 g
butter	250 g
caster sugar	450 g

1 Combine the flour and ginger in a bowl on the scales. Make a well.
2 Pour in golden syrup until the correct weight is reached.
3 Cut the butter into small pieces. Add the butter and sugar.
4 Mix together at a slow speed.
5 Divide into 4 even pieces. Roll into sausage shapes, wrap each in clingfilm and chill, preferably overnight.

6 Slice each roll into rounds. Place on a baking tray, spaced well apart.
7 Flatten each round using a fork dipped in cold water, keeping a round shape.
9 Bake in a pre-heated oven at 200°C until evenly coloured and bubbly.
10 Remove from oven. Allow to cool slightly, then lift off and shape over a dariole mould for a basket shape, or around a wooden spoon handle for a roll.
11 Stack the snaps, no more than 4 together, on a stainless steel tray and store.

158 Piped biscuits
(sablés à la poche)

energy	kcal	fat	sat fat	carb	sugar	protein	fibre	sodium *
993 KJ	237 kcal	15.2 g	8.2 g	23.3 g	8.4 g	3.4 g	0.8 g	0.2 g

Makes ⟩	20–30
caster or unrefined sugar	75 g
butter or margarine	150 g
egg	1
vanilla essence	3–4 drops
or	
grated lemon zest	
flour (soft), white or wholemeal	200 g
ground almonds	35 g

1 Cream the sugar and butter until light in colour and texture.
2 Add the egg gradually, beating continuously, add the vanilla essence or lemon zest.
3 Gently fold in the sifted flour and almonds, mix well until suitable for piping. If too stiff, add a little beaten egg.

4 Pipe on to a lightly greased and floured baking sheet using a medium-sized star tube (a variety of shapes can be used).
5 Some biscuits can be left plain, some decorated with half almonds or walnuts or neatly cut pieces of angelica and glacé cherries.
6 Bake in a moderate oven at 190°C for about 10 minutes.
7 When cooked, remove on to a cooling rack using a palette knife.

* For two biscuits

159 Almond biscuits
(biscuits aux amandes)

flour, nuts baking

energy	kcal	fat	sat fat	carb	sugar	protein	fibre
3361 kJ	800 kcal	53.5 g	4.2 g	62.4 g	62.4 g	21.2 g	14.4 g

	Makes ›	16–20
egg whites		1½
ground almonds		100 g
caster or unrefined sugar		50 g
almond essence		3–4 drops
sheet rice paper		1
glacé cherries, angelica or split almonds		

1 Whisk the egg whites until stiff.

2 Gently stir in the ground almonds, sugar and almond essence. Place the rice paper on a baking sheet.

3 Pipe the mixture, using a medium star tube, into shapes.

4 Decorate with neatly cut diamonds of angelica and glacé cherries, or split almonds.

5 Bake at 180–200°C, for 10–15 minutes.

6 Trim with a small knife to cut through the rice paper; place onto a cooling rack using a palette knife.

160 Shortbread biscuits

flour  baking

energy	kcal	fat	sat fat	carb	sugar	protein	fibre	*
507 kJ	121 kcal	7.0 g	4.4 g	14.1 g	4.6 g	1.2 g	0.5 g	

Method 1

	Makes ›	12
flour (soft)		150 g
salt		pinch
butter		100 g
caster sugar		50 g

1 Sift the flour and salt.
2 Mix in the butter and sugar with the flour.
3 Combine all the ingredients to a smooth paste.
4 Roll carefully on a floured table or board to the shape of a rectangle or round, 0.5 cm thick. Place on a lightly greased baking sheet.
5 Mark into the desired size and shape. Prick with a fork.
6 Bake in a moderate oven at 180–200°C for 15–20 minutes.

Method 2

	Makes ›	12
flour (soft), white or wholemeal		100 g
rice flour		100 g
butter		100 g
caster or unrefined sugar		100 g
egg, beaten		1

1 Sieve the flour and rice flour into a basin.
2 Rub in the butter until the texture of fine breadcrumbs. Mix in the sugar.
3 Bind the mixture to a stiff paste using the beaten egg.
4 Roll out to 3 mm using caster sugar, prick well with a fork and cut into fancy shapes. Place the biscuits on a lightly greased baking sheet.
5 Bake in a moderate oven at 180–200°C for 15 minutes or until golden brown.
6 Remove with a palette knife onto a cooling rack.

Method 3

	Makes ›	12
butter		100 g
icing sugar		100 g
egg		1
flour (soft)		150 g

1 Cream the butter and sugar thoroughly.
2 Add the egg and mix in. Mix in the flour.
3 Pipe on to lightly greased and floured baking sheets using a large star tube.
4 Bake at 200–220°C, for approx. 15 minutes.

* Using butter

12 Healthy eating

This chapter is relevant to the following units:

- Prepare, cook and finish healthier dishes (NVQ)
- Healthier food and special diets (VRQ).

Why healthy eating is important

Obesity and the related health problems have increased dramatically in the UK in recent years with an estimated 24 million adults classed as obese. There is also concern about the rising numbers of obese children.

Healthy eating is not just about reducing obesity, however. Research suggests that a third of all cancers are caused by poor diet. Diet can also be linked to high blood pressure, heart disease, diabetes, osteoporosis and tooth decay. Eating a balanced nutritional diet can help to protect us from these illnesses.

Increasing numbers of people now eat away from their own homes so those providing the food have a responsibility to be mindful of good nutrition.

What is healthy eating?

Food, nutrition and exercise are crucial to our health and well-being. There is no doubt that making the right choices of food and drink, combined with taking regular exercise, can protect against many western diseases and poor health. There are also many immediate health and lifestyle benefits to be gained from healthy eating.

Media coverage and advice on nutrition can seem confusing but the most reliable advice remains the same and is outlined in Table 12.1.

Table 12.1 Summing up healthy eating

What it is about	What it is not about	Immediate benefits
The bulk of the diet needs to come from starchy foods: preferably wholemeal bread, brown rice and pasta and potatoes Eating more fruit and vegetables Eating a little less of some food items Enjoying good food and making wise food choices Making small, gradual changes Feeling satisfied and good about food	Drastically cutting down on food Going hungry Depriving yourself of treats Spending more money on food Not enjoying food 'Brown and boring food' Just salads Making major changes Going on a 'special diet'	Better weight control Improved self-esteem Looking and feeling better Feeling fitter, with more energy Enjoying a wide variety of foods Not buying expensive 'diet' products Knowing that changes made today will have long-term benefits

The balance of good health

Foods are not 'good or bad' – it is the overall balance of the diet that matters. It means having a variety of foods, basing meals on starchy foods and eating at least five portions of fruit and vegetables a day. The balance to strive for is illustrated in nationally agreed advice (see the Eatwell plate).

The advice given is that the diet should consist of:

- **more starchy foods** – e.g. cereals, breads, pasta, potatoes, rice
- **more fruit and vegetables** – aiming for five portions per day

- **moderate amounts of food from the milk and dairy, and meat, fish and alternative proteins groups** – as a guideline, two to three portions from each group per day
- **very small amounts of foods containing fats and sugars, and drinks containing sugars** – selecting lower-fat options where possible; in addition, foods that are high in salt should be restricted.

The eatwell plate

Use the eatwell plate to help you get the balance right. It shows how much of what you eat should come from each food group.

FOOD STANDARDS AGENCY
food.gov.uk

Fruit and vegetables

Bread, rice, potatoes, pasta and other starchy foods

Meat, fish, eggs, beans and other non-dairy sources of protein

Foods and drinks high in fat and/or sugar

Milk and dairy foods

The Eatwell plate

Information on the portions of different types of foods that make up a healthy diet is given in the Eatwell plate from the UK government. For more information visit www.dh.gov.uk/en/Publichealth/Nutrition

Nutrients from food

Healthy eating is about selecting certain foods that provide the nutrients that are needed by the body in different amounts. If people choose foods in the advised proportions (as in the Eatwell plate), they should obtain all the nutrients they need in the quantities that promote good health. Nutrients perform different functions in the body and Table 12.2 summarises some of the key nutritional terms you will encounter, plus the current guidance for health.

Table 12.2 Key nutritional terms and current guidance for health

Foods provide …	For health …
Fat is a very concentrated source of energy. The same weight of pure fat has over twice as much energy as sugar or starch. Fat is present in foods in two main types: saturated fat in foods from animal sources such as butter, cheese, meat and milk, and fatty meats; unsaturated fat in foods from plants (e.g. oils, nuts and seeds) and oily fish (e.g. tuna, salmon, mackerel) sources.	We should cut down on fat intake, particularly the saturated types (usually from animal sources) that push up blood cholesterol, which is why it is important to switch to foods containing unsaturated fats. For example, using oils instead of butter and incorporating more oily fish like salmon in menu planning.
Carbohydrate may be one of two types: sugars, which occur naturally in certain foods such as fruit and honey but are added to many manufactured foods, particularly confectionery, cakes and biscuits; starches, found naturally in satisfying foods such as bread, breakfast cereals, rice, pasta and potatoes.	We should aim to get 50 per cent of our energy from starch, preferably unrefined starches, and cut back on sugars.
Fibre is found in plant foods and aids a healthy digestive system. Good sources include all wholegrain cereals, pulses, fruits, vegetables and nuts.	On current estimates we all eat around 20 g dietary fibre per day. The healthy goal is around 30 g per day.
Protein is the 'body-building' nutrient found in meat, fish, cheese and eggs, but also from vegetable sources such as cereals (e.g. pasta, breakfast cereals, bread) pulses and nuts.	Protein requirements are often overestimated. For example, adults need only between 35 and 50 g of protein per day. This can be provided by a 100 g portion of chicken plus a carton of yoghurt and 200 g of baked beans.
Vitamins and minerals are needed in minute amounts for many bodily processes. Since the body cannot make these essential micro-nutrients, they have to be provided by the diet.	Recommended daily amounts for 9 vitamins and 11 minerals are given in the government's report on Dietary Reference Values.
Salt is sodium chloride, which is involved in maintaining the body's water balance. Sodium is a type of mineral; sodium chloride is added to many manufactured foods and in particularly high amounts in cured and snack foods.	There is now stronger evidence that our salt intake is too high (estimated at about 8 g per day) and can lead to high blood pressure. The aim should be about 4 g of salt per day.
Energy comes from carbohydrates, fat, protein and alcohol. It is measured in calories or joules, which are so tiny they are usually expressed in kilocalories (kcals) or kilojoules (kJ).	We need to balance energy intake through food with energy output through activity; this is needed for good health and control of body weight.

The chef's role

Chefs have a vital role in making healthy eating an exciting reality for us all. Customer trends show that many people are looking for healthier eating options, particularly if they eat away from home every day. Interest in healthy eating is one of the major consumer trends to emerge in the last 20 years and represents an important and lasting commercial opportunity for chefs.

As well as escalating consumer demand, in some sectors, such as school catering, there are strict requirements relating to nutritional standards. Healthy options and nutruitinal information are now regularly included in contract catering menus.

Chefs can be highly influential in healthy eating. The ingredients and the proportion in which they are used, plus cooking and service methods chosen, can all influence nutritional content of a dish or meal. The most effective approach to healthy catering is to make minor adjustments to popular dishes which may involve:

- Small changes in portion sizes or adding a bread roll or jacket potato to a meal. This yields more starch in proportion to fat (effectively diluting the fat).
- Subtle modifications to recipes. For instance, make a pizza with a thicker base, add mushrooms and roasted peppers, top with less mozzarella than usual but add a sprinkling of Parmesan for flavour. Omit the salt, but rely on Parmesan, black pepper and chopped oregano to add flavour.

A healthy portion size: navarin of lamb

A traditional dish made healthier: Mexican bean pot and salad

Chefs are vital in developing healthier recipes that work. The skill is in deciding how dishes can be modified without losing quality. Some highly traditional dishes are best left alone whilst subtle changes can be made to others with no loss in texture, appearance or flavour. See 'Healthy eating tips' throughout the recipe sections.

The key to healthier catering is to:
- make small changes to best-selling items
- increase the amount of starchy foods
- increase the amount of fruit and vegetables
- increase the fibre content of dishes where it is practical and acceptable
- reduce fat in traditional recipes
- change the type of fat used
- select healthier ways to prepare dishes and be creative
- be moderate in the use of sugar and salt.

Nutritional information on menus

A number of outlets, such as restaurants, pubs, leisure attractions and cafes, have introduced nutritional information on their menus.

Many establishments have agreed to:
- display calorie information for most food and drink they serve
- print calorie information on menus
- ensure the information is clear and easily visible at the point where people chose their food.

> Take care when providing nutritional information on menus as there may be a danger of making misleading claims, which could break the law. If unsure, take advice.

Special diets

Vegetarian/vegan and other ethical diets

Vegetarians do not eat meat or fish, or any type of dish made with or containing the products of animals. Check for vegetarians who:

- occasionally eat fish and/or meat – semi-vegetarian or demi-vegetarian
- do not eat milk and dairy products – ovo-vegetarian
- do not eat eggs – lacto-vegetarian
- do not eat any food of animal origin (including honey, dairy products and eggs); such people are known as vegans (note that vegetables, fruits, grains, legumes, pasta made without eggs, soya products and other products of plants are acceptable)
- eat only fruit, nuts and berries – frutarian or fructarian.

Religious diets

Adherents of the religions listed below do not eat the following foods.

- **Hindu:** meat, fish or eggs (orthodox Hindus are usually strict vegetarians; less strict Hindus may eat lamb, poultry and fish, but definitely not beef as cattle have a deep religious meaning – milk, however, is highly regarded).
- **Jewish:** pork, pork products, shellfish and eels, meat and milk served at the same time or cooked together; strict Jews eat only Kosher meat; milk and milk products are usually avoided at lunch and dinner (but are acceptable at breakfast).
- **Muslim:** pork, meat that is not halal (slaughtered according to custom), shellfish and alcohol (even when used in cooking).
- **Rastafarian:** all processed foods, pork, fish without fins (eels), alcohol, coffee, tea.
- **Sikh:** beef, pork, lamb, poultry and fish may be acceptable to Sikh men; Sikh women tend to avoid all meat.

Medical diets

For medical reasons, the people on the special diets below do not eat the foods listed.

- **Dairy/milk free:** milk, butter, cheese, yoghurt and any prepared foods that include milk products (check label).
- **Diabetes:** dishes that are high in sugar and/or fat (low-calorie sweeteners can be used to sweeten desserts).
- **Gluten free:** wheat, wholemeal, wholewheat and wheatmeal flour, wheat bran, rye, barley and oats (some doctors say oats are permitted, the Coeliac Society advises against) and any dishes made with these, including pasta, noodles, semolina, bread, pastries, some yoghurts (e.g. muesli), some cheese spreads, barley-based drinks, malted drinks, beer, some brands of mustard, proprietary sauces made with flour (use cornflour to thicken; rice, potato, corn and sage are also acceptable).
- **Low cholesterol and saturated fat:** liver, egg yolks and shellfish (which are high in cholesterol), beef, pork and lamb (which contain saturated fats), butter, cream, groundnut oil, margarine (use oils and margarines labelled high in polyunsaturated fats).
- **Low fat:** any food that contains fat, or has been fried or roasted.
- **Low residue:** wholemeal bread, brown rice and pasta, fried and fatty foods.
- **Low salt:** foods and dishes that have had salt added in the cooking or processing (including smoked and cured fishes and meats, and hard cheeses) or contain monosodium glutamate.
- **Nut allergy:** nuts, blended cooking oils and margarine (since these may include nut oil; use pure oils or butter) and any dishes containing these (check label).

13 Maintain, handle and clean knives

This chapter is relevant to the following units:

- Maintain, handle and clean knives (NVQ)
- Health and safety in catering and hospitality (VRQ).

Knives are essential pieces of equipment in kitchens and have different styles and characteristics to deal with a wide range of culinary tasks. To achieve the best possible results from knives they must be well cared for, cleaned well after use and kept sharp. All chefs need to be trained in the best, safest and most efficient ways to use a range of knives and also cleavers, scissors and secateurs.

The types, availability and styles of professional knives have developed considerably in recent years. Quality knives are a good investment for a chef and should be chosen carefully.

You will need to consider:

- The tasks you are completing. For example, if you work in a fish restaurant a good quality filleting knife may be a good investment.
- How the knife feels to hold – they do vary in style, weight and balance.
- Ease of sharpening.
- The cost and what you are prepared to spend.
- Preferences in style and the materials used to make the knife.

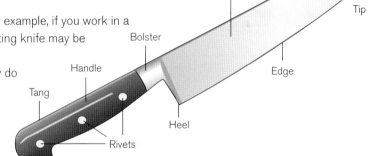

The parts of a knife

Knives and related equipment

The professional chef will use a range of knives in the kitchen. A very wide choice is available. The most commonly used knives are:

- **Chopping knife (cook's knife or chef's knife):** This will have a broad, rigid blade between 15 and 30 cm long, and a 'heel'. This is probably the chef's most useful knife and is used for a variety of tasks including, chopping, cutting, slicing, shredding of vegetables, meat, fruit, etc.

- **Paring knife:** A small multi-purpose knife used mainly for topping and tailing vegetables and peeling fruits and vegetables.
- **Filleting knife:** Used for filleting fish. This knife often has a flexible blade, which allows the chef to move the knife easily around the bone structure and between the flesh and bone of the fish.
- **Boning knife:** A short bladed knife with a pointed end used for boning meat. The blade is strong and

rigid and not flexible in order to get close to the bones, cut away the meat and manoeuvre between bones.

- **Palette knife:** A flat knife with a blunt, rounded end blade. It is used for lifting and turning food, scraping and spreading. It probably has most use in the pastry section but is also used in other kitchen areas.
- **Turning knife:** A small curved bladed knife used for shaping vegetables in a variety of ways.
- **Serrated edge knife:** This knife is used for slicing or for foods that are softer on the inside than the outside, such as crusty bread or tomatoes. It has a serrated blade, which is used in long strokes with a sawing action. It can also be used to slice foods such as meat or terrines into neat slices. This knife is not usually sharpened in the kitchen but is sent to a specialist company for sharpening.
- **Carving knife and fork:** A French carving knife has a long, thin blade and is also known as a tranchard. Long strokes with the blade enables neat and efficient carving of meat. A carving fork is two pronged, strong enough to support meats for carving and also for lifting them once carved.

Steels are used for sharpening knives. The metal shaft may be circular or oval; diamond steels embedded with abrasive diamond particles are considered to be the easiest and best to use. Steels usually have a guard to protect the hands and a handle similar to knife handles. To sharpen a knife, run the knife at an angle (usually 45°) along the steel edge.

Knives may also be sharpened in the kitchen by using a whetstone, pull-through sharpeners of various design and electric sharpeners. There is more information about knife sharpening below.

A palette knife

A turning knife

A carving fork

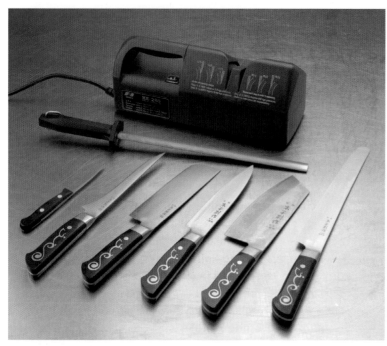

A selection of knives, a steel and an electric sharpener

Other tools used for cutting in the kitchen include:

- **Butchers' saws:** commonly used in butchery to saw through meat bones; they have serrated blades.
- **Meat cleavers (choppers):** usually used for chopping bones in meat. The heavy flat blade allows this to be done more easily.
- **Secateurs:** similar to scissors with two long pointed blades. Some secateurs have the handles set at an angle to the blades to allow for easy and efficient use. Secateurs have a variety of uses including cutting through chicken joints and trimming whole fish.
- **Kitchen scissors:** have a wide range of uses including snipping herbs such as chives, cutting lengths from filo pastry, cutting paper to line tins and moulds and opening bags and packets safely.

A butcher's saw

A meat cleaver

Materials used for knives

The materials used for knife blades include:

- **Carbon steel:** easy to sharpen and get a good edge but can rust and stain easily.
- **Stainless steel:** now very popular for chefs' knives. It is softer than carbon steel so will need sharpening more frequently but is resistant to rust stains.
- **High-carbon stainless steel:** a higher-grade stainless steel with a carbon content. These knives resist rust and staining and maintain their sharp edge for longer than standard stainless steel.
- **Laminated** blades are made with a hard steel and a more brittle steel sandwiched together to combine the advantages of both, producing a tougher blade that stays sharp for longer.
- **Ceramic** is the hardest material available for knife blades and will hold a sharp edge for the longest time. However, the blade can chip and may break if the knife is dropped. It also needs specialist sharpening. Ceramic knives tend to be lighter than steel and usually have plastic handles.

- **Folded steel** knives are of Japanese origin and have a strong and very sharp blade. The blade is made from numerous layers of soft and hard steel with a central layer of very hard steel forming the cutting edge. The layers are heated, folded and hammered to create soft layers that act as shock absorbers for the hard steel which tends to be brittle. The techniques used are labour intensive so these knives tend to be relatively expensive.

Knife handles were traditionally made from wood with the blade 'tang' secured by rivets; although wooden-handled knives are still manufactured, plastics have generally replaced wooden handles.

Knives made in one piece with a stainless steel handle and blade have become increasingly popular. They are forged with hard molybdenum/vanadium stainless steel, which retains a good edge and are considered to be hygienic in use because of the lack of joints. The handles are often of a hollow construction, which may be filled with sand for weight and balance purposes.

Using knives

Knives are essential tools for all chefs but they can cause serious injury to the user or to someone else if they are used wrongly or carelessly. Quality knives that are looked after and treated with care will give good service and will be less likely to cause injury.

Knives that are kept sharp are safer than blunt knives provided that they are handled with care. This is because a sharp blade will cut cleanly and efficiently through the food without the need for excessive pressure. A blunt knife is less easy to control. It will need more pressure and force and is likely to slip sideways, possibly causing injury as well as badly prepared food.

Knives need to be kept sharp by sharpening them frequently with a steel, whetstone or other sharpening tool. Take time to learn to do this properly and safely. Once a blade becomes really blunt it may need to be 're-ground' by someone specialising in doing this. An electric or manually operated grinding wheel is used to replace the lost 'edge' on the knife blade. Arrangements can be made for mobile units to visit your premises to re-grind knives or they can be sent away to be re-ground.

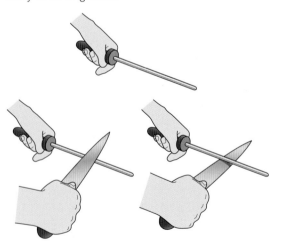

Sharpening a knife with a steel

All knives can be potentially dangerous if not used properly. If wrongly used serious injury can be the result as well as more minor injuries. By following a few simple rules and treating knives with respect, injury and accidental cuts should be kept

to a minimum. Use knives correctly at all times and encourage others around you to do the same. Any accidents/injuries that do occur when using knives must be recorded according to the establishment's operational procedure and reported to the relevant person (see Chapter 14).

Holding a knife

Generally, you should grasp a knife with your fingers around the handle (thumb and index fingers on opposite sides) and well clear of the blade edge. The exact way that you hold the knife will vary, depending on the size and design of the knife and the task being carried out. Grasp the knife firmly to give full control. Make sure that the fingers and thumb of the hand not holding the knife are well tucked in away from the blade edge to avoid cutting them.

Safety with knives

- If carrying a knife in the kitchen hold it down by the side of your body with the blade pointing down and backwards.
- Never run holding a knife and take care not to trip or slip.
- When handing a knife to someone else, offer them the handle while you hold the top (blunt edge) of the blade.
- Keep the sharp edge of the blade away from you when cleaning or drying knives and do not run your fingers along the blade edge.
- Do not have more than one knife at a time on the chopping board. When not actually using the knife place it alongside the board with the blade edge facing inwards.
- Never carry knives around on top of a chopping board; they could slide off.
- Do not allow knives to overhang the edge of the work surface; they could be knocked off or fall and cause injury. Never try to catch a falling knife – step back and wait until it reaches the floor.
- Never leave a knife with the blade pointing upwards. You or someone else could put a hand

down on the blade. (Many knives are now designed so it is impossible for them to be placed 'blade upwards'.)

- Keep the knife handle clean, grease-free and dry. If the handle is wet or greasy it can slip in use and could cause injury.
- Keep knives visible, i.e. not under vegetable peelings or a cloth. Store knives carefully; preferably in a box or carrying case with compartments to keep the knives separate and easy to find. Do not throw knives loosely into a drawer or locker.
- Any knives that have become damaged, badly worn or dangerous in any way should be removed from use immediately and reported to a head chef or supervisor.

Cleaning knives

Taking care to clean knives well will avoid cross contamination and make them safer to use (greasy knife handles can cause them to slip and cause injury). Good care and cleaning tends to make knives last for longer.

- Clean knives in hot water with detergent but keep hold of them and take care not to run fingers along the edge of the blade. Remember to clean the handle too.
- Do not leave knives in washing-up water where they are not visible. The blade could be grasped, resulting in cuts to the hand.
- Rinse and dry thoroughly and store in an appropriate place.
- Generally it is not recommended to clean knives in a dishwasher (the blade edge can be damaged).

Food safety and knives

A knife can very easily transfer harmful bacteria from one place to another or from one food to another, making it a vehicle of contamination. It is also very important to remember that an unwashed knife could cause allergen contamination. For example, if a knife is used to chop nuts then without thorough cleaning is used to slice cooked chicken the chicken will have traces of nuts, which could cause a severe reaction by someone who is allergic to nuts.

- Always make sure that knives and the cutting surface (such as chopping boards) are clean and sanitised before use to avoid possible cross contamination.
- Wash and dry knives thoroughly between tasks. Some kitchens have knives with colour-coded handles for use with nuts and other allergy-related foods.
- Do not use the same cloth to clean knives between tasks when you are preparing raw, high-risk or allergen-related foods.

- When knives have been used on raw meat and poultry make sure the knife is cleaned and disinfected before using on other tasks. Detergents used in cleaning will remove the grease but disinfectants or very high temperatures are needed to kill bacteria.
- When cleaning knives it is important to clean both the handle and blade well. A dirty handle could contaminate the hands.
- When you have finished working with knives, clean and dry them thoroughly before putting away. Bacteria will multiply on wet or dirty knives.

The knife is probably the most important utensil in the kitchen as it is essential for virtually all food preparation. A good sharp knife will help get the job done more effectively and with greater ease. Indeed, a good sharp knife is safer and easier to use than a knife with a blunt blade.

14 Maintain a safe, hygienic and secure working environment

This chapter is relevant to the following units:

- Maintain a safe, hygienic and secure working environment (NVQ)
- Health and safety in catering and hospitality (VRQ).

This chapter provides the necessary information for maintaining the required standards of personal hygiene, appearance, and cleanliness when working in a kitchen. It also covers the importance of reporting any illness or infection to a supervisor or manager, how minor first aid procedures should be dealt with and reporting more major injuries to the relevant authorities. The chapter also discusses how to recognise and deal with potential hazards so they do not cause injury or harm, following emergency procedures and matters of general safety and security.

Information is included to assist the chef/student to comply with the necessary legislation and procedures involved in working in a kitchen as well as provide useful information for successful completion of Professional Cookery qualifications.

Introduction

Every day people are injured at work; some of the injuries may be serious, disabling or even fatal. It is important to always work professionally with safety awareness to keep yourself and others that work with you safe. It is also very important to provide a safe environment for customers and visitors.

When you are working you must always follow the health and safety procedures that your employer has put in place, not interfere with safety equipment or procedure and report anything you consider to be a possible hazard.

Personal hygiene

All humans are a potential source of food contamination and everyone working with food must be aware of the importance of high standards of appearance and personal hygiene. As well as the important part this plays in avoiding food contamination it will reflect the professionalism of the individual as well as the establishment they work for, giving a positive impression to customers and guests.

All food handlers need to ensure that they have a daily bath or shower, clean underwear every day and use a suitable underarm deodorant.

Hands

Hands are frequently in contact with food and numerous other items; if not kept clean they can very easily transfer harmful bacteria to food, surfaces and equipment.

Hands must be washed thoroughly and frequently, particularly after using the toilet, before commencing work, during the handling of food, especially between different tasks and after dealing with waste. Hand washing must be completed using a basin just for this purpose. It must have hot and cold running water, suitable soap (preferably in a dispenser) and paper towels for drying hands.

Some establishments will also provide an anti-bacterial gel to apply after hand washing

There is more information in Chapter 15.

Fingernails

These should always be kept clean and short as dirt can easily lodge under the nails and be transferred to food introducing bacteria. Nails must kept neatly trimmed and nail varnish must never be worn in food areas.

Avoid excessive hand contact with food by using slices, ladles, tongs and spoons where possible and using disposable plastic gloves when appropriate. (Change these frequently, especially between tasks.)

Jewellery/rings/watches

The wearing of jewellery is not acceptable when handling food. Jewellery can trap particles of food and provide a warm damp environment for bacteria to grow; the bacteria can then be transferred to food being prepared. This is particularly relevant to Items worn on the hands such as rings and watches. Jewellery or parts of jewellery can fall into food especially as some food preparation involves plunging hands into water. (Body piercing items can also be a breeding ground for bacteria so remove them or completely cover before handling food.)

Hair

Hair must be washed regularly and kept covered with a suitable kitchen hat and/or net to prevent loose hair falling into food. The hair should never be scratched, combed or touched in the kitchen, as bacteria and loose hair could be transferred via the hands to the food and loose hair could also fall into food or food preparation equipment.

Nose

The nose should not be touched when food is being handled. If a handkerchief/tissue is used, the hands should be washed thoroughly afterwards. The nose is an area where there can be vast numbers of harmful bacteria; it is therefore very important not to sneeze on food, other people or working surfaces. If a sneeze or cough is unavoidable turn away and sneeze into the shoulder area.

Mouth

The mouth also harbours large numbers of bacteria, therefore the mouth or lips should not be touched when working with food. Do not use cooking utensils such as wooden spoons for tasting food, nor should fingers be used for this purpose as bacteria may be transferred to the food. A clean teaspoon (or disposable plastic spoon) should be used for tasting.

Ears

Ears too are a source of bacteria and should not be touched when handling food.

Cuts, burns and other skin abrasions

It is particularly important to keep all cuts, burns, scratches and similar abrasions covered with a waterproof dressing (e.g. a blue plaster). Where the wound has become infected there are large numbers of harmful bacteria that must not get into food; in most cases people suffering in this way should not handle food. Report any infected injuries to a supervisor before starting work.

Cosmetics

Cosmetics should be used very sparingly by food handlers, but ideally their use should be discouraged altogether. Cosmetics must never be applied in the kitchen.

Smoking

Smoking is now illegal in most buildings and certainly where there is food. If food handlers smoke at break times hands must be washed thoroughly afterwards because when a cigarette is taken from the mouth, bacteria from the mouth can be transferred via the fingers onto food.

Protective clothing

Protective clothing is worn to protect food from contamination by food handlers and to protect the wearer from such things as excessive heat, burns and sharp objects.

It is most important that food handlers should wear suitable protective clothing that protects the body and completely covers any other clothing being worn. Strong protective footwear should also be worn.

Clothing worn in the kitchen must be strong to make it 'protective' and withstand the hard wear and frequent washing needed. Clothing will also need to be lightweight, comfortable and absorbent to deal with perspiration caused by a hot kitchen.

Kitchen clothing must be clean, changed at least once a day and more frequently if it becomes soiled. It should cover any other clothing and only be worn in the kitchen area. Outdoor clothing, and other clothing that has been taken off before wearing whites, should be kept in a suitable locker.

According to the **Personal Protective Equipment (PPE) at Work Regulations, 1992**, employees must wear personal protective clothing/equipment suitable for the work they are involved in. For example, chefs wear protective chef's whites, but may add gauntlet gloves and eye goggles if cleaning an oven.

Jackets and trousers

Chefs' jackets are usually made of cotton or a cotton mixture, are double-breasted and ideally have long sleeves; these protect the chest and arms from the heat of the stove and prevent hot foods or liquids burning or scalding the body.

Trousers worn as part of a chef's uniform are usually made from a lightweight cotton or coated cotton. They should be loose fitting for both safety and comfort.

Aprons

Aprons are designed to provide extra protection to the body from being scalded or burned and particularly to protect the legs from any liquids that may be spilled; for this reason the apron should be of sufficient length with long ties allowing them to be wrapped around the body and tied at the front so if a hot spillage occurs the apron can be removed quickly.

Hats

The main purpose of the hat is to prevent loose hairs from falling into food and to absorb perspiration on the forehead. As well as the traditional chef's toque (tall white hat) a variety of designs are now available, some with an incorporated net to contain the hair completely. Lightweight disposable hats are now used by many establishments.

Footwear

This should be strong, and in good repair so as to protect and support the feet. As kitchen staff are on their feet for many hours at a time care of the feet is essential. Suitable, clean, comfortable kitchen footwear and socks need to be worn. Open-top shoes and 'trainers' are unsuitable; these would not offer protection from the spillage of hot liquids, falling knives or heavy items that could be dropped on the feet.

Personal health

To work in a kitchen good levels of health and fitness are required, so attention must be paid to maintaining good health with a good diet, adequate exercise and enough sleep and rest. Many employers now have an occupational health department to support and advise employees in health matters.

It is now a **legal requirement** for all food handlers to report certain illnesses they may have to their line manager/supervisor before starting work; they may be excluded from handling food. These illnesses include:

- diarrhoea, vomiting, or other symptoms of a food-borne illness. The food handler must not return to

food handling duties until they have been free from symptoms for 48 hours or more.

- any skin infections or infected cuts, boils, grazes or burns
- heavy colds and coughs, eye or ear discharges.

First aid

When people are injured or fall ill at work, it is important that immediate help is available and, in serious cases, medical assistance is called.

The arrangements for providing first aid in the workplace are set out in the **Health and Safety (First Aid) Regulations 1981**. Since 1982 it has been a legal requirement that adequate first aid equipment, facilities and personnel are provided at work.

All kitchen staff need to know who they should call or inform if there is an accident, where the first aid equipment is located and the procedures they should follow when there is an injury or incident no matter how small.

First aid equipment needs to be regularly checked, replenished and maintained and making this procedure part of a job role will ensure that the required items are always available.

All injuries, including minor injuries, must be recorded. This is usually done on individual recording forms that are then kept. Some organisations now record accidents on computer systems; these must also be kept for information and/or inspection.

A kitchen first aid box needs to include:

- first aid guidance card (this may have the details of who to contact in emergency, the named first aiders and emergency numbers)
- individually wrapped waterproof dressings (blue) – different sizes
- sterile eye pads (eye wash)
- individually wrapped triangular bandages
- safety pins
- medium-sized sterile individually wrapped dressings

- large sterile individually wrapped dressings
- disposable gloves.

These are the minimum contents and more items can be added to suit the needs of the establishment. It should be the responsibility of a named person to check the first aid box and keep it topped up.

Dealing with minor cuts and burns

Minor cuts, grazes and burns occur occasionally in kitchens because of the nature of the work being completed. Most minor cuts can usually be treated using the contents of the first aid box, maybe with the assistance of an appointed first aider. For more serious cuts and burns it is important to seek advice from the first aider and get medical help as soon as possible.

Minor cuts and grazes

Clean the cut/graze under cold running water, dry it thoroughly and apply a blue waterproof dressing of suitable size. If necessary, also wear a disposable glove. If the cut continues to bleed and is not being contained by the dressing seek further help.

Minor burns

Place the injury under cold running water and keep it there for a minimum of ten minutes. (An ice pack could also be used.) If the burn is more serious and/or the skin is broken, cover lightly with a sterile dressing and seek medical help. Do not let adhesive items, creams, antiseptics or kitchen cloths come into contact with the wound.

Working safely and legal responsibilities

There can be a number of inherent hazards when working in kitchen areas. For this reason, it is important to work in a safe and systematic way in order to avoid accidents or injury to yourself or anyone else.

The following are some common causes of accidents in the kitchen:

- slipping on a wet or greasy floor
- tripping over objects or walking into objects
- lifting objects wrongly or lifting loads that are too heavy
- being exposed to hazards such as hot or dangerous substances, e.g. steam, oven cleaning chemicals
- being hit or hurt by moving objects, such as being cut by a knife when chopping
- injury from machines such as vegetable cutting machines, liquidisers, mincing machines
- fires and explosions
- electric shocks
- not wearing suitable protective clothing or not wearing it properly
- incidents due to poor lighting
- ignoring or abusing the rules put in place for health and safety.

The Health & Safety Executive (HSE) is responsible for enforcing health and safety in the workplace.

- The HSE has the power to investigate premises, check, dismantle and remove equipment, inspect the records, ask questions, seize and destroy articles.
- It can give verbal or written advice, order improvement and prohibition notices and will, if necessary, prosecute, which can result in unlimited fines or even imprisonment.

Everyone working in a kitchen needs to know the laws on health and safety and how they will be affected by these laws. The **Health and Safety at Work Act 1974** gives employees and employers certain responsibilities they must adhere to within their working environment.

- All employees and employers must take reasonable care of their own safety and the safety of others they work with.
- Employees must inform their line manager/ supervisor if they see anything they think is unsafe and could cause an accident.
- Any procedure, equipment or protective clothing put in place for safety must be used correctly and never be modified or tampered with.
- Employees must cooperate with their employer on health and safety matters and procedures put in place to keep the working environment safe.

Employers must also ensure all staff are safe at work and not put staff in dangerous situations where they could injure themselves or others. They must provide safe methods of work for their employees. This includes:

- producing a workplace policy document on health and safety
- completing risk assessments for all equipment and procedures in the workplace
- providing safe equipment and utensils
- training and supervising staff in safe practices
- providing first aid equipment
- keeping an accurate record of all accidents.

The **Health and Safety (Information for Employees) Regulations (1989)** also require that employers provide Health and Safety information for their employees. This could be in the form of leaflets, posters, DVDs and information packs. A selection of these is available from the Health and Safety Executive.

RIDDOR (Reporting Injuries, Diseases and Dangerous Occurrences) Act 1996

The law says that all work-related accidents, diseases and dangerous occurrences must be recorded. However, some injuries must be reported under RIDDOR (Reporting Injuries, Diseases and Dangerous Occurrences) by informing the Incident Contact

Centre, Caerphilly Business Park, Caerphilly, CF83 3GG. Reports can also be completed online at www. riddor.gov.uk. Relevant paperwork and information can also be downloaded from this site.

The following are the injuries that must be reported:
- Any work-related injury lasting three days or more.
- Fractures (apart from fractures to fingers, thumbs or toes).
- Amputation (cutting off) of limbs – legs, arms, etc.
- Dislocation of a hip, knee or spine.
- Temporary or permanent loss of sight (blindness).
- Eye injuries from chemicals getting into the eye, a hot metal burn to the eye or any penetration of the eye.
- Any injury from electric shock or burning that leads to unconsciousness or the need to resuscitate the person or send them to hospital for more than 24 hours.
- Any injury resulting in hypothermia (when someone gets too cold), or illness due to heat, that leads to unconsciousness or the need to resuscitate the person or send them to hospital for more than 24 hours (e.g. an electric shock , or a gas flame blown back and causing burns).
- Unconsciousness caused by exposure to a harmful substance or biological agents (e.g. cleaning products and solvents).
- Unconsciousness or illness requiring medical treatment caused by inhaling a harmful substance or absorbing it through the skin (e.g. breathing in poisonous carbon monoxide leaking from a gas appliance).
- Illness requiring medical treatment caused by a biological agent or its toxins or infected material (e.g. harmful bacteria used in laboratories).

Control of Substances Hazardous to Health (COSHH) Regulations (1999)

The Control of Substances Hazardous to Health (COSHH) regulations state that an employer must not carry out work that might expose employees to substances that are hazardous to their health, unless the employer has assessed the risks and put relevant controls in place. These risk assessments must be recorded and available for inspection. All potentially harmful chemicals must be stored, used and then disposed of properly according to COSHH regulations. The hazardous nature of the chemical must identified on the packaging. Substances that are dangerous to health are labelled as very toxic, toxic, harmful, irritant or corrosive.

This includes the use of recognisable symbols.

Chemicals commonly used in kitchens include: detergents, disinfectants, sanitisers, degreasers, descalers, oven cleaners and pest control chemicals. These substances could cause injury if not used correctly by getting onto the skin, in the eyes, ingesting by mouth or inhaling through the nose or mouth.

People using these chemical substances must be trained to use them properly and safely. This will include:
- wearing the relevant protective clothing such as aprons, goggles, gloves and facemasks
- following the manufacturer's instructions correctly
- always storing chemicals in their original containers, away from heat with the lids tightly closed
- not allowing exposure to heat or to naked flames

Corrosive

Flammable

Harmful

Toxic

- never mixing chemicals
- knowing the first aid procedure
- disposing of used chemicals and empty containers correctly.

Manual Handling Operations Regulations (1992)

Working in a kitchen often includes the need to move heavy or awkwardly shaped objects. These could include deliveries of food and other items that need to be moved to another area, lifting heavy trays from ovens, manoeuvring large pieces of equipment, use of heavy cleaning equipment. Picking up and carrying heavy or difficult loads can lead to accidents and injury and long-term sickness if it is not done properly. Incorrect lifting or lifting something too heavy is a common cause of back injury. An employer must carry out a risk assessment on all tasks that involve lifting and put procedures in place to make it safe. Staff must then be trained in these procedures.

When dealing with lifting the general rules would include:

- assessing the load and not attempting to lift anything that is too heavy

- breaking the load into smaller units if appropriate
- using lifting equipment where available and also moving equipment such as trolleys
- requesting help with lifting.

When lifting, it is essential to use a safe lifting technique:

- Assess the load, plan how you are going to lift it.
- Position yourself with feet apart, back straight and knees bent.
- Grip the item firmly at the base or lifting handles.
- Lift in a smooth movement keeping the load close to the body.
- Walk carefully making sure there are no trip hazards.
- Lower or place the load still keeping the back straight and bending knees if necessary.

> In kitchens take extra care when lifting items that are also **hot**. These include large trays from ovens, roasting trays, large pans of liquids, oven or salamander shelves and a variety of other kitchen items that could be hot and cause burns. When moving a hot item be sure that you can do it safely and there is a clear space to put it down. Give others working around you verbal warnings. Wrap an oven cloth around hot pan-handles and do not allow hot trays to protrude over the edge of surfaces.

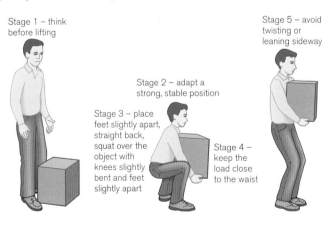

Stage 1 – think before lifting

Stage 2 – adapt a strong, stable position

Stage 3 – place feet slightly apart, straight back, squat over the object with knees slightly bent and feet slightly apart

Stage 4 – keep the load close to the waist

Stage 5 – avoid twisting or leaning sideways

Stage 6 – look ahead

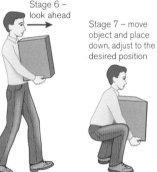

Stage 7 – move object and place down, adjust to the desired position

Hazards and risk assessments

> **Hazard** – Something that could cause injury, ill health or harm.
> **Risk** – The likelihood that the hazard will cause injury, ill health or harm.

A kitchen environment carries a number of potential hazards and it is now a legal requirement for all employers to carry out risk assessments for all of the procedures completed in the workplace to avoid risk of injury, ill health or harm. Health and Safety Legislation covers everyone in the premises including full- and part-time employees, agency staff, contractors, voluntary workers and those on work placement as well as customers and guests.

The more usual hazards encountered in a kitchen area would include:

- **equipment** – liquidisers, food processors, mixers, mincers, etc.
- **chemicals** – cleaning chemicals, disinfectants, pest control items
- **work methods** – using knives and equipment incorrectly and not following safety training and advice
- **work areas** – spillages not cleaned up, overcrowded work areas, insufficient work space, uncomfortable work conditions due to extreme heat or cold
- **poor storage** – boxes on floors causing trip hazards, knives and other sharp objects stored incorrectly, items stacked unsafely.

Slips, trips and falls

The majority of accidents in kitchens are slips, trips and falls. Therefore, floor surfaces must be of a suitable construction to reduce this risk. A major reason for the high incidence of this kind of accident is that water and grease can be spilt, making the floor surface slippery. For this reason, any spillage must be cleaned immediately and warning notices put in place,

where appropriate, highlighting the danger. Verbal warnings should also be given.

Falls can also be caused when items are left on floors and in passageways or between stoves and tables. People carrying trays and containers may have a restricted view and may not see hazards and so may trip over them. They may fall onto a hot stove, onto a sharp item or the item they are carrying may be hot. These falls can have severe consequences. Ensure that nothing is left on the floor that may cause an obstruction and be a hazard. If it is necessary to have articles temporarily on the floor, then they should be guarded to prevent accidents.

Kitchen personnel should be trained to think and act in a safe manner so as to avoid this kind of accident.

Remember! Kitchens can be dangerous places. Remain aware of hazards and potential hazards at all times. Report these immediately to a supervisor or line manager.

Hazard warning signs

Safety signs are used to control a hazard. They should not replace other methods of controlling risks.

Yellow signs/warning signs

These are to warn of various dangers, such as slippery floors, hot oil or hot water. They also warn about hazards such as corrosive material.

Blue signs/mandatory signs

These signs inform about precautions that must be taken, such as how to progress safely through a certain area. They are also used when special precautions need to be taken, such as wearing protective clothing.

Red signs/prohibition or fire fighting signs

Red signs tell people that they should not enter and are to stop people from doing certain tasks in a hazardous area. Red signs are also used for fire fighting equipment.

Green signs/safe signs

These are route signs designed to show where fire exits and emergency exits are. Green is also used for first aid equipment.

Electricity and gas

The majority of kitchens will have a range of electrical equipment and great care must be taken when dealing with electricity. Electrical equipment is covered by **Electricity at Work Regulations (1989)**; under these regulations all electrical equipment must be tested annually by a qualified electrician.

If a person comes into direct contact with electricity electric shock can occur, which can be very serious and sometimes fatal. If a person has an electric shock, switch off the current. If this is not possible, free the person using something that is dry and will insulate you from the electricity, such as a thick cloth, or something made of wood or rubber. You must take care not to use your bare hands otherwise the electric shock may be transmitted to you.

In the case of electric shock:

- Switch off the current.
- Raise the alarm.
- Call for medical/first aid help.

If trained in the procedure you can give artificial respiration where necessary

Gas is often the preferred fuel for industrial stoves and can be potentially hazardous. On leaving the kitchen, turn off all the gas appliances. It is important to report any gas leaks, faulty equipment or gas smell immediately to a supervisor or line manager.

In some kitchens there are central gas cut-off points used in emergency situations such as fire.

Fire safety

Every employer has a duty of care for the safety of employees in the event of a fire. The **Regulatory Fire Safety Order 2005** emphasises that measures must be taken to prevent fires. All staff must be trained in emergency evacuation with fire action plans clearly displayed to show the established evacuation routes for staff, customers and visitors. The fire evacuation procedures should be practised at least once a year, the procedure recorded and reviewed regularly to take into account staff changes and any changes to the premises.

Under current Health and Safety regulations it is now a requirement to:

- make sure that the fire precautions, where reasonably practicable, ensure the safety of all employees and others in the building
- complete a fire risk assessment of the premises and specific areas. This must be recorded and be available for inspection. Preventative and protective measures must be reviewed. A fire risk assessment will help to establish the likelihood of a fire occurring and highlight the dangers from fire in the workplace
- make sure suitable fire detection systems are in place and fire alarms tested weekly
- clearly sign all escape routes and make sure they are free from hazards that would slow down or prevent escape.

A fire requires heat, fuel and oxygen ('the fire triangle' – see below). Without any one of these elements fire will not start. Methods of extinguishing fires concentrate on cooling (as in a water extinguisher or fire hose) or depriving the fire of oxygen (as in an extinguisher that uses foam or powder).

Fire precautions

Effective measures in the prevention of fire include:

- removing all hazards or reducing them as much as possible
- making sure that measures have been taken to protect from the risk of fire and the likelihood of a fire spreading
- ensuring that all escape routes are safe and used effectively, they are well signed and easy to access
- provision of suitable fire fighting equipment and staff well trained in its use
- providing suitable ways of detecting a fire (e.g. smoke alarms) and instructions as to what to do in case of fire
- arrangements in place for what to do if a fire breaks out. Employees must be trained in what to do in the event of a fire
- all precautions provided must be installed and maintained by a competent person.

Fires are classified in accordance with British Standard EN2 as follows:

- Class A – fires involving solid materials where combustion (burning) normally forms glowing embers, e.g. wood.
- Class B – fires involving liquids such as methylated spirit or any kind of flammable gel used under a burner.
- Class C – fires involving gases.
- Class D – fires involving metals.
- Class F – fires involving cooking oils or fats.

There are different types of fire extinguishers that are suitable for different types of fire. Generally, portable fire extinguishers contain one of the following five substances:

- water
- foam
- powder
- carbon dioxide
- vaporising liquids.

| **Fuel** |
| Flammable gases, liquids or solids |

Ignition source	**Oxygen**
Smoking or naked flames	Always present in the air
Hot surfaces	Also comes from
Electrical equipment	oxidising substances
Static electricity	

The fire triangle

The most useful form of general-purpose fire-fighting equipment is the water-type extinguisher or hose reel. Areas of special risk, such as kitchens where oil, fats and electrical equipment are used, may need other types of extinguisher such as carbon dioxide, wet chemical or dry powder.

Ensure that you know the evacuation procedures in your establishment and follow the procedure shown to you. If you need to leave the premises because of fire the usual steps include:

- Raise the alarm and warn others verbally.
- Turn off gas supplies using a central cut-off point if possible.

- Do not put yourself and others in danger; only tackle the smallest of fires and only if you know how to do this.
- Leave by the appointed exits checking that others are also vacating the building. Guests, visitors and customers may need assisting and directing.
- Go to the appointed assembly point and await further instruction.
- Do not re-enter the building until you are told you can do so.

Incident/accident reporting

Health and safety must be monitored regularly in the workplace by the designated Health and Safety Manager/Officer. Any incidents or near misses must be recorded, even if no one is injured.

All accidents and potential accidents should be reported to your line manager, or supervisor. Each

accident is recorded in an accident book/file, which must be provided in every business. Below is an example of an incident report form showing all the details required.

Full name of injured person:			
Occupation:		Supervisor:	
Time of accident:	Date of accident:	Time of report:	Date of report:
Nature of injury or condition:			
Details of hospitalisation:			
Extent of injury (after medical attention):			
Place of accident or dangerous occurrence:			
Injured person's evidence of what happened (include equipment/items/other persons): Use separate sheets if necessary.			
Witness evidence (1):		Witness evidence (2):	
Supervisor's recommendations:			
Date:		Supervisor's signature:	
This form must be sent to the company health and safety officer.			

An incident report form

Emergencies in the workplace

Emergencies that might happen in the workplace include:

- serious accidents involving injury
- outbreak of fire or explosion
- threats such as terrorism or riots
- bomb scare
- failure of major system, e.g. water or electricity.

An organisation will have systems in place to deal with emergencies. Key staff are usually trained to lead the procedure in case of emergency and most organisations will have fire marshals and first aiders. These people will attend regular update meetings. Evacuation procedures will also be in place, which employees will need to practise (e.g. fire practice), and fire alarms will be tested regularly.

Security in hospitality premises

Security in hospitality premises always remains a high priority. In many hospitality establishments large numbers of people can be present in the building at any one time. These may include: staff, guests, customers, contractors, visitors and others.

As well as providing security and protection for all these people security consideration needs to be given to the buildings and grounds, fixtures, fittings and furniture, decor and decorative items, equipment, clothing, linen and stock.

The main security concerns include:

- **theft**: where customers' property, employers' property (particularly food, drink and equipment) or employees' property is stolen
- **burglary**: where the burglar comes onto the premises (trespasses) and steals customers' property, employers' property or employees' property
- **robbery**: theft with assault, for example when staff are banking or collecting cash
- **fraud**: false insurance claims; counterfeit money; stolen credit cards
- **assault**: fights between customers; assaults on staff by customers, violence or attacks on staff, verbal abuse
- **vandalism**: damage to property caused by customers, intruders or employees
- **arson**: setting fire to the property
- **undesirable individuals**: having people such as drug traffickers on the premises
- **terrorism**: bombs, telephone bomb threats.

The Health and Safety at Work Regulations require employers to conduct a risk assessment regarding the safety of staff in the business. Preventing crime is more efficient and less damaging than having to deal with it once it has happened.

Dealing with security

Everyone entering the premises should be monitored. Reception staff need to be trained to spot suspicious individuals and those likely to cause problems. Everyone who comes into the building should be asked to sign in at reception and, if they are a legitimate visitor, be given a security badge. It is also essential to make sure that any suspicious person does not re-enter the building.

- All contract workers should be registered and given security badges, and they may be restricted to working in certain areas.
- There should also be good security systems on all doors, those delivering goods need to report to the relevant person.
- All establishments should try to reduce temptation for criminals, for example by reducing the amount of cash that is handled. The use of credit and debit cards is now common and widespread and reduces the amounts of cash used, so reducing the risk of cash theft. However, credit/debit card fraud and crimes are also a problem.
- Staff who handle money should be trained in simple anti-fraud measures such as checking bank notes, checking signatures on plastic cards and so on.

- It is impossible to remove all temptation, so equipment (e.g. computers, fax machines, photocopiers) should be marked with some sort of security tag or identification.
- There are many simple and obvious security measures that can also be taken, such as locking doors and windows.
- Coded key pads on doors are effective in keeping areas safe. Keys should be kept securely and access to them restricted to those needing them.
- Good lighting is also important for security reasons – criminals are less likely to come onto the premises at night if they can be clearly seen. Regular checks should be made of the lighting in all areas. Lighting areas that can be seen by passers-by can also help.
- Closed-circuit television (CCTV) cameras with recordings are also used as a deterrent against crime.
- With regard to staff, the first step is to appoint honest staff by checking their references from previous employers.
- Staff are frequently provided with security swipe cards to enter the building; these may also carry a photographic image of the staff member.

- Some companies write into employee contracts the 'right to search'. This means that from time to time the employer can carry out searches of the employees' lockers, bags and other belongings.

Dealing with customers' property

In hospitality establishments customers' property often needs to be looked after, secured or cared for. Keeping customers' property safe whilst on the premises is dealt with by:
- locked rooms
- lockers and locking cupboards
- personal safes in rooms or a central safe customers can use
- cloakrooms with ticket/token systems
- items left in reception areas or concierge desks
- items given to staff for safekeeping.

When customers' property has been left behind by mistake the usual procedure is to report the left item to a supervisor, record the item left with a description and date and store the item securely. When the identity and whereabouts of the person leaving the item is known they may be contacted to inform them of their lost property.

Procedures

Most establishments will have definite procedures in place with regards to **risks, threats, and security**. Make sure that you are aware of these policies and carry them out correctly in line with the establishment's operational procedures.

15 Maintain food safety

This chapter is relevant to the following units:

- Maintain a safe, hygienic and secure working environment (NVQ)
- Maintain food safety when storing, preparing and cooking food (NVQ)
- Food safety in catering (VRQ).

This chapter provides the necessary information to enable you to prepare and cook food safely. It focuses on the key food safety control areas outlined by the Food Standards Agency, which are; cooking, cleaning, chilling and prevention of cross contamination. It also discusses food safety hazards and the necessary measures to control them from delivery of food up until the time it is served to the customer.

What is food safety and why does it matter?

Everyone consuming food has the right and expectation to be served safe food that will not cause illness or harm them in any way.

Food safety means putting in place all of the measures needed to make sure that food and drinks are suitable, safe and wholesome in all of the stages they go through.

Eating 'contaminated' food can cause harm and illness and in some cases even death.

The number of reported cases of food poisoning in England and Wales remains very high – between 70,000 and 94,000 cases each year. However, as a very large number of food poisoning cases are not reported no one really knows the actual number.

Food poisoning can be an unpleasant illness for anyone but in some groups of people it can be very serious or even fatal.

These high-risk groups are:
- babies and very young children
- elderly people
- pregnant women
- those who are already unwell or have immune system problems.

Although the main reason for adopting high standards of food safety is to prevent the possibility of food poisoning, there are many more benefits a food business can gain by keeping food safety standards high. These include:
- being compliant with food safety law
- reducing food wastage and improving efficiency
- return business from satisfied customers
- building a good reputation and receiving fewer complaints.

Food poisoning

Food poisoning is an illness of the digestive system that is the result of eating foods contaminated with pathogenic bacteria and/or their toxins. Food poisoning may also be caused by eating poisonous fish or plants, chemicals or metals. Symptoms of food poisoning are often similar and may include:
- nausea
- vomiting

- diarrhoea
- fever
- abdominal pain
- dehydration.

As well as food poisoning that is caused by pathogenic bacteria and viruses, illness associated with food or drinks may also be caused by: moulds, allergens, chemicals and physical contaminants.

It is therefore essential that great care is taken to prevent food poisoning and the Food Standards Agency has committed to reducing the numbers of reported food poisoning cases significantly in the UK.

How is food contaminated?

Food contamination can lead to food poisoning. It is important to understand how it happens and how it can be prevented.

Bacteria are all around us; they are generally present in the environment, on raw food, refuse, the human body, animals, birds and insects. When bacteria multiply in food or use food to get into the human body illness may result.

Chemicals can sometimes get into food accidentally and can then make the consumer ill. The kinds of chemical that can get into food can be cleaning fluids, disinfectants, machine oil, insecticides and pesticides.

Physical contamination is caused when something gets into foods that should not be there and may be one or more of a wide range of items such as glass, pen tops, paperclips, blue plasters, hair, insects and finger nails.

Allergens: an **allergy** is when the immune system in some people reacts to certain food. Reactions include swelling, itching, rashes, breathlessness and may even cause anaphylactic shock (a severe reaction often causing swelling of the throat and mouth that prevents breathing). **Food intolerance** is different and the immune system is not involved but there may still be a reaction to some foods. Foods usually associated with allergies and food intolerances are: nuts, dairy products, wheat-based products, eggs and shellfish.

High-risk food

Some foods pose a greater risk to food safety than others and are called **high-risk foods**.

They are usually ready to eat so would not need any further cooking that would kill bacteria. High-risk foods are usually moist, contain protein and require refrigerated storage.

High-risk foods include:
- soups, stocks, sauces, gravies
- eggs and egg products
- milk and milk products
- cooked meat and fish, and meat and fish products
- any foods needing handling or reheating.

Bacteria and food poisoning

Not all bacteria are harmful; some are very useful and are used to good effect in the manufacture of foods and medicines. Making milk into yoghurt or cheese may use bacteria in the process.

The bacteria that are harmful are called **pathogenic bacteria** and can cause food poisoning. Bacteria are very small, so small that you would need to use a microscope to see them; you would not be able to taste them or smell them on food. This is why pathogenic bacteria are so dangerous – you can't tell if they are in food or not. When bacteria have the conditions they need, i.e. **food, warmth, moisture** and **time,** they can multiply approximately every 10/20 minutes by dividing in half. This is called binary fission.

Some common food poisoning bacteria

Salmonella used to be the most common cause of food poisoning in the UK but since measures were put in place to reduce salmonella in chickens and in eggs, food poisoning from this source has reduced. The main source of salmonella is the human and animal gut and excreta but it is also on pests such as rodents, insects and birds and in raw meat and poultry, eggs and shellfish. Salmonella poisoning can also be passed on through human carriers (someone carrying salmonella but not showing any signs of illness).

Staphylococcus aureus is found mainly on the human body and can be present on skin, hair and scalp, nose, throat, etc. Cuts, spots, burns and boils will also be a source of this organism. When staphylococcus multiplies in food, a toxin (poison) is produced which is very difficult to kill, even with boiling temperatures. To avoid food poisoning from this organism, food handlers need to maintain very high standards of personal hygiene and report any illness they may have to their supervisor before beginning work.

Clostridium perfringens can be present in human and animal faeces and raw meat, poultry and vegetables, (also insects, soil, dust and sewage). A number of food poisoning incidents from this organism have occurred when large amounts of meat are brought up to cooking temperatures slowly then allowed to cool slowly. Clostridium perfringens can produce **spores** during this heating/cooling. Spores are very resistant to any further cooking and allow bacteria to survive in conditions that would usually kill them.

Bacillus cereus is another organism that can produce spores and can also produce two different toxins so is a very dangerous pathogen. It is often associated with cooking rice in large quantities, cooling it too slowly and then reheating. The reheating temperatures would not be enough to destroy spores and toxins. It has also been linked with other cereal crops, spices, soil and vegetables.

Clostridium botulinum is fortunately rare; the symptoms can be very serious, even fatal. Sources tend to be intestines of fish, soil and vegetables.

Toxins

Toxins (poisons) can be produced by some bacteria as they multiply in food. They are heat resistant and may not be killed by the normal cooking processes that kill bacteria so remain in the food and can cause illness.

Some bacteria produce toxins as they die, usually in the intestines of the person who has eaten the food.

Spores

Some bacteria are able to form spores when the conditions surrounding them becomes hostile, such as when temperatures rise or in the presence of chemicals such as disinfectant. A spore forms a protective 'shell' inside the bacteria, protecting the essential parts from the high temperatures of normal cooking, disinfection, dehydration, etc. Once spores are formed the rest of the cell disperses and cannot divide and multiply as before but simply survives until conditions improve, e.g. high temperatures drop to a level where the cell can re-form and multiplication can start again. Prolonged cooking times and/or very high temperatures are needed to kill spores. **Time** is very important in preventing the formation of spores. Large amounts of food such as meat for stewing, when brought slowly to cooking temperature, allows time for spores to form; these are then very difficult to kill. Bring food up to cooking temperature quickly – cool food quickly.

Food-borne illness

Some different organisms from the ones named above are said to cause **food-borne illness**. These pathogens do not multiply in food but use food to get into the human gut where they then multiply and cause a range of illnesses, some of them serious, including severe abdominal pain, diarrhoea, vomiting, headaches, blurred vision, flu symptoms, septicaemia and miscarriage. These organisms may be transmitted person-to-person, in water or airborne, as well as through food.

Food-borne pathogens include:
- **Campylobacter:** causes more food-related illness than any other organism. It is found in raw poultry and meat, sewage, animals, insects and birds.
- **E coli 0157:** is present in the intestines and excreta of animals and humans, raw meat and can be present on raw vegetables.
- **Listeria:** is of concern because it can multiply (slowly) at fridge temperatures, i.e. below 5°C. It has been linked with such chilled products as unpasteurised cheeses, pate and prepared salads as well as cook/chill meals.
- **Norovirus:** like all viruses, will not multiply on food, but it may live for a short time on surfaces, utensils and food and use these to get into the body. The most usual way this is spread is airborne, person-to-person, via water or sewage.

Poisoning from other items

Some foods can be naturally poisonous, such as some strains of mushrooms and undercooked red kidney beans. Some oily fish can develop toxins if stored at too high a temperature and occasionally some shellfish can cause illness when they have fed on poisonous plankton.

Some moulds can produce toxins as they grow; these are called **mycotoxins**. Mycotoxins can cause serious illness and have been linked with cancers. Do not use mouldy food. (Controlled moulds such as in blue cheeses are fine.)

Personal hygiene

All food handlers are a potential source of food poisoning bacteria so it is very important they take great care with personal hygiene and report any illnesses or infection they may have before starting work.

See the information on personal hygiene and protective clothing in Chapter 14.

Hand washing

Particular attention should be given to washing hands because contamination from hands can happen very easily. Hands must be washed frequently and thoroughly especially on entering the kitchen and between tasks.

1 Use a basin provided just for hand washing.
2 Wet hands under warm running water.
3 Apply liquid soap.
4 Rub hands together between fingers and thumbs.
5 Remember, fingertips, nails and wrists.
6 Rinse off under the running water.

7 Dry hands on a paper towel and use the paper towel to turn off the tap.

A nail brush may be used to aid thorough hand washing but always ensure this is clean and disinfected, for example, keep in a sanitising solution or consider using disposable brushes.

You should wash your hands:

- when you enter the kitchen, before starting work and handling any food
- after a break (using the toilet, in contact with faeces)
- between different tasks but especially between handling raw and cooked food
- if you touch hair, nose, mouth or use a tissue for sneezing or coughing
- after you apply or change a dressing on a cut or burn
- after cleaning preparation areas, equipment or contaminated surfaces
- after handling kitchen waste, external food packaging, money or flowers.

Hygienic working practices to avoid cross contamination

Cross contamination

Cross contamination occurs when bacteria are transferred from one place to another. This is usually from contaminated food (usually raw food), equipment or surfaces to ready to eat food. It is the cause of significant amounts of food poisoning and care must

be taken to avoid it. Cross contamination could be caused by:

- foods touching, e.g. raw and cooked meat
- raw meat or poultry dripping onto high-risk foods

- soil from dirty vegetables coming into contact with high-risk foods
- dirty cloths, dirty staff uniforms or dirty equipment
- equipment used for raw then cooked food, e.g. chopping boards or knives
- hands touching raw then cooked food, not washing hands between tasks, etc.
- pests spreading bacteria around the kitchen.

Controlling cross contamination

Separate working areas and storage areas for **raw** and **high-risk** foods are strongly recommended. If this is not possible keep them well away from each other and make sure that working areas are thoroughly cleaned and disinfected between tasks.

Vegetables should be washed before preparation/peeling and again afterwards. Leafy vegetables may need to be washed in several changes of cold water to remove all of the soil present.

Good personal hygiene practices by staff, especially frequent and effective hand washing is very important in controlling cross contamination and will avoid the significant amounts of contamination caused by faecal/oral routes. (This is when pathogens normally found in faeces are transferred to ready to eat foods resulting in cross contamination and illness.) An obvious way that this may happen is when food handlers visit the toilet, do not wash their hands properly then handle food.

Colour-coded equipment

Colour-coded chopping boards are a good way to keep different types of food separate. Worktops and chopping boards will come into contact with the food being prepared so need special attention. Make sure that chopping boards are in good condition, cracks and splits could trap bacteria and this could be transferred to food.

As well as colour-coded chopping boards some kitchens also provide colour-coded knives, cloths, cleaning equipment, storage trays, bowls and even staff uniforms to help prevent cross contamination.

The colour-coding system

Clean and sanitise

Clean and sanitise worktops and chopping boards before working on them and do this again after use, paying particular attention when they have been used for raw foods.

Chopping boards can be disinfected after use by putting them through a dishwasher with a high rinse temperature of 82°C. (High temperatures will kill bacteria.)

Small equipment, such as knives, bowls, spoons, tongs, etc. could also be the cause of cross contamination; it is important to wash them thoroughly, (once again a dishwasher does it well). This is especially important when used for a variety of food and for raw foods.

Take responsibility for food safety

As a food handler it is your responsibility along with those working with you to assist in the control of bacteria. Keep food areas clean and hygienic at all times, clean as you go and do not allow waste to build up, clean up any spills straight away. You need to be aware of protecting food from bacteria and preventing bacterial growth by keeping food clean, cool/hot and covered where possible.

Take great care with kitchen cloths, they are a growing area for bacteria. Different cloths for different areas will help to reduce cross contamination and it is certainly good practice to use different cloths for raw food and high-risk food areas. Use of disposable kitchen towel is the most hygienic way to dry utensils and food preparation areas.

If a tea towel is used, treat with great care: remember that they can easily spread bacteria so don't use as an 'all purpose cloth', don't keep it on the shoulder (the cloth touches the neck and hair, picking up bacteria).

Thorough cooking is one of the best methods available to control bacteria. Cooking to **75°C** and holding that temperature for at least **2 minutes** will kill most pathogens (but not spores and toxins).

Keep food being held for service above **63°C** or cool it rapidly and keep below **5°C**. Never put hot or warm food into a refrigerator or freezer; this will raise the temperature and put food into the danger zone.

Checking and controlling temperatures

Cooking food to a core temperature of **75°C** for **2 minutes** will kill most bacteria and these temperatures are important especially where large amounts are being cooked or the consumers are in the high-risk categories (see page 627). However, some popular dishes on hotel and restaurant menus are cooked to a lower temperature than this according to individual dish and customer requirements.

Table 15.1 Important temperatures when dealing with food

Food	Important temperature
Food stored in a freezer (no bacterial growth but does not kill bacteria, toxins or spores)	Store at −18°C to −23°C
Refrigerated food: Raw meat/poultry Raw fish and shellfish Cooked meats/meat products Cooked fish/fish products Dairy products/fats Eggs Salad items, herbs, leafy vegetables Cooked foods/high-risk items	Store at 1°C to 4°C*
Ambient stored food: Canned food Dry goods Grains General grocery items	Store at 10°C to 15°C in a cool, well-ventilated place
Cooked hot food (a temperature that will kill bacteria but not spores and probably not toxins)	Core temperature must reach 75°C
Cooked fish (EHO may advise a higher temperature)	Core temperature must reach 63°C
Reheated food	Core temperature must reach 75°C (82°C in Scotland)
Hot food being held for service	Keep at 63°C+

* Although the law says that 'foods which support growth of pathogens or formation of toxins must not be stored above 8°C, it is recognised best practice to store below 5°C.

Practical Cookery 12th edition

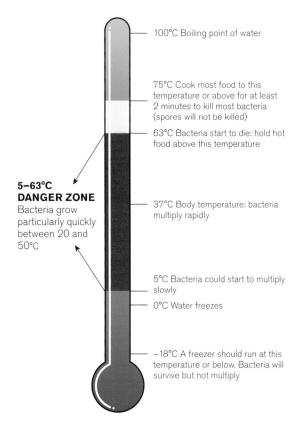

100°C Boiling point of water

75°C Cook most food to this temperature or above for at least 2 minutes to kill most bacteria (spores will not be killed)

63°C Bacteria start to die: hold hot food above this temperature

5–63°C
DANGER ZONE
Bacteria grow particularly quickly between 20 and 50°C

37°C Body temperature: bacteria multiply rapidly

5°C Bacteria could start to multiply slowly

0°C Water freezes

−18°C A freezer should run at this temperature or below. Bacteria will survive but not multiply

Important food safety temperatures

Electronic temperature probes are very useful to measure the temperature in the centre of both hot and cold food. They are also very useful for recording the temperature of deliveries and checking of food temperatures in refrigerators. Make sure the probe is clean and disinfected before use, (disposable disinfectant wipes are useful for this). Place the probe into the centre of the food making sure it is not touching bone or the cooking container.

Using an electronic probe

Check regularly that probes are working correctly **(calibration)**. This can be done electronically but a simple and low-cost check is to place the probe in icy water, the reading should be 0°C. Next, place the probe in boiling water and the temperature reading should be 100°C. In both cases **one degree** higher or lower is acceptable. If probes read outside of these temperatures they need to be repaired or replaced. When calibration of probes has been completed, record these temperatures and keep as part of the food safety management system.

Training

Food businesses must ensure that all staff who handle food are supervised and instructed and/or trained in food hygiene appropriate to the work they do. The person responsible for food safety management of a business must also be responsible for staff training. Appropriate training can take place in-house or with a training provider. Records of staff training must include the date, level of the training and topics covered. All records of staff training must be kept for possible inspection.

Food spoilage and food preservation

Most foods have a limited life and will eventually deteriorate due to: moulds, yeasts, enzymes or bacteria. Spoilage of food also occurs due to: exposure to oxygen, moisture or chemicals, damage by pests or by poor handling and bad storage.

Unlike bacterial contamination that is impossible to detect in a normal kitchen situation, food spoilage can usually be observed by sight, smell, taste, touch, etc.

Spoilage could include: mouldy, slimy, dried-up, over-wet fresh foods. Also, blown cans and vac packs and food with freezer burn. Different methods have been developed to prolong the natural life of various foods and keep them fresh. These include:

- **Use of heat** – cooking, canning, sterilisation, UHT, pasteurisation.
- **Use of heat and sealing** – canning, bottling, cooking then vacuum packaging.
- **Use of low temperatures** – chilling, freezing.
- **Exclusion of air** – vacuum packaging.
- **Changing gases surrounding food** – modified atmosphere packaging.
- **Removal of moisture** – dehydrated foods.
- **Use of acids, sugar or salt concentrations.**
- **Food preservatives** – e.g. nitrates.

Food preservation will often combine methods to ensure effective preservation, e.g. vacuum-packed fish will also be refrigerated and pasteurised milk will be refrigerated.

Use of heat to make foods safe and to preserve it is one of the most useful procedures available to those involved in food production and manufacture. Table 15.2 shows some commonly used temperatures.

Table 15.2 Temperatures used for food preservation

Process	Temperatures used
Cooking	Normal cooking, that is, to 75°C for 2 minutes at the core of the food will kill most pathogens and the food will keep a little longer.
Pasteurisation	This involves heating food to a temperature similar to cooking temperatures but for a very short time, i.e. milk is heated to 72°C for 15 seconds bringing bacteria to a safe level.
Sterilisation	Sterilisation of milk and other items involves heating to 100°C for 15–30 minutes by applying steam and pressure.
UHT	Ultra-high temperature. Used mainly for milk. It is heated under pressure to 135°C for just 1 second then cooled rapidly and sealed in sterile containers.
Canning	Very high temperatures are used to make sure the food is safe from all micro-organisms, toxins and spores. The typical time/temperature used is 121°C for 3 minutes.

Food deliveries and storage

For food to remain in best condition and be safe to eat it is essential that correct storage procedures are in place and fully understood by kitchen staff. Only approved suppliers should be used who can assure that food is delivered in the best condition, in suitable packaging, properly date coded and at the correct temperature. Suppliers need to be able to provide information on the product from source through to delivery (traceability).

- All deliveries should be checked then moved to the appropriate storage area as soon as possible and chilled/frozen food within 15 minutes of delivery.
- Use a food probe to check the temperature of food deliveries; chilled food should be below 5°C, frozen foods should be at or below −18°C. Record these temperatures and keep as part of the food safety management system.

- Many suppliers will now provide a printout of temperatures at which food was delivered (save these printouts in kitchen records).
- Dry goods should be in undamaged packaging, well within best before dates, be completely dry and in perfect condition on delivery.
- Remove food items from outer boxes before placing the products in fridge, freezer or dry store and remove outer packaging carefully, remaining fully aware of any possible pests that may have found their way in.
- Segregate any unfit food from other food until it is thrown away or collected by supplier. This is to avoid any possible contamination to other foods.

Storing raw meat and poultry

Wherever possible, store in refrigerators just for meat and poultry storage running at temperatures of 1°C–4°C. If not already packaged, place on trays, cover well with clingfilm and label. If it is necessary to store meat/poultry in a multi-use refrigerator make sure it is covered, labelled and placed at the bottom of the refrigerator running at 1°C–4°C and is well away from other items.

Storing fish

A separate fish refrigerator running between 1°C–4°C is best. Remove fresh fish from ice containers and place on trays, cover well with clingfilm and label. If it is necessary to store fish in a multi-use refrigerator make sure it is well covered, labelled and placed at the bottom of the refrigerator well away from other items. Remember that odours from fish can permeate other items such as milk or eggs.

Storing dairy products and eggs

Pasteurised milk, cream, eggs and cheese should be stored in their original containers between 1°C–4°C. Sterilised or UHT milk can be kept in the dry store following the storage instructions on the label.

After delivery, eggs should be stored at a constant temperature and a refrigerator is the best place.

Storing and defrosting frozen foods

Store frozen food in a freezer running at −18°C or below. Separate raw foods from ready to eat foods and never allow food to be re-frozen once it has thawed.

If you need to defrost frozen food, place it in a deep tray, cover with film and label what the item is, and the date when defrosting was started. Place at the bottom of the refrigerator where thawing liquid can't drip onto anything else. Thaw food completely (no ice crystals on any part), then cook thoroughly within 12 hours. Make sure that you allow enough time for this process – it may take longer than you think! (A 2kg chicken will take about 24 hours to defrost at 3°C.)

Storing fruit, vegetables and salad items

Storage conditions will vary according to type, e.g. sacks of potatoes, root vegetables and some fruit can be stored in a cool, well-ventilated store room but salad items, green vegetables, soft fruit and tropical fruit would be better in refrigerated storage. If possible, a specific refrigerator running at around 8°C would be ideal to avoid any chill damage.

Storing dry goods

Dry goods, including items such as rice, dried pasta, sugar, flour, grains, etc., should be kept in clean, covered containers on wheels or in smaller sealed containers on shelves to stop pests getting into them. Storage should be in a cool, well-ventilated dry store area and well-managed stock rotation is essential. Retain packaging information as this may include essential **allergy advice**.

Storing and handling canned products

Cans are usually stored in the dry store area and once again rotation of stock is essential. Canned food will carry **best before** dates and it is not advisable to use after this date. 'Blown' cans must never be used nor badly dented or rusty cans. Once opened transfer any unused canned food to a clean bowl, cover and label it and store in the refrigerator for up to 2 days.

Storing cooked foods

Foods that are purchased ready-cooked or cooked and then stored include a wide range, e.g. pies, pate, cream cakes, desserts and savoury flans. They will usually be 'high-risk foods' so correct storage is essential. For specific storage instructions see the labelling on the individual items, but generally, keep items between 1°C–4°C. Store carefully, wrapped and labelled and well away from and above raw foods to avoid any cross contamination.

Cooked food being held for service must be kept above **63°C (or below 5°C)**. If food is being cooled to serve cold or for reheating at a later time, it must be protected from contamination and cooled quickly, i.e. to **8°C within 90 minutes**. The best way to do this is in a blast chiller.

Any food that is to be chilled or frozen must be well wrapped or placed in a suitable container with a lid, (items may also be vacuum packed). Make sure that all food is labelled and dated before chilling or freezing.

The multi-use refrigerator

The following guidelines apply if a refrigerator is used to store various types of food.
- It is best practice to keep the refrigerator running at between 1°C–4°C (legal requirement 8°C).
- Food must be covered and labelled with name of item and the date.
- Always store raw food at the bottom of the refrigerator with other items above.
- Keep high-risk foods well away from raw foods.
- Never overload the refrigerator, to operate properly cold air must be allowed to circulate between items.
- Wrap strong-smelling foods thoroughly as the smell (and taste) can transfer to other foods, e.g. milk.
- Record the temperature at which the refrigerator is operating. Do this at least once a day, keep the fridge temperatures with other kitchen records.

Clean the refrigerator regularly.
- Remove food to another refrigerator. Clean according to cleaning schedule using a recommended sanitiser (a solution of bicarbonate

of soda and water is also good for cleaning a refrigerator).
- Remember to empty and clean any drip trays, and clean door seals thoroughly.
- Rinse then dry with kitchen paper.
- Make sure the refrigerator front and handle is cleaned and disinfected to avoid cross contamination.
- Make sure the refrigerator is down to temperature 1°C–4°C, before replacing the food in the proper positions. Check dates and condition of all food before replacing.

'First in – First out'

This term is used to describe stock rotation and is applied to all categories of food. It simply means that foods already in storage are used before new deliveries (providing stock is still within recommended dates and in sound condition). Food deliveries should be labelled with delivery date and preferably the date by which they should be used. Use this information along with food labelling codes (see below). Written stock records should form a part of a food safety management system.

Food labelling codes

- **USE BY** dates appear on perishable foods with a short life. Legally, the food must be used by this date and not stored or used after it.
- **BEST BEFORE** dates apply to foods that are expected to have a longer life, e.g. dry products or canned food. A best before date advises that food is at its best before this date and to use it after the date is still legal but not advised.

Examples of food labelling

Cleaning

Clean food areas are essential in the production of safe food and it is a requirement to plan, record and check all cleaning as part of a 'cleaning schedule'. Clean premises, work areas and equipment are important to:

- control the bacteria that cause food poisoning
- discourage growth of moulds
- reduce the possibility of physical and chemical contamination
- make accidents less likely, e.g. slips on a greasy floor
- create a positive image for customers, visitors and employees
- comply with the law
- avoid attracting pests to the kitchen.

The cleaning schedule needs to include the following information:

- **What** is to be cleaned.
- **Who** should do it (name if possible).
- **How** it is to be done and how long it should take.
- **When**, i.e. time of day.
- **Materials** to be used including chemicals, dilution, cleaning equipment, protective clothing to be worn.
- **Safety** precautions necessary.
- **Signatures** of cleaner and supervisor checking the work (also date and time).

As a food handler it is important to 'clean as you go' and not allow waste to accumulate in the area where you are working. This is because it is very difficult to keep untidy areas clean.

Cleaning products

There are different cleaning products designed for different tasks.

Detergent is designed to remove grease and dirt and hold them in suspension in water. It may be in the form of liquid, powder, gel or foam and usually needs to be added to water to use. Detergent will not kill pathogens (but the hot water it is mixed with may help to do this), but it will clean and de-grease so disinfectant can work properly. Detergents work best with hot water.

Disinfectant is designed to destroy bacteria if used properly; make sure you only use a disinfectant intended for kitchen use. Disinfectants must be left on a cleaned grease-free surface for the required amount of time, **contact time**, to be effective. Heat may also be used to disinfect, for example use of steam cleaners or the hot rinse cycle of a dishwasher.

Sanitiser both cleans and disinfects and usually comes in spray form. Sanitiser is very useful for work surfaces and equipment especially between tasks. It is usual to clean surfaces with hot water and detergent before spraying with sanitiser.

Items that should be both cleaned and disinfected include:

- all items that come into contact with food
- all hand contact surfaces
- equipment used for cleaning.

Cleaning procedure

Cleaning kitchen surfaces should be planned and all staff need to be trained in a suitable cleaning method such as one of the following.

Six-stage process for cleaning a surface:

1. Remove debris and loose particles.
2. Main clean to remove soiling grease.
3. Rinse using clean hot water and cloth to remove the detergent.
4. Apply disinfectant and leave for the contact time recommended on the container.
5. Rinse off the disinfectant if recommended.
6. Allow to air dry or use kitchen paper.

Four-stage process for cleaning a surface:

1. Remove debris and loose particles.
2. Main clean, use hot water and sanitiser.
3. Rinse using clean hot water and cloth if recommended on instructions.
4. Allow to air dry or use kitchen paper.

Cleaning is essential to prevent hazards but if not managed properly can become a hazard in itself. Do not store cleaning chemicals in food preparation and cooking areas and take care with their use to avoid chemical contamination. Make sure that items such as cloths and paper towel and fibres from mops do not get into open food (physical contamination). Bacterial contamination could occur by using the same cleaning cloths and equipment in raw food areas then in high-risk food areas or by using dirty cloths and equipment.

Dishwashing

Automatic dishwashing

The most efficient and hygienic method of cleaning dishes and crockery is the use of a dishwashing machine as this will clean and disinfect items that will then air dry, removing the need for cloths. The dishwasher can also be used to clean/disinfect small equipment such as chopping boards. The stages in machine dishwashing are:

1 Remove waste food.
2 Pre-rinse or spray.
3 Load onto the appropriate racks with a space between each item.
4 The wash cycle runs at 50°C–60°C using a detergent.
5 The rinse cycle runs at 82°C–88°C which will disinfect items ready for air drying.

Dishwashing by hand

If items need to be washed by hand the recommended way to do this is:

1 Scrape/rinse off residue food.
2 Wash items in a sink of hot water, the temperature should be 50°C–60°C which means rubber gloves need to be worn. Use a dishwashing brush rather than a cloth.
3 Rinse in very hot water, if rinsing can be done at 82°C for 30 seconds it would disinfect the dishes.
4 Allow to air dry, do not use tea towels.

Handling waste

Kitchen waste should be placed in waste bins with lids (preferably foot-operated). Bins should be made of a strong material, be easy to clean and be pest proof. They should be emptied regularly to avoid waste build-up as this could cause problems with multiplication of bacteria and attract pests. An over-full heavy bin is also much more difficult to handle and empty than a regularly emptied bin.

Pests

When there are reports of food premises being heavily fined or forcibly closed down, an infestation of pests is often the reason. As pests can be a serious source of contamination and disease, they must be eliminated for food safety reasons and to comply with the law. Pests can carry food poisoning bacteria into food premises in their fur/feathers, feet/paws, saliva, urine and droppings. Other problems caused by pests include damage to food stock and packaging, damage to buildings, equipment and wiring, blockages in equipment and piping.

Pests can be attracted to food premises because there will be food, warmth, shelter, water and possible nesting materials; all reasonable measures must be put in place to keep them out. Any possible signs that pests may be present must be reported to the supervisor or manager immediately.

Common pests that may cause problems in food areas are: rats, mice, cockroaches, wasps, flies, ants (Pharaoh's ants), birds and domestic pets. Pest management needs to be planned as part of the food safety management system. Regular visits from a recognised pest control company are advisable because they will offer advice as well as deal with problems arising. Companies conducting a regular audit will provide a pest audit report, which should be kept and could be used as part of the food safety management system.

Measures to keep pests out of the building are of great importance and need to be planned. Pest control contractors can offer advice on keeping pests out of the building and organise eradication systems for any pests that do get in. Some basic guidelines are:

- block entry – e.g. no holes around pipe work. Avoid all gaps and cavities where they could get in. Seal drain covers
- damage to the building or fixtures and fittings repaired quickly
- window/door screening/netting
- check deliveries/packaging for pests

Table 15.3 Signs of pest presence

Pest	Signs that they are present
Rats and mice	Sightings of rodent, droppings, unpleasant smell, gnawed wires, etc. Greasy marks on lower walls, damaged food stock, paw prints.
Flies, wasps	Sighting of flies and wasps, hearing them, dead insects. (Maggots.)
Cockroaches	Sighting (dead or alive) usually at night. Unpleasant smell.
Ants	Sightings and present in food. The tiny, pale coloured Pharaoh's ants are difficult to spot but can still be the source of a variety of pathogens.
Weevils	Sightings of weevils in stored products, e.g. flour/cornflour. Very difficult to see – tiny black insects moving in flour, etc.
Birds	Sighting, droppings, in outside storage areas and around refuse.
Domestic pets	These must be kept out of food areas as they carry pathogens on fur, whiskers, saliva, urine, etc.

- baits and traps
- electronic fly killer (EFK)
- sealed containers, no open food left out
- no build up of waste in kitchen
- outside waste not kept too close to kitchen
- planned pest management control, surveys and reports.

Flying insets cause problems as they can find their way in through very small spaces, or from other parts of the building. They can then spread bacteria around the kitchen and onto open food. To eliminate such insects as flies, bluebottles and wasps an EFK is recommended. These use ultra-violet light to attract the insects that are then electrocuted on charged wires and fall into catch trays. Do not position an EFK directly above food preparation areas and make sure the catch trays are emptied regularly.

Pest control measures can also introduce food safety hazards. Bodies of dead insects or even rodents may remain in the kitchen (physical and bacterial contamination). Pesticides, insecticides and baits could cause chemical contamination if not managed properly. Pest control is best managed by professionals.

Hygienic premises

Suitable buildings with well-planned fittings, layout and equipment allow for good food safety practices.

Certain basics need to be available if a building is to be used for food production.

- There must be electricity supplies and preferably gas supplies.
- Drinking water and good drainage.
- Suitable road access for deliveries and refuse collection.
- No risk of contamination from surrounding areas and buildings, e.g. chemicals, smoke, odours or dust.

Layout

When planning food premises a linear workflow should be in place. Delivery → storage → preparation → cooking → hot holding → serving. This means there will be no cross-over of activities that could result in cross contamination.

Clean and dirty, and raw and cooked, processes should be well segregated.

There must be adequate storage areas, proper refrigerated storage is especially important. Cleaning and disinfection should be planned with separate storage for cleaning materials and chemicals.

Sufficient staff hand washing/drying facilities suitable for work being carried out must be provided. Personal hygiene facilities must be provided for staff as well as changing facilities and storages for personal clothing and belongings.

All areas should allow for efficient cleaning, disinfection and pest control.

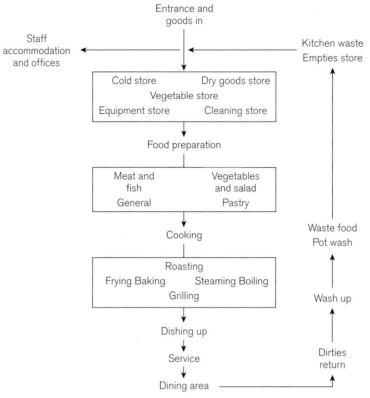

Workflow through the areas of the kitchen

Lighting and ventilation

Lighting (natural and artificial) must be sufficient for tasks being completed, to allow for safe working and so cleaning can be carried out efficiently.

Good ventilation is essential in food premises to prevent excessive heat, condensation, circulation of air-borne contaminants, grease vapours and odours.

Drainage

Drainage must be adequate for the work being completed without causing flooding. If channels, grease traps and gullies are used they should allow for frequent and easy cleaning.

Floors

These need to be durable and in good condition; they must be non-porous, non-slip, and easy to clean. Suitable materials are: non-slip quarry tiles, epoxy resins, industrial vinyl sheeting and granolithic flooring. Where the materials allow, edges between floor and walls should be coved (curved) to prevent debris collecting in corners.

Walls

Walls need to be non-porous, smooth, easy to clean, and preferably light in colour. Suitable wall coverings are: plastic cladding, stainless steel sheeting, ceramic tiles, epoxy resin or rubberised painted plaster or brickwork. Walls should be coved where they join the floor. Lagging and ducting around pipes should be sealed and gaps sealed where pipes enter the building to stop pests entering.

Ceilings

Ceiling finishes must resist build-up of condensation, which could encourage mould; they should be of a non-flaking material and be washable. Non-porous ceiling panels and tiles are frequently used and may incorporate lighting.

Windows and doors

Windows and doors provide possibilities for pests to enter the building so they should be fitted with suitable screening, strip-curtains, metal kick plates, etc. Doors and windows should also fit well into their frames, to stop pests gaining access.

Food safety management systems

In line with the Food Standards Agency's commitment to reduce food poisoning, all food businesses are required by law to have a food safety management system (since 2006) and this will be checked by Environmental Health Officers when they inspect premises.

Hazard Analysis Critical Control Points

All food safety management systems must be based on **Hazard Analysis Critical Control Points (HACCP)**. This is a recognised system that looks at identifying the critical points for stages in any process, the hazards that may occur and how these will be controlled. The system needs to provide a documented record of the stages **all** food will go through right up to the time it is eaten and may include:

- purchase and delivery
- receipt of food
- storage
- preparation
- cooking
- cooling
- hot holding
- reheating
- chilled storage
- serving.

Once the hazards have been identified corrective measures are put in place to control the hazards and keep the food safe.

The system must be updated regularly, especially when new items are introduced to the menu or systems change, and specific new controls must be put in place to include them, for example if a new piece of cooking equipment has been installed.

The HACCP system involves seven stages:

1 Identify hazards – what could go wrong.
2 Identify CCPs (critical control points) – i.e. the important points where things could go wrong.
3 Set critical limits for each CCP – e.g. temperature requirements on delivery of fresh chicken.
4 Monitor CCPs – put checks in place to stop problems happening.
5 Corrective action – what will be done if something goes wrong.
6 Verification – check that the HACCP plan is working.
7 Documentation – record all of the above.

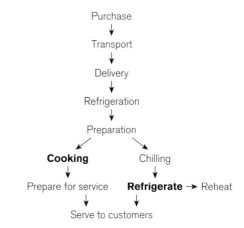

An HACCP flow diagram for cooking a fresh chicken

The example in this diagram relates to the cooking of a chicken. When dealing with a fresh chicken it is necessary recognise the possible hazards at all of the identified stages:

- **Hazard** – pathogenic bacteria is likely to be present in raw chicken.
- **Control** – the chicken needs to be cooked thoroughly to 75°C+ to ensure pathogens are killed.

- **Monitor** – check the temperature where the thigh joins the body with a calibrated temperature probe, make sure no parts of the flesh are pink and juices are running clear, not red or pink.
- **Hot holding** – before service, the chicken must be kept above 63°C. This can be checked with a temperature probe.
- **Or chill and refrigerate** – chill to below 8°C within 90 minutes. Cover, label and refrigerate below 5°C.
- **Documentation** – temperatures must be measured and recorded. Hot holding equipment should be checked and the temperature recorded. Record any corrective measures necessary.

Table 15.3 shows this example in more detail.

Table 15.3 An HACCP control chart for cooking a fresh chicken for later reheating

Process steps	Hazards	Controls	Critical limit	Monitoring	Corrective action
Purchase	Contamination, pathogens, mould or foreign bodies present	Approved supplier			Change supplier
Transport and delivery	Multiplication of harmful bacteria	Refrigerated vehicles		Check delivery vehicles, date marks, temperatures	Reject if > 5°C or out of date
Refrigerate	Bacterial growth Further contamination – bacteria, chemicals, etc.	Store below 5°C Separate raw and cooked foods Stock rotation	Food below 5°C	Check and record temperature twice a day Check date marks	Discard if signs of spoilage or past date mark
Prepare	Bacterial growth Further contamination	No more than 30 minutes in 'danger zone' Good personal hygiene Clean equipment, hygienic premises		Supervisor to audit at regular intervals Visual checks Cleaning schedules	Discard if > 5°C for 6 hours
Cook	Survival of harmful bacteria	Thorough cooking	75°C	Check and record temperature/time	Continue cooking to 75°C
Prepare for service	Multiplication of bacteria Contamination	No more than 20 minutes in 'danger zone'	2 hours	Supervisor to audit at regular intervals	Discard if > 5°C for 2 hours
Chill	Multiplication of bacteria Contamination	Blast chiller	90 minutes to below 10°C	Supervisor to audit at regular intervals	Discard if > 20°C for 2 hours
Refrigerate	Multiplication of bacteria Contamination	Store below 5°C Keep away from raw foods	5°C for 4 hours	Check and record temperature twice a day	Discard if > 5°C for 4 hours
Reheat	Survival of bacteria	Reheat to 75°C in centre	75°C (82°C in Scotland)	Check and record temperature of each batch	Continue reheating to 75°C

Safer Food Better Business

The HACCP system may seem complicated and difficult to set up for a small or fairly limited business. With this in mind the Food Standards Agency launched their **Safer Food Better Business** system for England and Wales.

This is based on the principles of HACCP but in an easy to understand format with pre-printed pages and charts to enter the relevant information such as temperatures of individual dishes. It is divided into two parts. The first part is about safe methods, e.g. avoiding cross contamination, personal hygiene, cleaning, chilling and cooking. The second part covers opening and closing checks, proving methods are safe, recording safe methods, training records, supervision, stock control and the selection of suppliers and contractors.

A copy of *Safer Food Better Business* is available from www.food.gov.uk.

Similar systems have been developed in Scotland (**CookSafe**) and Northern Ireland (**Safe Catering**).

Due diligence

'Due diligence' can be used as defence under food safety legislation when something relating to food safety goes wrong. It involves providing proof that a business took all reasonable care and precaution and did everything it could to prevent food safety problems, that is, exercised all due diligence. To prove due diligence, accurate and up to date written documents are essential and should include:

- staff training records
- staff sickness records
- temperature records (cooking and cold storage)
- pest control policy and audits
- cleaning schedules and deep clean reports
- equipment maintenance records
- CCP monitoring activities, changes made, corrective actions and recalls
- modifications to the HACCP system
- customer complaints/investigation results
- calibration of instruments
- lists of suppliers (traceability of food).

What the law says

The latest laws of importance to food businesses took effect from 1 January 2006.

They set out the basic food safety requirements for all aspects of a food business from premises to personal hygiene of staff, with specific attention to actual temperatures relating to food.

The main difference in the 2006 laws was the requirement to have an approved Food Safety Management Procedure in place with up to date records available.

Legislation concerning food safety covers a wide range of topics including:

- controlling and reducing outbreaks of food poisoning
- registration of premises/vehicles
- content and labelling of food
- preventing manufacture and sale of injurious food
- food imports
- prevention of food contamination and equipment contamination
- training of food handlers
- provision of clean water, sanitary facilities, washing facilities.

For further information on food safety legislation visit www.food.gov.uk.

Environmental Health Officers

Food safety standards and legislation is enforced in the UK by Environmental Health Officers (EHOs) or Environmental Health Practitioners (EHPs).

Enforcement Officers may visit food premises as a matter of routine, as a follow-up when problems have been identified or after a complaint. The frequency of visits depends on the type of business and food being handled, possible hazards within the business, the risk rating and any previous problems or convictions. Generally, businesses posing a higher risk will be visited more frequently than those considered low risk.

EHOs (EHPs) can enter a food business at any reasonable time without previous notice or appointment, usually when the business is open. The main purpose of these inspections is to identify any possible risks from the food business and to assess the effectiveness of the business's own food safety management systems; also to identify any non-compliance of regulations so this can be monitored and corrected.

The role of the EHO/EHP is to:

- offer professional food safety advice to food businesses on routine visits and provide useful information such as leaflets and posters
- advise on new food safety legislation

- investigate complaints about the business
- ensure that food offered for sale is safe and fit for consumption
- monitor food operations within a business and identify possible sources of contamination
- ensure food safety law compliance
- observe the effectiveness of the food safety management system
- deal with food poisoning outbreaks
- advise on Food Safety Training
- deal with non-compliance by formal action/serving notices. They have the power to:
  - close the business
  - seize/remove food
  - instigate prosecution
  - seize records.

Notices and orders for non-compliance

A Hygiene Improvement Notice will be served if the EHO (EHP) believes that a food business does not comply with regulations. The notice is served in writing and states the name and address of the business, what is wrong, why it is wrong, what needs to be done to put it right, and the time in which this must be completed, usually not less than 14 days.

A Hygiene Emergency Prohibition Notice is served if the EHO (EHP) believes that there is an imminent risk to health from the business. This would include serious issues such as sewage contamination, lack of water supply, rodent infestation, etc. Serving this notice means immediate closure of the business for three days, during which time the EHO (EHP) must apply to magistrates for a **Hygiene Emergency Prohibition Order** to keep the premises closed. Notices/orders must be displayed in a visible place on the premises. The owner of the business must apply for a **Certificate of Satisfaction** before they can re-open.

A **Hygiene Prohibition Order** prohibits a person, i.e. the owner/manager, from working in a food business.

Magistrates' courts can impose fines of up to £5000, a six-month prison sentence or both.

For serious offences, such as knowingly selling food dangerous to health, magistrates could impose fines of up to £20,000.

In a Crown Court unlimited fines and/or two years' imprisonment can be imposed.

The Food Standards Agency

The Food Standards Agency was established in 2000 'to protect public health from risks which may arise in connection with the consumption of food and otherwise to protect the interest of customers in relation to food'. The agency is committed to put customers first, be open and accessible and be an independent voice on food-related matters.

Scores on the Doors

Scores on the Doors is a strategy that has been introduced by the Food Standards Agency to raise food safety standards and reduce the incidence of food poisoning. When an EHO (EHP) inspection has been carried out a star rating will be awarded ranging from 0 to 5 stars:

★★★★★	Excellent
★★★★	Very good
★★★	Good
★★	Broadly compliant
★	Poor
No stars	Very poor

The intention is the given star rating will be placed in a prominent position on the door or window of premises but it is not mandatory to do so.

It is expected that the **Scores on the Doors** scheme will have a lasting positive impact on food safety standards.

16 Work as part of a team

This chapter is relevant to the following units:

- Contribute to effective teamwork (NVQ)
- Applying workplace skills (VRQ).

Teamwork

When working in a kitchen or in any hospitality role you will be working as part of a team. This may include:

- completing tasks on your own but as part of a wider team
- completing tasks with one or two other people as part of a wider team
- working as part of a large team that may be sub-divided into sections.

Teams will include: managers, supervisors (head chefs or sous chefs), as well as team members at various levels and those working at the same level as yourself. There will also be those providing support such as kitchen porters and clerical staff. Kitchen teams will vary in size and type depending on the establishment. A large hotel may have an extensive kitchen brigade with a formal structure but a small restaurant will have a smaller and less formal team.

Good teamwork is essential in all working environments and kitchen teams have traditionally worked closely together in an organised structure to ensure all work is completed to the required standards, on time, with all team members understanding their role and responsibilities. Working as part of a team can allow people to feel valued and learn from each other's skills and expertise. In a good team people feel supported in their role allowing for job satisfaction and team achievement. The work is completed on time to high standards and there is a positive and creative working environment.

Personal qualities of a good team member

An effective team needs certain qualities and levels of commitment from each team member. There are many such qualities required. These include:

- being reliable, dependable and always punctual
- taking a pride in personal appearance at work and always being clean, smart, tidy and well-groomed
- being a good communicator, listening to instructions and passing on relevant information promptly
- completing work on time, asking for help when it is needed and offering help to others when it is appropriate to do so
- being well organised, with the ability to think ahead and prioritise tasks as appropriate
- being open to feedback and always willing to learn new skills and techniques, as well as learning from experience
- having empathy with others and listening to the points of view of other team members
- being confident and assertive within the specific job role.

Sometimes negative behaviour is present in a workplace. This must be discouraged and dealt with promptly and effectively by someone managing or supervising the area.

Negative behaviour would include:
- poor time-keeping and being unreliable
- poor standards of dress and personal appearance
- being inconsiderate of others and unhelpful
- laziness; not completing tasks properly
- inappropriate language or swearing
- producing work that is not of the required standard or not produced on time.

Problems in working relationships

Sometimes in busy kitchens, the pressures, workload and different personalities can have negative effects on good working relationships within the team. It is important that you bring concerns of such problems to the attention of the line manager or supervisor. You will need to discuss: what the problem is and why you are concerned, giving specific examples where possible. Also state when the problems occur and the frequency. Try to remain constructive in your discussion of relationship problems so a solution can be planned in the most amicable way.

Signs of damaging behaviour within the workplace must be taken very seriously and needs to be reported. Examples of this kind of behaviour may include:
- **Intimidation** (deliberately making someone feel frightened)
- **Harassment** (annoying or unpleasant behaviour that takes place regularly, for example threats, offensive remarks or physical attacks)
- **Victimisation** (to single someone out and treat them unfairly)
- **Bullying** (hurting, frightening, threatening, persecuting or tormenting others or forcing someone to do something they do not want to do).

The above may take the form of:
- racist comments or gestures
- remarks about religion, belief, gender or sexuality
- remarks about personal characteristics or disabilities
- physical or sexual abuse
- belittling and undermining an individual's achievements

- ignoring individuals and making them feel isolated
- excluding individuals from information and what is going on
- threatening behaviour
- humiliating individuals in front of others
- setting of unrealistic or unachievable targets.

No employee should suffer any of the above and a solution to the problem must be found as soon as possible. Discuss any concerns that you may have with your line manager, supervisor or head chef.

Progressing as a team member

As your confidence as part of the team increases so should your teamwork skills and you may be allocated further responsibilities within the team, which may include:
- planning and organising
- ordering food and other goods
- setting targets
- mentoring others
- working across different roles.

Asking for help and offering help to others

Working as part of a team means that you will be working together with others to reach the desired goals within a specific time. Different requirements and pressures of work in different areas means that you may need to ask for help from others to reach the necessary targets on time. Equally it may be necessary for you to offer help and assistance to others. However, only do this when you have sufficient time and your own work will not suffer by helping others. If you are not sure about this ask your section chef, head chef or line manager.

Remember that it is the outcome and product of the team that defines a successful business or operation and it is less likely that those working in isolation will achieve the necessary goals.

'Teamwork divides the task and doubles the success.'

Planning and organising work

Kitchen work is generally more time-specific than many other areas of work. For example, if some office-based data entry was completed an hour later than planned this may not be too much of a problem but if someone ordered lunch that was an hour late the customer would rightly have cause for complaint and would probably not use the establishment again. To meet the time constraints of a busy kitchen, careful planning and organisation is essential.

The tasks to be completed by each kitchen section and each member of staff needs to be planned and organised so all work is completed efficiently, to the required standards and on time.

Kitchen tasks will vary in size, complexity and the amounts of time and skill needed. You will need to identify which tasks need to be given priority; larger tasks may need to be broken down into smaller parts.

Mise en place

Mise en place is a French term that means having 'everything in place'. In kitchen terms this became a popular notion around the time of Auguste Escoffier who is well known for his concepts of kitchen organisation and brigade systems as well as for his culinary expertise. The term 'mise en place' may be used for tasks such as:

- preparing meat or fish
- making sauces
- preparing garnishes and the various components of dishes
- preparing and blanching vegetables
- chopping herbs and preparing spices
- weighing/preparing ingredients for assembly, for example in a fruit cake
- preparing ingredients for dishes to be cooked to order
- having the correct equipment/utensils ready for use
- pre-heating ovens and other equipment.

Effective mise en place allows the chef to work efficiently in the busiest periods without having to spend valuable time assembling ingredients, garnishes or equipment and in completing basic preparation. It allows procedures and service to run smoothly within time constraints.

Keeping the work area clean, tidy and organised

It is important to keep your own work area clean tidy and well organised as you work. Completing tasks hygienically and protecting food from contamination are legal food safety requirements as well as allowing you to work efficiently and professionally. 'Clean as you go' must be standard practice in all food preparation areas.

Do not allow waste to build up in work areas; dispose of waste according to the policies practised by the establishment; for example, some items may be placed in specific containers for recycling. General waste should be placed in a lined waste bin with a foot-operated lid. Make sure this is emptied regularly.

Ensure that food contact surfaces such as chopping boards are clean and sanitised before use. Clean well and sanitise areas between tasks. Organise the equipment you will need and consider the best way to complete each task with maximum efficiency.

Put equipment and ingredients away in the proper places after use. Make sure that food items being put away into fridges, freezers and other storage areas are correctly covered or wrapped and labelled and dated according to the establishment's policy.

Working efficiently means that tasks are completed within the time allowed, in a well-organised, clean and tidy way without causing undue stress or tiredness. There have been many studies on the way people work best and the provision of working conditions that suit the people working with them. This is often referred to as **ergonomics**.

Avoiding waste

Careful preparation, storage and cooking methods, as well as good staff training, will help to avoid unnecessary kitchen waste. Waste needs to be avoided so that the calculated yield from ingredients will be achieved; also, disposing of waste is expensive

and will affect the overall cost of what is being produced.

Perhaps more importantly, we all need to be aware of food sustainability. There are ever-increasing demands on world food stocks, and efforts are being made to produce food that does not impose long-term harm on the environment, or endanger animal or fish species, but that does provide fair pay and conditions for agricultural workers. Reducing the amounts of food we waste will help to achieve these aims. We are also encouraged to decrease 'food miles' where possible, which means considering more local produce rather than similar produce imported from across the world. Doing this reduces waste on fuel, storage and often excess packaging too. Using more locally sourced food may also result in a high-quality, fresher product as well as adding local or regional interest to the menu.

How to reduce waste in the kitchen

Be aware of the quantities required before starting preparation. Also be aware of trends – the most popular menu items and special promotions. You may sell more of these, which will affect the amounts that need to be prepared. Take care to avoid unnecessary waste, which can be caused by:

- over-production
- wrong information or lack of information
- careless preparation, for example peeling vegetables too thickly
- poor cooking procedures, such as overcooking, causing excessive shrinkage or food to be completely spoiled
- poor storage and lack of stock rotation causing food to deteriorate
- allowing food to get contaminated so it then must be disposed of
- high-risk food at kitchen temperatures for too long (must then be thrown away)
- food contaminated by pests or dust.

All of the above must be avoided in a professional kitchen.

Following instructions

You will be given a number of instructions during your working day and it is important to complete these tasks to the best of your ability and with accuracy.

Instructions may be written down as a task list for you to complete or they may be given verbally. Whichever way you are given the instructions, read/listen carefully. If possible, confirm back what is required of you. Ask for further instruction if you don't understand what you are being asked to do.

With a list of tasks it will be necessary to prioritise which are the most important or need to be done first. Once again, if you are unsure about this, ask for guidance. Keeping a notebook to record the instructions given to you will help you to work efficiently and professionally.

Recipes

The recipe is one of the most important sets of instructions you will use and it is important to follow it accurately. Frequently, you will need to scale the recipe up or down (multiplying or dividing the amounts) to match the quantities you will need; take care to do this accurately. It is advisable to write down and double check the amended recipe amounts.

Read through the whole recipe at least once before starting the task and ask about anything you are unsure of.

Assemble the ingredients you will need before starting the preparation or cooking and also assemble all of the tools and equipment you will need. Take care to assemble the correct ingredients and tools needed. For example, if the recipe states plain white flour and you use self-raising flour instead the results will be very different. If the recipe states that a 20 cm diameter cake tin is needed and you use a 30 cm diameter tin different cooking times will be required and the results will be different.

Instructions for equipment and machinery

Always make sure you have been shown how to prepare and use equipment for specific tasks.

For example, does a dessert mould need lining with silicone film? Does a loaf tin need to be greased and floured? When the work you are completing requires the use of equipment or machinery and you are unsure of how to use it, always make sure you have had full instruction and training first.

Health and safety/food safety instructions

Follow the guidelines or training given to you by your employer and on any training courses you may have completed. Some of these instructions will also be legal requirements and it is your legal responsibility to comply with them.

Apart from following the necessary instructions, it is essential that you report anything that may cause problems in maintaining the required standards of health and safety or food safety. For example, it would be essential to report a refrigerator not maintaining the required temperature (food at the wrong temperature can be the cause of food poisoning) or an electrical appliance with a damaged flex (could be the cause of electric shock or fire).

Instructions about uniform and personal hygiene

Instructions on the required standards of kitchen uniform and personal hygiene must be followed precisely. This will give you pride in your own appearance and professionalism and will also maintain the standards and reputation of the establishment you work for.

You will have been given instructions about reporting any sickness or infection you may have before you start work. It is of the utmost importance and a legal requirement that you follow these instructions fully.

Emergency procedure instructions

You will have been given instructions on the procedure to follow in an emergency such as a fire. Be aware of the procedures and follow evacuation instruction correctly.

Standard Operational Procedure

Some instructions you are given about the way that you work and complete tasks will be specific to the individual workplace or a group of establishments. It means that all employees will be completing tasks in the same way and will be maintaining the same standards. This is called Standard Operational Procedure (SOP) and will detail the steps and activities of a process and the required quality and presentation of the finished product. An example would be the way a specific dish was produced, presented, garnished and served at a banqueting event.

Communication

Effective communication is essential to a successful kitchen team. There will be many different communication methods used between:
- individuals working together
- other kitchen sections and service staff
- other departments and management
- suppliers and contractors
- customers/guests.

Speaking and listening is the most widely used form of communication in a kitchen so it is important that it is carried out effectively.
- Speak clearly/listen carefully so the message is understood.

- Non-verbal gestures such as facial expressions and hand gestures may help to reinforce the message and will confirm understanding.
- Take time to communicate properly; avoid speaking from a distance or while walking past the other person.
- Avoid interrupting and avoid distractions; listen to what is being said then respond.
- Do not shout or use inappropriate language.
- When receiving verbal instruction, ask questions where necessary and summarise the instruction at the end.

However, there are many other ways that communication takes place in kitchens and they include:

- **Non-verbal gestures** such as a nod, a raised hand, 'thumb up'. These can be useful but make sure they are not misunderstood, especially when communicating between different nationalities and cultures.
- **Written communication** is very widely used, from formal letters to task lists and brief notes. Make sure they are clearly written in a way that the recipient will fully understand the meaning.
- **Pictorial communication** Pictures or diagrams are often used in instructions and signs used around the kitchen, especially for health and safety instructions. These are often standardised and are recognised internationally. A picture, diagram or sketch could also be used to convey meaning where there is a language barrier.
- **The telephone** remains a very widely used method of communication and there may be specific systems used in an establishment, such as land lines or mobile/smart phones.
- **Fax messaging** is now considered 'older technology' but still has numerous uses especially when exact copies, signed copies, drawings or diagrams need to be sent elsewhere.
- **Electronic systems** have become increasingly sophisticated and very popular. Frequently used systems include email, text messaging, QR (quick response) codes, electronic ordering systems, data logging systems and systems designed for specific company use such as 'Vocera', 'Maytas' or 'Opera'. Many employees are now given access to their own company email or other communication systems. Increasingly, communication takes place through 'social media', such as Twitter, Facebook, LinkedIn or Rehoba.

Passing on information to others

At some time in the day you may be left a message or given information that needs to be passed on to others. It is essential that such information is passed on quickly and accurately. Make sure that the person you are giving the information to fully hears and understands what you are telling them. Such information may include:

- A message from a member of staff saying they will not be in work or will be late. Record and pass on such details as: time of the call, how late they will be or the reason for absence and how long they expect to be away from work.
- A late delivery from a supplier or items that could not be supplied.
- Extra bookings or cancellations.
- Arrival of visitors such as maintenance contractors, inspectors or company representatives.
- Faulty equipment or supplies running low.
- Changes in the menu.
- Information about special dietary requirements.
- Changes in timing, for example, a buffet lunch required one hour earlier.

Use the most appropriate way to pass on the information, such as verbally, in a written message or by email.

Contributing to your own learning and development

Good employees will be keen to learn as much as they can about their job, as well as improving and refining their own knowledge and skills. Development within the job role will lead to progression and promotion and will also provide interesting challenges.

Improving your knowledge and skills is not only beneficial for you and your career progression but will help to raise the skills within the team and provide variety and diversity within the workplace. You may also encourage others working with you to develop their skills and knowledge too.

The ways you can develop and progress within your job role will include:

- asking questions of others as well as finding things out for yourself
- working with skilled and experienced colleagues
- attending training provided by an employer or asking about courses you are interested in
- attending a full-time or part-time college course
- completing a work-based qualification managed by a training provider or college
- asking for feedback and progression advice
- discussing progress with managers, supervisors and mentors
- actively participating in formal appraisal, discussing performance targets and progression
- producing or working to a learning plan (see below).

A learning/progression plan

A progression plan allows learning and development to be organised and progress/achievement can be monitored. The plan needs to have long-term aims of what you ultimately want to achieve and shorter-term aims that are the steps to get you there. Producing, developing and taking interest in your learning plan will show your employer that you are ambitious, proactive and well organised. Planning future progress is a good skill in itself and will help you to focus on planning your career.

A learning plan could be put in place by:

- the employer, human resources department or training department
- the head chef, supervisor or mentor
- a training provider or college managing your learning
- devising your own learning plan or simply keeping a notebook of your goals and achievements. These can then be discussed at appraisal or progress meetings.

SMART targets

It is considered desirable when setting targets for achievement to set 'smart targets'. SMART usually stands for Specific, Measurable, Attainable, Relevant and Time-bound, though other interpretations are sometimes used.

An example of how smart targets may apply in a kitchen is given in Table 16.1.

Reviewing your progress

The progress you are making may be monitored by:

- yourself (keep a record with dates in a suitable notebook or file)
- regular progress meetings with a tutor, head chef or mentor
- verbal and written feedback
- appraisals
- letters or emails
- logbooks, charts and electronic tracking systems.

Table 16.1 Using SMART targets in the kitchen

Term	Meaning	Example
Specific	Be clear about the actual skills and learning you wish to achieve; it may be helpful to outline how you think your specific targets may be achieved.	To achieve my targets of gaining skills in chocolate work I will need to spend some time training in the pastry section.
Measurable	This is being specific about how you will measure your achievements.	I want to have completed my NVQ Level 2 by the end of the year.
Attainable	Attainable means setting targets that are realistic and are actually achievable.	While in the pastry section, I want to become proficient at making puff pastry, choux pastry and sweet pastry.
Relevant	The targets need to be relevant to progression within your job role or college course while providing suitable achievement for you.	I would like to be able to run the vegetable section without supervision.
Time-bound	This refers to setting a realistic amount of time in which to achieve your goals. Being realistic about the time in which a goal can be reached probably means you will have the satisfaction of actual achievement.	In six months' time, I would like to be running the larder section and mentoring a new commis chef.

Performance appraisal

Appraisal is a method by which the performance of an employee is reviewed and evaluated, usually by a manager, supervisor or head chef. An appraisal is a part of guiding and managing career development and is a good opportunity for uninterrupted discussion between the employee and their line manager. Performance appraisal is a time to discuss recent successes, achievements, personal strengths and weaknesses, and suitability for promotion or further education/training. It is an excellent opportunity to discuss ways to progress and enhance career prospects.

Glossary

à la In the style of

à la française In the French style

à la minute Cooked to order

à la carte Dishes prepared to order and priced individually

Abatis de volaille Poultry offal, giblets, etc.

Abats Offal: heads, hearts, liver, kidney, etc.

Accompaniments Items offered separately with a dish of food

Agar-agar A vegetable gelling agent obtained from seaweed, used as a substitute for gelatine

Aile A wing (of poultry or game birds)

Aloyau de boeuf Sirloin of beef

Ambient Room temperature, surrounding atmosphere

Amino acid Organic acids found in proteins

Antibiotic A drug used to destroy disease-producing germs within human or animal bodies

Antiseptic A substance that prevents the growth of bacteria and moulds, specifically on or in the human body

Aromats Fragrant herbs and spices

Arroser To baste, for example during roasting

Ascorbic acid Known as Vitamin C; found in citrus fruits and blackcurrants; necessary for growth and the maintenance of health

Aspic A savoury jelly mainly used for decorative larder work

Assorti An assortment

Au bleu When applied to meat, this means very underdone

Au beurre With butter

Au four Baked in the oven

Au gratin Sprinkled with cheese or breadcrumbs and then browned

Au vin blanc With white wine

Bactericide A substance that destroys bacteria

Bacterium (plural: bacteria) Single-celled micro-organisms: some are harmful and cause food poisoning; others are useful, such as those used in cheese making

Bain-marie

- A container of water to keep foods hot without burning them
- A container of water for cooking foods without burning them
- A deep, narrow container for storing hot sauces, soups and gravies

Barding Covering the breasts of birds with thin slices of bacon

Barquette A boat-shaped pastry case

Basting Spooning melted fat over food during cooking to keep it moist

Bat out To flatten slices of raw meat with a cutlet bat

Bean curd Also known as tofu (see below); a curdled, soft, cheese-like preparation made from soybean milk; a good source of protein

Beansprouts Young shoots of dried beans, e.g. mung beans, alfalfa or soybeans

Beurre manié Equal quantities of flour and butter used for thickening sauces

Blanc A cooking liquor of water, lemon juice, flour and salt; also used to describe the white of chicken (breast and wings)

Blanch

- To make something white (referring to bones and meat)
- To cook but retain colour (referring to certain vegetables)
- To skin (referring to tomatoes)
- To make limp (referring to certain braised vegetables)
- To cook without colour, e.g. the first frying of fried potatoes (chips)

Blanquette A white stew cooked in stock from which the sauce is made

Blitz To rapidly purée or foam a light sauce, generally using an electric hand blender at the last moment before service

Bombay duck Small, dried, salted fish; fried, it is used as an accompaniment to curry dishes

Bombe An ice cream speciality of different flavours in a bomb shape

Bone out To remove the bones

Botulism A rare form of food poisoning

Bouchée A small puff paste case, literally 'a mouthful'

Bouillon Unclarified stock

Bouquet garni A bundle of herbs (e.g. parsley stalks, thyme and bay leaf), tied in pieces of celery and leek

Brine A preserving solution of water, salt, saltpetre and aromats, used for meats (e.g. silverside, brisket, tongue)

Brunoise Small dice

Butter

- Black butter (beurre noir)
- Brown butter/nut brown butter (beurre noisette)
- Melted butter (beurre fondu)
- Parsley butter (beurre maitre d'hotel)

Buttermilk Liquid remaining from the churning of butter

Calcium A mineral required for building bones and teeth, obtained from cheese and milk

Calorie A unit of heat or energy, known as a kilocalorie

Canapé Traditionally, a cushion of bread on which are served various foods, hot or cold; also used to describe small, attractive, well-flavoured dishes offered before a meal or at a drinks reception

Carbohydrate A nutrient; there are three types of carbohydrate – sugar and starch, which provide the body with energy, and cellulose, which provides roughage (dietary fibre)

Carbon dioxide A gas produced by all raising agents

Carrier A person who harbours and may transmit pathogenic organisms without showing signs of illness

Carte du jour Menu for the day

Casserole An earthenware, fireproof dish with a lid

Cellulose The coarse structure of fruit, vegetables and cereals that is not digested but is used as roughage (dietary fibre)

Châteaubriand The head of the fillet of beef

Chaud-froid A demi-glace or creamed velouté with gelatine or aspic added, used for masking cold dishes

Chiffonade Fine shreds, e.g. of spinach, lettuce

Chinois A conical strainer

Chlorophyll The green colour in vegetables

Ciseler To make slight incisions in the surface of a thick fillet of fish, on or off the bone, to allow even cooking

Civet A brown stew of game, usually hare

Clarification/to clarify To make something clear, such as stock, jelly or butter

Clostridium perfringens Food-poisoning bacterium found in the soil, vegetables and meat

Coagulation The solidification of protein; it is irreversible; examples occur when frying an egg or cooking meat

Cocotte Porcelain or earthenware fireproof dish

Collagen/elastin Proteins in connective tissue (e.g. gristle)

Compote Stewed (e.g. stewed fruit)

Concassé Coarsely chopped (e.g. parsley, tomatoes)

Confit Cooked meat, poultry or game preserved in good fat or oil

Consommé A simple, clear soup

Contamination The occurrence of any objectionable matter in food

Contrefilet Boned-out sirloin of beef

Cook out The process of cooking flour in a roux, soup or sauce

Cordon A thread or thin line of sauce

Correcting Adjusting the seasoning, consistency and colour

Côte A rib or chop

Côtelette A cutlet

Coulis Sauce made of fruit or vegetable puree (e.g. raspberry, tomato)

Coupe An individual serving bowl

Couper To cut

Court bouillon A well-flavoured cooking liquor for fish

Crème fraiche Whipping cream and buttermilk heated to 24–29°C

Crêpes Pancakes

Credit note Issued when an invoice contains incorrect details; credit is therefore given

Croquettes Cooked foods moulded into a cylinder shape, coated in flour and egg, crumbed and deep-fried

Cross-contamination The transfer of micro-organisms from contaminated to uncontaminated hands, utensils or equipment

Croutons Cubes of fried or toasted bread served with soup; also triangular pieces served with spinach, and heart-shaped pieces with certain dishes

Crudités Small, neat pieces of raw vegetables served with a dip as an appetiser

Cuisse de poulet Chicken leg

Danger zone of bacterial growth The temperature range within which pathogenic bacteria are able to multiply; from 10 and 63°C

Dariole A small mould, as used for crème caramel

Darne A slice of round fish (e.g. salmon) on the bone

Déglacer (to deglaze) To swill out a pan in which food has been roasted or fried, with wine, stock or water, in order to use the sediment for the accompanying sauce or gravy

Dégraisser To skim fat off liquid

Delivery note A form sent by a supplier with the delivery of goods

Demi-glace A brown stock reduced to a light consistency

Désosser To bone out meat

Detergent A substance that dissolves grease

Dilute To mix a powder (e.g. cornflour) with a liquid

Disinfectant A substance that reduces the risk of infection

Doily A fancy dish paper

Drain To place food in a colander, allowing liquid to seep out

Duxelle Finely chopped mushrooms cooked with chopped shallots

Eggwash Beaten egg with a little milk or water

Emulsion A mixture of liquid (e.g. vinegar) and oil, which does not separate when left to stand (e.g. mayonnaise, hollandaise)

Entrecôte A steak cut from a boned sirloin

Enzymes Chemical substances produced from living cells

Escalope A thin slice such as escalope of veal

Farce Stuffing

Fecule Fine potato flour

Feuilletage Puff pastry

Fines herbes Chopped fresh herbs (e.g. parsley, tarragon, chervil)

First aid materials Suitable and sufficient bandages and dressings, including waterproof dressings and antiseptic; all dressings must be individually wrapped

Flake To break something into natural segments (e.g. fish)

Flan An open tart

Fleurons Small, crescent-shaped pieces of puff pastry

Flute A 20 cm diameter French bread used for soup garnishes

Food-borne Carried on food

Food handling Any operation in the storage, preparation, production, processing, packaging, transportation, distribution and sale of food

Frappé Chilled (e.g. melon frappé)

Freezer burn Affects frozen items, which are spoiled due to being left unprotected for too long

Friandises Sweetmeats, petits fours

Fricassée A white stew in which the meat, poultry or fish is cooked in the sauce

Friture A pan that contains deep fat

Fumé Smoked (e.g. *saumon fumé* is smoked salmon)

Garam masala A combination of spices

Garnish Served as part of the main item; trimmings

Gastroenteritis Inflammation of the stomach and intestinal tract that normally results in diarrhoea

Gâteau A cake of more than one portion

Ghee The Indian name for clarified butter; ghee is pure butter fat

Gibier Game

Glace Ice or ice cream from which all milk solids have been removed

Glaze

- To colour a dish under the salamander (e.g. fillets of sole *bonne femme*)
- To finish a flan or tartlet (e.g. with apricot jam)
- To finish certain vegetables (e.g. glazed carrots)

Gluten This is formed from the protein in flour when mixed with water

Gratin A thin coating of grated cheese and/or breadcrumbs on certain dishes, which is then browned under the grill or in an oven

Haché Finely chopped or minced

Hors d'oeuvre Appetising first course dishes, hot or cold

Humidity The amount of moisture in the air

Incubation period The time between infection and the first signs of illness

Infestations Insects breeding on the premises

Insecticide A chemical used to kill insects

Invoice A bill listing items delivered, with the costs of the items

Jardinière Cut into batons

Julienne Cut into fine strips

Jus-lié Thickened gravy

Larding Inserting strips of fat bacon into meat

Lardons Batons of thick streaky bacon

Liaison A thickening or binding

Macédoine
- A mixture of fruit or vegetables
- Cut into 0.5 cm dice

Magnetron A device that generates microwaves in a microwave oven

Marinade A richly spiced pickling liquid used to give flavour and assist in tenderising meats

Marmite A stock pot

Mascarpone An Italian cheese resembling clotted cream

Menu A list of the dishes available

Micro-organisms Very small living plants or animals (bacteria, yeasts, moulds)

Mignonette Coarsely ground pepper

Mildew A type of fungus, similar to mould

Mineral salts Mineral elements, small quantities of which are essential for health

Mirepoix Roughly cut vegetables (e.g. onions, leeks, celery and carrots), often with a sprig of thyme and a bay leaf, used as flavouring elements

Mise-en-place Basic preparation before serving

Miso Seasoning made from fermented soybeans

Monosodium glutamate (MSG) A substance added to food products to increase flavour

Moulds Microscopic plants (fungi) that may appear as woolly patches on food

Mousse A dish of light consistency, hot or cold

Napper To coat or mask with sauce

Natives A menu term for English oysters

Navarin Brown stew of lamb

Niacin Part of Vitamin B; found in liver, kidney, meat extract, bacon

Noisette (nut) A cut from a boned-out loin of lamb

Nutrients The components of food required for health: protein, fats, carbohydrates, vitamins, mineral salts, water

Optimum Best, most favourable

Palatable Pleasant to taste

Pané Floured, dipped in egg and crumbed

Panettone A very light, traditional Italian Christmas cake

Parsley butter Butter containing lemon juice and chopped parsley

Pass To put through a sieve or strainer

Pathogen A disease-producing organism

Paupiette A stuffed and rolled strip of fish or meat

Paysanne Cut in even, thin, triangular, round or square pieces

Persillé Finished with chopped parsley

Pesticide A chemical used to kill pests

Pests Unwanted creatures that may enter food premises, e.g. cockroaches, flies, silverfish

Petits fours Very small pastries, biscuits, sweets, sweetmeats

pH value A scale indicating the acidity or alkalinity in food

Phosphorus A mineral element found in fish; required for building bones and teeth

Piquant Sharply flavoured

Piqué Studded clove in an onion

Plat du jour Special dish of the day

Poppadoms Dried, thin, large, round wafers made from lentil flour, used as an accompaniment to Indian dishes

Printanier A garnish of spring vegetables

Protein The nutrient needed for growth and repair

Prove To allow a yeast dough to rest in a warm place so that it can expand

Pulses Vegetables grown in pods (peas and beans) and dried; a source of protein and roughage

Quark A salt-free soft cheese made from semi-skimmed milk

Ragout A stew, for example *ragout de boeuf* is brown beef stew

Rare When applied to meat, it means underdone

Réchauffer To reheat

Reduce To concentrate a liquid by boiling

Refresh To make cold under running cold water

Residual insecticide An insecticide that remains active for a considerable period of time

Riboflavin Vitamin B2; found in yeast, liver, eggs, cheese

Rissoler To fry to a golden brown

Rodents Rats and mice

Roux A thickening of cooked flour and fat

Sabayon Egg yolks and a little water or wine, cooked until creamy

Saccharometer An instrument for measuring the density of sugar

Salamander A type of grill, heated from above

Salmonella A food-poisoning bacterium found in meat and poultry

Sanitiser A chemical agent used for cleaning and disinfecting surfaces and equipment

Sauté
- Toss in fat (e.g. *pommes sautées*)
- Cook quickly in a sauté pan or frying pan
- A brown stew of a specific type (e.g. veal sauté)

Seal To place meat in a hot oven or pan to colour the surface and retain the juices

Seared Cooked quickly on both sides in a little hot fat or oil

Seasoned flour Flour seasoned with salt and pepper

Set
- To seal the outside surface
- To allow to become firm or firmer (e.g. jelly)

Shredded Cut in fine strips (e.g. lettuce, onion)

Silicone paper Non-stick paper (e.g. siliconised paper)

Singe To brown or colour

Smetana A low-fat product; a cross between soured cream and yoghurt

Sodium A mineral element in the form of salt (sodium chloride); found in cheese, bacon, fish, meat

Soufflé A very light dish, sweet or savoury, hot or cold

Soy sauce Made from soybeans; used extensively in Chinese cookery

Spores The resistant resting phase of bacteria, protecting them against adverse conditions such as high temperatures

Staphylococcus A food-poisoning bacterium found in the human nose and throat, and also in septic cuts

Starch A carbohydrate found in cereals, certain vegetables and farinaceous foods

Sterile Free from all living organisms

Sterilisation A process that destroys living organisms

Steriliser A chemical used to destroy all living organisms

Stock rotation The sequence of issuing goods, so that the first into store are the first to be issued

Strain To separate the liquid from the solids by passing through a strainer

Sweat To cook in fat under a lid without colour

Syneresis The squeezing out of liquid from an overcooked protein and liquid mixture (e.g. scrambled egg, egg custard)

Table d'hôte A meal at a fixed price; a set menu

Tahini A strong-flavoured sesame seed paste

Tartlet A small, round pastry case

Terrine An earthenware dish used for cooking and serving pâté; also used as a name for certain products

Thiamine Vitamin B1; it assists the nervous system; found in yeast, bacon, wholemeal bread

Timbale A double serving dish

Tofu Low-fat bean curd made from soybeans

Tourné Turned, shaped in barrels or large olive shapes

Tranche A slice

Trichinosis A disease caused by hair-like worms in the muscles of meat (e.g. pork)

Tronçon A slice of flat fish on the bone (e.g. turbot)

TVP Texturised vegetable protein, derived from soybeans

Vegan A person who does not eat fish, meat, poultry, game, dairy products, honey and eggs, and who does not use any animal products (e.g. leather)

Vegetarian A person who does not eat meat, poultry or game

Velouté
- A basic sauce
- A soup of velvety or smooth consistency

Viruses Microscopic pathogens that multiply in the living cells of their host

Vitamins Chemical substances that assist the regulation of body processes

Vol-au-vent A large puff pastry case

Wok A round-bottomed pan used extensively in Chinese cooking

Yeast extract A mixture of brewer's yeast and salt, high in flavour and protein

Yoghurt An easily digested fermented milk product

Index of recipes

This index lists every recipe in the book. They are grouped by major commodity and by type of dish. There is a full topic index at the back of the book.

Index